D0990744

HERO OF BATAAN:

*The Story of General
Jonathan M. Wainwright*

HERO OF BATAAN:

The Story of General

Jonathan M. Wainwright

By DUANE SCHULTZ

ST. MARTIN'S PRESS
New York

Copyright © 1981 by Duane Schultz

All rights reserved. For information, write:
St. Martin's Press, Inc., 175 Fifth Ave., New York, N.Y. 10010.
Manufactured in the United States of America

Library of Congress Cataloging in Publication Data

Schultz, Duane P.
Hero of Bataan: the story of General Jonathan
M. Wainwright

1. Wainwright, Jonathan Mayhew, 1883–1953.
2. World War, 1939–1945—Campaigns—
Philippines-Bataan. 3. World War, 1939–1945—
Campaigns—Corregidor Island. 4. Bataan
(Philippines)—History. 5. Corregidor Island
(Philippines)—History. 6. Generals—United
States—Biography. 7. United States. Army—
Biography. I. Title.
E745.W32S38   940.54'26   81-8917
ISBN 0-312-37011-3   AACR2

To those who have drunk
from the same canteen

I hope that the story of what Americans suffered will always be remembered in its practical significance—as a lesson which almost lost for us this land we love.
Remember Bataan!
Remember Corregidor!

—J. M. WAINWRIGHT
September 10, 1945

Excelling in leadership and courage, throughout his forty-five years of distinguished service, he exemplified, in a conspicuously outstanding manner, the ideal combat commander. Through adversity and success his spirit never faltered. To his men, he was a tower of strength. . . . He will live in history as the hero of Bataan and Corregidor and as the commander who bought for this country the time needed for eventual victory in the Pacific.

—*General Orders*
Fort Sam Houston, Texas
September 2, 1953

CONTENTS

LIST OF PHOTOGRAPHS

Robert P. P. Wainwright, Major of Cavalry, 1852-1902.

J. M. Wainwright, First Captain of Cadets, U.S. Military Academy, 1906.

J. M. Wainwright, Colonel of Cavalry and Commanding Officer, Fort Myer, Virginia, 1937.

Commanding officer's quarters, Fort Myer, Virginia.

Col. J. M. Wainwright, Master of the Hunt, Fort Myer, Virginia, 1937.

"The Horse Is Man's Noblest Companion." Cavalry recruiting poster, 1920.

Skinny Wainwright and Douglas MacArthur, Fort McKinley, Philippine Islands, October 1941.

Wainwright and his aides on Bataan, February 1942.

Col. Joseph L. Chabot.

MacArthur and staff with Maj. Gen. Albert M. Jones during the USAFFE commander's only visit to Bataan, January 10, 1942.

Pile-type tank obstacles and double-apron fence entanglements on Bataan.

Philippine Scouts with war trophy.

Lt. Gen. T. J. H. Trapnell.

Lt. Gen. Masaharu Homma comes ashore on Luzon.

"Looks Like a Perfect Fit." Editorial cartoon, *The Washington Post*, April 4, 1942.

Brig. Gen. Arnold J. Funk.

Col. John R. Vance in finance department lateral, Malinta Tunnel.

Col. Stuart Wood.

Brig. Gen. Clinton A. Pierce questions captured Japanese soldiers.

Wainwright meets Homma to arrange the surrender of the Philippines, May 6, 1942.

Japanese drawing of Wainwright-Homma meeting.

U.S. forces surrender to Japanese troops on Corregidor.

Wainwright broadcasts surrender instructions from Manila, May 7, 1942.

"Corregidor Falls." Manila *Tribune*.

American generals in captivity, July 1942.

Schujo (post exchange) customers at Shirakawa prison camp, 1943.

Wainwright writes a postcard home, Formosa, 1944.

Wainwright and King take tea on a fishing trip arranged at Muksaq prison camp, 1944.

"Since Corregidor, Two Long Years." *Time* magazine cover, May 1944.

Adele Wainwright at home in Skaneateles, New York, October 1944.

Newly liberated Wainwright wearing shirt provided by Gen. Albert C. Wedemeyer, commander of American forces in China.

Wainwright, carrying a photograph of his wife, is helped into a car by Wedemeyer.

MacArthur greets Wainwright in Yokohama, Japan, August 31, 1945.

MacArthur with Wainwright and Percival.

Wainwright and Percival witness the signing of the Japanese surrender document aboard the U.S.S. *Missouri*, September 2, 1945.

Major Dooley, Lieutenant Colonel Pugh, Brigadier General Beebe, and Sergeant Carroll upon arrival in Manila.

Wainwright attends the Japanese surrender of the Philippines at Baguio, Luzon, September 3, 1945.

Wainwright receives his fourth star from Lt. Gen. Robert C. Richardson at Honolulu, September 7, 1945.

The Wainwrights are reunited at National Airport outside of Washington, D.C., September 10, 1945.

Wainwright addresses the U.S. Congress.

Wainwright receives the Medal of Honor from President Truman.

Wainwright enjoys a hot dog and cola at a baseball game at Washington's Griffith Stadium.

Wainwright's homecoming festivities continue with a ticker-tape parade in New York City.

Wainwright awards the DSM to Col. N. F. Galbraith

Wainwright cuts the cake at a surprise party hosted by Beebe at Fort Sam Houston, Texas, August 23, 1947, to mark Wainwright's sixty-fourth birthday and forty-fifth anniversary in the army.

LIST OF MAPS

U.S. Army Forces, Far East (USAFFE), December 8, 1941.
Withdrawal to Bataan, December 1941.
Bataan, January–March, 1942.
Corregidor Island (Fort Mills).

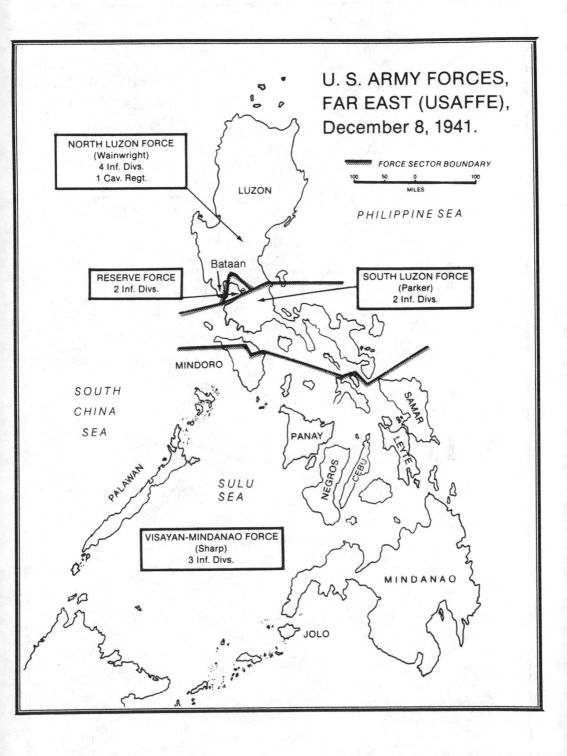

U. S. ARMY FORCES, FAR EAST (USAFFE), December 8, 1941.

FORCE SECTOR BOUNDARY

100   50   0   100
MILES

NORTH LUZON FORCE
(Wainwright)
4 Inf. Divs.
1 Cav. Regt.

LUZON

PHILIPPINE SEA

Bataan

RESERVE FORCE
2 Inf. Divs.

SOUTH LUZON FORCE
(Parker)
2 Inf. Divs.

MINDORO

SOUTH
CHINA
SEA

SAMAR

PANAY

LEYTE

NEGROS

CEBU

PALAWAN

SULU
SEA

VISAYAN-MINDANAO FORCE
(Sharp)
3 Inf. Divs.

MINDANAO

JOLO

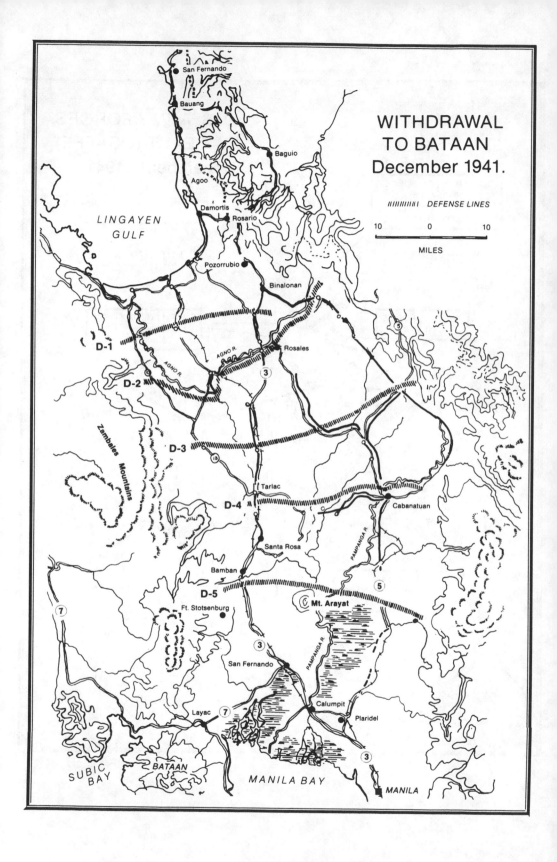

WITHDRAWAL
TO BATAAN
December 1941.

||||||||| DEFENSE LINES

10   0   10

MILES

San Fernando
Bauang
Baguio
Agoo
Damortis
Rosario
LINGAYEN GULF
Pozorrubio
Binalonan
D-1
D-2
AGNO R.
AGNO R.
Rosales
(3)
(5)
Zambales Mountains
D-3
(13)
Tarlac
D-4
Cabanatuan
Santa Rosa
PAMPANGA R.
Bamban
D-5
(5)
Ft. Stotsenburg
Mt. Arayat
(7)
PAMPANGA R.
(3)
San Fernando
Layac
(7)
Calumpit
Plaridel
SUBIC BAY
BATAAN
(3)
MANILA BAY
MANILA

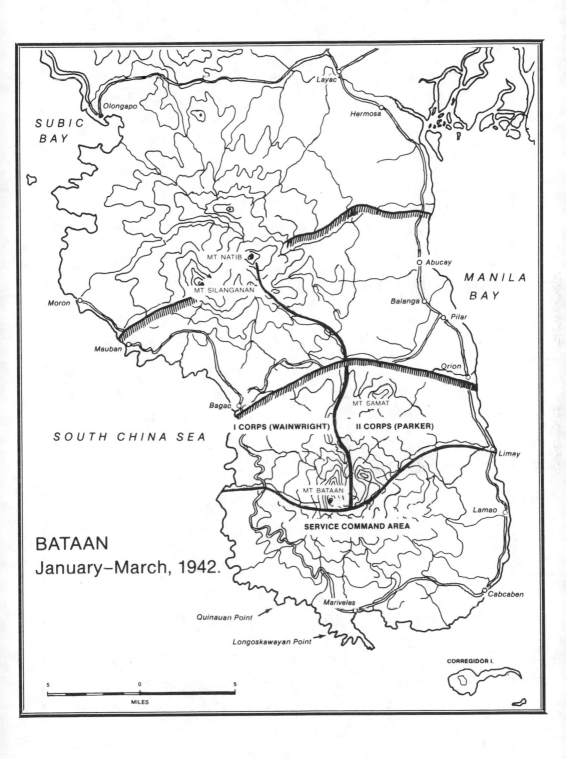

SUBIC
BAY

Olongapo

Layac

Hermosa

MT. NATIB

MT. SILANGANAN

Abucay

MANILA
BAY

Moron

Balanga

Pilar

Mauban

Orion

Bagac

MT. SAMAT

Limay

SOUTH CHINA SEA

I CORPS (WAINWRIGHT)

II CORPS (PARKER)

MT. BATAAN

Lamao

SERVICE COMMAND AREA

BATAAN
January–March, 1942.

Cabcaben

Quinauan Point

Mariveles

Longoskawayan Point

CORREGIDOR I.

5   0   5

MILES

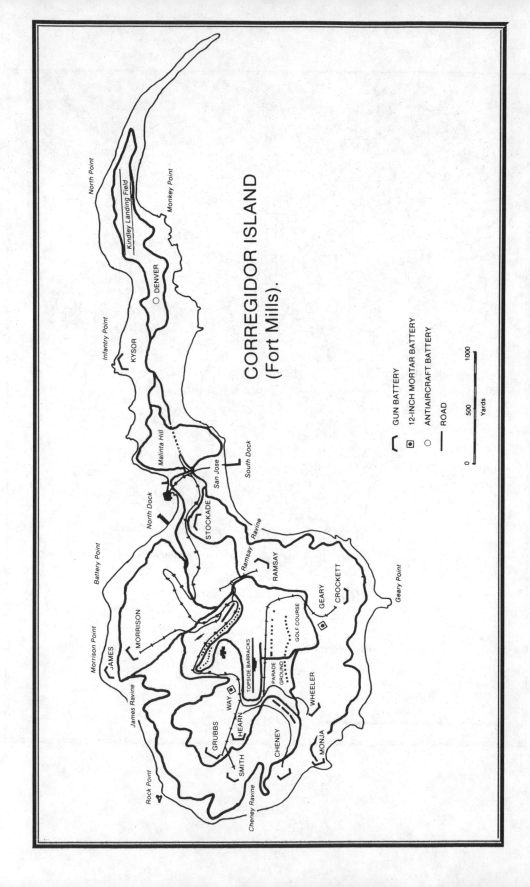

CORREGIDOR ISLAND
(Fort Mills).

GUN BATTERY

12-INCH MORTAR BATTERY

ANTIAIRCRAFT BATTERY

ROAD

0   500   1000

Yards

North Point

Infantry Point

Battery Point

Morrison Point

Rock Point

Cheney Ravine

James Ravine

Kindley Landing Field

Monkey Point

DENVER

KYSOR

Malinta Hill

North Dock

San Jose

South Dock

Ramsay Ravine

Geary Point

RAMSAY

CROCKETT

GEARY

GOLF COURSE

PARADE GROUND

WHEELER

MONJA

CHENEY

SMITH

HEARN

WAY

GRUBBS

JAMES

MORRISON

STOCKADE

TOPSIDE BARRACKS

HERO OF BATAAN:

The Story of General
Jonathan M. Wainwright

CHAPTER 1

"An Old-Fashioned Hero"

THE PLANES ROARED out of the east over the four-thousand-foot-high Mount Arayat. There were twenty-seven of them, twin-engine bombers, gleaming like silver darts in the bright noon sun. They were Japanese. The time was 12:25, December 8, 1941, ten hours after the American fleet had been wiped out at Pearl Harbor. The place was Fort Stotsenburg, fifty miles north of Manila, adjacent to Clark Field, America's largest air base in the Philippine Islands.

Bombs started to fall. Explosions and thick columns of smoke and flames leaped in the air. Unprepared men screamed in pain and in panic as they raced for shelter. Some of them glanced toward the large wooden headquarters building at one edge of the parade ground. There they saw a man standing quietly on the verandah, calmly watching the attack. He was tall, six feet, thin and gangly, and he stood erect as he surveyed the planes and the destruction. He was old, fifty-eight, and his face was craggy and sunburned. An outdoor man, he wore high shiny cavalry boots handmade in London, and twill cavalry breeches that flared over the tops of his boots. Hung low on his hip, in the style of the American West, was an old Colt .45. His khaki shirt was open at the neck, and on his head he wore an old-style broad-brimmed cavalry campaign hat.

The two stars of a major general adorned his collar. His name was Wainwright.

Another wave of bombers flew overhead. Wainwright walked down the steps from the porch, and started to cross the parade ground. He walked slowly and with a noticeable limp, the legacy of a fall from a horse years ago.

He might have been out for a leisurely stroll to the officers' club. He took little notice of the bombs and the shrapnel around him. A staff officer ran up and tried to push him toward a foxhole, but the general shook his head. He stopped next to an artillery emplacement just as one of the gunners was struck by shrapnel in the face. He knelt beside the boy and waved for the medics.

He straightened up again and stood still, as though defying the enemy bombs. More and more of his men were watching him now, drawing strength from his example, courage from his calm demeanor, as he hoped they would. Their own fears diminished. If the old man can take it, they thought, so can we.

Wainwright deliberately risked death that first day of the war to set an example, to lead his men personally by being out in front of them, taking the same chances, and more. That was his responsibility, his obligation, his definition of leadership.

His men loved him for it; they would have followed him into Hell itself. And they did.

Jonathan Mayhew Wainwright IV—he liked to be called by his West Point nickname, "Skinny"—was a hero in America's last age of heroes. A genuine, old-fashioned, flag-waving, gun-toting American hero. He was a soldier out of the army of the old West, the army of rugged frontier posts and lonely cavalrymen riding in columns of twos across the empty skyline. He grew up in a succession of stockaded forts. His father was a cavalryman, one of the tough, disciplined, colorful breed who loved a good time, and Skinny became one of the toughest and most colorful of them all.

He wore a gun of the old West, the Colt model 1873 single-action Army .45, the "Peacemaker." It wasn't showy or flashy, not like his friend Georgie Patton's twin pearl-handled nickel-barreled revolvers. The Peacemaker was a solid, reliable, no-nonsense weapon, like the man who carried it.

Skinny was a marksman who loved the feel of a fine gun. He was an expert horseman who loved the rough and tumble of polo and the excitement of the fox hunt, where he was privileged to wear the scarlet coat of a Master of the Hunt. He loved to drink and go to parties and sing "The Wide Missouri" and all the songs of the old cavalry.

Wainwright was one of those professional soldiers who came to maturity between the world wars, at once charming and profane, courtly and tough, a gentleman and a fighter, and a soldier to the core.

A genuine, old-fashioned American hero, he believed fervently in the virtues of the turn-of-the-century America in which he was raised: independence, self-reliance, dedication, hard work, and sacrifice. These weren't just words to him, they were part of his being, part of the fiber of the man, as characteristic as the way he sat a horse or held a cigar in his right hand to fluster young second lieutenants by returning their salute with his left.

He believed in the motto he learned at West Point: duty, honor, country. He was not ashamed to say that he loved his country, revered its ideals and its flag, and gloried in the medals it gave him for his service in its wars. And he had one aim in life, to be the best soldier he could in the service of his country.

Wainwright's opportunity came in 1941 on the broad open plains of Luzon, the jungles of Bataan, and the bomb-blasted fortress island of Corregidor. Faced with a hopeless situation, fighting against impossible odds, considered expendable by his country, Skinny Wainwright wrote one of the most glorious chapters in American history.

With his troops starving, their bodies shivering from malaria and ravaged by other tropical diseases for which there was never enough medicine, with no air force and no navy and with weapons from World War I, Wainwright fought a modern, well-equipped army to a standstill for almost five months. Elsewhere in the Pacific the Japanese were quickly victorious. Hong Kong fell on Christmas Day, Singapore on February 15. The American and British and Dutch navies were riddled with losses, the Dutch East Indies overrun. The Japanese were closing in on Australia.

But Bataan held. And after it finally capitulated on April 8, Corregidor hung on for another month. Wainwright had become, as *Time* magazine wrote, "the man left behind to preside at his country's worst military fiasco."

With no hope that reinforcements would breach the Japanese blockade, with no chance to win or escape, Skinny Wainwright led his ragged troops in a series of delaying actions that disrupted the Imperial Japanese timetable for the conquest of the Pacific. He accomplished this with little more than stubborn determination and sheer endurance. The last stand he directed on Bataan and Corregidor inspired a nation to ultimate victory at a time when defeat screamed from every headline.

A genuine, old-fashioned American hero, a soldier's soldier, a front-line general, he functioned best at the corps or division level where he was free to execute the quick bold strokes that were the hallmark of the cavalry, and where he could be in close daily contact with his men.

America had two kinds of leaders in World War II, the military managers and the heroic, martial fighters. Among the managers are Dwight Eisenhower, Omar Bradley, Hap Arnold, Douglas Mac-Arthur, Bedell Smith. Wainwright is with the fighters, with his friends Halsey and Patton, and Jimmy Doolittle and Curt LeMay. An officer in the Philippines wrote: "General MacArthur was Moses—commanding the waters to separate; General Wainwright was King Saul—fearlessly leading his people in battle."

Wainwright proved himself to be an outstanding field commander and a natural leader of men, who inspired and cared for his troops. He was a brilliant tactician, kind and generous, selfless and gallant. A larger-than-life character who drank and smoked and cussed, and who was moved to tears by the agonies his boys endured.

He was one of the few generals ever to be cheered by his men on the field of battle. When he knew defeat was inevitable, when he was suffering from beriberi and so badly undernourished that his right leg was nearly useless, he dragged himself along the dusty roads and through the jungle, leaning on his malacca cane, to be seen by his soldiers at the front. His men worshipped him and died for him because he was truly one of them. He shared their dangers, their privations, and their meager rations. Forty years later a staff officer summed up their feelings simply: "We loved the guy."

A genuine, old-fashioned American hero, Wainwright restlessly prowled the front lines on Bataan, risking death from Japanese shells and snipers, taking potshots at the enemy, talking to his boys in their foxholes. Not for him the safety of the command post where a battle is fought as a map exercise. He had to see it, and smell it, and be a part of it. On the long retreat into Bataan he had to be the last man across each bridge, making sure that all the troops were over before he gave the order to blow it up.

When the enemy established a roadblock behind the lines, he organized a motley platoon from the personnel on the spot, put them in a truck, and led them into battle like a lieutenant. He had to see everything firsthand, not on a chart or as described by a subordinate. He walked every yard of his front line, directing the laying of the barbed wire and the placing of the machine guns. And if there was trouble on the line, he flicked off the safety of his Garand rifle and fired with the rest of his soldiers.

Wainwright was everywhere, encouraging, cajoling, and sometimes threatening the untrained troops he had been left with. During a retreat that had turned into a rout, he placed himself squarely in the road, drew a line in the dust, and pulled out his old Colt .45. He claimed he would shoot any man who crossed the line. The troops stopped and turned around.

He came across a demoralized group of Filipino soldiers wandering down a narrow trail. Wainwright spied one who still carried his rifle and he put his arm around the boy, talking quietly to him for a few minutes. The others stopped to watch and listen to the thin old man and before long they were on their way back to the front.

He had a talent for picking good people for his staff and for getting the best from them. His headquarters in the Philippines were small and efficient, the men professional and dedicated. He was able to spend so much time visiting his troops because he was confident that the staff would handle the daily details that kept the army fighting.

Wainwright's courage and compassion were matched by his sense of humor and his ability to put things in a good light to keep up morale. At a gloomy staff conference he looked at his downhearted men and held up a medical report.

"That's the finest damn record I've ever seen," Skinny said. "Only one case of V.D. in the corps in a month!"

A genuine, old-fashioned American hero, yet at first glance an unlikely one. He was too old for a combat command. So ruled the War Department two years before, as it began to prepare for war. No officer over the age of fifty was considered eligible for combat.

Wainwright was also in an outmoded branch of service that was soon to be dismantled. In the coming war of airplanes and tanks, no one saw a future for the horse cavalry. But Skinny stubbornly clung to it, in danger of becoming obsolete himself.

There were other marks against him in those frantic days of planning for war. Wainwright had back trouble that caused him discomfort and pain. He limped and was hard of hearing in one ear. He wouldn't have the stamina for life in the field, Washington decided.

What was worse, he drank too much, some said, and it had become particularly apparent during the late 1930s when he was stationed in Washington, under the eyes of the chief of staff and the government. Rumors and gossip about his drinking—some true and some exaggerated—reached the highest levels of the War Department.

No, there were too many strikes against Skinny Wainwright, despite his admirable thirty-year record in the army. He was put out to pasture, given a pleasant assignment, one last post before retirement, and younger, more promising men were chosen for the top commands in the war that was sure to come, a war Wainwright could watch from the sidelines.

An old-fashioned American hero, but there was a limit to what even a fighter like Wainwright could accomplish. When Bataan fell and the Japanese closed their steel ring around tiny Corregidor and the island shook under the massive daily bombardments, Skinny was urged to leave on the last plane out.

"I have been with my men from the start," he said, "and if captured I will share their lot."

He raised the morale of his men to the last, just as he had done on Bataan. After each frustrating, nerve-shattering day he visited the wounded in the hospital, but not as a parade with aides trailing after him and photographers snapping pictures for the hometown papers. Rather, he wandered alone among the injured men, stopping by their cots to bum a match or a cigarette, to ask a hurt and frightened boy how he was getting along.

The end came to Corregidor on May 6, 1942, and Skinny wrote his final message to President Roosevelt on scrap paper. He did not even have an official message blank left.

"With broken heart and head bowed in sadness but not in shame, I go to meet the Japanese commander. Goodbye, Mr. President."

Hours later Wainwright returned from the greatest humiliation of his life, the surrender of his army. Slowly, painfully, he walked toward his headquarters in Malinta Tunnel on Corregidor, past several hundred of his men, now captives, unarmed, without food or water. They watched him come and as he got closer they rose to their feet and stood at attention. They saluted the general as he limped by and many reached out to him. They shook his hand and patted him on the shoulder and whispered a few words that brought tears to his eyes.

"It's all right, General," his men said. "You did your best."

Wainwright and his men spent three and a half years as prisoners of war. Although he was the highest-ranking American officer held by the Japanese, that did not protect him from privations and beatings and constant, gnawing hunger. In captivity as in combat, he shared the fate of his troops.

But Wainwright suffered a greater agony, the belief that he had let America down. He was haunted by the fear that he would be court-martialed for the surrender, and that the Wainwright name would be set down in history in disgrace.

He never imagined that he would come home to the cheers of the nation, to receive every honor his grateful country could bestow. Few Americans have been so celebrated. In 1945, the sight of Wainwright's drawn face and painfully thin body touched millions of people who lined the streets to catch a glimpse of this old-fashioned American hero. Their tears mingled with their applause and drove the thought of court-martial from his mind. Wainwright was home. His war was over. Now another ordeal would have to be faced.

CHAPTER 2
"Back in Harness"

On Saturday, September 14, 1940, the U.S. Army Transport *Grant* sailed out of New York harbor. On board were Brig. Gen. J. M. Wainwright, his old friend Brig. Gen. Edward "Ned" King, and several hundred officers and men. Once clear of land, the ship turned south, heading for Charleston and the Panama Canal on its forty-eight-day voyage to Manila in the Philippine Islands.

The U.S.A.T. *Grant* made four trips a year, ferrying army personnel and their dependents to and from duty spots in the Philippines. For the officers and their wives the voyage was relaxed and carefree, with plenty of good fun and companionship. It was like a seven-week vacation, with all the time in the world for sunning, for playing bridge and more vigorous deck games such as shuffleboard, for meeting new people and renewing old acquaintances, and for pleasant evenings in the bar, because drinking was always a part of life in the old army.

The first day at sea was sunny and warm and the waters were calm. Spirits were high. After dinner, the officers and their ladies assembled on the fantail to watch a new movie, *Boom Town*, starring Clark Gable and Spencer Tracy. Shortly before the show was due to start, a strong wind came up. The ship's crew was immediately ordered to hang canvas curtains from the deck above to shield the audience.

When the movie was over, the couples went off to the bar and back to their cabins while the sailors went about their work of removing the canvas curtains. One young seaman climbed up on the railing to get a better grip on the heavy, water-soaked canvas. Suddenly he lost his footing and plunged into the black waters far below. The captain ordered the ship to halt. Motorboats were lowered and parties searched for the man, but he was gone. The army officers and their wives, attracted by the commotion, lined the rails, waiting silently as the boats were hauled aboard. It was not a bright beginning for a cruise.

As senior army officer on board the *Grant,* Skinny Wainwright, with his wife Adele and his mother-in-law Mrs. Dwight Holley, widow of an army colonel, was entitled to the best quarters, a comfortable suite on the upper deck. General Wainwright was enjoying the leisurely days at sea and looking forward to his new command in the Philippines. It was the biggest and most important assignment of his long career, yet he was not entirely pleased with it.

War was coming—he was convinced of that—and the idea nagged at him that he was sailing in the wrong direction. "I think I'm going the wrong way," he had told a friend a few days before. He was afraid he would miss the real war by being "stuck away out in the islands."

Many others shared this belief. In 1939, an obscure lieutenant colonel by the name of Eisenhower had incurred the enmity of his chief, Gen. Douglas MacArthur, by asking to be sent from Manila back home to the United States. "I did so in the confident belief that should war break out the initial battles would be in the Atlantic Theatre," Ike said. Even if the Japanese did initiate hostilities in the Pacific, the professional soldiers knew that the fighting in Europe would be more important. The promotions and the medals would come faster there. War Department policy had decreed for years that in the event of a two-ocean war, the European theater would take precedence. No one—certainly not Skinny Wainwright— wanted to miss out on what was shaping up as the biggest war in history.

On the day Wainwright set sail from New York, the situation in Europe was grim. Virtually the entire continent was under the domination of Adolf Hitler. The fate of Great Britain was being decided at the same moment Wainwright's ship turned south for the Panama Canal. Hermann Goering's Luftwaffe was bombing England every day. The Battle of Britain was entering its deadly second phase, when the bombs were falling on London and other cities instead of on military targets. The country was hanging by the thinnest of threads, and many people, including U.S. Ambassador Joseph P. Kennedy, were saying openly that England was doomed. The end seemed only days away.

President Franklin D. Roosevelt was searching for ways to help the desperate British. He ordered the army to open up its warehouses of World War I weapons and ammunition, and to ship the goods to England. They were obsolete, but they were better than nothing. Most of the equipment of the British army was still on the beaches at Dunkirk.

Suddenly America was looking to its own military, neglected for so many years. Thousands of trainees poured into scores of new camps. Divisions, whole armies, were being created overnight, affording opportunities for regular officers that had not existed since 1918. Wainwright was not alone in realizing that these new armies and divisions would earn their glory on the battlefields of Europe, fighting the Wehrmacht, the greatest army the world had ever seen. But here he was on the *Grant,* sailing toward Manila, in the opposite direction.

The command Wainwright was getting in the Philippines was a good one, however. It was an opportunity to show what he could do and he was determined to make the most of it. After all, he had been a soldier for thirty-four years. He would obey his orders and do his duty as he had always done.

Something else was on Wainwright's mind as the *Grant* steamed southward. Although he thought he was going the wrong way for the war, he knew he was lucky to be going anywhere at all. Until a few weeks before, when the orders transferring him to the Philippines had come through, he had been convinced that his career was nearly over. Officers over the age of fifty, and particularly cavalry officers, were being purged.

In December 1938, Jonathan Wainwright had been sent to Fort Clark, Texas, which had the reputation as "the country's most somnambulant Cavalry post, where superannuated officers . . . were usually allowed a pleasant last fling before retirement." There a cavalryman could spend his days riding and hunting in the great outdoors, away from the scrutiny of official Washington, but free also from any further opportunity for advancement. Assignment to Fort Clark was like being put out to pasture, and it looked as though this would be Skinny's last post. The next step in his career would be a retirement ceremony.

But events were unfolding elsewhere in the world, in Europe and in China, at such a dizzying pace that they even intruded on the dusty Texas panhandle. The Nazi invasion of Poland, Holland, Denmark, Norway, France, and Belgium, and incidents in more remote places such as Nanking and Peking, stunned America's military leaders. Everywhere they looked, the Axis powers were crushing all the armies they opposed.

Slowly and tenaciously the man who would soon become the army's chief of staff, Gen. George Marshall, and other leaders, had been able to persuade a reluctant Congress that America needed a larger army, and it needed one quickly. Almost overnight, the army began to prepare for its next war. While German troops were overrunning France with their new *Blitzkrieg* tactics, the U.S. army went on full-scale maneuvers using trucks with the word "tank" painted on the side, broomsticks for machine guns, and bursting bags of flour for bombs.

The War Department combed the officer corps for seasoned leaders to train the flood of inductees, and in due course the file of Brig. Gen. J. M. Wainwright was reexamined. It was impressive—distinguished service in World War I, fine record on the General Staff, selection for every army command school. His efficiency reports were good. "Natural leader," they said, "magnetic personality, clipped speech, good disciplinarian, popular with officers and men, alert, forceful. Plenty of confidence in himself."

True, Wainwright was in the wrong branch of the service and too old to be considered for a major stateside post to prepare for the coming war with Germany, and he limped and was hard of hearing and he drank, but he would do nicely for a secondary assignment in the Philippines, where a brigadier general was needed. And so it happened that the man destined to become one of America's greatest heroes was plucked from the threat of an early retirement, put back in harness, and sent on his way to face the most trying and frustrating command of any American general throughout the war.

On paper, Wainwright's new command was impressive. He was to lead a division, the Philippine Division, the largest army unit in that distant American possession. He would soon learn that like the rest of the American army in the fall of 1940, the Philippine Division was woefully inadequate for the situation with which it was expected to cope.

Still, it was a division and the largest and most important command Wainwright had been given. After the isolation of Fort Clark, the opportunity did please him, even if it was on the wrong side of the world. There was always the hope that he could compile an outstanding record with his new division, and then be eligible for the big war, the one in Europe.

Also, Wainwright had a sentimental attachment to the Philippines. The assignment was bringing his career full circle. He had first seen combat there in 1909. It had been Wainwright's first war, and the last one for his father, who died there. If the Philippine Islands turned out to be the scene of Wainwright's third war, well, he would do the best he could. That was what being a soldier was all about.

Midway through the voyage to Manila aboard the U.S.A.T. *Grant*, on October 1, 1940, Wainwright received a radiogram from the War Department. Its contents pleased him greatly, bringing a characteristic broad grin to his face and a considerable amount of joy and satisfaction. He rushed to tell his wife and mother-in-law, and the three of them went up on deck to observe the ceremony marking the event. It was the day after the ship had passed through the Panama Canal and they were far beyond the sight of land. The westerly wind blew in their faces as proudly they watched a pennant with two stars on it being hoisted, announcing to all the passengers that Wainwright had been promoted to major general. Among those present was an eighteen-year-old army private, Richard M. Gordon, who would serve with Wainwright later on Bataan.

Skinny was indeed proud of the two stars he now wore on each shoulder. "Such things are deeply moving in the life of a regular army man," he said. "Promotions are an army man's life and sustenance; promotions and opportunities to distinguish himself." He celebrated enthusiastically that night, in the company of friends and well-wishers, and the congratulations poured as freely as the drinks. Perhaps the tour of duty in the Philippines would not be so bad after all.

Even if he were to rise no higher than two-star general, Wainwright had equaled the achievements of his distinguished ancestors, whose memory and heritage he revered. Had his career ended there, he would still have done the Wainwright name proud. He had already written an illustrious chapter in the family's history of more than a century of service to the United States.

The first Wainwright to settle in the United States was Peter Wainwright, a prosperous English merchant who came to Boston before the American Revolution. He and his wife, Elizabeth Mayhew, returned to England for the birth of their son, christened Jonathan Mayhew Wainwright. When the boy was eleven, the family came back to Massachusetts. Jonathan, General Wainwright's great-grandfather, graduated from Harvard College in 1812 and taught there for two years. He entered the seminary and was ordained in the Episcopal Church, rising to become Bishop of New York in 1852.* A prominent figure in church circles and in higher education, Jonathan Wainwright helped to found the institution that later became New York University, and he served as a trustee for Columbia College and on the examining board of Trinity College in Connecticut. He was a popular and beloved clergyman who published many articles and books, and also fathered fourteen children. One son was named Jonathan Mayhew Wainwright II.

This boy, General Wainwright's grandfather, entered the U.S. Navy in 1837 as a midshipman, and had a distinguished military career. By the time of the Civil War, he was a lieutenant, and in 1862 was given his first command, the *Harriet Lane,* flagship of a mortar flotilla. Wainwright saw a great deal of action in the Gulf of Mexico, off the embattled coasts of Mississippi, Louisiana, and Texas.

At Galveston, Texas, in 1863, the *Harriet Lane* was attacked by two Confederate warships. Rebel sailors swarmed aboard. Captain Wainwright led his crew in a valiant fight, but they were over-whelmed by superior numbers. Wainwright himself was wounded six times, brought down finally by a musket ball through his head. In recognition of his valor, a destroyer was commissioned the U.S.S. *Wainwright* in World War I.

Among the four children who survived him and his wife, the former Maria Page, were two sons, Jonathan Mayhew Wainwright III and Robert Powell Page Wainwright, both of whom would die for their country as their father had done. Jonathan entered the navy and was killed off the coast of Mexico in 1870, in a battle with pirates. The second son, Robert, General Wainwright's father, who married Josephine Serrell of New York, chose West Point and the cavalry.

On the other side of the family, Wainwright's maternal grand-father, Gen. Edward W. Serrell, was known for his contribution to military engineering. He developed the eight-inch Parrott gun known as the "swamp angel." During the blockade of Charleston in the Civil War, the gun was skidded across the swamps and set up on

---

*It is said that the bishop brought to New York some water from the River Jordan which was later used to baptize his great-grandson, J. M. Wainwright IV.

pilings, where it could fire its enormous 200-pound shells into the heart of the city, five miles away.

From the moment of his birth in Walla Walla, Washington, on August 23, 1883, Jonathan Mayhew Wainwright IV entered into a strong tradition of patriotism and public service. He was born in another century, a time when values and priorities were more different than the passage of one hundred years might suggest. The western frontier, with its spirit of individualism and personal freedom, was open and still being fought for. Only seven years had passed since Custer's last stand, and the United States gloried in the exploits of its blue-coated cavalrymen. Young Jonathan grew up on tales of the old West, though at the time the West was not so old. The newspapers often carried stories of fresh battles against the Indians.

In 1883 a band of Chiracahua Apaches under Chato raided settlers in the Southwest. The celebrated cavalry general George Crook set out with the Third and Sixth Cavalry regiments to do battle. Two years later Geronimo led another band of Apaches off the reservation, and once again the cavalry went into action. In 1890 at a place called Wounded Knee Creek, the Seventh Cavalry avenged Custer's Little Big Horn defeat with a massacre of 164 Sioux. The last battle with the Indians took place at Sugar Point, Minnesota, in 1898, when Wainwright was fifteen years old.

His father fought in these wars as a member of the First Cavalry, in which young Wainwright would later serve. The boy and his two older sisters were raised on the stories of the cavalry's deeds. He knew the army, the smells of horses and leather, the clanking of scabbards and canteens, the sounding of bugles. He grew up on war. He listened to glamorous accounts of massed charges across open fields into the guns of enemies who sometimes wore gray uniforms and sometimes blue ones.

The magazines, the newspapers, and the penny novels all glorified war, and always the most exciting branch of the army in which to fight was the cavalry. There was no doubt in the boy's mind about what he would do when he grew up. He would wear the dark blue uniform with the yellow braid down the trousers and sit tall on a horse and fight, just like his father.

The boy was every inch his father's son and in time he came to be like him—and more so. Tributes written about Robert Wainwright after his death can be used decades later to describe his son Jonathan. "He was a typical cavalryman," Major Wainwright's classmates wrote, "and was never happier than when engaged upon mounted duty. He was an enthusiastic sportsman; a great lover of horses and dogs and was never without them. . . . Throughout his career he displayed the highest characteristics of a soldier . . . he was at all times imbued with the true soldier spirit, and his hopes and his ambitions centered in the one never-failing idea of duty well performed. He was bred a soldier, thought as a soldier, and his highest ambition was to excel in his calling at all times and under all circumstances." Robert Wainwright would have been proud of how his son turned out.

The Indian wars gradually faded, replaced by a bigger and more gripping conflict, the Spanish-American War. This was more than just another war. It took on the trappings of a crusade. A new phrase, "manifest destiny," entered the national consciousness and a new mood imbued the people. The United States was undertaking its first exercise in imperialism.

A frenzy of pride, patriotism, and jingoism erupted into a passion for war, as well as the conviction that it was our God-given right and duty to spread the American way of life beyond our national borders. "Ambition, interest, land-hunger, pride, the mere joy of fighting, whatever it may be, we are animated by a new sensation," acknowledged *The Washington Post*. "The taste of Empire is in the mouth of the people even as the taste of blood in the jungle."

The bands played, the flags waved, and young men by the thousands rushed to join the colors, to emulate Teddy Roosevelt's charge and to expand, to conquer, to carry out what was being trumpeted as our holy destiny. From Indiana a firebrand political orator, Albert Beveridge, fanned the flames with words that sent the pulses of millions racing. "We are a conquering race. We must obey our blood and occupy new markets and if necessary new lands." Americans were a master race, superior to all others. Beveridge urged "American expansion until all the seas shall bloom with that flower of liberty, the flag of the great Republic." We must plant "American law, American order, American civilization" on foreign shores. So truly did Beveridge speak to the needs of the people in 1898 that he was elected to the U.S. Senate.

Young Jonathan Wainwright was as stirred as anyone else by these calls for a new American destiny. Fifteen years old when the war began and a student at Deerfield Township High School in Highland Park, Illinois, near Fort Sheridan, where his father was stationed, he wanted to join the volunteers, as many boys he knew were doing. His father forbade it. Wainwright was to complete high school and prepare himself for West Point. There would be other wars.

Captain Robert Wainwright left for Cuba with the First Cavalry. At the battle of Las Guasimas he led his Troop G into action and fought so bravely that he was given the brevet rank of major. "It is to Wainwright that the greatest credit is due," his commanding officer wrote. "It was Wainwright's steady forward movement, straight at the enemy's most formidable position, that disconcerted the Spaniards, and it is to Wainwright more than any other Regular officer that credit should be given for the brilliant success."

A few weeks later, in command of a cavalry squadron, Wainwright led a charge up the slope of San Juan Hill and won another brevet promotion, this time to lieutenant colonel.

His son followed the war news avidly, renewing his resolve to be as good a soldier as his father.

The fighting in Cuba ended, but the war in the Philippines was proving troublesome, requiring more and more American troops. This was a guerrilla war, a war of ambushes and small raiding parties and no fixed front line. The enemy attacked and faded quickly into the jungle.

Jonathan's father was sent there in 1902 and demonstrated that he could perform as well as a staff officer as he had as a combat leader, a feat later equaled by his son. He was appointed assistant to the Adjutant General, Division of the Philippines, under the leadership of one of America's greatest soldiers, Maj. Gen. Arthur MacArthur. The general also had a son, Douglas, who had wanted to enlist. Before Arthur MacArthur went to Manila he told his boy, "there will be plenty of fighting in the coming years, and of a magnitude far beyond this. Prepare yourself."

Douglas MacArthur's father eventually came home from the Philippines, but Jonathan Wainwright's father did not. He died there in 1902, not from an enemy bullet but from tropical disease, which had incapacitated more men than any action by the Filipino rebels. Skinny Wainwright would come to know its effects intimately forty years later.

In his grief over his father's death, Jonathan threw himself into his work at the U.S. Military Academy, vowing to become an outstanding cadet. His parents had instilled in him certain values— to work hard, to give of yourself, and to do your best.

When Wainwright arrived at West Point, New York, on July 31, 1902, the school was in a state of excitement. The month before, the centennial of its founding had been celebrated. Three days of ceremonies had seen the campus crammed with dignitaries and alumni from as far back as the Civil War. There had been elegant balls, athletic events, parades and reviews. The President of the United States, Teddy Roosevelt, had attended.

It marked a time of renewal for the passionate spirit of the academy, and the motto "Duty, Honor, Country" was spoken with a greater conviction than usual. The new cadets that summer were infused with the intensity of President Roosevelt's words. "No other educational institution in the land has contributed as many names as West Point has contributed to the honor roll of the nation's great citizens. Taken as a whole, the average graduate of West Point during this hundred years has given a greater sum of service to the country through his life than has the average graduate of any other institution in this broad land."

What a wonderful time to be an entering cadet! The second century of West Point, and the new century for America, promised to be even brighter than the last. Young Wainwright, like his fellow plebes, was caught up in the new spirit. During their first days they were taken to read the plaque that had recently been unveiled. "Let us pledge ourselves to our country that the best efforts of our lives shall be to make the record of the second century even more memorable than that of the first." If the entering class needed additional inspiration as it commenced the four long hard years of military training, it could be easily found in the fever of rededication and patriotism sweeping over West Point during that summer of 1902.

The spirit at West Point had been recharged, but the place itself and the ways in which its cadets were taught had changed little in one hundred years. The year before Wainwright entered, the Board of Visitors had called the academy's physical plant a disgrace, and recommended that most of it be torn down and rebuilt. Wainwright saw the evidence of this deterioration all around him, particularly in the barracks, which were "little better than those at the average county poorhouse."

But like all the plebes before and after him, Wainwright had no time to lament his surroundings. He was too busy trying to survive the severe hazing, an accepted but officially frowned-upon way of teaching plebes their manners. The upperclassmen, whose avowed duty it was to make or break new cadets during their first summer, made life a hell for Wainwright and his classmates.

The first days at the Military Academy have been described as "calculated chaos." Cadet Dwight Eisenhower wrote, "We were all harassed, and, at times, resentful. Here we were, the cream of the crop, shouted at all day long by self-important upperclassmen, telling us to run here and run there; pick up our clothes; bring in that bedding; put our shoulders back, keep our eyes up, and to keep running, running, running."

The senior men were after the plebes every minute, day and night, and there was more required than double-time marching and bracing one's shoulders. Some of the hazing was cruel; several cadets had died. Push-ups, strenuous exercise, standing on one's head at attention, or sitting at the dinner table with one's feet off the floor were some of the milder forms of harassment. More violent punishment included "chewing rope ends, eating soap and quinine, drinking tabasco sauce, picking up all the ants in a hill one at a time, permitting hot grease to be dropped on the feet," and other ingenious tortures designed to tame the wildest spirit.

As with every entering class, there were some who could not cope with it all, but Wainwright was not among the twenty of his classmates who dropped out at the end of the first year. It would take a lot more than pressure from upperclassmen to make him give up the dreams of his boyhood. He meant to be a soldier, and nothing was going to stop him. He double-timed and braced and recited nonsensical answers to nonsensical questions, and he kept his eye on one particular upperclassman, a third-year man who seemed to embody all the virtues and characteristics of the ideal soldier. His name was Douglas MacArthur, and Wainwright was determined to be as good a cadet as that slender and handsome, though arrogant, young man. In Wainwright's second year at West Point, MacArthur became First Captain of the Corps of Cadets. Wainwright set his sights on the same goal.

Like novitiates in a monastery, the plebes at West Point were secluded from the outside world. No contact was permitted with civilians; the army was their only home. There was no leave for Christmas or other holidays, and the only furlough allowed came during the summer of their third year. Cadets could be authorized to go off post on horseback, but they had to pledge that they would neither halt nor dismount for any reason.

The time was too full for them to be lonely or homesick, however. It was not that the program of instruction was so difficult, but with all the classes and drills and sports there was little time for the luxury of such feelings. And certainly not for Wainwright, whose determination to graduate as First Captain of Cadets grew stronger with each passing year. When asked if he had had enough time for sleep as a cadet, Wainwright said, "Not enough to press my trousers properly."

The curriculum for Wainwright's class of 1906 at West Point was essentially the same as it had been 100 years before when the academy was founded. Mathematics and the physical and natural sciences were stressed, along with civil and military engineering. The method of teaching these academic subjects had also changed little. Rote memorization of each day's assignment was required, and class time was spent in recitation or in writing the lesson on the blackboard.

Wainwright was not the best student at the school, though his grades were well above average. His least favorite subjects were "civilian" subjects—math, philosophy, and languages. He was always in the top third of his class, however, in subjects like practical military engineering or ordnance and gunnery. He ranked first in military efficiency and second in soldierly deportment and discipline, with a fifth in drill regulations.

In conduct he ranked eighth in the class of seventy-eight, receiving only forty-five demerits in his last year. The heaviest penalties—five demerits each—were for "smoking cigarette in sink about 9:30 P.M." and "profanity." In the precise Spencerian handwriting of the day his transgressions survive for inspection: "wearing patent leather shoes to supper formation," "dropping bayonet at drill," "rusty gun," "riding on road with coat unbuttoned."

The military side of the cadets' training had altered dramatically just before Wainwright enrolled. Prior to that time it was popular to say that a cadet learned close-order drill in his first six weeks, then spent the next four years performing it over and over. Wainwright was fortunate to receive a different kind of training, designed to expose cadets to every branch of the service in theory as well as in practice.

Wainwright learned how to fire mortars, Gatling guns, and larger artillery pieces; how to plan infantry and cavalry attacks; and how to mount picket and guard duty. He served in different command levels in infantry, cavalry, and artillery units. Previous classes of cadets did not have these experiences until after graduation. Also, in what at the time was considered a shocking departure from tradition, cadets could no longer use enlisted men to do their work for them on practice marches. Wainwright learned to take care of his own horse, to raise his own tent, and to clean his campsite himself.

He excelled at West Point not only militarily but also socially. From the beginning he was one of the best-liked and most popular cadets in his class. With his tall thin frame and his wrists sticking out of his cuffs, he was immediately dubbed "Skinny." He liked the nickname and it stuck with him all his life. Years later, when asked why he acquired the nickname at West Point, he replied, "because I was no bigger than a tight-rolled cigar." He also had another nickname, "Jim," which derived from his habit of signing his name "J. M. Wainwright," but the only person who persisted in using it was Douglas MacArthur.

Many cadets felt drawn to the lanky, quiet, modest Skinny, and he formed friendships that lasted a lifetime. One relationship that endured was with a thin, highstrung boy from California, who entered the academy two years after Wainwright. The younger cadet was overly sensitive and ambitious, and he alienated most of his classmates by his continual assertion that he would become the first general in his class. Wainwright liked him, despite his arrogance and the difference in their temperaments, because they shared a passion for the cavalry. The two cadets could often be seen racing across the campus or in the riding hall, along with the rest of a group known as the "cavalry fanatics." The boy did not become the first general in his class, but he did not do too badly; his name was George S. Patton.

Finally it was June Week of 1906, the long-awaited time of graduation. Skinny's mother came to the ceremonies, along with the pretty daughter of an infantry officer, Adele Holley, whom Wainwright had known since 1897, when their fathers were stationed near Chicago. They were both immensely proud of Skinny, but no more than he was himself. He was graduating with the highest honor a cadet can receive. Wainwright was First Captain of Cadets, joining the ranks of such notables as Robert E. Lee and John J. Pershing.

In the military academy yearbook, the *Howitzer*, Wainwright's classmates wrote: "Corporal, Sergeant Major, First Sergeant, First Captain, Hop Manager, Marksman, Toastmaster New Year's 1906. This is IT—the summit toward which the Pampered Pets of the Powers that Be continually do strive, the goal of every good cadet's ambition. Many honors have been heaped upon his head—so many that it's a wonder his slender frame has withstood their bending moment without any more damage than giving to his knees a permanent set.

"'Skinny' will long remember that awful Hallowe'en evening

when, just as he was making his most military salute and reporting 'A Company all quiet, Sir,' about a ton of brick dropped on the roof of the First Division. 'Skinny' collapsed on the spot and it took the O.C. a good hour's work with the sponge to bring him around."

As Wainwright marched at the head of the corps, past the reviewing stand, his chest swelled with pride and confidence in his future. Other than being the son of a general, he had the best possible start for an army career. Being First Captain tabbed him for higher things from the moment of graduation. This supreme accolade meant that he had the trust, respect, and affection of both the teaching staff and his peers. Although he stood twenty-fifth in his class of seventy-eight academically, he stood first militarily and socially. His chances of getting at least one star during his career were thought to be excellent.

And Wainwright was joining the one branch of service he loved best, the cavalry, commissioned a second lieutenant on June 12, 1906. How many times as a child he had heard the old song, "If you want to have a good time, jine the cavalry!" Here was the most glamorous part of the army, the most daring, the most heroic, capturing the public's fancy as the air corps would by the 1930s. And the cavalry was where his father had served.

Mrs. Wainwright had a special graduation present for her son, a dress sword with his name engraved on the blade. Many years later a Japanese general would wear it, but only for a while. Skinny treated himself to another graduation present, something he had wanted for a long time: a Colt model 1873 single-action Army .45, serial number 277996, which he purchased from William Reed and Sons, a gun dealer in New York City. It was the most popular handgun of the West, and it would serve Wainwright well in the years to come. Both of these graduation gifts would eventually, and circuitously, find their way back to the museum at Wainwright's beloved West Point.

Lieutenant Wainwright began his army service at Fort Clark and at other isolated posts in Texas, with names like Camp Eagle Pass and St. Filippee. Junior officers were barely paid a living wage during those years, but Wainwright never considered leaving the army. Duty to country was more important than the money that could be made in the civilian world. Besides, he was having fun. The old song was right—you did have a good time when you "jined" the cavalry. He had been assigned to his father's old outfit, the First U.S. Cavalry, a regiment steeped in glory.

Wainwright was able to ride as frequently and as hard as he

wanted and to exercise his marksmanship with hunting and target practice. The troopers under his command quickly came to respect him. He was demanding, but he was also fair and compassionate, becoming known as a good officer to serve under. At one of these early posts the men nicknamed him "Ducky," a popular term for an all-around good guy.

Wainwright drove his men hard, but he never expected anything from them that he would not do himself. On forced marches across the hot arid desert he shared their food and lack of comfort, and never looked to his own needs until he was sure that his men and his horses were taken care of. He continued to show this same kind of concern even many years later as a general.

Lieutenant Wainwright was also something of a hell raiser. His closest friend was another young cavalry officer, "Buckets" Briscoe, and the two were almost always in some kind of trouble. At a post in California Skinny and Buckets had motorcycles and liked to roar back into camp after midnight, waking everybody up.

One of his best-loved off-duty pastimes was poker. He would play for hours, until the night his straight flush was beaten, a loss that cost him three months' pay. He swore on the spot that he would never play the game again, and he kept his word.

But there were other ways to have a good time in the old cavalry. There were endless parties where the songs and the whiskey and the beer flowed freely. The cavalry had a well-deserved reputation as a hard-riding, hard-drinking outfit.

The favorite cavalry songs men had sung over the years celebrated that tradition. "Garry Owen" and "The Girl I Left Behind Me" tell of boozing, of gin and rye. "Fiddler's Green" describes the legendary place cavalrymen go after they die, located in that Valhalla "by a good old time canteen." There old troopers ride back to drink again, with friends at Fiddler's Green.

Drinking was celebrated in rhyme and story and ritualized in everyday life. An empty glass held on top of one's head was the signal for another drink. Drawing on the customs of fox hunting, one had a "heel tap," traditionally brought after a man was mounted up. The next drink was a "stirrup cup," and after that "one for the road." By then, one cavalryman recalled, "you were already under the table."

A man who didn't drink did not have much of a future in the cavalry, and Skinny Wainwright kept up with the best of them. He sang the old songs and told the old stories. One of his favorites was about the colonel who called in his officers to chide them about their overindulgence in liquor.

"Gentlemen," the officer said, "I don't mind an eye-opener in the morning. Everybody needs that. I can understand the need for a pick-me-up around ten-thirty and nobody's gonna hold a couple of drinks before lunch against you. I know you need something to keep you awake around mid-afternoon and of course you're entitled to a few drinks before dinner and a brandy or two afterwards. But, gentlemen, this constant sip, sip, sip all day long has got to stop!"

Skinny loved to startle outsiders with his description of a cavalryman's breakfast, "just a shot of straight whiskey and a cigarette." Another version was "cereal, the kind you drank," explaining to civilians, with a husky laugh, that beer was distilled from cereals such as barley.

A comrade of Wainwright's, who later served with him in the Philippines, captured something of this spirit in a story he wrote about Skinny arriving in heaven.

"'You were a pretty rough cavalryman,' the Lord God of Hosts says to him, 'and some of us here have a notion that the crown of a saint would look kind of funny on your head. What have you got to say for yourself, Jonathan Wainwright?'

"'I guess I did drink a little too much sometimes,' Skinny replied. 'But Your Honor, there is one question the answer to which I have always wanted to know. Begging your pardon, Sir, but if God didn't intend for us poor mortals to enjoy it, why did He permit such wonderful stuff as good Scotch and Bourbon to be made?'"

Yes, Wainwright had "jined" the cavalry and the times were good. Sometimes his body couldn't take the whiskey very well, though he had no trouble with beer, but he was in good company. The cavalry bred tough men who rode hell-bent-for-leather, and lived the way they rode.

He loved it.

In June of 1909 Wainwright's greatest wish was granted: a chance for combat. The guerrilla war in the Philippines was continuing, and so the First Cavalry was shipped across the Pacific to the sleepy Spanish town of Manila. Wainwright's unit was sent on to the island of Jolo to fight a hostile tribe of Moslems known as Moros. Vicious, fearless, masters of ambush, accurate with rifle or bolo, the Moros had a deservedly awesome reputation.

The governor-general of the Moro province, General John J. Pershing, had been trying to control them with a mixture of firmness and fairness, but the conflict was a rough, dirty war in which no American dared go out alone or unarmed. Shortly before Wainwright arrived, a Moro had attacked an American army captain, who emptied all six bullets of his revolver into the man. The wounds did not even slow the Filipino. He slashed the American with his knife and went on his way. An MP finally stopped him with his .45.

The situation was ideal for the mobility and the lightning raids of the cavalry, and it was very much like the wars fought against the Indians. Small patrols, led by a lieutenant, operated on their own for days or weeks. It was an exciting opportunity for young Wainwright, a chance to test his mettle against a determined enemy and to refine his considerable tactical and leadership abilities. He performed well. He fought bravely and commanded with imagination and vigor, earning high praise from his superiors and his men. The successful regiment sailed for home a year later, in February 1910.

The time between then and America's entry into World War I in 1917 was filled with personal and professional achievements for Wainwright. On the evening of Saturday, February 18, 1911, he married Adele Holley, whom he liked to call "Kitty," at the Post Chapel at Fort Douglas, Utah, where her father was stationed. The service was conducted by the dean of St. Mark's Cathedral in Salt Lake City.

Four months later, Skinny was asked to return to West Point to be an instructor in a subject that had not been his best—mathematics. It meant leaving his beloved cavalry, and that, Skinny quickly decided, was something he did not want to do. On June 11 he made his feelings known.

"I do not consider myself particularly well fitted for this duty, and that class of work is very distasteful to me. My entire interest is centered in Cavalry work, and I earnestly request that I be allowed to remain on Cavalry duty."

The superintendent of the military academy, Maj. Gen. Thomas H. Barry, agreed, but he felt that the young lieutenant needed a lesson in army manners.

"In respect of the request of Lt. Wainwright," he wrote, "it would seem well to remind him that he has been educated at the expense of his country and commissioned in its service to perform whatever duty may be assigned to him. We are all required to do duty and

work that at times may be distasteful, but the true soldier apprecia-
tive of his opportunities and obligations lends himself just as
cheerfully to doing that work as he does work of his own choice,
and, in my opinion, this young officer should shape his course
accordingly."

Wainwright remained in the cavalry and was never again asked to
teach at West Point.

The following year, on July 30, 1912, he was promoted to first
lieutenant, and on April 6, 1913, his son, Jonathan Mayhew
Wainwright V, was born. Skinny called the boy "Jack," the same
name he had chosen for his favorite horse.

The Wainwright family moved ten times in those seven years
before the war while Wainwright was stationed at posts in Idaho,
Vermont, Wyoming, Kansas, and California. One particularly
enjoyable post for Wainwright was Fort Yellowstone, Wyoming,
established in 1891 "to protect the park from vandalism, enforce
game laws, and guard natural wonders from despoilation." While
there, however, he suffered a fractured rib when he was accidentally kicked by a horse.

There was more schooling for Wainwright during these years. He
went to the Mounted Service School at Fort Riley, Kansas, on
September 25, 1912, but he didn't complete the course because, as a
classmate put it, "he broke one of those long skinny legs. We've
been expecting them both to break for fourteen years, but they're
doing pretty well with only one crack in all that time. He got it fixed,
but too late to get in all the fancy work." Wainwright made up the
basic course a few years later (1915-1916) and subsequently graduated from the Cavalry School's advanced course in June 1929.*

In the interim he was a member of the famed cavalry rifle team
and did exhibition duty with his unit, the "black horse" troop, at the
Panama-Pacific International Exposition Horse Show in 1915 in San
Francisco. He organized the First Cavalry's participation in the
competition and earned the appreciation of his squadron commander. "To your skill in handling men and horses, your tact in
dealing with official superiors and with Exposition authorities, to
your faithful attention to every detail, and the example of your own
splendid horsemanship are due more than to anything else the
creditable showing made by your regiment at which we are all
gratified. . . . in nearly two years of close association with you as

---

*The Mounted Service School became the Cavalry School in 1919.

your Captain and Major, you have been distinguished by an unvarying efficiency and attention to duty that indicates a fine future for you in your profession."

One rainy night in 1916 Wainwright rode his troop seventy miles in twenty-one hours over an unmapped road in pursuit of bandits in the Chiracahua Mountains of Arizona. His commanding officer called the action "a splendid example of leadership" and commended his good judgment.

This period was a prosperous one for those in civilian life, but not so for the military, where salaries were little above the pay during the Civil War. In addition, as happens whenever the country is not threatened by war, the army was held in disdain. Soldiers and officers were viewed with contempt, as incompetents who clung to secure jobs in the military because they could not make it in civilian life. Prejudice was openly displayed against army people and many public places posted signs reading "No Soldiers Admitted." These feelings spread so widely that Congress passed a law imposing fines on anyone found guilty of such actions.

To upgrade its image and efficiency, the army instituted tough new requirements for promotion and for continuance in the service. Men found to be lax in the conduct of their duties or who showed no potential for advancement were dismissed. Wainwright welcomed this tightening of standards. It cleared the service of a lot of deadwood and provided greater opportunities for those, like himself, who had outstanding ability. Under the new system of management, improved efficiency reports for officers were developed, to reflect more accurately a man's qualifications. Wainwright's reports were consistently superior and included such comments as "unusual zeal and devotion to duty . . . a young officer of unusual promise . . . the best officer of his grade known to me . . . high ideals and marked ability; of quiet unassuming manners and pleasing personality and temperament . . . the model of a smartly turned out cavalry officer . . . wrapped up in his profession and giving it all of his thought and time." In response to the question about the type of duty for which an officer was best suited in wartime, Wainwright's superiors wrote "command of troops." Shortly after the purge, on July 16, 1916, Wainwright's talents were recognized with a promotion to captain.

While Skinny was serving on border patrol duty in southern California in 1915 and 1916, he was keeping a sharp eye on Europe, which was now embroiled in the largest war the world had ever known. It was also more deadly than war had ever been. Huge armies were using modern weapons of technology—planes, tanks, poison gas, machine guns—and the fighting forces had become stalemated, unable to make the bold sweeping advances of the past. The combatants were underground, in dugouts and trenches, periodically going over the top to exchange thousands of lives for a few yards of ground.

Wainwright studied the bulletins from the front and tried to learn as much as he could about the new weapons and tactics, because he was convinced that America would soon be in the war. As a professional soldier, he expected to be a part of it. After all, that was why they had spent so many years in preparation, enduring the taunts of civilians, the budget cuts from Congress, and the slow promotions, while ignoring the enticements of the outside world. They would be ready when their country needed them.

America needed its professional soldiers the following year, when it suddenly found that the army was too small to engage in the war to which the government had committed itself. Overnight, hundreds of thousands of civilians had somehow to be transformed into soldiers. The officer corps had to be expanded almost twenty times, from 10,000 to 180,000.

Like most line officers, Wainwright longed for combat duty, but the army had other ideas for the young officer who had compiled such a distinguished record since entering West Point. In the year that it took the United States to prepare its enlarged army for combat in Europe, Wainwright served in a training and staff capacity. His first assignment was at Plattsburgh Barracks in New York, where he was adjutant of the First Officers' Training Corps. Almost as soon as he took the job as camp adjutant, fresh lettuce and fresh fruit showed up at the mess. In addition to his regular duties, Wainwright volunteered to give instruction on various aspects of horsemanship. His commanding officer wrote that "Captain Wainwright's lectures in these subjects were most carefully prepared and not only were they very instructive but they created an interest in horsemanship which could not have been attained except through his services."

At Plattsburgh and at several other such camps, civilians were turned into officers in less than three months of military discipline. Thousands of these "ninety-day wonders" were rushed through training and shipped overseas to lead the growing American army.

In August of 1917, newly promoted to major, Skinny Wainwright was sent to Camp Devens, Massachusetts, to serve on the General Staff of the Seventy-sixth Division. It was a signal honor, one of many that would mark his career in the coming decades. In February 1918 the division sailed for France, bringing him closer, he hoped, to his goal of a combat command. But for four months he found himself back in school, this time at the General Staff College established by the U.S. Army at Langres, France.

Only the best had been chosen for the General Staff College, and Wainwright was in good company. Others who attended were his friend from West Point, George Patton, along with Joe Stilwell, H. R. Bull (who would be Ike's operations officer in the next war), John S. Wood (who would command a division under Patton), and a number of others who would distinguish themselves in both world wars. The instructors were also outstanding and included George C. Marshall as well as British and French officers. Their job was to teach the younger men the complexities of staff work in a modern army.

It was a rigorous period of training. Classes began at 8:00 A.M., and the student-officers stayed at their desks until almost 5:00 P.M., with few breaks during the day. The instruction was so compressed and intense that the students collapsed on their beds every night, having pushed themselves into the early hours to finish their difficult assignments. There was so much to learn, so many aspects of contemporary warfare to master. It was no longer sufficient to know how to lead troops in combat. An officer now had to be able to administer, to organize, and to coordinate. This was a different kind of soldiering. Wainwright was preparing himself for the command of an entire army, with all of its attendant problems of logistics, communications, supplies, and the many other details with which a commander must be prepared to cope.

It wasn't combat, but it was rewarding, and Wainwright knew how valuable the training was for his career. He did well at the General Staff College and was given an immediate opportunity to put his new knowledge into practice when he was made assistant chief of staff of the famed Eighty-second Division. The division had served in defensive sectors in Toul and Pont-a-Mousson, and joined in the massive offensive drives at St. Mihiel and the Meuse-Argonne. It was known as the "all-American division" because it was composed of an assortment of southerners and foreign-born draftees from the big northern cities of the United States, and it had a reputation for being brawling and blasphemous. It got its baptism of fire at St. Mihiel as one of the sixteen divisions in the first American offensive of the war. The drive was successful, almost too easy, because the Germans had begun to withdraw the night before the attack. Nevertheless, it was costly—7,000 men were lost—but it provided training for the next and last major offensive of the war, the so-called "battle of a nightmare" at the Meuse-Argonne.

The attack at the Meuse-Argonne started off badly and one large unit of the Seventy-seventh Division—seven companies and two machine-gun sections—were cut off and surrounded behind German lines. All efforts to relieve this "lost battalion" failed, and other units—the First and Eighty-second Divisions—were ordered to attack the Germans east of the forest in hopes of relieving the pressure on the lost battalion. Wainwright's division commander had been on the job for only two days, and the problem he had been handed was complex. Within sixteen hours he would have to move two brigades a distance of eight miles over a road jammed with men and equipment of two other divisions. Once in position, in an area that he and his staff had never seen, they would have to attack.

The general assigned the planning to his staff. Working against time, Major Wainwright and the others devised a bold plan and drafted the attack order. The troops moved out at midnight on October 6, 1918, and continued their advance for two days, a yard at a time. One man in the outfit, Corp. Alvin York, would become a legend by singlehandedly breaking up a German battalion. Under pressure of the attack, the Germans finally withdrew. One hundred ninety-four of the 554-man battalion had been saved.

Skinny carried a legacy of the battle for the rest of his life, partial deafness in his left ear from being too close to an exploding shell.

A month later the war to end all wars came to a close, and American troops were clamoring to go home. By the following June, more than 2,700,000 soldiers had left Europe. Upon discharge, they were given a pair of shoes, a coat, a bonus of $60, and a helmet and gas mask as souvenirs.

Over a million men remained in Europe, however, and Wainwright, made a brevet lieutenant colonel on October 16, was one of them. Their duty was occupation, standing the watch on the Rhine. They were formed into the Third Army and stationed around Coblenz in Germany. Wainwright served as assistant chief of staff.

This was a satisfying period. He got wind of a plan to organize a ceremonial horse unit and he soon wangled the job of forming and commanding what became the Provisional Cavalry Squadron of the Third Army. The squadron's purpose was to add some pomp and pageantry to the occupying army's presence.

Skinny was able to pick not only the best of the officers and men available, but also the prize horses, including jumpers and polo ponies, from both American and captured German stock. He wanted hard riders and hard soldiers, intimating that he wanted hard drinkers too. This was to be a home for true cavalrymen.

It was also a sporting outfit, with lots of polo, jumping, riding to hounds, and an occasional review or parade, with the horses impeccably groomed, the brass trim gleaming. Wainwright also promoted other sports, particularly baseball. His team reached the championship playoffs, but the night before the final game, a rival outfit invited them to a party, hoping they would live up to their reputation as hard-drinking cavalrymen. They did, and at the game the next day they were clobbered.

As commanding officer, Skinny was also concerned with the education of his officers, and he decided that as long as they were in Germany they should all learn to speak German. He hired a professor and arranged formal classes, insisting that everyone attend and prepare for a written examination.

All the officers took the course seriously, concerned that their grades on the final examination would become part of their records. Therefore, the classes were well attended. Wainwright, however, kept finding excuses to miss them. Finally they all took the exam and the professor brought the results to Wainwright. And that was the last that was ever heard of the German class. Skinny never posted the marks or said any more about them.

These were great days in Coblenz, but they came to an end in October 1920, when Wainwright received orders to return to the United States.

He had served his country well during the war and had been honored for it. He had been a captain before the war; when it ended he was a lieutenant colonel. He wore with pride the Distinguished Service Medal, awarded to him with the following citation:

"For exceptionally meritorious and distinguished service as Assistant Chief of Staff, 82nd Division, First Assistant to Assistant Chief of Staff, G-3, Third Army, and later as Assistant Chief of Staff, G-3, American Forces in Germany. By his untiring energy, devotion to duty and exercise of intiative, he contributed in a large measure to the success attained by the commands with which he served."

Wainwright had also been given three Bronze Stars, the French Legion of Honor, and the Belgian Croix de Guerre.

But now it was 1920, and America was at peace again. It did not need its professional soldiers anymore. Nor did it want them. It was the same old story. There was an intense disenchantment with and opposition to war and to all things military. Pacifist organizations sprang up all over the country, each with a large and growing membership, and all arguing for the same thing—disarmament.

Soldiers were again the objects of scorn. The prewar contempt and prejudice reawakened. "No more war!" people shouted. And if there was to be no more war, then there certainly was no need for an army. Responding to this mood, the U.S. Congress emasculated the military.

Appropriations were reduced sharply and the officer corps was slashed from 15,000 to 12,000. Demotions in rank were the rule. Wainwright was reduced to his prewar rank of captain, as was his friend, Georgie Patton. Skinny was promoted to major a day later, on July 1, and spent nine years at that rank; Patton was a major for fourteen years. Demoralization swept through the armed forces and more than 2,500 officers who had fought in France resigned in bitterness.

These were dismal years for career military men. Prospects seemed worse for them than before the war because civilians were doing so well for themselves financially in the boom time of the roaring twenties. Those who stayed in the army seemed to be going nowhere, and the service was in danger of stagnating.

Brig. Gen. Paschal N. Strong, then an officer in the Corps of Engineers, described the army between the wars as a "Chocolate Soldier Army, a housekeeping Army. Its scattered garrisons were isolated on small posts, as much concerned with grass-cutting as with the arts of war."

It would have been understandable if Wainwright had become bored or idle, as many other officers did during those days. But he was saved from that by a series of challenging assignments over the next fifteen years, positions that indicated that his star was definitely on the rise. These were also tests for Skinny, once First Captain of Cadets, to see if he was truly fit to one day be a general. A prominent World War II general later echoed the judgment of Wainwright's superiors: Wainwright's "promotions and the type of duty assignments he received were recognition of outstanding ability," indicating that "he was considered in the potential General Officer group."

Major Wainwright's first trial came in 1921, a year after he returned from Europe. He was completing a tour as instructor at the Cavalry School at Fort Riley, Kansas, when he was ordered to Washington, D.C., to serve on the War Department's General Staff. For a man of the relatively young age of thirty-eight, Wainwright's assignment to the General Staff was an exceptional honor. This group of ninety-three officers served as the army's planning and operations unit. The position provided an immeasurable opportunity for a junior officer to see and be seen by the elite of the service, including the chief of staff. High-level command decisions were made by the General Staff, along with all long-range defensive plans.

One of the plans Wainwright was involved with related to the defense of the Philippines in the event of a war with Japan. The proposal developed was called War Plan Orange, that being the color code for Japan. Yellow had been the first choice, but it was changed out of concern that the Japanese would immediately suspect that it referred to them. The plan was predicated on the assumption that Japan would initiate hostilities with a surprise attack.

Once war began, the U.S. Army would go on the defensive in the Philippines. Manila, the capital city, would be abandoned and the American forces would withdraw into the Bataan peninsula of Luzon, where they would fight a delaying action. The forces on Corregidor, an island in Manila Bay two miles from the tip of Bataan, would be able to prevent Japanese ships from using Manila's harbor. Meanwhile, in this scenario, the powerful American naval fleet would steam out of Pearl Harbor to destroy the Japanese navy in a massive sea battle somewhere around Guam.

War Plan Orange required the army to hold out on Bataan and Corregidor for six months, at which time the garrison would be relieved. The same plan, with only minor modifications, was in effect twenty years later when the Japanese struck at Pearl Harbor, wiping out the fleet that was supposed to come to the aid of the army in the Philippines. At that time, Wainwright, who had helped to formulate the plan, would become a victim of it. But in 1921 he felt, as most army planners did, that the scheme was sound and that he was well qualified to be involved in its implementation. "I could do a good job when we have the Jap war," he told a friend. He wouldn't want to be the big chief, he added. He preferred to be the operational man. He would wind up being both.

Skinny worked on other plans to deal with potential enemies, contingencies designed to meet everything from an isolated skirmish to a war even larger than the one in which he had fought in France. His work on the General Staff was praised by his superiors at the end of his tour in 1923, and he was invited back for a second two-year hitch in 1925, spending the interim years with the Third Cavalry at Fort Myer.

From 1927 to 1934 Wainwright was selected for every army school of importance. These assignments were vital to his advancement. The work was always demanding. Skinny joked that he had "buckled down to studying for the next war."

Attendance at the Field Officers' Course at the Chemical Warfare School at Edgewood Arsenal, Maryland, and at the Advanced Course at the Cavalry School at Fort Riley, broadened his knowledge in specific branches of the army. The most prized schools, however, were the Command and General Staff School at Fort Leavenworth, Kansas, and the Army War College at Fort McNair in Washington, D.C.

The Command and General Staff School, known previously as the "school of the line," was a no-nonsense training program to prepare officers for higher command. The curriculum encompassed the planning of all aspects of hypothetical campaigns, the analyzing of Civil War battles, and the coping with problems of industrial mobilization of civilian industry in time of war. So important was attendance at this school that in 1928, two years before Wainwright was sent there, Congress passed legislation stipulating that no officer would be eligible for service on the General Staff if he had not graduated from the school at Fort Leavenworth.

Wainwright and his fellow students, including Harry Skerry, an engineering officer who would later serve him well on Bataan, worked hard at Leavenworth, but on weekends they "kicked up their heels" with riotous parties on Friday and Saturday nights. Skinny also tried to help his classmates with their study of Spanish, now part of the curriculum because President Hoover had warned of possible trouble with South American countries. In his zeal, Wainwright arranged for the post's radio station to broadcast the Spanish lessons and Spanish music. And before long all were heartily fed up with hearing so much of "La Paloma."

In the summer of 1933 Wainwright reached the pinnacle of his preparation for general officer rank when he was chosen to attend the prestigious Army War College. There, in the red-brick buildings of Fort McNair overlooking the Potomac River, he and his classmates—including Omar Bradley and Bill Halsey—worked diligently on a variety of problems ranging from the historical and contemporary to projections for the future. The files of the college show that he wrote on industrial mobilization plans for war, unit and individual training methods in World War I, developments in weapons and means of communications from the Napoleonic Wars to the present, studies of Gettysburg and of the German offensive on the Somme, and strategies for participating with allies of different nationalities in a future global war.

Two of his reports would later affect him personally—an intelligence estimate of the war potential of Japan and a study of the Orange plan for the defense of the Philippines, the same plan he had worked on eleven years earlier as a member of the General Staff. Before too long, Wainwright would be forced to implement it.

While Wainwright's professional life continued to be highly rewarding and stimulating, he suffered an immense disappointment in his personal life in the summer of 1933. His son was denied admission to West Point, having been judged "not qualified" on the basis of the competitive examinations. Friends have called it the greatest tragedy in Skinny's life. It appeared that the 100-year history of the Wainwright family's continuous service to the United States was at an end.* For Adele Wainwright the pain was even greater. She doted on her son; her friends say that this failure to be accepted at the military academy probably aggravated her own inability to deal with the great amount of drinking that characterized army life. It was a tremendous blow to them both, but life had to go on.

With his graduation from the war college in 1934, Wainwright's formal military education was complete. There were no more schools to attend. A comment made about George Patton when he graduated from the war college is equally appropriate for Wainwright. "If there was to be a next war," wrote Martin Blumenson, "[Patton] would be assured of a high and important place in it. Unless, of course, he failed somehow to measure up to the high standards he had set for himself or failed somehow to meet the high expectations of his superiors."

Promotions followed Wainwright's successful performances at the schools. On December 2, 1929, he had been made a lieutenant colonel; on August 1, 1935, a colonel. Remarkably, in that time of such slow promotions, he remained a colonel for only three years,

---

*J. M. Wainwright V entered the Merchant Marine as an officer and served with distinction in World War II, retiring later as a captain in the Naval Reserve. Skinny was very proud of his service.

receiving the single star of a brigadier general on November 1, 1938. General Malin Craig, then chief of staff and a former chief of cavalry, gave Wainwright his own stars to wear, a gesture of affection and respect from a senior to a junior officer.

So these too were good years for Wainwright professionally, the time between the wars. Life had not been spent only in the classroom. Wainwright was given the choicest assignments a cavalry-man could hope for, Director of Instruction and later Assistant Commandant of the Cavalry School at Fort Riley, and Commandant of the Third Cavalry at Fort Myer, Virginia. For a horseman there could be no finer duty.

At Fort Riley, Wainwright was concerned with the training of young cavalry officers, a task he approached very seriously. He knew everything there was to know about horses and the cavalry. "He was the greatest cavalryman ever," a friend from those days recalled. "He could do everything from shoe a horse to lead a division in battle." In quiet moments he would continue his study of military history. "Wainwright liked to sit in his big red leather chair," recalled a colleague, "reading the life of Robert E. Lee."

He wanted to make sure that the next generation of cavalry officers was as proficient as he was. He paid close attention to the curriculum and the daily instruction in everything from the care and training of a horse to tactics. But even more than that, he was concerned with the moral and physical development of his officers.

He prided himself on going on every hike and maneuver with his students, even though he was in his early fifties and they were in their twenties. He not only kept up with them, he surpassed them. He set a strong example to follow and kept himself in good physical condition.

After a typical day of hard riding over the windy Kansas plains, after they had had a bit of whiskey to warm the body and cheer the spirits, Wainwright would talk to his young officers seated around an open campfire. He tried to impress upon them what it meant to be an officer and a cavalryman. He stressed the need to live a simple, spartan life of dedication to duty and country, and the need to keep physically fit and ready for action at all times.

"When you young gentlemen get orders," Wainwright told them, "you should be able to move out at once. Just piss in the fire, call your dog, and get going."

Wainwright made a habit of expressing his appreciation to junior officers who performed their duties well. A former supply officer at Fort Riley, who was responsible for a mule-drawn wagon train, frequently supported the cavalry's outdoor training exercises. Wainwright never failed to thank him for his work and later tapped him for the advanced equitation class at the Cavalry School. "Wainwright looked out for young officers to better themselves," he recalled.

Of course, life was not all spartan dedication and hard work at Fort Riley. This was the cavalry, where the horse and its pageantry reigned supreme. General Strong and his wife Mary remember Fort Riley in the 1930s as "the number one cavalry post of the nation. It was said that if a horse entered your living room there, you offered it the best chair. I remember a bronze tablet at the entrance to the stables reading as follows: This area is sacred to the horses. Let no gasoline vehicle enter it except to save the life of a horse or its rider.

"Fort Riley was a paradise for anyone crazy about horses. Here the horse was truly enshrined. He dominated the conversation; he was the focal point of community thinking; he was, in fact, a way of life rather than a form of recreation. The post revolved around the horse shows, the weekly hunts—complete with hounds, master, whippers-in, et al., the schooling and training of mounts, the endurance rides, and the polo games."

The Cavalry School Hunt was conducted with all the panache and ceremony that could be found in the English countryside, as though Devonshire had been transplanted to dusty Kansas. As Master of the Hunt, Skinny Wainwright cut a dashing figure in his brilliant red wool coat with its gold collar and vest ornamented with gold C.S.H. buttons, white shirt and breeches, black velvet helmet, and black boots topped by a brown band. He carried a hunting horn in a leather case and held a black woven leather whip.

Never again would the army see such finery and ceremony. Never again would there exist such a breed of men. The last Chief of Cavalry, Maj. Gen. John K. Herr, wrote that jealousy arose among officers of other branches of the army "over the color and glamour attached to the cavalry, over the good times which the officers of that branch enjoyed in their sports at all the cavalry posts, and over the certain indefinable social prestige which the man on horseback, the cavalier, the *hidalgo,* the gentleman, had always had over the man on foot." It was a grand time to be in the cavalry, and it was the last time. The tank was noisily cresting the hill.

But while it lasted, there was no other life quite like it, and Skinny Wainwright would not have traded those days on bivouac or the polo field or riding to hounds for anything. Nowhere did life seem brighter than at fashionable Fort Myer, Virginia, where Wainwright served from July 1936 to December 1938, commanding the Third Cavalry, his last post before being put out to pasture.

Those who remember the army of the 1930s still talk about Fort Myer as a social post, a place where pomp and ceremony reigned. For excitement, drama, and color, no other military installation could match it. The several squadrons of the Third Cavalry stationed there were always in a state of spit and polish. They were constantly being called upon to provide escort for a funeral at the Arlington Cemetery next door, to parade before a visiting dignitary, or to put on a fancy full-dress drill for a group of congressmen and their wives.

Wainwright was happy at Fort Myer. He now had three horses of his own, including two prize jumpers, and he could ride whenever he desired, outdoors or in the huge riding hall.

Each winter there was a ten-week series of Friday afternoon drills and mounted spectacles known as the "Society Circus," in which Custer's Last Stand or the Charge of the Light Brigade or some other equestrian extravaganza would be reenacted. There were chariot races in which toga-clad cavalrymen, with laurel wreaths on their heads, raced around the riding hall with artillery caissons.

Every conceivable activity involving horses was shown at the Society Circus. One group dressed as Hungarian Hussars did the jumping, another dressed as Cossacks played mounted basketball. There were rodeos and gymnastics featuring stunts such as three men performing on a single galloping horse. There were tandem rides and waltzes on horseback. The lovely young debutantes of Washington society vied to participate. Each show was brought to a rousing finish by a race of six-horse teams pulling three-inch field guns around the hall at full gallop. It never failed to bring the audience to its feet.

The Society Circus was a major event in the Washington social season, and the hall was always filled with the social, political, and military elite of the country. President Roosevelt attended as often as he could; he and Mrs. Roosevelt loved the shows. She often came to Fort Myer to ride. After the horse shows the partying would begin, often lasting until the early hours of Saturday morning.

On Saturday afternoons, the officers from Fort Myer would join the fox hunts of fashionable Middleburg, Virginia, or the Potomac or Green Spring Valley hunts in Maryland. Saturday nights were for more parties, and on Sunday afternoons the officers took to the polo fields. Old-timers recall these days with great affection; today's army seems dull and tame to them by comparison.

One drawback to life at Fort Myer was that it was an expensive place to be stationed. One could not support such a lifestyle on the army pay of the 1930s, regardless of rank. Dress uniforms were required; Fort Myer was the only post in the country that demanded blue mess jackets. There were horses to maintain, proper attire for the hunts, uniforms for polo, and accessories of the highest quality. Boots were ordered from Peale of London, handmade to measurements filed with the company upon graduation from West Point. The boots cost $100 a pair and the boot trees were an extra $20. One of Wainwright's squadron leaders at Fort Myer did not get out of debt to Peale until after World War II.

Another disadvantage of Fort Myer was that the officers, particularly the commandant, were always visible to the highest powers of the army. Tommy Moffitt, a legendary first sergeant there, liked to say that "What you do at Myer stands out like a sore thumb." The chief of staff lived on the post and high-ranking officers from the War Department were always around, whether for an afternoon canter on their favorite horse or for drinks and dinner at the officers' club. The post was the showplace of the army, and officers were thoroughly screened before assignment there and were constantly under scrutiny. One had to ride well and to know how to behave properly at a fox hunt, a parade, and a dinner party. Certain codes of decorum and behavior were expected. An old army saying summed it up: "A man should be able to tell a good story, but he should not be a notorious braggart; a man should be able to drink a lot, but he should not be an alcoholic." At other posts more remote from Washington, faults and peccadilloes could be hidden from the War Department, but not at Fort Myer. Everything the commandant did or was rumored to have done became known very quickly. The Potomac River that separates Washington from Virginia, the War Department from the post, is not very wide.

Wainwright was drinking more heavily at Fort Myer than he had at earlier posts, but people who knew him then say he was not an alcoholic. He was not addicted to liquor, he didn't crave it, hide it in secret places, or drink on the sly. He often went for days without a drink and suffered no ill effects. "He just liked to drink," an old friend said. "If you offered it, he took it." His executive officer at Fort Myer watched over him carefully, "to make sure he didn't get tight at the wrong time or place."

There was a complicating factor, however, that may have exaggerated the stories about his drinking. A fall from a horse had caused a permanent injury to his left knee, and as he got older the joint pained him and caused him to favor it. He walked with a peculiar gait, limping and swaying, and sometimes he seemed to list to one side even when standing still. Those who didn't know about the injury and who saw him at a party, weaving about after only a few drinks, tended to assume that he had consumed more than was the case. Although Skinny liked to drink and took it whenever it was offered, his unfortunate walk only fed the gossip already reaching the War Department. "He can't hold his liquor," it was whispered. That much was true.

At the same time, forces of change were sweeping through the War Department, trying to fashion a modern army to deal with the menace of Adolf Hitler. On October 16, 1938, the man destined to mold the new army was appointed to a powerful position, deputy chief of staff. His name was George C. Marshall and he wasted no time initiating reforms he thought were required. His decisions, though necessary, were to end the careers of many officers and send others skyrocketing to fame.

Marshall's first criterion for success in the new army was youth. He was adamant on this point. No major commands were to be given to anyone over the age of fifty. Wainwright, already fifty-five, was declared too old for service in the army that would fight the second major war of the century. One of the few exceptions Marshall made was for Patton. He was fifty-three but he possessed something that Wainwright and most of the officer corps lacked: experience with the battle tank, which Marshall believed would be a crucial weapon in the coming war.

Wainwright was too wedded to the horse cavalry. It was, as far as Marshall was concerned, an outmoded branch that had no place in contemporary warfare. He had the rolls cleared of the older cavalry officers, and the most glamorous and colorful branch of the army faced extinction.

The chief of staff whom Marshall was slated to replace was Malin Craig, a cavalryman and close friend of Wainwright's. Craig got Skinny his star, but since he was due to retire soon he could do little else to protect Wainwright and his other friends in the doomed cavalry. Wainwright would be given one final tour of duty, in recognition of his past service. Orders were cut transferring him out of Fort Myer, so that Marshall could have Patton near him in Washington.

Skinny left Fort Myer in December 1938. His departure was much regretted by his officers and men. They held the customary formal parade to mark his leaving. He returned to his house for the

last time, and when he came out, he saw something that made him
realize how much the men of the Third Cavalry cared for him. He
stood on the front porch of his large red-brick house while the
entire garrison, mounted, still in dress uniforms, lined both sides of
the road from his quarters to the main gate of the post. Waiting to
escort him were four scout cars under the command of Capt. T. J.
H. "Trap" Trapnell, the former West Point football hero who was
one of Skinny's favorite junior officers.

The scout cars escorted Wainwright off the post and halfway
across Memorial Bridge. They stopped and Wainwright got out of
his car to bid farewell to Captain Trapnell and his men. In three
years' time, Wainwright would award Trap the Distinguished
Service Cross for his heroic action on another bridge.

Wainwright's new post at Fort Clark, Texas, where he was
assigned as commandant of the First Cavalry Brigade, was one of
the most isolated army posts in the country. At the head of Las
Moras Creek, the fort was opposite the town of Bracketville, which
had a population of less than 2,000. The next town was Eagle Pass,
even smaller than Bracketville, and that was forty-four miles away.
San Antonio was 143 miles distant, a major trip. The area was hot,
dry, and flat, filled with cactus, sheep, goats, and cattle.

Its very isolation created a unique social life on the post. The
officers and men had to be self-sufficient, to look to their own
amusement and entertainment. They formed a congenial group,
really one big family, with the commanding general and his wife as
"patriarch and matriarch."

Fort Clark was considered a good duty station for cavalry officers.
The opportunities for riding, mounted sports, and hunting and
fishing were ample. With a commander like Skinny, the post ran
smoothly and efficiently. He allowed his officers considerable
latitude in carrying out their assignments, and he always supported
them when outsiders were involved. If they did their job well, his
officers and men knew that he would look after their best interests.

He was always generous with praise for those who performed
well, and he was quick to recognize promise in his men. A second
lieutenant, fresh from West Point and then stationed at Fort Sam
Houston in San Antonio, was assigned to transport Wainwright's
horses and personnel by truck for large-scale maneuvers. Wainwright was impressed with the young officer's ability to get the task
completed quickly and smoothly. The man's name was Joseph L.
Chabot. When the job was done, Skinny called him over.

"Thank you, young man," he said. "I appreciate your moving us so efficiently." Later Wainwright sent a letter of commendation to Chabot's commanding officer.

In the Philippines Wainwright would meet Joe Chabot again, and would select him for his staff.

Every afternoon at Fort Clark the officers would meet at the club for "beer call," an occasion looked forward to by all. While they drank their cold beer, Wainwright and the other old-timers would tell stories of cavalry life. He loved to lead the conversation and he reveled in the camaraderie that bound the group together. He created an easy-going and relaxed atmosphere for the post, while maintaining a high standard of training and readiness.

Much of the time at Fort Clark was spent in the field, riding all day and sleeping out under the stars at night, free from paperwork and routine administrative chores. As at Fort Riley, Skinny stressed the need for a spartan life and set the example of physical conditioning by always leading his men on the hard rides and exercises. In the evenings he enjoyed the hours around the campfire, making small talk with his boys, singing old cavalry songs, and petting his dog, a Labrador retriever that followed him everywhere. (Mrs. Wainwright had named the dog Miss Seal of Featherstone.) The men got a kick out of watching the rawboned general doff his campaign hat, fill it with water, and place it gently on the ground for the dog to drink from.

Wainwright liked being a general. He delighted in the rank and the perks that went with it. On his first trip into the desert at Fort Clark his men set up his special snake-proof and varmint-proof tent, his personal washstand, and a "one-holer" in a shady spot. Wainwright walked all around the accommodations and grinned.

"If I knew generals were taken care of like this," he said, "I would have been a general a long time ago."

Another perk of being a general was having an aide. Skinny had brought with him from Fort Myer Capt. John Ramsey Pugh, who had all the qualifications of a good general's senior aide. "Social graces, wealth, and arrogance," his colleagues said. Pugh had served as a White House aide and had accompanied Mrs. Roosevelt on her morning horseback rides. Like Wainwright, Pugh was a baseball fan. His wife, the former Louise Myers, was an excellent horsewoman, and Wainwright admired her riding skills. Also with Wainwright at Fort Clark was a tall, lean Texan, Sgt. Hubert "Tex" Carroll, who would serve the general faithfully until his retirement from the army.

The days at Fort Clark passed pleasantly. Wainwright liked the outdoor life but he realized that it was a dead end. His career would close there. At his age there would be no more assignments, he thought.

Two years later, Maj. Gen. J. M. Wainwright was being given another chance. On October 31, 1940, the U.S.A.T. *Grant* passed between the tip of Bataan and the oddly shaped island of Corregidor, heading for the Philippine port of Manila. Skinny was back in harness, back where he had fought his first war thirty-one years before, back where his father had died, and back under the command of Douglas MacArthur, as he had been at West Point. He was facing the greatest challenge of his career. If he proved himself here, he knew he could be in line for bigger commands in the war that was sure to come. Wainwright's future looked promising again.

CHAPTER 3
"Days of Empire"

Life was good in Manila in 1940, so good that there was a waiting list for duty there. It was like having a two-year vacation with pay in a tropical playground. There were servants for everyone. A captain and his wife could hire a staff of four, and even a private, on his pay of $21 a month, could employ a Filipino to polish his boots and brass for the month for $1.50.

When Col. Dwight Eisenhower came back to the States in 1939 after a tour in Manila, a general asked him, "Have you learned to tie your own shoes again?" These were lazy, luxurious, and pampered days, and the white man lived like royalty, served well by his native subjects. These were truly the days of empire. The work hours were short, the duty easy, and there was little more to worry about than whether a rain shower would interrupt one's afternoon golf game.

Skinny Wainwright arrived during the closing months of America's occupation of the Philippines and was immediately swept into its enticing orbit. The partying that was so much a part of army life everywhere started as soon as the U.S.A.T. *Grant* docked at Manila's Pier Seven. The arrival of the *Grant* was always a social event. The ship was the primary contact with home, a distant 7,000 miles away, and its coming meant reunions with countrymen and an infusion of new blood for the tightly knit American community. It was cause for celebration, a holiday for all. Americans came from throughout the islands, even from southernmost Mindanao, to meet the passengers.

An army band was on the pier as the ship tied up and hundreds of people gathered to wave and shout at those lining the rail. General Wainwright, his wife Adele, and Mrs. Holley were the first to disembark, and they were engulfed by a swarm of old friends from other days and other posts. After the official greetings, they were whisked to their quarters at Fort McKinley, twenty miles south of Manila, where they barely had time to unpack their hand luggage before getting ready for their first party.

To entertain the general on his first night in the islands was an honor coveted by more than a score of cronies and junior officers. The invitations had been sent two weeks before in letters delivered to Guam, the ship's last port of call before Manila. Skinny leafed through the mail waiting for him at Agana, the tiny island's capital, and decided to accept the invitation from an officer in the Corps of Engineers and his wife, Lt. Col. and Mrs. Harry Skerry. Skerry had been a classmate of Wainwright's at the Command and General Staff School, and he and Margaret were delighted to be chosen.

The party at the Skerrys' house was a huge success, and the general and his lady were the center of attention. With close companions around him, Wainwright was relaxed and cheerful. He danced with all the ladies and lived up to his reputation as a good dancer. Those long legs moved him and his partners smoothly across the floor. He told amusing stories and joined in the spirited reminiscences that always marked such gatherings.

As the evening wore on and the drinking became heavier, Wainwright started to sing while someone pounded away on an old upright piano. A young lieutenant present, just six months out of West Point and on his first tour of duty, joined the fifty-seven-year-old general, thirty-four years out of West Point, in harmony. Wainwright was delighted.

"Isn't this something?" he said. "Two West Pointers almost forty years apart!"

Some sensitive ears might have shuddered at the general's singing, because he did not have a very good voice, but it was hard not to be affected by his enthusiasm. He thoroughly enjoyed his welcome to the Philippines that night.

Over the next days and weeks, Wainwright reacquainted himself with the country he had last seen in 1909. It had changed greatly in thirty-one years and he found little that was familiar. Then, most of the Filipinos had been hostile to the American conquerors or afraid of them. The rebellion had not yet been crushed, and the Americans were forced to live in armed camps.

By 1940 all that had changed. Although the United States was an imperialist power in the Philippines, it had been a benevolent one. Indeed, plans were already being formulated to return the islands to the Filipino people. Under a series of competent American governors, schools, roads, a sanitation system, and all the other accouterments of modern life had been provided, and the native population had been granted an ever-increasing role in self-government.

In 1934 the Tydings-McDuffie Act, which would grant independence to the islands in 1946, was passed by the U.S. and Philippine congresses. The act provided for the election of the first president of the Philippines, Manuel Quezon. Economically, politically, and socially, the Filipino people had prospered under American rule.

Nowhere was the progress more visible than in Manila, the showplace that served as the nation's capital. It was vastly different from when Wainwright had last seen it. Now a cosmopolitan city, its pleasures and beauty added to the delight of the Americans who were fortunate enough to be stationed nearby.

Manila was a major, bustling port, filled with ships from all over the world bringing their exotic cargoes to the shops of the city. One could find an unlimited variety of merchandise at prices so low that it was a shoppers' paradise, even for the poorly paid American soldiers.

The city was a curious and thrilling blend of the old and the new, of the East and the West. There were modern skyscrapers and wide boulevards crowded with automobiles, cheek by jowl with Filipino tribesmen in native dress and farmers with ox-drawn carts. There was even an exotic smell to the place, at once refreshing and nauseating, described as "a pungent mixture of jasmine, burning incense, garbage, and sewage."

A young army sergeant from New England, Walt Odlin, who would later serve as an orderly to the American generals imprisoned with Wainwright, detailed the excitement of the city in his diary.

"The old Walled City of portals, bastions, battlements, of balconies of exquisitely wrought iron overhanging narrow streets lined with unique shops, bazaars, saloons, and thronged with vari-costumed people from every corner of Asia. The pony-drawn cabs called calesas and caromatas; the Escolta, the combination Broadway and Fifth Avenue of Manila; the busy night-life of the town, the taxi-dancers at La Paloma, the fine restaurants; the band concerts in a park-way called the Luneta where Spanish senoritas promenaded with their duennas and beautiful Eurasian and Filipina girls strolled with their beaux. After the concerts' end the crowd drifted like white clouds over the dark lawn."

Despite its Spanish and Oriental flavor, Manila was infinitely an American city, and the military officers and their wives felt very much at home. They could buy nearly anything that had been available in the states, from Evinrude outboard motors, Harley Davidson motorcycles, Bell and Howell cameras, McGregor or Manhattan shirts, and Gruen wristwatches to Chiclets, Seven-Up, Nestlés chocolates, Mennen aftershave, and Camel cigarettes. They could shop in modern department stores geared to American tastes or through the Sears and Roebuck mail-order catalogue.

The latest American movies were at theaters throughout the city—*I Wanted Wings* with Ray Milland, *Blood and Sand* with Tyrone Power, *Meet John Doe* starring Gary Cooper, *In the Navy* featuring Abbott and Costello, and Orson Welles's *Citizen Kane.*

For the steak-loving Americans, there was an ample supply of excellent beef shipped frozen from Australia. At seventeen cents a pound, every officer's wife could afford it. Only fresh milk was in short supply. Every three months, when a ship from the U.S. arrived, it carried fresh milk in a refrigerated container. By the time it reached the officers' club, the contents had turned to pure rich buttermilk, a delicacy that sold for a dollar a glass. Then it was back to powdered milk again until the transport returned.

Manila was an idyllic setting—the architecture, the flowers, the friendly people, the glorious sunsets over Manila Bay and the South China Sea beyond. There was only one disadvantage: the climate. Only fourteen degrees above the equator, Manila was steamy and humid most of the year. Between July and October more than 150 inches of rain fell, stalling cars, washing away roads, and turning metal to rust in a day. Inside Wainwright's quarters at Fort McKinley the walls became so laden with moisture that electrical short-circuits were common. Shoes and other leather goods mildewed unless kept in a closet with a strong light always burning. Bed linens and clothing seemed never to dry out.

Skinny remembered from his last duty in the Philippines how

enervating the constant heat and humidity were. He saw its effects on newcomers, some of whom could not adapt and had to be sent home. "Men gasped for air during the hot season. Tempers frayed easily and troops lost weight. The sick-call rate rose sharply. Suicides began to occur, and commanders sought to identify persons developing mental and psychological aberrations."

Many Americans developed skin infections, particularly impetigo, and a variety of fungus conditions. And some, like Wainwright's father at the turn of the century, caught tropical diseases such as yaws, dengue fever, and malaria. Many died from them. The rate of hospital admissions among Americans in the Philippines was much higher than at any stateside post. Because of these difficult conditions, a tour of duty was limited to two years.

Partly because of the weather, but more because few people thought war would come to the Philippines any time soon, no one in the army worked very hard during the winter of 1940–41. General Wainwright often saw General MacArthur, who was then field marshal of the Philippine army, but their talk was not of war. Indeed, the issue of war with Japan rarely arose, and the contacts between the two men were largely social.

The good life of these days of empire had several more months to run before the threat of war ended them abruptly and for all time. During those comfortable and carefree times, the Wainwrights passed their days in the company of other Americans who were also living in a fading dream.

Fort McKinley was the most luxurious post in all the islands, a beautiful sprawling camp located in the hills above Lake Taal. The huge well-tended parade ground was its center, and ringing it on one side were the officers' quarters—roomy two-story houses with hibiscus and bougainvillea lining the walls.

The barracks were huge two-story buildings with steep overhanging roofs. There were no windows and the walls were low. The broad overhanging shutters allowed air to circulate freely and kept out the rain. Wainwright frequently visited the barracks and the nearby hospital to inspect the conditions of his troops.

Far enough away so as not to disturb the tranquility of the post were drill grounds and a rifle range. There was not much firing practice on the range. Bullets were expensive and the budget for such things was terribly low.

Military training was not something to get excited about during those months in 1940–41. It was too hot for much exertion of any

kind during the daytime. And since there was so little money for
training and no likelihood of war anyway, it was not deemed a
worthwhile way to pass one's time. Colonel Skerry of the Engineers
made himself unpopular when he tried to carry out training
exercises for his men on the golf course.

Anyway, there were comparatively few troops stationed at Fort
McKinley. Wainwright's Philippine Division was the largest American army unit in the islands, but it was not up to strength in 1940.
When Skinny took command, it contained about 7,500 men, most
of whom were Philippine Scouts. These scouts, with their high
standards of efficiency and toughness and their high morale, would
serve valiantly with the American army in the war that was to come.

The Philippine Division, though headquartered at McKinley, was
scattered in camps throughout Luzon, and so there had been few
opportunities for training as a unit. The largest outfit in the division
was the Thirty-first Infantry Regiment, the only army unit in the
Philippines composed entirely of Americans. The Thirty-first was
sometimes called the Thirsty-first because its men were known to
relish their liquor. The regiment had been organized in Manila
during World War I. Except for brief service in Siberia in 1920 and
in Shanghai in 1932, it had always been stationed in the Philippine
Islands. Further, it was the only American army unit that had never
been stationed in the United States. In 1940 it was based in Manila,
twenty miles from Fort McKinley.

There were two other infantry regiments in Wainwright's Philippine Division, the Forty-fifth and the Fifty-seventh, along with two
battalions of field artillery and the usual engineer, ordnance,
military police, medical, and quartermaster units. The quartermaster troops were in Manila, some of the infantry on Bataan, and most
of the rest of the division, including the artillery, at Fort Stotsenburg, fifty miles north of Manila. At Fort McKinley itself, where
Wainwright had his command post, there were hospital and medical
personnel, MPs, engineers, and chemical warfare troops. Therefore, the American complement at the post was quite small.

Wainwright made it his business to see and be seen by all the units
in his command, no matter where they were located. By this action
he quickly became a popular and respected division commander.
One of his staff at McKinley, Maj. LeGrande A. "Pick" Diller, said
that "Wainwright ran the post so smoothly that you weren't
conscious of being commanded. He did an excellent job. Everything

was run on a common sense basis."* As always, Wainwright was easy to approach and to get to know, informal, and very much one of the boys.

Other troops were stationed in the Philippines during that winter of 1940, but not many. The largest contingent was on Corregidor Island, two miles off the tip of Bataan peninsula, a short trip by boat through shark-infested waters. Some 6,000 men were there, manning the coast artillery and antiaircraft weapons. Their training was also limited by lack of funds. What little ammunition and targets existed were rationed. The antiaircraft units had enough gasoline to run their generators—which were essential for firing—only one hour a week. Most of the training consisted of dummy runs and make-believe firing at simulated targets.

Wainwright's favorite unit in the Philippines was the Twenty-sixth Cavalry Regiment, the only American horse cavalry unit to fight in the war. Skinny had a number of old friends in the Twenty-sixth Cavalry, including its commanding officer, the colorful Brooklyn-born Clinton A. Pierce. Wainwright and Pierce got together many times to talk about the old days when cavalry meant horses, not those noisy, smelly tanks.

The enlisted men of the Twenty-sixth Cavalry Regiment were Philippine Scouts; the officers were Americans. Like all the other units at the time, it was under strength, having a complement of 575 men in 1940, but it was one of the best-trained units in the army. Later, under Wainwright's command, these obsolete cavalrymen would prove to be the toughest outfit in the islands. Without their courage, the retreat into Bataan would have become a fiasco, and thousands of lives would have been lost.

One troop of the Twenty-sixth, F Troop, was stationed at Nichols Field, an Army Air Corps base south of Manila a few miles from Fort McKinley. In command was T.J.H. Trapnell, a favorite of Wainwright's from Fort Myer. They played polo together at Nichols Field, and when Wainwright ran maneuvers on the reservation between Nichols and Fort McKinley, he would assign Trap's troop of cavalry as the aggressor.

When Wainwright first spied Trap, shortly after his arrival in the

---

*Diller served as press relations officer to General MacArthur throughout the war.

Philippines, his greeting was, "Well, Trap, you walk into any more closets lately?"

The Old Man never let the young, athletic officer forget the incident that had taken place following a dinner party Wainwright, as commanding officer, had given at Fort Myer. Captain Trapnell had had a little too much to drink, but was doing his best not to show it. Standing stiff and ramrod straight, he bade his thanks to Colonel and Mrs. Wainwright in their foyer, pivoted smartly, opened the door, and marched straight into the coat closet.

Skinny loved to tell the story, with a hearty laugh and a grin of admiration.

Wainwright conducted as much training for his men as funds allowed, but there was no money for large-scale war games and maneuvers. He did what he could, stressing individual and small unit tactical exercises.

Every morning, two enlisted aides arrived at Wainwright's quarters with his three horses, beautiful bays, each about eighteen hands high, and he would join them for a ride around the parade ground. After they had made the circuit a number of times, Pvt. Richard Gordon, who had watched Wainwright's two-star pennant being hoisted on the U.S.A.T. *Grant,* would take the horses for exercise.

Skinny would return to his quarters for breakfast. While he was on his last cup of coffee, his junior aide arrived. He was Thomas Dooley, a likeable young officer from the Twenty-sixth Cavalry who had impressed Wainwright on their few meetings.

The general greeted Tom, got up from the table, and lit his first cigar of the day. He carried it in his right hand as a bit of devilment. He liked to see the consternation on the faces of officers and enlisted men when he returned their salutes with his left hand. It was a practice he kept up throughout his days on Bataan and Corregidor, and many a second lieutenant was flustered by it. If Wainwright didn't have a cigar with him, he carried his cane in his right hand.

Wainwright strode out the front door of his quarters to his waiting car, a 1936 off-green Packard, insisting that Dooley sit on his right side, to favor his good ear. This put young Tom in the place reserved for senior officers. Whenever anyone approached the big car to report to Wainwright, he would find the captain where the two-star general was supposed to be.

The workday began at 7:00 A.M. and ended at noon for both officers and enlisted men. The afternoon sun was too hot for continued work. Lunch was "soupsandwich," as the Chinese cooks called it, followed by exercise for the polo ponies and the traditional afternoon nap. Later activities included polo practice and games, riding, tennis, and swimming. Fort McKinley even had a private airport where army personnel could rent planes.

The Fort McKinley golf course in the center of the post was well used even in the midday sun. The links were within walking distance of Wainwright's quarters and he occasionally played, although he was not very good at the game. One afternoon he and Adele teamed up with Dorothy Brougher, the wife of Col. William Brougher, and Margaret Skerry, the wife of Col. Harry Skerry. Skinny let the three ladies tee off, and then he took his turn. He swung at the ball and missed. He swung again, and a third time, missing the ball on each stroke. As his anger mounted, his language got more colorful, and he never played another game with the ladies.

At 5:00 in the afternoon the cocktail or "calling" hour began, lasting until 7:00. Scotch was the favorite beverage. There was little bourbon available, but gin and rum were plentiful. A favorite pick-me-up, especially after a strenuous game of golf, was the rum-gum-and-lime, a concoction of rum, lime juice, and a simple sugar syrup.

The calling hour was an informal time and the conversation, drink, and laughter flowed freely. These were happy times to relax among good friends. Skinny added to the conviviality wherever he went. Col. Wibb Cooper, Wainwright's chief medical officer, and his wife remember that Wainwright sometimes arrived "well stocked up."

Skinny's drinking was much more controlled during the prewar days in Manila than it had been at Fort Myer. He limited himself to evenings and weekends and never indulged during duty hours, not even when the war drew nearer and duty hours extended well into the evening. His job as division commander was paramount, and he would not permit drinking to interfere with his duty.

Although hard liquor was definitely off limits during the workday, beer was not. But Wainwright had never had any difficulty handling beer. One of his first acts at McKinley was to "persuade" the PX sergeant to open an hour earlier so the commanding officer could have a cold beer at 10:00 A.M. instead of 11:00.

After the calling hour and dinner, it was time for the parties. And there were many of them. Post parties, regimental parties, cavalry parties, artillery parties, and on and on. Each year the Engineers held a Philippine party at which everyone wore native clothes. The parties were held in the officers' club on the post or at the Army-Navy club in downtown Manila overlooking the bay. These were gala events, with live bands, dress blues, yards and yards of taffeta, and a great deal of booze. Some of the bachelor officers ended the evenings on "drunkard's row," a long row of cots on the second-floor verandah of the club.

These were golden days, these days of empire in the winter of 1940–41, days in which the poorly paid professional army lived a life of ease, luxury, glamor, and fun. There may have been no other time or place quite like it, and there will never be again. It came to an abrupt end in the spring of 1941. Suddenly in Washington and in Manila the threat of war with Japan loomed, and the gay care-free days were over. Wainwright wrote that "the sparkle went out of Manila in the spring of 1941. War was coming and we all knew it."

The news was bad everywhere. In Europe Hitler was continuing his conquests. American attempts to halt Japanese aggression against China had met with no success. Despite economic restrictions against Japan, or perhaps because of them, the Japanese increased their pressure on the French and Dutch colonies in Asia.

To the War Department in Washington, the garrison in the Philippines seemed more vulnerable than at any time since the United States had taken possession of the territory over four decades before. Their weak position was underscored by decisions made in Washington in early 1941, policies that would certainly doom the Philippines in the event of war with Japan.

At a series of secret conferences between British and American military leaders held in Washington in January and February of 1941, a joint war plan called ABC-1 was adopted. It confirmed officially what had already been agreed upon privately as the basic American position: In the event of a war against both Germany and Japan, the United States and Great Britain would concentrate on the defeat of Germany while maintaining only a defensive posture in the Pacific area. The European front would have priority for money, men, and materiel.

At the same time, military thinking with regard to the old War Plan Orange, known as WPO-3, first formulated when Wainwright served on the General Staff in 1922, had changed. Although the plan to relieve the Philippine garrison within six months after the outbreak of war remained on the books, unofficially the idea had been quietly discarded. Army and navy planners estimated that if

Japan started a war, it would take at least two years before sufficient reinforcements could reach the islands, although they knew that the garrison could hold out no longer than six months. Thus, nearly a year before the war began with the Japanese attack on Pearl Harbor, the Philippine Islands had been written off, declared indefensible, and the American and Filipino troops had been condemned to death or imprisonment, caught in a hopeless situation.

The War Department faced a problem with this shift in policy. There were humanitarian, if not public relations, aspects to consider. It was one thing to declare professional soldiers to be expendable in wartime, but quite another for wives and children to be placed in that category. The dependents would have to be evacuated from the Philippines.

This news came as a shock to Wainwright and the other commanders. It meant that the threat of war was more serious and immediate than anyone there had suspected. The evacuation orders caused great emotional difficulties for the men and their wives. Separation in the peacetime army was rare, and, understandably, most of the wives were reluctant to leave. When would they see their husbands again? For the lucky ones like Adele Wainwright, whose husband would survive, it would be more than four years before they would be reunited.

There was much grumbling about the orders, especially about the fact that Mrs. MacArthur was being allowed to stay, but army wives are soldiers too. So they set about the task of packing and making ready.* This was the first time in U.S. Army history that such a large-scale evacuation had been necessary, and for awhile the authorities did not know how to go about it. At first they considered a seniority system, based on the length of time a wife had been in the islands. Those who had been there the longest would leave first. But they settled on a policy of sending the families home on the basis of where they were going in the states. Dependents who lived east of the Mississippi River were scheduled to depart for New York on May 5, 1941, aboard the U.S.S. *Republic;* those who would settle in the west would be sent to San Francisco on May 12, on the U.S.S. *Washington.*

---

*Furniture and personal effects were crated in native Philippine mahogany. Years later, the lumber used to ship the Wainwrights' things home was turned into a handsome bookcase for the library in Skaneateles, New York, Mrs. Wainwright's home town. Wainwright's name and shipping address, branded in the wood in 1942, are still visible.

Adele Wainwright and her mother left a month before the other wives. Skinny was very concerned about the imminence of the Japanese threat and was not about to take chances with his wife's safety. When Margaret Skerry asked him why Adele was leaving so soon, he replied, cryptically, "She doesn't want to live off rice." As he said goodbye to Adele, his beloved "Kitty," on their first real separation in thirty years of marriage, he told her, "If you're in San Francisco the first day of June I'll be much relieved."

There were grand though poignant parties to bid godspeed to the wives. They were called *despedidas,* the Spanish word for farewell. Everyone tried to be gay, to pretend that the separations would be short, but no one truly believed it and there were more tears than laughter.

When the last ship left on May 12, the men lined Manila's Pier Seven to watch as their loved ones passed out of view beyond the forbidding rock of Corregidor Island. Sharpening their sadness and loneliness was the feeling that a way of life had ended and that they were being left to face an uncertain future. The men of the Philippines were in for a greater ordeal than any of them could have imagined.

One of the men who watched the wives leave was Col. William Brougher, who foresaw, perhaps more clearly than anyone else, what the departure of the wives signified. He wrote a poem about it, ending with these prophetic verses.

> This place is doomed. Termites are boring in;
> A rift appears! I shall no longer stay,
> For I am old and have no single strength
> To pit against the thing that's sure to come. . . .
> A glorious buenvenida may be held
> One glad uncertain day, but some of us
> Who love this grand old Club will not be here.
> The whistle blows! I must be going now.
> Farewell, old Army and Navy Club, farewell!
> Perhaps you knew
> The Despedida to the ladies was
> Our Despedida too.

The end of family life brought a sense of crisis to the men of the Philippine garrison, a feeling that time was rapidly running out. A spirit of urgency was in the air and the mood turned serious. Workdays no longer ended at noon, the golf courses were empty during the week, the polo ponies got a shorter workout each day, and the men found themselves conducting training exercises, even in the heat of the midday sun.

Along with the new pressure to prepare militarily, there was a growing determination that the Japanese forces must be made to pay dearly for any attempt to capture the Philippines. The major obstacle to this goal was a lack of men, weapons, ammunition, vehicles, and other equipment—in sum, a shortage of everything needed to wage war against a modern, well-equipped enemy. Maj. Gen. George Grunert, commander of all military forces in the islands (the Philippine Department), pleaded for more materiel in the spring of 1941. He tried to point out how short his garrison was of its authorized quotas of every item.

The reply from Washington was terse. "There is nothing now in the offing." In response to his repeated requests for antiaircraft guns, ammunition, and airplanes, Grunert was told, "A sufficient number will be available in 1942"—a year away! Wainwright and the other commanders would have to make do with whatever was at hand.

In the meantime, the world situation was deteriorating. In July 1941, the Japanese army moved into Thailand and Indochina, bringing their forces substantially closer to Malaya, the Dutch East Indies, and the Philippines. Toward the end of the month, President Roosevelt instituted unprecedented economic sanctions against Japan. All Japanese assets in the United States were frozen, the Panama Canal was closed to Japanese shipping, and cargoes of steel and oil bound for Japan were curtailed. In the face of such measures taken by the U.S., it was no longer a question of "will there be a war?" but rather "when will the war start?"

These events forced a change in Washington's policy toward the Philippines. Instead of considering the islands a liability, territory to be abandoned in a two-front war, it now saw them as America's first line of defense against the continued expansionist moves of the Japanese Empire. General George Marshall decided that "If we could make the Philippines reasonably defensible, . . . we felt we could block the Japanese advance and block their entry into war by their fear of what would happen if they couldn't take the Philippines."

The first step was to institute a major change of command. General Wainwright found out about it at the end of July, when he and other senior officers were summoned to General Grunert's headquarters in Manila. Skinny greeted several old friends there, including Ned King, who had sailed with him aboard the *Grant,* and George Moore, a classmate from the Army War College, now in command of Fort Mills, the defenses on Corregidor Island.

General Grunert made a stunning announcement: General Douglas MacArthur was being recalled to active duty to become commander of a newly designated force, the United States Army Forces in the Far East—USAFFE—which would replace the old Philippine Department. In addition, the Philippine army would be inducted into the United States forces.

Wainwright, King, and the others were delighted with the news. The Filipino people idolized MacArthur and they would fight for him as for no other leader. Also, no one knew as much about the islands as MacArthur did or believed so confidently that they could be prepared and fortified to withstand a Japanese invasion. MacArthur's influence in Washington might mean greater success in getting reinforcements and equipment. With MacArthur in command, spirits rose, and pessimism turned to optimism.

A few days later, Skinny drove his big Packard up to MacArthur's headquarters in Manila to congratulate him and to find out what his new commander had in mind for him. MacArthur told Wainwright to continue with the training of his Philippine Division for combat, and he held out the promise of a larger command for Wainwright in the near future. He confided his plans for the development of the North and South Luzon Forces, each containing about three divisions of new Filipino troops. General Grunert would be given command of the northern force; the southern force would be Wainwright's.

Skinny was gratified by the trust MacArthur was showing in him. He would have charge of the second most important force in the islands, a unit at least three times the size of his present command. The future looked bright for J. M. Wainwright and for the entire Philippine garrison. On August 1, General Marshall stated bluntly that it was now "the policy of the United States to defend the Philippines."

While America geared up to start sending men and materiel to the Philippines, MacArthur was working on a new strategy for the defense of the islands, one that had Wainwright's full support. The new USAFFE commander opposed the passive stance of WPO-3, which called only for defensive delaying tactics with which to confront an invading force. Under that plan, all troops would withdraw into the Bataan peninsula as soon as the Japanese landed. There, together with the fortifications on Corregidor, they would be able to deny Manila Bay to the enemy until the American fleet could come steaming to the rescue and drive the Japanese out of the area.

MacArthur proposed—and the War Department accepted—a more aggressive plan. His troops would defend not only Manila Bay, but the entire Philippine archipelago. His army would not be concentrated only on the main island of Luzon, but would be spread throughout the islands, with almost half the troops deployed in the Visayan and Mindanao island groups far to the south.

It was assumed that the invasion would come on Luzon because it was the closest island to Japan and Formosa and contained the capital city of Manila. MacArthur decided to disperse his forces in such a way that they could be rushed to any invasion site and beat back the Japanese invaders on the beaches, throwing them into the sea. Wainwright agreed with MacArthur's idea. "A defense must be active, damn it, not passive!" he said. "It must involve counterattacks, to be the kind of defense I wanted." Consequently, he began to drill his troops in offensive rather than defensive tactics.

Both MacArthur and Wainwright were wrong, as it turned out, not because the plan was a bad one, but because when the Japanese attacked in December 1941 the USAFFE forces were unprepared. But at the time MacArthur's plan was conceived, few leaders in Manila or Washington had any doubts about its wisdom, primarily because they had such confidence in MacArthur himself. The official army history of the USAFFE forces reported it this way. "An optimist by nature, with implicit faith in the Philippine people, MacArthur was able to inspire the confidence and loyalty of his associates and staff. His optimism was contagious and infected the highest officials in the War Department and the government. By the fall of 1941 there was a firm conviction in Washington and in the Philippines that, given sufficient time, a Japanese attack could be successfully resisted."

Unfortunately, there wasn't sufficient time. The plan would fail. It was one of the most costly mistakes MacArthur ever made. That it did not result in an even greater catastrophe was because of the work of Wainwright.

The Philippines saw a whirlwind of activity during the late summer and fall of 1941. On August 15, General MacArthur

summoned Wainwright and the other senior commanders to
USAFFE headquarters in Manila to discuss his plans for mobilizing
and training the Philippine army. This was an enormous undertaking that would tax the ingenuity, patience, and energy of every
officer involved. Some 76,000 Filipinos would be inducted into the
army in the coming weeks, enough to form ten reserve divisions by
the end of November.

Camps and training facilities had to be built almost overnight;
training schedules were set out, and officers were detached from
their present units to carry on the training. The pace was grueling.
MacArthur set the example by working day and night, driving his
headquarters staff constantly. Wainwright and everyone else followed suit.

The task was difficult and frustrating. There was a serious
language problem between Americans and Filipinos and even
among the Filipinos themselves, who spoke a number of different
dialects. In addition to the shortage of training facilities, equipment
of all sorts was in short supply. The uniforms were old and most of
them unfit for wear. There were not enough blankets, mosquito
nets, tents, gas masks, or steel helmets to go around. There was a
severe lack of automatic weapons, and the artillery was of World
War I vintage. The ammunition was old. In one division, fully
seventy percent of the mortar rounds turned out to be duds. This
was the army that in four short months was expected to beat back
the Imperial Japanese Army on the beaches.

MacArthur had unlimited faith in his new Philippine army, but,
increasingly, Wainwright did not. While MacArthur sent glowing
reports about his forces to Washington, praising their combat
capabilities, Wainwright concentrated on trying to mold and discipline his units and kept his doubts to himself.

Meanwhile, the War Department was working urgently to send
men and supplies to the Philippines. The defense of the islands was
now a priority in Washington, and ships laden with troops and
equipment sailed from American ports in August and September.
The problem was that America's arsenal was bare in the fall of 1941.
The country's industry was just beginning to convert to war
production, and much materiel had already been sent to England
and to Russia. In addition, there was a serious shortage of ships.

Nevertheless, a small but steady flow of reinforcements began to
arrive in Manila. Two tank battalions of 108 light tanks were
shipped, along with an antiaircraft and a coast artillery regiment,

some ammunition, and additional troops. By October, 12,000 men were expected. MacArthur had been submitting endless requests for supplies, only some of which could be delivered. More was scheduled to be sent, but the lack of ships would cause fatal delays. By November, over a million tons of equipment was sitting on U.S. piers, waiting for ships to deliver it.

New aircraft did arrive, however, at an impressive rate, particularly the new heavy bomber, the B-17, in which General Marshall had so much confidence. By the time war broke out, more than half of all the B-17s in the air corps were based in the Philippines, along with fifteen percent of the U.S. fighter plane force. There were thirty-five B-17s and one hundred seven Curtiss P-40Es in the islands by December 1941. This was a formidable air force. Washington was convinced that its presence would cause the Japanese to reevaluate their position before launching an attack. Most of this fine air force would be destroyed on the ground on the first day of the war, right before Wainwright's eyes.

Gradually the defensive situation in the Philippines took a significant turn for the better, and so did Wainwright's career. In late September, while he was out on the Fort McKinley reservation overseeing a field exercise by his Philippine Division, a large black Chrysler pulled up. It was General MacArthur's car, and the USAFFE commander had brought some interesting news. General Grunert, commander of the old Philippine Department and the only officer under MacArthur to outrank Wainwright, had been ordered back to the states.

"That will make you the senior field commander," MacArthur said.

Wainwright nodded, and then MacArthur told him that he could have his choice of commands. If MacArthur thought Wainwright was too old or not aggressive enough, or if he had been dissatisfied with Wainwright as a troop commander or been concerned about his behavior in any way, he would not have hesitated to ship Skinny home, just as he was doing with Grunert. MacArthur did not keep anyone he did not want, and he certainly did not offer a choice among the top commands to anyone in whom he did not have complete trust and confidence.

Skinny thought for a moment and asked, "Which do you consider the most important point in the Philippines to defend? Where do you think the main danger is—the place where some distinction can be gained?"

"The North Luzon Force, by all means," MacArthur replied without hesitation.

"I'd like that," Wainwright said.

"It's yours, Jonathan."*

Wainwright believed, as everyone did, that the invasion would come on the island of Luzon. Now it would be his responsibility alone to drive the enemy into the sea. This was the most important command in the entire Pacific theater; they all knew that it was the Philippines, not Hawaii, that would be invaded by the Japanese.

Wainwright was anxious to take over his new command, but MacArthur told him to stay at Fort McKinley with his division until he had completed the plans for the first large-scale maneuvers ever to be conducted in the Philippines. They were scheduled for mid-December.

Throughout the fall of 1941 Wainwright had frequent meetings with MacArthur at USAFFE headquarters at Number 1, Calle Victoria, in the old walled city of Manila. The two men got along very well and they liked to argue back and forth in a friendly fashion about tactics and troop deployment and the schedule of training.

Skinny was one of the very few people who called MacArthur by his first name. An officer working in an adjoining office remembers overhearing these conversations as each tried to defend his position. "Now, Douglas," one would say; "Now, Jonathan," the other would reply. A hearty debate between two old West Pointers. There was never any rancor or animosity. That came later.

Training continued apace throughout the month of October, and more men and supplies arrived from home. Despite the deficiencies in the new Filipino troops that were now so readily apparent to Wainwright and the other field commanders, MacArthur continued to believe his own press releases about their progress. In a letter to General Marshall on October 28 he described the morale of his Filipino troops as "exceptionally high," and noted that their training had "progressed even beyond expectations." He had no doubt whatsoever that these hastily trained, raw recruits would stand firm in the face of the Japanese army. In less than a week,

---

*MacArthur gave command of the South Luzon Force to Brig. Gen. George M. Parker. Brig. Gen. William F. Sharp was to head the Visayan-Mindanao force.

events would be set in motion that would prove him disastrously wrong.

In Japan, the plans for the invasion of the Philippines had been initiated in early November. The Fourteenth Japanese Army, consisting of two divisions, a brigade, and supporting units—a total of 100,000 men—was assigned to the task. The commander of the Fourteenth Army, the man to whom Wainwright would ultimately have to surrender and who would himself end his career in disgrace, was Lt. Gen. Masaharu Homma.

Homma was five years younger than Wainwright and had compiled an equally illustrious record of achievement. He was sophisticated, well-traveled, and westernized in his outlook. An amateur playwright, he held what he called a "broad outlook" on life as a result of eight years of association with the British aristocracy. He opposed war with England and the United States. As a captain he had studied in England for three years during the First World War. He had come to England from the United States, sailing with a convoy of American troops. A few years later he was in India, attached to the General Staff of the Indian army. After service as an aide to the brother of the Japanese emperor, Homma spent two years in London as a military attaché. He had toured Europe, Canada, the United States, and the Middle East. His was an unusual background for a Japanese army officer.

Homma was to prove a formidable adversary for J. M. Wainwright. Yet he too would find himself to be a victim of circumstances. Both men would suffer for the coming events in the Philippines.

Japanese planners did not expect the Americans and Filipinos to offer much resistance. Their plans called for the capture of all of Luzon, including Manila and Bataan, in fifty days, by the end of March 1942. By then, the Fourteenth Japanese Army would be needed elsewhere, according to the Japanese timetable of conquest. They had accurate intelligence about the number of American troops in the islands and knew that the majority of them were in Luzon. They knew nothing, however, of WPO-3 and the plan to withdraw into Bataan. They assumed that the American and Filipino forces would make their last stand around Manila, where they could be easily defeated. The Japanese expected to conclude their war in the Philippines at Manila; Corregidor did not seem to figure in their plans at all. This turned out to be a grave miscalculation on their part.

War was edging closer, and Wainwright drove himself harder to prepare his forces for the December maneuvers. There were so many details to attend to, and always new units to incorporate into the training schedule.

In the middle of November Col. E. B. Miller, commander of one of the new tank battalions from the States, went to see the general to complain about his planned use of the tanks in the coming war exercises. Miller was an outspoken officer who never hesitated to criticize anyone, regardless of rank, who he felt did not appreciate the value of his tanks. As he strode into Wainwright's office at Fort McKinley, he was angry and ready to do battle.

Wainwright was busy, in no mood to have his orders for the tanks questioned. The stage was set for the classic confrontation in which a commanding officer chews out an unruly subordinate. Colonel Miller described the meeting:

"General Wainwright, tall and slim, received me very courteously. There was no stiffness about the visit and I felt at ease. It did not take long to come to the point. In essence, he told me it was absolutely necessary that the tanks be split for the maneuvers and that he would like me to go along with him without any further protests. He said that he would soon be taking command at Stotsenburg and that he would see to it, personally, that we received the type of training we so desired. In spite of my disappointment, as I left his office, I could not help but like 'Skinny.' He had let me say the things I had wanted to say and in my own words. He was not dictative in any way—merely firm in his decision. I had argued and lost."

On that same day in Washington another meeting was taking place, this one highly secret. Although no one in the Philippines then knew about it, what transpired directly affected all their lives. General Marshall had invited seven newsmen to his office in the Munitions Building and they had agreed not to publish anything about the talk. What he told them characterized the mistaken judgments of the time and revealed the kind of thinking that ultimately led to the downfall of the Philippines.

Marshall announced in a calm voice that "the United States and Japan are on the brink of war." He disclosed the nature of the reinforcements that had arrived in the Philippines and those that were on their way. He emphasized the capabilities of the thirty-five B-17s, naively believing them to be a force that would quickly destroy Japan's naval bases and major cities in the event of war. He said that once the Philippines had been fully armed and supplied, the president would tell the Japanese leaders about the air armada that faced them. The Philippines, Marshall predicted, would be secure by the middle of December.

The chief of staff had greatly exaggerated the potential power of the Flying Fortresses. They did not have sufficient range to reach Japan and return to their bases in the Philippines.

Marshall had not exaggerated the threat of war, however. On November 24 he approved a warning to be sent to all American naval commanders in the Pacific, adding the instruction that it be passed to army commanders as well: "There are very doubtful chances of a favorable outcome of negotiations with Japan. This situation coupled with movements of their naval and military forces indicate in our opinion that a surprise aggressive movement in any direction, including an attack on the Philippines or Guam, is a possibility." It was a clear warning of war.

MacArthur received the message the following day and immediately telephoned Wainwright at his headquarters at Fort McKinley.

"Jonathan," he said, "you'd better get up north and take command of that North Luzon Force now. Forget the maneuvers. How soon can you go?"

"I can go just as quickly as I can walk downstairs and get in my car," Wainwright said.

"Oh, that much rush isn't necessary. Wait a day or two, and then come down to Manila to see me before you go."

Skinny began at once to wind up his affairs at Fort McKinley and to arrange to take leave of his Philippine Division. He felt that the situation was more urgent than MacArthur had let on. He had his personal effects packed and he sent them, with his three horses, ahead to Fort Stotsenburg, his new command post.

Two days later MacArthur received an ominous message from Washington: "Negotiations with Japan appear to be terminated to all practical purposes. . . . Japanese future action unpredictable but hostile action possible at any moment."

When Wainwright called on MacArthur at his headquarters later that day to discuss the command of the North Luzon Force, he found that MacArthur was "considerably less eager and tense than I was." MacArthur wanted to discuss routine organizational and training matters. Skinny tried to explain the need for additional offensive combat training as soon as possible.

"Jonathan," MacArthur said, "you'll probably have until April to train those troops."

As Wainwright returned to Fort McKinley, MacArthur's April prediction was on his mind. But he knew, he wrote later, that "even if the Japs held off that long it would still be a tight squeeze. It takes time to turn a mass of conscripts into the kind of army we would need." He did not believe they would have enough time, and he was right.

That same afternoon, MacArthur repeated his assertion that they would have four more months to fortify the Philippines in a meeting with the U.S. High Commissioner, Francis B. Sayre, and Admiral Thomas C. Hart, commander of the Asiatic Fleet. MacArthur confided, Sayre wrote, that "the existing alignment and movement of Japanese troops convinced him that there would be no Japanese attack before the spring." Admiral Hart did not agree.

A mile away from USAFFE headquarters, on the campus of the University of the Philippines, the republic's president, Manuel Quezon, was giving a talk to the students. "Bombs may be falling on this campus soon," he said. There was laughter in the audience. Quezon raised his arm and shouted, "It can happen, I tell you."

The next day, November 28, while Wainwright was driving the seventy miles from Fort McKinley to his new headquarters at Fort Stotsenburg in the north, MacArthur was radioing an optimistic message to General Marshall in Washington: "Everything is in readiness for the conduct of a successful defense."

Readiness was not what Wainwright found when he arrived at Stotsenburg that afternoon. He was greeted by chaos and a state of almost total unpreparedness. Little organizational work had been done in advance for him, and there was virtually no staff to help run a large command of four infantry divisions and one cavalry regiment, his beloved Twenty-sixth. With this understrength and untrained force—the Twenty-sixth Cavalry was the only fully trained unit—Wainwright was expected to defend more than 600 miles of open beaches. The situation seemed impossible. Three hours after he arrived, he received orders from MacArthur to put the troops on a modified alert. Time was beginning to run out.

Hurriedly Wainwright assembled a staff, drawn chiefly from his own Philippine Division. He telephoned officers he knew he could count on and they rushed to Fort Stotsenburg to assist him in establishing a fighting command.

For his chief of staff Wainwright picked Col. William F. Maher, a thoroughly professional, ascetic, intelligent officer who had fought in World War I. Bill Maher had served Wainwright in the same capacity in the Philippine Division, and his abilities were a perfect complement to Wainwright's.

Maher kept meticulous track of every detail and ran a tight ship, setting up a small but highly efficient headquarters organization, in which he allowed no hangers-on. He was all business, with no time for extraneous sociability. More important, he knew Skinny so well that he could anticipate orders and maintain control of the liquor supply, which Skinny never seemed to mind. In the months of fighting ahead, Maher more than once cussed out officers of equal or higher rank for bringing booze to the headquarters for Wainwright. "Get that stuff outta here," he would yell, and he did not have to tell even brigadier generals more than once.

For his engineering officer Wainwright made another wise choice, Harry Skerry, an old friend from the days at Fort Leavenworth. To serve as assistant G-2 he picked the young infantry captain who had impressed him at Fort Clark, Joe Chabot. He had met Chabot again the previous July when he awarded him a trophy for winning the Fort McKinley golf tournament. He had complimented Chabot on his excellent physical condition. "We military people will need to be in good shape," Skinny had told him.

Assembling and organizing the staff to run a large fighting force, and to do so under the pressure of time, was a test of Wainwright's leadership ability, one he easily passed. He was at his best during those crucial days in late November 1941, displaying the qualities that had won for him such an excellent record of advancement. Those who witnessed Wainwright's work with the North Luzon Force have nothing but the highest praise for his skill as a tactician and a natural leader of men.

While the staff was settling in at Fort Stotsenburg, Wainwright went to visit the troops under his new command, to see firsthand how ready they were for war.

Wainwright's preparations on that day were being duplicated by the other senior commanders in the islands. On November 29, an American army lieutenant, Henry G. Lee, reflected the thoughts of many young men there in a letter he wrote to his parents.

"You've probably been wondering how we really feel over here about our situation and our chances. Truthfully, we are in a pretty bad spot over here—or will be if hostilities ever begin. Although troops and equipment have been pouring in for five months, we still lack much of the essential weapons of defense. We have not enough planes, for instance, to ward off an even moderate size bombing attack, and our anti-airplane ground defenses are non-existent. There is not one modern anti-aircraft weapon in the whole Philippine Islands.

"Also, the stories about the huge defense forces concentrated here, although true, do not convey the truth. A force of 50,000 men sounds large on paper, but when one considers that three-fourths of that force is untrained and poorly officered and equipped P. A. [Philippine Army] units, and that half of the remaining are Scout soldiers, still an unknown quantity under fire, then the 50,000 dwindles again to just two or three regiments of white troops and 2000 white officers scattered from Northern Luzon to the Sulu Sea.

"In talking to Navy officers, I have gotten the same reaction. The Asiatic Fleet, which looks so impressive in Manila Bay, is antiquated and under-manned, and the Pacific Fleet in Honolulu is seven days away under ideal conditions. In other words, if Japan wants these islands and wants them bad enough, she can have them.

"We all worry at times about our situation, but not for long, and we never discuss it among ourselves. We are here, and nothing can be done about that. We have no control over the situation, so we sit tight and don't worry too much."

The situation was growing more critical by the hour as November turned into December. War was now seven days away. On the first of December, Melville Jacoby, *Time* magazine's correspondent in Manila, cabled his office in New York: "The situation is even tighter this morning, is absolutely the closest war feeling yet. U.S. forces are straining and hurried military confabs are going on. Confidentially, two false alarms in the last twenty-four hours gave informed circles the jitters."

That night, the party to celebrate the Army-Navy game was held at Manila's Army-Navy Club. But what was normally the year's biggest social event was not so big in 1941. Few people came and the giant scoreboard that had been erected at the edge of the sea was blank. The radio broadcast of the game, relayed from the States, wasn't picked up because the navy ships in the bay had blacked out and gone on radio silence.

Carl Mydans, *Life* magazine's photographer, reported: "The guests who remained sat uneasily at their tables staring out past the empty scoreboard toward the dark sea beyond. For the feeling was strong upon us that somewhere out there in the distance the

Japanese fleet was moving and that war was just over the horizon."

On December 2, at dawn, a Japanese reconnaissance plane was spotted as it flew directly over Clark Field. No attempt was made to intercept it.

The following day, MacArthur sent Wainwright orders to protect all the airfields and to man the beaches to prevent enemy landings in North Luzon. The enemy was to be destroyed, the orders read, and the beaches held "at all costs." There was to be no withdrawal from the beach positions. Wainwright was instructed to prepare to carry out this mission and to direct his front-line units to put their heavy weapons in place and to make thorough reconnaissance patrols of their sectors.

Wainwright had to get word to his units, which were scattered all over Luzon, to move immediately to their assigned positions on the beaches. How was he to contact them? He had no radio communications. The only communications system was the public telephone, and Wainwright could use that only for the most routine of messages, for obvious security reasons. He never knew who might be listening. Out of necessity, Wainwright devised a secure but makeshift way of making contact with his far-flung troops.

He borrowed an old B-10 bomber from the air corps and called on his assistant G-2, Joe Chabot, to fly in it and drop messages at each camp, telling the troops where to go to establish their defensive positions. It was a day Chabot never forgot. He had just been discharged from the hospital after a bout with pneumonia and was still weak and under medication. The plane bobbed up and down as it flew low over the mountainous terrain, and in short order the captain was airsick. As the pilot located each camp, he would buzz it until someone came out on the parade ground. Then Chabot would roll up the message, put it in a hollow stick, and drop it.

It was a measure of how unprepared the Philippine defenders were that the commanding officer of the North Luzon Force had to resort to such a method to pass an order on to his troops.

By then Wainwright had visited all the units under his command and he knew the terrible truth about their condition. The Thirty-first Division, under the command of Brig. Gen. Clifford Bluemel, was in appalling shape. The infantry had had no more than a few weeks of training, and no combat training or practice. The artillery had never fired a shot from their obsolete weapons. There were no antitank guns, little transportation, and a shortage of hand grenades and of machine-gun and mortar ammunition. Their communications depended solely on public telephone lines.

Bluemel reported that his Filipino enlisted men could do two things well: (1) "when an officer appeared, to yell attention in a loud voice, jump up and salute"; and (2) "to demand three meals per day."

Wainwright's other divisions were just as ill equipped and inexperienced. The Eleventh Division, under the command of Brig. Gen. William Brougher, which was charged with the defense of the crucial coastline area of Lingayen Gulf, had to ask the local residents for help in fortifying the beaches. Native shopkeepers donated barbed wire and tools. Filipino civilians and soldiers together searched the woods and fields for bamboo and wood to build beach obstacles. Brougher and his officers went out on the roads and commandeered scores of civilian automobiles, trucks, and buses, "often with the drivers included."

Wainwright also had the Twenty-first Division, commanded by Brig. Gen. Mateo Capinpin, the Twenty-sixth Cavalry Regiment, one battalion of Philippine Scouts, two batteries of 155s, and one battery of 2.95-inch mountain guns. On paper his command included Brig. Gen. Clyde Selleck's Seventy-first Division, but this could be committed only on authority of USAFFE.

To Wainwright and the other officers it was a nightmarish way to prepare for war. The Philippine army was doomed from the beginning, Wainwright believed. "They never had a chance to win."

With determination and ingenuity, he did what he could. He improvised, innovated, substituted, cajoled, argued, and threatened. He did whatever was required to get his men as ready as possible. Once during those grim final days of peace he did some bargaining with his classmate from West Point, Brig. Gen. Henry B. Claggett, now head of Interceptor Command of the air corps. Skinny explained the problem—the maps of the extreme northern part of Luzon did not show the roads very clearly.

"I've got to get a reconnaissance up there to see how things are," Wainwright said. "You know, we might have visitors from Formosa up there one day."

"So?" Claggett asked, wondering what kind of deal Skinny was prepared to offer him.

"I'll trade one good airplane ride for that small building and some paint you're interested in," Skinny said, "provided—"

"—that I don't pilot the bomber," Claggett said.

"Exactly. Is it a go?"

"Born horse trader," Claggett grumbled. "You were the same way in school days at the Point."

The following day Claggett told a friend about the incident. "Yes, sir," he said, "a born horse trader. When Skinny doesn't trade any more—well, you'll know he can't!"

It wasn't long before Wainwright ran out of things to trade.

By the 4th of December Japanese planes were flying over the northern part of Luzon every night. Japanese ships were moving south, toward Malaya. On December 5 the commander of Britain's Far Eastern Fleet, Admiral Tom Phillips, came to Manila for meetings with Admiral Hart and General MacArthur.

MacArthur assured the American and British naval commanders that his forces would be ready by April.

"Doug, that is just dandy," Hart said. "But how defensible are we right now?" As far as Hart was concerned, war would be declared any day.

He asked Admiral Phillips when he planned to fly back to Singapore. "I'm taking off tomorrow morning," Phillips said.

"If you want to be there when the war starts," Hart said, "I suggest you take off right now."

On December 6, Melville Jacoby radioed his office in New York: "Informed sources this evening are seeing mounting chances of war."

That afternoon, squadron commanders at Nichols Field were called to the office of their chief, Brig. Gen. Harold H. George. Among them was Lt. Ed Dyess, a P-40 pilot.

"Men," General George said, "you are not a suicide squadron yet, but you're damned close to it. There will be a war with Japan in a very few days. It may come in a matter of hours."

In the evening Rear Adm. William R. Purnell told Army Air Corps Gen. Lewis Brereton that it was "only a question of days or perhaps hours until the shooting starts."

Back home, *Time* magazine reported that the odds on war with Japan were nine in ten. Columnist Walter Lippmann wrote that "The country is now really on the verge of an actual all-out war." *Life* magazine was wrapping up its December 8 issue. On the cover was a photograph of General Douglas MacArthur and inside was an article on the "showdown" between America and Japan. "The stage is set for war," *Life* reported, "a distant, dangerous, hard, amphibious war for which the American nation is not yet fully prepared."

The movie review of the week touted a new Errol Flynn film, *Custer's Last Stand*.

On the high seas in the Pacific, a convoy led by the heavy cruiser *Pensacola* was steaming for Manila, bringing fifty-two A-24 dive bombers, eighteen P-40 fighter planes, 340 trucks and jeeps, forty-eight 75mm guns, 600 tons of bombs, 3.5 million rounds of machine-gun ammunition, 9,000 drums of aviation fuel, and 4,600 men. These were major reinforcements. Wainwright and the other island commanders were counting on them to make a big difference in the fighting they knew lay just ahead. The convoy's arrival date was January 4.

Another ship was heading toward Honolulu, due to stop there briefly before continuing on to Los Angeles. This was the *Tatsuta Maru,* a Japanese ocean liner. Suddenly, with no explanation to the passengers, its captain reversed course. North of the *Tatsuta Maru,* a Japanese battle fleet was on course for Pearl Harbor.

Wainwright had done all that was humanly possible. His men were as prepared as they could be, given the limitations of the situation. There was nothing more he could do now. He took his horse "Little Boy" for a ride over to neighboring Clark Field and chatted awhile with Col. Eugene Eubank, who had recently led a flight of B-17s in on their long trip from the U.S.

Then Wainwright galloped back to Stotsenburg to inspect the Twenty-sixth Cavalry, a pack train, and a field artillery battery, the only units he had at the fort. At 11:00 that night he went to bed and slept soundly. In the years to come he often recalled that night.

"It was the last decent sleep I was to have for three years and eight months."

The next day was December 7.

CHAPTER 4
"The Cat Has Jumped"

W AR CAME TO THE Philippines in the early morning hours of December 8–December 7, Hawaii time. It came not through the sudden bursting of bombs to kill men in their sleep, but through urgent voices over the telephone.

Wainwright got the word in his quarters at Fort Stotsenburg at 4:35 A.M. The ringing phone in the next room broke into his dreams. He felt a sense of foreboding as he got out of bed and walked through the darkened bedroom.

He answered the phone and heard the calm voice of Col. Constant "Pete" Irwin, one of MacArthur's staff officers.

"Admiral Hart has just received a radio from Admiral Kimmel, Commander of the Pacific Fleet at Pearl Harbor, informing him that Japan has initiated hostilities."

That was all. No other information was available at the moment. Two and a half hours had elapsed since the beginning of the attack on Pearl Harbor, and the lives of Americans would never again be the same.

As soon as Wainwright hung up, he started to dress. He called his senior aide, Johnny Pugh, and told him what had happened. He used more cryptic words than the message Colonel Irwin had delivered.

"The cat has jumped," Wainwright said. Pugh knew immediately what he meant.

Fifteen minutes later Irwin called again to inform Wainwright that the naval and air bases at Pearl Harbor had been bombed, but he had no information on the severity of the damage. No one in the Philippines, not even MacArthur, knew that the Pacific Fleet lay in ruins. War Plan Orange was no longer viable. There were no ships to relieve the Philippine garrison in six months. The islands were foredoomed by the time the last Japanese plane wheeled away from the smoke and destruction at Pearl Harbor. They were on their own, cut off from any possibility of help.

Wainwright contacted Clark Field, the largest air corps base in the islands, to make sure they had been informed about the situation. The B-17s and P-40s stationed there would make tempting targets for Japanese bombers. He had often watched from the porch of his headquarters, only 1,200 yards from the edge of the airfield, as the graceful planes took off and landed, shattering the air with their powerful engines. Two days before, when he had ridden over to the field, he had seen them still unpainted and gleaming silver lined up wingtip to wingtip. He didn't want to see them destroyed on the ground now that the country was at war.

On other airfields, 500 miles to the north on the island of Formosa, anxious pilots stood by their bombers. The twin-engine planes, gassed and with full bomb bays, were part of the Eleventh Air Fleet of the Japanese air force. Their mission that morning was to bomb Clark Field in the Philippine Islands and the fighter bases at Iba, Nielson, and Nichols fields. The pilots had received word of the successes of their colleagues at Pearl Harbor in the Hawaiian Islands, and they were eager to launch their own attack.

But they were late, behind schedule because of a dense fog that had settled over Formosa during the night. Now they feared that the element of surprise was gone. The American forces would surely have learned about the attack on Pearl Harbor and would have their fighters waiting as the Eleventh Japanese Air Fleet flew over Luzon. The heavy U.S. bombers, the new B-17s, might already have been sent south to Mindanao, well beyond the range of Japanese air forces. Or worse, they might be taking off now for Formosa, arriving in time for the morning sun to burn off the fog, catching the fully loaded planes on the ground. The pilots looked around nervously, but the fog was so thick that they could not see the end of the runway.

In Manila and at every army and navy base in the Philippines the news of war was spreading. In the fashionable suburb of Malate, the editor and publisher of the largest Filipino newspaper chain, Carlos Romulo, was awakened by a telephone call from his city editor. The man told him about the Japanese attack in Hawaii.

"You're crazy," Romulo said. "Don't print anything as screwy as that!"

Romulo hung up on the editor and immediately dialed General MacArthur's private number. The USAFFE commander recognized his friend's voice at once.

"Carlos, it's here!" MacArthur said.

Three miles away at the U.S. Army's Sternberg Hospital in Manila, a pretty young nurse, 2nd. Lt. Juanita Redmond of Swansea, South Carolina, was finishing her tour of night duty. She made her rounds and planned an afternoon golf game. A friend telephoned with news of the Japanese attack. Nurse Redmond laughed.

"Thanks for trying to keep me awake," she said, "but that isn't very funny."

"I'm not being funny," her friend said. "It's true."

Redmond returned to the ward, shocked. Someone had switched on a radio and all the patients were listening. They wondered if Manila would be the next target.

Wainwright sat down at his desk and wrote out a list of the supplies and equipment he needed for his North Luzon Force. It was a long list but he was able to make it from memory. It included the same items he had been requesting for weeks. He summoned Johnny Pugh, handed him the list, and told him to get it to MacArthur's headquarters as fast as he could.

At some of the airfields on Formosa the fog began to break up at dawn. A portion of the bombing force, twenty-five army bombers, took off, heading south toward Luzon. Their targets were minor ones in the north of Luzon, some Filipino barracks and the Philippine government's summer capital at Baguio, where President Quezon was staying. The air force of 108 bombers and 84 Zeroes slated to bomb the American air bases was still grounded. The pilots were growing increasingly worried. They expected American planes overhead at any moment.

*   *   *

The early morning sun was bright and the sky was cloudless as the new day began in the Philippines, but word of the Japanese attack on Hawaii was sowing tension and fear. Friends phoned one another. Neighbors and strangers on the streets stopped to talk about it, finding comfort in the presence of others. By 7:30, there were few people in Manila who had not heard the news.

One who had not was T.J.H. Trapnell, promoted to major a few days before. He was on the beach on the outskirts of Manila schooling a horse, enjoying the privacy and quiet of the early morning. Someone called to him. Trap turned his horse and trotted over to the man, whom he recognized as Brig. Gen. Richard Sutherland, MacArthur's chief of staff. Sutherland told Trap what had happened and asked him how soon he could rejoin the Twenty-sixth Cavalry Regiment at Fort Stotsenburg. Trapnell raced back to Nichols Field, rounded up the men of his troop, and started on the hard ride north.

At 8:00 that morning Wainwright heard the B-17s at Clark Field starting their engines. One by one they lifted off the runway. Skinny wondered if they were going to Formosa to bomb the Japanese airfields. He knew that Brereton, the senior air force commander, wanted to undertake such a mission, and silently Wainwright wished him well. He did not know that the bomb bays of the Forts were empty. MacArthur had not granted permission for the raid. The planes were taking off only so they would not be caught on the ground.

Wainwright had more pressing concerns, dealing with the units directly under his command. He spoke on the telephone with all of his senior commanders, satisfying himself—and them—that the troops were as prepared as possible for whatever lay ahead.

Clint Pierce, commander of the Twenty-sixth Cavalry, stopped by Skinny's office, and the two men worked out the details of dispersing the regiment so that it would be reasonably safe from air attack. Most of the troops were moved to a concealed bivouac a mile and a half north of Stotsenburg. In less than three hours the troops were secure and ready to take to the field at a moment's notice. All its equipment and ammunition were at hand. The Twenty-sixth was ready for war.

By 9:00, radio station KMZH in Manila was making regular announcements about the war and broadcasting whatever skimpy news was available. But one of the many things that the announcer,

Don Bell, did not know was that a flight of Japanese planes had been sighted over northern Luzon. American P-40s from Clark and Nichols Fields took off to intercept them, but before they could reach them the Japanese had dropped their bombs on Baguio and other installations in the north.

At 9:25 A.M., the bomber commander, General Brereton, telephoned MacArthur's headquarters again, requesting permission to bomb Formosa. Again MacArthur refused. He would change his mind forty minutes later, but by then it would be too late.

A few minutes after the bombs fell on Baguio, Wainwright was informed of the attack and ordered to protect Fort Stotsenburg against a landing by Japanese paratroopers. He had few troops left at the base, but he was able to place an artillery battery at one end of the parade ground. He ordered the gunners to cut their fuzes to zero and to load their howitzers with shrapnel. If paratroopers did land, they would meet a hail of fire that few could survive.

That job done, he left his headquarters and walked across the parade ground to his house, to make his personal preparations for war. With the help of his Filipino houseboy, he started to crate up his clothing and the other items he would not need in combat, including the dress sword his mother had given him for his West Point graduation in 1906. He would not hold it in his hands again for seven years.

While Wainwright was packing his possessions, the second flight of Japanese planes roared down the runways of their airfields in Formosa. It was 10:15 and the pilots were worried about the outcome of their late start. Surely the Americans were waiting for them. As they headed south toward Luzon, the all-clear sirens sounded at Clark Field and the other American bases. Much of the tension of the morning disappeared.

The B-17s were ordered back to Clark Field to be loaded with fuel and bombs for the anticipated raid on Formosa. They landed one by one and taxied along the runways, lining up in neat, orderly rows. Less than a mile away, Wainwright's house shook as the planes came over and he had to shout his instructions to his houseboy. As soon as the bombers were safely on the ground, the P-40s, which had been covering them, also landed. The pilots and ground crews were calm. It was 11:30—lunch time—and as the men strolled to the mess halls they joked and talked about the weather and about the little damage the Japanese planes had done over Luzon. Everyone knew the Jap planes were no good.

The personnel in the plotting room at Nielson Field, in the suburbs of Manila, were more apprehensive. In the Air Warning Center at Nielson, reports of planes crossing the northwest coast of Luzon were coming in so fast that it was difficult to keep up with them. Col. Alexander Campbell, the aircraft warning officer, quickly evaluated the information and concluded that the planes were probably headed toward Clark Field. It was 11:45.

Colonel Campbell sent a teletype warning to Clark, but he could not get through. He tried to radio the field. No luck. The radio operator at Clark was out to lunch. Campbell picked up the public telephone and finally reached a junior officer, who said he would give the message to the base commander or to the operations officer, "at the earliest opportunity."

It was now 11:56, and air-raid sirens began to wail at all the airfields on Luzon, except at Clark Field. At the other bases the pilots rushed to their planes and by 12:10 every fighter was either in the air or on alert on the ground, with engines turning over and pilots in the cockpits. P-40s and the obsolescent P-35s swarmed over the island. Every airfield now had fighters patrolling overhead, except Clark. There the ground and flight crews were leaving the mess halls, ambling back to their neat rows of B-17s, while armourers loaded the planes with bombs. At the edge of the field eighteen P-40s had just been refueled. The pilots stood nearby, waiting to take off.

Inside one of the mess halls a group of mechanics and B-17 crewmen were listening to the news on the radio. "There is an unconfirmed report," announcer Don Bell said, "that they're bombing Clark Field."

The men laughed. The time was 12:25. "Since the only noise was the usual clatter of talk, dishes, knives, and forks, Bell's words were greeted with derision. Many of the men still refused to believe the Pearl Harbor reports, thinking it was probably some hare-brained general's idea of putting everyone on the alert."

At that moment, Skinny Wainwright finished his packing. He walked out on the wide front porch of his house and paused to look around at the post. It was beautiful. The houses were shaded by large tropical trees and the yards were full of flowering shrubs. The hibiscus and bougainvillea were in bloom and the sweet fragrances of ginger trees and gardenias filled the air. He glanced up at the Zambales Mountains to the east and the towering Mount Arayat, 4,000 feet high, which the natives called the top of the world.

A sudden movement caught his eye. A vee-shaped formation of twenty-seven planes was coming in over the mountains. The aircraft roared directly overhead, crossing the long parade ground that pointed like an arrow toward Clark Field. Before he could do anything, the first bombs were falling. Almost lost amidst the noise of the explosions was the mournful wail of the air-raid siren from the field, which he could just now make out. The ground shook and the bombs seemed to blanket the entire air base. Parts of planes and bodies flew high in the air and thick columns of fire and smoke leaped everywhere. Puffs of antiaircraft fire burst harmlessly several thousand feet below the enemy planes. The American gunners did their best, but their ammunition was more than ten years old and the fuzes were corroded. The gun crews were cursing loudly as they realized that no more than one out of every six shells they fired had actually exploded.

Wainwright's houseboy ran outside. He was wearing the general's helmet.

"Mother of God, General. What shall I do?" he shouted.

"Go get me a bottle of beer," Wainwright yelled.

There were scores of men all over the parade ground and Wainwright knew that for most of them it was their baptism under fire. They were watching him, looking to him for leadership, and he had to show by example how a soldier was supposed to behave. Joe Chabot, crouching in a sand trap, watched Wainwright standing out in the open, cool and brave as a lion, calming the young troops.

Chabot heard someone calling to him. It was Bill Maher, Wainwright's chief of staff.

"Answer your phone," Maher was shouting.

Chabot ran across the open field into his office and picked up the ringing telephone.

"We're being attacked," the voice at the other end announced. "Sound the alarm."

Wainwright downed his beer as another wave of bombers flew over. After a moment he put the bottle aside and walked out onto the broad parade ground, heading for his headquarters. Shrapnel was winging through the air all around him but he walked at a normal pace, as though he were out for a stroll. His engineering officer, Harry Skerry, ran up to him and tried to urge him into a foxhole. Wainwright shook his head.

"You won't get me in a foxhole when my men are out there," Wainwright said.

He continued across the parade ground and stopped beside one of the guns of the artillery battery. There he stood quietly, watching the destruction continue at the airfield. A noise next to him caused him to turn. One of the gun crew had been hit in the face by a piece of shrapnel. Wainwright bent over the man to examine him and ordered him taken to the base hospital at once.

While the wounded artilleryman was being carried away, a 1940 black Buick convertible, with the top down, sped up the perimeter road and skidded to a stop in front of the general. It brought his junior aide, Tom Dooley, whom Skinny had ordered up from Manila earlier in the morning. Wainwright smiled as the eager young man approached and spoke to him in a casual tone of voice.

"Hello, Tom. How was your courting?"

"I'm well up on it, General. It looks like it's a good thing."

"Are you nervous?"

"Certainly am. But I'm always nervous, General, even when I'm going to a dance."

Except for the fact that the two men were shouting to be heard over the explosions, it was a very ordinary conversation, which was precisely Wainwright's intention. He looked closely at Dooley and frowned.

"Tom, you didn't drive past Clark in this bombing, did you?"

"Yes sir," Dooley replied. "I got word to report to you as fast as I could."

Wainwright grinned and gestured for Dooley to follow him to the office. He sat down at his desk, grabbed a pen and a piece of paper, and wrote out a recommendation for a Silver Star for the young man.

The Japanese bombers were turning north, back toward Formosa. There was a momentary lull at Clark Field. Before anyone could help the wounded or assess the damage, however, thirty-four Zeroes appeared and crisscrossed the field, strafing everything in their path, particularly the remaining B-17s. One by one the big planes exploded in fiery balls as tracer bullets ignited their gas tanks. The carnage went on for over an hour. When it ended, the much-vaunted American air force in the Philippines had ceased to exist as an effective fighting force. Half of it had been destroyed on the ground in an attack that had caught the Americans by surprise, a full ten hours after the disaster at Pearl Harbor. Only seventeen B-17s remained operational, and fourteen of these were at Del Monte Field on Mindanao. Fifty-three P-40s at Clark and the other fields had been destroyed as well as thirty other aircraft, mostly old B-10 and B-18 medium bombers. The Japanese lost seven fighter aircraft.

The all-clear signal sounded. The stunned survivors at Clark Field were free to tend to the wounded and the dying. Wainwright called for his horse and he, Dooley, and Clint Pierce rode over to the ruined field to see what they could do to help. Skinny knew there would be more injured than the ambulances could cope with, so he had ordered that every available truck at Fort Stotsenburg get to Clark as fast as possible. Casualties were heavy—fifty-five killed and more than one hundred wounded. The trucks raced back and forth, with blood dripping from their sides, between the devastated airfield and the hospital at Stotsenburg.

Before long, the hospital was full, and the wounded were being taken on the long ride to Sternberg General Hospital in Manila where Lt. Juanita Redmond was still on duty. She played no golf that afternoon, nor for the next five months.

By 2:00 that afternoon the bombing victims were pouring into Sternberg not only from Clark Field but from Nichols Field as well. Redmond worked in the operating room for eight hours straight, until all the people had been treated. The young woman described the situation this way. The wounded "came in trucks, ambulances, buses, carts, anything that had wheels. They were brought in on blood-crusted litters; many of them still bleeding, some with shrapnel lodged in their wounds, or arms dangling, or partially severed legs. And many were dead when they reached us."

Around 3:00 that afternoon Wainwright returned to Fort Stotsenburg for a late lunch. A lot of stories were circulating at headquarters—some rumors, some factual—but none of them was encouraging. From the news services Wainwright learned that the Japanese were attacking Hong Kong and had sunk the Pan American Clipper, which only yesterday had been berthed in Manila. A message had been received from Shanghai but it ended ominously in mid-sentence. Bombs were falling on Singapore, Guam, and Wake Island. The Japanese were on the move throughout the Pacific.

From MacArthur's headquarters in Manila Skinny heard the only good news of that long tragic day. General Marshall had radioed MacArthur that the War Department would provide every possible assistance. To counteract this, however, Wainwright was informed that the only fighting unit in the Asiatic Fleet—a force of outdated cruisers and destroyers—was leaving the Philippine Islands and steaming south to Dutch Borneo.

By the time the sun set on the first day of the war with Japan, the destiny of the Philippines was clear. The navy was gone, the air force was effectively destroyed, and the Pacific Fleet, on which the Philippines was dependent for relief, was no longer available. The outcome of the war for these islands had already been decided. The only issue in doubt was how long they could delay the inevitable. Wainwright was determined to delay it as long as possible.

As darkness settled over Fort Stotsenburg he arranged to have a message sent by radio to his wife, back home in Skaneateles, New York, to tell her that he was all right. "I had thought of Adele a lot that first day of the war," Wainwright wrote some time later, and "had thanked God that she was out of it. But I missed her badly. There were so many things to say that cannot be said to anyone but a wife."

The next few days raced by in a blur of activity and discouraging developments. The greatest problem facing Wainwright was the shortage of supplies, especially transportation. There were not enough vehicles to move his forces rapidly from one point to another in the event of an invasion, or to bring supplies to a unit under attack. It was not a question of filling out forms to order a specified number of trucks from the central depot. The army in the Philippines did not have enough trucks to go around. Wainwright would have to make do with whatever he could get to defend the northern portion of Luzon.

He contacted two commercial bus companies and leased every bus they were willing to part with. He rented cars as well, or purchased them outright when they could not be obtained in any other way. As a last resort, he sent officers out to all the roads and highways with orders to requisition every usable vehicle that came along. Throughout the islands other commanders were doing the same. The army took over whole trucking companies. Every new and used car and truck up for sale was purchased by the Quarter-master Corps. The Signal Corps seized the Manila Long Distance Telephone Company and bought all the radio and telephone equipment it could find. The Medical Corps purchased all available medicine and bandages and commandeered buildings of all descriptions to serve as hospitals and medical storehouses. It was an inefficient and frustrating way to prepare for war, but there was no other way to do it.

Wainwright dispatched his signal officer to MacArthur's headquarters with a copy of a requisition form he had submitted weeks earlier. The request had gone unanswered. MacArthur's staffers shook their heads.

"We can't do very much for you," one said. "You'll have to improvise."

That, as it turned out, would be the watchword for the entire Philippine campaign.

While the army was girding for combat, Japanese bombers were taking an increasingly heavy toll of the defenders. Every day they roared over Luzon; they were almost unopposed. The American antiaircraft fire was still ineffective and the handful of P-40s dwindled after each raid. Associated Press reporter Clark Lee visited Nichols Field right after an attack and spoke to an angry sergeant who summed up the situation for everyone.

"For Christ's sake," he told Lee, "you people are reporters. Tell the people back home to send us some antiaircraft guns and some airplanes that'll fight those Jap fighters and climb high enough to knock down those bombers. All we can do now is sit here and take it and it's a hell of a lousy situation."

Every army and air force base on Luzon was struck repeatedly, and on December 10 it was the navy's turn. The huge naval base at Cavite, on the south shore of Manila Bay, was hit savagely by fifty-four planes in a two-hour attack. Nurse Redmond said she could see the fires from Manila, thirty miles away. After the raid, Admiral Hart reported to Washington that Cavite was finished as a base. If by some miracle relief ships could reach Manila, they would find no supplies or facilities for them there.

Wainwright went that day to inspect his scattered beach defenses at Lingayen Gulf. His main concern was to stretch his untrained forces over an area 625 miles long and 125 miles wide. The only unit he could spare for the entire northern coast of Luzon was the Eleventh Division, commanded by Bill Brougher. The division was not even fully mobilized yet. Its artillery was not ready. That thinly spread ill-trained force was all that stood between any invading Japanese and the rest of Luzon, and Wainwright was worried about how the men would react when the enemy finally appeared.

He did not have to wait long to find out. A small Japanese invasion force had been on their way since before the first Japanese plane bombed Clark Field. They had landed on the northern tip of Luzon on the morning of the 10th. MacArthur's plan to hold the enemy at the beaches would now be put to the test.

Japan's General Homma was almost as anxious about the invasion as was Wainwright, and for the same reason. He was concerned that the forces given him for his two initial landings—at Aparri and at Vigan in northern Luzon—were not large enough. His biggest unit was only the size of a regiment and the smallest no larger than a company. He knew that if the Americans launched an aggressive counterattack, his troops could easily be pushed back into the sea.

It was a risky venture and the hazards were increased by bad weather. At both invasion points strong winds and heavy seas interfered with the landings and upset Homma's complicated timetable. He need not have worried, however.

At Aparri, the beach defense consisted of one American lieutenant and some two hundred Filipinos with no weapons larger than a machine gun, and virtually no training. The lieutenant ran to the telegraph office and contacted his battalion headquarters inland. He was ordered to attack the enemy and drive them off the beach. Instead, he rounded up his men and headed south, without firing a single shot. The battle of Aparri was over. At Vigan there were no American or Filipino troops. Wainwright did not have enough men to cover the entire coastline.

Skinny was away from his headquarters when these landings occurred. He was inspecting the two divisions he had now placed along Lingayen Gulf, where both he and MacArthur believed the major invasion would come. As far as they were concerned, this was where their future would be decided, on the miles of open flat beaches.

When Wainwright learned about the Aparri and Vigan incidents, he decided that they were attempts to draw his troops away from Lingayen Gulf, and he refused to rise to the bait. His forces in the Lingayen area were already weak and he could not afford to divert any of them. Also, he knew that the only route south for the Japanese now on the island was through a valley in which he had a battalion in place. He reinforced it with some scout cars, but that was all he could send. It bothered him that enemy troops had already landed—"the rat was in the house," he said—but he knew that far more of them would come to Lingayen, and soon.

Just before noon reports reached Wainwright that Japanese paratroopers had landed about twenty-five miles northeast of Stotsenburg, in an area where he had no men deployed. If the messages were correct, the enemy soldiers could play havoc with his supply and communication lines. They had to be found and destroyed.

By telephone, he ordered Major Trapnell to lead a combat team into action. The force consisted of the Second Squadron of the Twenty-sixth Cavalry, reinforced by a platoon of tanks, self-propelled 75mm guns, and some scout cars. Trap led them out of Stotsenburg at the gallop, heading toward what he hoped would be the army's first chance to strike at the enemy.

Meanwhile, the invading Japanese had run into their first opposition. The remnants of the U.S. Air Corps hit them hard. Five B-17s, which had been flown up from Mindanao, covered by P-40s and P-35s, bombed the enemy ships lying off Vigan and sank a minesweeper. Two transports had to be beached, and a destroyer and a cruiser were damaged.

Two B-17s appeared over the Aparri landing site, one of them flown by Capt. Colin P. Kelly, Jr., shortly to become America's first war hero. Kelly attacked what he thought was the *Haruna,* a Japanese battleship. The *Haruna,* however, was several hundred miles away; the ship Kelly attacked was apparently a transport.

As the planes left the beach to return to Clark Field, they were attacked by Zeroes. Kelly's Fortress was shot up so badly that the control cables were shattered and the left wing burst into flames. He ordered the crew to abandon the ship. The plane took a steep dive. Down it plunged as all but Kelly bailed out. Below, Major Trapnell's men watched the airplane. It seemed to be heading straight for them, but it veered at the last moment and crashed a short distance away. "There was nothing we could do," Trap said, and he led his men at full speed past the burning wreckage.

The exploit of Colin Kelly, exaggerated by the press—it was said that he dove his crippled plane into the battleship—became an instant legend in the hero-hungry United States.

Trapnell's battle-ready cavalry force combed the area where the enemy paratroopers had been reported, but they found no sign of them. It had been just a rumor, one of many in those first confused days of war.

Wainwright returned to his headquarters at Stotsenburg from his inspection of the Lingayen Gulf beaches late that afternoon to discover that the fort had been heavily bombed during his absence. Only one man had died, but the buildings at Stotsenburg had been severely damaged and a number of the horses of the Twenty-sixth Cavalry had been killed in their stables. It was a sad sight for an old cavalryman. So far, December 10 had been a long, frustrating day, and it wasn't over yet.

That night, Wainwright, and everyone else in the Philippines who could get near a radio, listened to President Roosevelt's fireside chat, his first report to the people since the Japanese attack on Pearl Harbor. His words were grim, particularly for the hard-pressed Philippine garrison, which knew that the Japanese had landed on their island during the day.

"So far, the news has all been bad," the president said. "We have suffered a serious setback in Hawaii. Our forces in the Philippines, which include the brave people of that commonwealth, are taking punishment, but are defending themselves vigorously. The reports from Guam and Wake and Midway Islands are still confused, but we must be prepared for the announcement that all these three outposts have been seized.

"The casualty lists of these first few days will undoubtedly be large," Roosevelt went on. "It will not only be a long war, it will be a hard war."

The president did not tell the people about a meeting he had held earlier that day, which had a direct bearing on the men and women of the Philippines. Soldiers with loaded rifles were standing guard every 100 feet along the White House fence, blackout curtains had been ordered, and gas masks were being distributed as the president conferred with Secretary of War Henry L. Stimson, Army Chief of Staff George Marshall, and other high-level military and civilian leaders. Stimson had once been governor-general of the Philippines and had met both Wainwright and MacArthur.

Among the many urgent topics discussed was the *Pensacola* convoy, which had been on its way to Manila the day war broke out. On December 9 the Joint Army-Navy Board had ordered it to turn around and head back to Hawaii. Now Roosevelt decided to send it to Australia. From there, he argued, we might be able to get its supplies, airplanes, and ammunition to the Philippines. Orders were cut for the convoy to proceed at top speed to Brisbane, but valuable time had already been lost in the more than twenty-four hours since it reversed course. It would arrive in Australia too late to help the defenders of the Philippines.

Wainwright finally got to sleep late on the night of the 10th, only to be awakened shortly after midnight with the news he feared most—the Japanese were reported to be landing at Lingayen Gulf. The early communiques from the front were hazy, but by dawn, General Capinpin, commander of the Twenty-first Division, reported that the invasion attempt had been repulsed. Most of the Japanese ships had been sunk. It was said that "the bay was filled with floating bodies and the beaches strewn with Japanese dead."

At USAFFE headquarters in Manila and at Wainwright's bombed-out offices at Fort Stotsenburg, people were wildly excited. MacArthur's beach defense plan had worked. The Filipino troops had held their ground and beaten the enemy back. This was a great victory and cause for celebration!

Unfortunately, nothing of the kind had happened. The truth was that the untrained Filipino troops had panicked when they heard the sound of the one small motorboat the Japanese had sent into Lingayen Gulf to reconnoiter. The soldiers opened fire on the craft with everything they had. Col. Richard Mallonée, an artillery officer, wrote that "It was like dropping a match in a warehouse of Fourth of July fireworks. Instantly, Lingayen Gulf was ablaze." He could see flashes of artillery, "shell bursts, machine-gun tracer bullets, and small arms. . . . Thousands of shadows were killed that night."

Carl Mydans, a photographer for *Life* magazine, drove north from Manila to Lingayen Gulf as soon as he heard about the battle. He found nothing. No bodies, no destruction, no sign that any fighting at all had occurred. As he strolled along the deserted beach, an American army major approached him.

"Looking for bodies?"

"Well, that's what headquarters reported," Mydans said. "I heard there was a big battle here."

"Everybody wants to see the bodies and the wrecked boats," the major said. "There are no bodies and no boats, though God only knows why we aren't all dead. There was no battle. This is just a green division and they've been shooting the hell out of shadows all night long. First one let go and then another. Finally the whole division opened up and the whole gulf was blazing—but there never was any enemy."

Yet for days, newspapers in the Philippines and the United States trumpeted the story of the defeat the Japanese had suffered. When Wainwright found out the truth, he was all the more concerned about how his inexperienced troops would react to the real thing. Deep down, though, he knew the answer.

The next few days were filled with Japanese bombing raids, by as many as 200 planes at a time, amidst many more rumors and false reports. Wainwright and his senior commanders continued to try to give additional training to their Filipino troops. The only thing he knew for certain was that the Japanese were heading south from their beachheads at Vigan and Aparri. His troops had been unable to stop them. The battalion of Filipinos he had placed in the valley, which was the main route south for the Japanese, had retreated at the first sign of the enemy. They had put up no opposition. By December 12, the enemy had advanced fifty miles.

On that same day a new danger appeared from a different direction. Japanese forces made a successful and unopposed landing at Legaspi, part of General Parker's southern Luzon command. Now the enemy was in place on both ends of the island and moving toward the center, toward the prize of Manila. And still no resistance had been offered on the beaches.

MacArthur held an off-the-record news conference that day to explain his strategy. Editor-publisher Carlos Romulo attended. MacArthur admitted that despite his prewar beliefs, he could not possibly defend the entire coastline with the inadequate number of men under his command.

"The basic principle of handling my troops," MacArthur said, "is to hold them intact until the enemy commits himself in force. These small landings are being made to tempt me to spread out and weaken our defenses."

What the USAFFE commander did not tell Romulo and the others was the news he had heard from Wainwright. The Filipino troops, whom MacArthur had praised so highly to Washington before the war, were not doing well at all in the face of the enemy. Sometimes small units inland had held for a short time, taking a heavy toll among the Japanese before retreating, but all too often they had dropped their weapons and run at the first sign of the enemy, despite the best efforts of their officers. So far, the only major slowdown to the enemy advance had come when the Corps of Engineers had blown up bridges that the Japanese needed to cross. The problem was not with the courage of the Filipino troops; they simply had not had sufficient combat training.

Wainwright spent very little time at Stotsenburg during those days. He was almost always on the road in his dusty Packard, visiting his far-flung units. He frequently went to the front lines, to the consternation of his staff, to buck up morale and give lessons in tactics. He promised his men that he would try to get more supplies. He replaced some units, relieved some officers of their commands, and chewed out others. He appeared to be everywhere that first frantic week of the war, and no commander, general or lieutenant, was surprised to see his tall lanky figure bearing down. He would take the time to listen to each officer's problems as if they were the only ones he had to deal with.

And when the Old Man, whom they all fondly referred to as "Skinny" now behind his back, came to visit a unit, it was not only the officers he spoke to. He always had a good word for the enlisted men because he knew that ultimately, battles are won or lost by the private in his foxhole with his rifle, bayonet, and a few hand grenades.

It was during this period on Luzon that Wainwright earned a new nickname: "the soldier's general." He had the rare knack for instilling in his men the feeling that he cared about them and would look after them, that he understood and shared their problems and their fears. His men knew he was one of them.

One day he came across the remnants of a company of Filipinos in full retreat. They had been badly mauled and some had thrown away their uniforms so they could pass for civilians if they were captured by the Japanese. Some officers in Wainwright's party made loud and derisive comments about the Filipinos, but Skinny silenced them. He pointed to one man who still carried his rifle.

"Ah," the general said, "there's a Joe who still has his gun. God bless him."

Wainwright walked over to the man and began to talk quietly to him. As he patted the frightened soldier on the back, the other Filipinos stopped and gathered around the tall thin officer they had heard so much about. In a few minutes Wainwright had the whole group heading back toward the front line.

In the moments he could spend back at his headquarters at Stotsenburg, usually during the evenings, Wainwright pored over his maps, inventoried his diminishing supplies, fought for reinforcements, and grieved over the growing casualty lists. He was busier and more active than he had been in years, and he loved it. Just a month before, he had remarked to a friend, "We old boys are no good in the field. We can't take it." Every day Wainwright was proving how wrong that casual remark was.

That week a strange procession wended its way through the debris of Fort Stotsenburg to Wainwright's office. It was a group of Pygmies who lived nearby, led by their chief, King Tomas. They had brought something for the Americans—the severed head of a Japanese pilot. They did not say how the pilot had died, and no one wanted to know. The natives had killed one of America's enemies, King Tomas said, and they wanted as a reward six sacks of salt. They left carrying their salt, excited and pleased, but they refused to take the head with them.

On the 13th of December Wainwright decided that he had to move his command post out of Fort Stotsenburg. He needed better access to the front lines and he could no longer depend on the public telephone system to maintain communication with all of his units. He and his senior commanders were often resorting to couriers because the telephones were so frequently out of order. There was also the obvious security risk in discussing secret plans over the phone.

Wainwright moved his operations to Bamban, a small sugar refining town ten miles north of Stotsenburg. A major highway, the Manila North Road, ran through the town. The staff was pleased with the new and luxurious surroundings in the offices of the Bamban Sugar Central Company. The resident manager's home had tiled bathrooms, a sunken tub, and hot water. Tom Dooley, Skinny's junior aide, pronounced it a "delightful spot, like you see in the movies." It would be four years before any of them would see such luxuries again.

The next day Wainwright ordered the Twenty-sixth Cavalry Regiment to Bamban to serve as his primary reserve force, ready to move out at a moment's notice to fill any break in the lines. Judging by the rapid rate at which the Japanese were expanding their beachheads, Wainwright expected such a gap to occur at any time, along with the main Japanese landing. The Twenty-sixth was the only trained unit Wainwright could throw into the breach.

If the American and Filipino forces could just hold out long enough for reinforcements to arrive. Skinny knew about the *Pensacola* convoy. MacArthur's headquarters had notified him that it was expected to dock at Brisbane about December 19. It was comforting to know that help was on the way, that they had not been written off.

The question of reinforcements was on everybody's mind, especially since disheartening rumors about the Japanese successes sprouted by the hour. Most people did not know what to believe. "Rumor or fact?" wrote Juanita Redmond. "It was hard to tell where one began and the other left off. But we could all count the days until a convoy might be due; we could speculate endlessly (in our scant spare moments) when help would come. It didn't occur to us then to say, 'If help will come.'"

*   *   *

It was fortunate that on that day, December 14, neither Wainwright nor Redmond nor anyone else in the islands knew about a meeting that took place in Washington. It was a quiet meeting between two men to decide the fate of the Philippine garrison.

Two days before, in San Antonio, Texas, a newly promoted brigadier general, chief of staff for the Third Army, received a telephone call from the War Department in Washington.

"Is that you, Ike?"

"Yes," Dwight Eisenhower answered.

"The chief says for you to hop a plane and get up here right away."

The caller was Col. Walter Bedell Smith and the chief was Gen. George C. Marshall. Eisenhower guessed correctly why he had been summoned to Washington. It was because of his experience in the Philippines. Marshall wanted someone on the staff who was familiar with conditions out there.

It took Ike two days to get to Washington. There was heavy rain over Texas and all commercial flights had been cancelled. He caught a ride on an army transport to Dallas, where he connected with an eastbound train to Washington, arriving early on the morning of Sunday, December 14. The war was a week old. Ike's brother Milton met him at Union Station and drove him to the Munitions Building.

Marshall wasted no time once Eisenhower was ushered into the office. He talked for twenty minutes, outlining the seriousness of the events in the Pacific. He painted a grim picture. It would be many months before the Pacific Fleet could undertake any offensive operations. Also, the garrison at Hawaii had to be reinforced at once because they were extremely vulnerable to a Japanese invasion. Hawaii was just as liable to be invaded as were the Philippines, but the Hawaiian Islands were much closer to the west coast of the United States. Their capture by the Japanese would be disastrous. Therefore, said the chief of staff, reinforcements for Hawaii took priority.

The Philippine garrison was desperate. It had no navy, its air force had been effectively destroyed, and there were serious shortages of all commodities. The Japanese intended to capture the Philippines, and Marshall's problem, which he now handed to Eisenhower, was to decide what should be done about it.

"What should be our general line of action?" Marshall asked.

"Give me a few hours," Eisenhower said.

Ike left the office and walked down the corridor to the War Plans Division and his desk as the new deputy chief for the Pacific and Far East. He sat down to ponder the problem. He knew that he was being put to a personal test. His answer to Marshall's question would determine the course of his career. He was sure that the chief of staff had already decided on the best course of action and that he, Ike, was being judged. He would "drop to the bottom, be suspended in mediocrity, or rise to the top," all on the basis of what he recommended about the Philippines.

He stared for a long time at a map of the Pacific, then began typing his response with two fingers on a piece of yellow paper. The conclusions he reached were bleak, but he was convinced that there was no alternative. There was no way to save the Philippine garrison.

There were, however, two points to consider. The garrison must be encouraged to hold out as long as possible, and it must not appear—to the American people or to the rest of the world—that the United States was abandoning its outpost. A few hours later, that was what he told General Marshall.

"General," Eisenhower said, "it will be a long time before major reinforcements can go to the Philippines, longer than the garrison can hold out with any driblet assistance. . . . But we must do everything for them that is humanly possible. The people of China, of the Philippines, of the Dutch East Indies will be watching us. They may excuse failure but they will not excuse abandonment."

Ike went on to suggest that the United States prepare a base in Australia from which they might be able to send small amounts of supplies to the Philippines, and which would serve as a staging area for future aggressive operations against the Japanese.

Marshall listened to the suggestions in silence.

"I agree with you," he said finally. "Do your best to save them."

Eisenhower returned to his office to try to calculate how much time he had before the Japanese landed their main invasion force on Luzon.

That was also the big question in Wainwright's mind—when would the Japanese make their major landing?—but he had an additional concern. When the enemy came to Lingayen Gulf, it would be his responsibility, and his alone, to repulse them. Would his troops be up to it? Were they ready? Had he done enough? Could someone else have done more in the circumstances? There was little time for worry or speculation because a more immediate problem came to his attention. The situation in the north of Luzon was deteriorating. The Japanese forces that had landed at Vigan were pushing south toward Lingayen Gulf. Wainwright's raw Filipino troops had so far proved helpless to stop them.

Something had to be done, but Wainwright's options were limited. He had to keep the major forces around Lingayen Gulf intact. He could not afford to weaken them by sending assistance to the Vigan sector. The Twenty-sixth Cavalry, his only reserve, would have to go.

Wainwright called in Clint Pierce and gave him his orders. The Twenty-sixth, now at a strength of 699 men and 28 officers, was to move northward and take up a position at the town of Rosales on the Agno River. There they would be able to launch a counterattack if the Japanese force from Vigan broke through.

That same day, December 16, Wainwright received a welcome change of orders from MacArthur. He was no longer charged with the defense of all of northern Luzon. The area north of the town of San Fernando, La Union, on the island's west coast, was to be evacuated and conceded to the enemy. A new defense line would be established, running just north of San Fernando, La Union, to the east coast of Luzon.

As Wainwright plotted the complicated troop movements for the new defense line the next day, he became aware of one disturbing fact. San Fernando, La Union, was only twenty-seven miles north of Lingayen Gulf. When the Japanese invaded there, his troops in the north would be in danger of being cut off behind enemy lines. The old question haunted him. When would the main invasion come? He could not know that it was already on its way.

Japanese convoys had set sail on December 17 from Formosa and the Pescadores with 43,110 combat troops. Their destination—Lingayen Gulf in the Philippine Islands—was a mystery to all but a handful of Homma's men. It would remain concealed from them until they landed. Only a few officers were permitted to study the maps. The secrecy led to a sense of uneasiness among the troops and anxiety among the officers. Even Homma's staff members were nervous. So much depended on this operation. If the landing did not succeed, and on schedule, the Japanese timetable for the conquest of the South Pacific would be upset. The future course of the war depended on the outcome.

No one aboard the ships was more concerned than Homma

himself. He was worried that his force would not be large enough and he was unsure about how it would perform. This was the first taste of combat for his men. If they failed, he would, of course, be held responsible.

"During all my campaigns in the Philippines," General Homma wrote later, "I had three critical moments, and this was number one."

While the Japanese convoy steamed south at eight knots, panic spread among the Filipino civilians on Luzon. Terrified refugees streamed toward Manila from the north. Japanese planes swarmed overhead every day, virtually unchallenged. The people could see clearly how much damage had been inflicted. They had only to drive past Clark Field and the other American bases, or look across Manila Bay to the still smoldering wreckage of the great naval base at Cavite, or walk along the waterfront to spot the sunken ships in the bay.

Rumors, uncertainty, and alarm were growing, and MacArthur knew he had to do something to calm the populace. He telephoned his friend, Carlos Romulo, the newspaper editor.

"I'm calling you to active duty," MacArthur said.

Romulo hesitated, explaining that he would need some time to put his affairs in order.

"I'm not asking you," MacArthur interrupted. "I'm ordering you. Report tomorrow morning."

The next day Romulo showed up wearing the hastily tailored uniform of a major in the Philippine Army Reserve. MacArthur greeted him warmly.

"Carlos, my boy, congratulations! But who made you that terrible uniform?"

He told Romulo that his new job would place him in charge of all the news released to the press and the radio.

"Keep 'em warned," MacArthur said, referring to the Filipino forces, "but don't panic them."

Romulo settled down to work. It was a job he would continue to perform under Wainwright on Corregidor.

On the 18th, Skinny moved his headquarters farther north, near the town of Alcala on the Agno River, closer to where the invasion would take place. There were no luxuries about this command post. The staff lived in camouflaged tents under a grove of trees and Skinny moved into an old house trailer that would serve as his home and C.P. for the next three months. It was an aluminum trailer, eighteen feet long, that had been camouflaged with swathes of green and brown paint. The accommodations were spartan—an army cot, an old wooden table, and a few chairs.

That evening Wainwright found out that it was Tom Dooley's birthday. Amidst all the problems of preparing for the invasion, Skinny took the time to drop by Dooley's tent and extend his best wishes. The young man was pleased, and he recorded the visit in his diary that night.

"The general felt he must give me something, and he reached in his pocket and gave me a lucky piece from a convention he attended in Atlanta in 1930 of the 82nd Division [Wainwright's outfit during World War I]. He had carried the piece in his pocket since that time and was quite fond of it so it is a nice gift."

It was typical of Wainwright to be thoughtful and considerate of others, even in these difficult times. His actions help explain why his men went to such great lengths for him in the months ahead.

December 20 was a bad day for Wainwright, full of disturbing news. An aide awakened him at 2:30 A.M. with a report from USAFFE headquarters in Manila. An American submarine, the U.S.S. *Stingray*, had spotted a convoy of eighty enemy ships only forty miles north of Lingayen Gulf.

A few hours later he received news of a Japanese landing far to the south, at the port city of Davao on the island of Mindanao. By 3:00 that afternoon, the Japanese had taken control of that city and the airport, and were preparing to invade the neighboring island of Jolo, where Wainwright had fought his first war thirty-two years before. The capture of Jolo, which was a foregone conclusion, would isolate the Philippines from Australia. Jolo would give the Japanese forces an air base from which they could attack any American ships trying to bring help to the islands. The noose was closing.

Another disaster was reported that day, this one closer at hand. The two small Japanese forces that had landed at Aparri and Vigan ten days before had now linked up and were ready to take the coastal road south to Lingayen Gulf. Wainwright had to stop them.

He had two American-led Filipino battalions waiting, entrenched a few miles north of San Fernando, La Union, spread across the narrow plain through which the highway ran. To their left was the sea, to their right a mountain range.

When the Japanese struck, they hit hard, and the manner of their attack was unexpected. They made a massive frontal assault. In addition, a large number of troops slipped across the mountain range, thought to be impenetrable, and struck at the inexperienced defenders on their right flank. This was too much for the green Filipino troops. They broke and ran, dispersing in small groups into the mountains. Some of them did not filter back for two weeks.

The Japanese swarmed into the valley and in a very short time were in the town of San Fernando, La Union, itself. The east-west line Wainwright was supposed to defend had been breached. When the reports of the action reached him, he immediately planned a counterattack, committing his only reserve forces, the Twenty-sixth Cavalry.

Swiftly he sent the orders to Colonel Pierce. The troopers were to head north from their position at Rosales and do battle with the Japanese. Pierce's men were then several hours from enemy lines. They started out at once, but they never got there. A new emergency would soon send them elsewhere.

As usual, Wainwright got little sleep that night. In the early morning hours of December 21, while he was still trying to deal with the breakthrough at San Fernando, La Union, his attention was drawn to the vital beaches of Lingayen Gulf. Word had come from the little town of Bauang, just seven miles south of San Fernando, that Filipino soldiers had seen a Japanese trawler offshore. It had sailed slowly back and forth, taking soundings of the bay, and after a while it headed north. Not a shot was fired at it.

At about the same time, Wainwright received a report from MacArthur's headquarters that a convoy of 100 to 120 ships was expected to reach the mouth of Lingayen Gulf by evening. The news could mean only one thing. The main Japanese invasion of Luzon would take place that night.

The general and his staff pored over the troop deployments for the 120-mile coastline of Lingayen Gulf that he and MacArthur had worked out some time ago. No matter how many times he looked at his map, however, he still came to the same conclusion. The defenses were not adequate. He needed more troops, a larger mobile reserve, and many more artillery pieces. But none of these things existed. He didn't even have proper maps. Some were Spanish, from the last century, and others had been drawn in 1907, in insufficient detail for military operations. "Not one was worth a tinker's damn."

The entire coastline was held by two divisions of the Philippine army—the Eleventh and the Twenty-first. The southern curve of the bay, where everyone expected the landing to take place, was where the artillery of the Twenty-first had been placed—155mm guns. Four of them. That was all they had. The eastern shore of the gulf, as far north as San Fernando, was held by the Eleventh Division and the Seventy-first Infantry Regiment of the Seventy-first Division. The regiment, which had had only ten weeks of training, was attached to the Eleventh Division and headquartered at Bauang. The beaches around Bauang were the only part of the shoreline where the Filipino troops were actually dug in. One battalion was there, with one .50-caliber and several .30-caliber machine guns.

With the invasion imminent, Wainwright had to reconsider the position of the Twenty-sixth Cavalry. He could not now risk sending his only well-trained unit so far north. He sent a courier to Pierce with new orders, attaching the regiment to Brougher's Eleventh Division. The cavalry was to proceed to Rosario, where it would then be able to move either north or south, depending on where the Japanese came ashore.

In an effort to hold the Japanese advance at San Fernando, La Union, Wainwright ordered the Seventy-first Infantry Regiment, under Col. Donald Bonnett, to secure the Manila North Road against any further southward movement by the Japanese. Bonnett's men were Wainwright's greenest troops, but they were the closest to the scene and all he could spare for the job. He rounded up some buses for them and sent them chugging up the coastal road to do battle. Now there were even fewer troops to defend the coastline.

Impatient, tired, frustrated, dependent on messengers and the public telephone as his eyes and ears, Skinny Wainwright sweated through the long night, waiting for the signal that the Japanese invasion had begun.

CHAPTER 5
"A Bold Gamble"

W HILE WAINWRIGHT WAITED and worried through the night at his headquarters at Alcala, General Homma waited and worried aboard his headquarters ship in Lingayen Gulf. Both men were feeling the strain of events and both knew that the next few hours would spell success or failure for the entire Philippine campaign. They waited not only in darkness, but also in the absence of any solid information about what was happening. The events had been set in motion. The generals had done all they could. Now, cut off from their troops, they were powerless for the moment to do anything but wait. And that is always the hardest part of war.

At 1:10 A.M. on the morning of December 22, eighty-five Japanese transports began dropping anchor a mile or two off the northern coast of Lingayen Gulf. They were not landing where Wainwright and MacArthur had expected them to, on the southern rim of the gulf, where the bulk of the American and Filipino defenses were concentrated. But the Japanese were not landing where Homma expected them to, either.

The night was unusually dark, the seas heavy, and rain was falling intermittently. Because of the foul weather, the lead ship of the convoy dropped anchor eight miles from the landing site. This meant that all the invasion barges had to travel an extra eight miles in choppy seas before they could land.

The situation quickly deteriorated. The high waves made it

difficult to load the barges, and they bobbed around so much that the men and their equipment were soon soaked. The salt water knocked the Japanese radios out of operation, making it impossible to communicate with the ships of the convoy. Homma and his officers were out on the bridge, peering into the darkness, expecting American artillery to open up on them at any moment.

The landing itself was a disaster. The swells prevented the men from putting ashore their heavy equipment. Many barges overturned in the surf and others were tossed onto the beach so hard that they could not be used again for several hours, until the tide came in. As a result, the second wave of troops could not be loaded as scheduled. Part of the convoy sailed farther north to seek calmer waters, stretching the line of Japanese ships to fifteen miles. All that saved the initial landing from turning into a defeat was that there was no opposition on the beaches.

At 5:17 A.M. the first Japanese troops put ashore near the town of Agoo. At 5:30 another group landed at Aringay, and two hours later a third landing was made at Bauang. Only at Bauang did they meet any resistance. There, with a single .50-caliber machine gun, the Filipino battalion inflicted heavy casualties. Had they been more heavily armed, they might have beaten off the attack, but their gun jammed early in the action because of faulty ammunition.

Despite these losses, the enemy continued to swarm ashore at Bauang, and the plucky Filipinos were forced to withdraw. During the action, neither Wainwright nor Homma could get any news from the beaches. They did not know whether they were winning or losing.

In the early morning hours the Japanese convoy was attacked by American naval and air forces—one antiquated submarine, some of whose torpedoes were faulty, four B-17s, and a few P-40s. The sub sank a transport and the planes damaged several ships, though none severely.

At the same time, the increasingly rough seas forced a large portion of the convoy to seek the more protected waters at the southern end of the gulf, and here they came under fire from Wainwright's only artillery in the area, the four 155s. The gunners claimed two destroyers and three transports sunk, but they actually did no damage.

Fragmentary and occasionally conflicting reports reached Wainwright by dawn. He learned that the enemy was ashore at several places and pushing inland rapidly, but he was unable to get a complete picture of the situation. From the information he did have, however, he knew that the encroachment on the northern edge of Lingayen Gulf was serious. As he examined his maps, he realized that it was potentially disastrous.

The threat was not only that the Japanese had established several beachheads, it was where they had established them. The northern landing at Bauang was in a position to cut off Colonel Bonnett's Seventy-first Infantry Regiment, which Wainwright had sent north to San Fernando, La Union, to try to stop the combined forces moving down from Vigan and Aparri. By 11:00, Bonnett's force was in serious danger because the Japanese who had landed at Bauang had linked up with the northern force. By 1:00 the Seventy-first was almost completely cut off. Somehow, Wainwright had to save them.

His decision was complicated because Bonnett's force had been moving north in two segments. He ordered the southernmost portion to turn around and head south, to join the Eleventh Division. The larger group, now too far north to return directly to American lines, was ordered east toward Baguio and from there to rejoin American forces.

Wainwright's problems were increasing hourly. Although most of the Japanese troops were still aboard their ships, more had been landed, along with some tanks and artillery, and they were all pushing south along the coastal road to Manila. They had to be stopped. In late afternoon the enemy was reported to be ashore outside the town of Damortis. Now there were four beachheads covering a distance of almost twenty miles.

The Eleventh Division was being sorely tried. Its unprepared Filipino troops were giving way every time they confronted the enemy. At some positions they panicked. Any attempt to make an orderly withdrawal turned into a rout. There was no hope now of trying to turn back the Japanese. The only realistic goal for Wainwright was to try to prevent the enemy from advancing any farther south and to keep his men from being cut off on the beaches.

Again he called upon his only reserve, the remaining men of the Twenty-sixth Cavalry. He told his chief of staff, Bill Maher, "The Twenty-sixth are the only ones sure to stop them from being in Manila in a few hours."

Wainwright ordered Clint Pierce to lead his troopers north and to hold the enemy above the ten-mile-long road that ran from Damortis on the coast east to the town of Rosario. He knew that he was asking the impossible, but he had no other units capable of checking the enemy advance. To help his cavalrymen he decided to ask for a tank battalion from Brig. Gen. James Weaver's Provisional Tank Group, a unit which was not under his command, but under MacArthur's direct control.

Wainwright reached for the telephone and tried to get through to MacArthur. He reached the chief of staff, Dick Sutherland. Skinny was blunt, wasting no time on niceties. As a field commander he was not a politician, even when dealing with superiors.

"Give me a tank battalion," he told Sutherland, "or the Japs will be in Manila in no time. I have only the riddled Twenty-sixth to stop them while I get off the beaches."

"No," Sutherland said. He added a gratuitous remark about staying to defend our "sacred soil."

"I'm the corps commander," Wainwright said testily. "Let me fight as I see it or they'll be in your lap in a few hours. Give me permission to do what I can."

"I'll ask the general," Sutherland said, and he hung up.

A short while later he called Wainwright to report MacArthur's permission to use some tanks, but not nearly as many as Skinny had requested.

Weaver sent five tanks to accompany the cavalry. One was crippled by enemy fire immediately and the others were damaged soon after. It was all up to the men of the Twenty-Sixth.

The Japanese hit the thin line of cavalrymen with infantry, tanks, planes, and naval bombardment from the ships offshore. The fighting was savage and lasted more than three hours. The soldiers of the Twenty-sixth fought well, but in the end they were simply outgunned and were forced to withdraw toward Rosario. The regimental headquarters served as a rear guard, with Colonel Pierce himself leading the defense.

The cavalry unit suffered heavy losses and were being dogged by the Japanese tanks. The men moved along the road as quickly as they could. The battle became so confused at one point that the lead Japanese tank rode right into the middle of the regiment. Suddenly all hell seemed to break loose, and the Twenty-sixth Cavalry found itself in disarray. Terrified, riderless horses plunged about madly as the enemy tanks fired from point-blank range.

Now the rear guard was being led by Major Trapnell. Japanese tanks were right behind him as he came upon a wooden bridge spanning a stream with sides so steep that he knew the tanks would be unable to cross if the bridge were knocked out. Trap sized up the situation quickly and picked two other officers to come with him.

They got into the veterinary truck and drove out to the middle of the bridge. With Japanese machine-gun and cannon fire raging on all sides, Trap fired his .45 into the carburetor of the truck and set it afire, effectively blocking the bridge. The action brought the Distinguished Service Cross for all three men.

Later that night, when Skinny received a report of the regiment's actions, he was saddened by the losses his favorite outfit had suffered. Only 175 effectives could be found at the end of the day. Several hundred others had been cut off in small groups. It took three days before all of them were able to rejoin the regiment. Actual losses were about 150 killed and wounded. Wainwright ordered them out of the line and put the Seventy-first Division in their place. He wanted them to have time to regroup, but circumstances would force them back into action the very next day.

During that afternoon, Wainwright had had a more personal worry as well. His aides, Johnny Pugh and Tom Dooley, were missing. They had gone north with him to Rosario in the morning. There Skinny said he wanted to go on to Damortis, to check on the Twenty-sixth Cavalry. The staff tried to talk him out of it, concerned that he might be cut off by the invading Japanese forces. Pugh and Dooley volunteered to find the Twenty-sixth and report back to him.

Several hours later, when the men had not returned, Wainwright grew restless. He knew the area had been bombed and shelled and that the aides had risked their lives to protect him, to keep him from going into the threatened sector. He told his headquarters staff that before too long he intended to go north himself to try to find them.

Finally Pugh and Dooley were spotted by the general's orderly, Tex Carroll, as they approached the command post. Carroll rushed up to them.

"Lieutenant," he said to Dooley, "when you and Captain Pugh go off again for the Old Man, don't stay so long. He was about crazy. That general was afraid you two had been bombed and was about to go after you."

By the end of the day, Wainwright and his senior commanders knew that the war was going badly. No one seemed capable of stopping the Japanese. If Wainwright continued to try to fight the enemy on the plains of Luzon, his poorly trained units would be outgunned and outflanked at every turn. Surely it was time to put War Plan Orange-3 into effect and withdraw into the narrow confines of Bataan, where strong defensive lines could be established. But that was a decision only MacArthur could make. Wainwright had to contain the enemy in whatever way he could. If the Japanese broke through his meager defenses, the road to Manila would be open for them. He got very little sleep that night.

At USAFFE headquarters in Manila, General MacArthur also found it difficult to sleep. On his desk was a radio message from General George Marshall indicating that the *Pensacola* convoy had docked at Brisbane, Australia. In addition, three B-24s and B-17s were scheduled to leave for Australia every day until January 1. Pilots were supposed to ferry the B-17s from Seattle, Washington, as soon as they came off the assembly line.

Also on MacArthur's desk were reports from Wainwright on the extent of the Japanese invasion. He needed help right away— particularly fighters and dive bombers—which MacArthur had earlier suggested be brought in by aircraft carrier. MacArthur drafted a message to Marshall repeating his request. "Can I expect anything along that line?" he asked.

Then he began to work on a longer message outlining the events of the day and the size of the enemy force now on northern Luzon. He exaggerated the size of that force, reporting it as 80,000 to 100,000 men, considerably more than the 43,000 troops Homma had under his command. MacArthur also underestimated the size of his American-Filipino force as being only 40,000, when it was actually closer to 80,000. The reason for these statements was probably that MacArthur was finally considering the initiation of WPO-3, the very plan he had argued against so adamantly a few months before. He had not made up his mind yet, but he was building a case to Washington for its implementation—for the reason that his troops were outnumbered—should he later decide to revert to it. Everything depended on the troops of Wainwright's North Luzon Force. Would they be able to stiffen their resistance in the next day or two? If not, the only salvation lay in the extremely dangerous phased withdrawal into Bataan. And that would be Skinny Wainwright's job.

The next morning, December 23, Wainwright anxiously waited word on what was shaping up to be a crucial battle for his Seventy-first Division.

Given only ten weeks of training and equipped with old Enfield rifles, which few of the Filipinos had even learned to shoot, the division was now at Sison, four miles south of Rosario. Their mission was to prevent the Japanese from moving south on Highway 3, the Manila North Road. If the enemy broke through at

Sison, they would have a clear road to the capital and be in a position to outflank the Twenty-first Division on the southern edge of Lingayen Gulf. The Seventy-first had to hold, or at least to delay the Japanese advance as long as possible.

To help them, Wainwright ordered the Ninety-first Combat Team to reinforce the division, but they could not be in place before noon. The Japanese did not wait that long. They struck in the morning, but were unable to pierce the line, largely because of the deadly fire from the Seventy-first Division's artillery.

By twelve o'clock, the enemy still had not been able to advance, but then they tried again, this time with a massive frontal assault aided by tanks and planes. The attack was too much for the Filipino infantry. They broke and ran to the rear, through their own artillery.

At headquarters, Wainwright sweated out the retreat, still hoping that the Ninety-first Combat Team would arrive in time to stop the Japanese. They could not. The unit was held up at a bridge that the Japanese planes had destroyed, and were still far from the scene.

Wainwright was receiving frequent reports giving the details of the enemy breakthrough. Each message was more discouraging than the previous one. A new line would have to be established on Highway 3, to be held by some unit other than the Seventy-first, until that division had time to reorganize. Studying his map, he chose a spot near the town of Pozorrubio, four miles south of Sison, as the place to make his new stand.

The Ninety-first Combat Team was ordered to the line, along with the exhausted Twenty-sixth Cavalry, still reeling from their losses of the day before. Wainwright knew the plan was a stopgap measure at best. The Twenty-sixth and Ninety-first were too small to delay the enemy for long. The Japanese would probably break through them by nightfall, further menacing the Twenty-first Division on the southern edge of Lingayen Gulf. Something drastic was called for. A strong defensive line had to be set up immediately, or there would be no hope of preventing the enemy from overrunning all of Luzon. Wainwright had to take advantage of whatever natural barriers the terrain offered. There was only one such obstacle—the deep, wide Agno River, which was twenty miles inland from the Lingayen coast.

His decision made, Wainwright telephoned MacArthur's headquarters in Manila. Dick Sutherland came on the line. General Wainwright told him that it was impossible to continue to hold the beaches. He explained his plan to set up a defensive line along the Agno River. Sutherland agreed to the idea.

Then Wainwright mentioned another plan he had been formulating over the past few hours, to launch a counterattack once his forces had regrouped behind the Agno River. It was a daring and bold idea, but he knew it had no chance of succeeding with the troops presently under his command. They were too demoralized and poorly prepared. He needed a fresh division, one that was well trained and ready for combat. He wanted his old command, the Philippine Division, which MacArthur was holding in reserve to the south.

Sutherland told Wainwright to submit his plans for the attack to headquarters.

"I'll get my plans there as soon as possible," Wainwright said. "But give me an answer now on whether I get the Philippine Division."

There was silence on the line for a moment.

"It's highly improbable," Sutherland said.

This was a great blow to Wainwright. He was sure that with the Philippine Division he could surprise the Japanese, and perhaps cut off some of their southernmost units. But he could not do that with only the troops he had at present. Nevertheless, he continued to work out his idea for the counterattack. There was always the chance that MacArthur would change his mind.

But MacArthur didn't change his mind, and Skinny didn't get his Philippine Division. Quite the opposite. His request marked the beginning of a long retreat. Wainwright's plan to withdraw to the Agno River finally seemed to spur MacArthur to action, into making the decision to put WPO-3 into effect.

It was a decision that was made too late. MacArthur's delay in implementing the plan hastened, his biographer wrote, "the downfall of the American and Filipino defenders of Bataan more than did any subsequent action by Homma's troops."

That night, while Wainwright was at work designing his counterattack strategy, he received a telephone call from Col. Pete Irwin at MacArthur's headquarters.

"WPO-3 is in effect," Irwin said.

Wainwright said nothing for a moment. He was too disappointed to reply.

"You understand?" Irwin asked.

"Yes, I understand," he replied quietly.

The news was hard for him to take. He would not be given the chance to attack. His responsibility now was to hold back the waves of Japanese troops until the rest of MacArthur's forces had fled safely into Bataan.

The next day Skinny Wainwright came very close to being killed. He had spent the early morning hours at his desk, writing out the orders to all the units under his command, putting WPO-3 into effect. Accompanied by his aide, Lt. Tom Dooley, and by his G-3, Col. Frank Nelson, he got into his Packard and drove ten miles north of the Agno River to the town of Binalonan, which had been under heavy attack by the Japanese since 5:00 A.M. The Seventy-first Division was at Binalonan, and Wainwright wanted to see the division commander, Clyde Selleck.

There were two roads Wainwright could take to Binalonan—the main highway, number 3, or a secondary road parallel to it. He chose the secondary road. As they neared the town they saw a platoon of Japanese tanks rolling south on the main highway, no more than 200 yards to the left. Had they come up the highway, they would have run right into them.

Despite the danger and the realization that they might be cut off if the tanks went farther south, Wainwright pushed on for Binalonan without a moment's hesitation. At 11:30 they reached the center of town and were shocked to find it deserted. There were a few abandoned trucks and buses in the square, but not a single human being. There was supposed to be an entire division here!

Perplexed and angry, Wainwright drove toward the north-western outskirts of the town, toward the sound of heavy firing, and found the weary men of the Twenty-sixth Cavalry. They had been holding off the enemy for the last six hours. At one point the Twenty-sixth, now numbering 450 men, had launched a counterat-tack, only to be stopped by Japanese tanks.

Wainwright stopped the car when he saw Major Trapnell and asked him what had happened. The Seventy-first had evidently withdrawn to the Agno River during the night, leaving the embattled Twenty-sixth, which was supposed to have been out of the line regrouping, to serve as the rear guard.

Against the advice of Trap and the others, Skinny insisted on going to the regimental command post, even though it was under small arms and artillery fire from the enemy, who were no more than 400 yards away. With his characteristic calmness under fire, he ordered his car parked behind a shack nearby and walked on to talk to Colonel Pierce. As shells exploded around them and bullets whistled overhead, the two old cavalrymen discussed the situation.

Wainwright then ordered Pierce to send the wounded and his supply train south to the Agno and to withdraw slowly toward the river, fighting a delaying action all the while. It was a tough job, one that could not have been handled by any of the green divisions under Wainwright's command, but he was sure the Twenty-sixth Cavalry could do it.

Wainwright stayed at Binalonan for several hours, longer than was needed to take stock of the situation and to issue the necessary orders. The truth was that he was enjoying himself. This was where a soldier ought to be, at the front where the fighting is, not at a desk coping with a stack of papers. Wainwright knew it was good for the morale of his men to see him there, sharing their dangers. If there was any outfit that deserved his presence, it was his beloved Twenty-sixth Cavalry.

The men were delighted to know that the general was with them. One said that "word of his presence spread up and down the line like wildfire and the men settled down to their sharpshooting of incautiously exposed Japs with renewed confidence." A last, hoarded bottle of scotch was produced, and "we all had a quick shot and a toast." When it finally came time for him and his officers to leave, they did so "in the same leisurely manner in which they had arrived," in his defenseless Packard sedan. The regiment could not spare even a scout car to escort him, nor did he want one. He would take his chances like everyone else. He did not know if the enemy was behind him or if they had surrounded the town, but before he left he received a message from Major Trapnell that the road east of town was still clear.

The valiant Twenty-sixth held on until after 3:00 that afternoon, stopping the enemy with dogged courage. Their only antitank weapons were soda bottles filled with gasoline. Then, when Wainwright sent word for them to withdraw, "the troopers ran from their foxholes to their horses. Trotting five minutes, then walking five minutes, they headed for the Agno River."

Wainwright later described the actions of the Twenty-sixth Cavalry in his official report on the campaign. "I was personally present during a portion of this fight and cannot speak in too glowing terms of the gallantry and the intrepidity displayed by Colonel Pierce and all officers and men of the Twenty-sixth Cavalry on this occasion. This devoted little band of horsemen . . . had maintained the best traditions of the American Cavalry." The

Twenty-sixth Cavalry clearly lived up to its code name "mighty" that day.

Wainwright ran into another problem on the way back to his headquarters. As he drove along the banks of the Agno River, he saw that the bridge between the towns of Carmen and Villasis had been partially destroyed by Japanese airplanes. He stopped the car, got out, and stared at the wreckage. The bridge was the major escape route to the south for his Eleventh Division. They were scheduled to cross tonight. Without the bridge, the Eleventh might be lost.

While he stood there considering his options, his engineering officer, Col. Harry Skerry, appeared at his side. Skerry saved the day and, very likely, the Eleventh Division. He had already arranged to repair the bridge before nightfall and to blow it up once the division had crossed. Grateful that he had one less problem to deal with, Wainwright proceeded along the south bank of the river, checking his defenses, and making sure that everything was ready for the complicated maneuvers he would be undertaking to implement WPO-3.

That night an angry Clint Pierce came to his headquarters. He was furious with the commander of the Seventy-first Division for having pulled out his troops, leaving the Twenty-sixth on its own. Skinny listened to him quietly, letting him spend his frustration. Then he pulled a .45-caliber bullet from his belt and placed it on his desk in front of Pierce. He grinned at his old friend.

"You know what to do with him," he said.

Wainwright and his officers were familiar with the withdrawal plan. They had studied it before the outbreak of war and had carried out maneuvers over the terrain involved. The withdrawal to Bataan was to take place through a series of five defensive or delay lines, each one separated from the next by a distance that could be covered in one night's march. Each of the five lines had to be occupied before dawn and held until dark, at which time the bulk of the troops would withdraw to the next line. A small rear guard would stay in position until just before daybreak, when it would join the rest of the troops at the next line to the south. The last line was to be held longer than the rest, long enough to permit the South Luzon Force to withdraw behind it into the Bataan peninsula.

The Americans hoped that the Japanese would have to halt their advance in order to deploy their troops before each line. Thus, they would be delayed until the South Luzon Force had come north on

Route 3 to San Fernando, Pampanga, where they would meet Highway 7 to the west, taking them to Bataan. It was imperative that Wainwright's troops hold long enough for the 15,000 men of the South Luzon Force to reach Bataan. Otherwise they would be captured. Without these troops there would be little hope of holding Bataan for any length of time.

The difficulties facing Wainwright at this time were described by MacArthur's biographer, D. Clayton James. They were "so formidable that the plan was, indeed, a bold gamble. . . . Somehow divisions with only a third of their authorized strength would have to hold critical positions for long hours. Somehow companies and regiments that had collapsed during the first days of fighting, many of whose men were now wandering in rear areas, would have to be reorganized quickly and sent back to fill gaps in the front lines. . . . Somehow, despite enemy air supremacy, vital bridges would have to be protected until the USAFFE troops were across, and then be demolished before the arrival of enemy forces who often were close behind. Somehow the North Luzon Force, with its thinly manned lines stretched across the wide Central Luzon Plain, would have to guard its flanks from envelopment long enough for the South Luzon Force to complete its arduous movement from Tayabas Bay to Bataan. And finally, Wainwright's force would then have to disengage itself and back into Bataan in a danger-laden rearguard maneuver dependent upon precise timing. A more difficult operation than the planned retreat into Bataan, or one beset by more disastrous contingencies, had seldom been attempted in military history."

Whether it would succeed or fail depended entirely on Wainwright, a man put out to pasture only three years before.

While he made his last-minute arrangements for the phased withdrawal into Bataan on that afternoon of December 24, other men were trying to fortify Bataan to be defended. George Parker turned over command of his South Luzon Force to Brig. Gen. Albert M. Jones and went to Bataan to take charge. Because MacArthur had ruled out the use of WPO-3 before the war, little had been done to provide for the defense of the peninsula, and now it was far too late to do so adequately.

Supply officers worked around the clock to move food, ammunition, medical supplies, communications equipment—everything an army needed—into the dense, mosquito-infested jungles of Bataan. It was a huge logistical undertaking, all under the command of Brig. Gen. Charles C. Drake, Quartermaster, who had only 1,300

troops and seven days at his disposal to make provisions for as many
as 80,000 incoming men. Before the war, Drake had decided that
under the best of conditions it would take at least two weeks to
transfer the supplies to Bataan. Now he had only half that time and
the size of the force to be supplied was twice that planned for in
WPO-3. The job did not go smoothly, as Wainwright would later
learn. It was a nightmare, General Drake said, of "red tape,
stupidity, and panic."

The city of Manila was stripped of all military supplies, which
Drake had shipped to Bataan and Corregidor in 300 barge loads.
That part of the operation went fairly well, except that more
supplies were sent to Corregidor than to Bataan, even though
Bataan would house eight times as many men. It was on Mac-
Arthur's orders that more food was sent to Corregidor. Drake was
ordered to send no supplies at all to Bataan until the shipments to
Corregidor were completed.

This decision was unpopular with the men who found themselves
on Bataan. However, a staff officer for MacArthur, who later
served under Wainwright, wrote in his diary: "Our high command,
I believe, was prepared to sacrifice the Bataan forces to starvation
rather than to take the risk of being starved out on Corregidor. It
was a correct military decision, however heartless it might seem."

A major breakdown occurred in getting supplies from northern
Luzon to Bataan. At Fort Stotsenburg and other supply depots,
huge quantities of gasoline, fresh beef and other foodstuffs,
uniforms, ammunition, and equipment were abandoned because
the outposts had been evacuated prematurely.

In addition, the Manila railroad, which could have hauled a great
deal of the materiel, had no crews to run the trains. The civilian
workmen had deserted, and the Philippine government would not
allow American troops to take over. Government officials also
refused to permit U.S. forces to confiscate food stored in commercial warehouses, even those owned by Japanese companies. Even
Filipino-owned rice and sugar, which were stored in sizable quantities on Luzon, could not be moved to Bataan. A permit was
required to ship these commodities from one province to another.
The U.S. Army quartermaster officers, confronted by a bu-
reaucracy stunned by the suddenness of the onset of war, were
almost helpless. At one depot, some fifty million bushels of rice had
to be abandoned, only to be burned later by the Japanese army. Not
one sack of it could be moved to Bataan. As little as twenty percent

of that rice would have been sufficient to feed every soldier on Bataan for almost a year.

As a result of the government's confusion, and MacArthur's reluctance to order WPO-3, the American and Filipino troops on Bataan would soon be starving. And in the end, it was the lack of food more than the military efforts of the Japanese that would lead to the fall of Bataan. Lt. Harold K. Johnson, later Army Chief of Staff, confirmed this. "It wasn't the enemy that licked us; it was disease and the absence of food that really licked us."

If that were not enough, MacArthur's delay in implementing WPO-3 meant that there would be fewer troops available to defend Bataan. The plan had called for the forces stationed in the southern islands, at least three divisions, to be sent to Bataan when hostilities began. By December 24 it was too late to do that because the Japanese navy was in control of the seas.

Wainwright and his men were unaware of these things when they began their heroic withdrawal into Bataan. They did not know that they had been beaten by bureaucratic bungling, inefficiency, and the hesitant and reluctant actions of the USAFFE commander even before they set foot on the peninsula. Thousands would die and thousands more would suffer three and a half years of captivity because of these factors.

Wainwright returned to his headquarters late in the evening of December 24, after a long, tiring day. His aides reminded him that it was Christmas Eve. It was a sad time for all of them. Christmas had always been a joyous season in the Wainwright home. Skinny could recall holidays with huge gaily decorated trees, with presents beneath for his dear "Kitty" and their son Jack. He had never spent a Christmas apart from his wife and he missed her greatly. He thought for a moment, then put in a call to a friend at the RCA offices in Manila, and arranged to have a radio message sent to her back home in Skaneateles, New York.

Tom Dooley had a pleasant Christmas surprise for the general: a bottle of scotch. Wainwright's chief of staff, Bill Maher, had given his approval to the gift. It was, after all, a holiday. Wainwright invited Dooley to have a drink with him, and then they both went to the mess tent to join the rest of the staff for dinner. Their talk was of happier times and for a few hours, at least, Wainwright was able to escape the strains of the war.

For others Christmas Eve was a night they would prefer to forget. Major Trapnell and the remnants of the Twenty-sixth Cavalry were still in the process of withdrawing to the first defense line. They did get something to eat—canned corned beef, asparagus tips, hardtack, and coffee—their first meal in forty-eight hours. There was no water to drink, so the men pulled fresh turnips from the ground and ate them for the little moisture they contained.

To the south, in Manila, other Americans were on the move. They were leaving the city to the Japanese, as provided for in WPO-3. That afternoon President Quezon and U.S. High Commissioner Francis B. Sayre had sailed with their families aboard a small steamer to the fortress island of Corregidor. At 8:00 that night General MacArthur and his staff boarded the *Don Estaban* for the three-hour trip across Manila Bay to the Rock, as Corregidor was often called. The night was clear and bright with moonlight, now made even brighter by the one million gallons of fuel that had been set afire during the day. The gas was still burning. Occasionally an explosion could be heard as the engineers blew up another warehouse to prevent the supplies from falling into the hands of the enemy.

The lights of the Army-Navy Club in Manila twinkled on the waterfront, and some of the men on the *Don Estaban* thought of their wives and the final *despedida* last May, when they had last danced together. It seemed so long ago, part of another world, one that would never return. The officers sat on the deck talking quietly among themselves. Off to one side MacArthur sat alone, holding his head in his hands. Col. John R. "Jack" Vance, MacArthur's finance officer, reflected on the situation and wrote in his diary that the Philippines now seemed to him to be a "doomed garrison."*

Carlos Romulo waited in Manila with a handful of other officers in the blacked-out USAFFE headquarters. They were the rear echelon, unarmed in an open city with enemy forces so near that they could come through the door at any moment. Romulo and the others were to stay as long as possible, and then hope, somehow, to get out. The former newspaper publisher sat at his desk remembering MacArthur's final words to him a few hours before. "I'll be back, Carlos," the general had said.

One of the men broke the eerie silence. "Merry Christmas," he said wearily. "A helluva Christmas!"

At the town of Limay on Bataan, Lt. Juanita Redmond and fifty

---

*After the war, Vance wrote an excellent account of his experiences and entitled the book "Doomed Garrison" (Ashland, Ore.: Cascade House, 1974).

other nurses were settling into their new quarters, a dismal collection of dilapidated barracks. They were tired. They had made the long trip from Manila in open buses, passing hundreds of refugees and bombed-out barrios. Now on Christmas Eve they were busy assembling cots, scrubbing, and cleaning, trying to create a hospital out of their ramshackle facilities.

Nurse Redmond was hungry. There had been little time to eat during the day. The bus had stopped at a tiny village that afternoon. One of the enlisted men with them had done something unheard of; he ate some native-cooked wild rice.

"That stuff's contaminated or worm-infested or both," a nurse told him.

"Listen, sister," he said. "You'll be eating worse than this before the party's over, and be damn glad to get it."

The memory of this incident brought Lieutenant Redmond a chill. She and the others had laughed at the man. They did not know what a prophet he was.

In Washington, D.C., 20,000 people filed slowly past the army guards and into the White House grounds. The sentries diligently checked all packages. At 5:00 in the afternoon, President Roosevelt and his house guest, British Prime Minister Winston Churchill, came out on the portico. As the strains of "Hail to the Chief" faded, the sunset gun from Wainwright's old post, Fort Myer, was heard. The president pressed a button and the Christmas tree in front of him on the Ellipse exploded into a myriad of colored lights.

Roosevelt leaned forward and spoke his Christmas message into a microphone, to be carried to Americans everywhere, including those in the Philippines, where his words were borne by shortwave.

"It is in the spirit of peace and good will," he said, "and with particular thoughtfulness of those, our sons and brothers, who serve in our armed forces on land and sea, near and far—those who serve for us and endure for us—that we light our Christmas candles now across this continent from one coast to another on this Christmas evening."

Skinny Wainwright began Christmas day with bad news from MacArthur's headquarters on Corregidor. The Japanese had made another successful landing, this one on Lamon Bay, sixty miles southeast of Manila. There was no artillery to oppose it and only two Filipino infantry battalions in the area. This latest invasion posed a serious threat to the South Luzon Force. If they did not move quickly, the Japanese could prevent them from reaching

Bataan. The news was discouraging, but he had too many problems of his own in the north to spend much time worrying about it.

He climbed into his Packard and started off on another day of visiting as many of his units as he could. What he found cheered him. The first of the five lines of defense, D-1, had been successfully occupied the previous night and it had held securely despite persistent Japanese attacks. Wainwright rode up and down the line, cajoling, threatening, comforting, and inspiring his men at every stop.

By 11:00 that night, while the Twenty-sixth Cavalry was fighting another delaying action, all units reached the D-2 line behind the Agno River. Despite a good deal of confusion, to be expected with an operation on this scale, no units had been lost.

Christmas was not a particularly eventful day otherwise, just an ordinary day of war in which almost everything went as planned. Yet men died on that bright, sunny, holy day, some of them before the general's eyes. Lt. Henry Lee lost a friend and he wrote of his loss, and the losses of so many others, in a poem he called "Incomplete Epitaph."

> The waiting hearts to whom his heart belonged
> Know that he died one dusty Christmas Day
> "In action" the laconic message ran
> And "In the Philippines." They knew no more.
> His body knew no hallowed resting place
> He sleeps alone and lonely, as men sleep—
> As many men have slept—in many lands
> Since first the hairy clansman came to hunt
> Their rival clans with spear and axe and knife
> And take by force the gear they did not own.
> He is a name among ten million names
> A yellowed card filed in some dusty file
> A faded signature on fading notes
> A cherished pain burned on a few quick hearts
> The ageless tragedy of youth and war.

There would be many more ageless tragedies in the weeks and months ahead. The dying had only just begun.

On December 26 Wainwright's troops ran into trouble, which threatened to disrupt the whole carefully planned timetable of the withdrawal. Two Japanese thrusts breached the D-2 line, one through the right flank held by the exhausted Twenty-sixth Cavalry, and the other through the center of the line on Highway 3.

This closed off the road to the Eleventh Division, which was supposed to use it as an escape route that night. For the moment, the entire division was cut off.

The Twenty-sixth, which had been fighting all day, withdrew in perfect order ten miles southeast to the Ninety-first Division sector. One of the cavalry officers wrote that "It was a beautiful exhibition of careful planning, timing and execution by disciplined troops, permitting the last moment of delay to be extracted from the operation."

Wainwright ordered them on to Santa Rosa, but Colonel Pierce felt that his men and horses needed a day or two of rest. They had been on the move constantly for the last thirteen days. Pierce rode over to Wainwright's headquarters, but Skinny was away at the front. Pierce explained the situation to Bill Mahcr, who gave permission to withdraw south behind the final D-5 line. Perhaps now the Twenty-sixth Cavalry Regiment would get the respite they so sorely needed and greatly deserved.

At the time, Wainwright was trying personally to deal with the enemy breakthrough in the center of his front line. In late afternoon he was informed of the movement of the cavalry regiment. Sizing up the situation quickly, he sent orders for the Eleventh Division to withdraw through the town of Carmen to the D-3 line, but before the plan could be carried out, word came that Japanese soldiers had captured Carmen. In two hours the enemy had advanced three miles eastward, leaving only one line of retreat open to the Eleventh Division: the Manila railroad line.

The division commander, Brougher, rounded up a locomotive and some freight cars and rescued some of his units that had been trapped. He got the division safely to the new defense line. Although the day had brought more close calls and near disasters, by nightfall Wainwright's forces were entrenched behind the third defense line.

The next morning, December 27, found Wainwright at the weakest, widest, and least defensible of his five lines of withdrawal. It was a day menaced by catastrophe, but it turned out to bring him an almost unbelievable stroke of good fortune. The Japanese did not attack anywhere along his forty-mile line! The Japanese commander, Homma, had decided to halt his advance for the moment, to bring up more men and supplies and to consolidate his position.

By this time Homma could afford to take a day of rest. He knew that the American air forces had been wiped out, that there was no possibility of reinforcements reaching the Philippine defenders, and that Wainwright's three divisions facing him had been severely mauled. Homma was also aware that MacArthur had gone to Corregidor and that some troops were being shifted into the Bataan peninsula. On the basis of this intelligence, the Japanese commander concluded, incorrectly, that the American and Filipino forces planned only a minor delaying action in one small part of Bataan.

Homma consulted with his staff and decided to continue with the plan drawn up before the initial invasion, which called for the occupation of Manila as quickly as possible. Once the capital city had been taken by the Japanese, the remaining American and Filipino troops could be mopped up at leisure. Homma's staff believed that the withdrawal into Bataan was to their advantage because it made the capture of Manila that much easier. It was a conclusion they would later regret.

Wainwright used the lull in the battle that day to review his options. He stayed at his headquarters studying his maps with his staff, and assessing the condition of his troops and the progress of Jones's South Luzon Force in their exodus to Bataan. He knew it was vital that the road junction at San Fernando, Pampanga, and the Calumpit bridges over the Pampanga River, be kept open until the southern force had passed. If either of these points were abandoned too soon, the southern force would be lost.

Accordingly, Wainwright revised his plans for the next few days. In the original withdrawal plan, the D-4 line, the next one they had to reach, would be held for only one day before moving to the last line, D-5. The latter position would be defended for as long as it took the South Luzon Force to pass through San Fernando, Pampanga, and over the Calumpit bridges.

Now he had misgivings about that part of the operation. He saw that if his men were forced to retreat too quickly from the D-4 line, and if that action turned into a rout, they might not be able to hold the D-5 line long enough to save the South Luzon Force. He decided that his troops would have to make a stand at D-4, a twenty-five-mile path extending from Tarlac in the west to Cabanatuan in the east.

He planned the disposition of his troops on the new line and issued an order to his commanders. "D-4 will be held at all costs until ordered withdrawn. Maximum delay will be effected on each position."

Again Wainwright had done all he could. The rest was up to the soldiers in their foxholes. If they could not hold the line long enough, disaster awaited them all.

That afternoon, while Wainwright was drafting his new orders, bedlam erupted thirty miles to the south, at the San Fernando road junction he was trying to protect. Located ten miles northeast of the Calumpit bridges, the junction was formed by Highway 3 (the Manila North Road) and Highway 7, the only road into Bataan. As many as 80,000 troops would have to pass through San Fernando, Pampanga, and travel the narrow road twenty-five miles to Bataan.

By noon on the 27th, two forces had converged on San Fernando: a portion of Wainwright's men—as many as could be spared from the D-4 line plus some deserters—and the troop and supply convoys from Manila and other points south. To add to the chaos, approximately 20,000 Filipino refugees were trying to pass through San Fernando, Pampanga, to reach the apparent safety of Bataan. Before long, all movement came to a halt.

The streets of the town were clogged with vehicles of all kinds—ox-drawn carts, gaily painted Filipino buses, ambulances, private cars, and army trucks. The traffic jam extended three miles to the north and ten miles to the south. Not a single vehicle could move. The sun was hot and the sky clear. If Japanese planes spotted them, there would be a massacre. In addition, the road junction would be made impassable for days. Miraculously, no enemy planes appeared.

The confusion continued throughout the afternoon. Order was finally restored late that night when an MP detachment was able to get through. They were met by the blares of horns of several thousand stalled vehicles. Slowly they got the traffic moving. To those who were there it was a nightmare.

On the afternoon of December 28 Wainwright moved his headquarters again, this time to a convent, St. Mary's Academy, near the village of Bacolor. The building was 400 years old, damp and musty, but it was so overgrown with trees and shrubs that it offered excellent concealment from the air. A small, beautiful church was nearby. That evening, Wainwright heard the priest and the choir at services.

Wainwright's weakened men held the D-4 line for two days, but they were always uncertain about when and where the Japanese would attack. One part of the line broke sooner than the rest—the right flank at the town of Cabanatuan, held by the Ninety-first Division. On the 29th the Japanese hit the line hard and seized the town. They immediately pushed south and west, menacing the flank of the Eleventh Division, which was holding the center of the D-4 line.

At the western end of the line, the town of Tarlac also came under attack. The untested Twenty-first Division was there and the troops were standing fast. The Eleventh Division also held firm in the center, and one battalion counterattacked, which caught the Japanese by surprise.

Wainwright prowled up and down the line, encouraged by the way his center and left flanks were holding, but alarmed by the situation at Cabanatuan on the right. As fast as the Japanese were moving, in a very short time they could be in position to get behind the rest of the line.

By the night of Monday, December 29, he knew it was time to abandon the D-4 line. The Ninety-first Division had been routed, so he called up buses to take them south to regroup. But he wanted to hold the D-4 line a few hours longer. Every hour increased the likelihood that the South Luzon Force would cross the bridges at Calumpit, come through San Fernando, Pampanga, and go on into Bataan. Reluctantly he gave the orders to fall back to the D-5 line, from which there must be no further retreat until the southern force was out of danger. Wainwright's men had to hold or die there. There were no other choices. It was the most crucial point of Wainwright's withdrawal operation.

President Roosevelt sent a message of encouragement to the armies that Wainwright was leading into Bataan. It was broadcast to Manila via short wave, rebroadcast over local radio stations, and reprinted in almost every newspaper in the islands. There was not a soldier there who did not listen to or read or hear about the message and fail to be cheered by it. The president's words raised hopes greatly, though in vain. The message was untrue.

The broadcast contained the promise that reinforcements were on the way. "The resources of the United States," the president said, "have been dedicated by their people to the utter and complete defeat of the Japanese war lords. . . . I give to the people of the Philippines my solemn pledge that their freedom will be redeemed and their independence established and protected. The entire resources, in men and materiel, of the United States stand behind that pledge. . . . The United States Navy is following an intensive and well-planned campaign which will result in positive assistance to the defense of the Philippine Islands."

This was what Wainwright and his men needed to hear, direct

assurance from the president that help was on the way. At about the same time, the Philippines' Resident Commissioner in Washington, José Elizalde, sent a message to the islands, ending with the encouraging phrase, "help will be forthcoming." Surely there could be no doubt now, the men told themselves. All we have to do is hold out a little bit longer and we'll see the U.S. Navy sailing into Manila Bay!

The broadcast was a rash move on Roosevelt's part, and he realized his mistake almost at once. He called in his press secretary, Steve Early, in an effort to repair the damage. Early then told waiting reporters that they had misinterpreted Roosevelt's remarks by reading "too much of the immediate rather than the ultimate" into the president's statement.

The following day, Senator Tom Connally, chairman of the Senate Foreign Relations Committee, held a news conference. He said that things were "looking bad" in the Philippines, and that the islands had long been considered more of a liability than an asset. Arthur Krock of *The New York Times* wrote a long article about why reinforcements were not being sent to the Philippines and could not be sent in the near future. The War Department itself added the final touch. A spokesman announced that the public must realize how precarious the situation was in the Philippines, and that no reinforcements were being sent.

Thus, the message was clear in the United States in the closing days of 1941, but the word never reached the fighting men in the Philippines. As far as they knew, help was on the way. The president himself had told them so. He had given them hope. They would learn the awful truth soon enough.

By the last day of the year, Wainwright had successfully pulled his battered units back to the D-5 line. Approximately twenty miles long, this last line stretched from Bamban in the west to Arayat in the east. The line was flanked on the west by the Zambales Mountains and on the east by a swamp that extended for twenty miles. The only way the line could be breached was by a frontal attack, but Wainwright had only the remnants of two divisions—the Eleventh and the Twenty-first—with which to defend it. The important road junction at San Fernando, Pampanga, was only twenty-two miles south of the line, and the majority of the South Luzon Force had not yet reached it.

The men of the Eleventh and Twenty-first Divisions dug in to await the Japanese attack, but General Homma's attention was currently elsewhere. Instead of assaulting the D-5 line, he intended to bypass it completely. He sent his main force southward to Manila, along Route 5, which lay east of the swamp and so beyond the D-5 line. The road ahead of the Japanese was clear and it led to the town of Plaridel, from which another road went to the bridges at Calumpit, several miles away. If the enemy forces got to Plaridel and the bridges first, they could cut off the troops of the South Luzon Force below the river.

Units of Brig. Gen. Albert Jones's South Luzon Force were sent northeast of Plaridel, and Wainwright dispatched what meager troops he could spare. His force now consisted of a regiment of the Seventy-first Division, a battalion of field artillery, and the remainder of the battered Ninety-first Division; the Ninety-first was down to 500 men. They settled in at the town of Baliuag, six miles northeast of Plaridel, at daybreak of December 31. At 10:00 that morning Wainwright completed his plans for the defense of the Calumpit bridges and sent word to his men that they would have to leave Baliuag in time to reach the bridges by 4:00 A.M. By 5:00 the bridges would be destroyed. Any units that had not ossed by then would be left on the enemy's side of the river.

Shortly after Wainwright's orders reached his commanders, the Japanese launched their attack. By 1:30 in the afternoon they were in the outskirts of Baliuag and preparing for a massive assault on the town. Wainwright ordered the Ninety-first and Seventy-first units to pull out and drive for the bridge. He knew they had no chance of stopping the Japanese. Wainwright himself got in his car and raced the six miles from Baliuag to Jones's command post in a school house at Plaridel, arriving at around 2:00. He ordeed Jones to move his troops closer to the bridges and hold them as long as possible.

"No sir," Jones said. "My orders are to defend the bridge [from here] until all my people come through. If I fell back to the river I wouldn't have enough space to slow down the Japs."

Jones believed that if he gave up Plaridel, he would be writing off the rest of his troops to the south. Skinny was surprised by Jones's refusal to implement his orders.

"I'm giving you a direct order," Wainwright said.

Jones stared defiantly at Wainwright. "I've been ordered by Sutherland to take command of all troops below the Pampanga River."

Wainwright was stunned. No one had bothered to tell him of the change in command, even though MacArthur had ordered it four hours before.

"I'm not going to withdraw," Jones said with finality, and Skinny knew there was nothing he could do about it.

Wainwright stalked out of the room, got in his car, and drove west toward the Calumpit bridges. Now it was up to Jones's men to hold the line long enough for all the troops to get across.

Somehow, courageously, miraculously, they held on. At 1:00 on New Year's morning, Jones left his command post for the bridge, arriving just as the last of his Fifty-first Division was crossing. Only his rear guard, a Filipino brigade, and a small force holding Plaridel remained. Wainwright was waiting on the far side of the bridge, to make sure all the troops were safely across before giving the orders to blow it up. On the north side of the river, he was in command.

With him were Harry Skerry, his engineering officer, Jim Weaver, the tank commander, and Luther Stevens, commander of the Ninety-first Division. The men had been waiting through the long hours of the night, watching the ghostly span of the steel bridge stretching before them across the river, and its twin, the railway bridge, fifty yards to the west. There was a rumbling noise from the south. The small force of Filipino troops dug in around the officers' position tensed and peered anxiously across the river. Tanks were approaching: American tanks. They clattered over the long bridge and disappeared to the north, heading for San Fernando and Bataan.

Not long after that came the sounds of more motors approaching from the south. This time it was a convoy of trucks and commandeered civilian buses, Jones's Filipino rear guard. As soon as they crossed the bridge, Jones ordered the Plaridel force to retreat, and a little before 5:00 A.M. they too crossed the bridge.

Wainwright asked Skerry if everything was ready to blow the bridges. Skerry replied that it was, but he asked permission to delay. A platoon of Filipino engineers was south of the river, destroying installations between Manila and the bridge. Could Wainwright wait a while longer to allow this group to get across the river?

"All right," Skinny said. "Wait an hour."

Colonel Skerry, a highly skilled and conscientious engineer, walked out onto the empty bridge to check the four tons of dynamite that were in place. Then he went to the railroad bridge to inspect the three tons of dynamite on that span. Satisfied, he returned to Wainwright and the others.

By 5:45 there was still no sign of the Filipino engineers detachment, nor could anyone hear explosions to the south, which might indicate that the men were approaching. Wainwright told Skerry that they would give them another half hour.

Skinny had had no sleep and very little food. He was exhausted and had been on the move since the previous morning. Today promised no relief. He and Jones walked over to a civilian truck that had overturned near the road, hoping to find something to eat. Instead, they found a bottle of champagne. As the faint light of dawn appeared in the east, they opened the bottle and toasted the New Year and the safe withdrawal of their forces. The earlier confrontation had been forgotten. Wainwright never held a grudge against anyone for disagreeing with him, as long as he respected the man's fighting ability. Skinny and "Honus" (Wainwright liked to call him by the Spanish version of "Jones") shared the bottle and watched the sky brighten. Suddenly they caught the sounds of rifle fire coming from south of the river. It was growing louder by the minute.

"The situation is getting serious," Wainwright said.

He grabbed his binoculars and focused on the river bank. Japanese soldiers were approaching on the opposite side of the river. There was still no sign of the engineers and Wainwright could not risk any further delay. Destroying the bridges was the only way to stop the Japanese advance.

"Skerry," he said, the regret obvious in his voice, "we cannot wait any longer. Blow it now."

Colonel Skerry and his men approached the bridge abutment. Everyone else took cover. At precisely 6:15 the first charges exploded, then the second. Hunks of twisted metal, the wreckage of the two spans, plunged into the deep Pampanga River. Wainwright walked to the riverbank to watch. His men were safe now—the river was too wide to ford—but still he sighed. "It's too bad we had to destroy such costly and important structures," he said.

Wainwright's bold gamble had worked, although the men of Luzon had not yet all reached Bataan. He got back in his car and drove north, his weary mind busily calculating the final stage of the withdrawal.

Robert P. P. Wainwright, Major of Cavalry, 1852–1902.
U.S. MILITARY ACADEMY.

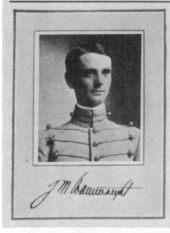

WAINWRIGHT, JONATHAN M., "Jim," "Skinny," Chicago, Ill. Corp., Sergt. Major, 1st Sergt., 1st Capt.; Hop Manager (3, 4); Marksman; Toastmaster, New Year's, 1906.

This is IT—the summit toward which the Pampered Pets of the Powers that Be continually do strive; the goal of every good cadet's ambition. Many honors have been heaped upon his head,—so many that it's a wonder his slender frame has withstood their bending moment without any more damage than giving to his knees a permanent set. "Skinny" will long remember that awful Hallowe'en evening, when, just as he was making his most military salute and reporting, "A Company all quiet, Sir," about a ton of brick dropped on the roof of the First Div. "Skinny" collapsed on the spot and it took the O. C. a good hour's work with the sponge to bring him around.

J. M. Wainwright, First Captain of Cadets, U.S. Military Academy, from the class yearbook, Howitzer, *1906.*

U.S. MILITARY ACADEMY.

J. M. Wainwright, Colonel of Cavalry and Commanding Officer, Fort Myer, Virginia, 1937.

U.S. ARMY SIGNAL CORPS.

Commanding officer's quarters, Fort Myer, Virginia.
U.S. ARMY SIGNAL CORPS.

Col. J. M. Wainwright, Master of the Hunt, Fort Myer, Virginia, 1937.

U.S. ARMY SIGNAL CORPS.

THE HORSE IS MAN'S NOBLEST COMPANION

JOIN THE

CAVALRY

and have a courageous friend

U.S. ARMY RECRUITING OFFICE:

"The Horse Is Man's Noblest Companion." Cavalry recruiting poster, 1920.

U.S. ARMY RECRUITING SUPPORT CENTER, CAMERON STATION, VIRGINIA.

Skinny Wainwright and Douglas MacArthur, Fort McKinley, Philippine Islands, October 1941.

U.S. ARMY SIGNAL CORPS; COURTESY MACARTHUR MEMORIAL.

Wainwright and his aides on Bataan, February 1942. From left: Tom Dooley, Johnny Pugh, Wainwright, Malcolm Champlin (naval aide), Hubert "Tex" Carroll. Photo is signed "To Tom Dooley From Battling Bastards of Bataan. Wainwright."

COURTESY COL. THOMAS R. DOOLEY.

Col. Joseph L. Chabot. Assigned by Wainwright as assistant G–2 of the North Luzon Force, Chabot (West Point, 1937) was instrumental in planning the phased withdrawal into Bataan. After the war he served in Germany and Korea and at the Pentagon, and was responsible for the expansion of Army reserve forces.

U.S. ARMY SIGNAL CORPS; COURTESY COL. JOSEPH L. CHABOT.

MacArthur and his staff with Maj. Gen. Albert M. Jones during the USAFFE commander's only visit to Bataan, January 10, 1942.
U.S. ARMY SIGNAL CORPS.

Pile-type tank obstacles and double-apron fence entanglements constructed by Philippine Army troops on Bataan, January 1942.
U.S. ARMY SIGNAL CORPS.

Philippine Scouts with war trophy, a Japanese officer's sword, taken after they cleaned out a Japanese assault force that attempted a landing on the west coast of Bataan.

CLARK LEE, ASSOCIATED PRESS.

Lt. Gen. T. J. H. Trapnell. A polo player and football star (West Point, 1927), Trapnell was awarded the DSC for his actions with the Twenty-sixth Cavalry on Bataan. He later served in Korea and Vietnam and commanded the Eighty-second Airborne Division, the Eighteenth Airborne Corps, and the Third Army.

U.S. ARMY SIGNAL CORPS.

Lt. Gen. Masaharu Homma, commanding officer of the Japanese Fourteenth Army, comes ashore on Luzon.

NATIONAL ARCHIVES.

Wainwright fills MacArthur's shoes. "Looks like a perfect fit." Editorial cartoon in The Washington Post, *April 4, 1942.*

DRAWN BY BRUCE HOUGHTON, AFTER COAKLEY; COPYRIGHT, THE WASHINGTON POST CO.

Col. John R. Vance at center of finance department lateral, Malin Tunnel, Corregidor. After the war, Vance (West Point, 1919) serve with Wainwright at Fort Sam Houston and later with the alli military government in Trieste, Italy.

U.S. ARMY SIGNAL CORPS; COURTESY COL. JOHN R. VANCE

Brig. Gen. Arnold J. Funk. A World War I veteran, Funk commanded the Fifty-seventh infantry on Bataan and rallied his troops to counterattack the Japanese forces. He was awarded the DSM and made chief of staff of II Corps.

U.S. ARMY SIGNAL CORPS; COURTESY MRS. ARNOLD J. FUNK.

Col. Stuart Wood. Fluent in the Japanese language, Wood (W Point, 1927) served as Wainwright's G–2 on Corregidor, and in t prison camps repeatedly risked his life to translate Japanese newspape and directives for his fellow officers. After the war, he served with t airborne forces at Fort Bragg, North Carolina.

U.S. ARMY SIGNAL CORPS.

Brig. Gen. Clinton A. Pierce (left), commanding officer of the Twenty-sixth Cavalry, questions captured Japanese soldiers on Bataan.
CLARK LEE, ASSOCIATED PRESS.

Wainwright meets Homma near Cabcaben on Bataan to arrange the surrender of the Philippines, May 6, 1942.

U.S. ARMY SIGNAL CORPS; CAPTURED JAPANESE WAR PHOTO.

Japanese drawing of Wainwright-Homma meeting.

U.S. ARMY SIGNAL CORPS; CAPTURED JAPANESE WAR PHOTO.

U.S. forces surrender to Japanese forces at Malinta Tunnel's west entrance, about 3:00 P.M., May 6, 1942.
    U.S. ARMY SIGNAL CORPS; CAPTURED JAPANESE WAR PHOTO;
COURTESY COL. JOHN R. VANCE.

Wainwright broadcasts surrender instructions over Station KZRH, Manila, May 7, 1942.
    U.S. ARMY SIGNAL CORPS; CAPTURED JAPANESE WAR PHOTO.

"Corregidor Falls." Front page of the *Manila* Tribune.
COURTESY COL. JOHN R. VANCE.

American generals in captivity, July 1942. Seated, left to right: Generals Moore, King, and Wainwright; two Japanese officers; Generals Parker and Jones. Standing, left to right: Japanese messenger; Generals Lough, Funk, Weaver, Brougher, Beebe, Bluemel, Drake, McBride, and Pierce; Colonel Hoffman (interpreter); two Japanese soldiers.

COURTESY ALBERT J. BLAND.

Schujo (*post exchange*) *customers at Shirakawa, Taiwan, prison camp, 1943. Col. John R. Vance takes canteen coupon in payment for a bottle of soya sauce. Col. James V. Collier holds package of* wakimoto *pills, a source of vitamins.*

NATIONAL ARCHIVES; CAPTURED JAPANESE PROPAGANDA ALBUM.

CHAPTER 6

"A Symbol of Forlorn Hope"

Wainwright and his orderly, Hubert "Tex" Carroll, headed north on Route 3 in the bright morning sun, keeping a sharp eye out for Japanese planes. It took over an hour to reach their destination—the next critical point in the withdrawal to Bataan—the road junction at the town of San Fernando, Pampanga. The bulk of Wainwright's North Luzon Force was still north of the town, and he had left a sizable force south of it to cover the nine miles from the destroyed bridges at Calumpit. If the enemy struck hard and fast, his weary and battered troops might not be able to hold out long enough to clear the vital crossroads.

The Packard weaved in and out of the heavy stream of traffic on the road to San Fernando, Pampanga. Every type of vehicle crowded around them, and though all were moving fairly well, they still presented a tempting target for an air attack. The sky was cloudless, the weather perfect for flying, and Skinny was sure that Japanese pilots could not miss spotting a nine-mile convoy. The thought was on everyone's mind, and all eyes warily searched the sky and the flat, open land on both sides of the road. There was no place to take cover.

When Wainwright reached San Fernando, Pampanga, he expected to find a bottleneck, such as had occurred several days before. But this morning traffic was flowing more easily. He stared down Route 7, the two-lane road that led to Bataan, and saw a line of jeeps, trucks, ambulances, and buses reaching far into the distance. The caravan filled the road for the entire sixty-two miles from San Fernando, Pampanga, to the tip of Bataan.

One of MacArthur's staff officers described it this way. "In addition to the mixed-up elements of the eight Philippine Army divisions, supply convoys and numerous special units, there were many civilian vehicles ranging from brand new motor cars to solid wheeled oxcarts. Those coming into Bataan were trying to avoid the Japanese by going with the Army, those leaving Bataan were trying to get away from the Army and the future battlefield." The movement continued all day and into the night. Some officers thought the exodus would never end.

Satisfied with the way things were going in San Fernando, Skinny went sixteen miles north to the D-5 front line to see how his troops were holding. The Twenty-first and Eleventh Divisions were on the line. The Twenty-first, holding the left flank behind the almost dry Bamban River, was hit early in the afternoon, but they beat off the initial attack and their artillery heavily shelled the enemy troops that were massing north of the river. The Japanese did not attempt to cross the river in force, and by nightfall the Twenty-first Division withdrew intact thirteen miles southwest to the town of Porac.

The Eleventh Division, on the right flank of the D-5 line, was attacked at 4:30 P.M. on New Year's Day. A battalion of Igorot troops fought fiercely and exacted a heavy toll on the enemy. By 10:00, the hour when Wainwright had ordered their withdrawal, the division slipped away from the D-5 line. They passed through the now nearly deserted town of San Fernando, Pampanga, and took up a position at Guagua. Wainwright's North Luzon Force now held a ten-mile-long line, where they waited for what they expected to be an attack by the entire Japanese army. To bolster the left flank of the new line, Skinny ordered the Twenty-sixth Cavalry Regiment to wait in reserve at San Jose, six miles behind the line.

During the afternoon, Wainwright had successfully extricated the Seventy-first and Ninety-first Divisions from their positions south of San Fernando, where they had been standing by in case the Japanese crossed the Pampanga River at Calumpit. The Japanese had tried, but the current was too swift. Wainwright ordered his men to withdraw. Both divisions were exhausted, so he sent them directly to Bataan, where they would have a chance to rest and regroup.

Now there were only two divisions and the Twenty-sixth Cavalry standing between the Japanese and the frantic preparations the

American and Filipino troops were making for the defense of Bataan.

Fortunately for Wainwright and his men, Homma was still unconcerned about the massed withdrawal into Bataan. He believed that victory lay in the occupation of Manila, now undefended and only twelve miles south of his main units. Once the city was in Japanese hands, Homma thought, the Philippine campaign would be almost over. The forces on Bataan and Corregidor could be captured in a few weeks. He was wrong—it would take more than four months—but on that New Year's Day, as his troops marched into Manila only nine days after their major landings on Luzon, it appeared to him that success was near.

Across Manila Bay, on the tiny island of Corregidor, the men at USAFFE headquarters shared Homma's belief in the imminence of a Japanese victory. American officers watched through high-powered binoculars as the Japanese flag was raised atop the Manila Hotel, where General MacArthur and his family had lived not too many days before. A pall of smoke hung over the capital city from the burning oil storage tanks. The American days of empire were truly at an end.

MacArthur drafted a message to Gen. George Marshall in Washington, outlining the situation and the dim prospects for the future. "The question of time is paramount," he wrote. "It is estimated that this garrison unsupported can survive serious attack for possibly three months at most although it is not possible to predict the date of such attack. Munitions and food are limited; there are only thirty thousand rounds of anti-aircraft ammunition; water supply is critical . . . I have no resources except as provided from the United States."

Carlos Romulo arrived on the Rock that day, having been evacuated with the rear echelon from Manila at the last moment. As he stepped onto the island that Skinny Wainwright would one day have to surrender, his thoughts were prophetic. "What a hole!" he said to himself. "We'll be trapped here."

The more Romulo saw of his new home, the more dispirited he became, particularly when he walked into what would be the army's last sanctuary, Malinta Tunnel. "The smell of the place hit me like a blow in the face," he wrote. "There was the stench of sweat and dirty clothes, the coppery smell of blood and disinfectant coming from the lateral where the hospital was situated, and over all the heavy stink of creosote, hanging like a blanket in the air that moved sluggishly when it moved at all."

It was also the smell of doom and impending defeat, and it pervaded the whole island.

When Romulo saw MacArthur, he was shaken by the change in the general's appearance. A week ago he had been jaunty and nattily dressed, "but now his uniform was unpressed, his hair shaggy, his face rough from the salt-water shaving. The lines creasing his face made him look like a tired hawk."

Romulo found himself alarmed by the confusion all around him. Everyone had assumed that Corregidor was well stocked and fortified, an impregnable fortress. Instead, it was the bleak last command post toward which Wainwright was moving inexorably as he brought his men into Bataan. And it would be much worse when he arrived to take command on Corregidor himself.

Wainwright spent the day of January 2 prowling his new line of defense, inspecting the positions of his hard-pressed troops for the attack that would surely come soon. He knew that Homma would not wait long. To the Japanese, said Lt. Gen. Sasumu Morioka, Wainwright's forces were like "a 'cat entering a sack.' General Homma fully intended to draw the string tight once the Americans were in the sack, thereby bringing the campaign to an early and successful conclusion. He was due for a painful disappointment."

The Japanese struck first at Wainwright's left flank at Porac. The enemy forces quickly broke through the front line of the Twenty-first Division and drove 2,000 yards before they were stopped. Wainwright ordered a counterattack to regain the lost ground, but it was dark before it could be mounted. All night long, the troops were alert, and Wainwright ordered the division's artillery to keep up a steady, harassing fire.

The right flank, held by the Eleventh Division, was not attacked that day, but Wainwright was worried about the weakened left flank. He laid plans for a counterattack to take place in the morning. At least he had held the line another day, and each day he could hold meant that much more time for the defenses on Bataan to be established. He had to hang on for a few more days, and then pull his two divisions into the peninsula. It was a demanding job for Wainwright and his men, but there was no choice. If the fortifications on Bataan were not ready when the Japanese attacked in force, the American and Filipino troops might be pushed all the way down that finger of land to its tip. Their orderly withdrawal could become a panicky rout.

Wainwright's adversary, Homma, received shattering news that day. New orders from Tokyo would serve to relieve some of the pressure on Wainwright's beleaguered soldiers in the coming weeks and give him the same problem Skinny was dealing with—too few seasoned troops. The message from Imperial General Headquarters informed Homma that the timetable for capturing Java had been advanced by a month because of the string of Japanese conquests already achieved so easily.

As a result, one of Homma's two divisions, the crack Forty-eighth, which was to have stayed in the Philippines until the end of the campaign, was now to be shipped out. To replace it Homma would get the Sixty-fifth Brigade, a poorly trained unit of 6,500 men, which had been formed only a year ago and had no combat experience. The brigade commander had pronounced his outfit "absolutely unfit for combat duty." Part of Homma's air force was also reassigned. He was left with one division, the Sixteenth, whose reputation was not very high.

Under these orders, Homma would have to do what Wainwright had been forced to do since the day the war began: fight as best he could with the inadequate resources available.

If developments in Tokyo on January 2 worked to Skinny's advantage, events in his own capital, Washington, D.C., would have been much less to his liking had he known of them. Secretary of War Henry L. Stimson had received MacArthur's radio message about the survivability of the Philippine garrison. Stimson described the cable as "most harassing and agonizing." He sent a copy of it to Roosevelt, but, surprisingly, the president was undisturbed by the news. Stimson saw clearly what the future held for the islands and realized that he would probably "have to go through the agonizing experience of seeing the doomed garrison gradually pulled down."

A reply was called for and the chore was given to Dwight Eisenhower, who was still making an effort, though unsuccessfully, to route some supplies to the Philippines. "Ships!" Eisenhower scribbled on his desk pad. "Ships! All we need is ships!" But there were not enough. There is, Ike wrote to MacArthur, "a marked insufficiency of forces for any powerful naval concentration in the Western Pacific at this time. . . . We are searching our resources. . . . Every day of time you gain is vital."

Wainwright knew this without being told, and as he endured another night with little sleep, he worked on the problem of how best to stretch his own slender resources of men and supplies to continue to hold on, yard by yard, hour by hour, and day by day.

On the morning of January 3, Wainwright received startling news from the Twenty-first Division, which had lost ground the day

before. Patrols reported that there were no Japanese units in front
of the division. It appeared as though the original defense line
might be regained, and he ordered his men forward. The advance
started well, but it was soon stopped by Japanese reinforcements
that had been brought up during the night. A heavy artillery
regiment began to pound Wainwright's Twenty-first Division with
105mm guns. When he was told about the artillery he became
alarmed and wrote out an order to "hold the line or die where you
are."

The Twenty-first did its best, but it could not stand up under the
heavy bombardment. The left flank began to crumble. The Japanese concentrated on the weak spot and drove a wedge between
two regiments. The division's artillerymen rallied, firing into the
faces of the enemy troops at a range of no more than 800 yards. For
six hours, they kept up their fire. When it grew dark, the Japanese
called off the attack. It had been a very close call for the American
forces.

That was not all Wainwright had to contend with. For the first
time, the Japanese attacked his right flank at Guagua, held by the
Eleventh Division. Supported by tanks and artillery, the men of the
Eleventh held their ground. By nightfall they had not retreated a
yard from their main line of defense.

Another twenty-four hours had been gained, and Wainwright
was heartened by the day's events. It was true that he was not on the
offensive yet, but following the long withdrawal, just holding on was
something of a victory. His untrained men were fast becoming
soldiers worthy of the name. If only he had more men and supplies,
they could win this war. Wainwright got a little more sleep that
night and felt a little more hopeful about the situation.

His optimism, however faint, was not shared in Washington.
Quite the opposite. There, another blow had been dealt to the
defenders of the Philippines. A few days before, President Roosevelt had asked the army high command about the possibility of
initiating a major relief effort for the area. On January 3, the head
of the war plans division, Brig. Gen. Leonard T. Gerow, sent his
answer. It could not be done. His final recommendation was that
"operations for the relief of the Philippines be not undertaken."

On Corregidor on January 3, the only assistance MacArthur
could give his men, and the people of the islands, was to try to raise
their morale. He wanted to establish a radio station that would
broadcast his news and propaganda throughout the Philippines. He
assigned the job to Carlos Romulo.

"Get it going, Carlos," he said. "I want the radio working in forty-eight hours."

MacArthur had thought of a name for the station. It would be called the "Voice of Freedom."

Wainwright had to abandon the defense line running from Porac to Guagua the next day, January 4. There was no action on his left flank but the other end of the line, held by the Eleventh Division, was hit hard by tanks and artillery. At 3:30 that afternoon he learned that the Japanese had reached the outskirts of Guagua. His troops were forced to fall back.

When he learned of the enemy breakthrough, Wainwright knew he would have to withdraw the entire line, including the Twenty-first Division at Porac. It now faced the danger of being outflanked. He gave the orders for both divisions to retreat during the night to a new position south of the Gumain River, a distance of six to eight miles. Despite heavy fighting and the confusion that almost always attends a withdrawal under fire, Wainwright's men succeeded. By dawn of the next day they were entrenched along a new defensive line.

General Wainwright had reason to be proud of what he and his troops had accomplished in the last few days. The official army history of the campaign records that their stand "on the Guagua-Porac line had earned large dividends. The Japanese had paid dearly for the ground gained and had been prevented from reaching their objective, the gateway to Bataan. More important was the time gained by the troops already in Bataan to prepare their positions."

But this new line was the last one before the entrance to the Bataan peninsula, only eight miles distant. Now Wainwright had to map out the trickiest part of the entire operation. He had to hold off the enemy at the same time he would be evacuating his forces to the safety of the units already in position on Bataan. Another bridge had to be crossed and defended until all units were south of it, and then blown up before the Japanese reached it. His exhausted and hungry men would have to fight and be on the move for at least another day.

While Wainwright was planning these intricate maneuvers, a meeting was being held in Malinta Tunnel on Corregidor. Its outcome would bear directly on his future and that of his men. The quartermaster, Charlie Drake, was reporting to MacArthur on a commodity that was soon to be in short supply—food. Drake's comments were bleak. Unless the Philippines were resupplied, he told MacArthur, the men on Bataan would have only enough food for approximately two months. Indeed, they could hold out that long only if they went on half rations immediately. That meant thirty ounces per day for each man. Food had been scarce for Wainwright's men during their trek into Bataan, and they were going to get a lot hungrier before the end. If Bataan was a refuge, it was fast becoming a barren one.

On the morning of January 5, Wainwright issued his orders for the final withdrawal into Bataan. It would begin at nightfall. More than 8,000 of his command would have to retreat a distance of eight miles and cross the steel bridge spanning the Culo River at Layac. The Eleventh Division had to withdraw southwest along Route 7, the road that led from San Fernando, Pampanga, while the Twenty-first Division had to march south along Route 74. Wainwright ordered the Twenty-sixth Cavalry, now down to approximately 650 men, to cover the left flank of the Twenty-first, and one battalion of the Twenty-first to cover the withdrawal of the Eleventh. The complicated operation required the utmost precision in timing.

As usual, Wainwright wanted to be at the front, to know exactly what was going on, and to pitch in—with advice or with his rifle—where needed. This time it almost cost him his life. He left for the front at 10:00 in the morning in an open Dodge command car. His Filipino driver, Sergeant Centivo, was at the wheel, and his aide, Tom Dooley, was riding shotgun. Skinny sat ramrod straight in the back seat.

They were looking for the command post of the Eleventh Division, but none of the soldiers they stopped along the road knew where it was. The morning was quiet. Only occasional small arms fire sounded in the distance. Wainwright began to gripe because they couldn't find the C.P. Each time they asked a soldier for directions, they failed to get a satisfactory answer. And each time the general shook his head and said, "Drive on, Centivo."

Finally they came across a Filipino lieutenant and two enlisted men. The officer knew where the Eleventh Division command post was—two kilometers back down the road. Wainwright was shocked to learn that they were now two kilometers ahead of their own front line, deep into Japanese-held territory.

"Drive on, Centivo," Wainwright commanded, "but to the rear!"

The Japanese did not attack in strength anywhere along the line of withdrawal that day. Only small, isolated skirmishes occurred, to Wainwright's immense relief. The maneuver itself was difficult under the best of circumstances. It could easily have turned into a rout if the enemy had kept up constant and heavy attacks.

As it was, the move was attended by a great deal of congestion and disorder. Units got lost, and individuals, companies, and battalions soon became entangled with others. "Everyone was in everyone else's lap," one observer wrote, "and the whole thing resembled nothing quite as much as the first stages of an old fashioned southern political mass meeting and free barbecue." Another officer commented that "it looked like the parking lot of the Yale bowl," as trucks, tanks, cars, horses, and men on foot passed through the tiny town of Layac.

There was nothing more Wainwright could do now. Even company and battalion commanders on the scene sometimes did not know where their men were. Communications were so poor that it was impossible for Wainwright to get a clear picture of the situation. He could only pace back and forth outside his temporary command post at Hermosa, hoping for the best. That afternoon he had had another close call. A flight of Japanese dive bombers attacked Hermosa. He continued to work until one plane broke off from the rest and began to strafe the command post. The general and his staff ran for the foxholes. As he approached one he saw that it was already occupied, by Col. Frank Nelson, his G-3. "Get over, Frank," Skinny yelled, and he jumped into the hole with him.

A little after 10:00 that night, Wainwright and his engineering officer, Harry Skerry, arrived at the north end of the Layac Bridge to watch as the exhausted men of the Eleventh Division stumbled across the narrow span. The evening was unusually beautiful, a tropical paradise, and the air was filled with the aroma of flowers, but soon the smells of sweat and fear were overpowering.

By 10:30, the last of the division disappeared in the darkness, heading gratefully into Bataan, and a few minutes later the Twenty-first Division began to cross the bridge. Skinny saw the division commander, General Capinpin, running up and down the column, urging his weary men on, sometimes with a kick. Wainwright grinned— General Capinpin had a reputation as a kindly man—and he ambled over to him to ask, "How many men have you shot today, Matty?"

It took two and a half hours for the Twenty-first Division to cross the bridge. By 1:00 in the morning, the only unit remaining on the north side of the river was the rear guard, a platoon of tanks. Col. Ray O'Day, the Twenty-first Division's American adviser, walked up to Wainwright and saluted smartly. Then he raised his right hand as though swearing an oath. "To the best of my knowledge and belief,"

O'Day announced, "all units of the Twenty-first Division have cleared the junction."

Wainwright sent orders for the platoon of tanks to move out, and then he and Skerry crossed the steel span together, their footsteps echoing in the silence. Skinny always insisted on being the last man over a bridge, not unlike a navy captain being the last to leave his sinking ship. Minutes later, the tanks clattered over the bridge. The tank commander dismounted, raised his right hand, and swore that all his tanks were now across the river. As the tanks headed down the road to Bataan, the sound of another motorized vehicle was heard approaching from the north. Were the Japanese already so near to the bridge? It turned out to be another American tank, a straggler, almost left behind on what was now the enemy side of the river.

When the lone tank cleared the Layac Bridge, Wainwright turned to Skerry. "Blow it," he said. At 2:00 A.M. a huge explosion toppled the span into the water. Wainwright shook Skerry's hand and got into his staff car. A moment later Major Trapnell of the Twenty-sixth Cavalry and Maj. Joe Ganahl, a polo-playing artilleryman and another favorite of Wainwright's, arrived and stopped to chat with Skinny. Ganahl mentioned that he had received a wire earlier that day from his wife in the States, announcing the birth of a son. Always ready for a celebration, Wainwright fetched a bottle of scotch from the trunk and the three men drank a toast to Ganahl's son.

For the moment, Wainwright's job was done. He had evacuated the North and South Luzon Forces—some 30,000 men, with their equipment and supplies—into Bataan, and had closed off the main road into the peninsula. Perhaps now he could get some rest. He thought he could certainly use it.

Wainwright's withdrawal into Bataan was a much greater success than anyone had thought possible, given the condition of the troops at his disposal. It was a tribute to his leadership and to the fortitude of his men that it had worked so well. Not a single large unit had been lost, and only once, on the right flank of the D-4 line, had a unit failed to hold long enough to cover the withdrawal as planned.

Losses had been high on both sides, however. The Japanese suffered some 2,000 casualties. The South Luzon Force arrived in Bataan with 14,000 men, a loss of 1,000. Wainwright's North Luzon Force, which saw the heaviest fighting, had greater losses. They had begun the withdrawal on December 23 with a complement of 28,000 men. By the time they crossed the Layac Bridge they were down to 16,000. Most of those lost were deserters, however: men who had slipped away to return to their homes. The number of casualties from combat remains unknown.

But on January 6, those who had survived were safe for the moment, more secure than at any time since the Japanese invaded the island of Luzon. As a result, an artillery officer wrote, "the morale was good. The general feeling seemed to be 'we have run far enough; we'll stand now and take 'em on.'" Most of the men did not suspect that, far from being a refuge, Bataan was a trap in which disease, starvation, and fatigue would eventually grind them all down. These proved to be deadlier enemies than the Japanese. Death or capture would be the only escapes from Bataan. It would become what Wainwright called "a symbol of forlorn hope."

Bataan was ideally suited for defense; at least it would have been had it been adequately supplied and equipped beforehand. Twenty-five miles long and twenty miles wide, the peninsula was "a kind of unfinished paradise, before it became hell." It was mostly jungle and mountains, crisscrossed by streams and impassable ravines. A chain of mountains stretched down the center of the peninsula, dominated by Mount Natib in the north, 4,000 feet high, and Mount Bataan in the south, almost 5,000 feet.

The terrain was rugged and covered with thick vegetation, which provided excellent cover from possible air attacks, but which also made it difficult to travel from place to place. One needed a sharp bolo knife to cut a path through it. The writer John Hersey described it this way: "There are great earthly hunches, precipitous rock walls, deep gullies cut by cold streams; thick groves of giant banyan trees with roots fanning outwards and trunks big enough for men to hack out hutlets underneath; clumps of trees of hard grain, the famous Philippine mahogany, the dao and the narra; great snakelike vines wrestling with trees . . . pure springs, quiet pools; thicklets of huge fern and tiny palm; grassy openings and outcroppings of rock and crowds of tropical bushes."

There were two roads on the peninsula. Route 110, a single-lane paved road, ran from Layac along the east coast to the town of Mariveles at the tip of Bataan. From there it wound northward along the west coast to Moron, about one-third of the way down the peninsula. The second road, the only way across Bataan, had a cobblestone surface and connected Pilar and Bagac, about halfway down the peninsula. Trails had been hacked through the jungle at several places, but these were unsuitable for tanks and trucks. An engineering officer said that these unimproved roads on Bataan were eight inches of dust in the dry season, eight inches of mud in the wet season.

The coastline of Bataan was narrow and hilly, particularly on the west coast where Wainwright made his headquarters. There the terrain was rugged, with cliffs and promontories jutting into the water.

Yes, Bataan was a good place to defend, but there was little to defend it with. Everything was lacking; food was in particularly short supply, and men can fight only so long on empty stomachs. More than 100,000 people were crowded into Bataan: 80,000 troops and 26,000 civilian refugees who had swarmed into the area to escape the invading Japanese. There was not enough food available to feed half that number adequately.

On the day Wainwright and his men crossed the Layac Bridge and entered Bataan, they found field rations to last for thirty days, canned meats and fish adequate for fifty days, enough flour and canned vegetables to last a month, and only twenty days' worth of rice, the staple of the Filipino diet. Such was the situation at its best, at the beginning of the siege of Bataan. It would soon get worse— much worse.

To try to stretch the meager food supply for as long as possible, MacArthur ordered half rations for the Bataan and Corregidor garrisons. The troops, already hungry when they reached Bataan, now found themselves trying to subsist—and to fight—on no more than 2,000 calories a day. It was, Wainwright said, "hardly enough to hold body and soul together." He set out at once to supplement the scanty fare by ordering his men to shoot every carabao they could find. The tough meat of the Philippine water buffalo had to be soaked overnight in salt water and pounded before being cooked. Though edible, it was always chewy and stringy. Still, it provided some nourishment.

Clothing, gasoline, trucks, engineering equipment, sandbags, barbed wire—virtually everything an army requires—was in short supply on Bataan. A serious problem was the lack of a proper communications system. One officer said, "Communications don't exist. Messengers get lost. Divisions can maintain only marginal contact with regiments. Some regiments can't find their battalions. We ran across companies that didn't know to whom they belonged. It's a mess!" There were no telephone lines and few radios. Wainwright had only two scout cars equipped with radios to keep in touch with all of his units.

On January 7, Wainwright took over his new command, the

western sector of what was now called the Bataan Defense Force. MacArthur had divided Bataan into two major commands: I Philippines Corps under Wainwright (about 22,500 men), and II Philippines Corps under Maj. Gen. George Parker (some 25,000 men). The tip of Bataan was designated the Service Command Area. In his I Corps Skinny had three divisions, the First, Thirty-first, and Ninety-first. He also had remnants of the Seventy-first Division as well as the Twenty-sixth Cavalry, a battery of field artillery, and a battery of 75mm guns. Parker's II Corps, on the eastern side of Bataan, included four divisions and the Fifty-seventh Infantry. It was at the eastern side of the peninsula, MacArthur believed, that the Japanese would strike first.

Under MacArthur's orders, the first line of defense, the Abucay-Mauban line, was established on January 7. This twenty-mile line began a third of the way down the peninsula and was organized for an in-depth defense. A forward outpost line was entrenched ahead of the main line of defense, and auxiliary defenses were prepared several miles behind the main line. Troops were placed along the beaches far to the rear of the main line, in case the Japanese attempted amphibious landings.

I and II Corps were both under MacArthur's direct authority. Although he remained on Corregidor, he established a forward command post on Bataan under Brig. Gen. Richard Marshall, through which he could control the fighting on Bataan. Thus, MacArthur was in administrative, though not actual, contact with the troops on Bataan. His statement to the War Department of January 7—"I am on my main battle line"—was a bit of dramatic hyperbole. It was Wainwright and Parker and their men who were on the main battle line that day, and every day of the three months that Bataan would hold.

Eight miles behind the front line was the rear battle position, the second and last line of defense on the peninsula. Stretching from Bagac on the west coast to Orion on the east coast, the defenses were just beginning to be prepared when the battle for Bataan began. Before the month of January was over, this position would become the front line, the place where the last stand on Bataan would be made. Wainwright's staff set up a new command post under a stand of trees south of Bagac.

On that day, January 7, Skinny was organizing and inspecting his half of the Abucay-Mauban line. It was about five miles long, ranging from the town of Mauban, overlooking the South China Sea, inland to the uncharted mountains in the center of the peninsula. Mount Natib divided his corps from Parker's and prevented the formation of a continuous line of defense. There was a five-mile gap between the two forces over rugged terrain, cliffs that at one point rose a thousand feet in a thousand yards. Between the right flank of Wainwright's line and Mount Natib stood Mount Silanganan, over 3,600 feet high.

All of Wainwright's line was hard to defend. On the left flank were the sea and a narrow beach. Not far inland, ridges up to seventy-five feet tall rose sharply, and the terrain from the ridges to the mountains was heavily wooded, so rugged and dense that his men needed bolos to cut their way through it. As a result, travel and communication between units and from front to rear were extremely difficult. The only road in the sector ran from Mauban south to Bagac. The shortage of supplies added to the problems of defense. Only the area around Mauban, on Wainwright's left flank, was protected by barbed wire. The rest of the line had nothing but jungle in front of it.

Wainwright had one advantage as commander of the Mauban-Mount Natib portion of the line; he was familiar with the territory. Before the war, as part of the preparations for the implementation of WPO-3, General Grunert, MacArthur's predecessor, had ordered the Twenty-sixth Cavalry to make a reconnaissance of the line. Based on their observations, Skinny had then prepared the plans for the defense of the very position he now held.

Satisfied that the line was as strong as it could be, Wainwright waited for the enemy to commence the battle of Bataan. He did not have long to wait.

In his headquarters in Manila, in sight of the peninsula of Bataan, the Japanese commander felt optimistic about the forthcoming battle. Although his best fighting unit had been reassigned and his new Sixty-fifth Brigade was poorly trained, General Homma believed that his men would meet little resistance on Bataan. He was wrong. He had based his strategy on erroneous intelligence reports on the condition and size of the American and Filipino troops, information that had relieved his concern about the inadequacy of his own forces.

According to Japanese intelligence officers, there were no more than 25,000 fighting men on Bataan, all of whom were supposed to be in poor physical condition. The Japanese knew that a large number of Filipino conscripts had deserted during the withdrawal into Bataan, and they were also aware of the cut in rations for the remaining troops. They concluded that the morale and stamina of the defenders had been weakened to the point where they would not have much will to fight. Japanese pilots had reported that there were no signs of any defenses being constructed. The jungle was so thick, however, that the pilots could not see what was taking place on the ground.

On the basis of this assessment, Homma believed that the American and Filipino soldiers could easily be pushed to the tip of Bataan, where those who remained would try to cross the two-mile stretch of water to Corregidor Island. A blockade of the island, plus air and artillery bombardment, would soon force that garrison to surrender.

Because he was sure that the fighting on Bataan would offer a quick and easy victory, Homma assigned the inexperienced Sixty-fifth Brigade to the task. They would move down the peninsula in two columns, one along each coast. By 6:00 P.M. on January 8, the brigade was in position south of the Layac Bridge. They would launch their attack the next day against Parker's II Corps and, at the same time, begin to advance on Wainwright's position.

The Japanese began the Battle of Bataan at 3:00 on the afternoon of January 9. Wainwright did not have to wait to be informed of the attack. He knew the instant it started because he could hear the heavy Japanese artillery bombardment, though the sound was coming from the far side of Mount Natib, miles away. Even with his slight deafness, he could feel the vibrations and sense the low rumbling. Throughout the afternoon, he constantly checked in with his forward positions, anxious for word of the strike that must surely come soon against his I Corps. But there was no Japanese offensive in his sector, at least not that day.

At 5:00 that afternoon Homma dispatched a small force westward from Layac, along Route 7 toward Olongapo on Subic Bay. They moved quickly down the undefended road. There was nothing to slow them down except the destroyed bridges. Even so, it would take them a week to cover the eleven miles of rough terrain that separated Olongapo from Wainwright's front line. Wainwright did not know that, of course. He believed the enemy attack could come at any minute, and he had cautioned his men to stay on the alert. That night he received word to gather his senior officers for an important meeting the following morning. MacArthur was coming from Corregidor. It would be the first time the two commanders had met since before the withdrawal from Lingayen Gulf.

The next morning, January 10, Wainwright and his commanders

waited in a clearing on the east-west road, a few miles from Bagac at the rear battle position, seven miles behind the front line. A convoy of four cars swept along the road from the direction of Parker's II Corps, which MacArthur and Sutherland had visited first.

MacArthur stepped out of his car and greeted Skinny warmly.

"Jonathan," he said, "I'm glad to see you back from the north. The execution of your withdrawal and of your mission in covering the withdrawal of the South Luzon Force were as fine as anything in history. And for that, I'm going to see that you are made a permanent major general of the Regular Army."

MacArthur walked along the line of the waiting I Corps officers and talked briefly with each. Then Wainwright asked MacArthur if he would talk with some of the troops. He knew it would be good for morale if the USAFFE commander visited some of the units in the area. A battery of 155s was nearby, and Skinny suggested that MacArthur come with him to chat with the men.

"No, Jonathan," MacArthur said. "I don't need to see them. I hear them."

MacArthur addressed the officers with great optimism and enthusiasm about the future of the fighting in the Philippines. What he told them was welcome, even astonishing, news. He reported that II Corps, which so far had received the brunt of the Japanese attack, would soon counterattack, and that Japanese air superiority was only temporary. New planes, MacArthur said, were coming from the United States. Crews from the American and Dutch air forces were now preparing airfields for them in Mindanao, from which bombers could attack the Japanese forces on Bataan. He also spoke of 20,000 troops on Mindanao that could reinforce the Bataan forces for an expected major counteroffensive that would enable them to reoccupy Manila in the near future. Finally, he impressed upon the officers how their resistance thus far had caught the imagination of the American people. It was truly an inspiring speech.

MacArthur and Sutherland held a long, private talk with Wainwright about the specific situation in I Corps. MacArthur wanted to know everything—the supply problems, the nature of the defenses, the morale and condition of the troops. Wainwright responded in blunt, no-nonsense terms.

As the two commanders and their staff mingled in the clearing, a young MP, part of the detachment assigned to protect the visiting brass, watched them intently. He was Richard Gordon, the soldier who had sailed to Manila on the *Grant* with Wainwright and who, in those balmy days before the war, had exercised Skinny's horses on the parade ground at Fort McKinley.

Gordon and the other enlisted men were upset, resentful of the great difference in appearance between Wainwright and the Bataan officers, and MacArthur's entourage. The visitors from Corregidor seemed "overdressed" in immaculate, out-of-place uniforms with neckties and smartly pressed pants. MacArthur was even wearing a jacket! In contrast, Wainwright and his officers looked like they had just come from the front line—which they had—in wrinkled khakis, stained with dirt and sweat. Not only in dress, but in bearing and manner as well, "it was Wainwright who impressed the troops at the C.P. with his command of the situation and the respect of the other senior officers present."

During the meetings that morning, Sutherland told Wainwright that he was alarmed by the five-mile gap between I and II Corps that he had seen during his inspection earlier in the day. He thought the Japanese might try to come down the center of Bataan, over the undefended Mount Natib. Skinny disagreed, saying that the terrain was too difficult for a large force to move through. It had taken his own patrols two full days to cross the gap with its deep gorges and dense jungles. Anyway, Wainwright pointed out, he did not have enough troops to defend the full line adequately. Sutherland was not satisfied. He told Wainwright, as he had earlier told Parker in II Corps, to shift some of his units to narrow the gap.

MacArthur and his staff returned to Corregidor that afternoon. The general was elated by what he had seen. He told Carlos Romulo that he was "very encouraged by the condition of the defenses." In conversation with President Quezon, MacArthur reported that there was no need to worry. He could "hold Bataan and Corregidor for several months without outside help." The morale of the troops was high. To his staff, MacArthur commented that, "Our 155s were music to my ears."

The day had been a successful one for MacArthur. It had been his first visit to the men of Bataan and it would be his only one. He never returned. Skinny did not see him again until two months later, just before the USAFFE commander left for Australia.

An ominous event attended MacArthur's visit to Bataan that day. Although they did not know that he was there, the Japanese sent him a message in the form of hundreds of leaflets that were dropped by airplane over the jungles of Bataan. It was a surrender ultimatum from Homma, the first of several. The Japanese general warned MacArthur that the end of the fighting was near and that the American and Filipino troops on the peninsula were doomed.

"The question is how long you will be able to resist. You have already cut rations by half. . . . Your prestige and honor have been upheld. However, in order to avoid needless bloodshed and save your . . . troops you are advised to surrender. . . . Failing that our offensive will be continued with inexorable force."

The Americans made no reply.

The next four days brought Wainwright a period of relative calm. He still spent every moment he could at the front with his men, encouraging them, seeking to improve his defensive positions, and waiting for the inevitable attack against his line. But there were no emergencies, no crises, no enemy breakthroughs, no disorganized units to whip back into shape. He was able to slow his hectic pace and get a little more rest, which, as an old field soldier pushing age fifty-nine, he could use.

He carefully followed the news of the fighting in the II Corps sector, which had been going on since the 9th. Parker's men were holding the enemy back and his artillery was exacting heavy casualties in every Japanese attack. The combat had been vicious, and several times it seemed that the enemy would break through, but with aggressive counterattacks, Parker's men maintained their position. There was a limit, however, to what they could do, and that limit would soon be reached.

On January 12, Wainwright had another visitor from Mac-Arthur's headquarters. Dick Marshall, head of USAFFE's forward echelon on Bataan, came to inspect the I Corps front line. He reiterated Sutherland's complaint about the gap between I and II Corps across Mount Natib. Skinny told him what he had told Sutherland two days before. The enemy surely could not attack in force over the mountain range. Also, he would have to weaken the main portion of his line drastically if he were to strengthen that area. Wainwright was wrong in his belief about the ability of the Japanese troops to move through the jungle. They did come through the undefended gap, and it almost spelled disaster for the entire front line.

Meanwhile, Homma was revising his plans for the conquest of Bataan. Because his attack against II Corps was not going well, he decided to increase by 5,000 the size of the force he had sent toward Wainwright's army, and then to attack in strength against both corps at the same time. He hoped to overwhelm the main line of defense and send the Americans and Filipinos scurrying toward the tip of Bataan.

On January 14, the Japanese began their march down the west coast of Bataan from Olongapo to Moron, just three miles in front of Skinny's forward position. Some of the enemy soldiers filed down a narrow trail. The rest headed toward Moron in small boats. From his own patrols and from friendly natives, Wainwright heard that the movement south toward his lines had begun. He immediately sent a force drawn from several units under his command north to Moron, to dig in and wait for the enemy. I Corps was back in the war again.

The next day, while Wainwright's men were preparing for their first battle on Bataan, they received a cheerful message from MacArthur, who had instructed his commanders to read it to the troops. MacArthur told the men on Bataan what they wanted to hear, what they desperately needed to hear.

"Help is on the way from the United States," the message said. "Thousands of troops and hundreds of planes are being dispatched. The exact time of arrival of reinforcements is unknown as they will have to fight their way through Japanese attempts against them. It is imperative that our troops hold until these reinforcements arrive.

"No further retreat is possible. We have more troops in Bataan than the Japanese have thrown against us; our supplies are ample; a determined defense will defeat the enemy's attacks.

"It is a question now of courage and determination. Men who run will merely be destroyed but men who fight will save themselves and their country.

"I call upon every soldier in Bataan to fight in his assigned position resisting every attack. This is the only road to salvation. If we fight we win; if we retreat we will be destroyed."

This was a stirring appeal, particularly to the Filipino troops. These men worshipped MacArthur; to them he could do no wrong. But most of the Americans knew better. A senior infantry officer then serving under Parker in II Corps referred to the message as "one of MacArthur's ghost stories."

Some U.S. soldiers laughed and jeered when the message was read to them. "Ample supplies?" wrote historian John Toland. "They were already on half-rations. Their grenades were no good; only one in four or five exploding. Their old Stokes mortars were more dangerous to them than to the enemy. Six out of seven rounds failed to detonate on landing and too often the ill-fitting shells burst the barrels." And how could help be on the way if the fleet had been destroyed at Pearl Harbor?

It was not heartening messages the men needed, but more food and ammunition, more weapons and planes, more of everything. But they would fight as MacArthur asked, not because of his exhortations, but because they had no choice. They had to try to postpone the inevitable. And who knows? some of them asked. Maybe MacArthur was right. Maybe help was on the way.

On the morning of the 16th of January, Wainwright's forward element met the enemy at Moron. At first the Japanese advanced quickly, crossing the Batalan River north of Moron against light opposition. The situation was perilous. Wainwright went to the front to take command of the fighting. He ordered the First Division, under Brig. Gen. Fidel V. Segundo, to counterattack, but they were repulsed each time. He called on his best troops, his old standby, the Twenty-sixth Cavalry. He had a composite of E and F Troops on hand.

Wainwright's cavalrymen moved out at once. In a bloody, savagely contested advance, the troopers drove the Japanese back to the north and west, but could not dislodge them east of Moron. The cavalry took heavy losses in men and horses, and, saddened by the casualties, Skinny ordered them to withdraw. He sent them far behind the lines to Bagac to rest and regroup, then dispatched the First Division to hold the ground the Twenty-sixth had won.

The First Division stood fast at Moron until late in the afternoon of the following day, when they were forced to withdraw one and a half miles south to a ridge that formed a natural defensive barrier. They dug in, under Wainwright's supervision, to prepare for the next attack. All through the night the defenders waited, alert for what the new day would bring.

That same day, MacArthur drafted a radiogram to the War Department. Its tone was dismal and pessimistic, far different from the hopeful message he had sent to the men on Bataan only two days before.

"The food situation here is becoming serious," he wrote. "For some time I have been on half rations and the result will soon become evident in the exhausted condition of the men. . . . I am having increasing difficulty in appeasing Philippine thought. . . . They cannot understand the apparent lack of effort to bring something in. I cannot over emphasize the psychological reaction that will take place here unless something tangible is done in this direction. A revulsion of feeling of tremendous proportions against

America can be expected. They can understand failure but cannot understand why no attempt is being made at relief through the forwarding of supplies. . . .

"I repeat that if something is not done to meet the general situation which is developing the disastrous results will be monumental."

Time was running out for the Philippine garrison. MacArthur in his Malinta Tunnel headquarters on Corregidor knew it. Officials in the War Department in Washington, D.C., knew it. And General Wainwright, spending the night on a jungle ridge in Bataan, knew it. Each day without proper food, each hour of waiting to be reinforced, brought them that much closer to the end.

Wainwright was forced to retreat two miles on the 18th. When his patrols reported to him on the size of the enemy force advancing on the ridge, he knew that his small force would not be able to hold. He withdrew to his forward outpost line, a mile and a half ahead of the main line of resistance.

He went up to inspect the new line that afternoon, to see how it was organized. He walked along it, with his two aides, his orderly, and his driver, going from foxhole to foxhole to speak words of encouragement to his men. Suddenly Wainwright saw five Japanese soldiers ahead of him. He flicked the safety off his Garand rifle and started firing. The Japanese ran into a haystack and he and the others poured fire into it. A moment later three enemy soldiers ran out and disappeared into the jungle. The other two were dead. "Not a bad day for a fighting general," Tom Dooley recalled.

A greater threat to Wainwright and his men was being planned that day by the commander of the Japanese force now opposing him, Maj. Gen. Naoki Kimura. When he learned that Wainwright's defense line stopped in the foothills of Mount Natib, he ordered a battalion of 700 men to traverse the mountain slopes and make its way behind Wainwright's front line. From there it could sever communications and the supply route to the front, and perhaps isolate the entire front line. The terrain did seem impassable, as Wainwright and Parker believed, but that evening the Japanese force tackled the job with a fanatical determination to get through. It would take three tortuous days, but they would succeed.

Unaware of the danger approaching from his right flank, Wainwright was busy with the main enemy force that was pushing hard against the left. Early on the morning of the 19th he ordered a counterattack forward of his outpost line. The drive gained ground, but slowly his men were repelled.

Later in the day, Wainwright and Tex Carroll drove out to visit another position of the line. Their old scout car was sighted by a Japanese Zero. The pilot cut his engine and glided silently down toward the road. Neither man in the car saw the plane descend. A string of machine gun bullets churned up the road ahead of them. Carroll slammed on the brakes and he and Skinny leaped out of the car and into a foxhole, the only protection in sight. The foxhole turned out to be an abandoned latrine. They stayed put while the Zero made two more passes over the road, then climbed out and tried to clean themselves off. Wainwright looked at his orderly, then down at his own fouled boots. "Who could ever imagine MacArthur in a mess like this?" he said.

That night the Japanese broke through the outpost line and began to hammer at Wainwright's main line of resistance. And all the while the Japanese battalion was hacking its way across the western slope of Mount Natib. Each step brought them closer to the rear of Wainwright's position.

In his office in the War Department in Washington, Dwight Eisenhower read MacArthur's gloomy radiogram about the situation in the Philippines. Ike was still having no success in getting them supplies. In his diary he recorded his thoughts. "In many ways, MacArthur is as big a baby as ever, but we've got to keep him fighting."

MacArthur was preparing yet another message for Washington, this one a letter from President Quezon. The Philippines leader was angry about the lack of assistance from the United States. "Thousands of the flower of the youth of the land are being killed and wounded and with the complete mastery of the air on the part of the enemy these boys will continue to be slaughtered. . . . I feel that with everything at stake we have the right to know if America's plan is to let the Philippines be conquered and not attempt to defend it except with the present American and Filipino forces."

Not only did Washington have to keep MacArthur fighting, it had to keep the Filipinos fighting as well, for as long as possible. Without them, there was no way to slow the Japanese.

Skinny was being confronted by another painful decision. His old friend Clint Pierce had come to see him, to talk about the outfit they both loved so much, the Twenty-sixth Cavalry. The troopers had been in almost continuous combat since the Japanese invasion and had fought the kind of war the cavalry fought best. They had displayed tremendous courage and skill and had carried on in the best tradition of that glorious old branch of the service.

Many were the times Wainwright wished he were back on horseback with them. But now it was clear that their days as horse cavalry were numbered. There was little fodder for the horses and the jungle terrain of Bataan was restricting the movement of the animals too much.

Sadly, Wainwright and Pierce agreed that the Twenty-sixth would have to be dismounted. The horses would be sent south to Mariveles and turned over to the Quartermaster Corps.

This decision marked the end of an era. Never again would a unit of the United States Army fight on horseback. The way of life that had characterized Wainwright's career was over. He tried not to think of the inevitable end for all those fine horses. If the men did not get more food before long, the animals would have to be eaten.

But Wainwright had little time to brood about this. The Japanese were continuing to press their attack against his front line. His weary soldiers might break at any moment. The news from Parker's II Corps was alarming; his front-line units could be overwhelmed at any time.

At 10:00 on the morning of January 21, the 700-man Japanese battalion emerged from the mountain range on Wainwright's right flank and set up a roadblock on the highway, the only road over which Wainwright's troops could be withdrawn to the south. The enemy force was in position only one mile behind the front line and had cut off the 5,000 men in the forward area. Wainwright's troops, under constant and heavy attack from the front, were now without an escape route. They were trapped.

CHAPTER 7

"And Nobody Gives a Damn"

EARLY ON THE MORNING of January 21, when Wainwright was on his way to the front, he learned about the Japanese roadblock in a very personal way. When he reached the command post of the First Division he was told that he shouldn't go any farther because enemy snipers had the road under surveillance. But that didn't stop him. He rounded up a scratch platoon, any personnel who could be spared from the C.P. He corralled a navy commander and two sailors, an air corps captain, and a number of Filipino soldiers—twenty men in all including Dooley, Carroll, and Centivo.

Wainwright grabbed his carbine, loaded his platoon into a truck, and led them north in his scout car. When they reached the roadblock, Wainwright found that a platoon of Filipino soldiers was already engaging the enemy. He took over command, leading his combined force in a two-hour assault. They were fighting in rugged terrain, filled with tall, densely packed trees and deep gorges, perfect country for enemy snipers who could be only yards from their victims and still remain invisible.

Wainwright was standing next to a high bank beside the road giving orders to a young officer. Suddenly Tex Carroll grabbed Wainwright by the seat of his pants and pulled him to the ground.

"Goddamn it, General," Carroll growled in his low, Texas drawl. "Get down or you'll get your damn head blown off!"

Heavy fire came over the bank where Wainwright had been an

instant before. It hit two Filipinos who had been standing with him, killing one and wounding the other. The bullets sprayed across the road and slammed into the trees, missing Tom Dooley by inches.

Shortly after noon, Wainwright realized that his force was too small to dislodge the enemy roadblock, and he drove north through the jungle to try to find reinforcements. Gradually he was able to pull together a few units from the Ninety-first Division, the Twenty-sixth Cavalry, and the One Hundred Ninety-fourth Tank Battalion. Placing Col. John Rodman, commander of the Ninety-second Infantry Regiment, in charge, Skinny told him to attack in force the next morning.

Wainwright now turned his attention to the front line and saw that his beleaguered First Division was showing signs of cracking. One battalion had already run from the line without firing a shot. The rest would not be able to hold much longer. If they broke and ran south, they would be heading right into enemy hands at the roadblock to the rear.

At 7:00 the next morning, January 22, Wainwright was back with the force he had hastily assembled to attack the roadblock. They had been unable to dislodge the enemy. The American tanks were repulsed by Japanese antitank guns and by mines that had been laid during the night. The battle raged all day and by evening the Japanese were still there, isolating the First Division.

This had been a busy and disappointing day for Wainwright. His troops on the front line were rapidly reaching the limit of their endurance, he hadn't been able to budge the Japanese to the rear, and now to compound his problems, he received orders from MacArthur to withdraw! Early that afternoon, Sutherland had come to Bataan to assess the situation for USAFFE headquarters. He visited Parker's II Corps on the east side of the peninsula and then met with Wainwright on the west. Sutherland did not like what he saw.

The Japanese had sent more troops across the mountains, through the undefended gap between the two corps, and there was growing enemy pressure on both front lines. Sutherland reached the inescapable conclusion that the Mauban-Abucay line would have to be abandoned. If they continued to try to hold, both corps could be bypassed around their flanks and surrounded. Sutherland told Wainwright to prepare to withdraw his men to the rear defense line, the one that stretched from Bagac to Orion. The withdrawal would commence the next day. Wainwright knew it would be a risky operation because the only road south for his I Corps was already in enemy hands.

That same day, unknown to Wainwright or to anyone at USAFFE headquarters, the Japanese unleashed a new threat against Bataan. They began a series of amphibious operations designed to land troops far down the west coast of Bataan, miles behind the new front line. If the landings were successful, the enemy would create chaos in the rear areas, disrupting supplies and communications and ending all hope of Wainwright withdrawing his I Corps to the tip of Bataan.

That night, at Moron, a battalion of Japanese troops was loaded onto landing barges that chugged out to sea and turned south, moving along the dark, mountainous west coast of Bataan. From the beginning, everything went wrong. The mission had been hastily mounted, the planning was inadequate, and the maps of the coast were so lacking in detail as to be useless. The sea was rough, the current fast and treacherous, and the men were packed uncomfortably in the swaying, bouncing barges.

At a point ten miles south of Wainwright's lines, the Japanese troops spotted a boat, low in the water, coming toward them. Was it one of their own, off course, or was it an American patrol boat? The Japanese flashed their identification signal but there was no response. A voice called to them in the darkness—in English. The Japanese immediately opened fire, which was returned just as promptly by four .50-caliber machine guns. The Japanese landing barge had run into a PT boat commanded by Lt. John D. Bulkeley, the man who would later take MacArthur and his staff to Australia.

Bulkeley sank the enemy barge, but the fire drew the attention of the American artillery on Bataan and he was forced to leave the scene. Less than an hour later he spotted another boat and opened fire. Before the barge sank, Bulkeley leaped aboard it and took three Japanese prisoners and a dispatch case containing military plans.

As a result of Bulkeley's attacks and the rough seas, the Japanese landing force had become divided and both groups were off course. The first landing party came ashore at Longoskawayan Point, ten miles from their objective and almost at the southernmost part of Bataan. The other group landed seven miles north of the first group at Quinauan Point. The operation was a success, however, because the Japanese achieved surprise at both positions.

They were met by an ill-prepared mixed force of grounded airmen and beached sailors on duty along that section of the coast.

None of them had fought on land before, but they would soon have their chance. Wainwright, too, would soon be fighting again. The Japanese were sending additional troops to menace the rear areas of I Corps. A bloody battle would rage for the next three weeks.

The situation on Bataan was bleak by January 23. Despite repeated attacks from Wainwright's soldiers, the enemy still blocked the road behind the front line. The First Division was holding the front line, but the Japanese were bolstering the forces they had arrayed against it. That night the division was scheduled to begin its withdrawal, leaving a covering force to keep the enemy occupied. The maneuver would have to be made on foot, along the rocky coast. If the Filipino rear guard broke, the Japanese would pour down the road and cut off the retreating division.

Farther to the south, American sailors and airmen were engaging the Japanese troops that had come ashore in the night. Wainwright was distressed about these landings. Even though they had not taken place in his sector—they were in the service command area, now under Clyde Selleck—they represented a direct threat to his men. If his forces reached the Bagac-Orion defense line intact, they would have the enemy not only to the front but also only nine miles to the rear.

On Corregidor, MacArthur was shocked by the enemy breakthrough. He sent a message of "impending doom" to George Marshall at the War Department.

"Heavy fighting has been raging all day," MacArthur wrote. "My losses during the campaign have been very heavy and are mounting. They are now approximately thirty-five percent. My diminishing strength will soon force me to a shortened line on which I shall make my final stand. . . . With its occupation all maneuvering possibilities will cease. I intend to fight it to complete destruction. This will leave Corregidor.

"I wish to take this opportunity while the army still exists and I am in command to pay my tribute to the magnificent service it has rendered. No troops have ever done so much with so little. I bequeath to you the charge that their fame and glory be duly recorded by their countrymen."

Wainwright ranged up and down the road during these two days, exhorting his men to move faster, untangling traffic jams, and once even threatening the troops. Lt. Samuel A. Goldblith was on the road on January 25, trying to move a 155mm gun that had gotten stuck in a ditch. He was attempting to maneuver his big ten-wheeled truck into position to pull the gun out of the ditch, but the fleeing troops kept getting in his way. Somehow, he had to retrieve that gun.

A command car drove up and Wainwright and his staff officers got out. Skinny strode up to the lieutenant and asked what the problem was. When Goldblith explained, Wainwright acted immediately. Barking out orders, he halted the retreating army. He took his cane, drew a line in the dust across the road, and planted himself in the center, facing the mass of tired men.

Then he pulled his old Colt .45 Peacemaker from its holster and announced that he would shoot any man who crossed the line before the 155mm gun was removed from the ditch. No one moved. The silence was broken only by the throaty roar of Goldblith's truck as he backed it up to the ditch and pulled the gun free.

Throughout the day and night the American and Filipino troops scurried down the road to their new position. Lt. Henry Lee was there and described the scene in a poem he called "Abucay Withdrawal."

> The order comes to withdraw at night,
> And the hungry, weary, half dazed men
> Stumble South to entrench again. . . .
> No time to falter or catch a breath
> For thought of future, for fear of death;
> No time for hunger or for a wound,
> No time for motors to be retuned.
> No time for sickness nor for the dead
> For the line is broken two miles ahead,
> And the crouching enemy waits to spring.
> There are trenches to dig and wire to string.
> Supplies to move and guns to sight,
> A whole new line must be built tonight.
> Another line in a losing fight. . . .
> Rifles spatter, machine guns spray
> As the weary doughboys take up the fray
> Bataan is saved for another day
> Save for hunger and wounds and heat
> For slow exhaustion and grim retreat
> For a wasted hope and a sure defeat.

In Malinta Tunnel on Corregidor, MacArthur called a staff conference on January 24. He was discouraged about the situation across the bay on Bataan and his attitude suggested to those present that he believed Bataan would soon fall. If it did, Corregidor was the last hope for the Philippines. The Rock had to hold, but to do so the garrison would need reinforcements—more food and more men.

He ordered the commander of Manila's harbor defenses, George Moore, to begin the transfer of food from Bataan to Corregidor, further depleting Wainwright's and Parker's already meager supplies. In addition, MacArthur told Moore that he planned to bring the Philippine Division to Corregidor before Bataan surrendered. It looked as though Bataan was being written off already.

But it was far from over to Wainwright. He was as unhappy about the withdrawal as everyone else, but he was determined to keep Bataan as long as he could. To accomplish that, he needed to get as many troops as possible into position on the new line of defense.

The Japanese were still holding the road south of his First Division. None of the attacks his men had made had been successful in breaking through. Meanwhile, the bulk of the First Division was on its way to the new line. Since they could not use the road, the troops had to scramble down steep, narrow trails to the beach, and from there to trudge toward Bagac. All their vehicles and artillery had to be destroyed. There was no way to get them out as long as the road remained blocked by the enemy. The loss of the guns left Wainwright's I Corps with only two 155s and four 75s.

By the morning of the 25th the division's rear guard, commanded by Col. Kearie L. Berry, was desperate. Ammunition was low, the food was almost gone, and the artillerymen had no shells left to fire. Berry had no choice. If he were to save his men, he had to pull them out, even though he had not received Wainwright's permission to withdraw. At 10:30 he gave the order and his exhausted, starving troops, carrying their wounded on improvised stretchers, made their way to the open beaches and the only route south.

"It was a gruelling march down the rugged coast in the pitiless tropical sun," Berry told John Toland after the war. "Many men threw away their guns and took off their uniforms. The sharp rocks cut the men's sneakers to bits. By dawn almost everyone, including Berry, was barefoot. Then the long line turned, climbing laboriously up a cliff, and headed for the coast road."

Berry stopped his men to let them rest while he went into Bagac to try to find someone who could tell him where to take his unit. A Packard came down the road toward him. Berry knew who it was;

there was only one car like that on Bataan. As he waited for Wainwright to get out, he was apprehensive about the general's reaction to Berry's withdrawal without orders.

"Berry," Wainwright said, "I'm damned glad to see you."

The colonel was much relieved, and he explained where his men were. Wainwright nodded and pointed southward.

"Keep going down the road to Trail 9," he said. "You'll take up position in there." Skinny smiled at the younger man and added, "I'll see that you're mentioned in orders."

The new defense line from Bagac to Orion was occupied by U.S. forces by the morning of the 26th. The withdrawal had been a success, despite the loss of vehicles and artillery in Wainwright's I Corps. No major fighting units had been lost. The Japanese had suffered many casualties while forcing the Americans and Filipinos back to their second line of defense. The enemy's Sixty-fifth Brigade had lost almost 1,500 of its 6,500 men, and the commander reported that his men had "reached the extreme stages of exhaustion."

MacArthur sent a message to the War Department, giving the impression that he was at the front. "In Luzon: Under cover of darkness I broke contact with the enemy and without the loss of a man or an ounce of materiel am now firmly established on my main battle position."

All during the morning hours Wainwright inspected his new line, examining it yard by yard to make sure the defenses were as strong as they could be. The Bagac-Orion line was approximately fourteen miles long, but in one respect it was easier to defend than the previous line. Although the Mariveles mountain range ran the length of the peninsula, there was no peak the height of Mount Natib to separate the front lines of I and II Corps. Here a continuous defensive line could be maintained from coast to coast. Also, because the land area to be defended was smaller, the American and Filipino troops could be deployed more effectively, both at the front and along the beaches.

The terrain, however, was just as fierce, the same mountains densely covered with trees and undergrowth. In Wainwright's sector, from the Pantingan River to the China Sea, the land sloped sharply on the extreme right flank all the way to the sea. There were no open fields of sugar cane here as there were in the II Corps sector.

The official army history concluded that "Nowhere on Bataan was the terrain less suitable for military operations. . . . It is hard to imagine heavier, more nearly impenetrable or bewildering jungle . . . It is covered with tall, dense cane and bamboo. On hummocks and knolls are huge hardwood trees, sixty to seventy feet in height, from which trail luxuriant tropical vines and creepers. Visibility throughout the area is limited, often to ten or fifteen yards."

If the territory made life difficult, the climate made it almost unbearable. The daytime temperatures averaged 95°, even in the jungle's gloomy shade. The mildest physical activity soaked a man with sweat in minutes. The heat was enervating, even to soldiers in peak physical condition. But the men on Bataan were not in good shape, given the fighting and the low rations. Travel on the road and on the network of trails slashed through the jungle behind the lines raised a thick cloud of choking dust that soon settled over everything. The dust and the heat were so annoying that Wainwright shaved his head in the hope that he would be a little less bothered by the conditions. At night the temperature dropped sharply, leaving the men shivering under their heavy army blankets. It was hell.

Wainwright's portion of the front was six and a half miles long, and he had three divisions with which to defend it—the Ninety-first, the First, and the Eleventh, plus the Second Philippine Constabulary. The only reserve force he had was the Twenty-sixth Cavalry. On the day the new line was being occupied, Wainwright received word from MacArthur's headquarters that his area of command would be enlarged considerably to include the whole of the western coast, from the front line to the tip of Bataan. Now he would be fighting a two-front war. The enemy was both in front and behind.

Clint Pierce, commanding officer of the Twenty-sixth Cavalry, was detailed to relieve Clyde Selleck in the service command area. Wainwright ordered Pierce to eliminate the Japanese beachheads that had been established at Quinauan and Longoskawayan Points.

Skinny wanted Pierce promoted when he took over his new command. MacArthur agreed. That evening Wainwright called Pierce to his headquarters.

"Colonel," Skinny said formally, "when I was promoted to be a brigadier general, the information was given me by General Malin Craig. He not only gave me the information but he reached up and detached two stars from the stars he wore on his shoulder. I now wish to inform you that you are from this moment on a brigadier general."

While he was speaking, his right hand had been clenched. Now he opened it and held out two shiny stars to the amazed and delighted Pierce.

"These are the stars that Malin Craig gave me," Skinny said to his old friend. "I want you to have them and wear them always—no matter how many more stars you get. Also, I want you to proceed to the west coast and kick hell out of the Nips who have landed there."

Homma, the Japanese commander, was pleased. He had pushed the Americans and Filipinos closer to the tip of Bataan. He was also worried, however, about how much longer this operation would take. It should have been easy to mop up the forces on Bataan. He was under pressure from his superiors in Tokyo, who were demanding to know why he had not been victorious. Now, on the morning of January 26, Homma thought Bataan would finally be his. The reason for his optimism was an American map that had been found by his troops in Manila. The secret document showed the defense plans for Bataan. Two red lines stretched across the peninsula, representing what were thought to be the outpost line and, five miles behind it, the main defense line. Either the map was incorrect or the Japanese misinterpreted it, because what they took to be the thinly held outpost line was actually the heavily fortified front line.

At 4:00 that afternoon Homma issued orders for an immediate attack along both coasts. The objective was to sweep away the forward outpost line and hit the main line. Homma was so confident that his captured map assured an easy triumph and so eager to strike before the American and Filipino forces became entrenched that he did not wait for his artillery. Within the hour, Japanese troops were advancing through the jungle. The second battle of Bataan was about to begin.

For two days the Japanese tried to break through Wainwright's left flank, the section held by the Ninety-first Division. By nightfall on the 27th the line was still intact. Skinny's real problem that day was not his front line, but rather the beaches to the rear, where the mixed force of airmen and sailors had been fighting for four days, in what came to be called the "battle of the points."

The Japanese were well dug in at their landing sites at Quinauan and Longoskawayan Points, and Wainwright realized that trained infantry was needed to clear them out. Under no circumstances could he allow the enemy to remain there. Their presence was too great a menace to the road, the only route between the service area at the tip of Bataan and the front. In one place the road was no more than a mile from a Japanese position.

The Japanese tried unsuccessfully on the 27th to reinforce their troops by sea at Quinauan Point. MacArthur believed that this indicated that a major Japanese effort to cut the road would soon be made. He ordered Wainwright to commit two Philippine Scout battalions to the area.

Wainwright focused first on Longoskawayan Point, the southernmost landing site and the one closest to the vital road. Sending in all the artillery he could spare, and enlisting the two giant twelve-inch mortars on Corregidor, he ordered a massive bombardment that lasted over an hour. Then Wainwright sent in the infantry. Despite the heavy American shelling, the Japanese resisted fiercely. Once they almost surrounded a portion of the attack force and by the end of the day they were still holding their ground.

The situation at Quinauan Point was no better. The Philippine Scouts kept the Japanese from advancing, but the enemy clung to the ground it already had.

A new threat loomed as the Japanese made a landing north of Quinauan Point. It was not where they had intended to go. The 200 men were reinforcements for the Quinauan Point group. Instead, they landed 2,000 yards to the north, between the Anyasan and Silaiim rivers. The beach there was held by the Philippine Constabulary troops, who ran as soon as they saw the enemy. When the sector commander, Clint Pierce, learned of the landing, he sent in his only reserves—grounded airmen of the Seventeenth Pursuit Squadron. As the ill-prepared pilots and ground crew set out for the coast, a few were overheard asking how to fire their rifles.

The enemy landings behind the lines had been a constant concern to Wainwright. He knew the havoc that could be caused if the Japanese were reinforced and able to break out of their beachheads. He also knew that it was impossible to hold the front line indefinitely against the enemy onslaught that would be increasing. If the Japanese to the rear could not be contained, Bataan would soon be finished. Wainwright studied his maps and reached the conclusion that the front line should be withdrawn even farther south, closer to the tip of Bataan.

He knew that such a move was in opposition to MacArthur's strategy and the long-held ideas detailed in WPO-3. Wainwright felt strongly that he was correct in his assessment, however, and he decided to tell MacArthur what he thought. At 4:30 on the afternoon of the 27th he dictated to Jesse Traywick, his assistant operations officer, a long memorandum for the USAFFE chief, outlining his views, and he sent the letter by courier to Corregidor.

Wainwright was careful to note that he was not making a recommendation, but rather a suggestion that "USAFFE consider withdrawing the front of both Corps to such positions as they may select so as to shorten the front and very greatly shorten the Coastal Flank; neither of which can, in my opinion, be adequately held by this Corps with the number and quality of troops available. My coastal flank is very lightly held, so lightly that the Japs appear to infiltrate through it at night at points selected by them. If I take troops off my front to thicken the Coast Defense, they will certainly crash through the front. . . . The landings on the West Coast, so far accomplished, can and probably will be handled. Our experience, however, indicates such landings to be only a prelude to landings of much greater force. With reliable troops, the situation would not be particularly serious but with the majority of troops available, it becomes distinctly serious. One battalion of the Philippine Army ran away last night from the front lines without having had a shot fired at it. It probably heard a little firing at its left and pulled out."

Having presented his estimate of the situation, Wainwright repeated that he was not making a recommendation to withdraw, but suggesting that if the front were shortened, then the defense of it and of the coasts could be greatly strengthened. Finally, he made it clear that unless he were ordered to withdraw from his present position, he would "hold here to the last."

The next day, while awaiting MacArthur's reply to his report, Wainwright focused on the most direct threat to his troops, the Japanese landings along the coast. If the enemy forces could not be thrown back into the sea, at least they had to be held where they were. This day would bring both success and failure.

That morning Wainwright drove south toward Clint Pierce's command post. Tom Dooley and Tex Carroll were riding on the running boards of the car to spot for enemy planes. For the past few days Japanese fighters and dive bombers had ranged over Bataan during the daylight hours, strafing and bombing at will. Before long, Wainwright and his men lost track of the number of times they had to leap from the car and jump into the nearest ditch for cover. No place was safe, not even headquarters. A bomb had landed so close that a piece of shrapnel had sliced through a tent and landed on Frank Nelson's desk.

They reached Pierce's C.P. without further mishap. The newly promoted cavalryman was limping, having been wounded three days before. He told Skinny it was an "ignominious wound." One of his toes had been shot off. The worst part to Pierce was that the bullet had ruined a perfectly good and expensive cavalry boot.

While Wainwright was there, a Japanese sniper was reported to be nearby. That was all the two tough old soldiers needed to hear. They grabbed their weapons and headed down the trail together, two generals in their fifties, tired and undernourished, Wainwright with his cane and Pierce with his bad foot, both delighted to be soldiering, doing what they loved best.

They had not gone very far when they were fired upon. Skinny raised his Garand and raked the tallest tree with automatic fire and the sniper fell to the ground. As they walked back to the command post Clint Pierce said he was going to recommend Wainwright for a Distinguished Service Cross. Skinny grinned and said he'd do the same for Pierce. Neither general received the medal. An officer on the promotions and decorations board on Corregidor confirmed that Pierce had indeed recommended Wainwright for the medal, but Wainwright's recommendation for Pierce never showed up!

The best news Wainwright received that day came from Long-oskawayan Point, the invasion site closest to the tip of Bataan. The 500 Philippine Scouts he had sent into action there fought bravely all day. By nightfall they had advanced about two-thirds of the way down the length of the point. If they could maintain their momentum they might be able to clear out the enemy in a day or two.

The action at Quinauan Point was less successful. Another Philippine Scout battalion, aided by 150 American airmen, was unable to make much progress through the jungle, although they kept up their attack throughout the day. By dusk they had advanced no more than one hundred yards. The battalion commander asked Wainwright for reinforcements, and from his meager reserve force Wainwright dispatched another company of scouts. It was all he could spare.

At the invasion site between the Anyasan and Silaiim rivers, a battalion of the Philippine Constabulary and the American Seventeenth Pursuit Squadron had advanced almost to the coast. The situation appeared promising, but that night, when it looked as if the Japanese were preparing to counterattack, the Filipino troops ran away, leaving the airmen on their own. The situation had suddenly turned serious. If the Japanese broke out now, they could easily cut off the road that was only 2,000 yards inland. Reinforcements were needed urgently. Wainwright ordered in another battalion of Philippine Scouts. He hoped that the enemy would not break through the American line during the night because the scouts could not reach the battlefield until the next morning.

There was a new problem developing along Wainwright's front line. For two days the Japanese had pushed against the left flank, but to no avail. The troops of the Ninety-first Division had held their ground. Because they were making no progress in that attack, the Japanese sent out patrols to probe the rest of the line for a weak spot.

They found one in the center of the line, in the area held by the First Division. The division was weak and disorganized and had not recovered from its harrowing withdrawal along the beaches from the first defense line. The men had been trying to prepare their new position, but the job was going slowly. All the men were exhausted, and they did not even have shovels or axes to work with. They were digging foxholes with their mess kits and clearing away the undergrowth with their hands and their bayonets.

Before they had a chance to get fully entrenched, they were attacked by 1,000 Japanese troops, who rapidly forced their way through the front line and kept on going. The infiltrators cut communication lines and panicked the rear-echelon troops. In the darkness it was hard to tell friend from foe.

Moving blindly through the jungle, the Japanese unit split into two groups. A small force, less than a company, took up position on the top of a hill 400 yards behind the front, at a place that would soon be known as the "little pocket." The larger Japanese force went eastward and stopped a mile behind the front line, close to the junction of two trails that U.S. forces had been using to move troops and supplies. This was the "big pocket."

Now Wainwright had three enemy forces to contend with: those pressing the front line, those who had landed by sea at the points to the rear, and the two pockets deep inside the forward position. He also had an answer from MacArthur about his suggestion to shorten the defensive line. It was an emphatic "no." MacArthur had also offered moral and tactical advice, and an admonishment to keep on fighting, something that Skinny Wainwright had never needed.

"Sooner or later," MacArthur wrote, "we must fight to the finish . . . we have now reached our last ditch. Our only safety is to fight the enemy off. He is not in great strength and if you can once really repulse him you will obtain relief from his pressure. . . . You must, however, hold on your front and there is no better place we can find than the one you are now on."

MacArthur went on to explain to Wainwright, the front-line commander, that he should constantly strengthen his position, organize his defense in depth, cover each beach and trail, and not let the enemy get through the front line. He added that every resource had already been committed, so Wainwright would have to rely on what he had in the way of men and supplies to achieve MacArthur's stated goals.

"Explain constantly to your officers and men," the USAFFE commander on Corregidor exhorted, "if they run they will be doomed but that if they fight they will save themselves. . . .

"Once again I repeat, I am aware of the enormous difficulties that face you. Am proud, indeed, of the magnificent efforts you have made. There is nothing finer in history. Let's continue and preserve the fair name that we have so fairly won."

MacArthur's advice was sound, of course, but the men of Bataan were in poor shape to carry it out. Two months of hard fighting, hunger, and disease were taking their toll, disabling the soldiers more effectively than enemy bullets and artillery shells.

The troops had been issued half rations or less for nearly four weeks, and the food supplies on Bataan were dwindling. By the end of January there was an eleven-day supply of meat and fish, a six-day supply of flour, and only four days' worth of vegetables. Sugar was a luxury. On a visit to the Twenty-sixth Cavalry, Wainwright confided to Trap Trapnell, "I don't worry about the Japs. I worry about the chow."

At headquarters, Wainwright and his staff usually had no more food than the soldiers on the front line. He prided himself on that. It was his habit to not expect his men to do with less than what he had. He ate only two skimpy meals a day, one at 8:00 in the morning and the other at 4:00 in the afternoon. There was no bread for the general, no sugar, butter, or margarine, though he still had a small supply of canned milk.

Occasionally Wainwright's diet was supplemented by gifts from well-meaning friends. One day an old cavalry buddy from Fort Myer, Virginia, Bill Lawrence, dropped by the command post for a chat. When he was about to leave, Lawrence asked Wainwright if he would like him to bring a ham the next time he came. Skinny hesitated, but his aide, Tom Dooley, nodded yes. "Imagine," Dooley recorded in his diary that night, "hesitation at the sound of ham."

The United Press correspondent, Frank Hewlett, made frequent trips between Bataan and Corregidor. Before one visit, a quarter master officer on Corregidor, Chester Elmes, gave Hewlett three

Edam cheeses. "Bring them to my good friend Skinny," Elmes said. No one on Bataan had seen a piece of cheese for a long time.

On his way to Wainwright's headquarters, Hewlett stopped to see Clint Pierce and decided to give him one of the cheeses. The other two he took to Wainwright.

Skinny was delighted, but after a moment he looked gravely at Hewlett and asked, "Hewlett, would it be all right with you if I gave one of these to Clint Pierce? Just a few days ago he was telling me how he would love a slice of cheese."*

Such luxuries were few and far between. As a rule, Wainwright and his staff ate the same rations as everyone else. They may have been better prepared, however. Skinny's Filipino cook, Francisco, had stayed with him since the days at Fort McKinley. Francisco showed great talent in preparing tasty food out of almost nothing. Some thought he even made carabao taste good.

There was a great deal of rice on Bataan, but it provided little nutrition. For the Americans, used to bread and potatoes, rice was a sorry substitute. For meat, which was available about every third day, the men had mostly tough, stringy carabao—water buffalo. The soldiers used their cunning to supplement this insubstantial diet with whatever else they could find. Dogs, monkeys, and even lizards were soon being eaten, and gratefully so.

One American soldier, Richard Mallonée, wrote: "I can recommend mule. There was little to choose between calesa pony and carabao. The pony was tougher but better flavored than the carabao. Iguana was fair. Monkey I do not recommend. I never had snake."

The wounded in the two hospitals in the rear area also had insufficient food. Juanita Redmond, a nurse at hospital #1, said that the soldiers complained more about their empty stomachs than about their injuries.

"Please, mum," they would say, "couldn't I have something to eat?"

"Can't you wait till breakfast? It won't be long."

"I'm so hungry. I haven't had anything to eat for days."

"For days? Wasn't there any food in your unit?"

"We were cut off. They couldn't get food to us."

---

*"There was nothing I could say but 'of course,'" Hewlett recalled, "but Pierce and I had several laughs about how he wound up with two of the general's three Edam cheeses."

And this was just the beginning of the battle of Bataan. The situation would grow worse in the weeks ahead.

Not only was there never enough food, but what was available was distributed unevenly. Some units had their own food supplies, appropriated during the retreat into Bataan. Other outfits had nothing but the standard ration. Some days they didn't even receive that. The troops in the front lines were farthest from the supply depots. As always in a war, those in the rear had better access to the food.

Some men and their commanders went to desperate lengths to get additional food. Trucks loaded with food were hijacked at gunpoint. Officers padded their strength reports to indicate that they had more men than they did so that they could draw more rations. One division with a strength of 6,500 got a food allotment for 11,000.

Particularly irksome to the men on Bataan was their belief that the garrison on Corregidor was better provisioned. They were correct. One day a detachment of MPs stopped a truck that was delivering food to the antiaircraft batteries on Bataan. Because the batteries were attached to the Harbor Defense Command, they were entitled to Corregidor rations. Word of the truck's contents spread quickly. To the Bataan troops starving in their foxholes it sounded like an incredible feast—ham and bacon, Vienna sausage, cracked wheat, raisins, peas, corn, tomatoes, peaches, potatoes, catsup, and 600 pounds of ice!

Wainwright was furious when he heard of the incident and ordered an inquiry. He was assured by the provost marshal that the troops on Corregidor were getting "approximately the same ration components. However, such is war." There was nothing Wainwright or anyone else on Bataan could do about the inequity.

Largely because of the inadequate diet, the health of the men on Bataan was deteriorating. Medical officers issued dire warnings to Wainwright and the other commanders that combat efficiency, already low, would sink even lower if the men did not get more protein. By the end of January, after only one month on Bataan, the incidence of malnutrition, avitaminosis, scurvy, beriberi, and amoebic dysentery had reached alarming proportions. Weight loss averaged fifteen to twenty-five pounds per man in some units. Soldiers were so weak that a minor illness would incapacitate them. Rapid movement caused an unusually fast heart rate and an attack of vertigo. By noon each day many men were already doubled over with the intestinal pain of beriberi.

The troops were on an official ration of 2,000 calories a day, half of what a fighting man needs. By March they would be reduced to 1,000 calories a day. On his daily tours of the front lines, Skinny saw the evidence of the lack of food—the swollen legs, the sunken cheeks, the thin and wasted bodies, the apathy and the irritability. He felt these symptoms himself. He was forced to support himself with a cane because his own legs were swollen and painful from beriberi.

Wainwright appealed to USAFFE headquarters for vegetables and fruit, vitamin concentrates, canned milk, and beef, but he received none of this. The food stocks on Corregidor, he was told, were needed there so that the fortress island could hold out until reinforcements arrived. Bataan's days were numbered, but with sufficient food the Rock could continue to frustrate Japanese plans for the conquest of the Philippines. That was the hope, but that policy meant no extra food for the defenders of Bataan.

In addition to malnutrition and the diseases it spawned, the men had to contend with malaria. The first signs had appeared in early January when the troops first reached Bataan, but so far it had been kept under control with regular doses of quinine. The supply of the drug was rapidly diminishing, however. Medical officers had enough for about one more month, at the present rate of use, and they were predicting large-scale epidemics of the disease by the end of February. The majority of the troops were already infected with malaria parasites.

A host of other medical problems plagued the Filipino troops because of abysmal sanitary conditions. "Lack of training in the elements of military hygiene was universal in the Philippine Army. Many of the Filipinos drank unboiled water from streams and pools and failed to sterilize their mess gear. Latrines were neither well constructed nor properly used. Kitchens were dirty and garbage buried near the surface. Huge flies, attracted by these malodorous dumps, swarmed everywhere."

As a result, diarrhea and dysentery were widespread and there was never enough medicine to treat them. Before long, the Americans came down with the same diseases, despite their better conditions of sanitation. Nurse Redmond treated a young American soldier for severe diarrhea. He thought it was caused by the water he had been forced to drink.

"We were cut off from our base," he explained to her. "Our canteens were empty and we were dying of thirst. We saw this carabao stream. It was awfully dirty but we just had to drink. You get so thirsty, you don't care what you gulp down your throat so long as it's wet."

Both of the hospitals in the service command area were swamped with sick and wounded men. The medical personnel were running out of medication, dressings, and everything else. Lt. Sallie Durrett, a nurse at hospital #2 near Cabcaben on the east coast, said that the situation was so bad that "our surgical gauze had patches on their patches." At hospital #1, a few miles away at Little Baguio, conditions were no better for Lt. Redmond and her colleagues. The disabled soldiers poured in every day of the week, straining the facilities and supplies.

Each hospital had been planned to care for 1,000 patients; by the end of January each had more than 3,000. By the end of March there would be 11,000 patients in the two hospitals. Events in the first week of April would swell that number to over 24,000. There was nothing that could be done to improve conditions.

Food and medicine were not, of course, the only things lacking on Bataan. The shortage of cigarettes was hard on the men, especially those at the front. There were never enough smokes. Many cases of cigarettes disappeared while being shipped to the front from the rear echelon supply depots. Men in the rear areas could buy all they wanted, on the black market, for five cents a pack. The men in the foxholes had to pay one dollar, when they could find someone to sell to them.

An officer from Corregidor reported that he had found a man who was willing to pay five dollars for a pack of cigarettes. Horrified, the officer gave the Bataan soldier his money back "and told him that if anyone ever wanted to charge him more than twenty centavos [ten cents] a package for cigarettes he should shoot them." During the three months of fighting on Bataan, only 400 cases of cigarettes were sent over from Corregidor, amounting to less than one cigarette per day for each man on the line.

Another hardship was the shortage of clothing and other personal gear. Most of the Filipino troops had no raincoats, blankets, or tents, and as many as one-fourth had no shoes. The rest of the men wore shoes that in normal times would have been discarded. The American soldiers were usually a little better off, but not much. Their uniforms had quickly become torn and ragged, and the men shivered on the bare ground during the cold nights. There were no replacements for the clothing or blankets. The situation got so bad that the uniforms of hospital patients were reissued to men at the front.

The men on Bataan were running out of everything save one vital ingredient: the will to fight. Despite hunger, disease, privation, and misery, they were determined to give a good account of themselves, to hold on as long as possible. Through the month of January many of the men maintained their hope that help was on the way from the United States. Each day that they held their ground against the Japanese gave that much more time for the convoys that must surely be heading their way to reach them.

Help *was* coming. That thought was the only frail reed they had to cling to. MacArthur himself had told them that reinforcements were coming, in his message of January 15. Lt. Henry Lee captured the mood of the men in a poem.

> MacArthur's promise in every mind,
> "The time is secret but I can say
> That swift relief ships are on their way
> Thousands of men and hundreds of planes—
> Back in Manila before the rains!
> With decorations and honors too,"
> MacArthur said it, it must be true.

Wainwright did everything he could to keep up the morale of his men. He visited the front lines often, to pass on words of encouragement to his troops and to try to inspire them by his presence. He also had to maintain the spirits of his staff. A friend remembers that he was "particularly remarkable at being able to seize on a tiny bright spot and exploit it to the fullest as a morale booster."

At a staff conference one morning the news had spread that the Japanese had just landed behind the lines on the beaches. Everyone was gloomy as Wainwright read through the latest reports, each one worse than the one before. Skinny looked around at the faces of his officers, then held up a piece of paper and grinned.

"That's the finest damn record I've ever seen," he said, referring to the medical report in his hand.

He went on to explain that there had been only one case of venereal disease in the entire I Corps area for the whole month of January.

"I wonder how that joker found himself a woman out here in the jungle," Wainwright said.

He chuckled.

"I bet you he was a cavalryman."

USAFFE headquarters also tried to keep up morale with broadcasts over the Voice of Freedom station three times a day. Carlos Romulo organized the programs beamed from Corregidor to Bataan and he played records and read optimistic news reports about the fighting. To the Americans on Bataan this propaganda was "so thick that it served no purpose except to disgust us and incite mistrust."

The United States also put radio programs on the air to keep up the spirits of the forces in the Philippines. The "Freedom for the Philippines" program was received every morning at 3:00 from station KGEI in San Francisco. News was reported in English and Tagalog, and the most popular radio shows of the day were sent— Jack Benny, Bob Hope, Bing Crosby, Eddie Cantor, Rudy Vallee. Toward the end of January, MacArthur sent a cable to Bing Crosby, asking the singer to dedicate a song to the soldiers on Bataan. On his next regular Thursday night show Crosby announced that the next tune was for the troops in the Philippines. It was "The Caissons Go Rolling Along."

Skinny and his men enjoyed the programs from home, but sometimes they damaged rather than helped morale. News correspondent Clark Lee was listening to the Bing Crosby radio show one night, but it was difficult to hear because the Japanese were jamming the music and the chatter. All they let through were commercials for cheese. "There had been one of the worst bombings that day," Lee said, "and nobody had much more than a piece of bread and a cup of coffee. Our reaction was, 'For God's sake, Americans, stop making cheese and make bullets and airplanes, because we need them fast.'"

KGEI's news announcer, William Winter, often angered the men. A colonel on Corregidor recalled: "We eventually came to dread his broadcast. From the security of the Fairmont Hotel in San Francisco, he would dare the Japs to attack Bataan and Corregidor. His taunts were usually answered by a heavier than usual bombing—or so it seemed to us."

There was plenty to listen to on the radio on Bataan. In addition to the programs from Corregidor and the States, there was a Japanese broadcast to the American soldiers on Bataan. It started every night at 11:45. American records were played, the songs carefully chosen to heighten homesickness. The theme song was clever too: "Ships That Never Come In." An officer on General King's staff said, "The damned Nips have got a new propaganda program that does not help our morale any. The men joke happily, but underneath they are disquieted."

The question of reinforcements was on everyone's mind. When are they coming? Will they arrive in time? Will I still be alive when they get here? As the days, then weeks, dragged on, it became harder for the men to maintain hope. Bitter wisecracks passed from one foxhole to another. An American enlisted man received a note from a friend on Corregidor announcing the birth of a baby on the Rock. "If they won't send reinforcements," he wrote, "we'll make our own."

This was a hellish war fought in a hellish place. And after a while the only thing that forced the men to drag themselves from one day to the next was the will to survive and the now slender hope that help was on the way. War in any place is a nightmare, but few places in few wars can compare with the situation on Bataan.

A young naval officer, Lt. Malcolm Champlin, who would soon join Wainwright's staff on Bataan, summed up the situation this way.

"It is hard to find adequate words to convey the horrors of battle to those who . . . have not been 'at the front.' To a soldier, or to any fighting man, the 'front' is his particular hell. It is not merely a soldier pointing a gun and firing that gun. It is not merely a shifting of groups face to face, first one giving ground, then the other giving ground. It is not merely a picture of men standing together and advancing, with a few dropping cleanly and noiselessly to the ground to be picked up later and given burial by their buddies.

"Not here, at any rate. Not on Bataan. Not in the jungle. It is sweat and filth and lice from the foxholes. It is unspeakable weariness and the fight to keep awake. It is, among other things, unclean. To those boys who have all known the small, perhaps unappreciated, luxuries of an American home, it is having to live in a ring of their own excrement and this because dysentery makes them too weak to stand, or danger too wary or justly afraid to leave the foxholes.

"It is hunger. Ever present hunger. It is the knowledge of a shortage of medicine. It is the knowledge that we ran out of grenades and that even when we had them only two out of every twenty-five went off. The Jap mortar always worked. But we know we have no mortars. The few we had, less than five out of twenty-five went off. All this was 1918 ammunition. This was the front line. This was the jungle. This was Bataan."

This was Skinny Wainwright's war as the month of January 1942 drew to a close. A hard, dirty, miserable, hopeless war in which he never had enough of anything to give to his troops. These were the conditions under which he fought hour by hour, day by day. Hold here, regain ten yards there, lead a meager unit of reinforcements to keep the line from giving way over there. The men worshipped him and held the line for him, though they were ragged, grimy with sweat and dirt, hollow-cheeked, with swollen legs and shrinking stomachs. Skinny spent every day with them and was brought almost to tears by their pitiful condition, which was a mirror image of his own.

These were what Skinny's good friend, U.P. correspondent Frank Hewlett, called the "battling bastards" of Bataan. And General J. M. Wainwright IV, the soldier's soldier, was one of them. He was entitled to say, along with the best of them,

> We're the battling bastards of Bataan,
> No mama, no papa, no Uncle Sam,
> No aunts, no uncles, no cousins, no nieces,
> No pills, no planes, no artillery pieces.
> And nobody gives a damn.

CHAPTER 8

"The End Here Will Be Brutal and Bloody"

WAINWRIGHT'S WAR never let up as the month of January came to an end. Each day, sometimes each hour, brought him a new crisis that demanded his attention or his presence on the scene. There was no time for rest. The lines and creases in his face grew deeper and his eyes became more sunken with fatigue. His grimy khaki uniform hung loosely on his increasingly gaunt frame.

Far into each night Wainwright studied the reports from his three-front war—the major defensive line to the north, the stubbornly entrenched pockets behind the lines to the east, and the Japanese landing sites on the points to the south. Each battle was a major one, and a major threat. Combined they became a nightmare of logistics, casualty lists, ground lost or gained, and a constant search for tired and hungry soldiers to reinforce those still holding on.

During the days, Wainwright and his staff, often accompanied by U.P. correspondent Frank Hewlett, were at the front. Usually they went north to follow the battle of the pockets. This enemy stronghold behind the front line had the greatest potential for causing chaos in the rear areas. If the Japanese were not contained, if they broke out and dispersed in the jungle, they could incite panic, destroy precious supplies, and sever vital lines of communication. They had to be checked and then annihilated, and soon.

The Japanese stood fast, however. Even the determined Philippine Scouts could make no headway against them, despite repeated savage assaults. The enemy was dug in well, with deep foxholes and trenches connected by tunnels, so that the men could move from one area to another unseen. They were invisible in the gloomy, almost impenetrable jungle. Even the dirt from their foxholes had been hidden and their positions were so carefully camouflaged that Wainwright's men sometimes stumbled over them.

Wainwright's artillery was useless in the jungle, even at a distance of only 200 yards. The shells exploded against trees, sometimes causing casualties among the American and Filipino troops, and not even reaching the enemy. The only way to clear out the Japanese was with rifle and bayonet, the dirtiest kind of war. Skinny was keeping up the pressure on the enemy, but by the last day of January his men had been able to make only scant progress.

At the same time, the individual battles of the points were raging, but there at least Wainwright had the satisfaction of some success. By the end of the month, one of the enemy forces, the 300 troops that had landed at Longoskawayan Point, had been wiped out. The action had required a thirty-minute artillery barrage, including the twelve-inch mortars on Corregidor and the guns from a minesweeper, the U.S.S. *Quail,* followed by three hours of heavy fighting by the tough Philippine Scouts. By January 31 it was over. Not a single Japanese soldier remained alive. Wainwright's troops had won an important victory.

The other battles at the points were not going so well. At Quinauan Point, despite many casualties, the U.S. troops had made only slight progress. The enemy held the cliff and the high ground 200 yards inland. Here too the jungle came to the aid of the enemy. Not a step could be taken without first slashing away the vines and creepers. The countryside hindered the advance of the American and Filipino forces, concealed the enemy, and made the use of artillery impossible. Wainwright knew that this would be a long and costly battle. Every foot of ground retaken would be paid for in blood.

At the third enemy invasion site, on the point between the Anyasan and Silaiim rivers, the Japanese had thrown back every attempt to dislodge them. One attack by Philippine Scouts was routed by its own artillery fire. The unit took twenty casualties. By the 31st, reinforcements were sent in and an attack was mounted to try to clear out the Japanese entrenched in the thickets and ravines between the two rivers.

Wainwright feared that these three landings at the points were preludes for larger enemy efforts to cut the road along the west coast and isolate his front-line troops. He was right. On that last day of January an enemy landing force consisting of a battalion of infantry was being loaded onto barges. Their destination was Quinauan Point, to link up with the troops already there and attempt to drive across the tip of Bataan. Their mission was to take the supply and communications center at Mariveles.

This time Wainwright was ready for them. His suspicion that the enemy would attempt another landing had been confirmed by a rare stroke of luck. A few days before, in the II Corps sector on the east coast of Bataan, a Filipino patrol had taken a set of orders from the body of a Japanese officer, revealing plans for the Japanese landings scheduled for around February 1. Now Wainwright had a chance to strike back. He made his preparations with care for a kind of battle never before fought on Bataan, a coordinated attack involving ground, sea, and air forces, committing every resource he could dredge up.

To implement his plan and to help him deal with future amphibious invasions, Wainwright did something unusual for those days of strong inter-service rivalry. He asked for help from the navy. He wanted a naval officer on his staff who could help him coordinate the land and sea operations. Rear Admiral Francis W. Rockwell sent his own aide, Lt. Malcolm Champlin, to Bataan. Skinny and Champ quickly became fast friends.

Champlin arrived on Bataan by boat from Corregidor early on the morning of January 31 and was driven from Mariveles at the southern tip of the peninsula four miles north to Wainwright's command post, now located in a grove of trees atop a hill. There was not much of a camp—a few tents surrounded by tables made of bamboo poles lashed together with jungle vines. Parked nearby was Wainwright's trailer. A dozen cots stood in the open, sheltered only by the trees. Mosquito netting of a strange dark color covered each cot. Back in the days when coffee had been available, the nets had been dyed with coffee grounds in an attempt to camouflage them. It worked—they were invisible from the air—but at night the dried coffee grounds often dropped through the mesh onto the sleeping men. Everything was covered with a thick layer of dust. Champlin found that his fresh uniform had turned gray from the dust in short order.

Wainwright was meeting with his staff when Champ reached the camp, and the navy lieutenant waited silently as Skinny questioned his aides about the fighting, while pointing with his cane to the various enemy positions on a map. When the general had finished, he turned around and was introduced to Champlin. Wainwright glared at him; he had been waiting four days for the navy to send him some assistance.

"What do I have to do?" Skinny growled. "Go through God Almighty before I can talk to the navy?"

Champlin stood at attention. He did not know what to say. Then Wainwright grinned and broke the tension.

"I'm glad to have you here, son," he said. "Come over for a chat in the trailer as soon as you are settled."

Champlin went to his assigned tent and unwrapped a package he had brought for Wainwright, compliments of Admiral Rockwell. When Tom Dooley saw that the gift was a bottle of scotch, he nearly fainted. Champ asked Dooley if he thought the general would be interested in it.

"Would he!" Dooley said. "Just come with me—and handle that bottle with care."

Champlin went along to the trailer and presented the whiskey to Wainwright.

"General," he said, "Admiral Rockwell sends his kindest regards and sent this along to cement some army-navy relations."

Skinny took the bottle and held it up to the light, turning it around slowly in his hands.

"Young man," he said. "Do you realize that you have here the finest liquor scotch there is, and that I haven't had a drink for three months?"

Wainwright invited Champlin to sit down and proceeded to explain to him why he had requested a naval aide. It was a long speech for Skinny, and it revealed to Champlin that here was no tradition-bound army man. Here was a general who realized the necessity of cooperating with what lesser men considered a rival service.

"We used to think, in the old days," Wainwright told him, "that an army could anchor one end of the line in the mountains and the other end of the line at the sea coast, but that concept does not apply here. The front which I must defend extends not only from the Pantingan River area in the center of Bataan down the Bagac Valley to the coast, but around that coast, including all of its small inlets clear to Mariveles Bay. We not only have the snipers behind our lines, who filter through, but also the snipers who have landed from boats in those inlets and on the little tongues of land clear back to Mariveles. It is essential that I have the closest possible liaison with the navy because of the navy's patrol of those coasts."

Liaison with the navy would be needed at once because the new Japanese invasion force was on its way.

February 1 was a day of waiting. Wainwright knew that the Japanese would not attempt their landing until after dark. But it was also a day of action on all three of his fronts.

Early in the morning Wainwright left his headquarters for another inspection tour of the front-line units. His aides, Johnny Pugh and Tom Dooley, were with him, along with Champlin. Skinny had invited the young naval officer to join the group and he had agreed immediately.

The four men piled into the open scout car driven by Sergeant Centivo. Tex Carroll hung on one running board and another sergeant rode on the other one, both keeping a lookout for enemy planes. As they neared the front, an American army officer stepped out into the road and stopped them. He advised Wainwright to be careful around the next curve because the road was on the exposed side of a hill, visible to enemy gunners. Wainwright ordered Centivo to go on as fast as he could. The officer jumped on the running board and came with them. They took the curve without being fired upon and Wainwright kidded the man about his warning.

"Wait and see," the man said. "When you come back this afternoon, be sure to make a quick trip around the curve."

He knew what he was talking about. As Wainwright's scout car approached the curve on the return trip, Centivo floored the gas pedal. At that instant they all heard the crack of artillery fire. A shell whistled overhead and exploded a hundred feet in front of them.

Before the next shell landed, seconds later, Centivo had swung the wheel hard. The open car bounced across the ground and skidded to a halt amid dense bushes. The men piled out and raced for the cover of a stand of trees twenty yards away. Shells burst along the road and in the clearing behind them. They ran through the woods and found themselves in the middle of a battalion command post.

While the enemy shells continued to whistle above them, each picked a foxhole to dive into, except for Wainwright. He had spotted the battalion commander and was chatting with him. Then he spied a cavalry captain who had served under him at Fort Myer, Virginia, several years before. He greeted the man warmly and guided him over to a row of sandbags to sit down. With the air heavy with dust and smoke and shrapnel, Wainwright and the captain perched on the sandbags with their backs to the exploding shells. They were the only ones exposed to the firing. Everyone else had sought cover.

For eighteen long minutes the bombardment went on. Wainwright and the cavalry officer reminisced about the halcyon days in Virginia and the horses they had trained as jumpers. Skinny mentioned that one of those horses was "Joseph Conrad," who was still with him here on Bataan.

Champlin watched Wainwright calmly wait out the attack, and later called it the "single most heroic act that I saw in my three years of combat." But while he admired Wainwright's bravery, he was also disturbed that the general should have taken such a terrible and, in his view, foolish risk. His death would surely sadden every man in the command and deprive the army of a valuable combat leader.

When quiet once again descended on the woods, Champ put the question to Wainwright directly, asking him why he had risked his life that way.

Wainwright smiled at the younger man and answered him slowly, choosing his words with care.

"Champ," he said, "think it over for a minute. What have we to offer these troops? Can we give them more food? No. We haven't any more food. Can we give them supplies or equipment or tanks or medicine? No. Everything is running low. But we *can* give them morale, and that is one of my primary duties. That is why I go to the front every day. Now do you understand why it is important for me to sit on sandbags in the line of fire while the rest of you seek shelter?"

Champlin did understand, and he has never forgotten the sight of the tired old man sitting straight and tall on a pile of sandbags while enemy fire burst all around him.

That night the Japanese came by sea. Wainwright's bold plan of cooperation with the navy had its first test and passed with flying colors. Champlin's first task after reporting to Wainwright had been to establish an observation post on a platform at the top of one of the tallest trees near the front line. He chose the site carefully. The three navy signalman he placed on duty there had an unobstructed view of all enemy ship movements in and out of Subic Bay, sixteen miles to the north. The signalman also had a direct telephone line to Wainwright's headquarters.

The night of February 1 was clear and moonlit, and the signalman on duty had no difficulty spotting the twelve Japanese landing barges as they chugged southward along the coastline. He telephoned Champlin, who ran to Wainwright's trailer at once to bring him the news. Wainwright proceeded to lay the trap. He alerted his artillery units along the coast and the heavy machine-gun sections on the cliffs overlooking the sea. He sent word to the navy and air corps. Two PT boats, under the command of Lieutenant Bulkeley, and the entire American air force—four shabby P-40s—were ordered into action.

First to strike the enemy were the airplanes, whose pilots could easily pinpoint the barges in the bright light of the full moon as they neared Quinauan Point. The planes roared in low over the water and dropped 100-pound antipersonnel bombs, and then they came over again for a strafing run. The artillery and machine guns opened up. The Philippine Scouts stationed on the beaches fired their rifles at the dark low shapes in the water. The Japanese could do nothing but crouch low in their barges, and they sustained many casualties.

Bulkeley's PT boats raced in for the finish, but an enemy minesweeper closed in and fired at them. Bulkeley's flimsy plywood boat was pinned by the searchlight like a bug. The PT boat crews fought back with their machine guns and torpedoes but were forced out of the area. Despite this setback, the Japanese landing force was beaten off; their attempt to land at Quinauan Point had been stopped. With half his men killed or dying the Japanese commander reversed direction and sailed north soon after midnight, leaving a trail of corpses and debris to wash up on the beaches.

Wainwright and his men were delighted. "For the Americans and Filipinos who witnessed the battle in the clear light of the full moon, it was a beautiful and heartening sight to see the remnants of the enemy flotilla, crippled and badly beaten, turn away." It was not often that Wainwright's beleaguered troops had scored a victory, and for a while that night they were able to overlook their hunger, tattered uniforms, and malarial chills.

But, sadly, though no one knew it until the next day, the battle was not the triumph everyone thought. The Japanese had been prevented from landing at Quinauan Point, but they had not returned to their base. They crept north about 2,000 yards and put more than 300 men ashore in the Anyasan-Silaiim area. The battle of the points was far from over.

Nor was the battle of the pockets over. There were days of brutal fighting ahead at both sites. On February 2 and 3 little progress was made despite the constant pressure kept up by the tired American and Filipino troops. Progress was being measured in yards. At Quinauan Point, Ed Dyess and seventy airmen of the Twenty-first Pursuit Squadron took over from the remnants of a Philippine Scout battalion that had been on the line since January 28. In six days the scouts had gained fifty yards but had lost half their men.

It was the same at the pockets. Nothing, not even tanks firing at point-blank range, seemed capable of dislodging the enemy. Wainwright went to the front every day. On the morning of the 2nd he was in the thick of the fighting and had another brush with death.

He went up to Maj. Adrianus Van Oosten, the local commander. The officer saluted smartly.

"I want to see what this situation looks like," Wainwright said.

"It's pretty dangerous, sir," Van Oosten said. "Better not go forward. There are still snipers in the trees."

"I'll take a look."

Wainwright moved off toward a trail that led into the jungle and had gone no more than ten steps when shots rang out. The officer accompanying Wainwright had his helmet and cartridge belt shot off, but Skinny was untouched and he continued along the trail. "You'd have thought he was walking to the club for a scotch," Van Oosten said. Soldiers raked the trees near Wainwright with tommy-gun fire and a Japanese sniper tumbled to the ground. His face had been painted green to blend in with the foliage.

While the fighting dragged on in the jungles of Bataan, decisions were being made across the bay at USAFFE headquarters on Corregidor and halfway around the world in Washington, D.C. These decisions would help to seal the fate of Wainwright and his men of Bataan.

In Malinta Tunnel on February 3 MacArthur was discussing his strategy for the time when Bataan would inevitably fall. He was talking with George Moore, the harbor defense commander. MacArthur repeated his intention to withdraw the Philippine Division to Corregidor when the collapse of Bataan seemed imminent. He ordered Moore to make sure that he had enough food on

Corregidor to feed 20,000 men on half rations until June 30. At present there were only 11,000 men on the Rock. MacArthur explained to Moore that he should not allow the food stock to fall below that amount by sending too much of Corregidor's reserves to the men on Bataan.

At that same time, Wainwright was receiving disturbing reports about the effects of the prolonged half-ration diet on his men who were fighting at the points and the pockets. He saw these effects for himself every day. The men were growing listless, apathetic, and it was becoming more and more difficult to make the front-line troops take action. Even the elite Philippine Scouts were being affected. And now the decision had been made that Wainwright and his men would receive no additional food from Corregidor.

On the night of February 4, an army officer assigned to the intelligence division of the War Department who had been caught in Manila at the outbreak of the war, left Corregidor on the submarine U.S.S. *Trout,* which had on board $10 million in gold and silver, the entire assets of the Philippine Treasury. The movement of the money was another indication of the expected fate of the garrison. The intelligence officer, Lt. Col. Warren J. Clear, a confidant of Secretary of War Stimson and other Washington leaders, had just spoken with MacArthur. The USAFFE commander and asked Clear directly how much help the Philippines could expect to receive from the United States.

Clear replied that President Roosevelt was committed to giving England and Russia priority. MacArthur's face reddened when he realized that no major relief effort for the Philippines was being undertaken. "Never before in history," he told Clear, "was so large and gallant an army 'written off' so callously."

MacArthur received a radiogram from General Marshall that further dimmed his hopes. The message was confidential, "to be seen by no one except the individual decoding it and General MacArthur." A veil of secrecy about its contents was also being maintained in Washington. "No record is being made of this message within the War Department," Marshall wrote, "and I have arranged that your reply labeled personal to General Marshall for his eyes only will come directly from the decoding clerk to me with no copy retained and no other individual involved."

Marshall had to make sure that no one else knew what was in his message because it could prove damaging not only militarily but politically as well. He was raising the possibility of MacArthur leaving the Philippines. If word got out, not only would the morale of the Philippines garrison plummet, but Roosevelt would be accused at home of abandoning the islands. In February of 1942, the men on Bataan were heroes to the American public. People proudly followed their valiant resistance on the front page of every newspaper in the country. Bataan was the only place in the Pacific war where the Japanese were being contained. It would not do for the people to know that Washington was considering evacuating the garrison's leader, a man who was an American legend.

"The most important question," Marshall wrote to MacArthur, "concerns your possible movements should your forces be unable longer to sustain themselves in Bataan and there should remain nothing but the fortress defense of Corregidor. Under these conditions the need for your services there might be less pressing than at other points in the Far East."

Marshall offered two courses of action to MacArthur. He could go south to Mindanao and stay there for a time organizing guerrilla operations before proceeding to Australia to assume command of all United States forces in the Far East. The other option was to go directly to Australia.

"The purpose of this message," Marshall said, "is to secure from you a highly confidential statement of your own views." He knew it would be difficult to persuade MacArthur to leave the Philippines and thus appear to be abandoning them. Therefore, Marshall made it clear that if MacArthur were to leave, it would be "by direct order of the president."

Thus the stage was set for MacArthur to depart and for Skinny Wainwright to take his place, to become the commander to preside over the surrender of the Philippines.

Wainwright knew none of this, and even if he had, he was too busy with the events of the moment to worry about it. On February 5 it appeared that he might finally make some progress against the Japanese who were holed up in the points and the pockets.

At 10:00 that morning Wainwright went to the command post of the First Division to meet with the senior commanders who were leading the continuing attacks against the pockets. A command problem there required his attention. The Japanese forces extended into several sectors, including the Eleventh and First Division areas, and both divisions were involved in the fighting. Skinny had decided that one reason for the failure to dislodge the enemy was the lack of a single overall commander on the scene to coordinate the attacks. This morning he would appoint one.

Waiting for him at the jungle command post were Bill Brougher, Albert Jones, Fidel Segundo, and Bill Maher. Wainwright came quickly to the point. He had selected the tough and aggressive Jones to be in charge. Although they had had their clashes in the past, Wainwright had never let personal feelings interfere with his work. He knew Jones was the best man for the job. Now he asked Jones how he would handle the campaign.

"They have to be pinched out," Jones said without hesitation. "First I'd isolate the pockets and throw a cordon around each one." He explained that he would wipe out the little pocket first before attacking the big pocket.

Wainwright nodded.

"All right, Honus," he said, once again reverting to the Spanish equivalent of "Jones." "You take charge." He told Jones to be ready to attack in two days, by February 7.

Satisfied that action would soon be taken to reduce the Japanese pockets, Wainwright turned his attention to the battle of the points. Here the situation was looking better, particularly at Quinauan Point, which the Americans had now renamed "quinine" point.

The previous day a concerted infantry and tank attack had driven the Japanese back to within fifty yards of the precipice at the tip of the point. Suddenly some of the Japanese soldiers seemed to go berserk. They screamed and tore off their uniforms. Some leaped off the cliff into the sea far below. The rest of the men scampered down the steep face of the bluff and holed up in caves and crevices. By the morning of the 5th, American and Filipino soldiers stood on the top of the cliff, looking down on the rocky escarpment where the Japanese would make their last stand.

Wainwright was pleased. The threat to the highway from this enemy stronghold was over. The remaining Japanese were in a hopeless position; they could not possibly escape. He ordered the local commander to give them the opportunity to surrender, certain that they would take advantage of it rather than face death. He was wrong. Americans had not yet learned that Japanese soldiers preferred death to surrender. The battle for Quinine Point was not yet over.

Still, it had not been a bad day for the U.S. forces. When correspondent Clark Lee caught up with Wainwright that afternoon, he found the general in an optimistic mood.

"Right now we have got the Japs stopped," Skinny told him, "and our position is more favorable than it has been since December eighth. If the United States will send me two divisions of American troops, or provide me with two trained Filipino divisions, and just enough airplanes to keep the Jap planes off our heads, I will guarantee to drive the Japs off Luzon in short order."

Later, as he was getting ready to head back to his command post, Wainwright spotted Lt. E. W. Stewart, who had distinguished himself in the battle of the pockets. Wainwright waved the young man over to his Dodge command car.

"You're doing a real good job," Skinny said. He opened up the luggage compartment of his car and pulled a bottle of scotch from a case that contained only four other bottles.

"This is the last of it," Wainwright said, and he offered the lieutenant a drink. Each man took a swig from the bottle. Then, Stewart recalled, "I thanked him and 'staggered' on."

On Corregidor, MacArthur was preparing a radiogram for General Marshall, asking for reinforcements. He made no mention of the chief of staff's earlier message raising the question of MacArthur's departure. Instead, MacArthur spoke of the opportunity that he believed existed to strike the Japanese a staggering blow. He called for the U.S. Navy to attack in force at the enemy's weak line of sea defenses. He said that if the Japanese fleet engaged the American navy and lost, the war would be over.

Both Wainwright and MacArthur were engaging in wishful thinking. The United States did not have two divisions to send to Wainwright or a fleet to send to MacArthur. The garrison remained as it had been since the day the war began, alone and doomed.

On the next day, February 6, the reality of warfare against the Japanese sank in. Wainwright was shocked. This war to the death defied everything he had been taught and believed in. The Japanese at Quinauan Point refused to surrender. The patrols sent down the face of the cliff took heavy casualties and had to retreat. It would be a merciless fight to the finish.

"The old rules of war began to undergo a swift change in me," Wainwright said. "What had at first seemed a barbarous thought in the back of my mind now became less unsavory. I thought of General U. S. Grant's land mine at Petersburg and made up my mind."

Wainwright would have to blast the enemy out of their positions. He asked his naval aide, Champlin, for help.

"Can't you send boats there and fire into the caves?"

Champlin explained that he'd have to see the color of the water first. If it were blue, the boats could come in close enough to the shore to bombard the caves. If the water were brown, the boats might get stuck on sand bars and be easy targets for Japanese airplanes.

Wainwright insisted that he wanted the bombardment to take place as soon as possible, but Champ said that he would risk losing thirty men if there were sand bars in the area.

"Hell," Skinny said, "I lose that many every morning. I want the thing done!"

Champlin went to Quinauan Point to see for himself. The water was blue. Wainwright sent a gunboat close to the base of the rocks to shell the caves and ordered his engineer, Harry Skerry, to take a platoon of his men to drop sticks of dynamite with thirty-second fuses over the edge of the cliff. One blast sealed fifty Japanese soldiers in a cavern. After the shelling and dynamiting had ended, Wainwright dispatched patrols on foot to work their way down the face of the cliff. They were fired upon. More drastic measures would be necessary.

At this moment Wainwright was presented with a new menace, an attack on the front line. Late on the evening of February 6 the Japanese launched a drive to reinforce their men holding on in the pockets. They broke through the main line of resistance of the Eleventh Division and headed down Trail 7. By midnight they had overrun a platoon holding a crucial junction and killed eighteen of the twenty-nine defenders in their foxholes. This left the way south to the big pocket open, and the Japanese streamed down the trail toward it unopposed.

Finally they were checked by American and Filipino forces only 800 yards from the big pocket, and some 600 yards behind Wainwright's front line. They were unable to link up with the men in the big pocket, but their presence formed *another* pocket, a long finger poking through the line. They also posed a threat to the flank of the main line. Wainwright thought it was like fighting a brush fire. As soon as a blaze was extinguished in one area, another leaped into life someplace else. He had no way of knowing where or when the next one would start.

On the 7th, while the last of the Japanese at Quinauan Point held on doggedly, the Japanese high command sent a fleet of thirty barges south. This time they were not trying to reinforce the previous landings, but rather to evacuate what troops they could, particularly those in the Anyasan-Silaiim area. Homma had decided that his beachheads were doomed.

The fleet was spotted by the navy signalmen in the treetop observation post. Champ passed the word to Wainwright, who quickly arranged a reception for the Japanese. With the help of two P-40s, American artillery and machine-gun units on the beach forced the enemy convoy to retreat. They failed to rescue a single soldier. It was another small but welcome victory for Wainwright's forces.

On the same day, using the plan Wainwright had approved two days earlier, Jones launched his drive to isolate the pockets and throw a cordon of troops around them. He did not succeed fully that day, but he made enough progress to give Wainwright the hope that these pockets of resistance behind his front line would soon be wiped out.

Wainwright received good news the next day. The Japanese at Quinauan Point had been eliminated. Success had been achieved in a combined army-navy operation that Wainwright had arranged the previous evening. At 6:00 in the morning the navy attack force had sailed from Mariveles. It consisted of two "warships," thirty-five-foot armor-plated longboats armed with machine guns and captured Japanese 37mm cannon. There were also two whaleboats carrying the landing party, twenty airmen of the grounded Twenty-first Pursuit Squadron, commanded by Ed Dyess.

At 8:00 the flotilla arrived off Quinauan Point and began to shell the enemy positions, which had been clearly marked by large white sheets hanging from the top of the cliff. After delivering a ten-minute bombardment, the whaleboats headed for the shore. Japanese dive bombers appeared overhead, swooped down, and dropped 100-pound fragmentation bombs. They hit both whaleboats and one of the gunboats, causing many casualties, but the survivors came ashore. While they were working their way to the top of the point, the Philippine Scouts started their descent on the face of the cliff.

By noon it was all over. All except one of the 600 Japanese troops who had landed there over two and a half weeks before was dead; one man was taken prisoner. American and Filipino losses were heavy. Wainwright was distressed when he received the final figures. Almost 500 of his men had been killed or wounded, but the threat to the west road had been eliminated. There was now one less battlefield for him to contend with.

Wainwright had no time to celebrate the victory at Quinauan Point. The fighting at the reinforced beachhead between the Anyasan and Silaiim rivers had dragged on for two weeks. Now, with the troops and artillery that could be released from the Quinauan Point fight, perhaps a difference could be made. But appearances were deceiving. The Japanese continued to fight for several more days, taxing Wainwright's tired and hungry troops to their limit. And still the pockets and the new thrust behind the front line menaced the rear areas.

Had Wainwright known of an event taking place at San Fernando that day, he would have rejoiced. There, at Homma's headquarters, an important meeting was about to produce a change in the battle for Bataan.

Wainwright was not the only commander facing problems. Homma also confronted a desperate situation on Bataan. He had lost nearly 7,000 troops in combat. Beriberi, dysentery, and malaria had weakened another 10,000. He had sacrificed two battalions in the coastal landings behind Wainwright's lines and another was apparently forfeited in the pockets. His attacks against the U.S. II Corps on the east coast of Bataan had been repulsed. The men sustained heavy losses and gained no ground. The Japanese forces had been reduced to three infantry battalions along the entire width of the Bataan line. If the Americans found out how weak his resources were, they would counterattack and probably defeat what was left of his army. This was his second critical moment.

Also, Homma was being pressured by Imperial General Headquarters in Tokyo to complete the conquest of Bataan within a few days. This was impossible and he knew it. Yet everywhere else in the Pacific the Japanese had quickly conquered their enemies. Guam, Wake, and Hong Kong had fallen, and the defeat of the British at Singapore was only days away. The Japanese army was victorious every place except Bataan. Homma's position was precarious.

He sat quietly, apparently lost in thought, while his staff detailed the situation and presented their recommendations. As the meeting wore on, two proposals took shape. One faction urged Homma to stop the offensive and to blockade Bataan until its defenders were starved into submission. The other faction insisted that the offensive should be maintained, but that it should focus on the east coast against II Corps instead of along the entire front line.

Homma could not agree with either position. He did not have sufficient troops for a major offensive, even against only part of the line. But he knew he would lose face and be relieved of command if he pulled back and waited for the Americans and Filipinos to collapse from hunger. That could take months, and Tokyo would not tolerate the delay.

Finally Homma told his aides of his decision. A new offensive would be launched, he said, but to do that he would have to request reinforcements. In the meantime, his front-line units would pull back to safer positions. Those at the Anyasan-Silaiim area and in the pockets would have to fend for themselves.

The Japanese leader was making an open admission of defeat, and tears streamed down his face as he made his announcement. As the meeting ended an orderly brought him a telegram from Imperial General Headquarters. Tokyo was displeased with his failure. The general read the message and fainted.

Wainwright was unaware of the temporary reprieve he was being granted and he continued to push his men aggressively against the infiltrators behind his lines. The Japanese at the Anyasan-Silaiim beachhead were nearly finished, as Wainwright learned on the 10th from captured Japanese orders. Messages in bamboo tubes had been dropped by plane to the soldiers at the beachhead and the Americans had found some of them.

The communication ordered the Japanese survivors of the landing to take to the sea on rafts, or to swim, if necessary. Wainwright stationed riflemen and machine gunners along the beaches and they slaughtered the fleeing Japanese as they floated past. Only 200 Japanese remained on shore. The last enemy beachhead was nearly obliterated.

Just behind Wainwright's front line, his men were at last winning the battle of the pockets. The little pocket had been reduced. Those who escaped had been trapped and killed, freeing Jones to focus on the big pocket. But as Jones was readying his forces to attack, the Japanese commander in the pocket received orders to abandon the position and to fight his way back to the main Japanese lines.

Despite the encouraging news from Bataan, there was gloom at USAFFE headquarters on Corregidor. A radiogram had been received from Roosevelt, in which he gave to MacArthur a "most difficult mission in full understanding of the desperate situation to which you may be shortly reduced. The service that you and the American members of your command can render to your country in the titanic struggle now developing is beyond all possibility of appraisement. I particularly request that you proceed rapidly to the organization of your forces and your defenses so as to make your resistance as effective as circumstances will permit and as prolonged as humanly possible."

Roosevelt noted that President Quezon and the Philippines cabinet would be welcome in the United States, and he hinted at the evacuation of MacArthur's family as well. MacArthur knew beyond all doubt that the Philippines had been written off, their value reduced to "a symbol of last-ditch resistance."

The following day MacArthur sent a reply to the president, stating that he would arrange for the evacuation of President Quezon and his government. As for his family, MacArthur said, "they and I have decided that they will share the fate of the garrison."

About the president's request that he hold out as long as possible, MacArthur noted that "My plans have already been outlined in previous radios; they consist in fighting my present battle position in Bataan to destruction and then holding Corregidor in a similar manner. I have not the slightest intention in the world of surrendering. . . . There has never been the slightest wavering among the troops. I count upon them . . . to hold steadfast to the end."

While Roosevelt and MacArthur were exchanging words about a last-ditch stand, the situation on Bataan was looking steadily brighter for Wainwright. By the middle of February the threats behind Wainwright's front line had been disposed of; the bloody battles of the points and the pockets were over.

On the 13th, the enemy force that had held the Anyasan-Silaiim beachhead was eliminated. A few had escaped by swimming out to sea but the rest were killed. The Philippine Scouts were reluctant to take prisoners, even though few of the enemy attempted to surrender. The scouts had seen the mutilated bodies of their own men who had been captured by the Japanese. The one enemy soldier who was captured and taken to battalion headquarters almost destroyed the place with a concealed hand grenade.

The Japanese lost an entire battalion at the beachhead, some 900 men, while the casualties among Wainwright's troops amounted to seventy dead and one hundred wounded. It had been a costly failure for the Japanese.

At the same time, the big pocket was destroyed. Less than 400 of the 1,000 Japanese who had infiltrated the lines on January 29 reached safety. They left behind, wrote John Toland, a "grisly battlefield. There were hundreds of graves, some curiously outlined with upright cigarettes, but many bodies were unburied and the stink of tropical decay was overpowering. Some dead men were holding hunks of raw horse meat in their hands, their only sustenance. Huge bluebottle flies rose from the bodies in clouds."

By the evening of February 14, Wainwright's troops had reduced the salient known as the upper pocket to an area only 350 yards long and 200 yards wide. By the 17th, this newest pocket ceased to exist. The ragged, diseased, and starving defenders of Bataan had beaten Homma's forces to a standstill. The Japanese army in this sector was no longer an effective force. Its Sixty-fifth Brigade had entered Bataan with 6,500 men; by mid-February 4,000 had been lost and many of the survivors were too sick and weary to fight. They were forced to go on half rations and were short of medicine and other supplies. The Japanese hospitals were overcrowded and understaffed. Homma was facing a situation remarkably similar to Wainwright's.

The U.S. and Filipino troops were physically weak, but their morale and fighting spirit were excellent by the middle of February. They not only had held the Japanese, but they had done the impossible—they had beaten them back.

Wainwright's morale was excellent too. "The general is in good shape and good humor these days," said Tom Dooley. When Wainwright heard on the radio that a Japanese submarine off the California coast had lobbed a few shells at Santa Barbara, he sent a cable, through navy channels, to the county sheriff, an old friend of his: "Be patient. The Bataan army is busy at the moment, but we will come to your aid as soon as we can."

One night they had a visitor from USAFFE headquarters, Col. Pete Irwin. No field commander likes a staff officer from higher up hanging around his C.P., looking for tales to carry back to the chief. Wainwright was no exception.

Irwin announced that he was spending the night at Skinny's command post. Wasting no time, Wainwright seized the opportunity to discourage future visits; he would make sure that Irwin got no sleep. "With a twinkle in his eye," Dooley recalled, Wainwright summoned his artillery officer and told the man to keep a nearby battery of 155s firing for most of the night! Wainwright had no more overnight visitors from MacArthur.

Wainwright was pleased to report to MacArthur in the middle of February that the morale of his men had never been higher. The troops were jubilant, optimistic, battle hardened, and ready to take the offensive. There was idle talk of launching a major attack to recapture Manila, but both Wainwright and Parker knew better than to mention this to MacArthur. Even if they could retake much of their lost territory, the gain would only be temporary. One major difference still existed between the Japanese and the Philippines garrisons. The enemy could count on being reinforced; the Americans could not. No new heights of morale or fighting spirit or combat experience could redress that imbalance.

No supplies of any consequence were getting through to the Philippines. The Japanese blockade was too tight. Attempts were made in Australia and Java to send ships with food and other supplies, but to no avail. An old friend of Skinny's even tried to send him a case of beer. Col. John A. Robenson, a West Point classmate, was stationed in Java, trying to recruit ships and crews who would, for a considerable sum of money, be willing to run the Japanese blockade. On February 11, Robenson had one freighter, the *Florence D.*, ready to sail. He and Skinny had "galloped many a dusty mile together" and polished off many a bottle of beer. He delivered a case to the ship's captain along with a letter for Wainwright. "This ship contains practically all the three-inch A.A. ammunition there is in the Far East," Robenson wrote. "You're doing a great job." The ship headed for Manila and was never heard from again.

Several times Wainwright discussed the problem of sending reinforcements and supplies to the Philippines with his naval aide, Malcolm Champlin. One evening he asked Champ point blank if the navy could get through the Japanese blockade. Without hesitation, Champ said no. As Admiral Rockwell's aide, Champlin was aware of the extent of the damage to the fleet at Pearl Harbor, and he told Wainwright the truth of the situation.

"Even if we had the ships," Champ added, "the United States doesn't have the troops to spare."

This was the first hard information Wainwright had, something beyond rumors and speculation, of just how bad things were for the U.S. beyond the war in the Philippines. He was momentarily stunned. He bowed his head and said nothing.

A lull settled over the battlefields of Bataan, a much-needed time of rest, a period of quiet. But it was merely the eye of the hurricane; the worst was yet to come.

Wainwright's war now became one of waiting and wondering

when the next attack would be launched. Neither he nor Mac-Arthur knew how desperate the Japanese were. USAFFE believed that a new offensive would be mounted any hour of any day, and vigilance had to be maintained. Every night Wainwright sent patrols across the no man's land that stretched the width of Bataan to scout for signs of an enemy buildup, for any evidence of an impending attack.

Front-line positions had to be strengthened, decimated units had to be reorganized or attached to other units and sent to fill in weak spots in the line. Communications had to be improved, supply lines shortened where possible, and, above all, morale had to be maintained throughout this period of waiting. Each day Wainwright visited as many units as he could, and he walked every yard of his line, supporting himself on his cane.

As always, it was important for him to see the situation first hand, to correct weak spots, to make sure that the men were well entrenched and concealed. And it was equally important for Wainwright to be seen, for his men to know that he was among them, sharing their lonely vigil and their scanty rations. More than once on these fatiguing inspections his men cheered as he came into view. His presence meant that they had not been abandoned. They were not forgotten. Their general was with them.

Wainwright needed to be at the front, to prowl around the lines, to visit the command posts. This was almost as necessary to him as food. "General Wainwright gets nervous and impatient when we stay in," Tom Dooley observed. And many evenings Skinny would say to his aide, "Tom, let's go visiting tomorrow." He wanted to be at the front with his boys, not back in his trailer bogged down with memos and reports. That was why he was always careful to pick good men for his staff, men who could efficiently administer the paperwork that was such an important part of war. Skinny knew he didn't have the patience for it. He craved the activity, the excitement, and the danger of the battlefield.

Several times during the simultaneous battles at the points and the pockets Wainwright had felt frustrated. Newsman Frank Hewlett noted that "Wainwright was downright miserable when he had battles going on in more than one sector of his command. This meant he would have to keep himself available at his command post for making decisions and couldn't be up front sharing the excitement."

Wainwright's war was a little less tense during the days that followed the Japanese withdrawal, but the days were still busy and full. He no longer had hourly crises to deal with—there were no more landing parties or infiltrations behind the lines—but a sense of urgency never left him. A new threat might appear at any time.

In addition to the constant inspection of his forces, Wainwright turned his attention to training. Lessons had been learned during the two months of fighting, learned the hard way on the field of battle. Now, taking advantage of the break, he saw to it that every soldier in his command was equipped for the next onslaught.

Some of the lessons involved simple things, yet many men had died for not knowing them, particularly the Filipino soldiers—the bulk of Wainwright's command—who had gone into battle with so little training. Those who had not deserted and who had survived the fighting were now battle-hardened veterans, but they still lacked training in some of the rudiments of jungle warfare.

They had to be taught that successful war in the jungle depends on speed and mobility, which is hampered by carrying too much equipment. Their kit was stripped to the essentials. They also had to be trained to remain under cover, something they would have learned before the war had there been time to teach them. Wainwright's training program soon bore fruit. "We are gradually getting the Philippine Army personnel to lie flat on the ground instead of cowering under trees," said one of the officers.

The men had to be told not to examine dead Japanese soldiers or their equipment; often the equipment was booby-trapped, or a "dead" enemy soldier would strike when you leaned over him. Also on the agenda were small-unit tactics, as well as how to advance through the jungle and how to coordinate infantry attacks with artillery and tanks.

Wainwright pushed his men mercilessly, as he pushed himself. He constantly stressed to his division commanders the need for more work during this quiet period and he warned them not to relax for a moment. Wainwright didn't. He restlessly checked on every detail of the defensive positions and even personally directed the laying of barbed wire. He knew that tough training and hard work now would save lives later and could easily mean the difference between winning or losing a battle. As to winning the war in that hot, stinking jungle? Well, he knew that without reinforcements there was little chance of that, but he was determined that the Japanese would pay dearly for every yard of territory they gained.

That was Wainwright's job. That was what he had spent a lifetime preparing for. Who could say what the future would bring? He was too busy to brood about what lay ahead. But to himself and his closest friends, Wainwright admitted that it did not look promising.

The staff at USAFFE headquarters across the bay on Corregidor did not view it as promising either. Gloom hung over the command post. On the morning of February 22, correspondent Clark Lee saw MacArthur in Malinta Tunnel and was appalled by his appearance. The general looked ill and appeared to have aged years in the past weeks. He seemed "drained of the confidence he had always shown." Lee asked some members of the staff what was wrong. They told him that MacArthur had just received an important message from the War Department.

It was the message MacArthur had been dreading. It brought him a step closer to being ordered out of Corregidor and meant that both Bataan and Corregidor were doomed.

"The president," George Marshall wrote, "is considering advisability of ordering you to Mindanao to continue your command of the Philippines from that locality." The chief of staff spoke of continuing the resistance in the southern islands, but made no mention of Bataan and Corregidor. It was easy to infer that they had been declared expendable and that no new supplies or reinforcements would ever reach them.

At the White House the president was conferring with Secretary of State Cordell Hull, General George Marshall, Admiral Ernest J. King, and presidential adviser Harry Hopkins. The topic was MacArthur. He could not be permitted to remain on Corregidor; everyone knew it would soon fall. If MacArthur—America's greatest hero—were killed or captured, it would be a tremendous blow to the home-front spirits. It would also have great propaganda value for Japan and help persuade the rest of the world that she was invincible.

Pressure had been applied to Roosevelt to save MacArthur. It had come from congressmen and senators and from other Americans who had written letters to the president. Hull, Stimson, and Marshall agreed that it was imperative to get MacArthur out of the Philippines.

But there were other considerations. If Roosevelt ordered MacArthur out, it would be a clear signal to the Philippines garrison, the American people, and the rest of the free world that the United States was abandoning its commitment to the islands. What would happen to the morale of the men on Bataan? Would they fold when they learned that MacArthur had left them? And what of the people at home? The stand on Bataan was the only spark of hope and pride in the whole dismal Pacific war, the only place where the Japanese had been stopped. Would the American people turn against the president for not saving it?

This was one of the most agonizing decisions Roosevelt had ever been forced to make. A presidential adviser, Robert Sherwood, said, "It was ordering the captain to be the first to leave the sinking ship."

Finally the president made up his mind. MacArthur would be ordered out.

At about the same time that the president was making his decision, MacArthur was talking to two war correspondents, Clark Lee and Melville Jacoby. They had been offered the chance to leave Corregidor on a small ship and they had come to ask MacArthur's advice. He told them to go and added that even if they should perish in the attempt, they should not regret having tried.

"The end here will be brutal and bloody," MacArthur told them.

On that hot and muggy Sunday afternoon most of the troops on Bataan still held the hope that U.S. ships were heading their way, loaded with men and supplies. They believed it because they needed to, and because that was what they were being told. In the daily broadcasts of Corregidor's Voice of Freedom station, Carlos Romulo promised that help was on its way. And even he believed the words he spoke.

Romulo often took the boat to Bataan. Wherever he went, from command post to foxhole, the question put to him was the same: When is help coming from America?

"Soon," he always answered. "President Roosevelt has sent word help is coming. Ships and planes must be on their way now."

The thought of help was becoming an obsession. In hospital #1, Lt. Juanita Redmond wrote about it. "Our feeling about help coming from home had gotten to be a constant, nagging, but almost unconscious thought in the back of our minds. Of course we talked about it; we talked about it a great deal. Every day the doctors, nurses, corpsmen, and patients made bets with each other as to how many hours, days, weeks—we didn't dare make it any longer than that—it would be before our boats reached us.

"And the men, and nurses too, would climb to the top branches of a tall tree on the hospital grounds, from which we could look out over the bay. If there were ships coming to our rescue we could see them from there. But I believe most of us were afraid to think about it alone with our minds; and we were very busy, we were working harder than we ever had, we couldn't spare the strength to face the real possibility that help might never come."

Very late on the night of February 22, the men and women on Bataan were forced to face that possibility. It was finally presented to them so clearly and directly that it could not be ignored, for it came in the distinctive voice of their commander-in-chief, Franklin D. Roosevelt.

His fireside chats were broadcast to the Philippines by the short-wave station KGEI in San Francisco. Tonight the president made a serious and wide-ranging speech and it seemed to some as though he were trying to prepare the American public for the worst. He made no mention of aid for the Philippines.

He spoke of the new kind of global warfare the U.S. was facing. He had requested that listeners have world maps in front of them to follow his talk. He explained about the vast distances over which men and materiel had to be moved, the gravity of the plight of the Western world, and the necessity of defeating the Nazi menace in Europe first. He set production goals for 1943 and 1944, but that meant little to men who needed hand grenades and mortars and airplanes now.

It was a stirring speech in the context of the total war and the ultimate victory that would be won by the Allies, but, one officer on Bataan wrote, "no hope for the relief of the Philippines could be inferred from his words." Another recorded in his diary: "It was the death knell of Bataan. He placed a large and emphatic period for all to see at the end of the handwriting on the wall."

Wainwright's war had not ended, but all hopes for Skinny and his men had been dashed. Their future would bring either death or capture. The soldiers were not bitter, however. Nor did they give up. They would keep on fighting, of that there was no question. Why? Few could have given a better answer than young Henry Lee.

> Yet, though the thrill, the zest, and the hope are gone
> Something within me keeps me fighting on.

CHAPTER 9

"They Are Leaving Us One by One"

WAINWRIGHT'S WAR remained one of watchful waiting for the rest of the month of February. The hot days dragged by without any sign of an enemy advance. Skinny didn't know it then, but when the Japanese finally attacked he would no longer be on Bataan. His days as a front-line general were numbered. Before long he would find himself confined to a desk in a musty tunnel, shaken by constant bombardment, while his men on Bataan carried on their last fight. It was not what he would have wished. He preferred to be on the line with his troops. But a soldier follows orders.

Even the most famous U.S. general in 1942, Douglas MacArthur, had no choice but to follow orders. And these came from President Roosevelt himself on February 23. The change of command from MacArthur to Wainwright had been set in motion and there would be no changing or stopping it.

"The president directs that you make arrangements to leave Fort Mills [Corregidor] and proceed to Mindanao. You are directed to make this change as quickly as possible. . . . From Mindanao you will proceed to Australia where you will assume command of all United States troops."

MacArthur read the radiogram at his desk and said nothing for a few minutes. Finally he asked an aide to fetch Mrs. MacArthur. When she arrived, MacArthur took her and his chief of staff,

Sutherland, outside Malinta Tunnel to talk over his dilemma. If he disobeyed the orders from the president he risked a court-martial. If he obeyed, some people would accuse him of deserting his men. Later that night he discussed the matter with his staff, and they tried to persuade him that he must leave. It would be for the good of the Philippine garrison, they argued. Only MacArthur could organize the American army that was in Australia and lead it back to the Philippines. He knew that they were right.

The next day MacArthur sent his reply to Washington, but he asked that his departure be delayed temporarily, "until the psychological time to leave.

"I earnestly hope that you accept my advice as to the timing of this movement. I know the situation here in the Philippines and unless the right moment is chosen for this delicate operation, a sudden collapse might occur which would carry with it not only the people but the government. Rightly or wrongly these people are depending upon me now not only militarily but civicly and any idea that might develop in their minds that I was being withdrawn for any other purpose than to bring them immediate relief could not be explained to their simple intelligence. At the right time I believe they will understand it, but if done too soon and too abruptly, it may result in a sudden major collapse. Please be guided by me in this matter."

Roosevelt agreed.

The right psychological moment for MacArthur was less than two weeks away. In the meantime, the exodus from Corregidor was beginning. U.S. High Commissioner Sayre and his party soon left. Carlos Romulo reflected on their departure and recorded a prophetic comment in his diary: "They are leaving us one by one."

For Wainwright and the men of Bataan the lull in the fighting continued as February drew to a close. An unnatural quiet lingered over the jungle, broken only by the sounds of shovels and axes as the troops worked to strengthen the defenses. Wainwright still spent his time walking along the line, examining the fortifications and encouraging his men. In the evenings he was able to relax a little and catch up on some much needed sleep. Whenever he could, he visited Clint Pierce, and the two old cavalrymen would swap yarns about faraway places and times and the fine horses they used to ride.

At night at his headquarters Wainwright often passed the time talking with his three young aides, Dooley, Champlin, and Pugh.

Once he indulged in a rare instance of criticism of the high command. First, however, he cautioned that his remarks were off the record. He described what he believed were three major mistakes that had been made in the conduct of the Philippines campaign.

The high command, Wainwright said, meaning, of course, MacArthur, should have visited the men in the front lines on Bataan. Wainwright knew the value to the troops of seeing their commander; that was why he was with them almost every day. Repeating the comments he had made to Champlin earlier that month, Skinny noted that all the officers could give their men was morale. There wasn't anything else.

Next, Wainwright faulted the USAFFE command for having placed too much confidence in the Philippine army in the months before the war. The simple fact was that the Filipinos had not been as ready for war as Washington had been led to believe. There had not been sufficient time to train them. In mid-1941 more American soldiers should have been requested instead of sending glowing reports about how well the Filipino soldiers could handle the job of defending the Philippines.

Finally, Wainwright was critical of the decision to discard the plan to withdraw immediately to Bataan as soon as war was declared. Trying to fight the enemy on the beaches was, he said, "a grandiose scheme, having only a paper army with which to do it."

This was one of the few times that Wainwright allowed himself the luxury of speaking so candidly. The frustration he was feeling about the kind of war he had been forced to fight must have been, at that moment, overwhelming.

Wainwright was not the only general on Bataan to criticize his superiors for their handling of the Philippines campaign. On the other side of the no man's land that separated the two armies, Homma was also upset about the kind of war he had been forced to fight. His situation was never more bleak than at the end of February. His army was almost nonexistent and in worse shape than Wainwright's. The Sixteenth Division, which two months ago had consisted of 14,000 men, now counted 712 combat-ready soldiers. Only 1,000 remained of the 6,500-strong Sixty-fifth Brigade.

As was the case with Wainwright's army, not all of Homma's losses had been suffered in battle. He too lacked sufficient food and medicine. Despite repeated requests, Tokyo had not replenished his food supply and his men were subsisting on twenty-three ounces a day; the normal Japanese army ration was sixty-two ounces. Disease was rampant. Homma had quinine only for the front-line troops and little medication for diphtheria or dysentery.

Thus, both generals, Wainwright and Homma, faced similar problems, but whereas Wainwright's would worsen, Homma's soon began to improve. In the last week of February the Japanese received reinforcements for the Sixteenth Division and the Sixty-fifth Brigade. A new division, the Fourth, also arrived, along with a large force from the Twenty-first Division and more artillery and planes.

Homma welcomed this assistance, but he was not pleased with his new Fourth Division. Once again it was apparent to him that Imperial General Headquarters considered the Philippines to be a low priority. Although the division numbered 11,000 men, it was under strength and poorly equipped. However, they were well fed, rested, and free of the diseases that had weakened his original units. And Homma knew that the Americans and Filipinos were not being reinforced at all. His greater force would be facing troops who were even hungrier and more disease-ridden than they had been during the earlier battles. With his new army Homma could take the offensive again. This time he would crush the defenders and soon all the Philippines would be his.

While the Japanese army was expanding, Wainwright's forces were dwindling because of disease. By the first week of March there was so little quinine on Bataan that it could no longer be given as a prophylactic, but was restricted to those who were already down with malaria. As a result, some 500 malaria cases were admitted to the hospital that week. And these were only the worst cases; the rest of the sick men stayed in their foxholes. By the end of the week more than one-third of the front-line troops had malaria.

Other diseases were also on the rise—avitaminosis, diarrhea, beriberi, dengue fever, hookworm, and dysentery. Hospitals #1 and #2 overflowed with 7,000 patients. By now they could take only those who required sophisticated surgical or medical treatment or whose period of recovery was expected to exceed three weeks. The rest had to be treated in substandard clearing stations.

The situation was difficult for the medical personnel and alarming to Wainwright. He often visited the hospitals and was increasingly appalled by the conditions and deeply concerned that as commanding officer he couldn't do more to ease the suffering of his sick and wounded soldiers. In early March at hospital #1 he saw native workmen building beds out of bamboo and stacking them three high. Some had to be placed out in the open.

Only one thing gave Wainwright a moment of satisfaction on that visit to the hospital: the sight of a table laden with war trophies taken from dead Japanese soldiers. The pile of sabers, helmets, flags, watches, uniforms, and mess kits was good for the morale of the patients.

The lot of those who were not yet sick or wounded was also very much on Wainwright's mind. On March 2, MacArthur ordered the rations on Bataan cut to three-eighths of normal. Both Wainwright in I Corps and Parker in II Corps protested, but it did no good. The men would have to try to hold off the impending Japanese attack with even less nourishment than before. One American officer wrote that he and his men were "so weak that we could hardly crawl from the foxholes and aim our rifles." Ed Dyess of the air corps said that "the chow line hardly ever formed that someone didn't collapse from hunger and weakness." It was getting harder for the men to supplement their diet. All the carabao had been killed and even monkeys and lizards were now scarce.

At Wainwright's command post one night, Tom Dooley, Joe Chabot, and a few others of the staff were talking about all the different foods they would like to eat again. Each man contributed his favorite, describing it lovingly and sometimes even supplying the recipe. Then the conversation turned to the restaurants they liked best in the States. The next morning Chabot complained of indigestion. Dooley and the others accused him of eating too much of the food they had talked about!

Wainwright knew that there was only one remaining source of food for his men on Bataan—the horses of the Twenty-sixth Cavalry. The idea grieved the dedicated old cavalryman, but he realized that sooner or later it would have to be. Whenever he could, he liked to slip away to the quartermaster depot where the horses were kept to pet his beloved prize jumper, Joseph Conrad. This magnificent animal with its beautiful, smooth, lustrous coat had won many ribbons in the United States. Wainwright missed the riding he had been able to do at Fort McKinley before the war.

Now Joseph Conrad was to become a victim of the war. The supply of fodder was running low and the horse had lost weight. It was beginning to show signs of malnutrition. Skinny felt as if he were watching a good friend slowly waste away.

By early March the decision had become inevitable. An officer from the quartermaster's outfit came to Wainwright to report that there was almost no fodder left.

"Yes, Captain," Wainwright said. "I knew this was coming. We have a lot of men here who are also short of food and horse meat is not so bad.

"Captain, you will begin killing the horses at once. Joseph Conrad is the horse that you will kill first."

Wainwright turned away and walked back to his trailer. His eyes were filled with tears.

Skinny was helpless to prevent even the death of his prized horse, much less of his soldiers, his men, his boys. There was nothing he could do to save them, no help he could give them in any material way. The knowledge tore at him. All those years of training and preparation, and now the best he could do as their commanding officer was to try to stave off the certainty of their fate a little while longer.

Across the bay on Corregidor MacArthur felt much the same way. Although he would soon be leaving, to try to arrange to bring help from Australia for the men on Bataan, there was nothing he could do for them now.

While the quartermaster on Bataan was butchering the first of Wainwright's horses, MacArthur was watching his small son Arthur, who was working with a tin can to make mud pies out of sand and water.

"Look, Daddy, at what I am doing."

"At least you have something to do," MacArthur said.

Wainwright had one consolation. He was still with his men. He could try to bolster their spirits and make sure that every yard of the front line was as strongly fortified as possible. His daily presence among them still gave them something to hold on to. But that was about to change.

The last stage of Wainwright's war in the Philippines started with a telephone call from Dick Sutherland on the night of March 9. Sutherland spoke tersely. The Old Man wanted Skinny on Corregidor the next day. A boat would be waiting at the dock at Mariveles. Wainwright was too tired to ask why MacArthur wanted to see him.

The 10th of March dawned clear and hot, typical of Bataan at that time of year. Wainwright and his staff were up early. Because he did not have to leave for Corregidor until noon, he had time to make another inspection tour of the front. This would be another routine visit to the line, Skinny thought, but he came close to death that morning, almost missing his historic meeting with MacArthur.

Wainwright corralled his aides—Dooley, Champlin, and Pugh—but before they all piled into the open scout car he handed Champ his Garand rifle, the one Skinny carried with him wherever he went. As they drove toward the front, Champ recalled, Wainwright "indulged in his favorite pastime of quizzing his aides on military strategy in general and cavalry tactics in particular. Except for distant firing, the war seemed far away."

Champlin slipped on his dark glasses to shield his eyes from the dazzling glare of the sun. He looked up at the sky and saw, "directly in front of the sun, a black speck was hurtling down in a direct line towards us and as I looked, the speck grew larger, second by second, and it grew wings, and the wings were dipping from side to side."

"Get the hell out of this car!" Champlin yelled. "Everybody out! Quickly!"

Wainwright, Dooley, and Pugh turned to look at him in surprise. Champ shouted at them again and leaned over to release the catch on Wainwright's safety belt. He leaped out of the car, carbine in hand, and ran for the cover of trees just beyond the road. The others were right behind him. A stream of bullets from the Japanese plane sliced up the road, tearing into the scout car.

"Bastard!" Champlin yelled. He fired the carbine until the clip was empty.

When the plane was gone, the others raised their heads and came out from behind the bushes. Tom Dooley went to examine the riddled scout car and counted seventy-two bullet holes in it. "Jesus," he said, "that was a close one."

Champlin glanced at Wainwright. The general had "an amused expression on his face and the twinkle in his eyes could not be mistaken."

"Well, you let off some steam, didn't you, son," Skinny said. "You kind of like that gun, don't you."

"Yes, General," Champlin said. "I guess I do."

"It's yours, son. Take it and thanks for spotting that plane. He'd have gotten us if you hadn't spotted him coming in out of the sun."

"But General," Champlin said. "This gun is ordnance issue."

"Who's fighting this war?" Skinny said. "The pencil pushers in Washington or you and I? Keep it, son. It's yours."

Wainwright took a small notebook out of his pocket, wrote a brief note on one of the pages, tore out the paper, and handed it to Champlin.

"If you get out of here," Wainwright said, "take that gun with you. When you get home, hang it over your fireplace and put these words on it."

Champlin did what the general asked. On the stock of the Garand is a brass plaque with the words Wainwright wrote down on that day on Bataan: "To Malcolm McGregor Champlin, United States Navy, from Lieutenant General Jonathan Mayhew Wainwright, United States Army, for saving my life in a strafing attack by a Japanese 'Zero' fighter on Bataan March 10, 1942."*

Wainwright completed his inspection around noon and headed for the dock at Mariveles. Pugh and Dooley were with him. They were met by an Elco cabin cruiser, appropriated by the army and commanded by Lt. James Baldwin, whom Skinny recognized at once. He had known Baldwin's family well in the peacetime army between the wars, and the two men exchanged reminiscences on the trip across the bay.

The boat tied up at the north dock on Corregidor and Wainwright went immediately to Malinta Tunnel. As he walked into the damp, gloomy, crowded corridor he never thought that it would one day be his headquarters—and his prison—during the final days of the battle for the Philippines.

He turned off the main tunnel into Lateral 3, USAFFE headquarters, where he was greeted by Dick Sutherland. The lateral was jammed with staff officers working at desks placed almost side by side. Sutherland led Wainwright to a quiet corner where they would not be overheard. Then the chief of staff told Wainwright the purpose of his visit.

"General MacArthur is going to leave here and go to Australia. He's up at the house now and wants to see you. But I'll give you a fill-in first."

Sutherland described MacArthur's plans to slip away by PT boat the following evening and go to Mindanao. From there the party would fly to Australia.

"Tell no one of this," Sutherland cautioned, "until the morning after next, the morning of the twelfth."

He also explained to Wainwright the changes in command that would become effective upon MacArthur's departure. The Philippines would be divided into four sectors, with MacArthur retaining overall command from Australia. Wainwright would command the most important sector, all of Luzon, which in reality meant only the

---

*Champlin used Wainwright's rank as of the time the plaque was commissioned; Wainwright was a major general at the time of the incident.

bottom third of the Bataan peninsula. Albert Jones would take over
Skinny's I Corps. George Moore would continue in command of the
islands in Manila Bay—Corregidor (Fort Mills) and the small
fortified islands of Fort Hughes, Fort Drum, and Fort Frank. For
the southern islands, the Visayans would be under Brad Chynoweth
and Mindanao under William Sharp. To make sure that Mac-
Arthur's orders were carried out, he had promoted a staff officer,
Col. Lewis Beebe, to brigadier general, and designated him deputy
chief of staff. Beebe would be MacArthur's link with Wainwright on
Bataan.

So Skinny was to stay on that dying peninsula, expected to hold it
as long as possible. He was to be left behind to conduct the last
stand of what the newspapers back home were calling America's
"newest Alamo." He and his men were clearly expendable. They
had only one mission—to fight until death or capture. It was a
soldier's ultimate and final duty.

The plan that Sutherland explained to Wainwright that afternoon of March 10 remained in effect no more than ten days. Events
in Washington altered it, much to MacArthur's annoyance, and
Wainwright came to play a bigger role in the final stages of the
campaign than MacArthur had intended. Skinny Wainwright
would be catapulted to fame and glory as a genuine old-fashioned
American hero.

When Sutherland finished describing the new command structure he stared at Wainwright for a long moment. He commented
that Wainwright looked hungry and he invited him to have lunch.
Wainwright was hungry, of course—all the men on Bataan were
hungry—but he declined the invitation. The men on Bataan didn't
have lunch; they hadn't in over two months.

"Nope, I think not," he said to Sutherland. "We eat only twice a
day over there."

Sutherland escorted Wainwright to MacArthur's home, a quarter
of a mile from the entrance to the tunnel. MacArthur came out on
the porch and greeted Wainwright warmly. Like Sutherland, he got
right down to business.

"Jonathan, I want you to understand my position very plainly.
I'm leaving for Australia pursuant to repeated orders of the
president. Things have gotten to such a point that I must comply
with these orders or get out of the army. I want you to make it
known throughout all elements of your command that I am leaving
over my repeated protests."

"Of course I will, Douglas," Wainwright assured him.

MacArthur sketched the new command structure he had devised, repeating what Sutherland had already told Wainwright. Then he turned his attention to the hopeless situation on Bataan.

"We're alone, Jonathan," he said, "you know that as well as I. If I get through to Australia you know I'll come back as soon as I can with as much as I can."

Wainwright replied that holding Bataan was his goal.

"Yes, yes, I know," MacArthur said. "But I want to be sure that you're defending in as great depth as you can. You're an old cavalryman, Jonathan, and your training has been long, thin, light, quick-hitting lines. The defense of Bataan must be deep. For any prolonged defense you must have depth."

Wainwright replied that he was aware of this. His defenses were as deep as the number and condition of his troops permitted.

"Good!" MacArthur said. "And be sure to give them everything you've got with your artillery. That's the best arm you have."

They fell silent for a moment and Wainwright thought of the meager resources he had at his disposal and the diseased and starving soldiers huddling and shivering in their foxholes. In the background he could hear the rumble of artillery from Bataan.

"You'll get through," Wainwright said quietly.

"And back," MacArthur said. But he was obviously worried about the impression his departure would make. He repeated to Wainwright the reason he had to leave and how he had resisted Roosevelt's order as long as he could. He told Wainwright who he was taking with him and why others were staying on Corregidor. They did not discuss why Wainwright was staying behind. There was nothing to be said about it. A soldier follows orders.*

---

*Wainwright never expressed any bitterness about being left in the Philippines, but Mrs. Wainwright did. After the war, reporter Bob Considine spent a month with the Wainwrights, gathering material to ghostwrite the general's memoirs. Considine wrote: "It soon was apparent to me that Mrs. Wainwright did not share her husband's dogged, if sometimes humor-tinged, loyalty to MacArthur. At dinner on two occasions, Mrs. Wainwright left the table at the first glowing reference to the Supreme Commander. It was abundantly clear that she felt MacArthur easily could have selected her husband among the fifteen top aides he took with him to Australia. . . . 'She always does that,' the general explained the first time his wife departed. The second time he shouted, 'Dammit, cut that out and come back to dinner!'"

The party leaving with MacArthur and his family was a large one—thirteen army officers, two navy officers, and a code clerk. Wainwright didn't know that only Sutherland had been authorized by Washington to go with MacArthur. The War Department expected that the rest of MacArthur's staff would stay behind to help Wainwright, Moore, and the other commanders with the final defense of the Philippines.

MacArthur walked down the steps of the porch with Wainwright and handed him two jars of shaving cream and a box of Tobaccolero cigars. One of those cigars would save his life a few weeks later.

The two generals shook hands.

"Goodbye, Jonathan," MacArthur said. "When I get back, if you're still on Bataan, I'll make you a lieutenant general."

"I'll be on Bataan if I'm alive," Wainwright said. It was a vow he always regretted that he was unable to keep.

Wainwright walked slowly down the hill toward the dock, thinking that he was now truly on his own and wondering how his men would react to the news of MacArthur's departure.

At 6:30 on the evening of March 11 MacArthur and his party left Corregidor. Carlos Romulo was one of the few people who knew about the departure. It was, he wrote, "the worst news I had heard since Pearl Harbor," and he was sure it would damage the morale of the troops. The same thing was on MacArthur's mind and he talked to Romulo about it.

"I'm placing Wainwright in command," he said, referring to Bataan. "He is the best soldier I have. Bataan can stand, but if any crisis comes and I am needed here, I am coming back, alone if necessary."

MacArthur offered Romulo the choice of staying on Corregidor or coming to Australia. Romulo wanted to leave the Philippines; the Japanese had put a price on his head because of the Voice of Freedom broadcasts he had made. If captured, he would be executed. Despite these feelings he made up his mind quickly.

"I'll stay," Romulo said.

"I knew you'd say that, Carlos," MacArthur said. "The Voice of Freedom can't be stilled. It must go on. Go to Bataan," he added. "Talk to the boys for me. Tell them that I had to do this and that they are to believe me when I say it's for the best. Tell them that my heart is with them."

Then MacArthur told Romulo that he had been promoted to lieutenant colonel, and he promised to get Romulo out if it looked as though Corregidor would fall. It was a promise that Wainwright would have to fulfill.

At Wainwright's headquarters on Bataan, his senior aide, Johnny Pugh, was recording his thoughts in his diary. "History is in the making tonight," he wrote, "as General MacArthur and his staff leave secretly for Australia. General Wainwright is left in command of all forces in Luzon. The latter is not a command to be envied surrounded as we are. If we can just hold out until our troops can work from Australia to us our place in the hearts of all loyal Americans will be secure.

"As I write from this dugout to the light of a Coleman lantern, I can't but believe our cause will win in the end. I don't know how we will hold, but know we will . . . There is no doubt in the mind of anyone here that the heathen Jap, whether he takes the Philippine Islands or not, is in for the licking of his life."

The next morning Wainwright assembled the senior officers of I Corps and told them that MacArthur had left for Australia. He watched their faces carefully as he explained the details of the new command structure, and he could tell that the news was unwelcome. "They realized as well as I what the score was," he said.

He turned over command of the corps to Jones and moved his headquarters south to a clearing outside of Little Baguio. He took with him Tom Dooley and Johnny Pugh, Malcolm Champlin, the enlisted men Carroll and Centivo, and Francisco the cook. The rest of the I Corps staff he left for Jones so that the new commander would have men around him who could keep the headquarters running smoothly. The staff gathered at the C.P. to bid Wainwright goodbye. They were sorry to see him go.

The new headquarters at Little Baguio gave Wainwright good access to the I and II Corps sectors, both now part of his Luzon command. He still intended to be visible to his men, at the front line with his troops as often as possible, without interfering with the authority of his senior commanders. He did not know that his days on Bataan were numbered. He would be there fewer than ten days.

Wainwright's new command was in pitiful condition. Parker reported that eighty percent of the men of II Corps were unfit for combat because of malnutrition, disease, and a shortage of clothing and equipment. Wainwright knew that at least seventy-five percent of I Corps were unfit for action. He commanded an army of the living dead. All that kept the men going was their spirit, and he was concerned about what MacArthur's departure would do to that.

The news of the change in command spread rapidly. On

Corregidor, MacArthur's new deputy chief of staff, Lew Beebe, wrote that "I knew by this time that there could be only one outcome. The Japs would ultimately take the Philippines and we would all be prisoners of war. . . . I had long been resigned to this fate."

Another Corregidor officer wrote to his wife that "The beaming faces of the departing members of the official family showed that they were not only leaving without regret but only thinly concealed the elation they felt at getting away from the scene of impending disaster. On the other hand, deep was the chagrin, bitterness, and disappointment of those members of the inner circle who were left behind. General MacArthur's departure indicated to everyone that the fate of Bataan and Corregidor was sealed."

Romulo confided to his diary: "I note everybody is depressed by the departure of the general." He added a simple, factual note to the page, recording another event of major importance to him. "I had a piece of cheese for lunch."

As Wainwright feared, the morale of many elisted men and junior officers on Bataan was severely affected. They looked upon MacArthur's departure with bitterness, with the feeling that they had been left aboard the sinking ship while the captain had sailed away in the only lifeboat. Bitter poems and sarcastic jokes passed from foxhole to foxhole, and the epithet "Dugout Doug" was born. It came from a song composed to the tune of "The Battle Hymn of the Republic."

> Dugout Doug MacArthur lies ashaking on the Rock
> Safe from all the bombers and from any sudden shock
> Dugout Doug is eating of the best food on Bataan
> And his troops go starving on.
>
> Dugout Doug's not timid, he's just cautious, not afraid
> He's protecting carefully the stars that Franklin made
> Four-star generals are rare as good food on Bataan
> And his troops go starving on.
>
> We've fought the war the hard way since they said the
>   fight was on
> All the way from Lingayen to the hills of old Bataan
> And we'll continue fighting after Dugout Doug is gone
> And still go starving on.

It is easy to understand the bitterness of the soldiers left behind, but the intimation of cowardice on MacArthur's part is malicious and untrue. Tales of his personal bravery under fire are so numerous and come from so many different sources that they cannot be questioned.

However, the anti-MacArthur feelings grew in the days and weeks that followed and were captured in a savage poem called "The Lost Leader," written by a Filipino survivor of the fighting on Bataan.

> Just for a handful of silver he left us,
> Just for a ribband to stick in his coat . . .
> Blockaded, unaided, we fight to the last,
> Though now we realize that all hope is past.
> Our leader has vanished like last summer's rose.
> "Gone to get help," he would have us suppose.
> May his medallion grow tarnished with tears,
> Now that his honor is built on our fears. . . .
> Let him go, let him go, we are the braver,
> Stain his hands with our blood, dye them forever.
> Recall, oh ye kinsmen, how he left us to die,
> Starved and insulted by his infamous lie;
> How he seduced us with boasts of defense;
> How he traduced us with plans of offense. . . .
> Recollect bonus boys gassed out by him;
> Remember Bataan boys sacrificed for him.
> Try him, Tribunal of Public Opinion;
> Brothers, condemn him throughout our dominion
> Then when he stands before Judges Olympian,
> Quakes at his final court-martial: oblivion!

This was typical of the attitude Wainwright had to contend with among his troops. From senior officers and old-line NCOs, however, professionals who had seen long service in the army, the reaction to MacArthur's departure was quite different. They realized that he would be more valuable to the war effort in Australia, where his considerable talents could be applied to the buildup of a large and modern army that would eventually defeat the Japanese. These men knew that MacArthur could do nothing more for them by staying on Corregidor. But there was a chance, though a slim one, that he might be able to organize shipments of food and medicine from Australia, which would enable them to hold out a little longer.

Also, they knew that if MacArthur were killed or captured on Corregidor, it would be a tremendous propaganda victory for Japan and a deep blow to American morale and prestige. So the senior Americans in the Philippines, at the time of MacArthur's departure, were not as bitter about it as were the lower ranks. But there was a pervasive feeling of resignation. A high-ranking staff officer wrote that "General MacArthur's departure left no one in doubt that the fate of Bataan and Corregidor was sealed. It put an end to any further talk of help being on the way."

There was one consolation for those on Bataan that helped to ease the sting of MacArthur's departure. Wainwright was now in command. Although the men knew he couldn't save them—no one could—they also knew that he would make the Japanese pay dearly for their victory. It was a comfort to have a familiar figure in charge, a man who was truly one of them.

Nurse Juanita Redmond echoed these thoughts. MacArthur's departure had brought some tension and confusion, but it was "mingled with satisfaction that General Wainwright, whom we all knew and loved, and who had been a familiar figure on Bataan, was at Headquarters."

And so the soldiers of Bataan now depended on the tall, tired, gaunt figure of Skinny Wainwright. Their lives depended on him now and he knew it. He also knew that he had to bear the heavy burden alone.

The next day, March 14, another officer left the Philippines. It was Wainwright's naval aide, Malcolm Champlin. Champ had been with Skinny only six weeks, but the two had become very close. That morning at Wainwright's headquarters Champlin received a telephone call from Capt. Ken Hoeffel, now commander of the remaining naval forces in the Philippines.

"Pack whatever you have, at once, and come to Corregidor. I expect to see you by six o'clock this evening."

Puzzled, Champlin asked for Hoeffel's chief of staff, Captain Ray, his usual contact at navy headquarters.

"He is not available. You are to come down at once."

"Aye, aye, sir," Champ replied.

He packed his few belongings in his musette bag, concerned that he was being relieved of his duty as Wainwright's naval aide. Had he been deficient somehow in his work for the general? There was only one way to find out. He walked over to Wainwright's trailer and told Skinny about the call, asking him directly "if this was in accord with his desires."

"Yes it is, Champ," Wainwright said. "I might as well tell you now something which Admiral Rockwell told me three days ago when I went to Corregidor to relieve General MacArthur. You are to leave for Australia tonight. You are still Admiral Rockwell's aide and I only borrowed you for a short period. You are to carry out your orders and I wish you luck."

Tears came to young Champlin's eyes as he shook hands with Wainwright. He saw a "slow, half-amused smile" spread over his face. "This was courage," Champlin said, "American courage, and it gave me the strength to turn and go."

At 10:15 that night Champlin boarded a tug that took him and several other officers out into the bay to meet a submarine. To his surprise, he saw Tom Dooley aboard. Dooley was going to the submarine to send out some letters and telegrams for Wainwright, and "to have a cup of real coffee with real cream." Dooley informed Champlin that Wainwright had awarded the naval officer two Silver Stars, one for inspecting the caves at Quinauan Point under fire, and the other for saving his life in the strafing incident.*

Wainwright was back in the lines again shortly after setting up his new headquarters. He was shocked at how fast his troops were fading. The number of combat effectives in his command was falling every day, even without any renewed Japanese attacks.

He saw the terrible condition of his men every day and it was confirmed in the reports of his subordinates. His engineering officer, Harry Skerry, inspected an infantry battalion and found the battalion commander so weak from dengue fever that he could barely walk. In another unit, said Col. Ray O'Day, the troops "were just able to fire a rifle out of the trench, and no more." It was the same in every outfit up and down the line and with the small reserve elements waiting behind the line. Even the Philippine Scouts, among the toughest and hardiest soldiers on Bataan, were now falling out of line on marches. It was a nightmare.

How could men in such condition ever be expected to hold when the enemy launched their next offensive, which surely must come soon? Something had to be done. The men had to have more food, but Wainwright was not in charge of supplies for Bataan. Mac-Arthur had placed them in the charge of Lew Beebe on Corregidor. On March 15 Wainwright took a launch to the Rock to ask for food

---

*A 1934 Naval Academy graduate and an attorney, Champlin was also awarded the Navy Cross for his service at Cavite. From 1967 to 1980 he was Judge of the Municipal Court in Oakland, California.

for his men from the stocks he knew were available on Corregidor. Although certain that his request would be turned down, he had to try. The sight of his men wasting away was too much to bear.

Beebe rejected his request. MacArthur had left specific instructions that no extra food was to be sent to Bataan. He had to make sure that there would be enough on Corregidor for it to hold as long as possible.

Rations on Bataan were sufficient to maintain the present starvation diet for only another three weeks, until April 10. After that date, Wainwright knew, there would be no more food.

Decisions then being taken in Washington and on Corregidor would soon alter Wainwright's life and place him in the most difficult and thankless situation in which any American general has ever found himself.

The events had been set in motion by MacArthur. Before leaving Corregidor he had explained to Wainwright, Beebe, Moore, and his staff the workings of his four-part command arrangement for the Philippines. Everyone concerned with the plan was fully briefed, but for some reason MacArthur neglected to inform the War Department and the Army Chief of Staff, General George Marshall.

As a result, Marshall assumed that Wainwright, the senior officer in the Philippines since MacArthur's departure, was commanding officer of the islands, and he began sending radiograms to Wainwright addressed as "Commanding General, USAFFE." This placed Lew Beebe in an awkward situation. He was MacArthur's designated representative on Corregidor and therefore Wainwright's superior.

Beebe decided to withhold the War Department communications from Wainwright and he notified MacArthur in Australia of the contents of each message. He asked his chief to inform Washington of the proper command structure. But soon more messages arrived for Wainwright, including one from the president telling of Wainwright's nomination for promotion to the rank of lieutenant general and expressing his confidence in Wainwright's leadership. Radiograms from Marshall requested that Wainwright submit daily reports on the fighting situation.

Beebe faced a dilemma. If he sent the messages to Wainwright he would be disobeying MacArthur's orders. If he withheld them from Wainwright much longer, he would be interfering with the wishes of the War Department, which had made it abundantly clear that Wainwright was now in command of the Philippines.

On March 18 Beebe sent a radio message to MacArthur.

"Following paraphrase of message received from Washington tonight. 'Commanding General USAFFE, Fort Mills, Philippine Islands. The Senate this afternoon confirmed your nomination to Lt. Gen. Acknowledge. Signed, Marshall.' This message is intended for General Wainwright as it was confirmed by another, and under the circumstances I will be forced to give it to him in the morning as it must be acknowledged. The War Department apparently intends that General Wainwright is to be in command here. Request instructions."

The next day Beebe sent another message to MacArthur. "Radio just received from the War Department signed Marshall paraphrase of which was sent to you indicates that General Marshall does not understand command setup in the Philippine Islands. The message was addressed to the Commanding General USAFFE. It is not clear to me who the Chief of Staff had in mind when the message was written. I am not delivering the message to General Wainwright but am acknowledging receipt by radio as directed, signed MacArthur. I do not know what information has been transmitted to General Marshall and consequently am at a loss in this particular situation. Request that if General Marshall has not been informed of the command setup here, he be so advised in radio to him personally in order that the situation may be clarified. Request instructions immediately so that I may know what action to take on General Marshall's order to render a daily report direct to the War Department."

On the 18th, unaware of his promotion and his new responsibilities, Wainwright went with Johnny Pugh to Corregidor on a personal matter. Wainwright did not see General Beebe that day. His business was with the finance officer, Col. Jack Vance. Wainwright wanted to arrange to increase his allotment of pay to his wife. The two men from Bataan stopped at Vance's desk in the crowded finance department lateral.

Jack Vance knew that conditions on Bataan were tough, but he wanted to know just how bad they really were. The picture Wainwright and Pugh painted for him was even worse than he had imagined. Also, Vance was surprised that they spoke so openly; everyone around them could easily hear their words.

Both Wainwright and Pugh were apprehensive about the situation on Bataan. "They stated that an hour or so of desk work brought on dizziness; a man moving about had to rest every few hundred feet; a man in a foxhole was too weak to climb out; and those suffering from dysentery lay in their own filth. Straggling had sprung up again; the men threw away their army equipment and even their uniforms; they were surly and were returned to their units only by the use of force."

Both men said several times that they expected to be either dead or prisoners within two weeks. Vance was shocked. "We on Corregidor felt the same way," he said, "but we never said it out loud." But Wainwright and Pugh spoke matter-of-factly, without emotion, of the impending disaster on Bataan. Obviously Wainwright believed that the end was almost at hand.

The following day hundreds of beer cans descended over the southern end of Bataan. Dropped from Japanese planes, they contained a message for Wainwright from Homma. The cans were decorated in the Japanese colors of red and white with long streamers attached. White labels bore the address: "To his excellency Major General Jonathan Wainwright, Commander in Chief of the United States Forces in the Philippines." Homma knew that Wainwright was now in overall command, even if Skinny did not.

The message in the cans was a surrender ultimatum.

Your Excellency:

We have the honor to address you in accordance with the humanitarian principle of Bushido, the code of the Japanese warrior. . . .

Since our arrival in the Philippines with the Imperial Japanese Expeditionary forces, already three months have elapsed during which despite the defeat of your allies, Britain and the Netherland East Indies, and in the face of immeasurable difficulties, the American and Filipino forces under your command have fought with much gallantry.

We are however, now in position to state that with the men and supplies which surpass both numerically and qualitatively those under your leadership. We are entirely free either to attack and put to rout your forces or to wait for the inevitable starvation of your troops within the narrow confines of the Bataan Peninsula.

Your Excellency must be well aware of the future prospects of the Filipino-American forces under your command. To waste the valuable lives of these men in an utterly meaningless and hopeless struggle would be directly opposed to the principles of humanity and, furthermore such course would sully the honor of a fighting man.

Your Excellency, you have already fought to the best of your ability. What dishonor is there in avoiding needless bloodshed? What disgrace is there in following the defenders of Hong Kong, Singapore, and the Netherland East Indies in the acceptance of honorable defeat?

Your Excellency, your duty has been performed. Accept our sincere advice and save the lives of those officers and men under your command. The International Law will be strictly adhered to by the Imperial Japanese Forces and your Excellency and those under your command will be treated accordingly.

If a reply to this advisory note is not received from Your Excellency through special messenger by noon, March 22nd, 1942, we shall consider ourselves at liberty to take any action whatsoever.

Wainwright sent no reply, but he was amused that the Japanese had sent the message in empty beer cans. "At least the Japs might have sent a couple of full cans," he said.

On the afternoon of March 20, while visiting the command post of the Twenty-sixth Cavalry, Wainwright got a phone call from his new chief of staff, Brig. Gen. Arnold Funk, who had recently won his star in combat. He had taken command of the Fifty-seventh Infantry Regiment in the II Corps sector and led a successful counterattack against the Japanese. Funk had good news for Wainwright. He told Skinny that the San Francisco radio station KGEI had just announced his promotion to lieutenant general.

That night Tom Dooley arranged a celebration dinner, complete with tablecloth and candles and drinks concocted from the native gin. The aides and the staff drank a toast to the general. "He was very happy about it all," Dooley said.

On Corregidor, Lew Beebe was growing increasingly concerned about the command problem. Who was his superior, MacArthur or Wainwright? He had received no clarification from MacArthur's headquarters in Australia, and he could no longer delay transmitting official War Department messages to Wainwright. That night he made his decision and he telephoned Wainwright on Bataan.

"I've got a nice piece of news for you, General," Beebe began, but there was so much static on the line that Wainwright couldn't understand him.

"I can't hear you," he shouted.

Beebe spoke again, but he still could not be heard. Wainwright called for Johnny Pugh to listen on the extension.

"Hello, what is it, General Beebe?" Pugh said.

"Tell General Wainwright that he has been promoted to lieutenant general and—"

Wainwright broke in and asked him to repeat it.

"A wire has just come in from the War Department promoting you—"

"Yes, yes. Go ahead," Wainwright said.

"—promoting you to lieutenant general. The troops in the Philippines are to be called hereafter the United States Forces in the Philippines [USFIP] and you're designated as commander in chief. Can you come over first thing in the morning? I'll send a crash boat for you."

"I'll be on the dock at Mariveles at eight o'clock," Wainwright said.

Early the next morning Wainwright turned over command of the Luzon Force to Maj. Gen. Edward P. King, formerly MacArthur's artillery adviser, along with his old trailer for King to use as his headquarters. At 8:00, Wainwright, Pugh, Dooley, and Carroll boarded the launch and headed for the Rock. Although pleased, of course, with his promotion, Wainwright mused that "a soldier could wish for a little more ceremony when he gets another star." He did have a clean shirt, however, with two white embroidered stars on each shoulder. The new third stars pinned next to them had been cut from a tin can.

Wainwright's spirits were high as the boat crossed the choppy bay. He was eager to take over his new command. Maybe there was still a chance that they could hold out until MacArthur organized the army in Australia to relieve them. It was all up to Wainwright now.

"Lee marched on Gettysburg with less men than I have here," he told his aides. "We're not licked by a damn sight."

CHAPTER 10

"The Troops on Bataan Are Fast Folding Up"

Wainwright's first thoughts as he landed on Corregidor the morning of March 21 and went to his headquarters in Lateral 3 of Malinta Tunnel were that at least things would be quieter and more peaceful here than they had been on Bataan. Perhaps now he could get some sleep; he hadn't had a full night's rest since the war began. With a little respite, he would be better able to cope with the awesome burdens MacArthur had left for him.

He was wrong. Life on Corregidor turned out to be as hectic and dangerous as the war-torn jungles of Bataan. He found that out within a few hours of his arrival. Every day, beginning at noon, Japanese bombers attacked the island for two hours. The Rock shook under the impact and the walls and ceiling of the headquarters lateral trembled with each explosion. Dust rained down as shock waves raced through the tunnel.

"Bataan is nothing at all," he remarked to the quartermaster, Charlie Drake. "It's quiet as a mouse. Corregidor is right in the middle of a bull's eye."

The next morning Wainwright had another brush with death. He and George Moore, commander of the harbor defenses, were driving along the south shore road of the island on an inspection tour. Air-raid sirens sounded and the driver quickly pulled off the road. Moore led Wainwright to the nearest shelter, which Skinny entered only after Moore insisted. As soon as they got inside, a string of bombs exploded at the entrance to the shelter, precipitating a landslide. If Wainwright had delayed another thirty seconds, he might have been killed.

At the first lull in the bombardment, Wainwright and Moore got back in the car to return to Malinta Tunnel. The driver raced up the hill and parked outside the east entrance, just as a new wave of Japanese planes came over the island. No sooner had they entered the tunnel when a bomb fell nearby, close enough to destroy their car.

Corregidor was indeed in the bull's eye, the center of the storm, and it would get worse in the weeks ahead. More than once, Wainwright would wish he were back on Bataan.

Another storm was beginning to break around Wainwright, this one political, and its instigator was MacArthur. Wainwright's first official act on Corregidor, undertaken on the morning of his arrival, was to formally announce his assumption of command of the newly designated United States Forces in the Philippines—USFIP. This was in accordance with the instructions from General Marshall that General Beebe had passed on to Wainwright. Skinny had appointed Beebe, who was officially MacArthur's deputy chief of staff, to be his own chief of staff.

When MacArthur received word from Wainwright about these changes in the command structure he had established, he was upset. He had never heard of USFIP. He radioed Wainwright and asked, testily, "on whose authority he had made the appointment." Wainwright radioed back a copy of his order from Marshall of March 20.

"With departure of General MacArthur, you became commanding general United States Forces in the Philippines. You are to communicate directly with the War Department in rendering daily operational reports which are to be dispatched over your name."

It was only then that MacArthur informed Marshall of the four-part command arrangement he had made for the Philippines, but it was too late. Events had moved beyond his control. Neither Marshall nor Stimson were in favor of a plan to conduct the Philippines campaign from 4,000 miles away. "This was in entire violation of all sensible policy," wrote the Secretary of War.

In a memorandum to the president, General Marshall expressed his fear that MacArthur's divided command arrangement would have "a very depressing effect" on Wainwright, "on whom we must now depend for the successful continuance of the fighting on Bataan." Marshall recommended to Roosevelt that MacArthur be told that his plan was unsatisfactory and that Wainwright would remain in command of USFIP.

Roosevelt agreed. A carefully worded message was sent to MacArthur making no criticism of his divided command structure. The message stated clearly, however, that Wainwright would retain his position unless MacArthur objected strongly. MacArthur bowed graciously to the inevitable.

"Heartily in accord with Wainwright's promotion to lieutenant general," he radioed to Marshall. "His assignment to Philippine command is appropriate."

Privately, however, MacArthur was not in accord with it at all, though neither he nor his staff spoke publicly about it. Some of MacArthur's staff, however, including Sutherland, were more critical among themselves. They did not believe Wainwright was qualified to take command.

On the surface, then, a potential crisis between Wainwright and MacArthur, now commander in chief of the Southwest Pacific area (CINCSWPA), had been averted. But underneath it had not, and it would fester and grow in the weeks ahead. Over the next few days Wainwright took several actions that led to fresh misunderstandings and controversies. These culminated in an angry radiogram from MacArthur to Marshall that was sharply critical of Wainwright. But by then Skinny was a prisoner of war with more important things on his mind.

It is usual for a new commander to inherit the smoothly functioning staff of his predecessor. Although he may later change some or even all of the staff, he normally can count on it to maintain the day-to-day details of the command during the transition. That was why Wainwright had left his I Corps staff for Jones on Bataan. But MacArthur had not left a staff for Wainwright; he had taken the key personnel with him to Australia.

"MacArthur," Secretary of War Stimson wrote, "in a pretty complete disregard of everything except his own personal interests had taken his entire staff away with him from Bataan, leaving Wainwright with the job of building up a new staff."

Thus, Wainwright did not find a smoothly functioning organization on Corregidor. He had to create one. As usual, he displayed his superb talent for picking good subordinates and for getting the best from them. The men he chose had all held subordinate positions on the large USAFFE staff, so each brought expertise in a particular area. In addition to his aides, Johnny Pugh and Tom Dooley, and his new chief of staff, Lew Beebe, Wainwright selected Pete Irwin, Nunez Pilet, Stu Wood, Jesse Traywick, and Nick Galbraith. He immediately promoted the lieutenant colonels to colonels, advanced Dooley to major and Pugh to lieutenant colonel, and put them all to work.

One of their first tasks was to sort through the monumental pile of uncompleted paperwork left by MacArthur's staff. For example, there were some 3,000 individual communications to deal with, most of them concerned with decorations and promotions, on which MacArthur's men had taken no action. Knowing how important these were for the morale of the troops, Skinny ordered his staff to expedite them.

Wainwright soon set to work acquainting himself with the responsibilities of his new command and familiarizing himself with his new home. The island of Corregidor, lying two miles south of the tip of Bataan, was three and a half miles long and one and a half miles across at its widest point, approximately the size of Manhattan Island in New York City. From the air Corregidor looked like a tadpole wriggling through the water, with a large, almost circular head and a narrowing curved tail.

Approached by boat from the Bataan side, one saw a lush, mountainous region with steep cliffs and jagged ravines and gulleys running down to the sea. The highest portion of the island, located at the head of the tadpole, rose 600 feet from the sea, forming a plateau about a mile in diameter. Christened by the Americans as "Topside," it looked much like any small army post during the years between the wars. Before the war, headquarters for Fort Mills had been there, along with officers' quarters, barracks for the enlisted meq, a huge parade ground, and the indispensable golf course.

A narrow neck of land connected the head and tail of the tadpole to form "Middleside." Here were the hospital, NCO quarters, additional officers' quarters, a service club, a stockade, several warehouses, and schools for the civilian children.

East of Middleside the ground dropped away sharply to "Bottomside." Only 300 yards wide, Bottomside contained two docks, one on the north side facing Bataan and the other on the south side facing the ruined American naval base at Cavite, seven miles away, and now in Japanese hands. Also at Bottomside were warehouses; shops; a power plant; and the town of San Jose, the base for several thousand Filipino civilian laborers brought to the island to build fortifications.

From Bottomside, toward the narrow tail of the island, Malinta

Hill rose to a height of almost 400 feet. This was the heart of Corregidor from a military standpoint, and the primary reason why the garrison held out as long as it did. Malinta Tunnel, completed in 1938, ran east and west for 1,400 feet from one side of the hill to the other. The main tunnel was thirty feet wide, crowned by an arched ceiling thirty feet high. Two trolley-car tracks ran the length of the tunnel and out to other parts of the island.

Branching off from the main tunnel were twenty-five lateral tunnels, each 400 feet long and fifteen feet wide and high. North of the main tunnel but connected to it was the hospital tunnel with twelve laterals. South of the main tunnel was the quartermaster storage tunnel with eleven laterals leading to four tunnels used by the navy.

USFIP headquarters was in Lateral 3, 150 yards from the east entrance. At its entrance was a modern drinking fountain that was constantly in use because the air in the tunnel was hot and sticky. Inside the lateral was a series of desks, staggered because the lateral wasn't wide enough to place them side by side. At the first desk sat Wainwright's adjutant general, Carl Seals. Next in line was Beebe, followed by Wainwright, some twenty-five feet in from the entrance.

The rest of the staff—Wood, Galbraith, Traywick, Irwin, and Pilet—had desks behind Wainwright's, and beyond these were the clerical staff. The office was always bustling with activity, the phones constantly ringing and people coming and going. Charts and maps were affixed to the walls and even on the vaulted ceiling; space was at a premium. Telephone wires were bundled together and strung along the walls, secured by circular hooks embedded in the concrete. More wires snaked across the floor. Wainwright had no more privacy there than any member of the staff.

The sleeping quarters for the staff were in Lateral 10, which was so packed with ammunition and explosives that the men had to be very careful about fire. There were fifteen double-decker bunks along the walls. Down one side of the lateral ran a seven-foot-high beaverboard partition, forming a three-foot-wide hallway on its far side. This led from the lateral entrance to a small ten-by-twelve-foot whitewashed room at the end. Wainwright found some privacy at the end of each day in this hideaway that had been constructed for MacArthur.

The tunnel complex was a hellish place in which to live and work, both physically and psychologically. Noisy, dirty, and crowded, it was, as one staffer said, "a gigantic beehive." Several thousand people worked and slept there, at desks crammed into every available space, end to end, and in cots stacked two and three high. There was little room to move around. There was no escape from the sight and sound and smell of other people, from the telephones, from the cries of the wounded in the hospital, or from the shaking of the tunnel during the frequent bombing and shelling attacks, when more people crowded into the tunnel to escape the exploding nightmare outside.

Along the walls of the main tunnel crates and boxes were piled as high as six feet, taking up every inch of wall space. Even when there were no raids there was a steady stream of people moving in and out, some on official business, others there in anticipation of the next attack. The place was always as busy and crowded as a New York City sidewalk at the peak of rush hour, with people scurrying back and forth like ants.

A thick layer of dust covered everything and the ventilation system was inadequate to deal with the smells of unwashed bodies, overworked latrines, and injured men. Insects added to the unpleasantness, vicious black flies that filled the air and bedbugs that crawled over everyone, general or private, throughout the night.

During and after the Japanese bombing attacks the ambulance sirens pierced the air in the tunnel, announcing the arrival of more wounded, and conversations ceased among those lucky enough to be inside when the ambulances raced down the main tunnel to the hospital. Often the screams of the wounded could be heard above the roar of the engines.

Life in the tunnel, however miserable, was at least safe. The bombs and shells could not reach those huddled against the walls, but that very safety produced its own psychological hazards. The men of Corregidor called it "tunnelitis," a disease of entrapment that developed from spending too much time underground. Once a soldier adapted to the confinement and security, it became difficult for him to leave it and go outdoors, where death could strike from the sky at any moment. It was particularly hard on those whose duties required them to come and go; some found it increasingly hard to leave the tunnel. As the bombardment grew more frequent and intense, more and more men succumbed to tunnelitis. Some of them did not see daylight until the island surrendered more than a month later.

Wainwright's war was now confined largely to the headquarters lateral of Malinta Tunnel, where a single naked lightbulb hung over his desk, the staff crowded around, and the sounds of telephones, typewriters, and urgent voices converged. This front-line general of Bataan, who loved nothing better than being with his boys, had to do his fighting from a desk. He left the tunnel every chance he could to visit the men at Corregidor's defensive positions and gun batteries, and twice he was able to get to Bataan. But the new responsibilities meant that his war had to be fought not with bullets but with paper.

An endless flow of reports, requisitions, and orders appeared on his desk. As USFIP commander Wainwright had to be informed of and to deal with everything that happened in the Philippines, from Luzon to the southernmost outpost in the islands. He had to prepare daily reports for the War Department and there were radiograms from Marshall and from MacArthur to respond to. Wainwright chafed under the isolation and confinement, but he never shrank from his duties. However much he wanted to be on the line, facing the enemy, he sat hunched over his messy, dusty desk, doing the best he could with what he had.

During his first days on Corregidor he spent much time inspecting the island and its defenses. Sloping down from the east entrance of Malinta Tunnel for more than a mile was a hilly ridge, and beyond that the land was fairly level, tapering to the tail of the island. A small landing strip, Kindley Field, had been built here, along with barracks and hangars.

The tip of the island was undeveloped except for a small cemetery, but it was also the point most vulnerable to amphibious landings. Thousands of yards of open beach edged this part of Corregidor.

During his inspection tours Wainwright paid particular attention to the Rock's defensive fortifications. He knew that if Bataan fell it would only be a matter of time before the Japanese attempted to invade Corregidor. The island bristled with firepower, fifty-six coastal guns and mortars designed to make the island impregnable to an attack by sea. Unfortunately, the weapons were of World War I vintage and were exposed to attack by air. They had been emplaced when the airplane was little more than a military novelty.

The big coastal guns were arranged around the rim of the island, concentrated on the cliffs around Topside. These batteries contained ten- and twelve-inch guns, the navy's biggest weapons at the time. They were of the disappearing rifle type, which on recoil sank below a parapet for reloading. They could not be seen from the sea, but they were unprotected from bombs, mortars, and shells. Turrets had been considered too expensive in the 1920s and 1930s when the fortifications had been established.

Corregidor also had two batteries of twelve-inch mortars dating from 1890 and 1908. Although old, they were accurate and reliable and could hurl a shell over 15,000 yards. These were the best weapons Wainwright had, but they too were open to the sky.

Lighter artillery, three- and six-inch guns, were permanently emplaced, and the garrison had a large number of mobile field pieces, including twenty-four 155mm guns and forty-eight 75mm guns, both drawn from the battlefields of World War I. For air defense Wainwright could call on twenty-four three-inch anti-aircraft guns, forty-eight .50-caliber machine guns, and five searchlights.

Three tiny islands south of Corregidor had been fortified with coastal artillery—Forts Hughes, Drum, and Frank.

This formidable array of firepower had persuaded the artillerymen in Wainwright's command that the Japanese navy would never be so foolhardy as to attack by sea. They were right. No Japanese ships were sighted from Corregidor, but the Japanese had no need to sail nearby. Their planes and their artillery at Cavite were tearing the island to pieces, and their final assault would come not from a naval fleet but from Bataan, just two miles away.

Wainwright realized soon after he arrived on Corregidor that his major weakness was not in firepower but in manpower. He did not have sufficient trained infantry to repel a major invasion attempt. Yet the island, and particularly the tunnel, was crowded with almost 12,000 people.

The problem was that most of these were not combat troops. Wainwright's only trained infantry was the Fourth Marine Regiment, 1,000 men who had been evacuated from Shanghai only days before the attack on Pearl Harbor. The marines, under Col. Sam Howard, were expected to defend the entire beach area, and they were fewer than half the number needed for an adequate defense. The only other combat-ready troops were 5,700 coast artillerymen, all of whom were needed to man the guns.

Few of the other people on the island were useful for defense. Some 2,000 were civilians, and many of the rest were support and administrative personnel who no longer had a military mission to perform.

The infantry and artillery spent their days on defensive preparations, but the people in the tunnel who had no clearcut duties were beginning to present a morale problem. They were helpless to do anything in their own defense, they were consuming precious food, and they were useless to Wainwright.

In peacetime Corregidor had been a beautiful island, a tropical paradise cooled by offshore breezes and alive with the fragrance and color of flowering shrubs and trees. Frangipani, bougainvillea, hibiscus, and orchids had bloomed in abundance. By the time Wainwright arrived, the signs of destruction were everywhere. The Rock was now ugly, scarred, and mutilated.

Wainwright saw the huge craters that dotted the island so uniformly that each one was no more than twenty-five yards from the next. The foliage had been blackened and trees mangled from fire and denuded of their leaves by the blasts of so many bombs. Some looked like macabre skeletons rising from the shattered surface of the earth.

The manmade structures lay in ruins and debris littered the landscape. Gone were the warehouses and shops, barracks and officers' quarters, and the hospital. The lush green parade ground and golf course at Topside were a pockmarked lunar surface. The island was being battered to its death. None of the big gun batteries had been knocked out, but their turn would come. The blasting of Corregidor was far from over.

As Wainwright settled in to his new command the people of Corregidor were coming to know him better. They were pleased with and grateful for what they saw. From officers in the headquarters lateral in Malinta Tunnel to privates in foxholes on the beaches at the tail of Corregidor, the same feeling was growing, the feeling that the men of Bataan had known. Skinny's a right guy. He's with us. The Old Man is one of us.

Wainwright's style of leadership—personal, intense, informal— was so dramatically different from that of their last commander, MacArthur, that Wainwright's presence provided an immediate improvement in morale. Whereas MacArthur had remained aloof and mingled only with his closest staff members, Skinny made time to chat with anyone who needed him, of whatever rank or job. "Wainwright was with us," his officers said, "and he was very popular. You couldn't help but like him. He was as cool and calm as a cucumber."

Lew Beebe was also impressed with his new commander, calling him "a gallant gentleman and a fine soldier." As chief of staff, Beebe had to work closely with Wainwright, and he saw every day how Skinny handled his difficult job.

"I liked the way he did business," Beebe said. "He doesn't hem and haw when he is called upon to make a decision. He has a mind like a steel trap and it acts just as quickly. When an officer asks General Wainwright for anything he had better be prepared for quick action, because he gets it. Likewise, when General Wainwright asks for anything one had better be prepared to deliver the goods with equal speed. He thinks like lightning and he can't tolerate people among his close associates who are mentally slow. He is a gentleman to his fingertips and is instinctively one of the kindest individuals it has been my privilege to meet."

Skinny's G-4, Nick Galbraith, who had served with MacArthur's forward echelon on Bataan, said, "The general was close to his staff, easy to get along with, and outgoing. He would give you a pat on the back and joke with you. MacArthur was stiff and formal. Wainwright would take things as they came and try to put them in the best light."

Stu Wood, the G-2, was also pleased with his new boss. He called Wainwright "one of the bravest men I have ever known," and he summed up the feeling of everyone on Corregidor when he said, in his characteristic Southern drawl, "we just loved the guy."

The admiration and respect felt for Wainwright was not restricted to the army. The Fourth Marines, a group that traditionally holds the army in disdain, could not have asked for a better commander than Wainwright.

The marines were pleased to see MacArthur depart; their relations with him had been bitter. Two days before MacArthur left for Australia he had recommended unit citations for every outfit on Bataan and Corregidor except the marines. Indignant Marine Corps officers complained to MacArthur's staff and were told, wrote Hanson Baldwin, "the marines had gotten their share of glory in World War I, and they weren't going to get any in this one." This attitude, plus MacArthur's failure to visit them on the beaches, and what the marines saw as his abandonment of them, had left a great deal of hostility. But the marines very soon knew that Wainwright was one of them.

This friendly, unpretentious new commander frequently visited their area, took cover with them during air raids, and seemed genuinely interested in their gripes. And when they heard a remark he made one day it further endeared him to them. Wainwright's comment reached almost everyone on the island, including many who felt that MacArthur had deserted them.

"If the Japanese can take the Rock," Skinny said, "they will find me here, no matter what orders I receive."

To men who could hold out little hope of escape, this vow represented "loyalty down" by their commander. They knew that whatever might happen, Skinny Wainwright would be with them to the end.

Reaction to Wainwright's new position as USFIP commander was also highly favorable back home. Newspapers from coast to coast trumpeted his name and dug instant biographies out of their files. Men who had served with him were interviewed, and his name and face became known in every household. With MacArthur out of the fighting, America found a new national hero in Wainwright.

An editorial cartoon appearing in *The Washington Post* of April 4, 1942, was typical. The drawing showed Wainwright standing in MacArthur's shoes. "Looks like a perfect fit," the caption read.

On Capitol Hill, congressmen reminisced about Wainwright. One said, "I remember distinctly the first time I saw a long, lean, lanky, then colonel, with his cavalry unit in action. Everything was spic and span. The men were tidy. The equipment and munitions were in first-class shape. Action and precision were manifested in every move. Yes, Lt. Gen. Jonathan M. Wainwright is a worthy successor of Gen. Douglas MacArthur as commander of our forces in the Philippines."

From his first day on Corregidor Wainwright set out to demonstrate that he was going to be his own man and run the outfit in his own way. He behaved with all the authority inherent in the Commanding Officer of all United States Forces in the Philippines. It was proper for him to set his own policies and not merely to continue the ways of his predecessor, even one with so formidable a reputation as MacArthur.

During his first week on Corregidor Wainwright reversed some of MacArthur's policies, and, what was worse in MacArthur's eyes, reported directly to Washington, as he was authorized to do, rather than to Australia. MacArthur, already unhappy that Wainwright had been appointed USFIP commander against his wishes, took this as more reason to be displeased with Wainwright. MacArthur thought he was tampering with his command and not even informing him of the changes. He protested to George Marshall. The chief of staff tried to soothe MacArthur's feelings by proposing a compromise. Wainwright would route all messages to the War

Department through MacArthur in Australia, except for the daily situation reports. These would be sent directly to the War Department but copies would be provided for MacArthur.

Another action Wainwright took early on was to try to help his men on Bataan by transferring food from Corregidor's stockpile to the beleaguered peninsula. This was contrary to MacArthur's decision to reserve food on the Rock sufficient to feed 20,000 men until June 1. Wainwright agreed with that basic policy—he was sure Corregidor would hold out longer than Bataan—but he also thought that Corregidor could spare some of its food.

He had been surprised to find that Corregidor was a land of plenty, compared to Bataan. The personnel on Corregidor were also on half rations and had only two meals a day, but they were losing weight more slowly than the troops on Bataan. At his first dinner on Corregidor Wainwright had been served champagne and ice cream. The practice soon disappeared, however. By April 1 Tom Dooley wrote in his diary, "I am always hungry these days—as is everyone."

The diet on Corregidor was a full half ration and included many items that were only memories on Bataan—bacon, ham, fresh vegetables, coffee, milk, and jam. Wainwright knew he had to keep enough food to maintain them until June 1, so he could not send as much to Bataan as he wanted to, but he knew that anything he could spare would be welcome.

Supplying his troops on Bataan occupied much of Wainwright's time during the last week of March. He was trying to devise ways for ships to get through the enemy blockade. On March 27 he wrote to MacArthur that "rations for troops on Bataan have been reduced to approximately one thousand calories which, according to the surgeon, is barely sufficient to sustain life without physical activity. I am holding a ration reserve for Fort Mills, as directed by you, to subsist troops there to June 1."

Wainwright noted that all attempts to ship food from Cebu in the southern islands had been unsuccessful because of the Japanese blockade, and he asked MacArthur for a squadron of B-17s to bomb the enemy ships and break the blockade, at least temporarily. There was a large supply of food and other supplies in Cebu that had been sent there from Australia, but the ships could not come farther north.

He closed the message on a dire note. "In the light of the obligation that the United States has assumed with reference to the Philippines, I deem it to be of paramount importance to save

Filipino troops from starvation or surrender if humanly possible to do so. With ample food and ammunition we can hold the enemy, in his present position, I believe, indefinitely."

Without food and supplies, Wainwright knew, there was no chance.

The question of food for Bataan was also worrying George Marshall and Dwight Eisenhower in Washington. They were doing everything they could, and indicated as much in a radiogram that Wainwright received on March 28. Marshall said that he was making arrangements for submarines to deliver medical supplies to Corregidor. He asked Wainwright if six converted cargo-carrying destroyers, then en route to Australia, could safely reach Corregidor.

"The gallantry of your troops," Marshall added, "has become a national symbol of determination to destroy the enemy's military power. I want you to feel that the president, the secretary of war, and I understand the immense difficulties of your situation. We realize how increasingly difficult your task has become. With the renewed bombardments of Corregidor the eyes of the entire country have focused on the ordeal through which you and your men are passing. My hourly concern is what we can do to help you. Radio me with complete frankness your desires and any information or comments you wish me to have. Our great desire is to employ every possible means to assist and strengthen you."

Wainwright replied immediately, asking that the cargo ships come directly to Corregidor. He noted his request to MacArthur for a squadron of B-17 bombers to attempt to break the Japanese blockade. "If the blockade could be broken for a day," Wainwright wrote, "we could move several thousand tons of badly needed subsistence from Cebu. Our most pressing need is subsistence as only a sufficient quantity remains on hand in Bataan to feed the troops there until April 15 at about one-third rations. . . . To be utterly frank, if additional supplies are not received for Bataan by April 15 the troops there will be starved into submission."

April 15 was little more than two weeks away. If Bataan were to be saved, help had to come soon.

This was grim news to Marshall. He knew that even if the cargo-destroyers ran the blockade, they would not arrive at Corregidor before April 15. Bataan was doomed. Marshall sent the gist of Wainwright's message to MacArthur and requested his reaction. He received it in short order, along with some thinly veiled criticism of Wainwright.

MacArthur said that he was trying to satisfy Wainwright's request for a bombing raid to disrupt the Japanese blockade, but that he had "only twelve serviceable B-17s, many of which are approaching exhaustion."

Then MacArthur disputed Wainwright's estimate of the food situation on Bataan, saying that he believed "the supplies on Bataan will last beyond the date of April 15. . . . When I left on March 11 it was my estimate that serious shortage would not develop at the earliest before May 1, allowing sufficient time for arrival of blockade runners from the United States."

MacArthur added, pointedly, "It is of course possible that with my departure the rigor of application of conservation may have relaxed."

He also took exception to Wainwright's statement that his troops would be starved into submission. Surrender was unthinkable to MacArthur. "I am utterly opposed, under any circumstances or conditions, to the ultimate capitulation of this command as visualized in General Wainwright's radio. If it is to be destroyed it should be upon the actual field of battle taking full toll from the enemy. To this end I had long ago prepared a comprehensive plan to endeavor to cut a way out if food or ammunition failed."

The plan, which MacArthur now outlined to Marshall, involved an audacious attack by the troops on Bataan that would carry them through the Japanese lines to capture Japanese supplies at Subic Bay. The American and Filipino troops would then "operate in central Luzon where food supplies could be obtained." If the attack were not successful, MacArthur noted, the men of Bataan could still escape north into Luzon where they could engage in guerrilla warfare.

MacArthur did not explain how men who could barely stand in their foxholes, who were shivering from malaria, and who had difficulty advancing a hundred yards, would be able to break through the reinforced Japanese line to fight their way through many miles of jungle and mountains. He had not seen the Bataan troops since January 10. Only Wainwright knew the shape the men were in.

After presenting his plan to Marshall, MacArthur said that he had not told Wainwright about it, "as I feared it might tend to shake his morale and determination." Implying that the plan might not succeed with the present leadership, MacArthur offered "to attempt myself to rejoin this command temporarily and take charge of this movement."

Marshall answered that it would not be necessary for MacArthur to return to the Philippines. "Should it become necessary for you to direct a last resort attack with the objectives you outlined, we feel sure that Wainwright and his forces will give a good account of themselves."

Learning about this plan some thirty years later, Col. A. C. Tisdelle, General King's aide, wrote that if MacArthur "had long ago prepared a comprehensive plan to endeavor to cut a way out if food and ammunition failed, then why didn't he carry it out before we were exhausted by malaria and starvation?" Concerning Mac-Arthur's statement that he had not told Wainwright of the plan because it might undermine his morale, the colonel wrote, "What the g—d— hell did he think Skinny was—a tenderfoot boy scout? To offer to return prematurely from his responsibility in Australia was to grossly insult the training and wisdom of both General Wainwright and General King, which he did with a puerile naiveté apparently unaware of the enormity of his affront to these two splendid soldiers."

Wainwright would learn about MacArthur's grand plan soon enough and would be forced to pass the order along to his weakened troops. In the meantime, Marshall sent him a copy of the no-surrender message Roosevelt had sent to MacArthur on February 9: "American forces will continue to keep our flag flying in the Philippines as long as there remains any possibility of resistance."

"I fully understand," Wainwright replied, "your instructions directing me to resist as long as it is humanly possible to do so. . . . While fully realizing the desperate conditions that are fast developing here because of shortage of supplies due to the effectiveness of the hostile blockade, I pledge myself to you to keep our flag flying in the Philippines as long as an American soldier or an ounce of food and a round of ammunition remains." It was a pledge he would be unable to keep.

While Wainwright's war was being fought with radio messages that last week of March 1942, his adversary, Homma, was preparing the final assault on Bataan. His reinforcements had arrived and were being given an intensive training program while his staff prepared the campaign. Once again Homma's intelligence information was faulty. He believed that the Americans and Filipinos were entrenched behind three lines of defense from Mount Samat to Mariveles at the tip of the peninsula. Actually there was only one defensive line, stretching from Bagac to Orion.

Homma expected the conquest of Bataan to take a month. "I do

not know," he wrote, "whether the enemy on Bataan will try to fight
to the end at the first and second line, whether they will retreat back
to Corregidor and fight, escape to Australia, the Visayans or
Mindanao, or give up at the right time, but I still propose to
prepare for the worst."

He scheduled the attack to commence on Good Friday, April 3,
and he envisioned long bloody weeks of fighting. He could not
know that Bataan would fall after five days.

Wainwright was unaware of Homma's timetable but he did expect
the next offensive on Bataan to come at any moment. His troops
were growing weaker every day and their ability to resist a major
attack was extremely low. He was helpless to do much more than
bombard the War Department with requests for assistance.

Carlos Romulo's work with the Voice of Freedom radio station
and with the preparation of news summaries brought him into daily
contact with Wainwright. "Those of us working now with Wainwright sensed his despair," he wrote. "He looked older and
unhappier. Within the space of two weeks, after leaving Bataan, he
had aged years. His hair had begun to grow out, so that it looked
like a bush on his head."

One afternoon Romulo was ordered to report to Wainwright in
the headquarters lateral, that "little place that looked and smelled
like a cave."

"Colonel Romulo," Wainwright said, "I know the position you are
in. If anything happens and you are found here you won't be safe in
Japanese hands. But we need you here, and while I think you
should leave, I wish you would keep on handling the press relations
and the headquarters propaganda."

Romulo said that he would stay.

"I'll see to it," Skinny told him, "that before it gets too hot here
you'll get away."

Romulo was gratified, but he wondered why Wainwright had
taken the trouble to assure him that he would be gotten out in time.
"Were things about to happen outside the knowledge of our press
relations section?" He was touched that Wainwright should express
concern about his safety when he had so much else on his mind.

Only Wainwright and his immediate staff knew how desperate
the situation was. Not even the War Department was fully aware of
the circumstances. They had been misled by MacArthur about the
number of troops in the Philippines garrison. When Wainwright
announced that he had 90,000 men on Bataan and over 11,000 on
Corregidor, Washington was astounded. Marshall asked Wain-

wright for verification. The figures were "greatly in excess of what we understood was there."

Secretary of War Stimson wrote in his diary that "the garrison is much larger than any of us had expected. We had all thought [the force on Bataan] was in the neighborhood of 40,000 men. Instead of that there are nearly 90,000 there. That adds to the difficulty and complexity. MacArthur kept his figures secret from the very beginning and everyone was astonished when Wainwright revealed the present roster."

This news further confirmed the hopelessness of Wainwright's situation. It had been difficult enough to try to get supplies for even a fraction of that number to the Philippines. Supplying over 100,000 troops was impossible. Still, the War Department tried to give the illusion of hope. Morale had to be maintained. Marshall radioed Wainwright to tell him that he should ask for any help he needed.

"It is a matter of continuing concern to me," Marshall wrote, "as to what additional measures the War Department might take to strengthen and sustain your gallant defense. . . . Your recommendations always receive my immediate personal attention."

Taking the chief of staff at his word, Wainwright sent him an eleven-page request for supplies, stressing food and quinine. There was little that Marshall could do, but he did try. He asked MacArthur to increase his efforts to send small boats from Cebu to Corregidor. He ordered the command at Pearl Harbor to send a shipload of 3,600 tons of food to the Philippine garrison. He ordered submarines to carry quinine and additional supplies and he directed Lt. Gen. Joseph Stilwell in China to explore the possibility of getting food to the Philippine Islands. Marshall did everything he could, but no more than a trickle of supplies ever got through, only a fraction of what was needed.

Wainwright too was searching for ways to pierce the Japanese blockade. He pressed MacArthur about the plan to send bombers to Mindanao and from there to attack the Japanese ships. MacArthur agreed. Wainwright worked out all the complicated arrangements for ships to sail north from Mindanao with enough supplies to support the men on Bataan for a month. But the planes didn't come and the ships lay idly at anchor. When the bombers finally reached Mindanao it was too late to help Bataan.

Each day, Wainwright received increasingly urgent and heartbreaking reports about conditions on Bataan. On March 29 he received the news first hand. A young army captain, John S.

Coleman, with the Twenty-seventh Materiel Squadron on Bataan, came to Corregidor on his own to try to get more food for his men.

Coleman went directly to Wainwright's headquarters. Such was the Old Man's reputation that the captain, who had never met Wainwright, was sure he could get to see him. Skinny put aside his paperwork and told his aide to show the man in. He stood up as Coleman approached his desk.

"Have a seat," Wainwright said. "I can tell you are from Bataan from that sunburned complexion."

To Coleman, Wainwright looked tired and worried, and he spoke spontaneously about his concern for the men on Bataan.

"I can see dust rising from different spots on Bataan during the day where the heavy bombers are operating in the area," Wainwright said. He talked about how the war was going and how he was making efforts to get supplies from the United States. Then he questioned Coleman about the condition of his men.

The captain replied that "they were slowly starving to death. They were so weak it took an extra effort for them to get out of their foxholes." Everyone had malaria, he added. If they sent everyone who needed treatment to the hospital, "we would have no one on the main line of defense." Coleman confirmed what Wainwright already knew, that "the next big push the Japs would make would be the end of the Bataan defense."

Then Coleman was silent for a moment. Finally he told the general why he had come to Corregidor—"to beg for food for my men."

Wainwright said that he could not give Coleman any more food, explaining that the War Department expected Corregidor to hold out after Bataan fell.

"If we furnish supplies to you," Wainwright said, "we would have to let the Filipinos have food too, to keep them fighting. This would deplete our supplies here on Corregidor too much. We just do not have the food to spare."

Although it was difficult for Wainwright to say this to the young man, there was nothing else he could do. He had pledged to Marshall and Roosevelt that Corregidor would hold until help came. But he couldn't let the captain go away empty-handed. Skinny wrote out an order for a 120-pound box of shredded coconut and a can of fruit cocktail. It was the best he could do. It was all anyone could do.

There was no possibility of getting help for the men on Bataan. The food was almost gone. Medical supplies were exhausted. There was no quinine. As many as fifty men a day were found dead in their foxholes from malaria. The troops looked like scarecrows. Their combat effectiveness was near zero.

At hospital #1 the chief nurse summoned her staff to announce that they were almost out of food.

"We've got to make what we have last," she said. "If necessary, we'll have one meal every two days. I know you won't complain."

"We could take it," said Lt. Juanita Redmond, "but what about the patients? They were weak; how could they live with anything less than they had?"

She knew, as did everyone else, that their war was nearly over. "Even our talk about convoys had stopped. What was the use? The Japanese had the islands sewed up; we could only hang on and do our jobs." She noticed a difference in the men on the wards; they were quieter, more thoughtful. Sometimes a young man would ask, "What will happen to us if help doesn't get here?" There was little comfort the nurses could give.

It was the same for Wainwright, across the bay in Lateral 3 of Malinta Tunnel. Whatever he could say to himself or his staff or a young soldier like Captain Coleman had little comfort in it. The Japanese were coming and the soldiers on Bataan would be unable to hold them off this time.

On the night of April 2 the Japanese were ready for what Homma hoped would be their last major offensive on Bataan. The front line was quiet. There wasn't even any patrol activity. The Americans and Filipinos fought off sleep as they lay in their foxholes and trenches staring into the jungle and listening for unusual sounds.

On the Japanese side of the line, 50,000 troops, rested, fed, and trained, tried to sleep, tried not to think about the battle that lay ahead. Over a two-and-a-half-mile section of the front, 150 heavy artillery pieces were aimed at the Forty-first Division of Parker's II Corps. In the morning they would unleash the heaviest artillery barrage of the war. At airfields on Luzon, Japanese pilots slept peacefully, secure in the knowledge that they would meet no American planes when they took off on their bombing mission in the morning. In his headquarters, Homma spoke to his senior officers about the importance of the upcoming offensive.

"The operations in the Bataan Peninsula and the Corregidor Fortress are not merely a local operation of the Great East Asia War. This battle has lasted for about three months as compared with our speedy victories in Malaya, Dutch East India, and other areas in the Philippines. As the Anti-Axis powers propagandize about this battle as being a uniquely hopeful battle and the first step toward eventual victory, the rest of the world has concentrated upon the progress of the battle tactics on this small peninsula. Hence, the victories of these operations do not only mean the suppression of the Philippines, but will also have a bearing upon the English and Americans and their attitude toward continuing the war."

The prestige of the Japanese empire was at stake, and so was Homma's career. If this campaign failed, he would be relieved of command and sent home in disgrace. The date he had chosen for the offensive was significant. To the Americans it was Good Friday. To the Japanese it was also a religious holiday, the anniversary of the death of their first emperor.

That night the Japanese made an announcement over the radio from Manila: "We are starting an all-out offensive in Bataan." When Wainwright learned of it he alerted his commanders on Bataan at once.

The attack began at 9:00 in the morning. One hundred fifty Japanese heavy guns started firing continuously in a barrage that reminded Wainwright and the older officers of the massive German artillery bombardments of World War I. At the same time, Japanese planes roamed overhead, dropping sixty tons of explosives on the section of the front where the infantry planned to attack.

The firing went on without pause for one hour . . . then two . . . then three. It did not stop until 3:00 that afternoon. Around noon a wave of bombers dropped incendiaries. The trees and vegetation leaped into flame and the troops panicked.

Toland described it this way. "Cover had been blasted away until most of the ground was as barren as No Man's Land of World War I. Shells again shrieked, exploding on all sides. They leaped into the bald craters. But soon, whipped by a sudden breeze, the fire leaped over the barren stretches to the lush jungle growth beyond. Hundreds were cremated. The others ran farther to the rear like frenzied animals, spurred by the smell of burning leaves, wood, clothes, leather and flesh."

At 3:00, when the artillery barrage ceased, Japanese infantry and tanks poured through the hole that had been blasted in the II Corps line. On Corregidor, Wainwright waited anxiously for fresh reports from Parker's headquarters. He itched to grab a carbine and rush to the line, but he could only pace back and forth in the tunnel, following the battle's progress through scratchy voices over the telephone. By nightfall he knew that the situation was serious. The enemy had broken through the line on a three-mile front and had penetrated deeply into the II Corps sector. Pitifully small reinforcements were sent to try to fill the gap as darkness settled over the battlefield. If the Japanese continued their advance tomorrow, they could outflank the other units on the front line and the entire main line of resistance would collapse. Bataan would be finished.

The events on Bataan worsened the next day. New Japanese thrusts increased the wedge driven through Parker's front line to over a mile. Wainwright traced the enemy penetration on his map. At this rate the Japanese would capture Mount Samat in a day or two and take the high ground dominating the entire American-Filipino position. They had to be stopped.

Wainwright had no combat troops to spare but he decided to send some food to Bataan. Perhaps that would help. He ordered rice to be taken from the Corregidor reserves and shipped to Bataan immediately, along with almost all the C-rations in storage. This doubled the rice ration for the troops from eight and a half to seventeen ounces per day. Overall, daily food intake increased to twenty-seven ounces a day, a substantial improvement, but still far below an army's requirements, even one in the best of condition.

In the afternoon, Wainwright received a radiogram from Mac-Arthur outlining his plan for the Bataan forces to launch a counterattack when their food had run out, and drive through the enemy lines into Luzon. Wainwright knew this was impossible. His men were not able to resist the Japanese attack. If they couldn't even hold their line, how could they be expected to attack?

Nevertheless, those were his orders. MacArthur also repeated the no-surrender order Wainwright had received from the president: "Under no conditions should this command be surrendered," MacArthur wrote.

There was only one thing to do, Wainwright decided. He would go to Bataan in the morning and assess the situation for himself.

The following day was Easter Sunday. On Bataan the troops bowed their heads in prayer at hastily conducted church services, then rushed away to fight and die on a bright hot sunny morning. Japanese planes swooped overhead, strafing and dropping bombs. Japanese artillery continued its merciless pounding of the lines. At 10:00 the enemy began the assault on the commanding heights of Mount Samat, and less than three hours later the men of Bataan saw the Japanese flag flying from Samat's peak.

Wainwright, Tom Dooley, and Tex Carroll crossed the open water between Corregidor and Bataan and proceeded to Ned King's headquarters outside of Mariveles. It was Skinny's second visit to the peninsula in the two weeks since he had gone to Malinta Tunnel to take command of USFIP. On March 28 he had met with all the general officers on Bataan at King's headquarters and had stopped to visit with Ed Dyess and his air corps unit as well.

This morning, Easter Sunday, Wainwright joined King and his staff for a solemn breakfast. "Morale seemed very low," Tom Dooley observed. "In my eyes DEFEAT was written all over them." After the meal, with Dooley driving "like a wild man," they headed northeast on the coast road to Parker's II Corps command post at Limay. There Wainwright learned that the Forty-first Division was reeling under a heavy attack. He listened quietly while Parker outlined a counterattack plan to try to regain some of their lost ground. Although Wainwright approved of Parker's plan, he was pessimistic about it. Given the condition of the troops, there was little chance of success. Still, they had to make the attempt or the entire II Corps sector might have to be pulled back, jeopardizing the I Corps position as well.

When Wainwright returned to Corregidor later in the day he turned his attention to MacArthur's order for a general offensive to thrust through the enemy lines. He composed a tactful reply. The idea, he radioed MacArthur, "has been under consideration by me for some time and I had about decided to adopt it if and when supplies became exhausted." But he went on to suggest obliquely that such an offensive would not succeed. "The troops have been on half rations for three months and are now on less than that amount which results in much loss of physical vigor and sickness. Nevertheless, before allowing a capitulation the operation you suggest will be adopted. I hope, however, that supplies will arrive in good time."

Wainwright knew that they would not. He would probably have to issue MacArthur's orders to his almost beaten men on Bataan, though he was well aware that they would not be able to carry them out. Though USFIP commander, Wainwright was still MacArthur's subordinate and had to follow MacArthur's command.

The atmosphere in the headquarters lateral in Malinta Tunnel was growing increasingly gloomy as more devastating reports came in from Bataan. "Wainwright pored over maps and reports," Carlos Romulo said, "his hair growing spikier, the circles around his eyes growing more pronounced. His aide, Colonel Pugh, was always with the intelligence and operations divisions, hoping for something cheerful that he could report to his chief. But there was never anything cheerful to report those opening days of April."

April 6 was a decisive day for Bataan, a day on which the fate of the garrison was irrevocably determined. With a deepening sense of frustration at being unable to be in personal and direct command of the troops, Wainwright paced his cramped cave of a headquarters for word of the II Corps counterattack.

When he heard what had happened he was not surprised. The counterattack had failed to make headway; it had run into a simultaneous Japanese attack. The American and Filipino troops were quickly thrown back and lost even more territory. The crucial day of decision ended as a day of disaster. By nightfall the entire left flank of II Corps had been pushed back and the enemy had penetrated 7,000 yards behind the main line of resistance.

That afternoon Wainwright broadcast a speech over Corregidor's Voice of Freedom radio station to commemorate Army Day. The talk was relayed to the United States and rebroadcast nationwide by NBC.

"Fellow Americans: It is an unusual privilege to address you from this far-off outpost of democracy. Our president has this year given a special significance to the celebration of Army Day by redesignating it as Total War Day. To the people of America this is appropriate, because you are engaged in a total war and there is no better way in which our president could impress this fact upon you than to set this day aside, to pay tribute to your army. No nation has an army more representative of its citizenry than the American army. Knowing this, our commander-in-chief has called upon the American people to dedicate all of their efforts and all their energy to support this army.

"Total war means total national effort. An army can be only as strong as the determination and the patriotism of the nation behind it. We who are privileged to be charged with the defense of this distant bastion of American democracy, find inspiration in the knowledge that we have the total support of the American people. Our duty is made easier by the knowledge that every man, woman and child in America is behind us.

"This whole-hearted support brought us victory in the World War. It will bring us victory in this total war. In 1918, I was in France. There I saw the American soldier, faced with almost insurmountable obstacles, fight his way through, because of that precious knowledge. I saw there sights which I have remembered through all of the intervening years, without the necessity of refreshing them in my memory. Your army is a good army; they are fighting a good fight.

"There is another picture which I should like to impress on my fellow Americans today. It is the picture which meets my eyes daily as I visit the front lines in Bataan and Corregidor. I see Filipino and American soldiers, side by side, shoulder to shoulder, stalwart young men ready to give up their lives in defense of the Stars and Stripes and that for which it stands. It is a stirring spectacle which should warm every American heart. It proves, as nothing else can prove, that we have won the friendship, the gratitude, and the affection of the Filipino people; that our deeds have convinced them of the nobility of our ideals and the sincerity of our purpose. A nation which, in forty years, wins such a place in the hearts of another people, is invincible. Its power rests on justice, righteousness, and the equality of mankind.

"Recently, I was entrusted with the command of the United States Forces in the Philippines. The responsibility is tremendous, but I am proud of this opportunity to give the best that is in me to the defense of my country. With the unfailing patriotism of our American soldiers, the unswerving loyalty of our Filipino troops, and the unlimited assistance of the United States, we will win."

Wainwright had written these stirring words to bolster the spirits of his soldiers. Morale was still the only thing Skinny could give to his troops. He knew, however, that the end was in sight and that he would soon have to issue MacArthur's orders for the suicidal attempt to break through the enemy lines.

The official army history of the battle for Bataan records that "The story of the last two days of the defense of Bataan [April 7–8] is one of progressive disintegration and final collapse. Lines were formed and abandoned before they could be fully occupied. Communications broke down and higher headquarters often did not know the situation on the front lines. Orders were issued and revoked because they were impossible of execution. Stragglers poured to the rear in increasingly large numbers until they clogged all roads and disrupted all movement forward. Units disappeared into the jungle never to be heard from again. In two days an army evaporated into thin air."

Wainwright called April 7 a "black day." Worried and upset, he searched for some way to halt the Japanese advance. In the afternoon he telephoned Ned King on Bataan with a desperate suggestion. Skinny's old I Corps, now commanded by Jones, had not been attacked; its half of the Bataan front line was intact. Could I Corps disengage itself from the line and move east, into the deep Japanese salient? If so, they could join forces with II Corps and try to form a new line along the Mamala River, running from the Mariveles Mountains down the spine of Bataan to Manila Bay.

What neither Wainwright nor King knew, so confused was the situation at the front, was that there was no longer any II Corps line for Jones's men to form up with. The idea was a last-ditch gamble, but Wainwright didn't know what else to try. He ordered King to launch the attack. King telephoned Jones and briefed him on the plan.

Jones said that it was impossible. His men were too weak to negotiate the terrain; they would have to scale a gorge. Even if they met no enemy troops, the men did not have the strength for the march. Nor could they transport the heavy equipment and artillery required for a major offensive. Also, Jones estimated that it would take at least eighteen hours for the division that would spearhead the attack to get out of the line and into position.

King was dismayed. He arranged a three-way telephone connection between his headquarters, Jones, and Wainwright. Jones repeated his objections directly to Wainwright and the talk continued for some minutes. Finally, with some annoyance evident in his voice, Wainwright said that he would leave the decision up to King, the field commander. After Wainwright hung up, King said that he agreed with Jones's analysis of the situation. He ordered Jones to withdraw I Corps to the south so that it would not be outflanked by the Japanese penetration on the eastern side of Bataan.

Later that day King sent a personal emissary to Wainwright on Corregidor. King wanted to make sure that Wainwright fully understood how bad the Bataan situation was in the wake of this latest full-scale Japanese attack. He sent his chief of staff, Arnold Funk, with instructions to give Skinny a full and honest account of the situation.

After the war, Wainwright wrote that Funk had told him that King might have to surrender. However, Funk maintained that King told him specifically not to mention the word "surrender" to Skinny; Funk's mission was only to report on the nature of the situation on Bataan.

Funk went to Wainwright's office in Malinta Tunnel, sat down opposite his desk, and began to talk. He thought that Wainwright looked worn and haggard and had a worried expression on his face.

Funk explained in detail the extent of the Japanese penetration in II Corps's sector and the terrible condition of Parker's men. He also told Wainwright of the overcrowded hospitals and the fact that approximately eighty percent of the combat troops were ill with malaria and seventy-five percent with dysentery.

Funk painted a grim, bleak picture. Wainwright knew that Arnold was not given to exaggeration. Both men knew that Bataan was lost, but Wainwright was under orders from Roosevelt and from MacArthur not to surrender. The latest radiogram from MacArthur forbidding surrender was on his desk at that moment.

"Arnold," he said, "you tell General King that there will be no surrender. He must attack."

Funk said nothing for a moment. The order saddened the tall, tough infantryman. Tears came to his eyes as he spoke.

"General," he said. "You know what the outcome will be." It was not a question but a simple statement of fact.

"I do," Skinny replied. "I understand the situation."

They stood and shook hands, and told each other what both considered to be a final goodbye. Wainwright's eyes were moist too and his voice barely above a whisper.

"God be with you and all of you over there," he said to Funk. "I have done all I can."

Wainwright's orders were never carried out. He and the other commanders knew that they could not be. Jones continued to withdraw I Corps farther south.

After Funk left Corregidor, Wainwright drafted a message to MacArthur, reporting on the catastrophic events of the day. Three Philippine army divisions had been eliminated as effective fighting units. Japanese artillery were emplaced on the heights of Mount Samat. Hospital #1 had been bombed, deliberately, three times. All reserves had been committed to battle.

When MacArthur received Wainwright's message he dispatched his own assessment of the situation to Washington. "In view of my intimate knowledge of the situation there," MacArthur wrote, "I regard the situation as extremely critical and feel you should anticipate the possibility of disaster there very shortly."

The disaster of which MacArthur spoke fell the next day, April 8. There was no longer any organized defense of Bataan, no cohesive main line of resistance. Communications were poor or nonexistent and many units existed only as pins stuck into a map. Order was gone; chaos reigned.

All morning Japanese planes bombed and strafed the American and Filipino troops. Some units had been trying to set up new defensive positions. Others were fleeing down the crowded trails and the east coast road. The Japanese pilots couldn't miss them. Soon the ditches were littered with the dead and the dying. The Thirty-first Infantry Regiment of the Philippine army was trying to dig in along the east road, but whenever enemy planes appeared the men fled into the jungle. After each raid it was increasingly difficult to force them back on the line. Officers threatened them at pistol point, but fewer returned after each raid. By 3:00 in the afternoon, before the Japanese infantry attacked, the line once held by the Thirty-first was deserted.

The road to the south was jammed with Filipino troops. An American officer said they were "like a mass of sheep. Thousands poured out of the jungle like small spring freshets pouring into creeks, which in turn poured into a river."

Wainwright telephoned King's headquarters frequently throughout the day. Each time the news was more disturbing. By early afternoon King told him that if he wanted to evacuate any troops from Bataan to Corregidor he had better do so now. Tomorrow would probably be too late.

Wainwright wanted to get the nurses from hospitals #1 and #2 off Bataan, and he needed the Forty-fifth Infantry Regiment of Philippine Scouts to bolster his beach defenses on Corregidor. Hurriedly he made arrangements for the evacuation.

Wainwright summoned navy captain Ken Hoeffel and ordered him to destroy any naval equipment at Mariveles that might be useful to the Japanese, and to transfer the food and ammunition stores to Corregidor. The Rock was going to need everything it could get.

Next Wainwright radioed a brief message to MacArthur, in which he gave the closest indication yet that Bataan was finished. "It is with deep regret that I am forced to report that the troops on Bataan are fast folding up." He hoped that when MacArthur learned how greatly the situation had deteriorated, he would rescind his order to launch an attack northward into Luzon.

At 4:00 Skinny sent for Carlos Romulo. Here was one promise he might be able to keep, to get Romulo to safety. As the press relations officer approached his desk and saluted, Wainwright pushed back a pile of papers on his desk and rose to greet him.

"Colonel Romulo, I'm ordering you out of Corregidor."

"What do you mean?" Romulo asked.

"Bataan is hopeless."

"By the way he said that," Romulo wrote later, "by the utter lack of expression on his frozen countenance, I realized he was a man who had gone beyond emotion. I know Wainwright wept for his boys on Bataan."

Romulo started to protest, but Wainwright waved him to silence. He explained that Romulo would leave Corregidor at 7:00 and go to Bataan, where a plane would take him south. Wainwright seemed abrupt and formal and Romulo was momentarily taken aback by his cold behavior. He saluted the general and said goodbye. Suddenly Wainwright visibly relaxed and came around the desk to shake hands.

"God bless you, my boy," Skinny said. "Tell President Quezon and General MacArthur I will do my best to the end."

At 7:00 that night Wainwright's orders to evacuate the nurses from Bataan were being implemented. At hospital #1 Juanita Redmond and the others were told to be ready to leave in fifteen minutes. Hurriedly they wrote out instructions for their patients and gathered their personal belongings. The doctors and corpsmen who were staying behind assembled to see them off.

"We'll be seeing you," they all said.

A similar scene was taking place at hospital #2, where Sallie Durrett and her companions boarded a bus for Mariveles. They too regretted leaving the doctors and corpsmen they had worked with for months. In addition, Nurse Durrett was leaving her fiance.

The nurses from hospital #1 had traveled only a short distance when they were finally told why they were leaving. The army officer in charge of their evacuation gave them the news, shouting to be heard over the engine of the bus. "Girls," he added, "there are going to be a lot of trucks, soldiers, civilians on the road. There'll be a great deal of confusion. Bataan has fallen."

The ride to the dock at Mariveles was hellish. Thousands of men were on the road, all heading south, trying to get away from the advancing Japanese army. "They banged on the sides of the bus," Nurse Redmond recalled, "pleading with us to take them, to carry them away before the Japanese caught them. It was horrible to catch glimpses through the dark of their pain-stricken faces, to hear them crying out to us over the roar of motors and the tramp of marching feet, and to know there was nothing we could do for them."

While the nurses were trying to reach the dock at Mariveles, Romulo was trying to leave it. He had come over on a motor launch from Corregidor and the car and driver that were supposed to meet him were nowhere in sight. Everything was confused. An American army major was shouting into a telephone, "I tell you, the show is over." He was crying. Finally another officer commandeered a car and told the frightened driver to take Romulo to the airfield.

"We can't get through."

"Get him there anyway," the officer said. "It's MacArthur's orders."

The car headed north, the only vehicle going in that direction, and slowly made its way through a mass of humanity. "Such a melange of vehicles swarming together was surely never before seen in this world," Romulo said. "Pouring out of the jungle came truckloads of soldiers. They looked like men of dust, limned in the red glare of the forest fires. They smelled of dirt and sweat and excrement. Some walked with spraddled knees, like old men, falling and rising and staggering on. Boys of seventeen and eighteen were dragging their guns and stumbling in the dust. I saw them fall, reel to their knees, stand and stagger a few steps, and fall again."

He passed the bus filled with the nurses from hospital #1. "I could not bear to look into their faces as we passed on that crowded road. I knew what was written on them. It was not fear. It was inevitability."

All through Bataan's last anguished hours Wainwright avidly followed the reports of the collapse that were coming in by telephone. The news was taking its toll on him. His sleep had long been limited to brief catnaps amid the noise and heat and confusion of the tunnel. He was thinner than he had been on Bataan and the creases in his face were deeper.

His aides and his staff were concerned about the Old Man and they tried to ease his burdens as much as possible. But no one could share his greatest burden, the responsibility of command. When Bataan fell, Wainwright would be the one held accountable for the largest surrender of American forces in the history of the United States.

As the night of April 8 wore on, Wainwright realized that the end was now only a matter of hours away. He kept waiting for a reply to his radiogram to MacArthur, hoping that MacArthur would release him from the senseless order to attack and break through the enemy lines. But no response came. MacArthur's orders were to attack before Bataan fell; Wainwright couldn't wait any longer. He had to issue the order.

At 11:30 in the evening he called Ned King.

"Launch an offensive with Jones's I Corps northward toward Olongapo," Wainwright said, explaining how that might relieve the pressure on II Corps.

Everyone understood the hopelessness of the situation, but King dutifully went through the motions, just as Wainwright had done. He contacted Jones and passed on the order.

"Any attack is ridiculous," Jones said. "Out of the question. My men are too weak."

King did not press the point. He knew that Jones was right. Even if an attack could be mounted it would only lead to needless slaughter, and so would continued resistance. King knew that Wainwright's hands were tied by MacArthur's orders; that was why he had instructed Arnold Funk to refrain from using the word "surrender" in his meeting with Skinny. The decision to surrender would have to be King's, a deliberate choice to disobey Wainwright's orders. This took great courage. King knew it could lead to his court-martial.

Shortly before midnight King asked Arnold Funk to assemble the staff. He called them to the flimsy timber and tarpaper shack that served as headquarters.

"I do not ask you here to get your opinion or advice," King said in a quiet and calm voice. "I do not want any of you saddled with any part of the responsibility for the ignominious decision I feel forced to make. I have not communicated with General Wainwright because I do not want him to be compelled to assume any part of the responsibility. I am sending forward a flag of truce at daybreak to ask for terms of surrender. I feel that further resistance would only uselessly waste human life. We have no further means of organized resistance."

King sighed and looked around the room at his officers. "I don't have a white horse," he said. "I don't have a saber. I don't have someone to ride up and down the front lines to rally the troops. There's just no way we can continue the fight."

"There was not a dry eye present," his operations officer recalled.

General King's war was over. Bataan had fallen. But on Corregidor Wainwright did not know it. He would not find out until six hours later.

While King was announcing his decision to surrender, Juanita Redmond and the nurses from hospital #1 were boarding a small open boat at the Mariveles dock. Sallie Durrett and the hospital #2 nurses were caught in a massive traffic jam. No one knew when they would get through. The boat to Corregidor could not wait any longer. They would have to take their chances.

Lieutenant Redmond looked out over the water and saw "streaks of flame leaping against the black sky. The bay seemed alive with shadowy forms of boats and native rafts, plying back and forth. Several were struck by artillery fire. Sick at heart we watched them sink and listened to the cries of the drowning grow faint and finally die away."

Several miles to the north, virtually in Japanese territory, Romulo reached the airfield at Cabcaben. Airman Ed Dyess was there, supervising the evacuation of every plane that could still fly—two fighter aircraft and one whose flight status no one was sure of. The latter was an old amphibious Grumman *Duck* J2F4. Its pilot, Lt. Roland J. Barnick, had just replaced a blown cylinder in one of the engines with a cylinder taken from a plane that had been sunk in Manila Bay on the first day of the war.

Dyess shoved Romulo and four other officers into the plane, which was designed to take only three, and Barnick, who had never flown that type of plane before, started both engines and eased down the runway.

At that instant, shortly after 1:00 in the morning, an earthquake shook the peninsula. The tremors, lasting more than a minute, were so violent that the submarine U.S.S. *Snapper*, 100 miles to the south, felt the impact. Its captain was sure they had run aground.

Then the whole tip of Bataan seemed to explode, the earth erupting like a volcano. The army was blowing up the ammunition dumps near Mariveles. The spectacle continued for four hours. Thousands of metal fragments from the exploding bombs and shells spewed out in all directions. Huge chunks of steel lashed the waters of Manila Bay, sinking small boats.

The nurses from hospital #1, in a small boat crossing the open water to Corregidor, were rocked by the blast, and the women huddled low as pieces of wreckage struck the craft's sides. On Bataan, where the nurses from hospital #2 were still on the road trying to get to the dock, Sallie Durrett saw that "the sky in the distance appeared to be on fire. It glowed with a bright yellow orange light."

Over Manila Bay, only seventy feet above the water, the passengers in the tiny, overloaded Grumman *Duck* couldn't see the explosions behind them, but they were aware of the bright light and the shrapnel striking the plane. They thought that American antiaircraft guns from Bataan were firing on them.

On Corregidor people stared in stunned silence at the hideous explosions and the fire illuminating the fleet of tiny boats trying to flee the inferno. The sight was fascinating, riveting and horrible, an almost theatrical end to Bataan.

Wainwright was unaware of the latest developments on Bataan. His only contact was the telephone, and communications were growing more difficult to maintain. His chief of staff, Lew Beebe, was on the phone constantly, trying to reach General King.* He couldn't get through. The demolitions at Mariveles had temporarily disrupted service to King's headquarters.

Finally Beebe reached Cliff Bluemel, who was trying to establish a last-ditch defense line along the Lamao River with the remnants of the Twenty-sixth Cavalry. General Bluemel, who for hours had worked to halt fleeing troops and make them take a stand, told Beebe of his frustration. He would not be able to hold his position.

Bluemel could hear Skinny talking loudly in the background. "Tell Bluemel to use his own judgment," Wainwright shouted, "and to take whatever action he deems best. Whatever he does will be approved by General Wainwright."

Beebe tried again to reach King, but had no more success. Wainwright asked him to try to raise Jones. The call went through and Beebe asked Jones if the counterattack had been launched. Jones replied that he had received no such orders from King.

"Well, stand by," Beebe said. "You'll probably receive instructions to attack at any minute."

"Why you silly ass," Jones shouted. "We've got *no* food left. My troops are withdrawing." He paused and added, "If you insist, I'll lead them to suicide." Then he hung up.

At 3:00 A.M. King learned of Beebe's conversation with Jones. He called Corregidor and spoke with Beebe.

"I want a definite answer," King said, "as to whether or not General Jones will be left in my command *regardless* of what action I may take."

Beebe repeated the question to Wainwright.

"Tell him he's still in command of all forces on Bataan," Skinny said.

"You bet, Skinny," King shouted into the phone. That was the last contact the two commanders had during that long night.

---

*Because of Wainwright's hearing loss, the staff almost always made his telephone calls.

True to his word, the gallant King had not involved Wainwright in any way in the surrender, taking the decision and the responsibility on his own shoulders. In their last conversation, Wainwright did not ask King about the attack he was supposed to have ordered Jones's I Corps to make.

For hours there was no further word from Bataan. Wainwright waited, pacing and worrying, but he had done all he could and he had issued the orders MacArthur had given him.

At 6:00 A.M. Wainwright learned the truth. King telephoned from Bataan and told the night duty officer at USFIP headquarters, Jesse Traywick, that he had sent emissaries to the Japanese to arrange for surrender.

Traywick rushed to Wainwright at once.

"Sir, General King is going to surrender!"

"Go back and tell him not to do it," Wainwright said.

Traywick ran back to his desk and spoke to King again. He returned to Wainwright and said, "It's too late."

"They can't do it," Wainwright shouted, overwhelmed by the events of the moment. "They can't do it!"

CHAPTER 11

"All Hell's Gonna Break Loose"

THE DEED WAS DONE, Bataan had surrendered, despite direct orders to Wainwright from MacArthur and the President of the United States to hold the peninsula at all costs. "There must be no thought of surrender," Wainwright had been told. For the first time in his long military career he had been unable to carry out his orders. The orders had been impossible to carry out—there was no way to save Bataan without outside help—but that did not alter the fact that he had disobeyed orders.

In the bleak early morning hours of April 9, when Wainwright learned of Bataan's surrender, he sat slumped at his desk, wondering how to tell MacArthur. On the one hand, Wainwright had to show his superior officer that he had done everything he could, that he had tried to execute his orders. On the other hand, he wanted to protect King, to indicate that he too had had no choice about the surrender, and to refrain from any criticism of him. Wainwright was well aware that King had faced an agonizing decision, to surrender against orders or demand the needless slaughter of his troops. King's decision was both sensible and courageous. At best his troops could have held only another day or so. In less than a month, Wainwright would confront the same dilemma.

Finally Wainwright wrote out a message for MacArthur.

"At six o'clock this morning General King commanding Luzon Force without my knowledge or approval sent a flag of truce to the

Japanese commander. The minute I heard of it I disapproved of his action and directed that there would be no surrender. I was informed it was too late to make any change, that the action had already been taken. Enemy on east had enveloped both flanks of the small groups of what was left of the II Corps and was firing with artillery into the hospital area which undoubtedly prompted King's action. . . . Physical exhaustion and sickness due to a long period of insufficient food is the real cause of this terrible disaster." Later he added, "The decision which [King] was forced to make required unusual courage and strength of character."

The radiogram was dispatched and Wainwright went out to inspect Corregidor's defenses, all the while awaiting MacArthur's reaction.

If only he had known. At the very time when the troops on Bataan were fast folding up, when Wainwright had been forced to issue those impossible attack orders to King, his own no-surrender orders were being rescinded in Washington.

On the morning of April 8 in Washington, Secretary of War Stimson was meeting with Warren Clear, who had left Corregidor by submarine several weeks before. Colonel Clear urged Stimson not to insist on a fight to the end on Bataan. He believed that the Japanese "would massacre everyone there."

After lunch, Stimson met with Eisenhower and with Maj. Gen. Joseph McNarney, who was acting chief of staff while George Marshall was in London. They discussed, in Stimson's words, "whether we shall order them to stand up to the bitter end or permit them to make a surrender." General McNarney then sent a memo to the president urging that the no-surrender order be revoked. The decision about the final actions on both Bataan and Corregidor should be left entirely up to Wainwright.

Roosevelt concurred but he directed that Wainwright's new orders be sent first to MacArthur, with instructions that he pass them on to Wainwright only if he agreed with them. The message for Wainwright said that the president was "keenly aware of the tremendous difficulties under which you are waging your great battle. The physical exhaustion of your troops obviously precludes the possibility of a major counterstroke unless our efforts to rush food to you should quickly prove successful. Because of the state to which your forces have been reduced by circumstances over which you have had no control I am modifying my orders to you as contained in my telegram to General MacArthur dated February 9 and repeated to you on March 23.

"My purpose is to leave to your best judgment any decision affecting the future of the Bataan garrison. I have nothing but admiration for your soldierly conduct and your performance of your most difficult mission and have every confidence that whatever decision you may sooner or later be forced to make will be dictated only by the best interests of the country and of your magnificent troops. . . . I feel it proper and necessary that you should be assured of complete freedom of action and of my full confidence in the wisdom of whatever decision you may be forced to make. Please acknowledge receipt of this message."

Roosevelt then asked MacArthur to report whether or not he was forwarding this message to Wainwright.

MacArthur read Roosevelt's cable carefully. He replied to the president that he did not advise sending the message on to Wainwright because Bataan had already surrendered. Later the War Department decided to send a copy of the message directly to Wainwright, overruling MacArthur's decision. The president's words were good for Wainwright's morale, but the circumstances surrounding the delivery of the message would lead to some bitter feelings.

On Corregidor Wainwright watched with his troops the last desperate attempts that soldiers and civilians were making to escape from doomed Bataan. Some, like the nurses from hospital #1, had reached the Rock before dawn. They had been taken into Malinta Tunnel and comforted, like the dazed survivors of a shipwreck. "It was good to be there," Juanita Redmond said, "to be greeted by friends, and given hot food and beds; to feel safe again."

Other who had been authorized to leave Bataan were less fortunate. The Forty-fifth Infantry of Philippine Scouts, which Wainwright wanted on Corregidor to bolster his undermanned beach defenses, never made it to the Mariveles docks. They could not get through the congested roads in time. All were taken prisoner.

The nurses of hospital #2 had been held up by the explosion of the ammunition dumps and did not reach Mariveles until daybreak. There was no boat for them. Tired and fearful, they sat down on the rocky beach, shared a single can of peaches, and looked wistfully at the haven of Corregidor only two miles across the bay. After a long wait, and because of much "vim, vigor, and swearing," General Funk was able to arrange for another boat and they were ferried to Corregidor, to be "greeted with tears and kisses by our sister nurses," Sallie Durrett said.

Many people who were not authorized to leave Bataan did so anyway. Wainwright and his staff watched them through binoculars as they put out to sea in anything that would float. Some lashed bamboo poles together to make rafts, others pushed off clinging to a board, and many started swimming through the oily and shark-infested waters. Japanese sniper and artillery fire picked them off by the dozens, but they kept coming. For most of the day Manila Bay was dotted with small boats and the bobbing heads of swimmers.

Most of them—no one knows how many—died in the water, but more than 2,000 made it across safely. Sailors, soldiers, and civilians, Filipino and American, came ashore on Corregidor that day, their emaciated condition grim evidence to the men of the Rock of what was likely to be in store for them. The survivors who struggled ashore were demoralized and defeated, sick, diseased, and starving. Few of them were combat troops and so were of no use to the Corregidor garrison. They were merely more mouths to feed from a dwindling supply of food.

Some of the refugees went into Malinta Tunnel and did not come out until Corregidor surrendered a month later. Army nurse Maude Williams said that they were "frankly tired of war. Gaunt, unshaven, dirty, wrapped in sullen despair, they squatted silently in the tunnel curbs by day. By night they stretched out on their scraps of blanket or on the bare cement, across the paths of trucks and cars. . . . it was impossible to clear them out for they had a certain tired stubbornness which defied command or insult."

To the men and women of Corregidor they represented a vision of the hell that awaited them. But there were no more places to escape to once Corregidor fell. Now they were truly on their own, completely surrounded by the enemy.

"There was little comfort to be found in looking ahead," Nurse Redmond wrote, "for though our underground fortress might be impregnable, supplying it was less than ever possible. If aid could not reach us while Bataan still held, we all knew (though the words were seldom spoken) that no relief could be hoped for now."

Around midday of April 9 Wainwright noted than an awesome and fearful silence had descended over Bataan. After five days of continuous artillery and mortar fire the sudden quiet was over-whelming, like being in the presence of a friend who has died. Men found themselves whispering as though respectful of the dead.

The silence was unnerving, and so was a procession they later saw from a vantage point high atop Malinta Hill. Peering through their binoculars, Wainwright and his aides saw long columns of captives walking north from Mariveles along the east coast road. These were the men of Bataan, Americans in their khaki uniforms and Filipinos wearing their blue fatigues. White flags of surrender dotted their lines.

Wainwright and the other observers did not know it then, but they were witnessing the greatest atrocity of the Pacific War, the Bataan Death March. Some 70,000 men began the trek north that day. Only 54,000 of them arrived at Camp O'Donnell, not far from Clark Field. Although the exact figures will never be known, it is estimated that between 600 and 650 Americans and 5,000 to 10,000 Filipinos lost their lives on the Death March. No one knows how many thousands of men—particularly Filipinos, who could more easily hide among the civilian population—escaped during the march.

Many of Wainwright's friends and comrades were walking the dusty road that day—Clint Pierce, Trap Trapnell, Bill Maher, Joe Chabot, Albert Jones, George Parker, Arnold Funk, Cliff Bluemel, and so many others he had known during the years between the wars. Some he would be reunited with when he became a prisoner himself, others he would meet after the war, but there were many he would never see again.

All the men shuffling along the road to the north, being kicked, beaten, bayoneted, and beheaded by the Japanese troops, or simply dropping from exhaustion, had been a vital part of Wainwright's war. Ed Dyess,* who had fought for him at Quinauan Point and had put Carlos Romulo aboard the last plane out of Bataan; Richard Gordon, who had sailed with him to Manila aboard the *Grant* so long ago and was a witness to MacArthur's single visit to Skinny on Bataan; Henry Lee, the young author of the haunting poems about Wainwright's war; John Coleman, the tough captain who had gone to Skinny on Corregidor to beg for food for his men; Walt Odlin, who was with General King when he made his last telephone call to Wainwright's headquarters; and hundreds of others who had once been cheered by the sight of the Old Man who walked the front line and stopped to chat with them, oblivious of Japanese shells and bullets. They were all part of those slow-moving columns that Wainwright watched from Corregidor that day, and he felt a heavy responsibility for their fate. Within a few hours this

---

*In 1943, Dyess escaped to Australia and brought to America the first news of the brutality shown by the Japanese.

feeling would force him to make one of the toughest choices any military commander has had to face.

Wainwright's adversary, Homma, wasted little time in preparing for the final stage of his campaign to capture the Philippines. Pleased that Bataan had fallen so far ahead of his schedule, he began to plan for the invasion of Corregidor. He had good reason for haste. He still feared that he would be relieved of his command because his operations were so far behind the overall Japanese timetable of conquest for the Pacific.

These time pressures forced him to consider invasion. Starving the Corregidor garrison into submission would take much too long. Before sending his troops to land on Corregidor's beaches, however, he intended to pulverize the island's defenses. He started the day Bataan surrendered.

Beginning at 4:30 on the afternoon of April 9, the Japanese air force made repeated sorties daily against the Rock, which had not been bombed since the end of March. On the 9th, ninety-nine planes ranged over Corregidor for four hours.

But the greatest threat to Corregidor came not from the air but from Bataan, from the Japanese artillery that was now within easy shelling range. Observers atop Malinta Hill watching the American and Filipino prisoners moving northward soon saw the first of the Japanese artillery, a 75mm battery, being set up near Cabcaben. By 4:00 it was firing. One of General Moore's staff officers, Col. Steve Mellnik, noted, "A drumbeat of artillery fire filtered through the tunnel."

As each Japanese artillery piece fired, its position was located and identified by a red pin on a large wall map of Bataan in Moore's harbor defense command headquarters. Moore decided that he would return fire in one hour, at 5:00.

Fifteen minutes before his artillery was due to open up, Wainwright walked into the lateral. He wanted to know what information harbor defense command had about the Bataan prisoners.

"Our observers haven't seen a white flag since noon," Moore told him. "We can only assume that the PWs are north of Cabcaben. Let me show you what we intend to do."

He pointed out the enemy artillery concentration around Cabcaben and explained to Skinny the details of the bombardment that he expected to unleash shortly.

"When the bombardment stops," one of Moore's officers said, "there won't be an operable cannon in the Cabcaben area. This shoot won't win the war, but it will buy time."

The opportunity to strike back at the enemy would also provide a much-needed boost in morale for the defenders of Corregidor. The excitement was clear on the faces of Moore's men, but not on the face of Wainwright. He looked thoughtfully at the red pins on the map and realized that they formed a circle around hospital #2. The evacuated nurses had told him that some 4,000 sick and wounded Americans and Filipinos had been left there. There had not been enough time for the Japanese to have moved them.

Here was the classic dilemma for the commanding officer. If Wainwright decided to return the fire he would risk the lives of the helpless patients in Bataan's hospital. If he withheld fire, the Japanese artillery bombardment would undoubtedly inflict casualties among the defenders on Corregidor and perhaps destroy some of its limited artillery, thus weakening the overall defense. From a military standpoint there was only one course: return fire, kill the enemy before he kills you, don't weaken your own chance for survival. But there were humanitarian considerations too, and Skinny was torn by the thought of his boys on Bataan. He looked at Moore and slowly shook his head.

"George, you can't fire on those artillery positions because four thousand of our soldiers are hospitalized there. I want you to hold off for three days and give the Japs time to evacuate the patients."

"We were dumbfounded by the decision," wrote Colonel Mellnik. "Understandably, General Wainwright had great sympathy for the patients he once commanded, and his responsibilities were wider than ours. But enemy fire was building up at an alarming rate. Besides we had no assurance that the enemy would ever evacuate the patients to a safer place."

It was an unpopular decision with the artillery officers, but Skinny's compassion for his men did save many lives. Although he was criticized at the time for his choice, postwar evaluations agree that "Wainwright's order, which stemmed from his sense of compassion, made little difference to the battle and doubtless saved lives."

The day Bataan fell had been long and exhausting for them all. As darkness settled over Corregidor it was time to write the tributes and the accolades, a moment for the words of inspiration and of sadness. Some were private; others were broadcast to the world.

Johnny Pugh, Wainwright's aide, confided to his diary that "The fall of Bataan has saddened me more than I can say. But no end of work was done there. For months we continued to improve our positions. Every inch of the front line was walked by General Wainwright . . . it is a tribute to General Wainwright that the lines of his old corps held, in spite of the debacle on the East Side."

In his headquarters in Melbourne, Australia, which he had named "Bataan," MacArthur was in tears as he wrote his tribute to the men of Bataan.

"The Bataan force went out as it would have wished, fighting to the end its flickering forlorn hope. No army has ever done so much with so little and nothing became it more than its last hour of trial and agony. To the weeping Mothers of its dead, I can only say that the sacrifice and halo of Jesus of Nazareth has descended upon their sons, and that God will take them unto Himself."

In Malinta Tunnel on Corregidor a tired Skinny Wainwright pored over the words of an announcement to be read over the Voice of Freedom radio station.

"Bataan has fallen. The Philippine-American troops on the war-ravaged and bloodstained peninsula have laid down their arms. With heads bloody but unbowed, they have yielded to the superior force and numbers of the enemy.

"The world will long remember the epic struggle that Filipino and American soldiers put up in the jungle fastnesses and along the rugged coast of Bataan. They have stood up uncomplaining under the constant and grueling fire of the enemy for more than three months. Besieged on land and blockaded by sea, cut off from all sources of help in the Philippines and in America, these intrepid fighters have done all that human endurance could bear.

"For what sustained them through all these months of incessant battle was a force that was more than merely physical. It was the force of an unconquerable faith, something in the heart and soul that physical hardship and adversity could not destroy. It was the thought of native land and all that it holds most dear, the thought of freedom and dignity, and pride in these most priceless of all our human prerogatives.

"The adversary, in the pride of his power and triumph, will credit our troops with nothing less than the courage and fortitude that his own troops have shown in battle. Our men have fought a brave and bitterly contested struggle; all the world will testify to the almost superhuman endurance with which they stood up until the last in the face of overwhelming odds.

"But the decision had to come. Men fighting under the banner of an unshakable faith are made of something more than flesh, but they are not made of impervious steel. The flesh must yield at last, endurance melts away, and the end of the battle must come.

"Bataan has fallen, but the spirit that made it stand—a beacon to all the liberty-loving peoples of the world—cannot fall!"

Millions of people in the Philippines and elsewhcre were moved by these words, perhaps none more so than an officer waiting at an airfield at Iloilo on the island of Panay, south of Corregidor. He stood beside the runway, tears running down his cheeks, as Wainwright's words came through the loudspeaker. He was Carlos Romulo, the last man to escape from Bataan. Wainwright had kept his pledge to get him to safety, and now Romulo was on his way to Australia. Three years later, in the shadow of the Washington Monument, he would finally express his thanks to Skinny Wainwright.

The message was received in the United States as well. When asked by reporters for his reaction, President Roosevelt said, "It makes one feel proud."

Corregidor took a heavy pounding from the Japanese artillery at the tip of Bataan the next day. "By noon," said one of George Moore's officers, "enemy shells were sweeping the island at a roll-of-drums tempo. They hit Malinta Hill with what sounded like a shower of exploding bombs." Many a gunner silently cursed Wainwright for his orders to withhold fire. Some pleaded with their commanders for permission to shoot.

There were few casualties, but water pipes, power lines, and telephone cables sustained heavy damage. It was unsafe to be outside around Malinta Hill. The men of the Rock knew that the bombardment would get worse because the Japanese were moving up more and heavier artillery pieces. They felt frustrated, knowing that the enemy guns were within easy striking range of theirs, but they had to wait two more days before they were allowed to return the fire.

Inside the headquarters lateral the continuous pounding caused the lights to flicker. The cement walls vibrated and dust settled on everyone's shoulders. Wainwright took stock of his situation. It was not promising. He knew that the 13,000 people on Corregidor were expendable, like a rear-guard unit left behind to allow the main unit time to regroup. Wainwright's duty was clear and he had done it well, holding up the Japanese for as long as humanly possible to give MacArthur time to organize a new army in Australia, a force that someday would retake the Philippines. Wainwright's was a bitter kind of duty; he knew that they were doomed, but they were expected to keep on fighting.

During the day, an announcement came over stateside radio

confirming Wainwright's promotion to lieutenant general. When one of the civilian women* in the tunnel offered her congratulations, Wainwright said, "It is an empty honor, Madam. I know *why* I am being promoted."

It was vital that Wainwright not show any bitterness to the men and women of his command. As had been the case on Bataan, the most important thing he could do for these people was to keep up their morale, their will to fight. He had to be out with his troops as much as possible. They needed to see him and to know that he was one of them, that he understood what they were going through because he was suffering the same privations and dangers himself.

That afternoon he issued a proclamation in an attempt to offset any anger or pessimism occasioned by the fall of Bataan.

"Corregidor can and will be held," Wainwright said. "There can be no question of surrendering this mighty fortress to the enemy; it will be defended with all the resources at our command. Major General George F. Moore, commanding general of Fort Mills, is whole-heartedly with me in the unalterable decision to hold this island together with its auxiliary forts.

"I call upon every person in this fortress—officer, enlisted man, or civilian—to consider himself from this time onward as a member of a team which is resolved to meet the enemy's challenge each hour of every night and day. All men who have served here before will remain at their posts, while those who have come from Bataan will be assigned to appropriate tasks and battle stations. It is essential above all that the men who have joined us from the mainland promptly rid themselves of any defeatist attitude which they may have and consider themselves as part of this fighting unit.

"Bataan has fallen—but Corregidor will carry on. On this mighty fortress—a pearl of great price on which the enemy has set his covetous eyes—the spirit of Bataan will continue to live!"

Brave words. Corregidor will be held! Corregidor will carry on! Wainwright knew how hollow and futile they were. Corregidor could carry on at best only until the middle of May, about five more weeks. Then their supply of diesel fuel would be exhausted and no

---

*There were several civilian women on Corregidor at the time, including an American woman and her debutante daughter ("who does not let you sit for one minute without mentioning same"), a navy wife who had avoided evacuation with the other wives, and an air corps wife who had been evacuated but who came back on a Norwegian freighter. Wainwright got the women to safety before Corregidor fell.

more water could be pumped from the wells. Then they would face surrender. Five weeks and it would be over, assuming that the Japanese did not invade first.

Wainwright talked with his staff about his options. Could he surrender even when they had run out of water? Would he be allowed to exercise his own discretion in the matter or would his hands be tied by the no-surrender orders from Washington and Australia, the same instructions that had forced him to order General King to counterattack when his troops were already beaten? Would Wainwright find himself having to disobey orders for a second time?

MacArthur had not forwarded Roosevelt's message of April 8, the message in which the president had given Wainwright complete freedom of action. But on April 10, Wainwright received from the War Department his own copy of that message.

The president and the War Department, concerned about public reaction to the fall of Bataan, desired to show the American people that they had confidence in Wainwright, the commander on the scene.

A new message was dispatched to Wainwright, to encourage him and to leave all future military decisions in his hands. Secretary of War Stimson decided to publish the message "to show that we had given the authority to handle the situation to the man at the front which was a proper and understandable position to take and then trust to Wainwright doing the right thing."

This latest message to Wainwright included a copy of the original message of the 8th—the one MacArthur had declined to forward— plus an assurance that any decision Wainwright had made or would make was understood to be dictated by the best interests of his troops. Roosevelt expressed the hope that Corregidor would hold, but he reiterated that Wainwright had complete freedom of action.

Wainwright replied at once to the president. He said that he had received no message from MacArthur concerning the president's radiogram of April 8. With regard to this new communication of the 10th Wainwright wrote:

"The kindness of your message and the confidence your Excellency places in my judgment in this desperate situation merits my heartfelt gratitude. I have left nothing undone in my efforts to hold Bataan but men who are starved, without air support and with inadequate field artillery are ill prepared to endure punishment that was inflicted by terrific plane and artillery bombardment. . . . I have been unable to obtain information concerning terms arranged by General King as all communications with Bataan have been severed. However the flag of the United States is still flying on this isolated island."

Skinny was annoyed that MacArthur had not sent him the president's cable rescinding the no-surrender orders. "Naturally, I was burned up," he said after the war. A close friend said, "the only ill feeling Wainwright bore toward MacArthur after the war stemmed from this incident."

After responding to the president, Wainwright radioed Mac-Arthur, informing him of the exchange of messages. He was still troubled about his authority to act in the current crisis. Although his new orders came directly from Roosevelt, the commander in chief, they had been sent first to MacArthur for his approval. By his silence, by his refusal to pass the message on to Wainwright, MacArthur had apparently indicated his disapproval.

MacArthur was Wainwright's immediate superior, a man Skinny had looked up to since his plebe year at West Point and too powerful a figure in the army to cross. He would not feel that he had autonomy until it was formally granted by MacArthur. Wainwright would have to wait for four more days before receiving the assurance he wanted, and then only after he had asked again.

Each day the Japanese bombardment grew in intensity and accuracy as the enemy trained more guns on the Rock. On April 11 the damage and destruction were serious. Casualties were still relatively light, but vital equipment and weapons were being whittled away. The antiaircraft batteries had been damaged severely, the heavy guns facing Bataan had been destroyed, and many small boats on the north side of the island had been sunk. At least now Corregidor's gunners could shoot back. Wainwright's prohibition against returning enemy fire had been lifted.

Despite the damage inflicted by the shelling, the island had an impressive display of artillery, particularly heavy mortars and mobile 155s, as well as the heavy guns of Fort Drum and Fort Hughes. At 10:00 on the night of April 11 they opened fire, forty cannon in all, with spectacular results. They hit ammunition and gasoline dumps, causing a brilliant fireworks display, and so surprised the Japanese that they did not respond for a full quarter of an hour. When they did react, it was ferocious. The Japanese bombed and shelled Corregidor for two hours.

Wainwright knew that he could safely leave the operation of the artillery in the capable hands of General Moore and his men. This left him free to concentrate on the administration of a command of now 13,000 people, and, more important, on conducting inspections and maintaining morale. He spent a great deal of time in the hospital laterals, comforting the wounded by his presence. His calm way of giving each patient a personal moment made these visits much appreciated by the soldiers and the staff alike. "Considering the almost intolerable strain under which every person on Corregidor was living," said one of the nurses, "there was extraordinarily little hysteria or complaining, and the general's own unfailing cheerfulness, the atmosphere of courage and friendliness he brought with him when he made his rounds, set the example for each of us."

It was not easy for Wainwright to display unfailing cheerfulness. He knew that the fate of every person he saw on his daily inspections was captivity or death. But he kept his feelings and his fears to himself because the younger officers and enlisted men still enjoyed the luxury of hoping that somehow they would be saved. Others were not fooled, however. "I could see in the eyes of the senior officers the thing that was in my own heart," Wainwright wrote. "They knew too."

Wainwright was also carrying a heavy burden of guilt over the loss of Bataan. In the privacy of his own mind he reviewed the events that led up to the tragedy and he felt responsible for it. He convinced himself that the army would hold him accountable. "I'm going to have to face this," he told United Press reporter Frank Hewlett, "and pay the price for our not being prepared." To another friend he confided, "I'll be the most disgraced officer in the history of the United States."

For the first time, the fear of court-martial entered Wainwright's mind. He was aware of the fate of Adm. Husband E. Kimmel and Lt. Gen. Walter Short, a longtime friend, who had been in command at Pearl Harbor. They had been relieved and sent home in disgrace, scapegoats for the Japanese surprise attack. Wainwright reasoned that a scapegoat would also be needed for the loss of the Philippines. "Don't be surprised if Wainwright is the fall guy," he told his staff shortly after the fall of Bataan. He could not shake this fear. It would stay with him and grow in intensity over the next three and a half years.

Wainwright spent as much time as he could at the beaches with Sam Howard's Fourth Marine Regiment. These were Skinny's kind of people, fighting men on the line, and they would bear the brunt of the inevitable Japanese invasion. The marines grew to love the

Old Man as much as any soldier did. They worked tirelessly for him to fortify the beaches as well as they could.

But it was a hopeless situation. The marines were too few in number and too poorly equipped to adequately defend the long open stretches. The regiment contained some 1,500 men, augmented by 2,500 others of doubtful usefulness. These were Filipinos and Americans, soldiers from support units, grounded airmen, and beached sailors, all of whom were in poor physical condition. None had been in combat before. And they were Wainwright's beach defense force, his front line.

The days quickly settled into a routine early in Wainwright's stand on Corregidor. Even the explosion of hundreds of shells and bombs all around every day can become routine. Wainwright awakened at 6:00 in the cubbyhole he used for sleeping, located at the far end of the barracks lateral. He shaved and dressed and walked outside for some fresh air, sometimes at the east entrance and sometimes at the west, stopping to chat with the soldiers on duty. He would look out over the island, mentally surveying the terrain, noting the destruction that had occurred during the night. After a meager breakfast of rice or a slice of bread and coffee, he went to his desk in the headquarters lateral to examine the reports that had come in from his commanders overnight.

At mid-morning Wainwright and George Moore made their inspection tour, paying particular attention to the crumbling beach defenses and the dwindling number of artillery pieces. They talked with the officers and the men, and Skinny continually tried to buck up flagging spirits.

Although they had many close calls from enemy shelling on these daily inspections, Japanese bombers were never a threat. Stu Wood's intelligence operation made sure of that. Wood, who spoke Japanese fluently, monitored the Japanese radio traffic from Manila and always knew when enemy planes were taking off for a bombing mission over Corregidor. "I'd hear them say, 'Get the carabao off the runway.'" The distance to the Rock from the Japanese airfields was not great, but the planes had to reach an altitude sufficient to avoid Corregidor's antiaircraft guns. Therefore, Wood could predict accurately their time of arrival over the island. The Rock never had a bombing raid they didn't know about in advance.

Wood kept tabs on Wainwright's whereabouts and would send out a warning when planes were expected. "General, you got fifteen minutes to start back."

Wainwright usually returned to the tunnel for lunch—typically some kind of soup—and went to work trying to reduce the mountain of paper accumulating on his desk. If he had made enough progress on the memos, reports, and requisitions, or if he just had to get away for a while, he took off in the afternoon for another morale-boosting inspection.

Each evening Wainwright wrote up a report on the day's activities, the catalogue of losses and destruction that had marked the previous twenty-four hours and the battles and actions that had occurred throughout the rest of his command—the islands to the south. One report went to the War Department in Washington and one to MacArthur in Australia, and they had to be sent every day.

Late at night, if the shelling was not too heavy around the tunnel entrances, Wainwright would walk outside again, perch on a rock or a piece of debris, and smoke a cigar, passing the time with whoever happened along, officer or enlisted man.

And so it went, day after day, each day bringing more death and destruction and less reason to hope. The end was drawing near, but until it came there was work to be done. It was Wainwright's duty to command and to fight as long as possible.

Wainwright had received no word from MacArthur about President Roosevelt's message rescinding the no-surrender order. Was MacArthur in agreement with the president or not? Wainwright still did not know.

MacArthur's feeling about the future of Corregidor was very clear: There was no hope for it. He indicated this in a message to George Marshall on April 13. "The life of this fortress," MacArthur said, "is definitely limited and its destruction certain unless sea communication can be restored. . . . You must be prepared for the fall of the harbor defenses."

But to Wainwright, MacArthur said nothing about the future and did not reply to his query. By the 13th Skinny was tired of waiting. He dispatched a more forceful message to his chief, reminding MacArthur that Roosevelt had directed him to pass on the no-surrender message to Wainwright if he, MacArthur, agreed with it.

"As I have had no reply," Wainwright wrote, "I assume that you do not concur." He noted that Roosevelt's message appeared to leave the ultimate decision about the surrender of Corregidor in Wainwright's hands. "If I am not correct in this assumption I hope you will so advise me. The fall of Bataan was a most severe blow to me but it was inevitable sooner or later in view of the effectiveness of the blockade. With men in full health and vigor, we could have held the enemy as we have on many occasions. . . . am now determined to hold my present position with God's help until a major diversion by you in some other theatre releases the pressure on us here. While my morale and that of my troops is still high in spite of adversity, a word of cheer and encouragement from you would be welcomed by all."

MacArthur had no words of cheer and encouragement, but at least he did answer Wainwright's question. "The message from Roosevelt to you transmitted here for delivery was not received until after the fall of Bataan and consequently was not forwarded as it referred entirely to the possibility of surrender on Bataan. Almost immediately thereafter the president's message came direct to you which has amplified the subject matter and now gives you complete authority to use your own judgment regarding the harbor defenses."

Now Wainwright had his answer. Whenever the time came, he and he alone was empowered to make the decision about surrender. His hands would not be tied, as they had been when Bataan was falling. His freedom of action also meant that any blame and punishment for the loss of Corregidor would be his too, a worry he would live with for a long time.

In addition to making clear the question of Wainwright's authority, MacArthur told him bluntly that there would be no relief for the Philippines garrison, despite his desire to provide assistance. "I cannot tell you how anxious I have been to bring you relief. My resources however are practically negligible. . . . I have represented to the War Department that the only way in which you can be relieved is by use of the Pacific Fleet. I have had no reply. If I had any real force at my disposal I think you know without my saying that no matter how desperate the chances of success I would move in an endeavor to reach you."

MacArthur had nothing to send, and even if he had, there were no ships in which to send it. He was as helpless to alter the situation as Wainwright was.

Secure on Bataan, Homma was far from helpless as he prepared for the invasion of Corregidor. His troops were in excellent physical and psychological condition and he had ample supplies, food, and medicine. Every day his observers reported that the defenses on Corregidor were crumbling. Under the combined Japanese air and artillery bombardment the Americans and Filipinos were being weakened as their artillery pieces were knocked out one by one.

Whenever Homma looked across the water to Corregidor he saw a pall of smoke and dust covering the island, the result of his air raids and round-the-clock bombardment from his 116 big guns located at the tip of Bataan.

Homma had only one problem, a possible shortage of landing barges. This reduced the number of troops he could put ashore in the first wave. The barges would have to be used as ferries, shuttling back and forth across the bay. That was why it was so important to destroy Wainwright's artillery before the invasion. If the barges were sunk, Homma would have no way of reinforcing the troops that might already have been put ashore.

The date for the invasion had not been set, but Homma knew it would be in the next few weeks. On the night of April 14 he sent a number of barges past Corregidor to the Manila Bay side of Bataan, covering the sound of their engines with an artillery barrage. No one on the Rock discovered them. During the next few nights Homma sent the rest of the barges through the same way.

Also on the 14th Homma began a concentrated effort to knock out the searchlights on Corregidor. He wanted to make sure that when his landing barges approached the island they would not be pinned down by the beams. Whenever a light shone anywhere on the Rock it was shot at by Japanese gunners in seconds. To test Japanese reaction time, an American crew turned on a searchlight for fifteen seconds. Shells roared in around the apparatus before the crewmen could run twenty yards. This was a clear indication to Wainwright, if any more were needed, that the invasion could not be far away.

April 14 was the day when Wainwright had to decide about the ration for his troops. His operations officer, Pete Irwin, urged him to increase the daily ration so that the troops might be better able to withstand the effects of the bombardment, which was no doubt going to increase in severity. The men had to be as strong as possible to meet the invasion.

Wainwright took stock of the food reserves on the island and calculated that if he doubled the present ration, supplies would be depleted within a month, by the middle of May. If they all remained on the half ration, the food could last through the end of June. They wouldn't be receiving any more food, but submarines might be able to bring in enough diesel fuel to keep the water pump going beyond May 15.

The crucial question was the date of the Japanese invasion. If the food ran out by mid-May, Wainwright would have to surrender, even if the enemy had not invaded. For this reason, he reluctantly turned down Irwin's suggestion and ordered that the troops continue on half rations. He had to hold out as long as possible. Increasing the ration would sentence them to no more than a month.

The days began to run together, each one indistinguishable from the one before. The shelling and bombing rarely let up. The explosives fell so frequently that it was impossible to keep facilities repaired. All structures above ground had been obliterated—shelters, beach defenses, buildings, ammunition dumps, food depots, and, one by one, Corregidor's big guns. Even the cliff faces were being shot away. The Japanese artillery fired every day with regularity and without interruption from just before dawn until noon. At 3:00 it would begin again and continue until midnight. Throughout the day the planes would come over, covering the island with fire and thick smoke, so that often the shoreline of Bataan disappeared from view. Most evenings the magnificent sunsets over the China Sea were obscured by the acrid black haze.

The topography of the island was being pounded and blasted into a new landscape, one that resembled the scarred battlefields of World War I. Wainwright remarked to Johnny Pugh that "he had seen many villages in France during the First World War which had been destroyed very badly, but he had never seen any destruction like that on Corregidor."

Associated Press correspondent Clark Lee wrote about Corregidor for U.S. readers. "The bombs didn't screech or whistle or whine. They sounded like a pile of planks being whirled around in the air by a terrific wind and driven straight down to the ground. The bombs took thirty years to hit. While they were falling they changed the dimensions of the world. The noise stripped the eagles from the colonel's shoulders and left him a little boy, naked and afraid. It drove all the intelligence from the nurse's eyes and left them vacant and staring. It wrapped a steel tourniquet of fear around your head, until your skull felt like bursting.

"Then would come the fires, and the heroism. Men and women dashing out and picking up the wounded while the bombs were still falling. They would carry the dead and the wounded to the hospital tunnel. You would hear the cars long before they reached the tunnel. The urgency of their horns, blowing all the way down the hill from Topside and then up the slope from Bottomside, told you they were bringing dead and those about to die and those who would be better off dead. The MPs would make the cars slow down as they drove into the big tunnel and they would stop at the hospital tunnel and blood would be dripping from the cars or the trucks. Then the stretcher bearers would gently lift out the bloody remnants of what had been an American soldier or a Filipino worker a few minutes before. They would lift out the handsome captain whose legs were bloody stumps. They would lift out carefully the eighteen-year-old American boy who would never again remember his name, or his mother's name, or anything else, but would just look at you blankly when you spoke to him."

Day by day, hour by hour, the island and its defenders suffered mortal wounds. Areas that had once been so heavily forested that the trees shut out the sun had now been stripped bare of every strand of vegetation. Huge craters pockmarked the ground, chunks of concrete and steel flew randomly through the languid air, claiming new victims wherever they fell.

The only place to hide was in the tunnel. The men of the beach defense and artillery units, whose work required them to be outdoors, would claw their way deep into their foxholes and trenches or huddle in bombproof shelters that might collapse at any minute. They never knew where the next barrage would strike. Any moving vehicle or congregation of troops could bring down a rain of shells in less than a minute.

Casualties were on the increase and daily life was becoming less and less tolerable. The outdoor kitchens had been destroyed and it was too dangerous to bring food around to the men at regular intervals or to have them line up for a meal. Eating, like life itself, became a haphazard thing, ruled by chance or circumstance or by where the next shell fell.

In the tunnel, though safe from exploding shells and bombs, men were under great emotional stress. The thick walls of the main tunnel and its many laterals formed a haven, but they were also a prison. The constant heat and humidity, the huge black flies and vermin, and the worsening smells of the hospital and the tightly packed unwashed bodies were the parameters of a world without sunlight or a cooling ocean breeze or a moment of privacy.

When the Japanese bombers flew over Corregidor the huge ventilator fans in the tunnel were turned off, to prevent smoke from being drawn into the laterals. The air quickly became stifling and there was a constant fear of suffocation. The lights flickered and went off, plunging the tunnel into a darkness so deep that nothing could be seen, not even a hand in front of one's face.

Tempers flared over trivial things. People were tense and

irritable. Even the nurses became brusque and snapped at each other and sometimes at the patients. The tunnel shook under each bombardment, loose objects rattled, and the wounded moaned. Unless you had a watch, who knew if it was day or night or if the sun had deserted the earth forever? Malinta Tunnel was a filthy dark hole.

Wainwright knew how the men and women felt and he was with them, trying to keep up morale, always displaying what someone had called his unfailing cheerfulness. The survivors of Corregidor remember this. It was not so much his heroic deeds or displays of courage, but that he was among them, sharing their lot.

"Skinny," an officer said, "would walk into a group of GIs and bum a match or a cigarette and sit down and bat the breeze with them." He was as tired and hungry and wary of the future as any of them, but he would not show it. Too many people depended on him.

One day Wainwright received a message that a fast cargo ship had left Hawaii and would try to run the Japanese blockade. He waved the message form at Frank Hewlett and announced that part of the ship's cargo was five million cigarettes, along with large quantities of food.

"Think what that will do for morale," Wainwright said. "With cigarettes and food, soldiers will bitch but they'll fight."

Wainwright did not expect the ship to reach them, but he knew that word of the attempt would be great for morale, and so he spread the news.

"Two days later the ship was diverted to Australia," Hewlett said, "but by then morale was up since everyone on the Rock knew that a big shipment of smokes was on the way."

Amid the monotony of the constant bombardment and the strain of daily life in the tunnel, several events stood out clearly in Wainwright's mind during the last two dismal weeks of April 1942. Most of them were disasters, but they were more memorable somehow than others that had become commonplace.

There was the time when a group of Filipino artillerymen dug an unauthorized and unreinforced shelter in the cliff behind their gun position. They had bombproof shelters built of reinforced concrete, but they felt safer in their hand-dug tunnel. One day a particularly heavy barrage collapsed the face of the cliff and sealed them in the tunnel. All seventy men died.

The next day a shell exploded in the mess hall of an artillery battery, killing nineteen.

Another evening a shell burst at the west entrance of Malinta Tunnel among a group of men who had walked outside for a breath of air. In panic the survivors rushed the gate to get back into the tunnel, but the concussion had sealed it. Suddenly another shell burst nearby.

Juanita Redmond was on duty at the hospital when the casualties were brought in. "We worked all that night and I wish I could forget those endless, harrowing hours. Hours of giving injections, anesthetizing, ripping off clothes, stitching gaping wounds, of amputation, sterilizing instruments, bandaging, settling the treated patients in their beds, covering the wounded that we could not move.

"I still had not grown accustomed to seeing people torn and bleeding and dying in numbers like these. When *one* patient dies it is agonizing enough; when you are faced with such mass suffering and death something cracks inside you; you can't ever be quite the same again."

After a score of close calls and near misses on Bataan and Corregidor, the war caught up with Wainwright one morning after breakfast. He was walking down the main tunnel toward the east entrance, planning to get some fresh air and to inspect a battery of artillery nearby. He stopped about forty feet from the entrance, where a barrier had been erected to keep shell fragments from entering the tunnel, to indulge in one of the few luxuries left to him—a good cigar. He took from his pocket a Tobaccolero, one that MacArthur had given him before he left Corregidor. He bit off the tip, struck a match, and got the cigar going.

Those few seconds saved his life. As he paused to light the cigar a shell exploded against the barrier at the mouth of the tunnel. The concussion raced through the tunnel and Skinny felt a searing pain in his ears. A moment later, being careful to keep the cigar lit, he passed through the shattered barrier and went outside. As he surveyed the damage at the entrance to the tunnel he realized that sounds seemed muted. He could see shells exploding, but could hear them only dimly. His left eardrum had burst and the right ear was also damaged.*

---

*When reporter Bob Considine was describing this incident after the war in his manuscript for Wainwright's book, he wrote, "as a result I have been quite hard of hearing ever since." Skinny objected. He crossed out the phrase and replaced it with "and the right ear since then has never been up to its old standard."

In the midst of death and suffering and tragedy there was also heroism and sacrifice. One afternoon Wainwright saw such an event and by evening everyone on the island knew about it. The American flag flew over Corregidor from a 100-foot pole located at the highest point on the island, the parade ground at Topside. It was visible to everyone on the Rock, to the conquered Filipinos in Manila, and to the Japanese on Bataan. "We will keep the flag flying," Wainwright had pledged to President Roosevelt, and every day it waved high above the smoke and flames.

Then the halyard was cut by a Japanese shell fragment. "Slowly, terribly," Wainwright said, "the flag began to descend down the pole as if drawn by some ghostly and prophetic hand, and most of those crouching in their batteries and holes looked at it as if it were the very sign of our doom." Down and down the flag came. Seconds before it touched the ground, Capt. Arthur Huff and three enlisted men of the coast artillery raced from their shelter. They gathered up the flag, fixed the halyard, and raised the colors to the top of the pole again while shells burst all around them. Wainwright awarded them the Silver Star for their courage.

By the end of April everyone knew that Corregidor could not hold out much longer. Wainwright read the daily damage reports and saw the look of defeat on the faces of his men. He was aware of the depletion of the stock of artillery ammunition and he knew that the situation could only get worse. He was particularly concerned about what the Japanese would do the next day. Wednesday, April 29, was Emperor Hirohito's birthday. Would that be the day of the invasion?

Skinny consulted Stu Wood, his G-2, who had been military attaché at the American Embassy in Tokyo before the war.

"What do you think is going to happen in the morning?" Wainwright asked.

"General," Wood said, "on the emperor's birthday all hell's gonna break loose."

He was right. All hell did break loose and it lasted for a solid week.

CHAPTER 12

"Goodbye, Mr. President"

THE EMPEROR'S BIRTHDAY brought Corregidor the most savage bombardment anyone had ever experienced. It began at 7:25 on the morning of April 29. Bombers took aim on the south dock and the entrances to Malinta Tunnel. Then the Japanese artillery on Bataan opened up and it too focused on the tunnel entrances.

Homma had decided to try to destroy the huge tunnel complex. Failing that, he would pound it so heavily that its inhabitants would become demoralized. His strategy did not work, but life inside the tunnel was a living hell. The rock and concrete walls vibrated so wildly that day that bottles stored on shelves crashed to the floor. Men trying to shave found the mirror dancing crazily in front of them.

Smoke pouring into the tunnel made everyone's eyes fill with tears. Soon it was hard to breathe. Thick dust settled everywhere so that the nurses and their patients had to wear wet gauze over their faces. People near the tunnel entrances were knocked off their feet by wave after wave of concussions.

On it went throughout the morning as the Japanese dropped over 100 tons of bombs and lobbed more than 10,000 shells on the tiny island. The few guns left intact on Corregidor returned the fire. Wainwright had ordered them to "fire like hell!"

Wainwright, his chief of staff Lew Beebe, and the other members of the staff sat quietly at their desks in the headquarters lateral, the floor shaking and moving beneath their feet. They were waiting for noon, the moment when Stu Wood had predicted that the Japanese would stop their attack to pay homage to the emperor.

"The silence will occur so suddenly," Wood told Skinny, "that it will hurt your ears."

Wainwright fiddled with an alarm clock Wood kept on his desk. He was always fascinated by mechanical gadgets and seemed greatly interested in the clock. Slowly the hands moved toward noon. As the second hand ticked off the remaining time, Skinny counted them aloud.

"Four . . . three . . . two . . . one."

Suddenly there was stunning silence. Everything was still. After more than four hours of crashing, booming noise, the quiet was overwhelming.

Wainwright looked at Stu Wood and grinned.

"Certainly dramatic, young fella," he said.

Years later Wood said that he had made a lucky guess. When he was military attaché in Tokyo before the war, "the emperor's birthday was an occasion of great celebration including plenty of beer and sake in the bars, so I suppose I figured it would carry over in combat."*

The silence ended all too quickly. Enemy shells and bombs poured anew on the Rock and by the afternoon there were fires all over the island. Ammunition dumps were ablaze and even the grass and undergrowth were burning. From Manila, thirty miles away, Corregidor seemed to have disappeared in a cloud of smoke and dust that rose high enough to obscure the sun. All afternoon ammunition from two dumps that had been hit continued to explode, showering the defenders with deadly steel fragments. All outdoor structures on Malinta Hill were flattened, including observation posts, the power plant for one of the searchlights, and an antiaircraft gun.

Drawn by curiosity about the effects of this massive assault, Nurse Redmond risked a quick look from the west end of the tunnel. "Trees were down," she said, "the roads were almost hidden under

---

*Wood had found himself in the Philippines by accident. While assigned to the American Embassy in Tokyo, he went to the nearest American military hospital, in Manila, for minor surgery, and was recuperating in the town of Baguio when war broke out. Had he been in Tokyo at the time, he would have been repatriated on the Swedish liner *Gripsholm*, with the rest of the embassy staff.

the debris, and there were great gaping craters in the earth. The air was heavy with dust and ground particles of wreckage swirling around in gradually diminishing arcs."

The assault continued until after nightfall, when the grim task of collecting the dead and wounded had to be performed by the ghostly flickering light of the dying fires. A massive sigh of relief was heaved when it was over, and people were sure they had survived the worst the enemy was capable of delivering. They were wrong. This was only the beginning.

While Wainwright sweated out the bombardment on April 29, Homma celebrated the emperor's birthday with an elaborate entrance into Manila. After a lavish parade and other festivities, punctuated by the sounds of explosions thirty miles across the water, Homma announced his plans to a group of Japanese and Filipino reporters.

He was going south to Mindanao to take charge of the fighting. As for Corregidor, he repeated his favorite line: "Time will settle everything." Homma wanted Wainwright to believe that the Japanese would not invade any time soon, that they were content to wait and starve him out. But Wainwright did not believe it. He knew Homma would invade, and soon.

Homma left Manila that afternoon but he did not go to Mindanao. Instead, he returned to his headquarters at Balanga to issue the invasion plans to his commanders and to observe the first day of amphibious training for his troops. His plan was simple, to take into account his shortage of landing craft. Only 2,000 troops could be put ashore at a time.

The first wave would land along the narrow, twisting tail of Corregidor at 11:00 P.M., an hour before the moon rose. They would be joined by another battalion at 4:00 A.M. The second major landing would take place at 11:00 P.M. the following night on the beaches below Topside and the two forces would link up in the Middleside area. The date was set for May 5, time enough for Homma's bombers and artillery to neutralize all of Corregidor's big guns, particularly the giant mortars of batteries Geary and Way. He did not want to send defenseless landing barges into the bay as long as those weapons were intact.

Homma had six more days to wait and to train and to rain fire and death on the defenders of Corregidor.

Wainwright was in the tunnel when a message arrived from MacArthur's headquarters in Australia. Finally he was getting something he had asked for, a means of escape for some of the people on the Rock. On April 17 Wainwright had requested that a navy seaplane bring medicines to Corregidor and take out some of the personnel. He wanted to evacuate the nurses, the few remaining civilian women, and some older American officers whom he believed could not stand the strain of the long captivity he knew awaited them all.

On April 29 Wainwright learned that two seaplanes, navy PBYs, would be sent. Together they could take about fifty passengers, a pitifully small number, but Wainwright was grateful for it. This might well be his last opportunity to get anyone out.

MacArthur had sent Wainwright a list of people he wanted. It included Stu Wood, whose knowledge of the Japanese people and language would be valuable for the long Pacific war he foresaw, and several highly trained cryptographers. The choice of the remainder of the lucky passengers was Skinny's. This decision could literally mean the difference between life and death.

Wainwright selected the civilian women, six old or ailing officers, and army pilot Bill Bradford, who had made a number of trips from Mindanao to Corregidor in a slow, lumbering, antique single-engine plane, bringing in medical supplies and taking out a few passengers each time. Major Bradford had crashed his high-wing Bellanca on take-off a few nights before at Kindley Field.

This left room for only thirty of the 150 nurses, to be chosen by the chief of nurses, Capt. Maud Davison. By six o'clock that evening she had made her decision and ordered the fortunate thirty to report to the mess hall.

Juanita Redmond was among them and she, like her colleagues, was torn between elation and sadness. Happy to be leaving the hellhole the tunnel had become, they also bore the guilt of feeling that they were deserting their post. They were sad at having to leave good friends with whom they had endured so much. A few asked to stay but Captain Davison turned them down. They were told to pack a musette bag and be ready to leave by 9:30.

That evening, while waiting for the seaplanes to arrive, Wainwright hosted a quiet party for his G-2, Stu Wood. He dug into his small supply of liquor, inherited from MacArthur, so that he and Wood could have a drink together. Wood, like the others who were leaving, had mixed feelings. Skinny knew how he felt and did his best to persuade the young man that his departure was for the good of the war effort.

"Stuart," Wainwright said, "you can do a lot more good down there. They need you more than here. Do your best."

Then Skinny got out his treasured handgun, the 1873 Colt Peacemaker he had carried since his graduation from West Point in 1906. He wanted MacArthur to have it, "as a token of my admiration and esteem, and in appreciation of our close personal relationship." Wainwright handed the gun to Stu Wood.

"Guard this with your life," Skinny said, "and give it to General MacArthur."

A little after 11:00 P.M. the two navy planes arrived. The sky was clear and as the planes glided in to land south of Corregidor the crews of several small naval vessels gunned their motors, from which the mufflers had been removed. Wainwright had ordered this as a cover. The racket could be heard over the entire bay and the planes came in undetected.

A procession of vehicles, led by Wainwright in a battered Chevrolet, drove slowly down the hillside from the tunnel to the shambles of the south docks at Bottomside. As the party got into the boats that were to take them out to the waiting seaplanes, the final, sad goodbyes were said. Wainwright shook hands with the men and hugged the nurses. Juanita Redmond kissed him on the cheek.

"Thank you, General," she said.

Bill Bradford gripped Skinny's hand.

"Wish you were coming with us," he said.

"I couldn't," Skinny said. "I have been with my men from the start and if captured I will share their lot."

Stu Wood wondered if he would ever see the Old Man again. He did, and it was a lot sooner than either of them expected.

Wainwright remained on the dock, watching through binoculars, as the passengers transferred from the small boats to the planes. He stayed there until both planes had taken off. As they disappeared in the darkness he offered a silent prayer for the men and women aboard, hoping that they would make it safely to Australia.

Only one of the planes got through. Stu Wood's plane struck a rock during a refueling stop on Lake Lanao in Mindanao and the passengers were stranded. Expecting to be captured, Wood wrapped Wainwright's Colt .45 in oil-soaked burlap and wax paper and hid it in the bole of a tree, carefully marking its location. After the war the gun was retrieved, but because of a series of administrative snafus it was never returned to Wainwright. Today it is part of the Wainwright exhibit at the West Point Museum, where "an etching of rust bears sad testimony to three years of erosion on a jungle island."*

The first few days of May brought a continuation of the savage Japanese bombardment of Corregidor. Casualties increased and many of the men began to crack. "The strain is beginning to tell," a coast artillery officer told Wainwright. For the first time cases diagnosed as shell shock and battle fatigue were admitted to the hospital.

Homma had ordered his gunners and pilots to crush and exterminate the island's defenders. On May 1 the shelling began before dawn and did not cease until midnight. In mid-afternoon the planes came over for the 274th bombing raid on Corregidor. They flew over three more times that afternoon; the entrances to Malinta Tunnel were the targets.

The pattern of shellfire that day revealed to Wainwright part of Homma's invasion plans. The tail of the island was struck repeatedly, along with James Ravine, which provided a path from the beaches to Topside. There were no installations in those two areas worth shelling, so Wainwright concluded that the Japanese were softening them up because they were the invasion sites.

The day dragged on, stressful, deadly, and discouraging. A staff officer returning to the tunnel that night found it gloomy as a morgue. No one saw any relief from the bombardment nor any hope of help.

Through it all the commander kept his characteristic sense of humor and his personal interest in those under his command. On May 1 he issued what the *Saturday Evening Post* later called the "most humane and considerate army orders ever given by any general."

Wainwright was concerned about the pay, allotment, and insurance records of his men, including those captured on Bataan. He wanted to be sure that proper benefits continued to be paid to families and survivors. That afternoon he ordered the radio facilities to be cleared so that the army could transmit names and serial numbers of some 30,000 men to Washington.

Later he learned that a submarine was expected to call at Corregidor in two days. He ordered his finance officer, Jack Vance,

---

*Wood also carried with him from Corregidor an Elgin watch belonging to navy captain Ken Hoeffel, who had asked him to give it to his wife. Wood kept the watch with him and returned it to Hoeffel in prison camp. "Hoeffel had worn it almost twenty-five years; he wore it twenty-five more."

to prepare the financial records for shipment—eighteen trunk lockers full.

Vance thought he saw a chance to get another finance officer, Royal Jenks, who was old and ill, to safety. Vance had tried to get Jenks off Corregidor before, but without success. He went to see Wainwright to suggest that a senior officer who was familiar with the financial records, and understood their value, should be sent on the submarine with them. Thus, the officer would be able to ensure that they reached the appropriate office in Washington.

Wainwright nodded his agreement and grinned.

"By God, Jack," he said, "*you're* not going! You're going to stay here with us."

The second day of May was worse than the first. Wainwright wrote in his official report to George Marshall that "Corregidor and the other Fortified Islands subjected to continuous shell fire, the heaviest concentration yet experienced by Corregidor. . . . During a five-hour period, twelve 240mm shells had fallen per minute for a total of 3,600 hits in the Geary-Crockett area at Topside."

Wainwright and George Moore calculated that enough shells had fallen in that five-hour period—one shell every five seconds—to fill 600 trucks. The entire day's bombardment lasted from 7:30 in the morning until almost 8:00 that night, with only a few lulls.

Again the Japanese concentrated on the north side of the island, where they expected to invade, and on the heavy mortar batteries. And on this day they finally destroyed battery Geary. Early in the morning gunners observed that the enemy artillery fire was slowly creeping along the streetcar tracks that led to battery Geary. "At the rate it was moving," Jack Vance wrote, "it would reach Geary early in the afternoon. And that was just the way it happened."

Enemy shells penetrated the center magazine, where 1,600 powder charges, each weighing sixty-two pounds, were stored. The blast was earsplitting. The island shook as if in the throes of an earthquake, and even in the deepest recesses of Malinta Tunnel people knew that something disastrous had happened. The entire battery was demolished. The ten-ton barrels of the mortars were tossed in the air as though they were weightless. One landed 150 yards away and another was blown through a three-foot-thick reinforced concrete wall. A six-ton slab of concrete was hurled a thousand yards away, where it sliced through a four-foot-thick tree. Twenty-seven men were killed and many more injured.

Homma had now accomplished his mission; he had eliminated the threat of the mortars to his landing craft. Before the day was over his gunners had destroyed all eight mortars in battery Geary and had effectively reduced the mortars in battery Way to one.

By evening the tail of the island was invisible to Wainwright and the other men watching with him from Topside. Only smoke and dust could be seen, dotted by the flames of many small fires. Anything that could still burn flared up, even scarred stumps of trees. The exhausted and shaken men of the beach defense had to double as fire fighters.

As the island continued to reel under one disastrous explosion after another, Wainwright's staffers were urging him to leave Corregidor and set up a new headquarters in Mindanao to the south. Lew Beebe and George Moore, as well as Skinny's senior aide, Johnny Pugh, told Wainwright what he already knew: Corregidor could not hold out much longer. They pointed out that when it inevitably came time to capitulate, the Japanese would force him to surrender the entire Philippines, his whole command, not just the fortified islands in Manila Bay. In that event, the American and Filipino units in the southern islands and in northern Luzon, who had so far avoided capture, would have to surrender as well, instead of hiding in the mountains to operate as guerrilla forces. If Moore were left in charge on Corregidor, the Japanese could demand of him only the surrender of the Manila Bay islands, the extent of his harbor defense command.

The argument put to Wainwright was prophetic. Just four days later he would be made to surrender the entire Philippines command. Although it might have been better had he left, Skinny would not budge. In truth, he could not leave Corregidor without specific orders to do so. It would have been a clear act of desertion.

"This was General MacArthur's headquarters," Wainwright told his staff, "and this is where I will stay."

Lew Beebe decided to take matters into his own hands. He contacted Dick Sutherland, MacArthur's chief of staff, to see if MacArthur would order Wainwright out.

"I am sending this unofficially," Beebe wrote, "to give you off the record information which I believe should be in your possession." He painted a pessimistic but accurate picture of the situation on Corregidor and noted that Mindanao and the other southern islands would soon be in Japanese hands. Then he brought up the matter of Wainwright.

"As the situation is now developing there remains very little that can be accomplished by the staff of the USFIP. General Moore will be in command of the fortified islands and there will be no duties for this staff to perform which could not be handled by other officers. It is therefore my considered opinion that General Wainwright, with as many of his staff as can be accommodated, should be evacuated to Australia where they can be of further service to the government. . . . since it is likely that American prisoners will be held for the duration of the war, I feel that the interests of the government would be served best if this staff were moved to Australia."

For some reason, Beebe did not mention the most persuasive argument for Wainwright's evacuation: that as commander of all U.S. forces in the Philippines he would be forced to surrender more than just Corregidor. Instead, Beebe based his plea on Wainwright's experience in fighting the Japanese.

"I am sending this," Beebe continued, "because General Wainwright believes he should go down with the ship. However I do not believe that he should be permitted to fall into the hands of the Japs. His experience and knowledge of Jap tactics are too valuable to the government to be lost. . . . I do know from various conversations that he expects to remain here to the end, and surrender himself with the troops if the necessity arises. Since he is a soldier, he will move only if he is ordered to do so. It is my fixed belief that he should be ordered to move with such members of his staff as can be accommodated, in the near future."

Twenty-four hours would pass before Beebe would receive a reply to his suggestion.

The Japanese attack went on and Wainwright recorded in his official USFIP report for May 3 that "Corregidor experienced its two hundred and eighty-seventh bombing since the beginning of the war." By now there was no more antiaircraft fire from the Rock; all the guns had been destroyed. Shells and bombs pounded and blasted the island throughout the day and casualties mounted among the artillerymen and the beach defense troops. There were few places intact in which they could take shelter.

In his headquarters, Wainwright bent low over his desk writing out a message for MacArthur. Beebe had shown him his message to Sutherland of the previous day, and Skinny was concerned about how it might be received. He told MacArthur that it was "prepared without my knowledge or consent. It was shown to me prior to its dispatch but I neither authorized nor prohibited its dispatch. The conditions he predicts have actually occurred."

Wainwright reported to MacArthur on additional Japanese encroachments in the southern islands and described the current conditions on Corregidor. "Situation here is fast becoming desperate. . . . The island is practically denuded of vegetation and trees leaving no cover and all structures are leveled to the ground. Communications and utilities are almost impossible of maintenance. Casualties since April 9 approximate 600."

In a final reference to Beebe's message, Wainwright said, "whatever your decision may be it will be fully and cheerfully carried out."

Later that afternoon Beebe received a reply from Sutherland. It was emphatically negative on the question of evacuating Wainwright and the USFIP staff. MacArthur and Sutherland were still smarting over Marshall's decision to place Wainwright in command of USFIP, overruling MacArthur's plan to retain command of the Philippines from Australia. They still believed that Wainwright and Beebe had double-crossed them.

"General Wainwright was assigned to his command by the War Department," Sutherland told Beebe, "and General MacArthur has no repeat no authority to relieve him therefrom."

As to the evacuation of Beebe and the USFIP staff, Sutherland wrote that he and MacArthur had hoped that Wainwright would have chosen to send out Beebe and the others. "We still hope that such may be the case. Best regards."

MacArthur had never hesitated to ask by name for individuals he wanted transferred to his command in Australia—Carlos Romulo, Stu Wood, and the cryptographers were a few—but now he was leaving all such decisions to Wainwright.

The question of who was to leave and who was to stay would soon be only a mental exercise, because the night of May 3 was the last chance for anyone to leave Corregidor. The submarine U.S.S. *Spearfish* lay submerged on the edge of the minefield at the entrance to Manila Bay. Wainwright had arranged for it to stop on its way back to Australia from a patrol, to pick up as many passengers and records as it could cram aboard.

That afternoon Wainwright again had to make the life-and-death decision about which of his people to evacuate. The sub could take twenty-five passengers, and Wainwright chose thirteen nurses and twelve army and navy officers.

This was the first time any American submarine would have so many women aboard for such a long voyage; their presence would create problems for the skipper, Lt. James C. Dempsey. Everyone adapted well to the cramped quarters, however, and the story of the voyage became the basis for the movie *Operation Petticoat*, starring Cary Grant.

Not everyone Wainwright selected agreed to go. One senior nurse refused, as did Johnny Pugh. Wainwright had told Pugh of his choice just a few hours before departure. He planned to promote Pugh to colonel and give him the responsibility of carrying the headquarters records to the War Department in Washington. Pugh refused both the promotion and the chance to leave, saying that he was too young for the rank and that it was his duty to stay with Wainwright. This was a courageous decision and reflected Pugh's loyalty to the man he had served since 1938.

The men Wainwright was sending out had valuable experience, knowledge, and records that the War Department could ill afford to lose. One of those going was Pete Irwin, ordered off Corregidor not only because of his experience, but also because of a severe case of stomach ulcers. He would not have lasted long in a Japanese prison camp.

Wainwright talked to Irwin that evening about a growing worry: How would MacArthur and the American people react to the surrender of the Philippines? What would they think of him? Skinny told Irwin to go straight to General Marshall in Washington to try to make him understand how hopeless the situation was on Corregidor and why he, Wainwright, would probably have to surrender.

Irwin assured Skinny that everyone would "understand the necessity of his actions," but Wainwright was not convinced. He would not believe it until three and a half years later when he was finally released from imprisonment.

Despite his uncertainty about his place in history at this moment, Wainwright maintained his concern for the men who would go down with him. He gave Irwin a roster of the Corregidor garrison as of May 3, plus a list of all those whom he had recently promoted. Had Wainwright not sent out that information for the War Department, the dependents would not have received their higher allotments.

Now Wainwright had done everything he could for his men except one thing—to save them from captivity. That, to his regret, was beyond his power. But he could still fight, delaying the inevitable a little longer. As he was bidding goodbye to the last submarine passengers, he said, "They will have to come take us. They will never get this place any other way."

*   *   *

On the next day, May 4, the Japanese artillery bombardment was so severe that the rapid fire sounded, Wainwright said, "like a continuous drum-fire of bursting shells." In twenty-four hours some 16,000 shells exploded on the island, churning up the debris and wreckage that was all that remained outside the tunnel. There was nothing left to destroy on Corregidor except morale, and finally that too shattered for many men on that long, hideous day.

"The troops began to crack," wrote Jack Vance. Wainwright heard about it from his staff and saw it for himself as he made his rounds. Many of the soldiers had reached the limit of their endurance and their behavior made a bad situation worse. Some of the men hid out, away from their assigned positions, and officers had to chase them from the tunnel or from caves and crevices and force them back into the line.

There were self-inflicted wounds and more than a few suicides. Exhausted men smashed the stocks of their rifles and walked away in a daze, oblivious to the shells bursting around them. Beach defense troops developed a hatred of the "tunnel rats" and turned bitter over their lot. "Almost everyone was overwhelmed by the psychosis of doom." What was the point of sticking it out any longer? They were finished and they knew it.

Life in the tunnel was made more unbearable by the presence of several thousand Filipino civilian laborers who had been living on the island. Now they crowded into the main tunnel, jamming the entrances, and refused to move. "They relieved themselves where they stood. For food they were issued canned goods, and the empty and dirty containers were added to the human filth on the pavement. Dirty clothing was discarded on the spot. Several dead lay on stretchers at the end of the hospital section, awaiting a lull in the bombardment for burial."

The tunnel lights failed several times a day, sometimes for as long as a half hour. Water was in such short supply that no one was allowed to bathe. Drinking water was issued only a few times a day.

All across the island, all day long, the shells continued to fall and enemy planes flew back and forth almost leisurely releasing their bombs. Then came the word Wainwright had been expecting. That afternoon observers spotted fifteen landing barges off the coast of Bataan. It would not be long, he knew, before they headed for Corregidor.

A clerk brought Wainwright a message from General Marshall: "Please give me direct your very frank estimate of the situation.

Start your message 'To be seen only by decoding clerk and General Marshall.'"

Wainwright hunched over his desk and wet his pencil with his tongue. Slowly he wrote out his reply.

"Hostile Air Corps has been bombing Corregidor relentlessly since March 24. Following fall of Bataan on 9 April enemy immediately replaced artillery on south shore of peninsula and has since then subjected our defenses to artillery fire. Beginning 29 April (Emperor's Birthday) the fire of hostile artillery increased in intensity and has continued at that tempo to present date. The hostile bombing has been relatively ineffective but artillery fire from large caliber guns (240 mm) has resulted in destruction of large percentage of coast defense and beach defense artillery and small arms. Continual bombardment has resulted in about 600 casualties since April 9, and has lowered morale of troops. Morale difficult to maintain at best because troops have been constantly under or subject to air or artillery attack since December 29 and have been receiving half of poorly balanced ration since January 8. However, morale amazingly good considering conditions under which troops are now operating. Persistent reports from our operatives indicate that enemy is planning to launch an assault against Corregidor. He has prepared a large number of motor boats on which weapons are mounted, and has also constructed a large number of smaller boats to be used in transporting troops. I have nothing on which to base an estimate of present hostile troops strength on Luzon. However, enemy has recently taken Cebu and Panay, using about ten thousand men in each operation, and is now engaged in attack on Mindanao. I estimate that at least ten thousand are now engaged in operations on Mindanao.

"Unless troops have been withdrawn from the Philippines I believe that a sufficient force remains on Luzon to undertake an operation against Corregidor. Enemy forces will soon be in possession of all important areas bordering on coast of Mindanao and our troops will be confined to mountains. Thereafter enemy can clean up Visayan islands and Mindanao at leisure. In my opinion the enemy is capable of making an assault on Corregidor at any time. The success or failure of such an assault will depend entirely on steadfastness of beach defense troops. With morale at present level I estimate that we have something less than an even chance to beat off an assault.

"In accordance with your request I have given you a very frank and honest opinion as to the situation here as I see it."

Wainwright decided it was time to issue the final orders to his garrison, to initiate the measures that would signal the end. All code books and secret files were to be destroyed. The Japanese must not find anything of value when they reached Malinta Tunnel.

From his headquarters in Melbourne, Australia, MacArthur dispatched a gloomy message to the War Department.

"You must be prepared for the collapse shortly of the Harbor Defenses in Manila Bay. The generally optimistic tone of reports from there do not repeat not reflect an accurate military estimate of the situation. The occupation of Bataan definitely condemned these fortresses and enemy guns of large caliber located there are rapidly destroying our fixed fortifications. Personnel losses have not been great aggregating about six hundred since April ninth of which approximately two thirds are wounded. It is apparent to me however that morale is rapidly sinking and the end is clearly in sight."

"By May 5," wrote a staff officer, "Corregidor was broken and blasted; the lovely green-capped hills now lay bare and naked, the earth scourged and flayed and ulcered." But there was no letup in the brutal pounding. It started at 4:30 A.M. and lasted throughout the day, with only a few short interruptions. Waves of planes bombed the island again and again. At 2:47 that afternoon the Rock suffered its 300th air raid.

"There was a steady roar from Bataan," another officer recorded in his diary, "and a mightier volume on Corregidor. A continuous pall of dust and debris hung over everything. There was a feeling of doom mingled with wonder."

There was little answering fire from Corregidor. Almost all the guns, big and small, of the once impregnable fortress had been destroyed. The beach defense guns were gone, along with the searchlights, barbed-wire entanglements, and machine-gun emplacements. There were almost no beach defenses remaining on the north side of the island, the side closest to Bataan.

Communications facilities had been obliterated and the telephone lines were being torn up faster than they could be repaired. The only way for one unit to contact another was by runner, a suicidal job when shells were dropping every five seconds. By the afternoon of the 5th the dust and smoke were so thick that observers on Topside could barely see Bottomside and the tail of the island had disappeared.

In the afternoon Wainwright received a report by radio from one of his operatives behind the Japanese lines. The message contained discouraging but unsurprising news. The Japanese Fourth Division had completed its amphibious landing training on the coast of Bataan. Also, the Japanese had built a large number of bamboo ladders, just what they would need to scale the cliffs below Topside. Reading the report, it occurred to Wainwright that there would be a full moon all week. He had learned on Bataan that the Japanese preferred to attack by the light of a full moon. The invasion would come any night now, he knew—perhaps even tonight.

At his headquarters on Bataan, Homma watched the 2,000 troops of the first wave of his assault force board their landing barges. It was a little before 9:00 P.M. As he watched them sail out of the tiny harbor at Lamao he heard his artillery open up again in one mighty roar as they continued to pulverize the north beach landing areas. It was, Homma wrote, the third critical moment of his Philippines campaign.

In his cramped living quarters in Lateral 10 of Malinta Tunnel Wainwright suddenly straightened up in his chair when he heard the Japanese artillery. His face bore an uneasy expression and his voice was grim.

"I don't like the sound of that, Lew," he said to Beebe. "It isn't customary for the Japs to pound us so heavily at night. They can't observe their fire in the dark and they don't like to waste ammunition."

Wainwright fell silent and listened intently for a while; then he stood up.

"I don't like this at all," he said again. "I'm afraid we're in for it. This sounds to me just like artillery preparation before an attack. Come on. Let's go up and see what Moore thinks about it."

As Wainwright and Beebe were walking down the main tunnel to George Moore's harbor defense headquarters lateral by the east entrance, Homma's invasion plans began to go awry. Almost as soon as they had left Lamao, the Japanese troops found themselves in trouble. The barges of the second wave drifted to the right of the barges of the first wave. They were supposed to be on the other side. As a result, the second group did not land until a full hour after the first, a potentially disastrous delay.

Then, as the small flotilla got out into the bay, they realized that the tide, which flowed to the west near the Bataan coast, was moving eastward in deeper water. The barges were being forced more and more off course. Each yard of drift to the east took them farther from their assigned invasion sites.

Moore got up from behind his desk when Wainwright and Beebe entered the office.

"George," Skinny said abruptly, "what do you make of this shelling?"

"It doesn't sound good to me," Moore replied. "I have already phoned to the beach defenses and I was told that the Japs are shelling all of the coves on the northern side of the island."

"Well," Wainwright said, "what does that mean to you—if anything?"

"I'm afraid that I think just what you are thinking. It looks like the Japs are getting ready for an attack at some time during the night."

Wainwright sighed and sat down in a chair facing Moore's desk.

"I knew that's what you would think," he said with a grin, "but I had to hear you say it."

Wainwright lit a cigarette, took a few puffs, and said, "What steps are you taking to meet it?"

For the next half hour they discussed the few options open to them and the defense measures the garrison could take.

"I guess we can do nothing but wait for developments," Wainwright concluded. "We are as ready as we'll ever be. But it's hard to sit here and wait."

They did not have long to wait.

By 10:30 P.M. the landing barges were in sight of Corregidor. Shells continued to strike the north shore of the island. At 10:40 the artillery switched to white phosphorous shells that burned the earth with their eerie silver glow. Suddenly the barrage shifted from the tail of the island to Malinta Hill, giving the U.S. Marine Corps regiment on the beaches a chance to raise their heads and scan the dark waters of the bay.

Aboard the barges there was confusion as Japanese commanders sensed that they were lost. They did not see the landmarks they had expected. They were approaching the wrong beaches. Swept by the tide, they were heading for landing sites thousands of yards east, much farther from Malinta Tunnel, which they were supposed to reach by daylight.

At 11:10 the boats were spotted heading toward the shore. "Here they come!" someone yelled, and the marines opened up with rifles, machine guns, and other small arms, everything they had.

A USFIP staff officer rushed into Moore's lateral to announce the battle.

"The Japs are making a landing on the tail of the island," he said.

Wainwright dashed off a brief message for General Marshall: "Landing attack on Corregidor in progress. Enemy landed North Point. Further details as the situation develops."

Wainwright followed the battle closely through the fragmentary messages that came in to Moore's command post, either by runner or by one of the few telephones still in operation. There was nothing else for the Old Man to do. It was all up to his troops on the beaches.

The marines were slaughtering the Japanese invaders. There was no other word for the strength and fearlessness of their defense. The sea ran red with blood. A Japanese observer said that it was a "spectacle that confounded the imagination, surpassing in grim horror anything we had ever seen before." Another called it a "dreadful massacre." The enemy suffered seventy percent casualties while still in the water. Every Japanese unit lost at least half its men. One report estimated that only 800 of the 2,000 who had left Bataan got ashore on Corregidor. But the survivors *were* ashore and slowly, doggedly, they regrouped and began to move eastward toward Malinta Hill.

The tension was heavy in the harbor defense lateral as reports filtered in to Wainwright from the beaches. By midnight it was clear that the enemy was making progress, despite the determined resistance of the American and Filipino troops. Reserve units from all parts of the island were being sent into battle, but they were unable to push the enemy back.

Shortly after midnight Jack Vance went to the command post. As finance officer, he had more than two million Philippines pesos and he wanted to know if the situation was serious enough to warrant destroying it. Wainwright and Moore were deep in conversation, so Vance approached Lew Beebe with his question.

"What do you think?" Beebe asked Moore.

"They have started to land," Moore told Vance. "They wouldn't attempt it if they did not have sufficient force to succeed."

No one spoke for a moment and Vance's question remained unanswered. It would take several hours to dispose of the currency, he explained, so perhaps he should get started. Beebe agreed.

In Washington, Wainwright's announcement that Corregidor had been invaded was on everyone's mind. They expected the island to fall within a few hours and agreed that some message must be sent to Wainwright in the president's name. George Marshall asked Ike to write it.*

Wainwright received the message at 2:30 A.M. in the clear, uncoded. When the radio operator on Corregidor took it down he had to write it on a piece of ordinary lined paper. He had run out of official message forms. Wainwright was deeply moved by the words and he managed to keep the paper throughout his years of imprisonment.

"During recent weeks, we have been following with growing admiration the day by day accounts of your heroic stand against the mounting intensity of bombardment by enemy planes and heavy siege guns. In spite of all the handicaps of complete isolation, lack of food and ammunition, you have given the world a shining example of patriotic fortitude and self-sacrifice. The American people ask no finer example of tenacity, resourcefulness, and steadfast courage. The calm determination of your personal leadership in a desperate situation sets a standard of duty for our soldiers throughout the world. In every camp and on every naval vessel, soldiers, sailors and marines are inspired by the gallant struggle of their comrades in the Philippines. The workmen in our shipyards and munitions plants redouble their efforts because of your example. You and your devoted followers have become the living symbols of our war aims and the guarantee of victory."

The message was signed "Franklin D. Roosevelt."

Victory seemed a long way off to the people in Malinta Tunnel. Before Wainwright could draft a reply to the president, more discouraging reports of the fighting reached him. The Japanese had reached battery Denver, no more than one mile east of the tunnel. More reserves were being committed to the battle, including gunners from the coastal and antiaircraft batteries.

One large unit of reserves was drawn from Topside. To reach the battlefield they had to cross an open stretch of 200 yards through artillery fire and pass through Malinta Tunnel from west to east. The group lost twenty percent of its men before it got into the tunnel. There were few reserves left.

Wainwright knew they had only hours now, so he phoned Jack Vance and told him to destroy the currency and coins. "We did not waste any words," Vance said. "General Wainwright was in full

* Ike later recorded in his diary: "Corregidor surrendered last night. Poor Wainwright! He did the fighting in the Philippine Islands, another got such glory as the public could find in the operation."

control. Mentally each of us was aware of the inevitable. If this Jap landing was beaten off, we were still a beleaguered garrison that would soon run out of food." They would have no need of the money.

Then Skinny returned to his lateral and took a moment to reply to President Roosevelt's message.

"For the President of the United States. Your gracious and generous message of May 4 has just reached me. I am without words to express to you Mr. President my gratitude for and deep appreciation of your great kindness. We have all done our best to carry out your former instructions and keep our flag flying here as long as humanly possible to do so. At 10:30 P.M. May 5 the enemy effected a landing here following such terrific air and artillery bombardment of the beaches during the past seven days that the beach defense organization was completely obliterated and a great many weapons were destroyed. As I write this at 3:30 A.M. our patrols are attempting to locate the enemy positions and flanks and I will counter attack at dawn to drive him into the sea or destroy him. Thank you again, Mr. President, for your wonderful message which I will publish to my entire command."

Both generals, Wainwright and Homma, were in what the latter referred to as an "agony of mind" during that long night, and for similar reasons. They did not know exactly what was happening on the battlefield. Neither could get a clear picture of the situation and each feared he was losing the fight.

Homma had good reasons for his pessimism. Up to two-thirds of his landing craft had been destroyed. He had only twenty-one barges to resupply the troops already ashore and to launch the second night's invasion. He was unsure about where his men were, though he did know they were a good distance from Malinta Hill. The timetable called for the occupation of the hill by dawn, less than an hour away. It seemed certain that they would not make it. Without control of Malinta Hill, Homma might have to postpone his second landing.

In addition, Homma's troops on Corregidor were running short of ammunition and attempts to replenish their supply had failed. The staff reported that the invasion force would be out of ammunition by 11:00 in the morning, just over six hours away. "When I recall all this," a Japanese officer said, "I cannot but break into a cold sweat."

Homma became convinced that his attack force would be wiped

out, ending his career. He would be sent home in disgrace. "I had plenty of troops on this side of the sea," he recorded, but he could not send reinforcements with the few boats he had left. When he learned that the Americans had launched a counterattack at battery Denver, Homma fell into a state of depression. "My God," he said, "I have failed miserably on the assault."

"Dawn broke upon the wreckage of a fort. On Corregidor not a stick was standing; the beaten earth was pulverized, and grim-faced, bearded men, bleeding from their wounds, crept from crater to crater.

"Exactly what happened that night and early morning on the shell-shattered eastern slopes of Corregidor will never be known in full detail, for most of the men who could tell are dead. And even those who lived saw only segments of action; the fighting was inchoate, wild, vicious."

The American counterattack had been checked and there were no more reserves to send in. Wainwright had no more options, no more choices, and very little time. He would have to decide soon whether it made any sense to continue the fighting, to spend more lives to buy a few hours or days more.

At 4:00 in the morning he had received a final message from General Marshall: "Never has so much been done with so little. The nation will be forever grateful."

Casualties had been heavy during the night and many wounded men had been left out on the line to die. There were no more stretcher bearers and it was impossible to get the wounded to the hospital through the heavy enemy fire. Many injured men tried to reach the tunnel on their own, but very few of them made it. As many as 800 had already been killed; the wounded were thought to number up to 1,000.

Japanese bombers flew over the island as soon as it grew light, and a fresh avalanche of shells descended over the American-held portion of the island. Steve Mellnik, one of General Moore's officers, wrote that conditions in the tunnel were frightful. "The floor heaved; bursting shells played a tattoo. . . . Many lights went out in a shower of sparks; only two remained to illuminate the smoke-filled tube. Then a giant hammer pounded the roof over our heads.

"About ten o'clock a particularly violent explosion shook Malinta Hill; I thought the hill would collapse on us! Waves of almost solid sound reverberated through the tunnel and made the top of my head flutter. Dust rose; pieces of concrete dropped from the ceiling."

At the same time, Wainwright received dire news: the Japanese had put tanks ashore. He had no antitank weapons whatsoever. He was powerless to stop them. The image of the massacre that could result from a tank firing down the length of the tunnel formed in his mind; it was unthinkable. Wainwright could wait no longer. He paced the narrow aisle between the desks for a few moments, and then stopped and looked at Beebe.

"Lew," he said, "this thing has got to be stopped during daylight hours. We are going to have to surrender sooner or later and we might as well face the facts now. We might hold on two or three days longer but what good would it do? The Japs are working around both sides of the east entrance to the tunnel right now. If they break into this tunnel there will be all hell to pay and no pitch hot. There are more than a hundred nurses in the hospital and over a thousand patients . . . and I hate to think of what would happen if the Japs ever got in this place. What do you think about it?"

"I believe we should send a flag of truce through the lines right now," Beebe said. "We must do it today or wait until tomorrow morning. We couldn't get a flag through the lines during the hours of darkness . . . Tomorrow would be too late. The Japs would have the tunnel by that time."

"Right," Wainwright said. "Send for George Moore."

It took Moore only a few minutes to reach the headquarters lateral. As soon as he walked in, Wainwright said, "Should we surrender now or wait?"

Moore did not hesitate.

"There should be no delay," he said.

The matter was decided.

Wainwright was calm as he gave Beebe and Moore instructions on the surrender procedure. He ordered Beebe to broadcast the surrender message that had already been prepared. Skinny's communications officer, Col. Theodore "Tiger" Teague, had kept the message taped to his chest for the last few days.

"Tell the Nips that we'll cease firing at noon," Wainwright said.

Then he instructed Moore to initiate Plan Pontiac, the destruction of all weapons greater than .45 caliber. The arms were to be destroyed by noon and precisely at that hour the American flag would be lowered and a white flag run up in its place.

Wainwright called in the quartermaster, Brig. Gen. Charlie

Drake, and several other senior officers. He told them about the surrender and the measures for its implementation.

"I'm surrendering on account of the nurses and the wounded," Wainwright said. "If it gets dark, it'll be nothing but a holocaust."

No one protested or expressed surprise and all agreed that it was the only thing to do.

Wainwright ushered them out and went back to his desk. He pulled out a piece of paper and quickly started writing. There were several last-minute messages he had to prepare, farewells to President Roosevelt and to MacArthur, and a brazen attempt to restrict the number of troops he would have to surrender, to salvage something from his capitulation.

While Wainwright prepared his radiograms, Lew Beebe was broadcasting over the Voice of Freedom transmitter.

"Message for General Homma. Message for General Homma or the present commander-in-chief of the Imperial Japanese forces on Luzon.

"Anyone receiving this message please transmit it to the commander-in-chief of the Imperial Japanese forces on Luzon.

"For military reasons which General Wainwright considers sufficient, and to put a stop to further sacrifice of human life, the commanding general will surrender to Your Excellency today the four fortified islands at the entrance to Manila Bay together with all military and naval personnel and all existing stores and equipment.

"At twelve noon, local daylight saving time, May 6, 1942, a white flag will be displayed in a prominent position in Corregidor, at which time all firing from the harbor forts will cease unless a landing by Japanese troops in force is attempted without flags of truce, in which case they will be taken under fire.

"If all of your firing and aerial bombardment has ceased at twelve noon, local time, the commanding general will send two staff officers by boat, flying a white flag, to the Cabcaben dock to meet a Japanese staff officer, whom the commanding general requests that Your Excellency have there, empowered to name the tim and place for the commanding general to meet Your Excellency in order that he may make the formal surrender and to arrange all details.

"Upon the return of his staff officers the commanding general will proceed by boat accompanied by some of his staff to such place as may be designated by Your Excellency. The commanding general's launch will fly a white flag and his party will consist of five or six persons. He requests that motor transportation meet his party at the landing point designated by you."

When Beebe finished speaking, a Hawaiian-born army sergeant who spoke Japanese repeated the message in that language.

Wainwright had devised a simple and straightforward plan for the details of the surrender, and everyone expected it to go off smoothly. To make sure that Homma received the message, Beebe repeated it three times, at 11:00, 11:45, and 12:30, in both English and Japanese. Unfortunately, Homma never heard it. Wainwright's attempt to arrange an orderly surrender to begin at noon turned into a debacle that was not concluded until midnight.

Wainwright finished his message for Bill Sharp, commander of all forces in the Visayan-Mindanao area far to the south. Although the Japanese had won much of the territory under General Sharp's command, he still had units intact that were ready to withdraw into the mountains and undertake guerrilla warfare. They expected to harass the enemy until MacArthur's forces could return to the Philippines.

Wainwright hoped that he would be able to save Sharp's troops. He did not want to have to surrender them along with the Corregidor forces. He radioed Sharp that he was releasing him from the USFIP command and he instructed Sharp to report to MacArthur for orders.

"I believe you will understand the motive behind this order," Wainwright said.

The surrender message Beebe was transmitting referred only to the islands in Manila Bay. If Wainwright could convince Homma that he no longer commanded the units beyond Manila Bay, he would not be held accountable for their surrender. Wainwright's gamble did not pay off and the attempt to release Sharp's forces from his command came close to wrecking the surrender negotiations.

Other messages, official and unofficial, were being sent from Corregidor that morning. Ken Hoeffel dispatched a final radio to the Navy Department. "Our few remaining ships being sunk," he said. "Now destroying all military equipment. 172 officers and 2126 men of the navy send last expression of loyalty and devotion to country, to families, and to friends. Going off the air."

Melvyn McCoy, the navy's communications officer, scribbled a few words on a piece of paper and handed it to his radioman. "Beam it for Radio Honolulu," he said, "and don't bother with code."

"Going off air now," the message read. "Goodbye and good luck."

An army radio operator, Corp. Irving Strobing of Brooklyn, New York, broadcast an official message: "Notify any and all vessels headed toward this area to return to their home ports."

Strobing had been on duty for thirty hours and was exhausted, but he couldn't relinquish his precious contact with the outside world. "I was afraid to let them go for even a second," he explained. "I had to keep sending."

And he did—a rambling, moving, and dramatic personal account of the last moments on Corregidor. His words brought America to tears when they were published in newspapers and magazines all over the country.

"They are not near yet," Strobing said. "We are waiting for God only knows what. How about a chocolate soda. Not many. Not near yet. Lots of heavy firing going on. We've only got about an hour twenty minutes before—We may have to give up about noon, we don't know yet. They are throwing men and shells at us and we may not be able to stand it. They have been shelling us faster than you can count—

"We've got about fifty-five minutes and I feel sick at my stomach. I am really low down. They are around now smashing rifles. They bring in the wounded every minute. We will be waiting for you guys to help. This is the only thing I guess can be done. General Wainwright is a right guy and we are willing to go on for him, but shells were dropping all night, faster than hell. Damage terrific. Too much for guys to take, enemy heavy cross shelling and bombing."

Wainwright had received no response to the surrender message and he was becoming worried. Beebe had broadcast it twice now. The shelling from Bataan continued without letup and the Japanese troops on Corregidor were advancing on Malinta Tunnel.

The order to execute Pontiac had gone out. Hardened marines, veterans of the First World War and of the "banana wars" in Latin America in the 1930s, wept openly when told about the surrender order. The adjutant of the Fourth Marines, ordered to burn the regimental colors, stood with tears streaming down his face. Col. Sam Howard, the commanding officer, said, "My God, and I had to be the first marine officer ever to surrender a regiment." And still the shells exploded and the fighting continued.

At his desk in Lateral 3 Wainwright wrote out the final sentences of his farewell to MacArthur.

"We have done our full duty for you and for our country. We are sad but unashamed. I have fought for you to the best of my ability from Lingayen Gulf to Bataan to Corregidor, always hoping relief was on the way. . . .

"Goodbye, General, my regards to you and our comrades in Australia. May God strengthen your arm to insure ultimate success of the cause for which we have fought side by side."

At the far end of the tunnel, Corporal Strobing continued to tap out his last message.

"Men here all feeling bad, because of terrific strain of the siege. Corregidor used to be a nice place. But it's haunted now—Can't think at all. I can hardly think. Say, I have sixty pesos you can have for this weekend. The jig's up. Everyone is bawling like a baby. They are piling dead and wounded in our tunnel. Arms weak from pounding key long hours, no rest, short rations, tired—"

The soldiers in the tunnel were confused and frightened. They knew that the surrender message had been broadcast three times, but Japanese artillery continued to pound the island. They had destroyed their weapons and they could hear the sounds of battle drawing closer to the east entrance of the tunnel. A few were openly bitter, but most were dazed, lacking the energy to be angry at their fate. Some went to sleep, others sat with their backs against the rough cement walls, staring vacantly into space.

The few men waiting near Lateral 3 saw Lew Beebe hurry down the main tunnel from the Voice of Freedom transmitter. He went into Wainwright's headquarters. It was 11:50 A.M. He told Wainwright that there had been no answer to the surrender broadcasts.

Wainwright was confronted by a terrible possibility. What if the Japanese refused to honor the flag of surrender that would be hoisted in ten minutes? Suppose they did not cease firing at noon? His men had been almost totally disarmed and could not keep the Japanese away from the tunnel. If the enemy came in shooting it would be a massacre. Hastily he worked to finish his last message, the one to President Roosevelt.

"It is with broken heart," Wainwright wrote, "and head bowed in sadness but not in shame, that I report to Your Excellency that I must go today to arrange terms for the surrender of the fortified islands of Manila Bay."

"I know how a mouse feels," Corporal Strobing tapped out on his key. "Caught in a trap waiting for guys to come along and finish up—My name is Irving Strobing. Get this to my mother. Mrs. Minnie Strobing, 605 Barbey Street, Brooklyn, New York. They are to get along O.K. Get in touch with them as soon as possible. Message. My love to Pa, Joe, Sue, Mac, Joy, and Paul. Also to my family and friends. God bless them all, hope they be there when I come home."

"There is a limit of human endurance," Wainwright continued, "and that limit has long since been past. Without prospect of relief I feel it is my duty to my country and to my gallant troops to end this useless effusion of blood and human sacrifice. If you agree, Mr. President, please say to the nation that my troops and I have accomplished all that is humanly possible and that we have upheld the best tradition of the United States and its Army. May God bless and preserve you and guide you and the nation in the effort to ultimate victory."

"Tell Joe wherever he is," young Strobing tapped, "to give 'em hell for us. My love to you all. God bless you and keep you. Sign my name and tell mother how you heard from me. Stand by."

"With profound regret," wrote Lt. Gen. J. M. Wainwright, "and with continued pride in my gallant troops, I go to meet the Japanese commander. Goodbye, Mr. President."

There were no more messages from Corregidor.

CHAPTER 13

"I Have Taken a Dreadful Step"

A T NOON ON May 6 Wainwright issued the most heartrending order of his long military career, to haul down the Stars and Stripes and raise the white flag of surrender. He summoned Paul Bunker of the Coast Artillery and told him what he had to do. The 210-pound, barrel-chested colonel, an all-American football player at West Point and a classmate of MacArthur's, did his duty like the professional soldier he was.

Accompanied by his exec, Lt. Col. Dwight Edison, and a bugler, Bunker marched stiffly from the west entrance of Malinta Tunnel to the base of the flagpole on the parade ground at Topside. Shells exploded around them and a heavy pall of smoke hung over the area, but nothing would deter Bunker from carrying out his orders in the proper military manner. Against the backdrop of the ongoing attack, the bugler played the mournful notes of "Taps" while the two officers stood at attention. Bunker lowered the flag, gathered it carefully in his powerful arms, and raised a white bedsheet in its place. The awful deed was done.

Bunker burned the flag, but he kept a small piece and sewed it into the sleeve of his shirt. That swatch of red cloth measuring two by three inches survived the war and the prisoner-of-war camps (although Bunker himself did not) and is on display at the West Point museum.

Wainwright waited in his cubicle in the tunnel, watching the minute hand of his wristwatch move past twelve. The suspense was hard to bear. The surrender message had been broadcast three times, the garrison's weapons were being destroyed, and now the flag of surrender flew over the compound. Yet the Japanese shelling had not lessened. Wainwright thought his worst fear was about to come true. The enemy would ignore his attempt to surrender. They would press their attack until the Corregidor defenders had all been killed, including the helpless wounded men jammed in the hospital laterals.

At 12:30 Wainwright ordered General Beebe to repeat the surrender broadcast. Fifteen minutes went by, then twenty, and the only response from the Japanese was salvo after salvo of shells. Several reports reached Wainwright that Japanese troops were advancing steadily on the tunnel, firing as they approached. Some marines were trying to hold them back with nothing more than .45s and a few rifles, but even these courageous men could not repulse the Japanese tanks. If the enemy did not cease firing soon, they were all doomed. For Wainwright, every moment was agony. The old field soldier could take no action; he could only wait.

Across Manila Bay at his headquarters on Bataan, Homma was also waiting. Like Wainwright, he believed he had failed, that he had too few boats to launch the second wave of the invasion or to evacuate the troops already on Corregidor. They might be pushed back into the sea at any moment.

He had neither heard nor been informed of the four surrender messages Beebe had broadcast from the Rock. Homma believed he had to keep up the pressure on Wainwright, so his gunners continued to pour round after round into Corregidor. Shortly before 1:00 he received word of a miracle. Through the smoke and haze a white flag had been spotted waving in the breeze. The Americans were surrendering!

Out of seeming disaster had sprung victory. After four months of brutal fighting Homma had finally succeeded in carrying out his mission. He had conquered the Philippines. Only the formalities of surrender remained. Quickly he sent word to his senior operations officer on Corregidor, Motoo Nakayama, to send Wainwright to him. He cautioned Nakayama that the American commander must be prepared to surrender all of his forces in the Philippines, not just those on the fortified islands in Manila Bay. That was exactly what Skinny Wainwright was determined not to do.

Homma settled back to wait for Wainwright, but he did not order an end to his attack on Corregidor. The Japanese guns would keep firing and the troops would continue their advance on Malinta Tunnel. Despite the appearance of the white flag, Homma was not giving the Americans any relief.

By 1:00 Wainwright decided that he could not wait any longer. He had to make contact with the enemy to arrange a cease-fire and to begin the surrender process. The radio messages had not worked. He would have to send someone to the enemy lines. He chose a young Marine Corps captain, Golland L. Clark, for the hazardous mission. While Japanese artillery rumbled overhead, Wainwright told Clark what he wanted him to do. He was to find the highest-ranking Japanese officer on Corregidor and escort him to Malinta Tunnel to work out the details of a cease-fire.

Clark took Lt. Alan Manning and a bugler with him. The three marines left the tunnel entrance and marched down the war-scarred hill, picking their way around craters and debris, but unable to avoid the sight and stench of death that seemed to be everywhere they looked. Manning waved a sheet that was tied to a long pole. When they reached the American lines the bugler sounded off and the trio crossed the no man's land to meet the Japanese. The enemy troops held their fire and the three marines disappeared from view down the slope of a hill.

Wainwright and his staff had another long hour to wait before Clark reported back. The news he brought was not good.

"He won't come to see you, General," Clark said. "He insists that you go and meet him."

Wainwright nodded and stood up. He thanked the marines and announced that he would go. He unbuckled his holster belt that contained a government-issue .45 and laid it on his desk. Then he gathered a small group of men—his aides Pugh and Dooley, plus General Moore and his aide Bob Brown—and left the tunnel, following Captain Clark. They affixed a white flag to Moore's battered Chevrolet and drove part of the way to the enemy lines.

At the foot of Denver Hill, not far from the heavily damaged Kindley Field, they left the car. Clark led them to the top of the steep hill where two Japanese officers were waiting. The younger officer was Lieutenant Uemura. He stared at the Americans for a moment, his arrogance clear in the expression on his face, and walked up to Wainwright.

"We will not accept your surrender unless it includes all American and Filipino troops in the whole archipelago," he shouted.

There it was, the ultimatum Wainwright had feared, the demand to surrender the entire force. He decided to stall, to get the

Japanese to stop firing while he tried to negotiate the surrender terms. He told Uemura that he would not discuss the surrender with him and he demanded to speak with the highest-ranking officer on the island.

At that point the second Japanese officer approached Wainwright. He was Col. Motoo Nakayama, Homma's senior operations officer, the man who had taken General King's surrender of Bataan four weeks ago. Nakayama did not speak English, but with Uemura acting as interpreter Wainwright told him that he would surrender only the islands in Manila Bay.

Nakayama loosed a torrent of angry words and his manner became hostile. He was adamant: Wainwright had to surrender all forces in the Philippines. Wainwright was equally stubborn.

"In that case," Wainwright said, "I will deal only with General Homma and with no one of less rank. I want an appointment with him."

Nakayama agreed to take him to Bataan.

Wainwright turned to his staff and quickly issued orders. Moore and Brown would return to the tunnel and take charge until Wainwright returned from Bataan. Pugh would go back to Skinny's quarters and pack a bag for him and bring it to Bataan. Beebe and Tex Carroll, Skinny's orderly, were to come over with Pugh. Dooley would stay with Wainwright.

The two Japanese officers escorted Wainwright and Dooley toward the north dock where the general's launch was berthed. They never made it. A fresh artillery barrage blanketed the area between Denver Hill and the tunnel and the north dock was right in the middle of the fire. Nakayama stopped and crouched to protect himself, refusing to go on because of the shelling.

"Why the hell don't you people stop shooting!" Skinny yelled. "I put up my white flag hours ago."

"We have not accepted any surrender from you as yet," Nakayama said.

After a few minutes the Japanese thought it was safe to proceed. Nakayama rose and led them away from the shelling toward the landing beaches at Cavalry Point. From there he radioed Bataan and ordered a boat to come for them. They sat down on the ground and waited in silence, all four men staring across the water at the tip of Bataan, where Wainwright suspected a greater humiliation was to come.

Wainwright reached Bataan at 4:00 that afternoon, when the small, slow Japanese boat finally tied up to the 400-yard-long dock at Cabcaben. Tired, hungry, and anxious about what lay ahead, Wainwright set foot again on the peninsula he had fought so hard to hold. It appeared to him to be almost idyllic now, a quiet and tranquil setting. Tall, graceful coconut palms grew down to the water's edge, sheltering several nipa thatched huts. Two small frame buildings perched at the end of the dock. It could have been peacetime, except for a barricade the Japanese had erected between the two buildings.

By contrast, Corregidor was in its death throes. At that moment the Japanese launched a vicious air raid. Enemy planes flew the length of the island from east to west, their bombs sending columns of dirt and smoke high in the air. They circled leisurely and returned, covering the Rock with more sprays of explosives. Within minutes the island had disappeared again under a thick pall of smoke. This was the first time Wainwright had seen Corregidor from this vantage point. It was awful. He was reminded that his actions in the next few hours would determine the fate of 13,000 men and women trapped under that smoke.

He did not know it at the time, but the fate of the Corregidor defenders was even more precarious. As the air raid ended, three Japanese tanks broke through the last-ditch American line to the east entrance of Malinta Tunnel. They lined up side by side no more than ten yards from the opening and angled their machine guns down the length of the tunnel.

Eight Japanese soldiers moved out in front of the tanks and deployed themselves across the entrance. They were dressed and hooded in heavy asbestos suits and they pointed the nozzles of their flamethrowers into the main tunnel. All was deathly quiet. No one spoke. The hatch of one of the tanks clanged open and an officer climbed out. He peered into the tunnel, took off his goggles, and pulled out his revolver. Using hand gestures he stationed two men to stand guard at the entrance and took the other six with him. As they entered the tunnel the soldiers' fingers tightened on the release valves of the flamethrowers.

Far back in the tunnel, in the hospital lateral, the nurses were being issued Red Cross armbands and numbers. Sallie Durrett wore number P-1177. She wondered what life as a prisoner would be like.* So did everyone else. They did not know that they were not

---

*The nurses—those "angels of Bataan"—were interned in Santo Tomas, a civilian prison camp on the grounds of the national university in Manila, and were liberated in February 1945.

yet prisoners of war. They were hostages, pawns to be used against Wainwright to force him to surrender all of the U.S. troops in the Philippines.

At Cabcaben dock, Nakayama commandeered a car and took Wainwright and Dooley north toward Cabcaben airfield. They drove over the dusty road for less than a mile to a small, primitive, wood-frame house hidden in a forest of mangrove trees. The house was the only structure still standing and the effects of the fighting were evident in the bullet and shrapnel holes that dotted its sides. It had once been painted blue, but that had been a long time ago, and now the house was faded and peeling.

Wainwright and Dooley were ushered onto a porch along the rear of the house, which opened into the kitchen. Their view was of Manila Bay. Nakayama sat down at a small wooden table, but Skinny lingered near the door, looking out at the water. A strong wind blew in from the sea, raising a dense cloud of sand and dust. The floorboards trembled and vibrated from the explosions on Corregidor. All through the long afternoon and evening Wainwright would hear and feel the continuing destruction of his helpless command.

At about 5:00, only a few minutes after Wainwright had arrived, he and Dooley were joined by Lew Beebe, Johnny Pugh, Tex Carroll, and Bill Lawrence, his administrative assistant and friend from the days at Fort Myer. Everyone was hot and thirsty. Beebe glanced into the kitchen and gestured to a Japanese soldier that they would like a drink of water. After a wary look at Nakayama, the guard reluctantly brought the Americans some.

There was no sign of Homma. Nakayama refused to say when he might come. The waiting was getting on everyone's nerves and the Americans were painfully aware of the constant sounds of war across the bay.

Some Japanese cameramen and reporters came to the house at 5:30. Wainwright and his party were ordered out to the front lawn to have their pictures taken. Skinny turned his back to them, refusing to be photographed. The head of Japanese army propaganda, Colonel Katsuya, ordered him to turn around. Wainwright weighed his options and decided not to risk jeopardizing the upcoming negotiations over such a small matter. The cameramen made the most of their opportunity to photograph the high-ranking American officers. "They posed us this way and that way,"

Beebe said, "measured distances, changed positions several times, and finally shot a few pictures."

One of the Japanese newsmen standing on the lawn that afternoon was Kazumaro Uno—"Buddy" to his American friends, who referred to him as "an American in a Japanese uniform." Uno was a native of Salt Lake City, Utah, and he had gone to Japan because of the prejudice he had experienced in the United States.* Now he stared at the captives lined up in front of the house and recorded the scene for his readers.

"It was easy to tell which one was the American C-in-C for he was the eldest, tallest, and most distinguished looking in the party, despite the tired, haggard, frightened look on all their faces." He described how Wainwright leaned heavily on his cane, looking "worried and bewildered."

At 6:00 Homma arrived. Three cars roared up the road from the south, turned sharply in front of the house, and stopped. From the lead car, a Cadillac, Homma stepped out, dressed in a spotless uniform complete with decorations and sword. His staff was outfitted even more elegantly, with a bright gold sash running diagonally across each man's chest. The contrast between the Japanese and American officers was striking. Some of the newsmen remarked loudly in English, for Wainwright's benefit, that the Americans "should have dressed up for the occasion."

The difference in physical appearance between Wainwright and Homma was even more pronounced. Barrel-chested, muscular, and almost 200 pounds, Homma was a formidable figure. He was well rested and his face showed no sign of strain or worry. Wainwright's face was pale and drawn and deeply lined. Down to 160 pounds, he was "thin as a crane," a Japanese observer wrote, and "made a pathetic figure against the massive form of General Homma." Skinny's eyes were sunken and his hair short and spiky. He wore no decorations on his simple khaki shirt and had to support himself on his cane when he walked. Wainwright was at that moment a weary and defeated old man.

But he and his party stood at attention and saluted when Homma

---

Life photographer Carl Mydans described Uno as a "tortured soul." When Mydans was later interned near Shanghai, Uno brought him gifts and described an incident that brought tears to Uno's eyes. As a 13-year-old Boy Scout, trying to be a model American citizen, he had been denied admittance to a club while on an outing with his troop.

approached them. The Japanese general scarcely looked in their direction when he passed by. His hand moved lazily to his cap in a casual and contemptuous salute. "It was apparent at once," Beebe wrote, "that he was pompous and overbearing." Wainwright thought it was not a promising beginning.

The Americans followed Homma onto the porch and took seats on opposite sides of the table, with the two generals facing each other. There were no opening courtesies, no polite preliminaries on Homma's part. The meeting was to be all business, blunt and brutal.

Homma stared at Wainwright, saying nothing, waiting for him to begin. Wainwright reached into his pocket and pulled out a piece of paper. It contained a statement of surrender, but only for Corregidor and the other islands in Manila Bay. Wainwright had already signed it. He leaned across the table and handed it to Homma, but the Japanese commander did not even glance at it. Although he was fluent in English, he passed the document to his interpreter, who translated it aloud into Japanese.

When Homma heard the statement, he responded harshly through his interpreter. His message was short and clear. He would accept no surrender unless it included all American and Filipino forces in the Philippine Islands.

"Tell him," Wainwright said to his interpreter, "I command no forces in the Philippines other than the harbor defense troops."

Wainwright explained that the forces in the southern islands—Mindanao and the Visayans—were under the command of General Sharp, who reported directly to MacArthur for his orders.

Homma was angry. He knew that Wainwright was lying.

"But you are the C-in-C of the American Forces in the Philippines," he said. "Even the latest Washington reports confirm your position, General Wainwright."

Wainwright tried again, repeating that he no longer commanded Sharp's forces in the south.

Homma pressed the point. He asked Wainwright when Sharp's troops had been released from his command.

"Several days ago," Wainwright said. He added that even if he did still have authority over Sharp he could not communicate with him because all radio transmitters on Corregidor had been destroyed.

Homma brushed aside that argument, saying that he would supply an airplane to take one of Wainwright's officers to Mindanao to see Sharp.

The negotiations reached a stalemate as both commanders repeated their positions. Wainwright insisted that he commanded only the forces in Manila Bay. Homma refused the surrender on these terms and said he would continue his assault on Corregidor. Back and forth they went for fifteen minutes until Homma and his officers held a brief, excited conference. Homma brought the group to silence by pounding on the table. He rose and glared at Wainwright.

"At the time of General King's surrender in Bataan I did not see him," he shouted. "Neither have I any reason to see you if you are only the commander of a unit of the American forces. I wish only to negotiate with my equal, the C-in-C of American forces in the Philippines. Since you are not in supreme command, I see no further necessity for my presence here."

Homma got ready to leave. Newsman Buddy Uno thought Wainwright looked "cruelly flustered" at that moment. Skinny "unconsciously started chewing the cigar he was smoking to a pulp, and puffing out the smoke quickly."

For an instant the Americans were shocked. No one knew what to say. Then Johnny Pugh cried, "Wait!" and he leaned over to speak to Wainwright. Beebe joined them. After a short and frantic discussion Wainwright addressed Homma in a subdued voice.

"In face of the fact that further bloodshed in the Philippines is unnecessary and futile," he said, "I will assume command of the entire American forces in the Philippines at the risk of serious reprimand by my government following the war."

Homma listened intently as Wainwright's words were translated.

"You have denied your authority," Homma replied, "and your momentary decision may be regretted by your men. I advise you to return to Corregidor and think this matter over. If you see fit to surrender, then surrender to the commanding officer of the division on Corregidor. He in turn will bring you to me in Manila. There is no point in continuing this discussion. The conference is terminated."

Homma turned away abruptly and left the porch, got in his car, and was driven away.

Wainwright and his staff sat speechless, too surprised to move. The surrender had been rejected and the Japanese on Corregidor would not be stopped from attacking the defenseless American forces. There was little question in Wainwright's mind about what to do now. Homma's departure, he said, "left me in the position of having all my people in the fortified islands slaughtered, or accept his terms."

But the problem was how to surrender. Homma had gone. Every

minute of delay meant more deaths on Corregidor. Time was critical. Not only were the Japanese advancing, but it was already beginning to get dark. Wainwright was well aware of the difficulty of arranging a surrender on the battlefield at night.

"We can't leave things this way," he told his men. "I'll see the interpreter and ask him what we are supposed to do."

He limped down the steps and walked around to the front lawn. Homma's staff had also departed. Only Nakayama and Uemura from Corregidor, and the Japanese newsmen, were there. Wainwright approached Nakayama and asked what he should do.

"I don't give a damn what you do," Nakayama said. "You can go back to Corregidor and fight. The attack on Corregidor will continue."

"But we have destroyed all our weapons," Wainwright said. "We are in no position to continue to fight."

"That is none of my business," Nakayama shouted. "You had a chance to surrender and you refused it. Now you can go back there and do as you please."

Nakayama turned and walked away, leaving Wainwright in the humiliating position of having to plead to be allowed to surrender. Again and again in the fading daylight he approached Nakayama and his interpreter, trying to work out some way of surrendering. A Japanese newsman wrote that Wainwright "followed them importunately, out to the road, tediously repeating the same words, and begging that they intercede with General Homma. What a pathetic figure!"

This was no time to stand on pride, not with the lives of 13,000 people hanging in the balance. No matter how much it hurt him, Wainwright had to keep trying. A white flag had flown over Corregidor for several hours and his troops could no longer fight. Finally, desperately, Wainwright told Nakayama that he would surrender all forces in the Philippines.

Wainwright thought he was complying with the Japanese demands but now Nakayama told him that his capitulation was not enough to arrange for another meeting with Homma. Instead, Nakayama said, Wainwright would have to surrender to the commander of the Japanese forces on Corregidor, a colonel. Here was the final blow, a three-star American general forced to surrender to someone of much lower rank. Wainwright had no choice but to agree.

Nakayama said he would take Wainwright and his party back to Corregidor, where, in the morning, the surrender could be carried out. He rounded up a car and a truck for them and they proceeded to the Cabcaben dock, accompanied by reporter Buddy Uno. The shelling and bombing of Corregidor had ceased, but fires could be seen dotting the island. As they waited for a boat Wainwright wondered what he would find when he got back to Malinta Tunnel.

In USFIP headquarters in Malinta Tunnel, Wainwright's staff officers as well as George Moore and other army officers were worried about Wainwright's prolonged absence. They had received no word since he and Dooley had gone to Bataan with Nakayama, some time after 2:00 in the afternoon.

Japanese troops had entered the tunnel. At first all was bedlam. Moore, his aide Bob Brown, and Carl Engelhart, a finance officer who spoke Japanese, had gone to the tunnel entrance to try to prevent the enemy from shooting. The Japanese soldiers spreadeagled Moore and Brown against the wall at bayonet point while Engelhart tried his best to explain about the surrender.

The Japanese did not believe him. They ordered all troops to leave the tunnel within ten minutes. The Americans were frantic; they knew it was impossible to evacuate so many people in such a short time. Then Charlie Drake and Ted Kalakuka of the Quartermaster Corps arrived. Kalakuka, fluent in Japanese, Russian, and Spanish, finally made the Japanese understand that Corregidor had surrendered.

The American officers were able to arrange an orderly evacuation of the tunnel. The soldiers and civilians were herded outside. Nurses, the wounded, and some high-ranking officers were permitted to remain in the tunnel.

So far the occupation had been peaceful, but the situation was tense and delicate. Late in the afternoon Paul Bunker and two other officers stormed into Moore's office. They had been robbed of their watches and valuables by some Japanese soldiers. The fiery Bunker urged Moore to protest this violation of their rights as prisoners of war under the Geneva Convention.

General Moore urged caution.

"Until Wainwright formalizes this surrender agreement with General Homma," he explained, "the latter can treat us as captives and not as prisoners of war."

And captives, as they well knew, enjoyed no rights or protection. Everyone on the Rock that night was a captive, not a prisoner, and they knew that the slightest action on their part could spark a massacre. They had to accept whatever treatment the Japanese meted out.

In the quartermaster's lateral in Malinta Tunnel Charlie Drake sat on the edge of his cot, elbows on his knees and his chin in his hands. A Japanese sergeant who had helped him clear the tunnel wandered in again.

"You sing?" he asked Drake.

"Yes."

"You know 'Old Black Joe'?"

General Drake nodded and began to sing while the sergeant stood in front of him. When he finished, the Japanese soldier sat down next to Drake on his cot, placed his rifle on the floor, and laid his sword across his knees. He gestured for Drake to begin again and this time sang along with him. When Drake reached the line "gone are the days," he paused and said softly, "They sure are."

The ride across the bay was rough and choppy. Wainwright sat quietly, trying to figure out if there were some way of avoiding the surrender of Sharp's troops in the south. The terrain on Mindanao was especially suitable for guerrilla operations and close enough to Australia to be supplied with food and weapons. Also, the island could serve as a staging area for MacArthur's army when it was ready to retake the Philippines. Wainwright knew that Sharp's forces, divided into small teams, might be able to hold out for months, even years, in the jungles and mountains. He hated the thought of having to include them in the surrender.

On the other hand, Wainwright knew he would have to pay a terrible price to keep Mindanao in American hands, nothing less than the lives of all the people on Corregidor, that dark shape now looming ahead of him. For the compassionate and humanitarian Wainwright, there could be only one answer. Too many lives were at stake. His troops were his primary responsibility. He would have to reassume command over Sharp and order him to surrender. And then he would have to pray that Sharp would recognize and understand Skinny's dilemma and comply quickly. If not, they were all in for a bad time.

Nakayama was less truculent on the ride back to Corregidor, magnanimous now that he was the victor. He offered the Americans bottles of Japanese grape-flavored soda. Lew Beebe accepted one and within a few minutes felt seasick.

The Japanese officer then reached into his pocket and pulled out a small paper bag. "This is what the Japanese soldier eats in place of candy," he said through his interpreter. He gave the bag to Buddy Uno, who passed it to Wainwright. Skinny took a few and handed the sack to Johnny Pugh. Johnny ate one and pronounced it "not bad." Beebe did not take any. Uno thought they were something like dog biscuits, "less tasty, perhaps harder." But Nakayama seemed to enjoy them, munching "as if they were chocolates."

Suddenly the boat lurched and stopped. It had run aground some fifty yards from shore. The crew tried to maneuver the boat free, but nothing worked. Dooley and Carroll were ordered over the side to push the boat, but that did not help either. Finally Nakayama jumped into the chest-high water.

"You walk—when you can!" he shouted.

The others followed him, except for Beebe and Wainwright, whom the Japanese colonel ordered carried to shore. Carroll and a Japanese soldier hoisted Wainwright out of the launch and started for the beach. They tripped and down Skinny went into the water. He got up and waded the rest of the way. Beebe was also dunked before he reached the shore.

Once they all reached the beach Nakayama ordered everyone to sit down and rest. He passed the biscuits around again and seemed concerned about Lew Beebe's condition.

After about ten minutes the Americans were formed into a column of twos and marched under Japanese guard to Malinta Tunnel, a mile and a half away. Uno led the parade with a flashlight, playing it over the terrible desolation and a great many bodies, both American and Japanese. Along the way they stumbled over some sleeping Japanese soldiers, who were astonished to see the strange procession.

At a road junction about 500 yards from the tunnel they stopped again. Japanese artillery emplaced at the eastern end of the island had opened fire on the western end. Wainwright knew he had to put an end to the shooting. Now that he had seen how much of Corregidor the enemy already occupied, he asked Nakayama to take him at once to the local Japanese commander to surrender. It was vital that he arrange it now; the Japanese might launch another attack in the morning.

Nakayama agreed and he led Wainwright and his party down the hill to Bottomside, to the demolished town of San Jose. Here Col. Gempachi Sato, in command of the invasion force, had established his command post. Here, in dim and flickering lamplight, the long bloody battle for the Philippines formally ended. Sato drew up a surrender document. There was no discussion of its terms. The surrender would be unconditional and total and it would include all United States forces in the islands.

Details were prescribed; nothing was left to chance. The towns on the southern islands where the forces should report to lay down their arms were specified and the process was to be completed within four days. The last two paragraphs of the document were short and ominous. Until all the terms of the surrender had been met, the Japanese would continue their military operations. There would be no formal cease-fire yet.

Wainwright signed the surrender document at midnight and was taken under guard to Malinta Tunnel. As he approached the west entrance he saw a pathetic sight. Hundreds of his soldiers—tired and hungry, their uniforms in tatters, and many of them wounded—were resting on the ground. When they saw him coming, those who were able to got to their feet. They struggled to attention out of respect and affection for the Old Man, the commander they had come to love. As Wainwright walked among them they reached out to pat him on the shoulder. Others shook his hand.

"It's all right, General," they said. "You did your best."

Skinny's eyes were wet with tears by the time he entered the tunnel. He walked slowly down the long main corridor, now strangely empty and quiet, to George Moore's headquarters. The two men talked briefly. Wainwright explained what he had done and Moore agreed that there was no other course open to him.

"But I feel I have taken a dreadful step," Wainwright said.

Nothing Moore nor anyone else could say would ease the pain and the dreadful sense of defeat Wainwright felt that night, the sense that he had let his country down.

Followed by a Japanese guard, Wainwright and Johnny Pugh went to the general's living quarters. A few minutes later Lew Beebe joined them. Skinny slumped in a chair near the ventilator grating, trying to cool off in its faint breeze. The heat in the tunnel was oppressive. His face and clothing were dirty and streaked with sweat and his trousers were still wet from having to wade ashore. He managed a tired smile.

"Hello, Lew," Wainwright said. "Feeling any better? Come in and cool off."

"I'm better," Beebe said, "but I feel like going to bed and getting some sleep for a change."

They said goodnight and Wainwright went over to his cot and lay down. He had not slept in two days and he wouldn't get much rest tonight. Too many thoughts were racing through his mind, foremost among them his despair at being responsible, so he felt, for two surrenders. First Bataan and now Corregidor. Together the largest capitulation in the history of the United States. This terrible burden would plague Wainwright throughout his long years of captivity.

In Australia MacArthur was expressing his disappointment that Corregidor had not been able to hold out longer. "I didn't think it would come so soon," he told his staff. His disappointment would shortly turn to anger.

All across the United States the fall of Corregidor was viewed with shock and sadness. For a brief time the nation went into mourning. The heroic defense had been recorded in the daily newspapers. Commentators compared it with the stand at the Alamo. The American people had pride in its sons and daughters. The British had lost Hong Kong and Singapore early in the war and the Dutch had lost Java. But Corregidor had held and many believed that it would go on holding until the legendary MacArthur returned with a new army. "Corregidor" and "Wainwright" had become household words, and the tall, lean figure of the old cavalry officer had stared resolutely from the front page of nearly every newspaper in the country. Skinny was a new American hero.

But now he and his men and the Philippines were lost and everyone knew it would be a long time before they returned, if they ever did. The loss was felt keenly in the small, picturesque town of Skaneateles in upstate New York. There Adele Wainwright received the bad news.

Reporters called at the family home but she could not see them. Her daughter-in-law, young Jack's wife, received them and explained that Mrs. Wainwright was in "a highly nervous state." She was "naturally very worried, as we all are. She feels there is nothing to say, and that there is nothing anyone can say."

Adele Wainwright, the general's beloved "Kitty," would also become a victim of the war. Her husband's years of captivity would affect her for the rest of her life.

At dawn on May 7 Wainwright was visited by Homma's intelligence officer, Col. Hikaru Haba, who had come over to work out the details of the surrender agreement signed only a few hours before. The most pressing problem was arranging for the surrender of the largest intact force in the Philippines, the Visayan-Mindanao Force commanded by General Sharp.

Wainwright called for his operations officer, Jesse Traywick, and told him that a Japanese plane would take him to Mindanao to deliver a letter to Sharp. Wainwright then sat down to dictate the letter, outlining the situation and informing Sharp that he, Wainwright, had been forced to surrender all the islands.

"You will therefore be guided accordingly," Skinny wrote, "and *will* repeat *will* surrender all troops under your command . . . This decision on my part, you will realize, was forced upon me by means beyond my control."

He authorized Sharp to inform MacArthur of the contents of the letter. However, Wainwright concluded, "let me emphasize that there must be on your part no thought of disregarding these instructions. Failure to fully and honestly carry them out can have only the most disastrous results."

When he finished with the letter Wainwright thought that would be the end of the matter, but the Japanese were not satisfied. Haba informed him that he would be taken to Manila that afternoon to broadcast his order to Sharp. He would also have to reach two commanders, Col. John Horan and Lt. Col. Guillermo Nakar, whose small units were operating in the mountains of northern Luzon. Wainwright chose Col. Nick Galbraith, his supply officer, and Lt. Col. Ted Kalakuka, the assistant quartermaster, for that job.

Wainwright objected to the broadcast in the strongest possible terms. He knew that the transmission would undoubtedly be picked up in the States. On reflection, however, he realized that the broadcast would give Sharp additional time to consult MacArthur because he might hear it at least a full day before Traywick could bring him the written instructions.

Wainwright and his staff waited in the lateral until Haba returned for them at 5:00. The Japanese officer led them out the west entrance of the tunnel, where a large number of Skinny's defeated troops were waiting. He later described that intensely emotional moment.

"They were standing there in the blazing sun in the area where I had seen them the night before. Obviously, they had not been fed or given any water during that terrible time.

"They were in very bad shape. But as I walked through them they all got to their feet. Some stood at attention and saluted as I passed, and I raised my hand to my old sun helmet. Others just stood, took off their hats, and held them across their chests.

"Again I felt the tears welling up in my eyes and could do nothing to stop the emotion."

When Wainwright described the experience for reporter Bob Considine, who was ghostwriting the general's story, he read over the manuscript, took his pencil, and added the following line. "I am a student of the Civil War, but not until then did I know how General R. E. Lee felt after Appomattox." Officers in Wainwright's party and enlisted men in the group outside the tunnel have confirmed the poignancy of the moment and the wealth of feeling for the general.

The party crossed from Corregidor to Bataan on a Japanese landing barge that chugged and sputtered across the bay on an engine made in 1902. During the ride Wainwright issued his orders to Colonel Galbraith on how to effect the surrender of the troops in northern Luzon. The rest of the time Skinny sat quietly, looking all around, as though memorizing the scene. They landed at Lamao on the east coast of Bataan, six and a half miles north of Cabcaben. They were left for two hours in the front yard of an elementary school and given a little food—rice and fish with a lot of bones in it—their first food, other than Nakayama's "dog biscuits," in two days.

While they were waiting Wainwright reviewed his instructions to Traywick. He couldn't predict how Sharp would react, so he tried to impress upon Traywick the importance of his mission.

"Jesse," he said, "I'm giving you complete authority to handle this situation."

He handed Traywick a handwritten note and told him to use it only as a last resort if Sharp continued to refuse to surrender. The note gave Traywick authority to arrest Sharp if he did not carry out Wainwright's instructions.

"Jesse," Wainwright repeated, "I'm depending on you to carry out these orders."

At about 7:30 that night Wainwright and his group were herded into a large touring car that sped north along the coast road. It was getting dark and the guards drew the curtains over the windows, so the passengers caught only brief glimpses of the towns they passed through, points Wainwright and his soldiers had fought over during the retreat into Bataan—Layac, Lubao, Guagua, the road junction at San Fernando, Calumpit.

They reached Manila shortly before 11:00 P.M. Wainwright was very tired. He had been awake since dawn and had slept fitfully for only a few hours the night before. Haba insisted, however, that the broadcast be made that night. The car stopped outside radio station KZRH, where they were met by Lt. Hisamichi Kano of the Japanese propaganda corps. Kano, who had been educated in the United States, treated Wainwright and his men courteously, escorted them inside, and brought them some watermelon.

Wainwright reviewed the speech that had been written for him, but he had some difficulty understanding it because the language was awkward and stilted.

"General," Kano said, "I can straighten it out for you," and he disappeared into an office where he refashioned the speech in more natural English.

When everything was ready Wainwright was taken to the main broadcasting studio and seated at a round bamboo table with a microphone in the center. Behind him was a bandstand with an upright piano and music stands, a reminder of earlier and happier times. It was 11:43 P.M. They were on the air. In the control booth a Filipino announcer started to speak.

"How do you do, one and all. This is Marcelo Victor Young speaking to you from the main studio of KZRH, the voice of the Philippines, and calling the attention of everyone everywhere. Everyone, everywhere, all Filipinos in America and all over the country and all you Filipino and American officers and men, listen to a speech.

"Listen to your commanding general. From the bomb-spattered, all-wrecked sectors of Corregidor and through the hot dusty roadways of Bataan and several other provinces he has made his way to this city, accompanied by high-ranking officers of the Japanese army. He has come to speak to all of you, to give you his own message in his own words from his own lips. Listen now to General Jonathan M. Wainwright."

Skinny slipped on his glasses and began to read from the prepared text, moving the fingers of his left hand down the page line by line. His voice was heavy with weariness and it sounded unusually deep as he tried to suppress his emotions.

"This is Lieutenant General Jonathan M. Wainwright. I have a message for General William F. Sharp, commanding the Mindanao forces. For General Sharp, commanding in Mindanao. Anyone receiving this message please notify him.

"By virtue of the authority vested in me by the President of the United States, I, as Commanding General of the United States forces in the Philippines hereby resume direct command of Major General Sharp, commander of the Visayan and Mindanao forces, and all troops under his command. I will now give a direct order to General Sharp. I repeat, please notify him. The subject is surrender. To Major General William F. Sharp, Jr. This is the message: To put a stop to further useless sacrifice of life on the fortified islands, yesterday I tendered to Lieutenant General Homma, commander in the Philippines, the surrender of the four harbor defense posts in Manila Bay. General Homma declined to accept unless the surrender included places under your command. It became apparent that they would be destroyed by the airplanes and tanks which have overwhelmed Corregidor.

"After leaving General Homma with no agreement, I decided to accept, in the name of humanity, his proposal and tendered at midnight to the senior Japanese officer on Corregidor the formal surrender of all American and Filipino troops on the Philippine Islands. You will, therefore, be guided accordingly and will, I repeat, will surrender all of your forces to the proper Japanese officer.

"This position, you will realize, was forced on me by circumstances beyond my control."

Wainwright announced that his assistant chief of staff for operations, Colonel Traywick, would personally deliver a letter to Sharp. General Sharp was to repeat to MacArthur the contents of the letter and the broadcast.

Wainwright read the speech again, this time addressed to Horan and Nakar, commanders of the small units operating in the north of the island of Luzon.

Wainwright paused before continuing. His voice was breaking and choked with emotion.

"The Japanese army and navy will not cease their operations until they recognize the faithfulness of execution of these orders. These orders must be carried out faithfully and accurately, otherwise the Imperial Japanese army and navy continue their operations. If and when such faithfulness of execution is recognized, the commander in chief of the Japanese forces in the Philippine Islands will order that all firing be ceased."

The implication was obvious. If Sharp and the others refused to surrender, the lives of all those who were now captives might be forfeit.

The general coughed, unable to talk for a moment.

"Taking all circumstances into consideration, and—"

Wainwright could not go on. There was a long moment of silence and then the announcer broke in.

"You have been listening to a special broadcast of Manila Station KZRH, in which General Wainwright delivered a message to his men."

Skinny was numb and drained of all feeling. The propaganda officer, Kano, took him and his staff into an office and produced a bottle of scotch. Kano poured drinks for them all.

The battle for the Philippines was over. The broadcast was Wainwright's last official act as commanding general of the United States Forces in the Philippines. The fighting part of his war had ended, the kind of war he had trained and prepared for all of his adult life. Now he was faced with a different kind of struggle, one for which neither he nor anyone in his command was prepared: a war of cruelty, starvation, disease, humiliation, and privation. A war that would last for three and a half years and be fought in isolated camps in the Philippines, Formosa, Japan, and Manchuria. A war in which victory would be measured in simple terms, in terms of sheer survival. In many ways it was much tougher than the conflict just ended, and it began immediately after Wainwright's radio speech was finished, at 1:00 A.M. on May 8.

Skinny had expected to be taken back to Corregidor once he had made the broadcast. That was the plan Colonel Haba had announced when he'd come to take the Americans to Manila. For that reason, Wainwright had left his trunk in Malinta Tunnel. Also, he hoped he could do something for his troops if he returned. He was concerned about how they were being treated, especially the nurses and the wounded.

But the plans had been changed. Wainwright and his officers were driven from the radio station to their first place of confinement, the University Club Apartments on Dewey Boulevard, which bordered the beach along Manila Bay. The club occupied the top two floors of the building. The four lower floors contained apartments in which many American and British civilians had lived before the war. He was lodged in one apartment and the staff in separate rooms.

They managed only a few hours of sleep. Periodically they were awakened by the thump of hobnailed boots as Japanese guards strode the corridors and burst into each room to check on the prisoners. Early in the morning Wainwright was roused by Colonel Haba. It was time for the three American officers to leave with Wainwright's letters of instruction—Traywick to Sharp, Galbraith to Horan, and Kalakuka to Nakar. The fate of the Corregidor garrison depended on them.

Wainwright had no way of knowing that his radio broadcast had unleashed a storm at SWPA headquarters in Australia. MacArthur was irate that Wainwright was trying to force the surrender of the southern islands. If only the War Department had accepted MacArthur's four-part command structure, Wainwright would not be in this position. The SWPA commander was bitter.

MacArthur's anger was directed not only at Washington but also at Wainwright, and he held it against him for some time to come. Three years later, when discussing the surrender of Sharp's forces with Lt. Gen. Robert L. Eichelberger in March 1945, MacArthur said, "I ordered them to keep on fighting and Skinny ordered them to surrender while he was a prisoner. It was not a very creditable thing." Apparently MacArthur did not realize the conditions on Corregidor and the threat Wainwright was under. After the war General Marshall commented that MacArthur's animosity toward Wainwright was "tremendous."

But now MacArthur had to decide what to do about Sharp. When he first learned of Corregidor's surrender, before he heard Wainwright's radio broadcast, MacArthur had notified Sharp that he, MacArthur, was resuming command of the Visayan-Mindanao force. Sharp was ordered by MacArthur to "communicate all matters direct to me."

When Sharp heard Wainwright's speech he was placed in a difficult situation. Wainwright had released him to MacArthur's command and MacArthur had made it plain that Sharp would report only to him. Now Wainwright had countermanded his orders and was again taking command of Sharp's troops. Sharp, it seemed, had two commanders.

Sharp relayed Wainwright's surrender message to MacArthur and asked for instructions. They were not long in coming, but they did little to clarify Sharp's confusion. MacArthur said that "orders emanating from General Wainwright have no validity." He urged Sharp to separate his force "into small elements and initiate guerrilla operations."

Then MacArthur added the following: "You, of course, have full authority to make any decision that immediate emergency may demand. Keep in communication with me as much as possible. You are a gallant and resourceful commander and I am proud of what you have done."

Sharp decided to wait and hear what Traywick had to tell him about conditions on Corregidor before deciding what to do.

Meanwhile, MacArthur dispatched a radiogram to the War Department that was highly critical of Wainwright.

"I have just received word from Major General Sharp that General Wainwright in two broadcasts on the night of [May] 7/8 announced he was reassuming command of all forces in the Philippines and directed their surrender giving in detail the method of accomplishment. I believe Wainwright has temporarily become unbalanced and his condition renders him susceptible of enemy use."

Others also believed that Wainwright's orders to Sharp had no validity. There was even some doubt that it was Wainwright who had made the broadcast. In a War Department meeting in Washington George Marshall spoke of "the attempt of the Japanese to put over a false order from Wainwright by the radio to compel the surrender of the others." The psychological warfare branch of Army Intelligence made a recording of the speech, which had been picked up by a San Francisco radio station. They offered the following analysis:

"This alleged broadcast can carry no weight whatever, for many reasons. First, it was apparently not General Wainwright's voice, his manners of speech, his diction, nor his pronunciation of familiar Filipino names. The record of the broadcast was played for intimate officer friends of General Wainwright who are familiar with his manner and way of speaking, his phraseology, and particularly, pronunciation of Filipino names that he has spoken many times to these officers. It did not have the tonal qualities, inflections, characteristics of pronunciation of Wainwright's voice.

"Certainly the wording of the statement was not American, as phrases used, techniques of expression employed were identical with standard propaganda coming from Tokyo.

"It is known that before General Wainwright surrendered he had radioed the commanders of the American-Filipino troops elsewhere in the Philippines, releasing them from his own immediate control and directing them to report to [MacArthur].

"Furthermore, General Wainwright had surrendered the day before, and therefore had no troops of which he could resume command and give orders.

"From the time of his surrender he could no longer under any circumstances issue orders."

No one in a position of authority outside the Philippines was ready to go along with Wainwright's plea for the surrender of the forces under Sharp and the north Luzon commanders. Everything depended on the three local commanders and how persuasive Wainwright's emissaries would be. If Sharp and the others sided with MacArthur and the War Department, Wainwright and his troops would be in grave danger.

The days passed slowly for Wainwright at the University Club Apartments. Three days went by without any word from the outside world. He had no idea what had happened to his men. Then, on May 11, Jesse Traywick returned with good news. Sharp had agreed with Wainwright's assessment of the situation and had surrendered his forces.

The same day, Lew Beebe, Bill Lawrence, and Tex Carroll were brought over from Corregidor. Their arrival gave Wainwright his first chance to learn about conditions on the Rock. They were bad, but so far there had been no casualties. Sergeant Carroll brought Wainwright's shaving gear and the first clean clothes he had had for four days.

The captives soon established a routine. Their treatment during the month they were held at the University Club was fair. Beebe recorded in his diary that "During this period we received the best treatment accorded us as prisoners." The food was the best they were to have until their release in 1945 and their quarters were the most comfortable.

Wainwright and the others were permitted to visit one another in the two apartments they occupied and they had access to the club library. They were permitted to go up to the roof each day after breakfast and dinner for sunshine, fresh air, and exercise. From there they could look out over Manila Bay to the desolate island of Corregidor and the green jungles of Bataan.

The guards were not inconsiderate. Lieutenant Uemura from Corregidor was "very kind to us all," according to Tom Dooley, and Lieutenant Kusimoto occasionally brought them ice cream and cigarettes.

What was difficult to bear was the boredom, the mind-numbing sameness of each day. The entries in the diaries of the Americans repeat the word "routine." Every day was similar to the one before. Playing bridge, reading, washing clothes, walking back and forth on the roof. Weather and food were the major topics of conversation. If it rained, they could not go up on the roof. When they got ice cream or real coffee, or when Tex Carroll baked a raisin pudding for the general, these were events worth recording. And so were days like May 18, of which Dooley wrote, "all hands ravenous— dress at clatter of dishes."

Boredom, routine, monotony, broken only by three events in that long first month of captivity. On May 14, at 11:05 P.M., the general's old friend Bill Lawrence died of pneumonia. Like so many others to come, the death could have been prevented with proper medical care. But the Japanese had refused to provide any assistance, even though one of their doctors had diagnosed Lawrence's condition the day before.

On the 15th the Americans were taken to Wainwright's former post, Fort McKinley, to bury Major Lawrence. Skinny saw the quarters where he had lived with his wife, the parade ground on which he had ridden every morning, and the ghosts of so many people who had filled those distant days of empire. And he saw the Japanese flag flying over the base and Japanese soldiers lounging in the quarters. The sights depressed him.

The second break in the routine occurred on Friday, May 29, when Japanese intelligence officers questioned them. Wainwright was interrogated first, early in the morning, and the others took their turns in the afternoon. The Japanese received no information from the Americans, but to the latter it was a welcome change of pace. The Japanese were frustrated when their captives claimed to be totally ignorant of almost everything.

After three hours of questioning Tom Dooley, the Japanese intelligence officer threw up his hands. "I cannot see how you are the general's aide," he said, "and know so little."

The American officers on Corregidor were also being interrogated. When asked about the whereabouts of the American and Philippines treasury, the finance officer, Jack Vance, answered "I don't know" to each question. Finally, in exasperation, the intelligence officer said to the translator, "Ask him if he knows the Japanese army is on Corregidor."

The third disruption in Wainwright's routine at the University Club Apartments, and the most depressing, occurred on Sunday afternoon, May 24. Skinny had received so little information about the troops he had been forced to leave behind on Corregidor that he was becoming increasingly worried. That afternoon he saw them again, from the window of his apartment, as they were marched down Dewey Boulevard. Looking like "a great line of tattered beggars," the American contingent from Corregidor was led from the beach through the city to Bilibid Prison. The Japanese planned the parade as a form of humiliation for the defeated Americans and it came to be called the "gloat march."

Wainwright could see from his window that the men were in

terrible shape. They had been confined for two weeks in an area the size of two city blocks in a basin east of Malinta Hill, an area formed when the bombing and shelling had destroyed a coast artillery motor pool garage. There, with no shelter from the sun and little food or water they had waited, with nothing to do but shoo away the huge biting and swarming flies.

On the 23rd they had been put aboard three ships and jammed so tightly together that they had to stand. They were given no food or water. The next morning the ships took them to Manila where they had to wade ashore on the beach.

Skinny recognized many old friends in the long column and his heart ached for them. He spied Jack Vance and Charlie Drake and several others. "Many of these men were so sick and weak they could scarcely drag themselves along. Hundreds were obviously suffering from the effects of the heavy aerial and shore battery bombardment they had received for days prior to the surrender. Scarcely any seemed to be in good condition. A few had hats. Most had dirty towels or torn shirts over their heads to protect them from the terrific heat of the tropical sun."

Filipino civilians along Dewey Boulevard and other city streets tried to pass food and water to the men, but the Japanese guards beat them back. They were no less brutal to the helpless men in their charge. Stragglers in the column were beaten with the flat end of a sword or prodded with the point of a bayonet.

It took a long time for the column of fours to pass out of sight of the University Club. Wainwright had already heard stories about the brutality shown toward the Bataan prisoners on their march to Camp O'Donnell, and there were rumors that the survivors of that march of death were even now dying at the rate of 400 a day. These stories, combined with the sight he now witnessed, brought Wainwright and his men a new awareness of the nature of their enemy. This inhumanity and callous disregard for human life was unknown to them. It angered them, and it made them all the more alarmed about their future.

Wainwright had good reason to be concerned about the fate of his men, because he still had not fulfilled all of Homma's surrender demands. The disposition of Sharp's forces had been settled, but there had been no word from Galbraith or Kalakuka, the two officers sent into the north of Luzon.

Kalakuka was never seen again.* Galbraith, after a series of

---

*An American officer who hid out as a guerrilla throughout the war reported that Kalakuka died in a Japanese jail.

nightmarish difficulties and narrow escapes, was able to accomplish his mission. He hiked through the mountains for several days before locating Horan. He persuaded the colonel that he would have to surrender to save Wainwright and the men being held hostage, and then set out to find Horan's guerrilla units, which were spread all over the area. They had no radio, telephone, or roads linking them.

In the company of a truculent Japanese officer, Galbraith combed the rugged country to contact as many of Horan's men as he could. Even if he could not find all of them, he reasoned, his actions might persuade Homma that every effort had been made to carry out the terms of the surrender.

Galbraith's conscientiousness and diligence paid off and the Japanese were convinced of the sincerity of his efforts. They even commended him "for his strenuous endeavors." After the war, Wainwright recommended Galbraith for the Distinguished Service Cross for his actions, but the War Department reduced the decoration to a Bronze Star.

On the morning of June 9, 1942, more than a month after the Japanese came ashore on Corregidor, and six months from their commencement of the Philippines campaign—which was scheduled to last only fifty days—Wainwright's surrender was accepted. Lieutenant Uemura came to Wainwright's apartment with a letter written in Japanese. Uemura translated it for him.

"The troops under your command have now surrendered; your high command ceases and you now become a prisoner of war and will today be conducted to a prisoner of war camp at Tarlac."

CHAPTER 14

"Sold Down the River"

WAINWRIGHT HAD LAST SEEN the town of Tarlac at the end of December when it had served as the western end of his D-4 line of defense on the withdrawal from Lingayen Gulf. His troops had held there for three days and the town had taken terrific punishment from Japanese artillery and bombs. When he pulled out, Tarlac had been a battlefield, its buildings and streets a shambles.

It looked a little better on the early afternoon of June 9, 1942, when Skinny and his staff arrived after a long ride in two cars and a truck. It was a very hot day. Tarlac was eighty-five miles north of Manila and the road was the same one Wainwright's North Luzon Force had fought on six months before. Along the way, he saw how the war and the Japanese occupation had ravaged the countryside and the towns.

Wainwright passed through places whose names were seared in his memory, places where he had lost friends, where his troops had sometimes fought bravely and sometimes melted into the jungle. The places were all associated with defeat, points he had been forced to yield to the advancing Japanese. Calumpit, where he had destroyed the beautiful bridge. San Fernando, where the retreating troops had created a colossal traffic jam. Bamban, the western anchor of his D-5 line, where he had been headquartered early in the war. Santa Rosa, San Miguel . . . It was like reliving a bad dream to see them all again while on his way to a prisoner-of-war camp. Wainwright said nothing during the ride.

At 1:30 in the afternoon they arrived. "What a shock," said Lew Beebe, "when our car stopped in front of a bare, wooden, two-story building which had been used as a Philippine Army Training Center!" It was a grim-looking place.

Although the quarters were depressing, Wainwright and his party were pleased to find so many comrades there. The barracks housed close to 200 generals and colonels, including those who had been on Corregidor—George Moore and the rest of the officers—as well as the men of Bataan, of whom Wainwright had heard nothing since the peninsula had fallen two months ago. Now Skinny was reunited with Ned King and Arnold Funk, Parker, Jones, Brougher, and Bluemel, and Clint Pierce from the Twenty-sixth Cavalry. These Bataan officers were in terrible shape; some did not even have shoes.

But Skinny was pleased to see them again, to know that they were alive. Their weakened condition saddened him, however, because he felt responsible for their fate. He was their commanding officer and he had not been able to save them from imprisonment.

Wainwright's momentary bitterness was reflected in a comment he made to Lt. Col. Charles Lawrence of the quartermaster corps, who had once commanded the supply depot at Tarlac. An air corps sergeant, whom good luck had made an orderly to the Bataan generals, overheard him.

"We were sold down the river," Wainwright said, "by the people in Manila. The Philippine army didn't even have stones to throw."

This was one of the rare times Wainwright was heard to voice criticism of USAFFE, and it was a statement with which no one present would have disagreed. They all knew how true it was.

The men in the Tarlac barracks crowded around to greet Wainwright and the other new arrivals. In the crowd Skinny spotted Arnold Funk, who had come to him on Corregidor the night before Bataan fell to tell him for General King how bad their situation was. Skinny shook hands with him and grinned, then shook his head sadly.

"Arnold," he said, "sure is good to see you. This is a hell of a situation for two old field soldiers to be in. I didn't expect to see you again."

It was hard for them all to keep back the tears.

Once inside the barracks Wainwright got his first indication of prisoner-of-war life at Tarlac. It was not reassuring. The building was so crowded that there was barely enough room between the bunks to turn around. The officers lived on the second floor, which was filled with cots for the generals and two-tiered bunks for the colonels.

There were no mattresses, blankets, mosquito nets, sheets, or pillows, and the men had to fend for themselves and help one another. Skinny gave Lew Beebe a blanket and he provided his young aide, Tom Dooley, with a large piece of canvas from a bedroll he had carried with him for the last thirty-two years. Dooley tore out the wooden slats of his bunk and replaced them with the canvas to make it more comfortable.

The first floor of the building contained two rooms, a small one converted into a primitive hospital and a larger one for the mess hall. That night Wainwright found out how poorly the prisoners were fed.

"For dinner that night we had just rice," Lew Beebe said. "Plain boiled rice and nothing more." The newcomers were amazed to see the old Bataan hands go back for second and even third helpings. "How anyone could eat three mess kits full of plain boiled rice was beyond my comprehension. Before many days had passed I discovered that I must learn to eat rice or starve. I preferred to eat the rice, although I vowed that no one could make me like it. Before I was released I not only ate it—I liked it."

The rice was of poor quality, full of small pebbles and dust, indicating that it was sweepings from the warehouse. It was not sufficient food to sustain life for long, not for men who had been on half rations or less for several months. Some people already showed signs of malnutrition and it was obvious to Wainwright that he would have to do something to try to improve their diet.

Jack Vance and others had come to the same conclusion. Vance had composed a letter addressed to Homma saying that since the men were now considered prisoners of war rather than captives, they should be supplied with toilet articles, clothing, food, and pay, as provided by the Geneva Convention. Jack took the letter to Wainwright and asked Skinny if he would give it to the camp commandant over his signature.

Wainwright read the letter slowly.

"I'm not begging him for anything, am I, Jack?"

Vance assured him that he was not.

"Leave it here," Wainwright said. "I think I can sign it."

Two days later each man was given a cake of soap, a toothbrush, and some toothpaste. The food did not improve, but at least the men could clean up. It felt good to be able to soap up and go out in the rain to rinse off.

Because Wainwright's petition through formal channels did not bring any improvement in their diet, the men resorted to informal and irregular means—free enterprise. The Japanese sergeant of the guard was offered a commission on anything he could purchase and bring into the camp for the men. Wainwright and the officers from Corregidor pooled their money, sharing it with the penniless officers from Bataan, so that all of them could buy whatever the sergeant had to offer—mangoes, bananas, candy, cigars, and cigarettes. There was never enough, but the system was an improvement. When the men left Tarlac they looked back on these days with nostalgia because there they had eaten so relatively well.

Occasionally they managed to get some Philippine coffee and would hoard the small supply, saving it for Sunday morning when each man would be given one cup. Most of the officers had not had real coffee for months. As a result, the caffeine in a single cup produced a not unwelcome feeling of intoxication.

One officer remembered, "When we sat down to eat our rice on those mornings everyone was glum and silent. Nothing was to be heard but the click of spoons on mess-kits. Then the coffee began to take effect, and within fifteen minutes every officer's tongue was limbered up and going full speed ahead."

Wainwright managed to find something stronger to drink in Tarlac, courtesy of Al Bland, the orderly to Generals Pierce and Bluemel. Bland worked in the camp kitchen for a while, where part of his job was to take the garbage to a dump by the perimeter fence. One day he found a note in an empty trash can from a Filipino in the town of Tarlac asking if there was anything the prisoners wanted. Bland asked for something alcoholic to drink.

Every three or four days for the several weeks that Bland worked in the kitchen he found a bottle of San Miguel gin in the trash can. He took the booze to Tex Carroll, Wainwright's orderly. When Skinny's aides, Pugh and Dooley, found out where the general was getting the gin, they told Bland to stop.

"Don't pay any attention to them," Carroll told him later. "Any time you can get it, do."

The faithful Sergeant Carroll watched over Wainwright "like a mother hen," doing all he could to make the general's confinement easier. He realized that to go from a commanding general in the U.S. Army to being a slave of the Japanese was the ultimate humiliation. The severity of this demotion in status had been made clear to Wainwright and the others from their first day in Tarlac.

The Japanese rules were strict and simple, designed to be as degrading as possible to Wainwright and the American officers. A captive general in the American army was inferior to the lowest Japanese private and had no more rights than a coolie. Why? Because he had surrendered.

By surrendering, Wainwright and his men had violated the Japanese code of *Bushido,* the way of the warrior. A fundamental tenet of *Bushido* is that a soldier never surrenders. To do so is to commit the ultimate disgrace to one's country, family, and self. It is far more honorable to die in battle or commit suicide than to allow oneself to be taken prisoner. There is no greater shame for a soldier than that.

To the Japanese, their captives were unworthy individuals who had dishonored themselves. They were shocked that the Americans wanted their names sent to their government so that their families would know they were alive. Why would they want loved ones to know of their shame? During the surrender of Bataan, when some Japanese officers offered pistols to their captives so they could kill themselves, the Americans had refused. The Japanese were stunned.

In the early days of his imprisonment, Wainwright was often asked by Japanese interrogators why he had surrendered. "Why didn't you kill yourself?" they wanted to know. He had surrendered, he told them, to save lives, and he had not taken his own life because he hoped to return to his family.

Stanley Falk, in his history of Bataan, wrote, "The Japanese soldier, in General Homma's words, 'despised beyond description' his fellow countrymen who allowed themselves to be captured. Since this was so, the Japanese looked upon an enemy who had surrendered with even stronger contempt. The brutality with which a Japanese soldier treated his subordinate in the normal course of events would hardly seem excessive to him when dealing with a disgraced enemy prisoner for whom he had little love in the first place."

Wainwright and his officers could expect no mercy or compassion. There would be no restraints on the Japanese guards against brutality and no deference to rank and age. Every American was made to salute any Japanese soldier. If the American was not wearing a hat, he had to bow low to all Japanese he encountered and to snap to attention whenever a Japanese guard entered the barracks.

It was embarrassing for Wainwright, forty years a soldier and four a general officer, to salute and bow to the rawest private of an enemy army. When he was first instructed in the proper way to bow, he said it made him feel like throwing up.

The Japanese also had a strict policy about infractions of the rules. The Americans were grouped into ten-man punishment squads. If any member of a squad broke a camp rule, all the men in the squad would be punished.

Anyone who tried to escape would be executed, and the Japanese insisted that the officers sign pledges that they would not escape. They discussed the matter for several days, "then we all signed with the mental reservation that since it was signed under duress it had no validity."

The Japanese collected the signed statements, but they were taking no chances. Wainwright was informed that as senior officer he would be held personally responsible if any of his men escaped. His punishment would be immediate execution.

"I won't tell you what to do," Skinny said to his men, "but if your desire for freedom in the jungle is so great you can't resist, come by and take me with you!"

Many of the men were bitter during the weeks they spent at Tarlac. The bitterness was brought on by many factors: the boredom of endless days with nothing to do, the opportunity to compare war experiences with men from other units, and the revelations of the bestiality displayed by the Japanese on the Bataan Death March. The men were also affected by the shock of surrender and imprisonment and the bleak prospects for the future.

"It all happened so fast," a colonel said. "How did we wind up our careers being treated like coolies?"

Wainwright and his officers talked frequently about what had happened to them and, more important, who was to blame. Some blamed the navy for leaving the Philippines only a few days after war began. Others blamed the air corps for losing most of its planes on the first day of the war. But above all they blamed MacArthur for his belief that his Philippine army was ready for war, for his conviction that the Japanese would not invade until April 1942, for his delay in implementing the War Plan Orange withdrawal into Bataan when he saw that the Philippine army was disintegrating, and for his failure to stock the Bataan peninsula with food and supplies well before the siege began.

Paul Bunker, the man who was a classmate of MacArthur's and who had had to run up the white flag on Corregidor, recorded in his diary on June 16 that "Bitterness and contempt of MacArthur seems to be universal . . . also contempt for his staff. We try hard to be optimistic and think that our tour of this dog's life will be a short one, but if MacArthur's staff is now blundering as it did at Corregidor then our prospects are dismal indeed. And every day is so precious to me: I haven't so many of them left, at my age."

The officers could readily agree with Wainwright's comment that they had been sold down the river. In this spirit, many of them contributed freely to an essay written by General Brougher that enjoyed a wide circulation at Tarlac.

"The small group of Americans in the Philippines were 'sold down the river,' committed to a hopeless task from the beginning. Why? Perhaps just a colossal military blunder. There was no fairness or common sense in committing a small group of Americans to a hopeless task that had no chance to wind up any other way for us.

"Who had the right to say that 20,000 Americans should be sentenced without their own consent and for no fault of their own to an enterprise that would involve for them endless suffering, cruel handicap, death, or a hopeless future that could end only in a Japanese prisoner of war camp in the Philippines? Who took the responsibility for saying that some other possibility was in prospect? And whoever did, was he not an arch-deceiver, traitor and criminal rather than a great soldier? Didn't he know that he was sentencing all his comrades to sure failure, defeat, death, or rotting in a prison camp?

"A foul trick of deception has been played on a large group of Americans by a Commander in Chief and small staff who are now eating steak and eggs in Australia. God damn them!"

A few times Wainwright joined in this criticism of the high command, but he never publicly uttered a word against MacArthur.

As the generals and colonels rehashed the Philippines campaign they conceived the idea of forming a veterans' organization after the war. Membership would be restricted to the senior officers who served in the Philippines. Brougher proposed that it be further limited to those who were in the Philippines after April 1, 1942, to keep out the "MacArthur gang," all of whom had left by then.

When Skinny heard about it, he "raised the devil."

"You can't do that!" he said.

He felt it would be too public a rebuke to a commanding officer. Their grievances had to be kept among themselves, not spread to the world at large.

The bitterness festered and turned to anger, but at first it had no suitable target. The prisoners couldn't fight their guards, nor could they strike back at MacArthur. That left only one another. For a short time, the tension in the crowded barracks was high.

Arguments flared up at the slightest provocation, real or imagined, particularly among the colonels. There were quarrels about whose bunk was in the way and there were allegations about unfairness in the food distribution from the kitchen to each of the ten-man squads. Some charged that others were getting more than their share. Occasionally the confrontations became violent, though the men were so weak that most of their blows were harmless.

After a few days Wainwright had had enough. He called a formation of the colonels and delivered a stinging reprimand, accusing them of acting childishly.

"You gentlemen have had an easy life for some years. Now you taste some hardship and it is apparent that some of you cannot take it well. I want no more behavior of the sort that has occurred recently."

That was all that needed to be said. The squabbling dropped off immediately; they all knew that Skinny meant business. They may have been prisoners but he was still their C.O. Despite his own emotional burdens and apprehensions, his bearing remained "olympian." Walt Odlin, General Funk's orderly, wrote that "General Wainwright was always the commander. There was no mistaking that."

Wainwright's men loved and respected him and they knew he would always do his best to look out for them, but they also knew he would tolerate no unmilitary behavior and allow no dissension in front of the Japanese. They might be poorly clothed and fed, treated like slaves by their captors, but they were still in the U.S. Army. When their commander gave an order it had better be obeyed. As Sergeant Bland put it, in the language of the old army,

"When General Wainwright said 'squat,' you squat."

With a few close friends and old comrades, however, he could unbend and reveal his fears. Wainwright was convinced that he was in disgrace, his career was finished, and he would be court-martialed for having surrendered. He would not be dissuaded from these depressing thoughts throughout his three and a half years of captivity.

His friends tried to ease his burden, but many of them also believed they would be court-martialed. Some tried to cheer him by suggesting duty assignments Wainwright would be qualified for after the war, but Skinny wasn't interested.

"My career is over," he said. He cited examples from his wide knowledge of military history to support his belief, officers in the War of 1812 and the Civil War who were court-martialed for surrendering. He pointed out that those cases involved small numbers of troops, nowhere near the size of the force he had surrendered. The man responsible for the largest capitulation in America's history was certainly not going to be hailed as a hero when he returned.

"I'm going to be tried when I get back," he said to General Pierce and the others.

Sergeant Odlin overhead him telling one of the colonels, "You must visit me in San Antonio after the war, if I am not too much in disgrace." Wainwright also worried that his wife would have no money to live on, thinking that his allotment would be stopped because he had surrendered. He was despondent a good deal of the time, and Al Bland's gifts of San Miguel gin were a welcome balm. They helped, for a while, to take his mind off his bleak future.

While Wainwright worried about being sent home in disgrace, his adversary in the Philippines, the Japanese general Homma, was relieved and ordered back to Tokyo. Less than two months after Wainwright had surrendered to him, Homma's career was over. It is a handsome irony that the man who won the war in the Philippines finished his days ignominiously while the man who lost became a national hero.

Homma's victory had provided him with only a short-lived triumph. His military reputation had been stained because Wainwright and his American and Filipino forces had held out so long on Bataan and Corregidor. Also, Homma's conduct of the occupation came under criticism. The problem was not that Homma was too strict or brutal in his administration of the Philippines, but that he was too lenient. His superiors in Tokyo believed that he was going too easy on the Filipinos. He had ordered his troops not to consider the natives as enemies or to interfere with their religion or customs. He refused to occupy the presidential palace and planned to release thousands of Filipino troops he had captured.

In addition, Homma defended the policies the American government had pursued during its tenure in the Philippines and he refused to distribute a propaganda leaflet accusing the U.S. of exploiting the people.

"The Americans never exploited the Philippines," Homma said. "It is wrong to make such false statements. They administered a very benevolent administration over the Philippines. Japan should make better and more enlightened supervision."

The final embarrassment for Japan took place during the victory parade Homma had arranged in Manila shortly after Wainwright was transferred to Tarlac. It was intended as a triumph for the Japanese army, and long columns of troops passed before Homma's reviewing stand. The conquered Filipinos watched the passing troops in silence until a Philippine army band marched by. When the people heard what the band was playing—"The Stars and Stripes Forever"—they broke into wild applause.

Shortly thereafter Homma was stripped of his command and ordered home. In Tokyo he learned that he would not be permitted to report to the emperor, an honor accorded every returning commander, and he spent the rest of the war as a civilian. In 1946, after Wainwright had returned to the United States, acclaimed as a hero, Homma was executed as a war criminal. His death sentence was formally approved by MacArthur.

A routine was established at Tarlac and, boring though it was, it gave some form if not meaning to Wainwright's days. The prisoners rose at 6:30 A.M., had roll call ten minutes later, and breakfast at 7:30. Sick call was at 9:00, lunch at noon, supper at 6:00, roll call at 8:00, and lights out at 10.

They tried to curtail their talk about their own war, now past, and the acrimony and blame that went with such discussions, and look to the future instead. What would happen now in the Pacific war? That theater, not Europe, was their overriding concern. How long would it take for MacArthur to return to the Philippines? How long before Japan would be defeated? How long before they would be freed?

There were many debates about how long the war would last.

The navy officers were always the most optimistic. "The navy will come get us in a year, at most," they said.

The army officers disagreed. More likely, they thought, it would be two years.

"All of you are wrong, gentlemen," Wainwright said. "This will be a longer job. I believe we'll be here about four years." His estimate, as it turned out, was the correct one.

Among the talk and that mainstay of peacetime military life—bridge games—there was little else to do at Tarlac. The lack of activity and the absence of knowledge about the world beyond the prison camp were almost as hard to bear as the insufficient food and degrading treatment. The diaries of the generals and colonels record these stresses in terse lines.

"Dull routine with little to read," wrote a navy doctor, Capt. Robert Davis. "Days long and dull. Same routine daily."

"The days go along. Same routine."

"New rules keep us inside after eight P.M."

"Beds are twelve inches apart. Noisy, but get some sleep."

"Here we sit with no news of outside world. Hate to see generals saluting privates."

"Dull hours with no reading. I have an old *Geographic* today. Hungry for news."

"Peculiar situation with no outside world, so we just exist and wait."

Occasionally the Japanese conducted interrogations or made strange requests. Shortly after Wainwright arrived at Tarlac the Japanese camp commander, Colonel Ito, distributed forms on which the prisoners were to list their bank accounts, stocks and bonds, real estate, insurance, and the net worth of their relatives. The purpose was to arrive at an amount for which they could be ransomed.

"Your government will pay much for you," the commandant told the prisoners.

The action caused a brief flurry of excitement and hope, until Wainwright pointed out that the United States government would never pay a ransom for prisoners of war. Nor should it, they all knew.

In their second month at Tarlac the Americans were instructed to write essays on topics chosen for them by the Japanese. None of the men took the effort seriously, but it gave them something to do. The papers were dutifully completed and nothing more was ever heard about them.

Any diversion, any break from the routine, was enough to spark a holiday atmosphere, and the event would be talked about for days afterward. On June 27 Colonel Galbraith arrived, returning finally from his long mission for Wainwright in the mountains of north Luzon. No one had heard from him for nearly two months. Now here was a man who had been outside the camp, and he was deluged with questions about the war.

Wainwright greeted Galbraith with his "usual elan."

"Where've you been?" Skinny asked, grinning. "Glad to see you back," he added.

Two weeks later, on July 11, fourteen colonels arrived from the southern Philippine islands. Among them was Colonel Stuart Wood, Wainwright's G-2 on Corregidor, who had planned to deliver Skinny's Colt revolver to MacArthur before his ill-fated PBY struck a rock in the waters off Mindanao. The prisoners were so excited to see new faces that they leaned out the barracks window, shouting their greetings. The newcomers brought some precious things—stories to tell and hash over and a fresh mixture of news and rumors.

July 4, America's Independence Day, was recognized by the Japanese. They allowed the prisoners an extra hour's sleep in the morning and distributed a small amount of milk and some bananas. They also permitted the men to sing patriotic songs. "A big day," Tom Dooley wrote in his diary.

The men found amusing moments too at Tarlac, and any funny incident or story would sweep through the ranks within hours, to be repeated for days before dying out. One night Col. Jack Vance, who seemed never to be without a cigar, had the latrine trench collapse under him. As he climbed out, Skinny said, "Jack, are you sure that's a cigar in your mouth?"

Wainwright liked to tell the story Walt Odlin had brought him about a Japanese guard with whom Odlin had been discussing the war. America could not possibly win the war, the guard said. "Why not?" Odlin had asked. "Americans can't do anything in the war," the Japanese repeated. "We have all your generals and colonels right here!"

Then there was the day the Japanese gave the prisoners some sorely needed protein in the form of meat on the hoof, a mangy carabao.

"Here is meat," the guard said, leaving the poor beast in the middle of the camp. While the men scrounged for something with which to kill it, the buffalo broke free and began to run wildly around the grounds. Everyone with enough stamina for the exertion chased after it, shouting.

Although the Japanese guards hurried to close the camp gates, the carabao raced through them, and so did a group of American enlisted men. The guards stared at them, open-mouthed, as they followed the animal until it headed back into the camp. They tailed it inside again, more concerned with food than with escape.

One of the men had been a cowboy—Staff Sgt. Harry B. Greenleaf—and he borrowed a length of rope from a Japanese soldier and neatly lassoed the animal. The officers had unearthed a sledgehammer with which to kill the carabao, but the veterinarian, Josiah "Doc" Worthington, issued a warning. First, he cautioned, he would have to make sure the animal wasn't diseased before he could allow them to eat it.

Wainwright stuck his head out the barracks window and hollered at Greenleaf.

"Hit that thing between the eyes before it gets away again. If Doc Worthington rejects the carcass as unfit, hit him between the eyes too!"

Tragedy struck Tarlac on July 17 when death claimed an American colonel. As with the death of Major Lawrence at the University Club in Manila, this was caused by neglect on the part of the Japanese. An ordnance officer, Col. Edwin Barry, awoke one morning complaining of a sore throat. Col. Harold Glattly, an army medical corps doctor, examined Barry and requested medicine to treat the infection he had diagnosed. The Japanese refused.

By 8:00 that night Barry could hardly breathe. Using a rusty razor blade and a tube from an enema bag Glattly performed a tracheotomy, but it did not help. Barry died two hours later and was buried the next day. Wainwright led the mourners at the brief services.

Despite such cases of brutality, the commander of the prison camp did on occasion show himself to be considerate. He was the only camp commander that the men would later describe as kind and humane.

Col. Ito was particularly concerned about Wainwright's health. He sometimes brought Skinny extra food—candy, mangoes, and milk. Toward the end of June Ito gave Wainwright a case of beer and some sardines. "Not enough of anything to go around," commented Col. Mike Quinn, who had been Wainwright's chief of transportation on Bataan, "but the Old Man can certainly use it; he doesn't look good."

Wainwright and his men even found a kind of beauty at Tarlac, a tranquility provided by the camp's setting. Twenty miles to the east Mount Arayat soared nearly 4,000 feet, and fifteen miles to the west was an equally high range of mountains. Gently rolling countryside lay in the foreground. Facing westward was a grassy bank on which the men congregated in the evening. "No one who was there," said Walt Odlin, "will ever forget the many evenings we all sat on that bank and watched the most glorious sunsets men can see."

July 31, 1942 was a special day for Wainwright, marking his fortieth year of army service, a record of which any man could be proud, under normal circumstances. But these were far from normal circumstances. Young Tom Dooley and other friends came to Skinny to congratulate him on that day, but the occasion only served to remind him how much he had let down the army and the country.

Had Wainwright been aware of what was occurring at that moment at the War Department in Washington, he would have felt much better. General George Marshall had just sent a radiogram to MacArthur recommending Wainwright for the highest award the United States could bestow, the dream of every career soldier, the Medal of Honor.

Marshall had been deeply touched by the spirited defense Wainwright had put up in the Philippines, and he wanted to recognize Wainwright's efforts by asking Congress to award the medal. He collected statements from three officers who had served with Skinny in the Philippines, men who had been sent out before the end. They were Col. Milton Hill, inspector-general, Col. Arthur Fischer, intelligence officer, and Col. Thomas Doyle, infantry.

These men had nothing but the highest praise for Wainwright's efforts on Bataan and Corregidor. Doyle, who had commanded the Forty-fifth Infantry Regiment on Bataan, wrote that he frequently observed Wainwright "on the trails of Bataan with the advance elements of his command. He visited my front line which was under heavy enemy fire. He was armed with a rifle and on several occasions joined the firing line. His own staff attempted to dissuade him from taking the personal risks involved, but without success. I observed that his visits were a decided factor in the maintenance of high morale in my command.

"The troops became so accustomed to seeing General Wainwright," Doyle said, "that on days when he did not appear, it was assumed that he was visiting other portions of the front."

Doyle noted that after Wainwright took command on Corregidor, he spent much of his time visiting the "emplacements and positions and encouraging the personnel, frequently under aerial bombardment and shell fire. He utterly disregarded his own safety on all occasions."

Colonel Fischer agreed. Wainwright "was on the firing line daily," he said, "and units were so greatly impressed that they reported to me in terms of eulogy what General Wainwright was doing to develop seasoned troops in the field."

Milton Hill was equally lavish in his praise of Skinny's conduct, reporting that it was only because of Wainwright's influence and "outstanding leadership" that morale among the troops did not plummet after MacArthur left. "On various occasions, I have observed General Wainwright clad in overalls, armed with a rifle, up in the front lines. His fearlessness in directing the fighting in the extreme forward elements of his command was well known. When I left Corregidor [May 3, 1942], General Wainwright was in good mental and physical condition, although he had lost considerable weight. He was cheerful, calm, and collected under very trying conditions."

Based on these first-hand accounts and guided by his own respect for Wainwright—and his compassion for the old soldier's fate—Marshall believed that Skinny should have the Medal of Honor. All he needed was MacArthur's endorsement, because he was Wainwright's immediate superior, which surely, Marshall thought, would present no problem.

MacArthur himself had been awarded the Medal of Honor on March 25, 1942, after his escape to Australia. It had been given to offset the propaganda unleashed by the Japanese, accusing MacArthur of cowardice and charging that he had deserted his troops on Bataan. Also, the medal met with popular approval on the home front, where MacArthur was being hailed as a hero. The citation mentioned MacArthur's heroic conduct of defensive and offensive operations on Bataan—which he had visited only once—and the inspiration of his troops while under heavy fire. On this basis, obviously Wainwright was at least equally deserving.

Marshall sent the proposed citation for Wainwright's decoration to MacArthur on July 30 (July 31 in the Far East), and asked for his remarks and recommendations. They were quick in coming and they were hardly what Marshall expected.

Marshall's commendation for Wainwright read: "Lieutenant General Wainwright (then Major General) while in command of the American Forces on Bataan, and later the U.S. Army Forces in the Philippines, distinguished himself conspicuously by gallantry and intrepidity at the risk of his life above and beyond the call of duty, in action against Japanese Forces on the Bataan Peninsula, and on Corregidor Island, Philippines. He frequently visited the extreme forward elements of the troops under heavy fire and on several occasions joined the firing line with a rifle and engaged in fire action. He masterfully conducted the withdrawal of the Northern Luzon Force into Bataan with a minimum of losses. By his fearlessness and demonstrated outstanding ability as a military leader, he was an example to all ranks and was responsible for a high state of morale in the American Forces under extremely trying and adverse conditions."

This was a straightforward and factual statement of Wainwright's combat record and leadership on Bataan and Corregidor.

Marshall did not realize that MacArthur's animosity toward Wainwright had not diminished in the three months since Corregidor had fallen. Indeed, it had intensified. By the end of the summer fragmentary accounts of the Bataan Death March had reached MacArthur, and he blamed Skinny for this great loss of life. If Wainwright had ordered King to carry out MacArthur's planned counterattack northward, to capture Japanese supplies at Olongapo, most of the Bataan troops would now be guerrillas instead of prisoners. MacArthur believed that Wainwright's failure to press this attack was directly responsible for the deaths of so many American and Filipino soldiers. He did not seem to recognize that King's troops were in no condition to carry out such an operation and that they had completely run out of food. Also, MacArthur still resented Wainwright for forcing Sharp to surrender the Mindanao forces, and for, as MacArthur saw it, undermining his four-part command structure.

Obviously, MacArthur was in no mood to recommend the nation's highest honor—a medal that both he and his father had received—for the likes of Wainwright. It has also been suggested by D. Clayton James, MacArthur's biographer, that MacArthur disliked the fact that "Marshall presented him with the proposed citation, which had been drafted without MacArthur's counsel." His reply to the chief of staff reflected his hostility.

"The citation proposed," radioed MacArthur, "does not repeat not represent the truth. I am recommending General Wainwright and a number of other officers for the Distinguished Service Medal and for the Legion of Merit but I do not repeat not recommend him for the Medal of Honor. In order to avoid the inclusion of my adverse observations and opinion and certain facts into his record which would now serve no useful purpose I am not including in this message an enumeration of these circumstances which could properly preclude such an award but will do so if it is your desire. It was my complete knowledge of this officer's part in the Philippine campaign that impelled me to prepare upon my departure a command setup which would have limited his responsibilities.

"As a relative matter award of the Medal of Honor to General Wainwright would be a grave injustice to a number of other general officers of practically equally responsible positions who not only distinguished themselves by fully as great personal gallantry thereby earning the Distinguished Service Cross but exhibited powers of leadership and inspiration to a degree greatly superior to that of General Wainwright thereby contributing much more to the stability of the command and to the successful conduct of the campaign. It would be a grave mistake which later on might well lead to embarrassing repercussions to make this award."

MacArthur had written here a damning indictment of Wainwright, full of mysterious innuendoes and the suggestion that Wainwright's conduct of the campaign had been ineffectual. He offered no support for his charges. This he could write of the man he had selected for the most important command in the Philippine Islands before war broke out—the North Luzon Force. This of the man whose successful conduct of the withdrawal into Bataan had been characterized by MacArthur himself as being "as fine as anything in history." This of the man who in MacArthur's own proposed four-command arrangement for the Philippines had been assigned to Bataan, the most vital command of all.

MacArthur had had confidence in Wainwright then, but now he was vilifying him with words strong enough to ruin his career. MacArthur implied that it was because of Wainwright's "part in the Philippine campaign" that he was "impelled" to propose a command arrangement that would have limited Wainwright's responsibility. Why? Because he had performed poorly? Obviously not. MacArthur had praised him. And far from limiting Wainwright's responsibilities, MacArthur's command arrangement would have increased it from one to two corps. Perhaps MacArthur was letting the surrender cloud his judgment; he felt the loss of his beloved Philippines as a personal betrayal.

Marshall was greatly surprised and distressed by MacArthur's response, and he brought the matter to the attention of Secretary of War Stimson. He also asked his Deputy Chief of Staff, General McNarney, to look into the affair and make a recommendation.

Stimson was unequivocal. "I told him," Stimson recorded of his conversation with Marshall, "that if the papers showed that Wainwright deserved it, as Marshall thought they would, I favored giving it to him regardless of MacArthur's objection."

Marshall waited for McNarney's report. MacArthur had raised some bothersome questions. What were the "embarrassing repercussions" that might follow the awarding of the medal to Wainwright? Had there been some personal clash between the two men? Had Wainwright done something unbecoming of which Washington was unaware? Something that would be made public if the medal were given? Something that could be embarrassing to the army?

Or was MacArthur engaging in his familiar theatrical posturing, piqued at the prospect of sharing the limelight with Wainwright, the man who had surrendered? MacArthur saw himself as the hero of Bataan and Corregidor. For Wainwright to receive the same high award could make him a rival for popular acclaim.

McNarney made his report the next day. It was simple and direct, three short paragraphs.

"General Wainwright's commanding officer states flatly that the proposed citation does not represent the truth.

"Personally, I question General MacArthur's motives and my emotional reaction is to award the decoration.

"I also question General MacArthur's judgment where matters of personal prestige are concerned and believe both General Wainwright and the Army would suffer from a public airing of the case. Recommend no further action at this time and that no record of the exchange of cables be placed in General Wainwright's 201 file."

Reluctantly, Marshall agreed with the recommendation. He was unwilling to risk exposing Wainwright or the army to the possibility of scandal, however unsubstantiated it seemed to be. Also, the prospect of further antagonizing MacArthur was not pleasant. He was idolized by the public and sorely needed in the Southwest Pacific to spearhead the drive for victory over Japan.

Wainwright's Medal of Honor proposal was quietly shelved, though Marshall was determined to see that some day Skinny would receive it. But even when the issue was raised after the war there was concern about how MacArthur would react.

MacArthur's comments about Wainwright were not placed in his personal file and the War Department kept the affair secret for almost twenty years. Every page of the file is stamped "super secret." On MacArthur's message to Marshall, John R. Dean, secretary to the General Staff, wrote: "The master copy, file copies and stencils from which this was prepared have been destroyed— This is the only copy in existence." In 1942, the War Department could take no chances that MacArthur's feelings about Wainwright would become public knowledge.

Marshall was always mindful of the plight of Wainwright and his fellow prisoners of war. There was nothing he could do for the men directly, but he made every effort to notify the families of any information he received. He tried to be supportive of Mrs. Wainwright, who was living with her mother in Skaneateles, New York.

On May 7, 1942, the day after Corregidor fell, Marshall had sent to Adele Wainwright a copy of the last messages exchanged by Wainwright and the War Department, along with a personal letter.

My dear Adele;

You have been in my thoughts pretty constantly for a long time, and I have wanted to write to you, but since there was nothing encouraging I could tell you regarding the probable outcome of the fighting around Manila Bay, I did not force the task. Now, however, I want you to know that you have had our deepest sympathy.

There is little that I can add to what has already been published to the world regarding Wainwright's superb fight to the end. There must be a great deal of consolation to you at this time in the knowledge that he has made for himself a great place in history. . . .

I will keep you informed of any further news we receive, and if there is anything I can do for you, please do not hesitate to communicate with me.

Faithfully yours,
G. C. Marshall

Mrs. Wainwright replied a few weeks later, thanking him for his kindness. Things were not going well for her, she told him. "Each day of my life seems worse than the last as I look into the future." In addition to her anxiety about her husband, Adele was worried about their son Jack, now chief officer aboard the merchant ship *Henry Grove* of the American South African Line. "My son's ship is two weeks overdue in an African port and no word up to this morning."

Marshall immediately offered his help, "on a strictly confidential basis, of course," in trying to determine the time of arrival of her son's ship. "Difficult as your situation is," he wrote, "I am confident that you can keep your chin up for that is just what Wainwright would want you to do."

Marshall kept his word. On August 13 he wrote to Adele again. "I have checked up on your son's boat and find that it arrived safely at its destination and is on its way back. I hope this will be of some reassurance."

On that same day, Wainwright was also aboard a ship, a Japanese freighter sailing north from the Philippines to Formosa. Two weeks earlier the prisoners at Tarlac had been told they would be moved, but their destination was a secret. Rumors swept through the camp: They would be taken to Japan! That meant only one thing; they would remain prisoners until Japan was defeated.

When they found out that their next camp would be on the island of Formosa they were relieved, but the departure saddened them as well. They knew that the farther they were from the Philippines, the longer it would take for U.S. forces to liberate them.

Before the Americans left, Colonel Ito, Tarlac's commander, asked Wainwright if he would assemble the general officers for a group picture. Skinny agreed. He hoped that any photographs that were taken would have a chance of reaching the newspapers, so the families of the men held here would know at least that they were alive.

The generals gathered outside the barracks and posed for the photographer. No one smiled, not even the Japanese with them. Wainwright folded his arms and stared straight into the lens. Ito was pleased, however, and showed his appreciation by giving the men some food and two bottles of scotch.

The day before the prisoners were scheduled to depart, the Japanese announced that they would have to sign a pledge not to escape while they were traveling. Wainwright objected and said that they would not sign unless the agreement was amended so that their promise would not be binding if they came in the vicinity of

American forces. The Japanese agreed, and everyone in the camp signed.

On August 11 the prisoners were awakened at 3:30 in the morning to prepare for their long journey. The men packed their belongings, cleaned the barracks and latrine, and quietly ate their usual inadequate breakfast. At 6:40 they were formed into a column and marched through the gate to the railroad station. Along the route cheering Filipinos made the V-for-victory sign with their fingers, and a fourteen-year-old boy whistled "Auld Lang Syne."

Wainwright and his men were leaving the security of the known and familiar, heading for a strange place where there would be new guards and new rules, new physical surroundings, a different climate. Would the new camp bring them better treatment or worse? More food or less? So far, Ito and his guards had treated them tolerably. A few men had been slapped for disobeying rules, but no one had been beaten or tortured.

At Tarlac the Americans had worked out an accommodation with their captors. They knew which guards were kind, which ones were to be avoided, and which could be counted on for favors. There was some predictability about their lives that brought a measure of security; a man knew what he could and could not do. Now that was ending. As Wainwright led them down the road, already hot from the morning sun, they dwelled on the uncertainties that lay ahead.

The trip got off to an excellent and memorable beginning. During the six-hour train ride from Tarlac to the central railway station in Manila, the prisoners ate better than at any other time since long before their imprisonment. At every stop native vendors rushed to the open windows of the train to sell food. The Japanese guards made no attempt to stop them.

Skinny and the others purchased fried chicken, sausages, bananas, small cakes, and other delicacies they had forgotten existed. They even bought eggs. Lew Beebe said that "none of us had seen an egg for at least five months." They had a feast, and it was a long time before they would eat so well again.

At the railroad station in Manila, Wainwright and the others were loaded into captured American trucks. The driver of Skinny's vehicle, an American POW, had exciting news for the general. The U.S. was on the move in the Pacific. Marines had landed in the Solomon Islands at a place no one had heard of—Guadalcanal. Wainwright gladly passed the information along. It was great to

hear that America was on the offensive, but the Solomons were a
long way from the Philippines, and even farther from where they
were now going.

The trucks took the men to Manila's Pier Seven, a huge covered
platform that brought back memories of home. It was here on this
pier that these men had stood back in May of 1941, watching the
ships depart with their wives and families, carrying them back to the
States. How long before they would see them again?

The prisoners had to wait for more than an hour in the hot,
steamy shelter. They were ordered to face away from the ship,
kneeling and with heads bowed, so that they would not see the
many small white cardboard boxes the Japanese were bringing on
board. They contained the ashes of Japanese soldiers who had
fallen in the long battle for the Philippines.

While they were waiting, Wainwright saw a familiar face. It was
Lt. Kusimoto, a Japanese officer who had been kind to Wainwright
and his small party during their time at the University Club
Apartments in May. Kusimoto had brought a present for Wainwright, a carton of Lucky Strike cigarettes. Skinny very much
appreciated the gesture.

Finally they boarded the modern, diesel-powered freighter, the
Nagara Maru. Skinny and King were assigned a cabin with a
porthole, but the rest of the prisoners were not so fortunate. Two
hundred of them were packed below decks in the cargo holds.
Double-deck sleeping benches had been built so close together that
the prisoners had to crawl into them on their hands and knees.

The ship remained at the pier all that night and most of the next
day. The sun heated the steel above their heads so it was too hot to
touch. The men were bathed in sweat. The air was suffocating. At
dusk the ship edged out into Manila Bay, passing between Corregidor and the tip of Bataan.

Conditions improved once the ship was at sea. During the two-
day voyage to Formosa the men were allowed up on deck and were
fed fairly well. The diet was still only rice, but at least there was
enough of it, along with hot tea to wash it down. "We never ate half
as well afterward as we did on that voyage to Formosa," said Walt
Odlin.

They arrived at the harbor of Takao on the southwest coast of
Formosa at 9:30 in the morning of August 14. By now they were
anxious to get off the crowded ship, but the Japanese were in no
hurry. The day grew hotter and there were no cooling sea breezes

to bring relief. They spent the whole day aboard, "very hot and miserable," Tom Dooley recorded in his diary.

At 3:00 the following afternoon Japanese prison guards disinfected the men and led them off the *Nagara Maru* and right on to another ship. The new one, a "small rusty, dirty little tramp of a coastwise steamer" was the *Otari Maru*, and the men were crammed aboard with even less room than they had had before. Wainwright and King were shoved down into the hold with the others.

The trip was a short one, overnight, around the southern tip of Formosa. At 8:00 in the morning they anchored at the small port of Karenko. There was another long, frustrating wait before they were herded off the ship, and it was noon by the time they all assembled on the pier. The sun blazed overhead and there was no food. The Japanese formed the prisoners into a column of fours with Wainwright at the head, and led them off through the streets of the town.

The Japanese had declared a holiday and had brought most of the native population into town to gawk at the American captives. People lined both sides of the road, staring silently at the long line of men marching westward through and out of the town on a hot asphalt highway.

The prisoners were a pathetic sight, said one, gaunt, with "clothes faded and tattered—not washed or shaved since leaving Tarlac—shoes coming apart—some men limping from blisters."

Wainwright was leading a ragged army of ghosts.

Wainwright is permitted to write a brief postcard home, Formosa, 1944.

NATIONAL ARCHIVES; CAPTURED JAPANESE PROPAGANDA ALBUM.

Wainwright and King take tea on a fishing trip arranged by Colonel Sazawa at Muksaq prison camp in the spring of 1944.
NATIONAL ARCHIVES; CAPTURED JAPANESE PROPAGANDA ALBUM.

TIME

THE WEEKLY NEWSMAGAZINE

GENERAL WAINWRIGHT
Since Corregidor, two long years.
(Army & Navy)

"Since Corregidor, Two Long Years." Time *magazine cover, May 8, 1944.*

REPRINTED BY PERMISSION FROM TIME, THE WEEKLY NEWS-MAGAZINE; COPYRIGHT TIME INC. 1944.

Adele Wainwright, with a photo of her husband, at home in Skaneateles, New York, October 1944. She has just received news of U.S. landings in the Philippines.
◄ WIDE WORLD PHOTOS.

Wainwright, carrying a photo of Adele, is helped by Wedemeyer into a car. Brig. Gen. Lewis C. Beebe is at right.
NATIONAL ARCHIVES.

Newly liberated Wainwright, on arrival in Chungking, China, August 28, 1945, wearing shirt provided by Gen. Albert C. Wedemeyer, commander of American forces in China.
◄ NATIONAL ARCHIVES.

MacArthur greets Wainwright at the New Grand Hotel, Yokohama, Japan, August 31, 1945, their first meeting since they parted on Corregidor more than three years before.

U.S. ARMY SIGNAL CORPS.

MacArthur with Wainwright and Lt. Gen. A. E. Percival, the British commander at Singapore, at the New Grand Hotel, Yokohama, Japan, August 31, 1945.

U.S. ARMY SIGNAL CORPS.

Wainwright and Percival witness MacArthur's signing of the Japanese surrender document aboard the U.S.S. Missouri, *September 2, 1945.*
U.S. ARMY SIGNAL CORPS.

From left: Tom Dooley, Johnny Pugh, Lew Beebe, and Tex Carroll upon arrival in Manila.

U.S. ARMY SIGNAL CORPS.

Wainwright attends the surrender of the Philippines by Japanese General Tomoyuki Yamashita at Baguio, Luzon, September 3, 1945.
U.S. ARMY MILITARY HISTORY INSTITUTE.

Wainwright receives his fourth star from Lt. Gen. Robert C. Richard-son at Honolulu, Hawaii, September 7, 1945.

U.S. MILITARY ACADEMY.

The Wainwrights are reunited at National Airport outside of Washington, D.C., September 10, 1945.

U.S. MILITARY ACADEMY.

Wainwright tells the U.S. Congress, "It is good to stand on American soil again."

UNITED PRESS INTERNATIONAL.

Wainwright receives the Medal of Honor from President Harry S. Truman at the White House, September 10, 1945.

HARRIS AND EWING.

Wainwright enjoys a hot dog and cola at a baseball game at Washington's Griffith Stadium.

U.S. MILITARY ACADEMY.

Wainwright's homecoming festivities continue with a ticker-tape parade in New York City.

WIDE WORLD PHOTOS.

Wainwright awards the DSM to Col. N. F. Galbraith in 1946 for his wartime mission to North Luzon. A graduate of The University of Chicago and a World War I veteran, Galbraith commanded a battalion of field artillery (PS) and served as G–4 for MacArthur and Wainwright.

U.S. ARMY SIGNAL CORPS.

Wainwright cuts the cake at a surprise party hosted by General Beebe at Fort Sam Houston, Texas, August 23, 1947, to mark Wainwright's sixty-fourth birthday and forty-fifth anniversary in the army.

U.S. ARMY SIGNAL CORPS.

CHAPTER 15

"I Am Hungry All the Time"

WAINWRIGHT LED HIS bedraggled column of men into the barbed-wire enclosure of the prison camp at Karenko, which would be his home for the next nine months. He was ordered to stop on a drill field in front of a large, two-story barracks building and to form the men in three ranks. By now they had been prisoners long enough to know that the Japanese would keep them standing there for a long time. It was one of their ways of demonstrating their absolute power over the Americans.

The men took advantage of the enforced wait to look around and get acquainted with the surroundings, and they were impressed with what they saw. Karenko did not look like a typical prison camp. The grounds were nicely landscaped and maintained, and the buildings appeared attractive from the outside.

The barracks had gray cement walls and a black tile roof and were better constructed than anything at Tarlac. A cement porch encircled the ground floor and a wooden porch reached around the second floor. The windows were spotlessly clean, giving the men hope that their quarters inside would be equally clean. That would be a welcome change.

Behind the barracks was a park with banyan trees, shrubbery, and a neat gravel path. Nearby were the cook house and bath house, and some distance beyond them was a barracks for the Japanese guards. They could hear the sound of a rushing stream not far away. About five miles to the west a solid wall of mountains rose to a height of 9,000 feet.

After Tarlac and the awful ship voyages to Formosa, this new camp looked almost like a paradise, and the men dared to think that their lives as prisoners of war would take a turn for the better. They were wrong.

Karenko's camp commander, Captain Imamura, a sickly-looking middle-aged man who soon became known to the men as "The Dyspeptic," approached the prisoners. He was followed by an interpreter, equally sickly-looking, skinny, and short. The officers who had escorted the prisoners from the harbor called them to attention—*"Kioski!"*—and formally turned them over to the camp commander. The ceremony ended with a series of bows, each party trying to give the final one.

That done, the prisoners were ordered to bow to their new keeper at the command *"Kirei!"* Imamura saluted the prisoners and shouted *"Yasume!"*—at ease. He mounted a table and made a long speech. Wainwright and his men waited patiently for the translation.

When the commandant had finished, the interpreter climbed up on the table and spoke in a language that only vaguely resembled English. It was impossible to follow his words, and the prisoners were confused about what was happening and what was expected of them. But they knew not to interrupt with questions.

It wasn't until a few days later that they found out. The interpreter passed around a copy of the commandant's speech—in English—and it made for interesting reading.

Previous to the present war of Greater East Asia Nippon ardently desired peace over the Pacific and made her best efforts to settle the problems peacefully. In spite of such diligent effort of Nippon, the United States and Britain had constantly challenged Nippon and drove her to the most difficult position to keep her prestige and to solve the question of life or death. Nippon, therefore, has taken up arms with most heroic determination for the sake of her self defense and the permanent peace of the world. Nippon indeed stood up at the risk of her existence, together with her history for the last three thousand years.

One hundreds millions of the people have united themselves firmly under the August Virtue of His Majesty, the Emperor, and have desperate determination to strike down our enemies, the United

States and Britain which have been molesting Greater East Asia. Heaven always sides with justice. Since the outbreak of the war Nippon has annihilated the Pacific Fleets of the United States and Britain and Australia the past six months, and has captured all the Dutch East India, Hong Kong, Malay, Singapore, etc. And now the occupation of Australia is imminent. Such brilliant results of the war has never been recorded in the history of the wars in the world. Now not only on the Pacific but on the Indian Ocean not a single war ship either of the United States or of Britain is seen. Their aerial forces, too, are almost entirely annihilated. And now not an air plane of them is seen flying over our domain.

It is entirely the gracious gift of His Majesty, the Emperor, that you, who crossed over the death line, being assured of the safety of your life, can enjoy peaceful living.

I hope that you will enjoy the peaceful life in this camp and return to your dear families after the restoration of peace which I hope will not be very long. The following are general principles that I require you to seriously observe:

1. Everyone who does not observe the Nippon military discipline shall be severely punished, and the life of such prisoner shall not always be assured.

2. To be loath to labor or to express dissatisfaction for food, clothing and habitation is prohibited. Everyone of the country is willing to endure all sorts of hardships and fighting for the final victory of the war, you must understand therefore, that it is nothing but natural that you are not allowed to lead an idle life.

3. The American and the English are not allowed to hold the haughty attitude over the people of Asia or to look them down which have been their common sense for a long time. If there is any such attitude at all on your part you shall be severely dealt with.

The statement sobered Wainwright and his men because it indicated without doubt that life would not improve for them at Karenko. Rule number one was enforced especially stringently by the Japanese guards. The slightest infraction of their military discipline meant harsh punishment, as they all soon found out.

When Imamura and the interpreter had finished explaining the camp rules, the prisoners were called to attention and commanded to bow again as the commandant left the drill field.

The Japanese guards ordered the prisoners to strip to their underwear. Not one of the generals and colonels, or their aides and orderlies, had any underwear to speak of anymore. It had long since worn out. They wore nothing but G-strings fashioned out of strips of cloth. The men made a pitiful sight—old and young, general and corporal—standing in three rows with their tattered clothing and meager possessions piled at their feet. As they glimpsed the emaciated condition of their neighbors, each was reminded of just how wretched he was.

The guards pawed diligently through the prisoners' belongings and took pens, notebooks, cigarette lighters, rusty razor blades, flashlights, and the few surgical instruments the doctors had been hoarding.

Then the Japanese collected their shoes. They systematically labeled each pair and carted them away. Skinny wondered if they were expected to go barefoot. Presently the guards returned with piles of clogs and told the prisoners to get dressed.

The men were tired. They had been standing in the sun for more than two hours, having marched two miles to the camp. They had not been able to wash or shave since leaving Tarlac five days before. Above all they were hungry. No food had been distributed since early in the morning.

At 6:00 the processing was completed. The men were formed into squads and led inside the barracks to their assigned spaces. They all had difficulty walking in the uncomfortable clogs, particularly when negotiating the stairs. Many of the men were so awkward and clumsy that they silently cursed their captors for humiliating them in yet another way.

The interior of the barracks was a disappointment. Wainwright and King got a tiny room to themselves, and the squad rooms, measuring fifteen by eighteen feet, were to house from eight to a dozen men each. The bunks were made of iron and the mattresses, stuffed with straw, were "as hard as the floor, and probably no cleaner." The pillows were heavy, firm sacks of rice. Each room was lit by a single dim bare bulb that hung over a crude wooden table flanked by benches. The thought of sleeping and eating and passing their days in these cramped quarters for months, perhaps years, was depressing, but worse was to come.

After the men settled in to their new quarters, they were ordered to designate members of each squad to be food carriers and servers. At last they would get something to eat! The carriers went to the cook house and returned with dinner in large wooden pails. The servers' job was to parcel out the food, being careful that every man got the same amount.

"Our first meal gave us an indication of what was to come," said Lew Beebe. The time at Karenko was "the worst period of starvation we were to endure as prisoners of war." Dinner that night consisted of a teacup of rice and a bowl of thin watery soup, actually hot water in which a few vegetables had been boiled. The rice was plain. "There was nothing in it or on it—except, of course, the rice worms and weevils." The hungry men gulped down the rice, worms and weevils included. At least the insects would supply some protein. But the men still had some hope that things would improve. They went to bed their first night in Karenko sure that they would be fed better the next day. This meal was scanty, they thought, only because the camp had just been established and had not yet received adequate supplies. Tomorrow would be better.

Breakfast, lunch, and dinner the next day were exactly the same—a single cup of rice and a bowl of hot water. "This menu did not vary for the next two thousand meals," wrote finance officer Jack Vance, and soon it took its toll on the men, physically and mentally.

The prisoners began to waste away. They could see the changes in one another when they took their weekly baths. They were being "reduced to skin and bones. With most body flesh gone, loose skin could be folded on the arms and legs and it hung down from the buttocks." Wainwright and others who were thin to begin with suffered acutely. "We used to get awfully hungry," Wainwright said after the war. "We would dream up visions of juicy steaks and tempting roasts and vegetables—until we realized that we must forget the things we could not have."

Wainwright complained to Imamura, the camp commander, and later to the commander of all Japanese forces on Taiwan. "If you're trying to keep us alive," he told them, "then give us enough to keep us alive. We're not asking for luxuries." His pleas did no good. The Japanese replied that if the prisoners were given meat, next they would want women. "Ridiculous!" commented a Corregidor officer. "A prostitute would have starved at Karenko. You could write a book about POW sex life in less than a page. All we wanted was food."

Everyone became food-conscious. They thought, talked, and dreamed about food. They filled page after page of their diaries and notebooks with recipes, and exchanged notes on the preparation of their favorite foods. They prepared detailed cookbooks and compiled long lists of notable restaurants in cities they had lived in or visited. Food became their obsession. "I am hungry all the time," Tom Dooley wrote.

Lew Beebe agreed. "During the starving process one is *always* hungry. The first thought on waking in the morning is food. The last thought at night, or the last sensation, is one of hunger. A bowl of soup and a cup of rice, such as we received, appeared only to intensify the craving for more food. Long since I had learned to like rice—I loved it, in fact. I felt that I could eat my weight in plain boiled rice."

The Japanese cooked the rice for themselves in huge cauldrons, and some of the grains would solidify on the walls of the pot. A few lucky prisoners who had access to the cook house would scrape off the golden crust and bring it to Wainwright and King, so the older men would have a little more to eat.

The men tried to supplement their diet as best they could. They spent hours wandering over the grounds hunting for snails and picking papaya leaves to add to the soup. Occasionally the guards gave them an orange or a banana, and these precious gifts were recorded in one's diary, a memory to be treasured.

On Thanksgiving day of 1942 the Japanese provided a treat—rabbit for the soup. They supplied twenty-nine rabbits to be shared among 317 men, so "we barely detected the odor in our soup," scoffed navy doctor Robert Davis. "Some contrast to a Thanksgiving at home."

Months later, in March of 1943, when the Japanese finally allowed the Americans to receive food from Red Cross packages, a brisk traffic in foodstuffs and tobacco sprang up. Prices were highly inflated by peacetime standards, but money meant little compared to survival. For those who did not have cash, sellers took checks written on plain pieces of paper to be cashed after the war. A can of corned beef sold for $25, a one-pound can of powdered milk for $30. A single American cigarette could bring up to a dollar.

Some of the prisoners hoarded their Red Cross items instead of eating them. One man, who weighed less than 100 pounds, was admitted to the hospital with a diagnosis of malnutrition. He had consumed none of the life-saving food from his Red Cross packages, saving every ounce in the belief that sooner or later the Japanese would cut off all their food.

Shortly after their arrival at Karenko the prisoners began to receive pay, in accordance with the Geneva Convention. The pay scale was that of the Japanese army and ranged from 395 yen a month for a general officer to less than 20 yen for a sergeant. Only twenty-five yen was given in cash. The rest, minus the cost of their food and clogs, was credited to their accounts.

The Japanese opened a *schujo*, a post exchange, where the prisoners could spend their money, and Wainwright selected Jack Vance to run it. Various items of food were made available—sugar, salt, curry powder, and a sweet syrup to mix with the rice. The Japanese also provided clothes hangers and shoe polish; although the prisoners had neither clothes nor shoes, they bought these items too!

The constant gnawing hunger affected many of the men psychologically. "Hungry men," observed Walt Odlin, "are irritable, unstable, confused men. Such men cannot govern themselves or live in a civilized manner. Among us, tempers were short. Fighting words often passed between fellow prisoners."

Scuffles broke out between officers and between enlisted men, often over trivial incidents. One night after lights out two officers were discussing the time difference between Washington and Karenko. Their voices rose and one said something the other didn't like. Their language grew foul and tempers flared. The offended officer jumped from his bunk, switched on the light, and was ready to settle the matter with fists.

Two men who had served together on Corregidor worked hard at Karenko to grow a tomato plant, and they eagerly awaited the first result of their efforts. At last a small green tomato appeared and daily grew larger and larger. They talked constantly about how good it would taste when it ripened. One day, unable to wait any longer, one of them ate the tomato. When the other found out they got into a fight on the barracks porch, but soon fell to the ground, exhausted.

None of the altercations lasted long. The men were too weak to carry on more than a brief struggle. If a disagreement threatened to go beyond that, Wainwright would step in and stop it. Skinny "kept everyone under control," the colonels said. "All he had to do was say, 'Cut out your bitching,' or 'That's enough,' and everyone obeyed."

Wainwright was still troubled by his own problems and was having difficulty keeping up his spirits. Plagued by his fear of having brought shame upon himself and his family and by his certainty of a court-martial if he returned home, his morale rose and fell. His orderly, Tex Carroll, ever sensitive to the general's moods, did all he could, as did his aides Johnny Pugh and Tom Dooley, but sometimes their efforts were not enough.

Like his fellow prisoners, Skinny was weak from the improper diet and sometimes he too became short-tempered and irritable. But at Karenko, as on Corregidor, he was still the commanding officer, and he was always conscious of his duty to set an example for his men.

His roommate, Ned King, occasionally annoyed him. General King was suffering great remorse over his surrender of Bataan, and he was often so depressed that he sat for long periods with his head in his hands. "It bugged hell out of Wainwright," one colonel said, but Skinny never rebuked King because he understood the man's feelings all too well.

After a month at Karenko Wainwright and the other prisoners learned the meaning of rule number two in the camp commander's "greetings" speech. "To be loath to labor . . . is prohibited. . . . You are not allowed to lead an idle life."

Captain Imamura called Wainwright to his office and told him that the prisoners would be given the opportunity to work in a garden and could keep any produce they raised. The idea of extra food was tempting to a starving man, but Wainwright refused, pointing out that the Geneva Convention forbade work by commissioned and noncommissioned officers. Nothing more was said. The commander dismissed Wainwright without further comment. But the pressures on Skinny to comply started the following day when the food supply was reduced. The soup was more watery and there was less rice for each meal.

This treatment continued for a month. The men grew progressively weaker, and many were convinced that the Japanese planned to starve them to death. That was not their intention, however; it was only to starve the Americans into submission, to the point where they would volunteer to work in the garden.

Toward the end of October Wainwright was summoned to Imamura's office and told that if the prisoners worked, not only could they keep the food they raised, but they would also be given an extra cup of rice for every workday.

Skinny returned to the barracks and discussed the matter with his generals. They all agreed that they had no choice. It was work or starve. Imamura was pleased. He had won this test of wills with Wainwright through the simple expedient of threatened starvation. The Americans had been forced to capitulate, suffering a further humiliation.

On October 26 Tom Dooley wrote in his diary: "Everyone started work today." Wainwright and his officers were given the Japanese version of a hoe, a short-handled implement. Wainwright and the taller prisoners had to stoop awkwardly to use it. The farming was exhausting for the undernourished men, and was made doubly hard because they were still unused to the uncomfortable clogs on their feet.

Six days a week the men cleared away grass, brush, rocks, and trees, and dug the hard soil to a depth of six inches. Wainwright worked with Jack Vance to clear a small patch of land on which they planted sweet potatoes. As they labored, they wondered aloud if they would live long enough to taste the results of their work.

The Japanese hoes were crude, poorly constructed tools, and they broke faster than new ones could be supplied. The farming proceeded slowly. The smallest physical effort sapped what little strength the men possessed. Prison guards prowled among them and pounced on any man they considered a slacker, yelling, slapping, and threatening him with bayonets.

The work was hard and humiliating, and the promised spring harvest—if anything would grow in the rocky, barren soil—was a long way off. And the extra rice they had been promised for their chores was less than they had been led to expect. Half the time they received no work rice, and when it was provided it amounted to no more than half a teacup per man. To starving men, however, anything additional was welcome, and that tiny supplement could mean the difference between life and death.

Eventually Wainwright, the senior generals, and every officer over the age of sixty were taken off farming detail and assigned the easier task of tending the goat herd. Twenty-five small black goats were brought into camp every day, and the American officers were charged with keeping them confined to an area designated by the Japanese.

Skinny knew horses and mules, but he didn't know anything about goats. Fortunately, Harry Greenleaf—the Cowboy—did, and he was placed in charge of the herd and the herders. Every day, the elderly three-star general reported to the young sergeant for one hour of duty. Skinny and Greenleaf got along well and passed many a pleasant hour together, talking about their shared love of horses.

Occasionally they discussed the war and the thought of liberation. Wainwright told Greenleaf what he had told all the others: They were destined to remain in captivity for a long time. He also mentioned an idea that had occurred to him several times recently. He told Greenleaf that he thought a war between America and Russia was inevitable, and that the men from Bataan and Corregidor would remain prisoners until that conflict was settled.

When Wainwright's goat-tending duty was over, he would limp back to the barracks, leaning on his cane, looking every inch a tired old man. Another day had passed in the seemingly endless string of similarly dreary days that stretched far into the future. Beyond that lay the chilling prospect of public disgrace and shame. To Wainwright the future appeared every bit as grim as the present.

Inevitably, there were a few breaks in the routine, some pleasant and others tragic, and at Karenko as at Tarlac all were faithfully recorded in the prisoners' diaries. One of the most welcome events came in September of 1942 with the arrival of new prisoners. The first batch appeared at 10:00 on the night of September 8 and consisted of 357 British and Dutch officers and enlisted men, as well as some high-ranking civilian officials, all of whom had been captured in Hong Kong, Singapore, Borneo, or the East Indies.

Lt. Gen. Arthur E. Percival, commander of the British forces at Singapore, led them into the camp. An old friend of Wainwright's was along too—Lt. Gen. Hein ter Poorten, commander of the Dutch army in the East Indies. He had visited Wainwright at Fort McKinley in the Philippines before the war, and the two men had become instant friends. The civilians in the group included the governors of Hong Kong, the Straits settlements, the Netherlands East Indies, and Sumatra, plus two British chief justices.

Now the group at Karenko was the largest and most important collection of prisoners held by any country during World War II. "In that forsaken spot," recorded Bill Brougher in his diary, "was assembled probably the most impressive array of allied 'brass' and high-ranking officials gathered together at one place."

The Dutch prisoners looked well fed. Some were even fat, and Wainwright felt sorry for them, knowing how hard it would be for them to adapt to the pitifully small rations at Karenko. In just a few weeks their clothes would be too big for them and they would become as preoccupied as everyone else with food.

The British were as emaciated as the Americans, "skeletons like ourselves," one wrote, but they had managed to hold on to a great many of their possessions. Wainwright watched in amazement as they trooped into the camp carrying tea caddies, dress uniforms, chess sets, hundreds of books, a phonograph with a large collection of records, and an anvil!

The British made a spectacular entrance, those wraiths laden with the trappings of a civilized life. One officer from Hong Kong entered the compound looking gaunt and weary, his clothing in tatters. But he was smiling, and under one arm he carried a highly polished teapot. "And in its cheerful shining face," Brougher wrote, "I read the history of his race."

For a time, these newcomers revitalized the spirits of the Americans. "They brought news," Walt Odlin said, and "the blessing of new ideas, views, and personalities to freshen our drab lives. Before their arrival our original group from Tarlac had exchanged all our stories, interests, and hopes many times over. We had told each other about our families so often that any of us knew dozens of relatives of our comrades as well as their own neighbors did. Now we were refreshed and exhilarated as we plunged into this stream of newcomers from England, Holland, Australia, and Java that poured into the somewhat stagnant water that our own society had become."

A second contingent of prisoners arrived on September 27. This group consisted of General Sharp, commander of the Visayan-Mindanao force, three other American generals, twenty colonels, and sixteen enlisted men, all taken captive in the southern islands of the Philippines. They too carried with them a fresh batch of news—rumors and stories of their part in the Philippines campaign. Many of the men had served with those in the original group on earlier posts, and there were a number of happy reunions.

Skinny found more old friends to greet among the newest contingent of prisoners, but their arrival was also a reminder of his humiliation at Homma's hands. These were the men whom he had been forced to surrender. Wainwright knew that if he had not had to do that, many of these soldiers would now be fighting as guerrillas.

The next morning Wainwright spoke to Brad Chynoweth, who had been in command at Panay and Cebu. "In utter abjection," General Chynoweth said, "he apologized to me for having ordered us all to surrender. The surrender was a bitter blow to me. But I assured him, from the depth of my heart, that I did not blame him for his actions."

Tom Dooley recorded in his diary that night: "General Wainwright very down in spirits."

The great increase in the number of prisoners brought about two significant changes in the camp routine. Regular Sunday morning church services were instituted. For one all-too-brief hour the men were able to regain a measure of dignity, as long as they did not look around at the ring of machine guns the Japanese set up before each service.

The devotions were conducted by American and British officers using the prayer book of the Episcopal Church, similar to that of the Church of England. A particularly moving service was conducted on the morning of October 25 by a popular and respected British officer from Singapore, Maj. Gen. M. B. Beckwith-Smith. Ordinarily the services were held outdoors, but today it was raining. The Japanese gave the men permission to use a large building close to the barracks.

Beckwith-Smith, the model of the aristocratic officer one would expect as commander of the Coldstream Guards, chose to read "A Prayer For Our Loved Ones."

> Holy Father in Thy mercy
> Hear our anxious prayer
> Keep our loved ones now far distant
> 'Neath Thy care . . .

His voice rolled on, reminding all present of the ones they had left behind. To a man they wondered if they would see their loved ones again. Each prisoner was filled with his own thoughts of home.

Suddenly Beckwith-Smith stopped. He glanced at the sea of thin sad faces before him and tears streamed down his face. He tried to continue with the prayer but he could not. He turned his back to the congregation for several minutes and stood straight and still until he regained his composure. Rain pounded on the roof, but there was no other sound. No one spoke and few men dared to look at any other, so overwhelmed with emotion were they all. Finally Beckwith-Smith turned around and finished reading the prayer. The last line echoed the hopes of every person there as they thought of their families, so far away in time and place.

"Bless them, guide them, save them," he read. "Keep them near to Thee."

A month later Beckwith-Smith died of strep throat and malnutrition.

The other welcome and civilizing change introduced by the new arrivals at Karenko was the phonograph concert. A. M. L. Harrison had brought his portable wind-up Victrola and a sizable collection of recordings. For an hour or so, many evenings, Wainwright and the other officers could be transported beyond the walls of the camp and their lives as captives and slaves of the Japanese. The music was mostly classical—Beethoven, Schubert, Brahms, and Mozart—but there was also Gershwin and light Strauss waltzes.

These moments brought some relief from the realities of daily existence. As the time in Karenko wore on, the men had greater and greater need for any escape they could find. Their captors were becoming more vicious.

During Wainwright's first weeks at Karenko the Japanese frequently slapped any prisoner who violated a camp rule, but no one had ever been seriously beaten, and the punishment had always been related to a specific infraction. The situation changed in late September when the Japanese civilians who had been interned by the U.S. and Australian governments at the beginning of the war were repatriated. These people reported that they had been badly mistreated; the ones from the United States said that Japanese-Americans there had been stripped of their property and taken to concentration camps.

The Japanese prison camp administrators were outraged. The officials at Karenko immediately summoned Wainwright and the senior British and Dutch officers to appear before them. The camp commander, Imamura, said that unless they wrote to their governments to demand that they discontinue the poor treatment the Japanese-Americans were receiving, none of them could hope for better treatment at Karenko. Soon thereafter, Imamura lined up the guards and addressed them. "What he said I don't know," Wainwright said, "but I do know that right after that they commenced knocking people around—hitting them over the heads with guns, kicking them and putting on a regular reign of terror which lasted for a long, long time."

Few prisoners escaped injury during the time of brutality that followed. The Japanese guards had no respect for rank or age. That very night Wainwright angered a guard, who proceeded to "knock the hell" out of him. Skinny had gone to the latrine, which had guards stationed at both entrance and exit to check the prisoners in and out, and he had absentmindedly left by the entrance door. A guard was waiting for him. Wainwright bowed low, as every prisoner had to do, and when he straightened up the guard struck. The Japanese private lashed out with his open hand and delivered several sharp, stinging blows to Wainwright's face. Then he strolled away.

Confused and dazed, Skinny spotted General Funk standing nearby and limped over to speak to him.

"What did I do, Arnold?" he asked. "What did I do?"

"You used the wrong door, General."

On another visit to the latrine, Wainwright's bowlegged stance, typical of a cavalryman, aroused the interest of a guard nicknamed "Toad." Colonel Mallonée wrote that Toad "jerked [Wainwright] to attention, got his heels together, and then roared about his knees being apart, tapping them with his bayonet. Skinny got his knees together, but of course had to move his feet and then toe in. This caused another roar and his heels came back together as his knees spread. . . . the guard knelt and held Wainwright's knees together with his hands to show what he wanted. As he removed his hands the knees bounced apart. Those who were there, also at attention, fully expected him to work Skinny over then.

"Instead, a puzzled expression crossed his face. He again held the knees together. As he released them they again bounced apart. A pleased grin replaced the scowl. . . . For the next five minutes or so, as a child would play with a jack-in-the-box, this moron played with the knees of the lieutenant general commanding the United States Forces in the Philippines."

Two nights later Wainwright was not so fortunate when a guard outside the latrine beckoned to him. Confident that this time he had not violated any camp rule, Skinny approached him. Before he could bow or ask what the guard wanted, the man slapped him across the face repeatedly. With each blow he shouted, "For Japanese in America!" The beating of Wainwright was his retribution for the treatment of the Japanese who lived in the United States.

Every time the man hit him Wainwright felt his legs grow weaker, but he forced himself to remain upright until the maddened guard "doubled up his fist and hit me under the jaw and knocked me down." Skinny lay still for a moment, then slowly hauled himself to his feet. The Japanese guard had vanished. The old man dragged himself to the washroom and splashed cold water on his face. He made his way back to the barracks and told a friend what had happened. It was the blackest moment of his life.

This incident still rankled after the war when Wainwright related it to Bob Considine. The two men had become friends and were on a first-name basis, and Considine asked, "What else went through your mind as you lay there, Skinny?"

"Wainwright slowly stiffened in his chair. His shoulders, which had drooped as he told the story, squared off. He fetched a newly laundered handkerchief from his pocket, dusted the tears from his cheeks and eyes, blew a thunderous blast from his nose, and regarded me coolly. 'I'll tell you what else went through my mind as I lay there, *Mr.* Considine,' he said curtly. 'And this is it: a private should never strike a lieutenant general!'" "I never dared call him 'Skinny' again," Considine said.

After the war Wainwright talked about the Japanese brutality with the army war crimes investigators. "Hitting people like that just became the rule," he said. "We stayed there at that camp [Karenko] for a total of seven and one-half months. I should say for five or five and a half months that thing went on almost continuously. I have seen this happen after evening roll call at eight o'clock when people would go out to the latrine and come back to go to bed. I have seen men consistently beaten for a period of four or five minutes. The Jap sentinel would just haul off and hit him for no reason at all." Wainwright tried to get the beatings stopped. He and Percival sent a letter to the camp commandant, who replied that he could do anything he wanted with the prisoners, even shoot them.

Some of the American enlisted men were beaten so frequently that they always seemed to have blackened eyes and bruised faces. Some nights at the latrine a guard would line up everyone who happened to be there and walk up and down the column punching each man with his fist.

Wainwright saw guards crush a man's toes with the butt of a rifle and whip another over the head with a bayonet. Beckwith-Smith was beaten about the face, and he never recovered from the effects. Heath, another Singapore officer, was hit over the head with a rifle barrel. Then the guards rammed the butt of the weapon into Heath's useless right arm, from which a portion of bone had been removed following a wound in World War I.

On and on it went, day after day. "I saw so many different

things," Lew Beebe wrote, referring to the beatings, "that I don't remember all of them." No matter where a man was or what he was doing he was never safe from a beating. Skinny wasn't even protected in the small room he shared with Ned King.

The morning after Wainwright's second beating, he and King were cleaning their room, preparing it for an inspection. The door was thrown open and a guard burst into the room, yelling at them in Japanese. Skinny was so startled that he accidentally knocked a porcelain mess bowl to the floor, shattering it.

The guard was irate. He lunged at Wainwright and hit him several times across the face. As he did so, the rifle in his left hand slipped, and the bayonet jabbed Wainwright in the wrist. He ordered Wainwright out of the room and led him across the parade ground, in full view of the prisoners, to the guardhouse. There a Japanese sergeant sent Wainwright to the hospital.

Wainwright's war had become more cruel than anything he had encountered on Bataan or Corregidor. With the coming of winter, even these dismal conditions would grow worse.

Wainwright and his fellow prisoners said they had never felt as cold in all their lives as they did during the winter of 1942–43 at Karenko. Skinny had spent the last two years in the tropics, where his blood had thinned in adaptation to the warm climate. The Americans from Bataan and Corregidor had only the remnants of their light tropical uniforms, and the barracks were unheated. The troops were so thin and undernourished from their starvation diet that their bodies were incapable of manufacturing heat on their own.

Bitter winds blew constantly from the northeast. Wainwright shivered from the cold as he tended his goats each day. He did not possess sufficient energy to keep himself moving around to get warm. At night he shivered under the four blankets the Japanese had issued to each man, and he always wore all the scraps of clothing he owned. He and the other men would wrap towels over their heads and burrow under the blankets. "I thought sometimes that I would never be warm again," wrote Lew Beebe.

The constant cold drained what little strength the prisoners had left and made them more susceptible to illness. Wainwright took sick in mid-December. He lay on his bunk, tossing with chills and fever. There was nothing the American and British doctors could do for him. The Japanese would not provide any medicine. For several days Sergeant Carroll was constantly at the general's bedside, wiping his fevered face with a water-soaked rag and trying to keep the old man warm. Wainwright showed some improvement after a few days and by Christmas was able to leave his bed.

Skinny also suffered from a disease that afflicted almost all the prisoners at Karenko—beriberi. It was easy to tell who had beriberi because its effects could be heard whenever a man walked barefoot across the floor. He made a distinctive sound, what the men called the "foot slap." The person with beriberi loses control over the muscles that govern the toes. Instead of lowering the toes to the floor, the way one walks normally, the toes and the sole of the foot fall under their own weight, making a characteristic slapping sound.

There was a simple cure for the disease—vitamin B-1, which is contained in, among other things, unpolished rice. But the Japanese fed the prisoners only polished rice and the number of beriberi cases grew rapidly.

Wainwright was lucky. He had the dry form of the disease. Wet beriberi causes the ankles and then the entire body to swell. It results in prolonged illness and sometimes death.

Death was no stranger to the men of Karenko that winter. The first man to be claimed was Beckwith-Smith. He had survived Dunkirk and Singapore, but he could not survive a strep throat and malnutrition and the lingering effects of the beating he had suffered. He died at 7:30 on the morning of November 11, Armistice Day, a date of significance for Wainwright and for many American and British soldiers who had fought in World War I.

At 11:00 that morning, the hour when the guns had stopped on the battlefields of France twenty-four years before, the prisoners observed a two-minute silence in honor of Beckwith-Smith. The body was cremated and the ashes buried in the campground, with Wainwright and the senior British and Dutch officers attending a simple ceremony. Brougher eulogized Beckwith-Smith in his diary: "He shared our bondage with commanding grace."

In February of 1943 another popular prisoner died, American army sergeant James Cavanaugh. His death could also have been easily prevented, but again the prisoners had no medication for strep throat, and there was insufficient food to prevent malnutrition. Wainwright had been particularly fond of Cavanaugh. "Everyone dreadfully depressed over his death," Tom Dooley wrote.

At the end of February Col. Paul Bunker, the man Wainwright had sent to raise the flag of surrender over Corregidor, died of wet beriberi. His body had swollen to enormous proportions. Bunker asked to see Wainwright, but he did not recognize him. Skinny sat with him during his final hours. The next day Skinny and most of the other prisoners made out their wills. No one knew whose turn was next.

Life went on for the survivors. They tried to keep their minds occupied as best they could through numerous homely activities. They fashioned tiny decks of playing cards from scraps of cardboard; caught minnows for an "aquarium"; and taught each other poetry, songs, and foreign languages. They listed in their diaries the names of fellow prisoners and of favorite books read, and some recorded their history of the Philippine campaign. One officer set down the dollar value of each item of clothing and personal gear, including his golf clubs, abandoned at Fort Stotsenburg at the outbreak of the war. When the men could find a needle and unravel a piece of cloth for thread, they made mittens and caps with earflaps for warmth. Wainwright stitched up a small canvas notebook as a gift for Tom Dooley; bound inside were several sheets of flimsy U.S. airmail stationery.

In this way, days were endured, hunger was tolerated, and numbing cold and stinging beatings were accepted as routine. Despite their privations the men still had hope to sustain them, hope that someday the war would be over and they would have lived through it. Their optimism was fed by two things, rumors and the little hard news they could find. Rumors cropped up constantly, sweeping through the camp as quickly and completely as the chill winds blowing from the northeast. The men devoured the tales as if they were food; in a way they were—they nourished the soul.

The most persistent rumor was that they would soon be exchanged for Japanese prisoners of war. They would be sent home or interned in a neutral country for the duration. Chile was settled upon as the most likely country for their confinement.

Shortly after their arrival at Karenko the prisoners had been fingerprinted. This action fanned the stories of their imminent repatriation. Periodically someone announced that a ship was in the harbor, ready to take them out. The addition of the British and Dutch contingent in September 1942 further convinced the Americans of the coming exchange. Why would the Japanese gather so many high-ranking officers and civilians of different nationalities in one place if not to make an exchange? The idea made sense to men grasping for any way out of a desperate and humiliating situation.

Wainwright was never taken in by these rumors. He knew that

they would remain prisoners until Japan was defeated, or perhaps until the war he foresaw with Russia was over. He listened to the stories and saw the temporary light of hope in the eyes of his men, but he never believed them.

"General Wainwright told us repeatedly that our hopes were in vain," Walt Odlin remembered. Skinny was right. The Japanese never had any intention of exchanging their prisoners of war. They were there for the duration, however long that might be.

News was difficult to obtain in the early weeks at Karenko, and the lack of information about the war added to Wainwright's sense of isolation. For some time there was no world beyond the walls of the camp. Nothing existed out there.

Late in the fall the Japanese provided old copies of an English-language newspaper, the *Nippon Times,* prepared by the Japanese propaganda office in Tokyo. It reported that the Japanese were triumphant throughout the Pacific, a statement which, throughout 1942, was not so inaccurate. The paper did present a truer picture of events in the European theater.

Sometimes it was possible to see through the enemy propaganda. According to the *Nippon Times,* the U.S. Navy had ceased to exist west of Hawaii, and the battles of Coral Sea and Midway were described as complete Japanese victories. Yet in a later edition of the paper the Japanese admitted that "despite our losses at Midway, we have an adequate fleet." Although the prisoners could not tell how many enemy ships had been lost, it was obvious to them that Midway had not been a victory for the Japanese.

Wainwright and his men followed the *Nippon Times* version of the Japanese conquest of the Aleutians, the Solomons, and New Guinea. Everywhere the Japanese were apparently winning. Even though the men of Karenko did not believe all they read, the fact that the Japanese were fighting so far to the south indicated what rapid progress they had made since their capture of the Philippines. The Solomon Islands and New Guinea were not so far from Australia. The men knew that the farther south the Japanese advanced, the longer it would take for the U.S. forces to win the war and set them free.

The news from the other side of the world was more promising, but it also engendered much bitterness among the prisoners. In November of 1942 Wainwright learned of the American invasion of North Africa, including details of the number of ships and men involved. The operation soon became a heated topic of conversation among the officers. If America had so many men in uniform and a fleet large enough to launch a major invasion, why hadn't they been sent to the Pacific to reinforce Bataan and Corregidor? Why was everything going to the European theater? The obvious Europe-first policy angered them. They knew that no amount of victories over the Germans and Italians would hasten their own day of liberation.

One American officer spotted a small item in the *Nippon Times* about Mrs. Wainwright. She had attended a celebration in Hartford, Connecticut, for "Wainwright Day." The man brought the news to Skinny right away, sure that it would boost his morale and convince him that he was not in disgrace back home. He was being honored!

Wainwright read the article slowly, but he refused to believe it. He was sure that the Japanese had planted the story in the paper as a trick. Nothing his friends could say changed his mind. He was convinced that he would return home in shame.

Like most of the other men in the camp, Wainwright was thirsty for news. He was especially keen on learning about the Pacific war, his part of the war. Events in Europe did not interest him nearly as much. Stu Wood, who read and spoke the Japanese language fluently, constantly risked his life at Karenko—and at other camps later—to smuggle in Japanese newspapers in an effort to get more news for Skinny and the others. Thirty papers, a month's supply, could be gotten in exchange for a wristwatch.

Wood translated the articles and spread the news through the camp, choosing his contacts carefully. One day he passed Wainwright on the drill field. "The ocean is sweet with sugar," he whispered. Skinny was delighted. Wood's cryptic phrase meant that Japanese ships were being sunk by American submarines!

As Christmas of 1942 neared, the first Christmas in captivity, most of the men became depressed. But they pulled themselves together and decided to have as much of an old-fashioned Christmas as they could manage. Skinny's old cavalry buddy, Clint Pierce, organized a committee to ask the Japanese for permission to arrange a celebration. It was granted, and a wave of joyful spirit swept through the camp. The men made plans and carried out their preparations with vigor, determined to make Christmas a truly festive day.

Skill and ingenuity were applied to the decorations. The barracks were gay with branches, boughs, and ferns hung on the walls and arranged on the tables. Cigarette packs and cartons were cut up to obtain pieces of red and blue paper, which were used to form the words "Merry Christmas" and "Happy New Year." The bright, colorful letters were pasted on the windows with thick ricewater. Foil from packages of tea was cut into shiny stars. Long chains of colored paper were tied together and hung throughout the rooms and hallways. A gifted whittler carved a small Santa Claus doll out of a block of wood. The dingy rooms took on a cheerful atmosphere and spirits rose dramatically.

There could be no proper Christmas celebration without music, and so a group of choral singers, the Octette, was formed. Col. William Braly, one of General Moore's staff officers, had managed to keep his violin. He gathered the group behind the pigpen and rehearsed them in the traditional Christmas carols. The Octette was directed by Lew Beebe and included Charlie Drake, Tom Dooley, Eddie O'Connor, Ted Lilly, Gurden Sage, and T. M. Cornell, plus William Wilterdink and Robert Davis from the navy. They developed a smooth professional style and brought much pleasure to the men during that holiday season and the many months that followed.

Two general officers—one British and the other Australian—tried to concoct a special drink for the holidays. They mixed potato peelings from the garbage dump with rice and a little sugar in their tea caddy, and set the brew to boiling. A little while later the stuff exploded and most of the liquor was lost. The generals and their American confederates each got three swallows, with which they toasted the holiday, the king, and the U.S. president.

The weather on Christmas Eve was beautiful. A full moon illuminated the compound and the mountains beyond, and the temperature was comfortably warm. After the 8:00 P.M. roll call the Octette strolled through the barracks singing the familiar music of the holiday season. During these wonderful moments Wainwright and his men, remembered one, "completely escaped from the present time and place . . . our deeply stirred emotions erasing all that was ugly and disagreeable from our thoughts."

Wainwright stood in the center of the barracks for a while, hearing the songs, lost in the memory of past Christmases and of home. He went into his room and closed the door. As the carolers approached they sang a favorite of his, "Hark, the Herald Angels Sing." It was too much for Skinny. He put his head in his hands, grateful that no one could see him. But he was not alone; many an old soldier cried that night.

Christmas morning was bright and sunny. The men joyously

exchanged handshakes and simple presents they had fashioned from whatever they could find.

"Next year we'll be long gone from this place," some said.

"You bet!" others replied.

They would say the same thing next Christmas, and the one after that.

After the morning church service, conducted by Generals King and Percival, the prisoners discovered that the Japanese had arranged a surprise—extra food. Each prisoner was given an orange and an apple, a small cake made from sweet-potato flour, and a six-ounce loaf of bread, the first bread they had had since leaving the Philippines. This was a feast, and they all ate heartily. The noon meal brought another treat; there was pork in the soup.

So festive did some prisoners feel that they drew up elaborate menus recording the day's meals. Decorated with drawings of holly wreaths and Christmas bells, the menus were signed by the members of the squad and kept as souvenirs for many years.

Breakfast: Green Vegetable Soup
                Rice and Barley with Salt
                Cigar
                Tea

Dinner: Green Vegetable Soup with Pork Fat
                Rice, Barley, and Pork with Salt
                Bread, Orange, Banana
                Sweet Potato Cake, Raw Peanuts
                Cigar, Tea

Supper: Bean and Vegetable Soup
                Rice and Barley with Salt
                Cigars

Two of the senior Japanese guards, nicknamed by the Americans "Boots" and "Baggy Pants," wandered through the squad rooms politely bidding everyone a merry Christmas. They expressed regret that they could not supply more good things to eat. It was truly a day of miracles.

The next day brought back the old, dismal routine, but the prisoners' holiday feelings lingered because New Year's Eve was coming. The Japanese had granted permission for them to put on a program of entertainment, and plans were afoot for a long and rollicking show. Throughout the camp enthusiastic performers rehearsed songs, skits, and dramatic readings.

What a show! The Octette sang a medley of favorites—"Take Me Out to the Ball Game," "Smiles," and "Sweet Rosie O'Grady." A magician did tricks, four Australian soldiers offered an outrageous skit complete with mining camp songs, and, for the highlight of the evening, Skinny got up on stage to recite "General Gas 'n' Oil," a satirical poem about an old cavalry general who objects to the newfangled noisy, smelly monsters called tanks.

"Our general's participation in the program was a splendid example of leadership," Walt Odlin wrote, "for even as he stood there making us rock with laughter, we knew he was still not fully recovered from a severe beating." The cheers he received that night were loud and long, deep from the heart of every man. Wainwright was still one of them, a soldier's soldier.

The men went to sleep content that night—those hungry, weary, tattered men of Karenko—hoping that the new year would be better than the last.

"Outlook for 1943 much brighter," wrote Tom Dooley in his diary.

It did not turn out that way.

CHAPTER 16

"How Long, Oh Lord, How Long?"

Day by day, week by week, month by month, with agonizing slowness, time labored on, each day much like the one before. There was never enough food to assuage the hunger, never enough medicine to cure the sickness, never enough news from the outside world, never enough heat during the long cold winter. The harassment from the guards continued, though less violent than before, but a man could still be slapped for the slightest offense—or for no offense at all—and another shred of dignity stripped from him.

As the hunger weakened the men's bodies, so the boredom and ever-declining hope for a quick release attacked their souls. They might record the passage of each day in their diaries, or scratch another day off on the pine board over their bunks, or take note of birthdays or wedding anniversaries or years in the service, but that told them only that another day or month or year had passed. These were records of time spent, past, lost, but they gave no indication of how much more time lay ahead.

There was news of victories in Europe and there were rumors of successes in the Pacific, but did that mean the war would be over next year, or in two years, or not for five? And what was happening at home? Wainwright worried about his wife. How was Adele getting by on her own? And what of Jack? He was the right age for military service. Where was he? Was he still alive? For many long months neither Wainwright nor anyone else received news from home. The isolation was hard to bear.

How long before they would see their families again? Would they ever see them again? What would their own fate be when—if—they returned home? Were their careers finished? Skinny knew his army days were over. If, somehow, he escaped a court-martial, the best he could expect was a forced retirement, branded for the rest of his life as the man responsible for the largest surrender in his country's history. Would he ever be able to hold his head up again?

The uncertainty, the waiting, the endless, pointless, repetitive days took their toll. Day by day, week by week, month by month, Wainwright and his men asked the same haunting question: How long? General Brougher captured their growing fears and torments in a poem he read to them all one night. He called it "How Long, Oh Lord, How Long?"

> How long, oh Lord, can men endure the fate
> Of blasted hopes, defeat, and vengeful hate?
> How long can spirit live, can will survive,
> And keep the flickering flame of faith alive?
> In thralldom dark, depressed with cank'ring care,
> How long can hope contend with black despair?
> How long, oh Lord, how long? Foredoomed to share
> We're waiting still for help that never came . . .
> How long, oh Lord, how long? For all I know
> My loved ones may be dead long months ago.
> No letter comes, no word of love and cheer,
> For weeks, for months, and now another year.
> How long, oh Lord, before the callous grow
> On tender spots where heart-aches pain me so? . . .
> How long, oh Lord, how long? While ships delay
> My precious years run out, my powers decay.
> My birthright lost, by ruthless time's decree
> To lads who learned their alphabet from me.
> A rusting sword upon a garbage heap . . .

On the date that marked the end of Skinny's first full year of captivity—May 7, 1943—he was no longer in Karenko. A month before, he and 116 of the other highest-ranking officers and civilians had been taken from the security of the known and familiar, the comradeship of old friends, and sent thirty-six miles south to a new camp at Tamazato.

*   *   *

The day Wainwright left, April 2, 1943, had been hectic and exhausting, a day of sad farewells. All the colonels were staying in Karenko. The new camp was for generals, governors, and chief justices only. Those who were staying came to Wainwright to say goodbye, and Skinny wondered if he would ever see these men again, men who had been through so much for him—Tom Dooley, Nick Galbraith, Jack Vance, and so many others.

At 8:00 A.M., Wainwright and the others were marched into the railroad station at Karenko and herded aboard tiny cars. The train reminded Lew Beebe of the Toonerville Trolley. The tracks were no more than two feet wide and the wooden cars looked so flimsy that the men wondered what kept them from falling apart.

The journey was long and slow, more than eight hours, and the men were packed so tightly together that they could barely move. They had been provided a little food—some bread, sugar, and a few rice cookies—and Wainwright had some additional luck. Brougher shared the tomatoes he had grown at Karenko. They were delicious.

At 4:30 that afternoon the tedious journey ended at the town of Tamazato. The men were led to a barbed-wire enclosure some 300 yards from the station. This was Wainwright's third prison camp, but it was not to be his last. Before the war ended he would be moved three more times.

No sooner had they marched into the compound when Japanese officials sent them back to the station to unload the tables, chairs, bunks, and mattresses they had brought from Karenko. The setting at Tamazato may have been new, but their camp equipment was the same.

By the time they finished it was dark and very late. The Japanese guards gave them hot soup for supper and assigned them to squads. Wainwright was put in the twenty-man Third Squad, along with his Dutch friend, ter Poorten, and most of the American generals—King, Brougher, Pierce, Bluemel, Funk, Jones, Moore, Beebe, and the others. Although Wainwright was the ranking officer and therefore entitled to be squad leader, he assigned the task to General King, as he had at Karenko. Skinny knew that his hearing was not good enough for the job. Sometimes he missed hearing Japanese orders. It was dangerous when an individual failed to hear a Japanese command, but he knew it would be unfair if all the members of his squad were punished because he had not heard an order.

Conditions at Tamazato turned out to be an improvement in

many ways. For some reason—and neither Skinny nor any of the other prisoners knew why—his group had been singled out for preferential treatment. "Our situation is in many ways much more pleasant," Brougher wrote. "It is a quiet, restful place, with delightful climate. We are reasonably well fixed here—for the duration, if necessary."

No work was required of the men and for the first time they were allowed a degree of independence in the running of the camp. They were even permitted to take over the kitchen, with Lew Beebe in charge. A remarkably talented cook, Staff Sgt. G. E. Brown (General Percival's mess sergeant and a former assistant chef at Claridge's Hotel in London), prepared all the food. The men not only had more food, but food that was more to their taste.

Two weeks after arriving at Tamazato, and almost a year after they had been captured, the prisoners received Red Cross packages. "There is a Santa Claus after all!" Brougher wrote. Wainwright and his squad stared in disbelief as they unpacked items they had almost forgotten existed. Corned beef, liver paste, cocoa, salt, bacon, marmalade, chocolate, cheese, crackers, candies, and even American cigarettes. The tobacco was so strong in comparison to the Japanese cigarettes that some of the men got high on just two puffs.

"I can't describe properly our sensations when we received these boxes," Lew Beebe said. "But have you ever been so happy you wanted to cry?"

At first the men could barely prevent themselves from wolfing down everything in sight, but in a day or two, after considerable diarrhea from overindulging, common sense prevailed, and they consumed the food more slowly. Sergeant Brown did wondrous things in the kitchen with the new "civilized food" and many of the men made up their own interesting combinations, such as "rice pudding," a mixture of chocolate and rice.

Within a few days the men began to put on weight, and in just one week the physical effects of the extra food were pronounced. Wainwright had gained seven pounds. Their overall health improved and they began to feel stronger. Soon they were able to take some exercise. It wasn't much—walking a mile in the morning and another in the afternoon—but a week before they had been unable to do it.

The generals suffered no beatings at Tamazato, though some guards kept up mild harassment and hazing. The same rules were in effect, however, particularly the requirement that all prisoners must bow low before every Japanese soldier, no matter what his rank.

In early June of 1943, the prisoners met with a Swiss representative of the International Red Cross. Prior to the meeting, the camp commandant had briefed the men carefully on what they could and could not say to the visitor. None of the prisoners was allowed to speak to the Red Cross official in private. A Japanese officer was always at his side, paying close attention to all conversations. As a result, no complaints could be voiced about the beatings and the diet at Karenko, or about their failure to receive Red Cross packages until recently. The representative was given a complete tour of the camp and could therefore report in all honesty that the conditions were not bad. The men had adequate food, were allowed to administer the camp by themselves, and showed no signs of torture or beatings. Wainwright was annoyed that he could not tell the man what they had suffered for nearly a year, but he knew it would do no good. The Japanese would take reprisals against them so it was not worth the risk, not when conditions were so much better now.

Physically the men were growing stronger, and their morale had improved as well, but they were still haunted by the same question: How long would it go on, this life as prisoners of war? They were still cut off from all other human contact.

The fears they had labored under at Karenko nagged at them. Had they been forgotten, written off by their families and their country? Did anyone out there even know they were alive? Wainwright had been permitted to write three brief letters to Adele, but he didn't know if the Japanese had mailed them. Perhaps Adele and their son Jack thought he was dead.

Skinny had not heard from his wife. He knew she would have written if she thought he were alive. Obviously the Japanese were not permitting the letters to get through.

And so the days passed at Tamazato. The men were stronger but emotionally they lived in a vacuum, deprived of news from the outside world. Now that they were no longer worried about starvation, their concern turned to their families. What was happening beyond the barbed wire that encircled them?

In Skaneateles, New York, Adele "Kitty" Wainwright did know that her husband was alive, or at least that he had been six months before. In early December 1942, Skinny had been asked by the commandant at Karenko to broadcast a short radio message to his wife. He jumped at the chance, though he was not optimistic that the message would reach the United States.

It was heard on December 12 and the War Department immediately notified Mrs. Wainwright. This was her first word from Skinny since April 1942, before Corregidor fell.

"From Lt. General Wainwright to Mrs. J. M. Wainwright, Skaneateles, N.Y. Am well and cared for. Notify my cousins, Jack and Jimmy Ulio, and Jenny. Have written you regularly, try to write to me."

It wasn't much, but Adele treasured that brief message during the hard months ahead, and she continued to write to him, sending a long letter at least once a week.

General George Marshall was informed of the radio message and wrote to her that same day.

"The War Department has already notified you of the radio message received from Wainwright but I wish to confirm it and to tell you how glad I am for you. I know that direct word from Skinny must be of great comfort to you, as it is to all of us."

Before too long, Mrs. Wainwright had an opportunity to send a radio communication to Skinny. For a program called "Eyes of the Air Force," she recorded her thoughts at a station in Syracuse. The message would be transcribed and broadcast from the closest American radio station to Formosa. No one knew if it would reach him, but she wanted to try.

"Everything at home is fine," Adele Wainwright told her husband. "I keep very busy. I am an airplane spotter and serve regular shifts on the observation post in Skaneateles. So many of your friends wanted to be remembered to you it would be impossible to name them all. But Johnny especially asked me to say hello. He wanted me to be sure and tell you that he is well and happy and that he has his own ship now. So 'hello' from our son, Captain Johnny." Wainwright never received the message.

Mrs. Wainwright also took part in two celebrations in Wainwright's honor during 1943. The *Nippon Times* news item that Skinny refused to believe had been correct. The city of Hartford, Connecticut, held a formal ceremony for Wainwright Day. Charles McKew Parr, Hartford's delegate to the state legislature, was a West Point classmate of Wainwright's. Governor Raymond Baldwin read a resolution passed by the general assembly expressing the state's "Heartfelt gratitude and deep admiration for the heroic defense of Bataan and Corregidor Island." Adele was so overcome with emotion that she could hardly speak.

A few months later she went to Governors Island, New York, to receive an Oak Leaf Cluster for Wainwright's Distinguished Service Medal. Mayor Fiorello LaGuardia of New York City spoke at the ceremony, which was attended by several high-ranking American and Filipino military officers and by a representative of Skinny's West Point class.

Other information about Wainwright reached Washington during his first year of captivity. It came informally, through a member of MacArthur's staff, and Secretary of War Stimson found it disagreeable because it maligned Wainwright. In MacArthur's official family, Skinny had not been forgiven for surrendering the Philippines.

The information came on Thursday, February 25, 1943, in the person of Col. Joseph Stevenot, who before joining MacArthur's staff had been a telephone company executive in Manila.

"He brought me some very pleasant messages for myself from MacArthur," Stimson wrote in his diary, "but he struck the wrong note when he told me of some things against Wainwright of an unpleasant character during the strenuous times of Corregidor. I asked him sharply whether MacArthur had asked him to give that message to me and he was very much taken back and said no. Then I told him that I had never heard anything against Wainwright but on the contrary thought he made a very gallant defense after MacArthur left. It made a bad impression on me. I fear there is a bad atmosphere around MacArthur's staff."

Although several members of MacArthur's staff traveled to Washington during the war, they carried no more criticisms of Wainwright to the War Department. Indeed, in late January 1943, the War Department had asked for and received some kind words from MacArthur for the occasion of the awarding of Wainwright's Oak Leaf Cluster. MacArthur dispatched the following.

"Please tell Mrs. Wainwright of my sincere hope that before too long a time elapses I may have her husband back on active service again under my command. His rescue is ever in my thoughts."

Regardless of his personal feelings, MacArthur was sensitive to the country's admiration for Wainwright.

It was not only at awards ceremonies that Wainwright's name was being kept alive. People throughout the United States saw his picture—one taken before the war in dress uniform—on the cover of *Collier's Magazine*, July 10, 1943. A second picture inside, on page 16, showed a defiant Wainwright staring into the camera of a Japanese photographer. This one had been taken in front of the little house on Bataan in which he had met with the Japanese general Homma.

In a highly romanticized article entitled "But Not Forgotten," the magazine's readers were treated to a Hollywood-style version of Wainwright's capture and his days as a prisoner of war.

"In the tropical hills of Formosa, a tall skinny guy strides along jungle paths, swishing at weeds with a carved bamboo cane. At the end of the path, the cane sings against taut barbed wire, and the man, halting suddenly, swears softly under his breath. He flicks the dust from his faded old American Army uniform, with three silver stars on the shoulder, and strides back along the path.

"Not so long ago, his name was headline—famous all over the world. It was in the Emporia Gazette, the Berliner Tageblatt, and the Sydney Bulletin; in Nicki Nicki and the London Express and Pravda and Il Popolo d'Italia. The headlines called him a hero and a firstclass fighting man—even the enemy headlines did that. But there on the jungle path, caged behind the wire, he might have wondered a little wryly if people had forgotten. There had been so many names in the headlines since May, 1942.

"When he was first brought to the hills more than a year ago, he raged bitterly against the little yellow men who held him captive—and who had to tilt back their heads to look up into his craggy sunburned face. They respected him, these cocky little yellow men, as a man and a soldier. But as the days passed, he fought himself to a calmer frame of mind; he was too old a warrior to waste his strength, sapped by hardship and too little food, in vain anger and hatred. . . .

"That would be Lieutenant General Jonathan Mayhew Wainwright, hero of Bataan who so inspired his men that they changed the name of Corregidor to Wainwright's Rock. That would be 'Skinny'—the boy from Walla Walla, who refused to escape from the battered, bloodstained fortress at the entrance to Manila Bay. That would be the weary, sweat-soaked soldier who told his curious Japanese captors on May 6, 1942, 'I'm here with my men because my conscience would not let me leave them.'

"They stood stiffly at attention and saluted him for that—this exhausted, defeated-but-not-beaten battler who had, for months, fought their overwhelmingly superior forces to a standstill. They broadcast his words in their own chant of victory, paying tribute to his fortitude."

The writer went on to describe Wainwright's early army career and his last days on Corregidor in a glamorized mixture of a little fact and a lot of fiction. Had he not already been a genuine hero, based on his own accomplishments, articles such as this one were guaranteed to create a heroic image of him.

"Some day," the article concluded, "before too long, there will be consternation among the little men guarding the barbed wire high in the Formosa hills. There'll be shots and shouting and to Skinny's ears will come the cheering of American soldiers, charging in to set him free.

"That'll be a great day for Skinny—and for America, too."

At least the closing line was true, and despite its hyperbole the article showed that America had not forgotten Wainwright, the soldier of Bataan.

Wainwright knew none of this, of course, as he continued to pass the days as a captive. By July of 1943, when the *Collier's* article appeared, his situation had changed again, this time for the worse. He had been moved to a different camp and now he was lonelier than he had ever been.

On June 1, 1943, the Japanese had lined up the prisoners for an inspection and told them they would be divided into two groups. A small group would stay and a larger group, eighty-nine prisoners, would be sent to an unnamed destination. Wainwright and twenty-seven others—King, Moore,* Percival, ter Poorten, a few other top British and Dutch officers and civilians, and fourteen orderlies, including Tex Carroll—would remain at Tamazato.

Wainwright's familiar world was growing smaller. He bade goodbye to many good friends—Arnold Funk, Clint Pierce, Lew Beebe, and others. He had passed many pleasant hours with these men and their presence had helped ease the pain of imprisonment. Four days later the American brigadier generals and their group departed at 9:30 in the morning. Guessing correctly that they would be returning to Karenko, Wainwright took out a half sheet of brown lined paper and penciled a note to his aide Tom Dooley. One of the generals delivered it to young Dooley that afternoon.

Dear Tom:—
Some of us are staying here for the time being at least; the majority are leaving—We hear that you and Johnny [Pugh] will leave Karenko

---

*Lt. Gen. Wainwright and Maj. Gens. King and Moore were the three highest-ranking American prisoners.

with those who are leaving here today—I often wonder how your appetite is being satisfied. If you were here with me I could help you as I get more to eat than I want and give Carroll some each day—I can't tell you how much I miss your cheerful smile and your daily visits, but it won't be long now——

Best luck to you Tom, and every good wish—I long for the day when we can get together again.

J. M. W.

The camp seemed empty with so many comrades gone, and Wainwright felt even more isolated and out of touch with the rest of the world. The large group had meant more people with whom to pass the time of day, more rumors to chew on, more bridge partners, more opportunities for diversion. The problem of boredom grew more acute for Wainwright now.

Two and a half weeks later, Wainwright's party was ordered to pack their meager possessions. It was time to move on. Again they were struck by the uncertainty that accompanied every move. Life at Tamazato had been dull, especially since the departure of the others, but the men had been well fed and housed and there had been no beatings. Would their new camp be better or worse?

The following day they found themselves on the narrow-gauge train heading back to the town of Karenko. When they sensed their destination, they were delighted. Karenko had been unpleasant, but at least they would be rejoining their friends. But when they were ordered off the train at Karenko station, Wainwright and the rest of his small party were marched to the dock and herded aboard a small, filthy freighter.

The hot sun baked the steel deck of the ship. The men were packed into a long narrow hold with barely enough room to stand or to sleep. The cargo hatch was shut and fastened above their heads, and then they could feel the ship vibrate as the engines were started. They remained in the stifling, grimy hold until the next morning when the ship docked at Keelung, on the extreme northern coast of Formosa.

Wainwright led them off the ship and through the streets of the town, a strange procession of fourteen men whose average age exceeded sixty, fourteen others who were thirty to forty years younger (the orderlies), and one duck. Tex Carroll had raised the duck at Tamazato, feeding it whatever scraps of food he could scrounge, and now he was bringing "Donald" to their new home. Wainwright had told him that the duck was the only member of the group who looked healthy and fit.

The prisoners boarded a rickety train that took them about twenty miles inland, where they were loaded onto a truck. They drove another five miles into the interior of the island to a camp near the tiny village of Muksaq. Here Wainwright would spend the next sixteen months, a succession of days filled with restless idleness. How long, oh Lord, how long?

Muksaq did offer one advantage. The officers were treated at least as well as they had been at Tamazato. Indeed, often the treatment was better, although the Japanese had an ulterior motive.

The rooms in the Muksaq barracks were small, but each man had a chair, a table, and a reasonably comfortable cot. The camp was built on a hillside overlooking a pleasant valley, and was sufficiently high to offer an attractive view.

Their good treatment began at mealtime on the first day, when the Japanese distributed to the prisoners an enormous amount of rice. They also received vegetables with their meals and were promised fruit as well.

The officers were not required to work, and they were provided with many English-language books that had been captured from the British. This was paradise! Comfortable quarters, ample food, and no forced labor. It was enough to make a man suspicious. And Skinny was. He knew the Japanese were up to something. They would not provide such luxuries without expecting something in return.

A few days later Wainwright found out what it was. The commander of all the POW camps on Formosa paid a visit to Muksaq. Colonel Sazawa—"that son-of-a-bitch," Wainwright called him—oozed charm and good will toward the prisoners. There was nothing he would not do to make the prisoners' stay more comfortable. Whatever they wanted, he said, they had only to let him know.

Wainwright listened to him dumbfounded, unable to respond to such pleasantries after more than a year of callous treatment. For the next several weeks, Colonel Sazawa and other Japanese officials paid frequent visits to the camp, ever smiling and benevolent. Finally they revealed their purpose. They were softening up the high-ranking prisoners before beginning a campaign to pressure them into contacting their governments. The prisoners were to persuade American, British, and Dutch leaders that they had no chance of winning the war against the Japanese empire.

A member of Sazawa's staff came to Wainwright's room. "What do you want most in life?" he asked the general. "All I want,"

Wainwright said, "is for the war to be successfully terminated and get home."

"You can get the war stopped if you want to," the officer said. "If you will write a letter or broadcast a statement to President Roosevelt that the United States has no chance to win the war, and that they had better stop it—the war will stop."

"I do not care to continue the discussion," Skinny said coldly. "I want you to get the hell out of my way."

The officer persisted. Wainwright should tell Roosevelt that it was in the country's best interests to stop the fighting at once.

Wainwright refused to speak to him, and after a while the officer left.

"I had resigned myself," Skinny said. "I didn't care what happened to me—I wasn't going to let them talk to me like that."

The Japanese tried the same approach with the British and Dutch personnel but had no more success. But they were not ready to abandon their plans.

The more Wainwright thought about the Japanese proposal, the more he believed that the war was going badly for Japan. He could not know for sure, of course, because here at Muksaq he received considerably less news of the outside world than he had at Karenko or Tamazato.

A continuous stream of Japanese officers now descended on Wainwright and the others, trying to overwhelm them with statistics showing that Japan could not be defeated. Sometimes they seemed so plausible that it was difficult for men so far removed from their own world not to accept them. The Japanese bombarded the men with figures of American and British losses and insisted that the war was going badly for the Allies, and continued to urge them to write to their governments, insisting that they end the war.

Desperate hope and a suspicion of the enemy propaganda encouraged Wainwright's belief that the tide of the war had turned in the Allies' favor. But comforting as the thought was, it brought him no closer to liberation. No allied force was close enough to Formosa to free them, and if troops did get close enough, the Japanese would move them farther north, even to Japan itself. There were rumors that the Japanese would kill the prisoners if the Allies were winning. Wainwright was destined to remain enslaved for a long time to come.

Colonel Sazawa stepped up his efforts to win them over. He proposed picnics and fishing expeditions in the mountains, and the prisoners always agreed to go along. The excursions meant extra food and a break in the routine.

Sazawa's first picnic backfired, however. He had arranged a feast, and it had been a long time since the prisoners had eaten so well. They felt almost content until Tex Carroll informed Wainwright that they had just eaten Donald, their pet duck. After that, Sazawa's propaganda appeal met with a stony silence.

Sazawa was stubborn; he refused to give up. He asked Wainwright and King if they would agree to be filmed by newsreel cameras, allegedly for the Red Cross. After some discussion about the comments they were asked to read, the two men agreed. If the movie managed to reach the United States, their families would be able to see that they were in fairly good condition, though seriously underweight.

In late spring of 1944, after Skinny had been at Muksaq for almost a year, Colonel Sazawa made one more effort to use him and the other men for propaganda purposes. He escorted them all on a fishing trip up in the mountains. Photographs were taken of this holiday, idyllic scenes showing Japanese guards politely handing their high-ranking prisoners cups of tea and tasty snacks.

After the picture-taking and a good lunch, Sazawa stood before his guests and made what Wainwright called "a perfectly scurrilous and insulting speech about the United States—he didn't have any better sense than to do that." It was a variation of the speech he had made many times and it was followed by a request that the prisoners write to their governments to report the fine treatment they were receiving from the Japanese.

None of the prisoners said a word. Sazawa looked at them imploringly and they stared back at him until he turned away. The prisoners were taken back to camp, and Sazawa knew they had won. But the prisoners had lost the diversion afforded by his efforts.

The twenty-eight men in Wainwright's party spent a lonely Christmas season in the long, cold winter of 1943–44. They had no entertainment or carol singing or excitement, as there had been last year with the larger group at Karenko. Skinny ate Christmas dinner in his room with Carroll. Their spirits were not high. Also, the realization that this was their second Christmas in captivity was depressing. How many more bleak Christmases would there be? He had passed his sixtieth birthday in August, and he looked and felt older than that. How many more birthdays would go by before he was free? How long, oh Lord, how long?

Two events during those long months at Muksaq proved to

Wainwright that he had not been forgotten. In November of 1943 he was reading a six-week-old copy of the *Nippon Times* and was startled to see his name in a report out of Washington. The article said that President Roosevelt had promoted him and four others to the permanent rank of major general. Wainwright was in good company. Two of his old friends were on the list—Joe Stilwell and Georgie Patton. Skinny was excited and flattered by the news, but he was also confused. He had expected to be court-martialed. Now, it seemed, his brevet rank was being made permanent.

The more Wainwright thought about it, the more he lost the fear of a court-martial. Yet he remained certain that if he ever returned home, it would be as a soldier in disgrace. What future could there be for a man, regardless of rank, who had surrendered such a large force? It was a terrible burden to live with.

But there were formalities and procedures attendant upon his promotion, and as a soldier Wainwright intended to deal with them properly. Although he was a prisoner of war, he still had to follow army rules. The rules said that his promotion had to be accepted formally, in writing. He went to see the camp commander and, after some argument, received permission to write a brief message to the War Department. The man agreed to send the note to the United States through the Red Cross.

Six and a half months later Wainwright's acceptance of his promotion arrived in Washington. General Marshall sent a copy to Mrs. Wainwright at once, along with greetings from himself and his wife.

"Received message appointing me major general, Regular Army. Appointment accepted. Please inform American Red Cross and through them inform Mrs. Wainwright at Skaneateles, New York, that I am well."

"Katherine joins me in the pleasure of passing to you this encouraging news, and both of us send our affectionate regards."

Two weeks later Adele replied from Nantucket, Massachusetts, where a friend had placed a house at her disposal for six weeks.

"Thank you very much for sending me the message from Skinny. The very last word from him was written August second last year so you can know how glad I was."

The second happy occurrence in Wainwright's life at Muksaq took place in May 1944, when he finally received a letter from his wife. Although Adele had written often, this was the first letter to reach him in twenty-nine months. He was overjoyed to hear from her. He read the letter so many times that he knew it by heart, and he no longer felt quite so alone and forgotten.

The American people hadn't forgotten Wainwright. On May 8, 1944, his drawn and tired likeness appeared on the cover of *Time* magazine. He wore three stars on his collar and his hair was short and bristly, but the artist had made his face too full. Skinny was much thinner than that by the second anniversary of his capture. A grid of barbed wire was superimposed on the painting, and a sword hung over Wainwright's head. The caption was simple: "General Wainwright. Since Corregidor, two long years."

Wainwright would have been pleased by the accompanying story. It was fitting praise for his courage and fortitude and his life of service to his country.

"The man left behind to preside at his country's worst military fiasco, waits for death or liberation on Formosa, according to Jap reports. Three vague hand-printed messages have come from him. That is all. Whether he is well or ill treated is not known. The Japanese look with scorn on the defeated.

"But those who knew Wainwright knew that he would accept his fate with the stoicism of a professional soldier. Though he might look back on the events which had landed him behind barbed wire with bitterness, he could look back on the life of Jonathan Mayhew Wainwright without shame."

An account of his career up to the war followed, and then a glowing report of his fight for Bataan.

"He was ravaged by beriberi, emaciated. He could barely use his right leg; he dragged himself along with a cane.

"His faded breeches shrank up his legs. His shirt was ragged. His steely eyes were sunken with fatigue. But his tours among the starved, tattered, forgotten men of Bataan were almost triumphal. They cheered him on the field. Behind his back they reverently called him 'Old Skinny.' . . .

"Some day in the not too distant future the humiliation of the Philippines will be avenged. Wainwright and his soldiers wait. If they live they will learn that the nation has not forgotten the Philippines' gaunt and ghostly men."

Skinny had not been forgotten, not by his family or his country nor by the families of all the men from Bataan and Corregidor who were awaiting their day of liberation. In Charlotte, North Carolina, two army wives, Marie Grimes and Hat Diller, started a newsletter, *Philippine Postscripts,* for the POW families. Wives and mothers wrote in if they had any news of their men or sent excerpts from postcards or letters to be shared with all. Adele Wainwright had a letter printed in the March 1, 1944, issue.

"Three letters and one card have come from Skinny since May of 1942. The first letter was almost all about business, no address but dated August 1942. It reached me last June. The next was a card of February and then a printed letter of twenty-five words. Christmas Eve I received one written in August 1943 but no address. Said he had a cable from me in February 1943 and no letter since November 1941. Also that he was better than the past year, weighed 125 lbs., and that the living conditions were a little better. I went down to Panama City, Florida, in August. There was a Liberty Ship launched at the yard in Panama City on Skinny's birthday. The shipyard was named for him. The Red Cross use my large living room for surgical dressings and keep all sewing and wool there. My days are filled with work and so they pass."

Skinny would have been proud of the shipyard and the many streets and plazas, parks and schools all over the United States that now bore his name. He would have been prouder still of the exploits of his son. In January 1944, Captain Jonathan Mayhew Wainwright V was awarded the Distinguished Service Medal of the Merchant Marine for heroic action at Salerno. Jack Wainwright's ship, carrying a cargo of high-octane gasoline, had been bombed and set afire in the harbor. He gave orders to abandon ship, and he and the crew went over the side. Then he learned that there were still wounded men aboard, and the ship was likely to explode at any moment. Wainwright and a crewman went back on board and got the wounded off safely.

Captain Wainwright was carrying on the 100-year tradition of the Wainwright family, serving their country well. In Skinny he had had a good mentor.

On October 20, 1944, American troops invaded the Philippines. MacArthur had kept his promise to return. There was no doubt now. America was winning the war.

When news of the invasion was released, reporters in the United States immediately phoned Mrs. Wainwright. Her mother, Mrs. Holley, fielded their questions. "My daughter is too excited to make any comment," she told them, and she went on to say that they were packing to move to Washington now so that Adele could be closer to her friends. "We have been there on Leyte Island," she continued, "at the very place where they are landing now, and we're positive the invasion will be a success." It was a success, and Wainwright's moment of liberation suddenly seemed a lot closer.

American forces were now less than 200 miles from Formosa.

The problem was that by October 20, 1944, Wainwright was no longer on Formosa. He had been taken from Muksaq two weeks before to a place deeper inside enemy territory, in the cold wastelands of Manchuria.

On October 5, the fourteen high-ranking prisoners and their orderlies made a twenty-four-hour train ride to the southern end of Formosa and stayed overnight at a camp near Heito. The next day Wainwright and the others were flown to Japan, to the southern island of Kyushu. Another long and uncomfortable train journey followed. At 5:00 in the morning they stopped at Beppu and were taken by bus to the most exotic accommodations they had known since their capture—a resort hotel.

Here, to Skinny's great pleasure, were the rest of the American generals he had not seen since Tamazato back in June of 1943. They had been brought to the hotel four days earlier and were well settled in to their unaccustomed luxurious surroundings. There were joyous greetings all around that morning as Wainwright, King, and Moore met old friends. Skinny was delighted to be surrounded by comrades again. Some of the Dutch and Britishers with whom he had been confined for so long had begun to irritate him, he confided to them. Now he was back among friends. To them Skinny looked thin and tired.

The group spent only two more days at the hotel at Beppu, but they were pleasant days, and Wainwright remembered them fondly during the darker days ahead. Conversation was lively. The men exchanged stories and rumors and items of news. The beds were comfortable, with good mattresses, and a sheet and comforter for each man. There was also good food to be savored. "A grand spaghetti dish for supper," Bill Brougher wrote, "tasted like human food." They were permitted to bathe, ten at a time, in a large tank of hot water piped in from a nearby mineral springs.

The men talked for hours, speculating about the location of their next camp—probably in Japan, they thought—and about when the war would end. The fighting in Europe was going well for the Allies, who were breaking into Germany itself, but the prisoners knew little of the war in the Pacific, though they eventually learned of MacArthur's landing in the Philippines. They were occupying their time the way they had for more than two years, indulging in rumors and guesses, though at Beppu at least they could talk in relative comfort.

It was too good to last. Wainwright knew that the Japanese would not let them remain in a hotel. Two days after Skinny arrived the group departed at 11:15 in the morning. Two cooked meals were given to each man, and they spent all day on a slow-moving train headed north. At 9:00 that night they reached the port town of Kokura and were packed into a ship's hold. There was almost no ventilation.

The men got little sleep that night. At 9:00 the next morning the ship got under way, and at 5:15 they docked at Pusan in Korea. They were marched to the Pusan Railway Hotel, and were given a complete dinner. The feast provided by the Japanese was amazing to behold. The prisoners dined on soup, fish, meat, macaroni with tomato sauce, cauliflower, cornstarch pudding, and real coffee. They slept comfortably on straw mats on the floor. The good treatment unleashed a new flood of speculation and suspicion about their future. They had no illusions that they would suddenly be freed, but perhaps the tide of war had turned so heavily against Japan that it planned to give its prisoners better care.

The considerate treatment continued the next day. The men were awakened at 5:30, fed a good breakfast at the hotel, and led to a comfortable train, which at 8:00 A.M. began a journey north. They ate well during the day, "very good and plenty," recorded Brougher in his diary, but by nightfall the weather turned cold. The Japanese issued each man a blanket and an overcoat, but there was no heat on the train. Still in a weakened condition and used to the tropics, the Bataan and Corregidor officers weren't prepared for such cold weather. As the train sped even farther northward, Wainwright and the others began to suspect that they were being taken to Manchuria, as far away from Allied forces as it was possible to get.

Wainwright was allowed off the train briefly the next morning at Seoul. He and his men were permitted to exercise and to wash. They collected box lunches and hot tea for their breakfast. At 3:00 the following afternoon, October 14, four days after leaving Beppu, they arrived at their new home, a prison camp on the outskirts of Chengchiatun in western Manchuria.

It was an isolated and desolate place, a former Russian army post, and to some it seemed the end of the world. Hundreds of thousands of black crows filled the air, and the sky was a dirty yellow. Fierce winds blew dust and sand from the Gobi Desert. Wainwright led his men in formation and waited through the inevitable address by the camp commandant.

"The commandant arrived in a four-door sedan of about 1930 vintage," recalled an American officer. "There was no glass in the windshield and no glass in the windows. There was no engine. The motor power was supplied by two little Manchurian ponies. The ponies were driven by a soldier in the right front seat. The car was steered, using the auto steering wheel, by another soldier in the left front seat. The commandant was almost buried under furs in the back seat. As he was slowly driven down the front of our line to inspect us, all we could see of him was a pair of magnificently waxed mustachios. He immediately became Colonel Handlebars."

The prisoners were asked to sign another pledge not to escape, and were issued seven blankets apiece, giving an indication of how cold it was expected to get. The men were already shivering now in the middle of October. What would it be like during the winter?

Wainwright and King were assigned to a tiny room and their first task was to try to figure out how to operate the clumsy Russian stove. Even when it was running they felt cold. Keeping the fire going would be a continuing battle, but at least it would give them something to do. Boredom became their greatest problem at Chengchiatun.

They had no books to read, no work to do, and the fierce winds and cold temperatures kept them indoors. The Japanese prohibited Sunday church services so there was not even that small diversion to look forward to. And on November 8 it started to snow. The stuff was pretty to look at—Wainwright hadn't seen snow in five years—but the blizzard added to his sense of isolation, and it also lowered the temperature drastically. Standing next to the stove failed to ease his constant chill.

One month after Wainwright's arrival at Chengchiatun, 259 new prisoners arrived—all the American colonels, whom Skinny had not seen since he left Karenko in April 1943. The men were a welcome source of excitement, though they were in terrible shape, having spent two weeks locked in the hold of a ship with little nourishment.

Their arrival brought vitality and spirit into the camp, but it also meant lower rations. The food provided now had to sustain many more people. This situation was maddening to the prisoners. They knew that a shipment of more than 3,000 Red Cross parcels, enough for nine boxes per man, had arrived on November 16, but the Japanese refused to issue them.

Thanksgiving Day of 1944 was bleak in both weather and spirit. The abundant Red Cross packages were still locked away, and the men were brought even less food than usual. "So what do we have to be thankful for?" one wondered. "We have nothing and we know nothing."

But at least they were all together again, the American officers who had begun their terms as prisoners so long ago at Tarlac in the Philippines. The companionship was good for Wainwright's morale—he was pleased to have his men with him—but he was not to enjoy it much longer.

On November 28 Wainwright was summoned by the camp commandant and told that in three days he would be moved farther north, to a more isolated camp, more miles distant from the nearest Allied troops. This would be his sixth prison camp. The thought of another move to another unknown place brought back to Wainwright all the doubts and questions such a move entailed. Would there be enough food? Warm clothing? Something to do? Would he get any life-sustaining Red Cross packages there? Any news? Would there be harassment and beatings again?

Worse, Wainwright was once again being separated from his men, the American generals and colonels with whom he had so recently been reunited. Ned King, George Moore, and Sergeant Carroll would go with him, but the rest of his party would be the same British and Dutch officers and civilian government officials he had been with at Muksaq. Such a small group again, these fourteen men and their orderlies. It was a terrible blow to Wainwright.

His friends saw the change come over him when news of the imminent move spread. Skinny seemed to withdraw into himself and become quiet and morose. One by one his men came to wish him well. They tried to be cheerful. They told him the war couldn't last much longer, that he would soon be free, but it made little difference. His spirits had plunged drastically. He felt his sixty-one years of age, his two and a half years in captivity, the effects of the poor diet and the boredom and the humiliating treatment. Doubts about his future tormented him afresh. The surrender and the idea of a court-martial resumed their importance in his mind.

Jack Vance talked to Skinny about duty with the American Battle Monuments Commission, a post General Pershing had held after World War I. Colonel Vance had served with Pershing on the commission writing the history of the war, and he thought this would be good duty for Wainwright. He knew Skinny's love of military history, and he pushed the idea, hoping to cheer the Old Man up.

"It's a fine job for you, General," Vance said. "You're an authority on the Far East. Give it some thought."

"No," Wainwright said. "My career's over. I'm out of it."

"Wainwright doesn't look good at all," Col. Mike Quinn wrote.

"He is emaciated and seems to have lost a tremendous amount of weight. He never had too much to spare anyway. It seemed to me that I could see a deadening of his spirits. Well, that can hardly be held against him."

Quinn tried to cheer him up by passing along what little news he had heard from his wife. It was a mistake. He mentioned that his wife and a friend had seen two members of MacArthur's staff in the States. Skinny was not surprised. "This is the only time I have ever seen Skinny bitter, and he really was. After all, they certainly left him a baby to handle and all pulled out."

Before Wainwright's party left Chengchiatun, his roommate, General King, fell and injured his hip. The American doctors in the camp could do little for him without x-ray equipment, and the Japanese refused to take King to the hospital. He was in great pain and couldn't walk. The doctors made a crude splint for him and carried him to the train on a stretcher. Skinny walked beside him, trying to muster the stamina to console him. He walked bent over against the bitterly cold wind, and turned around for a last look at the friends he was leaving behind. He thought he had never felt so low. How long, oh Lord, how long?

Almost two weeks later, after Wainwright had been in Manchuria for nearly two months, the War Department believed he was still on Formosa. On December 12, 1944, George Marshall wrote to Adele Wainwright to pass along an optimistic (and largely untrue) report of the conditions in the Formosa prison camps, information obtained from the Red Cross.

We have received some further information on the Japanese prisoner of war camps in Formosa, and since General Wainwright is being held in one of these camps, I know you will be interested in the following summary taken from the report. Please consider this as confidential, for your private information only.

Conditions in these camps are reported to be better than average, with the food "adequate," medical attention generally available, and morale high. The bulk of the diet is rice, but the prisoners get meat and vegetables, and are allowed to purchase sweets at their canteens. Many prisoners of war have gained weight. In some of these camps the officers have a choice of pastimes such as tennis, swimming, volley ball and hiking. Camp entertainments are allowed. General officers . . . are afforded a small private room, with bed, table and chair. . . .

Treatment and morale, in the words of General Wainwright, are "as good as can be reasonably expected." No reports of brutality have been received, though this should not be construed as conclusive.

Mrs. Wainwright replied on February 9, 1945, from Miami Beach, where she was staying with friends.

Thank you very much for your letter with the Red Cross information about Skinny. It was most kind of you to send it as I am, as you can imagine, always eagerly waiting for news. Three letters and a card came here in the last few days. His last letter was written on August 23 of '44 which was his 61st birthday. It is the only one ever sent with a heading. It said "Taiwan." There are endless rumors about his being taken to Japan.

The rumors were more up to date than the Red Cross report. It would be another six months before the War Department found out that Wainwright was being held in Manchuria.

Wainwright was spending the worst Christmas of his life in a prison camp near Sian in northeast Manchuria, a hundred miles from the city of Mukden. He and the small band of prisoners there had made little attempt to initiate any gaiety or holiday atmosphere befitting the season. They were too cold, hungry, and depressed.

The Japanese had promised to issue a Red Cross package for each man on Christmas Day, so the men could at least look forward to the candy and cigarettes and extra food their bodies so sorely needed. But the enemy did not keep the promise. The Japanese guards doled out only a portion of a package to each prisoner, very little food and no candy or cigarettes. They announced that because the prisoners had received these gifts, there would be less available for them in the future.

"Christmas, hell!" Skinny said.

Sian was an unpleasant camp. The nine months that Wainwright spent there were a mind-numbing agony of cold, hunger, and boredom in the winter and unbearable heat, hunger, and boredom in the summer. Now the temperature dipped to 45° F below zero and the tiny stoves were ineffective. Again Skinny slept in all his clothes, and still he woke up shivering. In summer the sun baked the barracks and cracked the dry earth.

The food was never sufficient and the taste was poor. Wainwright got a kind of sour mush for breakfast, a thin watery soup for lunch, and vegetables and soybean curd for supper. The menu rarely changed and Red Cross packages to supplement his diet were few and far between. He weighed less than 130 pounds, a significant drop from his prewar weight of 160, and he looked terrible.

The Japanese guards did not beat the prisoners at Sian, but there was constant harassment of a different kind. The camp commander, Lieutenant Marui, was not too bad, Wainwright thought, compared to other camp commanders. "He treated the senior officers and the civilians with a considerable amount of consideration except he was a nagging little devil."

Marui carried out frequent inspections of the barracks, and he had precise rules about how and where things had to be kept. Wainwright was required to jump to attention and bow low when Marui came to his room, then remain at attention while the commandant prowled about the tiny quarters. If Wainwright's shoes had spots on them, or if his trash box wasn't clean or was an inch out of place, Marui would get upset. He would bellow at Wainwright, loudly enough for everyone in the barracks to hear, belittling and humiliating the old general.

There was little for Wainwright to do at Sian, no vegetables or goats to tend, so few people to talk to. Walking around the camp grounds for exercise was difficult because of the winds and the weather. Skinny spent his long slow days playing solitaire, whittling any small piece of wood he could find, and sharpening the razor blades of the other prisoners. He honed the blades on the inside of a drinking glass that Col. Ray O'Day had made for him from a bottle.

There was no news of the war. The Japanese refused to give the prisoners newspapers. Wainwright tried repeatedly during his nine months there to get newspapers but with no success, and he spent a lot of time speculating on when the war would end. He was convinced that he would not be liberated until after an invasion of Japan itself, and he figured that it would take at least another full year before such an invasion could even be mounted.

Another year! And then how long after that before the Japanese agreed to surrender? That could take an additional year. That would be 1947—five years of captivity. Two more years to wait. The thought was intolerable.

Wainwright's physical strength and spirit ebbed during those months at Sian. The years of inadequate food, of humiliation, of declining hopes had taken their toll. The three American generals—Wainwright, King, and Moore—all became despondent. Would they live long enough to see the Japanese surrender? How much more could they take? How long, oh Lord, how long?*

---

*General Moore took his own life in 1949. Expressing the feelings of all the prisoners of war, Gen. Albert Jones said, "We who went through similar experiences and who find we are unable to remember things and get the shakes, etc., can sympathize with the viewpoint that he feared he was losing his mind."

August 16, 1945, was another brutally hot day. Wainwright sat at a table in his cubicle, stripped to his shorts, playing another game of solitaire. He had dealt more than 8,600 hands so far. Corp. T. J. Willard, one of the American orderlies, knocked and stuck his head in the open door. He was smiling. Wainwright looked up at him, puzzled.

"Let me congratulate you, General," Willard said.

"Really?" Wainwright asked. "Upon what?"

"The war is over."

Skinny was stunned. He had waited for this moment for 1,200 days, but now his mind reeled, unable to accept it.

"I don't believe it," he said. "How do you know?"

Willard explained that a Japanese interpreter had reported that Russia had invaded Manchuria, and that Japan had offered to surrender.

"Was he drunk or sober?" Skinny asked.

"Well, he'd had some sake," Willard replied.

"Well, I don't believe it anyway," Wainwright said. He could not immediately comprehend the fact that the war might be over, that he had survived, and that he would finally be going home.

There was nothing for him to do but wait for official word from the Japanese commandant. Maybe it was only a wild rumor or a cruel hoax. Wainwright couldn't sleep that night. He lay awake in his bunk, wondering if his prayers had been answered.

CHAPTER 17
"Day of Glory"

WAINWRIGHT'S WAR *was* over and he had won. But he didn't know it yet. All he knew was that he had survived. Now he would face the moment of truth he had been worrying about for three and a half years. How would he be received at home? Was he condemned to a life of shame and disgrace? Had the Wainwright name been dishonored by his actions?

He would have to wait two more days before beginning to get an answer to these tormenting questions. Although the war was over and the Japanese had agreed to surrender, no one knew where Wainwright was. At the War Department in Washington, George Marshall and his staff were greatly concerned about Wainwright, worried that the Japanese might have executed him at the last moment in a fanatical act of reprisal.

Throughout China and Manchuria, teams of OSS personnel parachuted into every known POW camp, sometimes arriving before the camp officials had learned of their country's surrender. There were tense confrontations, but none of the OSS teams was harmed.

On the morning of August 17, OSS Maj. J. T. Hennessey and four members of his rescue team arrived at the Japanese camp at Hoten, just outside of Mukden in Manchuria. A number of Wainwright's friends were there—men he had last seen at Cheng-chiatun—and they bombarded the OSS men with questions about the war. Breaking away with difficulty from the crowd of exultant prisoners, Hennessey went to the commandant's office to inquire about Wainwright. He was told that Wainwright was 100 miles away, at Sian. At last he had been located; now he had to be freed. Hennessey summoned two of his men—Maj. Robert F. Lamar, a flight surgeon, and Sgt. Harold Leith, a specialist fluent in Russian and Chinese. They made plans to leave for Sian in the morning.

In Skaneateles, New York, Adele Wainwright "collapsed with hysterical joy" when she heard of Japan's surrender. But then word came from the War Department that Skinny's whereabouts were unknown. Adele had not heard from him since April, when Radio Tokyo, without revealing his location, quoted him as saying he was "well and comfortably housed."

"It takes about a year to receive a letter from him," Mrs. Wainwright told a reporter. "I wrote him one card in reply to the Japanese radio message which answered his question as to whether we had received it."

Wainwright never received that card because American censors refused to clear it. They returned it to Adele and informed her that she "should not mention the Japanese broadcast, because it would give information to the enemy that their radio propaganda broadcasts were being heard in this country."

Mrs. Wainwright and the other officers' wives could do nothing but wait. After so many years of waiting, the next few days would seem intolerably long.

The waiting was difficult for Wainwright too. When he awoke on the morning of August 18, groggy from having slept poorly, he still did not believe what Corporal Willard had told him. It seemed too good to be true. With the long years of hardship and disappointment so fresh, he could not suddenly accept the possibility that they were over. The camp buzzed with excitement, the captives keyed up and tense, all wanting to believe the news but not yet able to do so.

After the morning roll call, the camp commandant, Lieutenant Marui, stood in front of the prisoners and read from a piece of paper. Wainwright and the others waited impatiently for him to finish so the interpreter could tell them what he was saying. They watched his face carefully as he spoke and listened to the tone of his voice, but they provided no clues. Finally Marui stopped and signaled to the interpreter.

"By order of the Emperor of Japan," the interpreter said, "the war has been brought to an amicable conclusion."

The prisoners looked at one another and exploded with laughter. They embraced and pounded each other on the back and shook hands vigorously. But most of all they laughed. The commandant's words provided a relief of tension, of uncertainty, of anxiety, such a needed relief that they could not control themselves. Even if Japanese troops had run at them with drawn bayonets at that moment, they probably could not have stopped laughing.

Marui, his interpreter, and the guards looked on in silence. No one made any attempt to quiet the prisoners. After several minutes they fell silent. The interpreter looked at them sternly and reminded them that they were still prisoners of war. The men started to snicker. Roll call was over. Wainwright would never have to attend another one. "We returned to the barracks," said General King, "silent and thoughtful. We sat down on our cots, General Wainwright and I, both offering silent prayers of thankfulness."

Marui called Wainwright to his office and told him that two Americans from Mukden would arrive at Sian later in the day. Wainwright passed the word to the others. All through the hot afternoon they restlessly prowled the fence, watching for the first sign of their liberators. No one came. Drained of emotion from the high spirits and excitement of the morning and the letdown of the afternoon, they went about their routine and ate their skimpy prison fare that evening, feeling very much still prisoners of war. Outwardly nothing had changed. The guards were in place, carrying their weapons. Marui wore his sword. The prisoners had to bow whenever they passed a Japanese guard. Everything was just as it had been, and the same dull numbness of their lives, so habitual now, crept back over their minds as darkness fell. No one had come to set them free.

OSS Major Lamar and Sergeant Leith reached Sian at 3:30 on the morning of Sunday, August 19. Lamar stationed Leith outside the camp; the major would go in and see what kind of reception awaited them. If the Japanese were hostile, there was no point in risking both lives. The guard at the gate notified the camp commander, who got dressed and received Lamar graciously in his office.

Marui offered the major a cup of tea. Lamar thought things were off to a smooth start, until he asked to see the prisoners. He had to make sure that Wainwright and his party were indeed at Sian and that they were alive. Marui refused. Lamar would have to wait until daylight. Lamar pressed the point, demanding to see them at once. He threatened Marui with reprisals and the two men argued for some time. Then the Japanese offered a compromise. Lamar could see Wainwright now and the others in the morning. Lamar agreed, and Marui sent a guard for Wainwright. The two men waited in silence.

A few minutes later a tall emaciated figure appeared in the doorway. He looked like a scarecrow in his tattered garments. Lamar had trouble recognizing the man as Wainwright from the prewar photographs he had seen. Wainwright waited obediently at the door; a prisoner did not enter the commandant's office without permission. He stared at Lamar and spoke in a voice barely above a whisper.

"Are you really American?"

Lamar nodded and introduced himself. Wainwright remained in the doorway until Marui beckoned him into the room. He stepped across the threshold, stopped, and bowed low to the Japanese commandant. Lamar rose and offered Wainwright his chair. The gesture offended Marui. Prisoners did not sit in the presence of a Japanese.

"He must remain standing," Marui shouted.

Lamar began to argue with him again. Wainwright stood quietly to one side, saying nothing. Finally Marui relented and Wainwright sat down in the same room as a Japanese soldier, the first time he had been allowed to do so in three and a half years.

"General," Major Lamar said, "you are no longer a prisoner. You're going back to the States."

Wainwright looked at him for a moment, and then in a hoarse voice he asked the question that had tormented him for so long.

"What do the people in the States think of me?"

Lamar answered without a moment's hesitation.

"You're considered a hero there," he said. "Your picture is even in *Time* magazine."

Wainwright seemed skeptical but he said no more about it. He returned to his barracks a few minutes later, still unconvinced, still worried about the kind of reception he was going to get.

A few hours later, Lamar and Leith had breakfast with Wainwright and the other prisoners. There was no elation around the crude wooden table on which they ate, no sense of celebration, no excitement that freedom was at hand. Instead, they very "carefully counted out each bean for the soup so that no one would be cheated," just as they had done every other morning.

Lamar and Leith talked about the war. They told them about the dropping of the two atomic bombs and about Russia declaring war on Japan, but nothing seemed to spark their interest. The meal continued in silence. The OSS men were appalled at the "general lethargy that dulled the spirits of the men sitting at the table."

They realized that Wainwright and his men had to be gotten out of the camp quickly, not only for their emotional well-being, but also for their physical safety. Many Japanese units were still operating in Manchuria, and Lamar feared that they might kidnap this highest-ranking group of prisoners in the Far East and use them as hostages, or kill them. He and Leith couldn't protect them. He had to get them to the larger camp at Mukden as soon as possible.

Lamar tried to contact his superior at Mukden, Major Hennessey, but his radio was out of order. He was unable to get through by telephone because the lines had been destroyed by the Russian troops who were advancing throughout Manchuria. Lamar was cut off. His only course was to go to Mukden himself and return with a convoy of vehicles to take the Sian prisoners out. He would leave Sergeant Leith behind. If the Russians arrived, Leith could communicate with them in their own language. Lamar explained the plan to Wainwright and said he would return in two days.

During the day, the prisoners' spirits began to rise as the realization that the war was over finally took hold. They began to pack their belongings so that they would be ready when Lamar returned. Their preparations took little time; they had so little they wanted to take with them. Wainwright was finished in about an hour, and he wandered about restlessly, wondering what to do with himself.

All that day he waited, and all the next day as well, expecting at any moment to see a convoy of American trucks roll up to the camp gate. No one came, and again life gradually settled down into its dreary routine. Skinny was no longer a prisoner, but here he was still confined in the same place. He didn't dare leave the camp because he might run into a Japanese army unit, which would shoot on sight. And so he waited, back in his room, playing solitaire hour after hour. All that had really changed was his diet. The Japanese had distributed all the Red Cross parcels they had been hoarding. Many of the men stuffed themselves with food and chain-smoked American cigarettes.

The third day came and went, and still there was no sign of Major Lamar. Wainwright began to worry. Had he been killed before he reached Mukden? No one else knew where the prisoners were. Morale sank again. How much longer would they have to wait?

Major Lamar had gotten to Mukden and had been trying for two days to arrange transportation for Wainwright's group. He had to deal with the Russians, who had taken over the city, but was having no success. The Russian troops had discovered the Japanese commander's liquor supply, and were boisterously and dangerously drunk. They had no interest in a group of prisoners a hundred miles away, no matter who they were. Major Hennessey, Lamar's superior, was powerless. The Russians were in charge.

By the morning of August 24, Wainwright was desperate, and he decided that they could not wait much longer. If help didn't reach them soon, he was determined to get to Mukden on his own. He sought out Lieutenant Marui and other Japanese officers and asked them to find a local guide who would lead them to Mukden.

"I'll give a guy five hundred dollars U.S. and five hundred Manchurian yen if he'll guide us out to Mukden."

There were no takers.

Finally, at noon on the 24th, the prisoners saw a convoy approaching—at last, American jeeps and trucks! The men crowded the camp gates, anxious for a glimpse of the Americans who were coming to rescue them. As the convoy got closer, they were startled to see that the vehicles, American lendlease equipment, were decorated with large red stars. This was a Russian unit.

The Russian soldiers, dirty and unkempt, drove through the gates and stopped. Wainwright went to greet the convoy commander, a ferocious-looking colonel with a full beard. With OSS Sergeant Leith interpreting, Wainwright explained to the Russian colonel about their predicament and asked for his help in getting to Mukden.

The colonel listened intently. He said he was on his way to Mukden. If the prisoners could furnish their own transportation and be ready in one hour, they could join his convoy. The habit of command instantly came back to Wainwright, and he quickly organized the expedition, ordering Marui to supply two buses and a truck.

Marui, afraid of the Russians, who were armed with tommy guns, said "Yes sir." It shocked Wainwright to hear these words from a Japanese soldier, after serving so many years as his slave. Skinny decided that the experience made him feel very good.

At 6:00 that evening, the Russian colonel led the convoy of troops and prisoners out of Sian prison camp. Wainwright was happy to be on the move. He expected to arrive at Mukden before morning, but it was to take a lot longer than that. Nothing about Skinny's liberation was coming easy.

The trip to Mukden was a nightmare. Barely out of sight of the Sian camp, the convoy got lost. Hour after hour, all through the night, the men wandered up and down the roads and trails of Manchuria, backtracking, making circles, becoming stuck in dead-ends, getting nowhere.

At dawn on the 25th they reached a tiny village, and the Russian colonel stopped to try to get his bearings. Apparently he was unsuccessful because he promptly got lost again. In the afternoon it rained heavily, turning the dirt roads into quagmires. The prisoners' buses frequently got stuck in the mud. Everyone had to get out, unload the luggage, and try to push the buses free. They forded fast-flowing streams, and once they crossed a high, rickety railroad bridge that swayed dangerously as they bounced over the wooden railroad ties.

When darkness came they still had no idea of where they were. They had been traveling more than twenty-four hours and were tired, dirty, and hungry. One of the buses was mired again and this time it was impossible to rescue it. Wainwright thought he had reached the limit of his endurance when the Russians threatened to abandon the prisoners on the spot.

Then they had their first stroke of luck. Someone spotted a narrow-gauge railroad line. A native Chinese told them it was a spur that joined the main tracks to Mukden at a point no more than twenty miles away. The prisoners did not know if the spur line was still in use, but they decided to go no farther with the Russian convoy. They would wait where they were for a train. As though on command, a small engine hauling three cars came along just minutes later and the Russians flagged it down. There was a heated discussion, and the Russians brandished their tommy guns, but finally the Japanese train crew agreed to transport Wainwright and his party to the main railroad line.

The prisoners loaded their baggage onto one of the cars and bade farewell to the Russians. The little train started off but before it had chugged out of sight of the convoy the engine jumped the track. The Russian colonel drove up to Wainwright and said he would go ahead to the main line and see if he could find another train to send back for them.

Wainwright and the others spent the night on the derailed train, getting little sleep on hard wooden benches. They had no food and no idea of their position, nor were they confident that the Russian officer would send help. How much longer would it take before they were safe in American hands? So far, their liberation had become a cruel joke.

At American army headquarters in Chungking, commanded by Gen. Albert C. Wedemeyer, people were frantic with worry over Wainwright's whereabouts. Lamar had recounted his problems to headquarters and a plane had been dispatched to fly over the Sian camp. The pilot reported that the camp was empty. Search planes were sent out over most of Manchuria looking for the prisoners, but there was no sight of them. Wainwright had disappeared. A rumor began to circulate that the Russians had kidnapped him and taken him to Siberia.

At daybreak on August 26, a train arrived, which, in a few hours, brought Wainwright and his party to the main line to Mukden. Surely today, Wainwright thought, they would reach the Americans at Mukden. Then he was told the bad news. There would be no train to Mukden until late that evening. They would have to spend the day waiting at the railroad junction. After a while the Russian colonel grew tired of waiting. He commandeered a train that was bound for another destination and put the prisoners, his troops, and his jeeps aboard. At 7:00 P.M. they departed, reaching Mukden at 1:30 on the morning of August 27. It had taken three days for Wainwright to travel 100 miles.

The men were too exhausted to wander around the city in darkness looking for Major Lamar, so they went to sleep where they were, in their car in the middle of the railroad yard. While they slept, Sergeant Leith found Lamar and reported that Wainwright's party had arrived safely. Lamar went to the train at once, arriving a little before 3:00 A.M.. He knew that Wainwright was exhausted, but he thought the general would forgive him for awakening him.

Arrangements had been made, Lamar told Wainwright, to fly him to Chungking in a few hours. And in six days' time, Wainwright and Percival would go to Tokyo, at the invitation of the War Department and General MacArthur, to witness the formal surrender of the Empire of Japan.

"Wainwright was overjoyed. He waved the cane given to him years before by MacArthur, and stepped off the train and away from the past."

Later at the Mukden airport Wainwright was reunited with many of his old friends. His aides—Tom Dooley and Johnny Pugh—were there, along with Beebe, Bluemel, Brougher, Funk, Jones, Pierce, and others. At 11:00 they boarded a C-47 and headed south. The men talked the entire way, comparing stories about their final months of imprisonment, when most of the American officers had been separated from Wainwright, King, and Moore.

At 4:30 that afternoon the plane landed at the first American base they had set foot on since 1942, an OSS airfield in northern China near the city of Sian, a place that bore the same name as Wainwright's last prison camp. They stayed overnight, relishing the food that was available to them, especially the ice cream and real coffee, things that had existed for three and a half years only in their dreams.

"My, what a wonderful feeling!" General Brougher wrote in his diary that night. "Cigarette issue, chocolate issue, a quart of good American bourbon whiskey." The men went to the movies on the air base that night, to see Jack Oakie in a documentary film called *That's the Spirit,* which showed the American army in action all over the world.

The scenes Skinny saw were from a new age, one that he knew nothing about. So much was different from his army of 1942—the uniforms, the helmets, the tanks, guns, and planes. Even the label given to the American soldier—the G.I.—was new. How much the army had changed! His troops and his equipment on Bataan and Corregidor, indeed, his own experiences leading his men, seemed part of another war. He felt himself to be a bit obsolete and outdated, a veteran of a past war.

The following day, August 28, Wainwright and his group left at 11:00 A.M. for a two-and-a-half-hour flight to Chungking, the headquarters of General Wedemeyer, who had directed the OSS operations to find Wainwright and the other POWs held throughout Manchuria.

The plane touched down at Chungking airport and taxied to the spot where Wedemeyer and a large crowd were waiting for what Tom Dooley called "a Royal Reception." The door was opened and Wainwright exited first, a frail, thin old man leaning heavily on his cane. At the bottom of the steps, the two generals saluted and shook hands.

"My God, Al," Wainwright said. "It's great to see you. I can't thank you enough for what you've done." Then he asked the question that still haunted him. "What do people think of me, Al?"

"You're a legitimate hero, General," Wedemeyer said. "We all admire you here—everybody does."

"I thought I was going to be court-martialed," Wainwright said, shaking his head in wonder.

As they drove to Wedemeyer's quarters, Wedemeyer did his best to convince Wainwright that he would return to the U.S. as a genuine hero, but the idea was hard for Skinny to accept.

Wedemeyer's thirty-room house sat on a cliff overlooking the Yangtze River. To Wainwright it was a palace, with a wide verandah running the width of the building and a large courtyard filled with flowers. Wedemeyer gave Skinny his own bedroom with a private bath, and outfitted him in his own uniform. The best gift of all was a photograph of his wife Adele, which had been transmitted by the wirephoto service, another technological innovation that hadn't existed in 1942. On the picture was a note in her handwriting.

"I am very happy today," Adele Wainwright had written. "Waiting impatiently for your return. We are all well. Best love to you. Kitty H. W."

Wedemeyer arranged for Wainwright to send his own photo to her that afternoon. Across the lower left corner of the picture Wainwright wrote, "Kitty Darling: My devoted love to you always. Am well and hope to be home soon—to Manila, Aug. 30, then to Tokyo."

Wainwright had another message to send that day, reporting his return to duty to General Marshall at the War Department. As soon as Marshall received it he sent a personal reply.

"I was profoundly moved a few moments ago to receive your first message dated August twenty eighth and I have already repeated the substance of it to Mrs. Wainwright. A more detailed response will follow later. Meanwhile, I reaffirm the expressions of my last message to you a few hours before the fall of Corregidor in deepest appreciation of all that you did and have done for the honor of the army."

Wainwright was deeply touched by Marshall's words, particularly the reference to his last message before Corregidor fell. He had kept throughout his imprisonment the paper on which the message had been recorded, and he had read it so many times that he knew it by heart. "Never has so much been done with so little. The nation will be forever grateful."

Wainwright's doubts had been dispelled. He did not have to worry any longer about how the country would receive him. He sat down at the desk in Wedemeyer's bedroom and wrote out another message for Marshall.

"Your personal message of August 28th leaves me without words to express adequately the gratitude which I feel for your considera- tion and sympathetic attitude. Your last message to me at Cor- regidor was received at 4 o'clock in the morning when the fall of the Island was imminent. The sentiments which you expressed at that time afforded me the greatest consolation during the trying experiences of that day and throughout my long period of captivity. The original copy of that message has been in my personal possession since it came to my hand and it will always be one of my most cherished possessions. I look forward to the day when I can thank you in person for your many kindnesses, and I thank God that our country possessed a soldier of such distinction to lead her armies through the difficulties which beset an unprepared nation to final and glorious victory. I leave here morning of August 30th to join MacArthur in Manila to accompany him to Tokyo to witness the formal surrender. My highest personal and official regards to you."

At 3:30 the next afternoon, a simple but dignified and impressive ceremony took place on the lawn outside the American headquar- ters at Chungking. Wainwright, Jones, and Moore were awarded the Distinguished Service Cross. Wainwright's medal had been approved by MacArthur in late January 1942, for his conduct of the withdrawal into Bataan, but there had not been time to present the medal formally. Wedemeyer read aloud the three-year-old citation.

"For extraordinary heroism in action in Northern Luzon, Philip- pine Islands, during the period from 21 December 1941, to 5 January 1942. As Commander of the North Luzon Force, General Wainwright repeatedly visited the points of most severe conflict throughout his command, displaying outstanding courage and indifference to danger. By his presence and soldierly bearing during the severe enemy aerial bombardment and strafing attacks, and during attacks by infantry and tanks, he stimulated and inspired the troops of his command."

Wedemeyer stepped up to Wainwright and pinned the medal to his shirt. Skinny could not hold back the tears and they coursed down his craggy cheeks. He stood tall and proud, but made no effort to hide his emotion. He had been vindicated. He was going home a hero.

At 8:00 A.M. on August 30, dressed in Wedemeyer's hat and shirt sporting the China-Burma-India theater patch, Wainwright took off from Chungking airport. With him were Percival, Beebe, his aides Dooley and Pugh, and the patient Sgt. Hubert Carroll, who had been at his side throughout the war. Wainwright brought these four men of his own staff with him for a special reason, as he had explained to MacArthur.

"All of this party were with me on the tragic day when I was forced to surrender and I am particularly anxious that they be present when you accept the surrender of the Japanese Nation."

After about ten minutes they landed at the huge American air base at Peishiyi, where they transferred to a four-engine plane, which was too large to have flown into Chungking. The new plane, U.S. Army Air Corps Lt. Gen. George Stratemeyer's converted B-17, was a "luxury craft," according to Tom Dooley.

They flew over Hong Kong, which was still in Japanese hands, and the pilot made a leisurely loop around the city. Wainwright and Percival peered out at the infamous Stanley prison camp, where a large number of British POWs were still being held.

At 5:30 they landed at Nichols Field outside Manila. There to greet Wainwright was the new president of the Philippines, Sergio Osmena, whom he had known before the war. As they drove into Manila, Wainwright was appalled by the destruction. The city lay in ruins. The Japanese had not declared Manila an open city, as MacArthur had done in 1941, but had fought for it yard by yard. The familiar landmarks Wainwright had known so well were gone. The party stopped at the Admiralty Apartments for the night. Wainwright had expected to see MacArthur in Manila and travel with him to Tokyo, but MacArthur's plans had changed and he had already flown to Yokohama.

MacArthur had left one of his aides, Col. Sid Huff, to take charge of Wainwright. And take charge he did, caring for him throughout the next week until he reached the United States. Huff produced the general's favorite foods and a limited but adequate supply of liquor. Unobtrusively, he rationed Wainwright's drinking, never providing more than his weakened body could tolerate.

Whenever Wainwright's spirits seemed to flag, Huff was there to cheer him up. Occasionally Wainwright became depressed about the surrender, and Huff would remind him of the recognition he was getting and the honors he was sure to receive at home. During one of these pep talks Huff blurted, "Why, General, when you get back to the States, you're going to be promoted to four-star general." Wainwright was delighted to hear that. He did not know that Huff had made it up on the spot, acting under the assumption that it would happen.

The first night in Manila Huff summoned a barber for Wainwright and a tailor to cut down Wedemeyer's uniform until it fit Wainwright's gaunt frame a little better. Then Huff gave Wainwright a .32-caliber revolver and holster. Skinny put it on at once and said he felt complete again.

The next morning Wainwright and his party got up early. They were whisked out to Nichols Field, where they climbed aboard "a beautiful ship," a C-54 transport plane. It was the largest, fastest, and most comfortable airplane any of them had ever seen. They stopped for lunch at Okinawa, then took off for Japan.

At 5:30 on the afternoon of August 31 Wainwright's plane landed at Yokohama. The field that not very long ago had been used as a training base for kamikaze pilots was ringed with Japanese antiaircraft emplacements. The men were taken in old Japanese army cars the fifteen miles into the city, passing boarded-up shops, windows with their blinds drawn, and nearly deserted streets. The few Japanese they saw bowed low as the cars passed. What a difference from the first time Wainwright had arrived in Japan, as a prisoner of war.

The cars pulled up to the imposing New Grand Hotel, built after the earthquake of 1923. It had suffered no damage during the war. Several of MacArthur's staff were waiting on the front steps, including "Pick" Diller, who had served with Wainwright at Fort McKinley before the war. They told him that MacArthur was having dinner, but that he wanted to see Wainwright as soon as he arrived.

As Wainwright walked through the lobby toward the dining room, an aide rushed ahead to notify MacArthur, who immediately got up from the table. He started for the lobby, but before he got far the door swung open and Wainwright entered the huge dining room. Everyone fell silent as MacArthur rushed forward to greet him.

MacArthur was shocked by Wainwright's appearance. "He was haggard and aged," he said. "His uniform hung in folds on his fleshless form. He walked with difficulty and with the help of a cane. His eyes were sunken and there were pits in his cheeks. His hair was snow white and his skin looked like old shoe leather."

Wainwright gave a weak smile as MacArthur embraced him. Both men were close to tears. Wainwright tried to speak, but no words came. Even MacArthur, known for his elegance of expression, could say nothing except, "Jim, Jim," in a voice barely above a whisper. "Jim" was an old West Point nickname for Wainwright used only by MacArthur.

They sat down to dinner, and Wainwright told MacArthur something of his life as a prisoner of war. In the course of the conversation, Wainwright mentioned how tormented he had been over the surrender of Corregidor and how he believed that his career had reached a disgraceful end.

MacArthur was surprised to hear of his worries and he sought to ease his mind. He asked Wainwright what assignment he would like now.

"I want command of a corps," Wainwright replied, "any one of your corps."

"Why, Jim, you can have command of a corps with me any time you want it," MacArthur told him. That offer meant as much to Wainwright as any honor he had thus far received. It relieved him of the fear that his former chief held the loss of the Philippines against him.

The reunion was memorable for both Wainwright and MacArthur. Years later, writing about that dinner with Wainwright, MacArthur said, "The emotion that registered on that gaunt face still haunts me."

MacArthur had difficulty sleeping that night. "Something in the dining room reunion troubled him, and he couldn't put his finger on it," wrote William Manchester. "Then it came to him. It was the brown walnut cane with the curved handle. He had given it to Wainwright in prewar Manila, expecting him to use it as he had used his own—as a commander's stage prop, a swagger stick. Instead it had supported the dwindling weight of a whipped man, suffering torments of shame through those years of humiliation when he had been unable to lean upon anything else, not even pride."

Reporters were waiting in the lobby of the New Grand Hotel for Wainwright to emerge from his meeting with MacArthur. One of them wrote, "Thin and haggard and leaning on a cane, Wainwright nonetheless had a sparkling eye." They asked him to say a few words.

"The shoe is on the other foot," he told them. "It's one of the greatest thrills of my life to come back to witness the surrender. The last surrender I attended, the shoe was on the other foot.

"It's good to be back a free man and an American soldier wearing a gun again," and he patted his new .32-caliber pistol in its gleaming leather holster.

To his astonishment, Wainwright was going home not only a hero, but a wealthy man as well. He received a cable from the United States that the King Features Syndicate wanted to buy the newspaper rights to his story. They offered him $155,000, more money than he had ever seen in his lifetime. In addition, Doubleday offered a $25,000 advance for the book rights. A well-known reporter, Bob Considine, would ghostwrite the story for him.

Considine was paid $5,000 for writing the forty-two-part newspaper syndication that formed the core of the book.

Skinny slept soundly that night. Things were going so much better than he had ever dared hope. He felt that he was living a dream.

Wainwright was up early on the morning of September 2. After a hearty breakfast, he and his party—Percival, Beebe, Pugh, Dooley, and Carroll—were taken to the dock at Yokohama, where they boarded the destroyer *Nicholas*. The air felt cool, almost chilly, as they headed out into the bay, and low-hanging clouds colored everything slate gray.

Skinny was in good company. Also aboard the sleek destroyer were Courtney Hodges, Joe Stilwell, and Robert Eichelberger. These generals had all been in the Pacific war and eagerly shared their stories with Wainwright. He was hungry for news about the fighting he had missed.

They reached the mighty battleship U.S.S. *Missouri,* anchored eighteen miles offshore, in about an hour. Wainwright stared in awe at the U.S. fleet, more than 250 warships spread out before him. To a man whose navy had consisted of four wooden PT boats, the power here in Tokyo Bay was dazzling. He knew that he was seeing only part of America's naval might. What they could have done in 1942 with just a fraction of the fleet that lay anchored around him now!

The *Nicholas* anchored near the 45,000-ton *Missouri* and the men were transferred aboard by launch. Wainwright had never seen a ship so large. He was almost transfixed by its size. He looked up from the gangway and saw an old friend from his War College days back in 1933-1934: Bill Halsey. "I could not trust my voice," Halsey said. "I just leaned over the rail and grabbed his hand."

As Wainwright came on deck, he recognized more of his colleagues among the hundreds of officers lined up facing the small table on which the surrender documents would be signed.

At 8:55 A.M. the Japanese delegation boarded the ship, led by the foreign minister, Shigemitsu, a man with a wooden leg who had a difficult time negotiating the gangway. The Japanese wore tall silk hats and cutaways, a marked contrast to the tieless, khaki-clad Americans who covered every inch of the ship to watch this moment of retribution.

Four minutes later the chaplain read a brief invocation, the national anthem was played over the loudspeaker, and MacArthur, flanked by Admirals Nimitz and Halsey, walked toward the table. As MacArthur passed Wainwright and Percival he gestured for them to come forward, to stand in a place of honor two paces behind him.

MacArthur made a brief, eloquent speech, and invited the Japanese representatives to sign the surrender document. Eighteen minutes had elapsed. MacArthur sat down and took five fountain pens from his pocket. He lined them up on the table in front of him, picked up the first one, and started to sign his name. He stopped, part of the way through, and turned around to beckon to Wainwright. MacArthur handed Skinny the pen. The second pen he gave to Percival. Everyone who witnessed this powerful gesture was touched, but none more so than the two old ex-prisoners of war who had suffered so greatly for so long.

At 9:25 the documents were signed by representatives of the eight other nations that had been at war with Japan. Then MacArthur rose and announced that the proceedings were closed.

At that moment the sun came out from behind the clouds, and the sound of aircraft could be heard from the south. A giant air armada—400 massive B-29s and 1,500 navy fighters and dive bombers—droned over the *Missouri*. The planes made a long graceful turn and disappeared over the mainland of Japan.

World War II was over.

After the ceremony, Wainwright and his party were invited to join the senior officers of the Pacific war in Admiral Halsey's wardroom. The men drank coffee and munched doughnuts and cinnamon rolls, pedestrian fare for the occasion, but in its way uniquely American. They talked calmly about the war they had just concluded and the types of weapons with which they would fight the next one.

After no more than an hour, MacArthur left, taking Wainwright with him. They transferred by launch to the destroyer *Buchanan*, which took them back to Yokohama. During the hour-long voyage

Wainwright asked MacArthur for a favor. His son was in the States, but he had heard that Jack's ship was expected to sail any day for the Pacific. Wainwright asked MacArthur if he could arrange for young Wainwright to meet him in San Francisco and travel with him to Washington and New York for the homecoming celebrations.

MacArthur took immediate steps to see that Wainwright's son was given enough leave to be with his father during the next two weeks. That taken care of, the two men chatted about the war, and MacArthur brought up something that had been on his mind for a while.

"Well, Jonathan," he said, "I hear that you've been offered a lot of money for your memoirs."

Wainwright said that he was correct.

"Bully!" MacArthur said. "You write them, then send them to me and I'll check them and send them on to the War Department."

A month later, when Wainwright recounted this exchange to Bob Considine, he grinned and said, "I didn't do any such thing." Wainwright had no intention of allowing MacArthur to alter his version of events.

At 2:00 that afternoon, Wainwright was on another plane, pursuing a schedule of activities so hectic it would have exhausted a man half his age, even one who had not just spent three and a half years in prison camps. The demands were taking their toll, but Wainwright kept up the pace and did not allow himself to skip a single event that was planned for him. After what he had been through, he wouldn't have missed any of the forthcoming events for anything in the world.

Wainwright and his party were on their way back to Manila to witness the surrender of the Philippines, which was to take place the following morning. The plane landed at Iwo Jima at 5:30, where they had a quick dinner and a briefing on the costly fighting for that island. At 6:30 they took off, reaching Manila at 2:00 in the morning.

Wainwright got no more than three hours sleep that night. Up at 5:30, he was whisked to Nielson Airport on the southern outskirts of Manila, where a C-47 was waiting. The transport flew north over some of the territory on which Wainwright had fought his delaying tactics on the retreat into Bataan so long ago. It landed at a small airfield, and the party was driven to Baguio, the summer capital of the Philippines.

This once beautiful town looked desolate and deserted now,

except for the First Cavalry Division guard of honor that lined the road. It was fitting that the First Cavalry should be on hand to greet Wainwright; he had served with them on his first tour of duty in the Philippines nearly forty years before, after his graduation from West Point. The car stopped at one of the few remaining buildings of Camp John Hay, the former residence of the U.S. high commissioner.

A comrade spotted Skinny as he got out of the car. He was Gen. William C. Chase, who had last served with Wainwright in 1936 at Fort Riley. "He was just skin and bones," Chase said. "I wanted to tell him about his old cavalry brigade, the First, and about how my brigade officers mess was always called Wainwright Hall. He seemed too done in even to recognize me, an old friend."

Inside the high commissioner's house, Wainwright and Percival were seated at a large table on which had been placed the swords turned in by the Japanese commander of the Philippines and his staff. The other American officers took their seats, and the Japanese officers sat down opposite them. The Japanese commanding officer's name was well known to the Americans and the British. Lt. Gen. Tomoyuki Yamashita was the man who had conquered Singapore in 1942, and to whom Percival had been forced to surrender. Percival stared at him now without any visible emotion. Yamashita was very surprised to see him.

When the surrender document was signed, the American officer in charge presented the first pen to Wainwright and the second to Percival. The proceedings concluded, Wainwright was driven back to the airfield for the return flight to Manila. On the way south the pilot obligingly circled low over Fort Stotsenburg and Clark Field, where Wainwright's war had begun. He saw the crater-filled runways of Clark Field and the parade ground next to the ruins of his old headquarters at Stotsenburg, from which he had watched Japanese planes roar over the Zambales Mountains.

Back at the Admiralty Apartments in Manila, Wainwright topped off the eventful day—a day on which the islands he had surrendered had been formally returned to American control—by watching a Shirley Temple movie.

Manila is halfway around the world from Washington, D.C., and it took Wainwright six days to travel that distance. But what glorious days they were for him. Old friends trooped to see him at every stop, reporters and photographers besieged him every time he got off the plane, and he was wined and dined royally everywhere he visited.

He left the Philippines for the last time at 8:00 on the morning of September 5, flying in the C-54 that had been placed at his disposal in Japan. The pilot, Capt. Morris M. Perkins, and his crew would fly Wainwright and his party all the way to Washington, making several stops along the way. At 5:30 they arrived on Guam, an island Wainwright had last seen in 1940 when it was a sleepy tropical paradise with a defense force of less than 100 marines.

In 1945, Guam had one of the largest and most impressive naval and air bases of any country. Wainwright marveled at the ten huge airfields on which were parked hundreds of B-29s, the largest bombers in the world. He saw a new fighter plane, the P-51, and was startled to learn that it could fly faster than 500 miles an hour. What a change from the P-36s and P-40s of his day.

The next morning they left Guam and headed for Kwajalein, reaching that island at 6:30 in the evening. Again Wainwright saw the evidence of America's might all around him. That evening, while Wainwright was enjoying a steak dinner, a junior officer came into the dining room and handed him a radiogram. The soldier was smiling broadly, and in a moment so was Wainwright. The message said, "President has submitted to the Senate nomination for temporary appointment as General, Army of the United States."

Four stars! The dream of every career officer since the plebe year at West Point. But for so long Wainwright had thought it was an impossible dream because he had spent the war as a prisoner. If his career ended now he was well satisfied. He did not yet know what awaited him in Washington.

At the next stop, Honolulu, Skinny was pleased to receive the personal congratulations of MacArthur. "We are all so happy, dear Jim, at your promotion. May you live long to enjoy it."

In Washington, D.C., military and civilian leaders were busy preparing for Wainwright's arrival. The official reception was planned as one of the biggest celebrations in the city's history. Wainwright may not have realized how much of a hero he was to the American people, but the citizens of Washington did. For each of the six days Wainwright was en route from Manila, readers of the capital city's newspapers were bombarded with articles about the general and the tribute in store for him. Maps showed the route of his motorcade, timetables detailed his activities, and the many events scheduled in his honor were described again and again.

Wainwright's name was front-page news every day. Interviews with colleagues told affectionately of "the man who won his rank with a saddle, a saber, and a pair of yellow braid pants," a man who was "as fondly remembered here as commanding officer of Fort Myer as he is revered for his stand on Corregidor." Reporters reminded readers that "When MacArthur arrived in Australia he said he had left behind a modern soldier with enough 'horse-soldier tradition' to hold that line if it could be held."

By the time Wainwright's plane left San Francisco on the evening of September 9, it carried a new and welcome passenger, Capt. Jonathan M. Wainwright V, U.S. Merchant Marine. Father and son had had a joyous and tearful reunion. Captain Wainwright had proudly taken Skinny on a tour of his ship. The 100-year Wainwright tradition of continuous military service to the nation was being well carried on.

San Francisco, a city Wainwright loved—he could recite the names of all the streets from Market to the Presidio—celebrated his return with a large noisy parade up Market Street. It was a double celebration, for Wainwright's return and for the anniversary of California's statehood.

And now Wainwright was on the last leg of his flight. George Marshall had specified that the plane should land at Washington's National Airport at exactly 12:30 P.M. on the next day, the 10th. The pilot, who did not want to be late, made sure he allowed plenty of time for the cross-country flight. It was good that he did because Skinny developed a toothache not long out of San Francisco. The pain was intense and his jaw was becoming swollen. Clearly, he needed emergency dental treatment.

The pilot radioed ahead to Omaha and when the C-54 set down at 2:30 in the morning, an army dentist, Maj. John Kish, was waiting. He treated Wainwright as best he could under the circumstances, and gave him an ice pack to keep on his jaw for the rest of the flight. Interviewed by reporters the next day, Kish said that Wainwright was a "hell of a swell fellow—felt bad about having to get people out of bed."

Wainwright had not lost his compassion for his men. His status as a national hero had not turned his head. He remained what he had always been, a soldier's soldier. Everyone he came in contact with on his long trip home felt that he was one of them. Staff Sgt. Earnest H. Prescott, the radio operator on Skinny's plane for the journey, said, "The General's a real 'Joe'; he's G.I. all right—finest general I ever saw."

The hardships of Wainwright's war hadn't destroyed his basic human touch. His concern for others remained a part of him through all the days of glory and tragedy that lay ahead.

Monday, September 10, 1945, was hot and sticky, as the nation's capital so often is, even in the late days of summer. The temperature was expected to reach 89° and thunderstorms were predicted for early in the day. The planners of the day's activities hoped it wouldn't rain during the afternoon.

At 11:00 a brief cloudburst drenched a corner of the Washington Monument grounds, soaking some of the people who were already waiting, but the rain spared the stand from which Wainwright would speak. The growing mass of people, which had started forming three hours earlier, tried to sit in the shadow of the monument to avoid the sun. As the sun shifted, so did the crowd, gradually moving east in a body.

Portable refreshment stands had been set up and many persons had brought their own lunches. By noon the monument grounds were jammed and more spectators were coming. Workmen were putting the finishing touches on the reviewing stand and erecting a huge red heart decorated with a gold key and the words "Welcome, Skinny."

At the nearby Memorial Bridge over the Potomac River, gateway to the city from the airport, two fire engines parked at either end. They raised their ladders, wrapped in red, white, and blue bunting, to form a giant inverted vee across each end of the bridge. Firemen climbed the ladders and strung an enormous American flag and a banner saying "Welcome." Every lamppost across the bridge bore a "Welcome, Skinny" poster with the general's photograph.

In a suite at the Shoreham Hotel on Calvert Street off fashionable Connecticut Avenue, Mrs. Wainwright nervously made ready for her husband's homecoming. She had arrived from Skaneateles the day before and had slept little during the night. She had eaten almost no breakfast and declared to friends that she was too excited to have lunch. She put on a black dress trimmed with light blue around the neckline, a string of pearls, a black straw hat, and white gloves. On her shoulder she pinned a single orchid. When the wait had become too hard to bear, Adele insisted on leaving for the airport, arriving a little past noon, twenty-five minutes early.

From the Pentagon and other offices around Washington, General Marshall and other invited dignitaries were being driven out to National Airport. Buses brought the army's honor guard and band. On the monument grounds the crowd had swelled to such a size that it could no longer follow in the shadow of the sun. The sloping green lawn was covered with 400,000 people. As many as 300,000 others lined the streets over which Wainwright's motorcade would travel, sweating in the hot sun for a glimpse of the nation's hero. An elderly woman fainted on the monument grounds but revived as attendants were about to place her in an ambulance. She refused to be taken away. "I've just got to see that man," she said over and over.

Red Cross buses drove as close as they could to the grandstand. One hundred disabled veterans from nearby hospitals got out and were helped to front-row seats. Eighteen of them were amputees; none of them could walk. The crowd cheered for each man as he was carried to his seat.

A contingent of the American Legion marched up to the grandstand and formed a line across its width and along each side. At the rear of the grandstand an artillery crew checked over their field gun one last time.

Everything was ready for the day Wainwright would call "the highlight of my whole life."

Captain Perkins, the pilot of Wainwright's plane, was ahead of schedule, so he took Wainwright and his party on a sightseeing tour over the Great Smoky Mountains of Tennessee and North Carolina. Even with the detour, however, he arrived early, landing at 12:26. Skinny peered through the windows as the plane taxied up to the line of waiting dignitaries. He had eyes only for his beloved Kitty, whom he had not seen in more than four years. The C-54 stopped and its engines were switched off. The stairway ramp was wheeled into place. The door opened and Wainwright stepped out, and the crowd roared. The army band played "Ruffles and Flourishes" as he slowly descended the stairs, leaning on his cane.

He looked terrible, even to those who hadn't known him before the war. His legs wobbled, his shirt collar was much too big for his neck, and his face was drawn and gaunt. Yet there was a sparkle in his eyes. When he grinned he looked like a different person.

"He looks as if he might topple over any minute," a radio commentator told his audience at that moment, "until he smiles. And then you know he would not topple over—now or for some time to come."

Adele Wainwright looked up at George Marshall, who was standing by her side. He smiled and nodded, and she ran forward, arms outstretched to embrace her husband. Tears were streaming down her cheeks.

"Hello, darling," she said.

Skinny kissed her once, then again, but was too overwhelmed to say anything. Behind them the airport crowd cheered. Photographers and reporters swarmed around the couple and asked Mrs. Wainwright to repeat her welcoming kiss. Firmly but graciously she refused. For a moment the milling crowd separated her from him. Alone, she bowed her head and wept openly.

General Marshall made his way forward to shake Wainwright's hand, and he led them both to a car that was waiting to take them to the Pentagon. Wainwright was amazed at the size of the building, but even more surprised by the welcome that awaited him inside. In the large open courtyard, forty-seven veterans of Bataan and Corregidor applauded when he came into view. He plunged among them, greeting many who had shared the bad times, including Sam Howard, commanding officer of the Fourth Marines on Corregidor, and Carlos Romulo, now a brigadier general, whom Skinny had gotten out on the night Bataan fell. Wainwright was visibly moved by the sight of so many men who had fought with him.

"You, my friends of Bataan and Corregidor," he said, "I am glad to see you here. It is too bad that all of you are not here but more are coming. They are on the way."

The Wainwright party was taken next to the office of Secretary of War Henry Stimson. The two old acquaintances greeted each other warmly. "I had a good talk with him," Stimson wrote in his diary that night. "He was a fine upstanding man and I liked him very much. . . . He was very simple in his attitude and in what he said, but he had been deafened by concussion of some explosion and was rather hard to talk to. But I sat and chatted informally while the others did likewise around the room and just at the end I said a few words expressing our greeting and our joy at having him with us."

A motorcade of limousines, a dozen jeeps, and cars bearing reporters, photographers, and radio broadcasters, passed under the red-white-and-blue arches on Memorial Bridge, through enthusiastic crowds that grew ever larger as Wainwright approached the Washington Monument. The grounds were covered by a sea of people and they overflowed Constitution Avenue, where the police set up barriers to try to keep them back.

The field gun behind the monument opened up with a nineteen-gun salute as Wainwright's car turned into the monument grounds, but its booming sounds were almost drowned out by the roars of the 400,000 people. They continued to cheer as Wainwright and his party mounted the steps of the grandstand. With Skinny and Adele were Brig. Gen. and Mrs. Lew Beebe, Col. and Mrs. Johnny Pugh, Lt. Col. Tom Dooley and his mother, and Sgt. Hubert Carroll and his sister.

Carlos Romulo stepped up to the microphone to deliver a welcoming address. His words reflected his personal gratitude toward Wainwright.

"We who last saw General Wainwright within the tunnel of Corregidor saw a leader bent under the tragedy of impending doom, a man left holding in his helpless hand the honor of America.

"He was the emblem then of our defeat.

"This man, this American eagle taken captive, is now our emblem of unceasing watchfulness and our standard for the eternal battle for universal peace and security. Let us thus remember him for the rest of our human history as the symbol of vigilance and of victory.

"Without his sacrifice we could not have been stimulated towards so glorious and swift an end. Without that haunting picture of an heroic man bent under grief in a rock tunnel in the Philippines, under a single swinging electric bulb that lighted the damp walls, and his bleak look that saw so much ahead of horror and hopelessness, we would not have shared his struggle with so high a sense of dedication.

"Do not doubt that even then he saw ahead this inevitable victory of justice. He was an American officer in that hour that was the blackest in the history of the United States, he was patriot and soldier, and he refused rescue and liberty to make that last stand on Corregidor and share torture with his men, knowing what it meant for himself in personal suffering but knowing, too, what his sacrifice would teach Americans who were safe and secure when they learned the full story of that tragedy of Corregidor.

"Through surrender he won this war. Through his delaying action on Bataan he speeded forward the coming of V-J Day, the last day of the earth's longest and most terrifying struggle for freedom.

"Bataan was his heroism, and his martyrdom was Corregidor. Heroism and martyrdom are combined in the person of this single man.

"General Wainwright could not hold Corregidor, but he could hold fast to the standards of American decency, American honor, and American courage. Not once did he let the standards down; not even under Japanese torture did he let America down. Without his personal suffering, our victory would be less satisfying and less triumphant. He was America on that bitter rock in Manila Bay. Now in this hour of flying flags and triumphant drums, he is the vindication of our democracy. He is *your* America and *my* America set free."

Throughout Romulo's speech, Mrs. Wainwright sat nervously on the edge of her chair. She twisted her handkerchief, dabbed at her eyes, and turned repeatedly to look at Skinny, who had been seated five chairs away. When Romulo referred to Wainwright as "this American eagle taken captive," she broke down and sobbed.

Wainwright slowly rose and walked over to the microphone. An almost mournful hush fell over the audience as he pulled out his prepared remarks and put on his glasses. He looked out at the crowd for a moment and began to speak.

"Thank you, all of you, for this great reception. My comrades and I will remember always the warmth of this hour [the sweltering audience applauded and laughed] and the honor you have bestowed in welcoming us today. I am proud to accept these special honors from you, Mr. Commissioner: the key to the city and this scroll. They are symbols of the spirit which has brought this huge assembly together.*

"I am happy to accept the membership, so graciously offered me, in the Disabled American Veterans. I accept it in the name of all my comrades who suffered in battle and in the cruel months of captivity that followed.

"I still find it hard to believe that I am really here, back among my own people. We lived in a blacked-out world during our prison days. One of the least, and the greatest, of the cruelties practiced by the Japs was to keep us from frequent contact with home. We seldom knew what had happened to our loved ones.

"From the poverty of our existence out there, we have returned to find America strong and great. Even before we first set foot on the American Continent at San Francisco last Saturday, we knew how this country had rallied from our defeat at Corregidor.

"We saw the strong, seasoned American troops who had defeated the Japanese in campaign after campaign. We saw the wealth of air power in great planes which were hardly blueprints in the days when we anxiously scanned the skies for the relief that did not exist. We saw the mighty naval armada, risen from the grave of Pearl Harbor, stretched out across the waters of the Pacific to menace the now cringing Japs. The power of America was assembled out there, and we thanked God for it.

"The men who fought on Bataan and Corregidor were never beaten in spirit. Exhausted by thinning supply and the ordeal of terrific pounding by siege guns and bombers, it was useless to continue the struggle. We surrendered as honorable soldiers.

"You know what happened after that. The rights and privileges

---

*The District of Columbia Commissioners also presented Mrs. Wainwright with a silver tea service.

which civilized nations have agreed to grant prisoners of war were denied by the Jap. Many brave and gallant soldiers died under the torment and starvation they were forced senselessly to suffer.

"The tables are now completely turned. No humane person could desire that the Japs be forced to endure what many of our men went through. Yet I know that Americans will insist that the full meaning of Japan's surrender be brought home to every subject of the Emperor. These truculent men must be forced to realize the folly of their ambitions. Until the Japanese people display sincerely a desire for peaceful ways, we must not abandon our watch.

"It will be many days before I shall feel that I know my country fully again. You cannot realize what it is like to return home after years spent without the day-to-day happenings which you learn from the press and radio.

"Yet there is one thing apparent on every hand—the deep sincerity with which this country has devoted itself to avenging what we suffered in the early days of Bataan and Corregidor. I am grateful for it. Nothing can restore the men who died to their loved ones. Yet their sacrifice, living on in the thoughts and deeds of America, can protect this nation from the lack of practical foresight which brought about those tragic events.

"As I stood on the deck of the *Missouri*, at the right hand of General MacArthur, watching the signing of the surrender document, I fervently wished every American could feel the full significance of that moment. Nearly four years had elapsed since the Japs launched their attacks on Pearl Harbor and on the Philippines.

"That moment of surrender in Tokyo Bay had been bought with the blood of more than a million Americans who died or were wounded in the struggle. Billions of dollars and countless hours of work by Americans at home had been required to bring that little party of beaten Japs to the *Missouri*'s deck. All because for a while we were careless of the nation's safety. We let down our guard.

"It is over now, and we are at peace. But in the name of all my comrades who suffered with me, I pray that this nation will never again neglect the strength of its defenses; in all the joy I feel on returning to my own land, there is the memory of the last days of Corregidor and of the awful months that followed.

"Those memories can never be erased from my mind. I hope that the story of what Americans suffered will always be remembered in its practical significance—as a lesson which almost lost for us this land we love.

"My comrades and I have been profoundly touched by all these evidences of your great regard. I thank you in their name and in my own. This is truly such a welcome as a man dreams of, locked away behind barbed wire and the bayonets of cruel jailers. It is the surest evidence I could have that you still keep before you the words which I know fired you to great effort after our sorrowful defeat: 'Remember Bataan! Remember Corregidor!'"

At these words the crowd went wild with excitement, the applause and shouts loud and fervent, continuing as Wainwright left the platform and headed for his car. He and Adele climbed into the back seat of an open Packard, which slowly began to drive away. The police had difficulty keeping back the well-wishers. A woman slipped through the cordon and jumped on the car's running board. The Wainwrights shook hands with her and she burst into tears. "I'll never forget this day," she told them.

The procession moved along Constitution Avenue past more cheering throngs, and drove on to the grounds of the Capitol, where almost 8,000 people were waiting. Wainwright stood up and waved, and smartly saluted one of the military guards.

Here he was scheduled to make two brief speeches, one to the House of Representatives and the other to the Senate. At 2:50 he was escorted into the House chamber. The congressmen gave him a standing ovation. The Speaker of the House, Sam Rayburn of Texas, introduced him.

"We are honored today by the presence of one of the outstanding heroes of the earth. His name will be permanently inscribed on the tablets of fame. It is my high privilege and great pleasure to give you General Jonathan M. Wainwright."

Once again the members stood and applauded as Wainwright walked to the dais. He looked at them with a solemn expression on his face, then cast a glance and a thin smile to his wife in the gallery.

"Mr. Speaker and Members of the House of Representatives:

"Now I feel that at last I have come home to my country—all the way. I thank you from the bottom of my heart for the generous impulse which moved you to call me here.

"In receiving the honor of a reception by the Congress, I can express my gratitude to all the American people for the welcome which they have given me and my comrades since our liberation.

"In greeting us, I know that our countrymen intend to show some measure of their feeling for all those who fought through the last weeks on Bataan and Corregidor. Many survived the pounding of Jap guns only to suffer more cruelly later on under the inhuman treatment given them in prison camps. As their commander, I can tell you it was the memory and hope of America that sustained them through darkest days.

"During the last year we were kept from all sources of news by our captors, yet we contrived to learn, by rumors and scraps of information that reached us, of the growing military might which must someday restore us to the rights of free men in our beloved land.

"We knew that our country had developed great power. Yet when my comrades and I were rescued from our captivity, we were not quite prepared for all we saw. A great new Army with new weapons and endless supply had made America what her citizens hope she may always be—invincible in battle.

"To men who have faced overwhelming power without the means to meet it, as we did in the Philippines, there was deep satisfaction in seeing how completely the odds had been reversed. How we longed for some of that offensive power on Corregidor. Had this nation been able to send it through the Jap blockade, tired as we were, there would have been no fall of Corregidor.

"From desperate days, we have returned to a world at peace. I thank God for our liberation and for the sympathy and high respect in which you have held us throughout the long ordeal which is now at its end."

Wainwright nodded his thanks to the assembled legislators, who were on their feet again, and turned to shake hands with Speaker Rayburn. His speech had taken five minutes.

Wainwright was led through the rotunda of the Capitol from the House wing to the Senate. Scores of people in the corridors clapped as he walked by.

Senate Majority Leader Alben Barkley and a committee of senators, including Warren Magnuson of Wainwright's home state of Washington, escorted Wainwright onto the Senate floor amidst the applause of the standing senators. He was introduced by Kenneth McKellar, president *pro tempore* of the Senate, and began to speak in slow, measured tones.

"Mr. President and members of the Senate:

"My comrades and I have just come from a reception by the House of Representatives. I want to express to you, as I have to the members of the House, the deep gratitude which all of us feel for the honor you have conferred in bringing us here today.

"Since the hour when we were restored to our countrymen in Chungking, we have been overwhelmed with kindness and consideration on every hand. It has been a moving experience. It has been such a spontaneous welcome as only the warmth of America could bring forth.

"Through it all has run the sadness of remembering the brave men who fell not in battle but died in foul prison camps of their captors' cruelty and neglect. It is a pitiful story, gentlemen. Some of it has already been told. I hope it may be revealed in all its ghastly detail.

"The American people must realize fully the nature of the enemy we knew so well. Only on a just consideration of his nature as it was revealed to us will we be able to decide such measures as must be taken to insure our future security from his lust for power.

"I am still living in a world of wonder. Out there in the Pacific since my liberation I have seen the strength of an aroused America arrayed against the Jap. It has been a pleasant sight.

"You will understand, I feel sure, if I say that I gloried in it and in the humiliation of the Japanese leaders who surrendered abjectly on the deck of the *Missouri*. Nothing could have moved me more than the invitation to be present at those ceremonies, and I hold as one of my treasured possessions the pen which General MacArthur first touched to the document of surrender.

"Later, I had an almost more personal triumph when I stood at Baguio on Luzon while General Yamashita surrendered all the remaining Jap forces in the Philippines. My only regret was that General Homma could not have been present. It was to him that I was forced to surrender the remnants of the gallant American Army which had fought him on Bataan and Corregidor.

"It is good to stand on American soil again and, in this chamber, to thank you and the American people for all you have done to welcome us back. Through these receptions and ceremonies we realize how well you remembered us during the bleak years when we were allowed to have no word of your warmth and anxiety. In the name of all my comrades, I thank you."

He shook hands with Barkley and the others on the podium and with every person on the Senate floor, including seven congressmen who had followed him from their chamber to hear him speak again.

Wainwright's energy was flagging now. His legs had begun to wobble and he was leaning more firmly on his cane. His eyes had dark heavy pouches beneath them. He obviously needed rest, but his day of glory was not yet over.

From Capitol Hill, the motorcade traveled down Pennsylvania Avenue, which was bordered by cheering crowds all the way to the

White House. Adele Wainwright beamed with pride as she walked by her husband's side through the White House lobby. Reporters waiting nearby applauded them both.

President Truman was waiting in his office. He was concerned about Wainwright's physical condition and had told a reporter that he didn't want to "kill him with kindness." The president had instructed General Marshall to see that Wainwright underwent a minimum of physical exertion.

But things had gotten out of hand. There were too many cities and too many people who wanted to pay homage to Wainwright, to shower him with gifts and awards and to express their appreciation for all he had sacrificed for his country. Truman was no exception, and he had planned a special ceremony at the White House. It was a secret, known only to a few intimate friends.

The Wainwrights were ushered into Truman's office. The president, wearing a seersucker suit and his honorable discharge button from World War I, came across the room to greet them. The two men shook hands and Truman handed Mrs. Wainwright a huge basket of flowers. They chatted for a few moments and then Truman suggested that they all step outside to the Rose Garden.

A bank of microphones had been set up in the garden and a large corps of reporters and photographers was waiting. About a hundred people stood behind a low hedge, mostly White House aides and clerks. Skinny nodded to them and recognized two famous faces—Rosalind Russell and Walter Huston. At that moment, however, he was more famous and more sought after than any movie stars.

President Truman stepped up to the microphones, took a piece of paper from his pocket, and cleared his throat. He smiled quickly at Wainwright and began to read his prepared remarks. Wainwright listened politely to what he was sure would be another flowery speech of praise, but suddenly he realized what the president was saying. The old soldier visibly straightened, squaring his shoulders, and his eyes sparkled, though he almost could not believe what he was hearing.

"General Jonathan M. Wainwright, 02131," President Truman said in his nasal voice, "commanding United States Army Forces in the Philippines from 12 March to 7 May 1942. He distinguished himself by intrepid and determined leadership against greatly superior enemy forces. At the repeated risk of life above and beyond the call of duty in his position—"

And that was the moment when Wainwright realized that he was about to receive the highest accolade any soldier could hope for.

"—he frequented the firing line of his troops where his presence provided the example and incentive that helped make the gallant efforts of these men possible. The final stand on beleaguered Corregidor, for which he was in an important measure personally responsible, commanded the admiration of the Nation's allies. It reflected the high morale of American arms in the face of overwhelming odds. General Wainwright's courage and resolution were a vitally needed inspiration to the then sorely pressed freedom-loving peoples of the world."

Truman put away the paper and turned to Wainwright.

"And so," he said, grinning broadly, "it gives me more pleasure than most anything I've ever done to present General Wainwright with the Congressional Medal of Honor—the highest honor in the land."*

An aide handed Truman a small, highly polished wooden box. The president took the blue-ribboned gold star from the box and placed it around Wainwright's thin neck. Tears filled Wainwright's eyes. He took the president's hand in both of his, and the crowd roared its approval. Flashbulbs popped. Skinny's aides crowded around him, and Sergeant Carroll, who had rarely left his side throughout the war, was the first to congratulate him. The gesture was fitting. Carroll was an enlisted man, like Wainwright a soldier's soldier.

---

*The award, first proposed three years before by Marshall and aborted because of MacArthur's reaction, had been brought up again by Marshall just five days before, on September 5. The following evening Secretary of War Stimson read over the 1942 recommendation and supporting papers. "It is a sharp issue," he recorded in his diary, "and has come up between him and MacArthur . . . Marshall went through it and had told me yesterday of some of the difficulties and dangers of the situation and the possibility of a row coming up between MacArthur and Wainwright which would stain the memories of the present war. He therefore wanted me to make the decision. I went over the papers last night and finished the last of them this morning very carefully, and after analyzing them I have decided on what I think is good evidence that MacArthur's objections were untenable and in fact on their face untrue, and I decided we should give the Medal of Honor. Marshall was much relieved." Truman was much in favor of making the award. He had met Wainwright some years before and had always held him in high regard. A few months earlier the president had written in his diary: "I don't see why in Hell Roosevelt didn't order Wainwright home and let MacArthur be a martyr. . . . We'd have had a real General and a fighting man if we had Wainwright and not a play actor and a bunco man as we have now."

Wainwright was overwhelmed with happiness and gratitude. He had been vindicated and honored by his country as few men have before or since. This moment was the realization, he said, of "every dream of glory" a soldier could have. He told Truman that he had expected to come home in disgrace. The president assured him that he was "a leader and a hero" to the American people.

The sun glinted on the medal, highlighting the American eagle and the words "Valor" and "United States of America." Beebe, Pugh, and Dooley, along with Adele and their son Jack and his wife, alternately laughed and cried as they gathered around to shower Skinny with congratulations.

Wainwright's future had not appeared so bright and promising in a long time. There was no hint on that warm September day of glory of the personal tragedy that lay ahead.

CHAPTER 18

"Alone in His Hero's Cage"

THOSE WHO KNEW Skinny Wainwright during the final years of his life—the eight years he lived after his liberation—talk about that time with a slow shake of their heads and sadness in their eyes. They talk about a man whose status as a war hero and celebrity caused him to be used and taken advantage of by others. A man whose appearance at a restaurant generated so much hysteria that he had to be whisked away for his own safety. A man whose stars were pulled from his uniform by people desperate to have a part of this living legend.

They talk about a man deluged with invitations, hundreds of them, who felt obliged to accept all of them he could, believing he had to repay the adulation and affection that was heaped on him. A man run ragged by parades and speeches and celebrations. Once he wrote to Ike, "Do I *have* to accept all these invitations?" Yet he continued to accept, out of gratitude—and duty.

Old friends remember a man who sometimes hid out in an attic refuge provided by a comrade from Bataan, to escape the constant demands on his time. "Alone, in his hero's cage," a West Point classmate said, "he worked for other men and made their speeches!" They never left him alone, these hangers-on, these sycophants riding on the coattails of the great. They were even in his hospital room at the moment he died. Only then was Wainwright free of them.

They talk about his loneliness, these true friends who worried about Skinny and tried to protect him during those years. His beloved wife, whom he had waited so long to be reunited with, was no longer at his side. Adele, too, was a victim of the war and of his status as a hero. "The strain of the long wait," a friend said, "the worry over his treatment as a prisoner, the lack of positive information as to his whereabouts, and finally the terrific excitement of his return amid the wild acclaim of our people, continuing for so long, brought on a serious collapse." She fell into an emotional turmoil and tried to find solace in drink. Various treatments were tried and she returned to him from time to time, but never for long. Finally she went to a hospital in Colorado Springs, and Skinny was alone.

And then Wainwright's friends talk about his drinking, which grew so much worse after his retirement. There was always a party somewhere, "an endless round of parties," and receptions and rodeos and speeches—and always someone to put a drink in his hand. Skinny never turned it down. A shot of whiskey eased his loneliness, for a while. It relieved the constant pressure from an adoring public, for a while. It dulled the pain of leaving the army, his career, his life, for a while.

This was a different kind of war that Wainwright fought during his last years, a much more personal war. It was a war he lost.

Wainwright's day of glory—that wonderful day when he received the Medal of Honor from President Truman—was only the beginning of the tribute paid him by a grateful public. Everybody wanted a piece of the hero.

He was mobbed and cheered the next day at Washington's Griffith Stadium, where he went to watch a baseball game. He loved baseball, and, between shaking the hands of hundreds of well-wishers and signing autographs, he managed to see a bit of the play as the Washington Senators beat the Cleveland Indians.

The following day Wainwright went to the dentist, received a check for three years and nine months back pay, lunched at the Army-Navy Club, and made a national radio broadcast from the National Archives, during ceremonies to place the Japanese surrender documents on public display.

The Wainwrights went on to New York City for the biggest

reception of all. Four million people turned out for his parade, second in size only to Eisenhower's. The crowd strewed the twenty-two-mile path of the parade with nearly 500 tons of confetti.

Something special set this victory parade apart from all the others that great city had seen. A *Newsweek* reporter wrote: "To the welcome given General Jonathan M. Wainwright . . . something new was added: the tribute of tears. Along the entire parade route, eyes glistened and throats were stilled at the sight of the gaunt, wrinkled soldier. Plainly, New Yorkers felt the impact of one American's sacrifice."

The speeches, the awards, the banquets were scheduled without letup. There were parades and honors in Adele's home town of Skaneateles and in Skinny's birthplace of Walla Walla, honorary degrees from more than a half dozen colleges and universities, keys to cities, honorary memberships in more organizations than he could remember, and a grueling 14,000-mile victory bond tour with scores of stops in towns from one end of the country to another.

Through it all, friends and classmates say, Wainwright remained modest and unassuming. "In spite of all the adulation and the cheers and the flags, he is still his own true self all the time." A Bataan officer added, "Skinny is apparently taking all the popular acclaim without turning his head."

Wainwright recognized the dangers of fame and tried to be careful of his public remarks, not pontificating on matters of which he had no knowledge. In a speech given at the Waldorf Astoria Hotel in New York, less than two months after his homecoming, he voiced this concern.

"By some process which I do not clearly understand, a military man who achieves notice—perhaps I should say notoriety—in war time is sometimes looked upon as a sort of oracle or soothsayer capable of uttering words of wisdom on almost any subject and gifted with power of prophecy.

"If he is not careful, he finds himself making ponderous observations on religion, sociology, art, economics. I almost said politics. Sometimes he talks too much.

"I am going to guard against any impulse to prophesy in this brief address, and I am going to try not to talk like an oracle."

Wherever Wainwright spoke, he limited his comments to a subject he knew something about, from personal experience, and about which he felt strongly: military preparedness.

"We must remain strong and great in spirit, fixed in our

determination to keep the peace of the world. Peace is a militant state, which is not secured by wishful thinking. If we are to be sure of our liberty, we must preserve the peace through full cooperation with other peace-loving nations. We must be ready to fight for it, if necessary. Until we can be certain that our security is safe from such treachery as we have suffered at the hands of the Japanese, we must keep our defenses impregnable. That is the lesson of Bataan. That is the trust of all those who suffered from the defeat at Corregidor."

He argued consistently and articulately for a strong defense force, for universal military training, for the crushing of militarism in Japan, and for never again being caught as we had been at Pearl Harbor. In a speech on the fifth anniversary of the attack on Pearl Harbor Wainwright said, "Pearl Harbor and Bataan were a needless waste." He even favored merging the army and navy into a single defense force to eliminate inter-service rivalry, a position not popular with his fellow generals. In 1951 he spoke out in support of a congressional bill to reactivate the mounted cavalry, a proposal that grew out of the army's early experiences in Korea, where a motorized force was having difficulty operating in a country with few roads.

Wainwright felt it was his duty to speak out like this, but the work took its toll on his health and spirit. "It was hard to take," he said of his situation. "The welcome was overpowering."

Despite his status as a celebrity, Wainwright was still a soldier, and he had no intention of retiring. The army agreed. It was good public relations to have a hero on active duty, particularly a general who was such an effective spokesman for the army's interests.

The chief of staff wanted a major and visible command for Skinny, and in January of 1946, after his victory bond drive, he found it. On the 19th of that month Wainwright was ordered to Fort Sam Houston, in San Antonio, Texas, to become Commanding General of the Fourth Army.

Wainwright approached his new command with vigor and excitement. It was good to be back in harness again. He called on a number of men from his Philippines command to round out his staff—Lew Beebe, Arnold Funk, Nick Galbraith, Jack Vance, Tom Dooley, and others, and, of course, Sergeant Carroll as his trusted orderly. One of Wainwright's first activities was to push for promotions and decorations for those who fought for him in the Philippines. He especially wanted to recognize the contribution of the Philippine Scouts.

Wainwright tried to cut down on his speaking engagements, but it was impossible. Too many people and organizations wanted to see the hero of Bataan, and he still felt it his duty to go, particularly for a veteran's organization. And there were many of these who wanted to claim him as one of their own.

He was honorary president of the U.S. Cavalry Association, Commander of the Disabled American Veterans, and spoke before the National Association of Barbed Wire Clubs, the American Convention of Ex-POWs, the Bataan Relief Association, Federated Organizations for Bataan Relief, American Legion, Military Order of the Carabao, Military Order of the World Wars, and on and on. Skinny could be counted on to be the drawing card for every veteran's group.

Each Decoration Day, Armistice Day, V-J Day, and Army Day brought scores of new invitations. There were plaques and scrolls and more medals than he could keep track of.

There were also the West Point reunions. Wainwright received a standing ovation when he attended his fortieth reunion in 1946, and at the forty-fifth reunion banquet he entertained his classmates with poems of the old cavalry.

One honor that particularly touched him was a telegram read at the American Legion Banquet in Chicago to commemorate Army Day on April 10, 1948. It was from Douglas MacArthur.

"It is particularly appropriate," MacArthur wrote, "that your American Legion Post should commemorate the historic role of the American Army in the shaping of American destiny on April tenth with General Wainwright as your distinguished guest. For on that day six years before, the American Army with its staunch Filipino allies concluded in dignity and honor one of the most glorious actions in the defense of Bataan. General Wainwright brought to an able close a campaign which, in its every phase, bore the influence of his brilliant and courageous leadership."

Everywhere Wainwright went, there would be someone from Bataan or Corregidor to remind him of those dark days. Whenever he found such a man his eyes would mist over and he would grip the soldier's hand and talk quietly with him for a few moments, ignoring the rest of the crowd.

Every year brought a reunion of the Wainwright Travelers, a group started by the generals and colonels in the prison camp at Tarlac. These were usually happy, joyful occasions, but they were times for tears as well. The Octette got together again and sang the old songs they had performed in the camps. Skinny listened, recalling the hard times, and told a reporter how much the group meant to them. "They were a hook," he said, "upon which the prisoners could hang their lives in those dark days."

Once the Travelers met at Wainwright's home in San Antonio. The dining room was decorated with palm fronds and tropical vegetation, reminiscent of the Philippines. The men and their wives sat down to a meal of rice and soup, spooned into tiny cups from galvanized iron buckets. Just like the camps. It was good, Wainwright thought, to be reminded of how bad things had been, so you could appreciate what you had now. The soup was followed by a meal of roast turkey and duck.

Reunions of Bataan–Corregidor survivors were always emotional times for Wainwright. He went to Milwaukee on July 26, 1946, for the 192nd Tank Battalion that had fought for him on Bataan. A thousand people greeted him at the airport, among them sixteen survivors of the battalion from Janesville, Wisconsin. They stood to one side as a group and watched Wainwright step jauntily off the plane. He shook hands with the members of the reception committee and stood stiff and straight as the national anthem was played. Then the master of ceremonies brought the tankers up to meet him.

"The general took a step forward," wrote a local newsman. "He halted momentarily, his eyes filled with tears, but he fought them back. His voice choked. As the Janesville men and several tankmen from other parts of the State marched in columns of twos toward him, the general motioned to them to open ranks. He went in among them, threw his wiry arms around the leaders and as many more as he could gather in a single clasp. With his voice shaking with emotion, he told his men, 'Boys, I want each of you to know how much I appreciated what you did under me.'" He walked slowly among them, grasping the hand of each man in both of his, and repeating his words of thanks.

Later Wainwright told reporters, "Frankly, when I saw those men—only a handful left of that great tank battalion—my eyes filled with tears. It gave me a shock to see how few were left."

"General Wainwright had all the guts of a great soldier," one of the tankers said. "We like him. We admire him. He's a real man. We'd do it again and die for him."

The wives and mothers of those who didn't come back also wanted to meet him. "Our boys died under him," one said, "and we just want to be near him." A woman who lost her twin sons on Bataan said, "We just feel we owe a lot to General Wainwright. We want to shake his hand."

There were so many people who wanted to shake his hand, to touch him, so many survivors and relatives of survivors, and he believed he owed it to them to go wherever they asked him.

But the memories were painful. Wainwright's tears were real. He was never far from the past. One night in San Francisco he was having dinner at Omar Khayyam's in the company of Malcolm Champlin, his young naval aide from Bataan. At a nearby table sat two men wearing uniforms of the Dutch navy. They recognized Wainwright and summoned the waiter, who returned in a few minutes and handed one of them a saucer of rice. The sailor rose and walked over to Wainwright's table. Without a word he knelt, placed the rice under Skinny's chair, and stood and saluted. Wainwright looked up at the boy and they both started to cry. He jumped up and clasped the sailor by the shoulders.

"What is your name?" Wainwright said. "I remember you."

"My name is not important," the man said. He saluted once more and left the restaurant with his companion. Skinny reached down and brought the saucer of rice to the table. He stared at it for a long time with tears streaming down his cheeks. Then in a husky voice he told Champlin what it was all about. For a time some Dutch sailors had been interned in one of Wainwright's prison camps. Whenever they could, they would take a portion of their work rice, place it on a saucer, and slip it under the barbed wire for Wainwright and the other high-ranking prisoners. The young man in the restaurant had been one of those sailors.

When Wainwright would return to San Antonio after these physically and emotionally exhausting trips, it was to a large, empty house. Adele was gone now, permanently hospitalized in Colorado. But his house didn't stay empty for long. As soon as word spread that Skinny was back in town, the parties quickly resumed.

"The drinking parties at his residence were endless," a friend recalled. "These sorts of parties were common among a large percentage of the military, but not so extensively as in Wainwright's case. Everybody barged in constantly, sort of a 'hanging on the coattails' syndrome."

Every night—and many an afternoon—was open house at Wainwright's quarters. The liquor flowed freely, and Wainwright's continued drinking, especially after his retirement, made him more susceptible to those who wanted to use him. There is no question that people took advantage of him, and sometimes he was not competent to hold off the people who were preying on him. There is also no question that he died an alcoholic, unable to cope with the demands of his fame.

Soon he began to drink heavily when he was away from home. Those who knew him during those difficult and lonely years admit with great reluctance to seeing him "under the influence" at public affairs. At Mule Day festivities in a small Tennessee town, Wainwright—and the state's senator, Estes Kefauver—were guests of honor. Skinny drove a four-mule team down Main Street. "Are you sure you can drive this thing, Skinny?" an old Bataan friend asked. "I could drive it with eight mules," he replied. Off they went, stopping every block or so to take another sip.

For years people clamored for his presence, desiring to buy him a drink or take him to dinner, to ask him to grace this affair or that celebration, so they could be in the presence of the hero.

Often, when the pressures became too great, Wainwright took refuge in a quiet attic room, a place of retreat where he could hide out from the people who were pestering him. Sergeant Carroll would drive up an alleyway not far from Wainwright's home, checking to make sure no one had seen them. Wainwright would then slip from the rear of the car into the kitchen of a large three-story house and up the back stairs, while Carroll drove away before anyone could spot the general's car.

The house belonged to Arnold Funk, Wainwright's old comrade from Bataan. General Funk was the commanding officer of Fort Sam Houston. He and his wife kept a small, plainly furnished, top-floor room in their house for Skinny. There he had a couch, a table and chair, and a radio. There was no telephone and no one would bother him. The houseboy, Masuda (who preferred to be called "George" because, he said, he wanted to atone for the actions of his countrymen), brought Wainwright coffee and a snack, usually custard, and Skinny napped or read mystery stories. Late in the afternoon he would come downstairs, sometimes to ask, shyly, "May I have dinner with you?" At these times all he wanted was a quiet, home-cooked meal with good friends who didn't want anything from him. Here he found peace and contentment. It was the closest he could come to a home and a family.

It was inevitable that rumors and gossip would spread about Wainwright's drinking, reminiscent of Fort Myer in 1938. Some of the stories were true, but some were exaggerated. They reached the highest level of the army, however, and disturbed the chief of staff, Dwight Eisenhower.

"He drank too much," Ike said. "I tried everything. I gave him a high command in Texas. I gave him an aide to look after him. But he wouldn't stop drinking."

Wainwright's friends worried about his reputation, fearing that he might embarrass himself—and the army—because of his drinking. Then he might be forced to resign under a shadow, compromising his brilliant career. They needn't have worried. Skinny had the same concern. He knew it was time to get out honorably.

On August 31, 1947, after forty-five years of continuous service, J. M. Wainwright, age sixty-four, retired from the army he loved and had served so well. He was the last of the West Point class of 1906 to retire. More than 10,000 spectators turned out in the blazing Texas sun to see Skinny "read himself out of the army."

Some 3,000 troops marched past the reviewing stand and thirty planes from Brooke Field roared overhead. Wainwright rose and walked slowly to the podium, polished his glasses on his coattail, and began to speak. In this his last speech as a soldier his theme was again the country's military preparedness.

"For an old soldier to say that it is a pleasure to take his last review is, in my mind at least, a stretch of the imagination and a far cry from the truth.

"Military men are not imperialists. They are not war mongers or savage killers. They are profound lovers of peace who believe that it can be obtained and maintained through an efficient military organization as an important part of a peaceful government."

With sweat pouring down his face, Wainwright reached the end of his farewell address.

"As I hang up my saber I look with confidence at these younger soldiers in whose hands the destinies of the army and the nation will rest. They are strong, capable hands, eager to do a job and do it well.

"Thank you, goodbye, and God bless all of you."

The army band marched onto the field, formed the letter "W" in front of the reviewing stand, and played a favorite song, "Auld Lang Syne." A sophomore student from Trinity University sang the sad words in a clear, ringing voice. Wainwright gripped his cane, squared his shoulders, and stared straight ahead. The last note rang out over the field and hovered a moment before dying. It was over.

*   *   *

"There's nothing deader than an ex," a Corregidor officer said. "Even an ex-general."

A month later Wainwright wrote to MacArthur. "I have retired, bought a home in San Antonio, and entered into one or two lines of business here. I have been wearing civilian clothes now for a month but cannot say that I have gotten used to them yet."

His large house, which he named "Fiddler's Green," after the old cavalry song, was as full of parties as his quarters on the post had been. Wainwright was still the hero, the celebrity, and retirement did not decrease the number of people who wanted to be associated with him.

He was the honored guest or the featured speaker at horse shows and hunts and rodeos and charity functions. The state of Texas adopted him as a native son, and he always tried to satisfy the demands of the local populace. Their gift, a lavish saddle, filled a corner of his living room.

"By now you are in Texas," Clint Pierce wrote to a mutual friend, "and have probably seen 'Tex' Wainwright. It is not any longer de rigeur to call him 'Skinny.' He has been adopted by the state of Texas, and he uses a new nickname."

Wainwright threw himself into what was for him a new world, that of business. He became vice-president of a chain of food stores, and president of a life insurance company and chairman of the board of another. He didn't know any more about life insurance than he did about supermarkets, but he didn't have to. It was his name, not his expertise, that was wanted.

The insurance companies with which he was associated specialized in policies for American military personnel and dependents throughout the world. This was a new and potentially lucrative market, and what better way to enter it than through the contacts of one of America's best-known generals. Wainwright's name opened doors; he was good for business.

He wrote letters to friends and colleagues, including MacArthur, asking for their help, and his companies extended their reach to Europe and Japan. He flew around the country in a company plane, visiting men still on active duty. He sent company executives to contact old army men. Some of these people found it embarrassing.

But Wainwright approached the business world with all the enthusiasm and diligence that had served him so well in the army. And he remained willing to answer the call whenever a veteran's organization wanted his presence or someone offered him a forum to speak out on military preparedness.

There was a brief fling with politics, in support of Douglas MacArthur. Wainwright still believed that MacArthur could do no wrong, and he was incensed, as were most career soldiers, when Truman recalled MacArthur from the Far East in 1951. Wainwright said that MacArthur "will forever stand as one of the great captains of history."

When there was a groundswell of support for MacArthur to run for president at the 1948 Republican convention in Philadelphia, Wainwright was there to help his former chief. In his hotel room he pored over the nominating speech he had been asked to deliver, polishing and sharpening the words. He wanted to be as forceful and persuasive as possible, to convince the delegates that America needed MacArthur. But many in the Republican Party did not agree, and they dominated the convention. Wainwright waited impatiently in his hotel room as the proceedings dragged on. His speech had been scheduled early enough to make the morning newspapers, but it was not to be.

The hours passed. Midnight, 1:00 A.M., and still the convention chairman postponed the nominating speeches. At 3:40 in the morning Wainwright entered the hall to a smattering of applause. The reporters had gone and so had most of the delegates. Skinny made his speech to row upon row of empty chairs.

Skinny Wainwright died on September 2, 1953, eight years to the day after he witnessed the signing of the Japanese surrender in Tokyo Bay. He suffered a stroke on August 13 and lapsed into a coma, from which he never recovered. During the last two weeks of his life there was always a crowd in his hospital room and in the corridors outside. People still clung to his coattails, even as he lay dying.

At noon on the 2nd of September, The Reverend Paul Osborne, rector of St. Paul's Episcopal Church, stopped by Wainwright's suite at Brooke Army Hospital. "There were a number of persons in the room, none of whom I knew. The General's breathing was very labored so I placed my hand under his head to hold it up so that breathing might be easier. I felt his pulse beat stop, and said to the officer next to me, whom I believed to be a Medical Officer: 'Colonel, the General has just died.' He asked me what time it was and I looked at my watch and said, 'It is 12:23 P.M.'."

There was a long moment of silence in the room. One of the visitors stepped up to the foot of the bed and stared at Wainwright. "Look at that mask on his face," he said. "Just like Napoleon's." How ghoulish it was, these leeches still clinging to the dead hero. Finally Wainwright was free of them.

The nation mourned Wainwright, and tributes appeared in many newspapers and magazines.

"General Wainwright had something of the rocky quality of the island fortress he defended," wrote *The Washington Post*. "He was the epitome of the old type, ramrod-straight cavalry officer, and he sought to protect his men during the period of captivity at the expense of personal torture and indignity at the hands of the Japanese."

"Jonathan Mayhew Wainwright was a soldier of the old U.S. Army," said *Time* magazine. "A lean, bowlegged cavalryman, he spent his happiest days in the hard-riding, spur and saber atmosphere of the vanishing Army posts of the West. In an age that produced Army men of many talents—generals who could double as diplomats, showmen, orators and businessmen—'Skinny' Wainwright, a fine horseman, a crack shot and an all-round good officer, was never anything but a soldier. . . . his men believed in him, and they followed him to the limit at Bataan and Corregidor."

Never anything but a soldier. That was all Wainwright had ever wanted to be, not a celebrity, not a hero, just a soldier. That was enough of an accolade.

Tributes poured into San Antonio from all over the world, from the great and the unknown, from those who knew him and those who knew of him, from all who were saddened by his passing.

"General Wainwright was one of our greatest soldiers," wired MacArthur to the family, "and one of our greatest patriots. We shall mourn him as a life-long friend and true gentleman."

General Eisenhower wrote, "I have just learned with the deepest regret of the passing of my old friend General Wainwright. His example of courage, fortitude, and unshakable patriotism, all exhibited in the face of the most discouraging conditions, will long be an inspiration to Americans and free men everywhere."

Heroes are not buried simply. The services for Wainwright were among the army's most elaborate and moving. They began in San Antonio, in the Post Chapel at Fort Sam Houston, where his body, dressed in the winter uniform of "pinks and greens," with rows of ribbons on the jacket, lay in state for two days. Hundreds of people, among them many survivors of Bataan and Corregidor, filed past the casket to pay their respects to the old soldier.

On September 5 a private service was held in the Post Chapel, attended by Wainwright's son and daughter-in-law and a number of old friends. Adele did not attend; she was not even told of his death for some time.*

The casket was carried outside while the Fourth Army Band played Wainwright's favorite hymn, "Nearer My God to Thee." The procession wound slowly through the post to the strains of Chopin's Funeral March. Alongside the hearse walked six comrades as honorary pallbearers—Herbert Brees, Courtney Hodges, William Simpson, John Leonard, George Grunert (Wainwright's first commanding officer in the Philippines), and Walter Krueger (who had led the troops that recaptured the Philippines in 1945).

Behind the hearse came the traditional riderless horse draped with a black blanket adorned with a light-colored border and four stars. Wainwright's highly polished boots were reversed in the stirrups, a farewell salute to a cavalryman, and in the scabbard was the sword his mother had given him upon his graduation from West Point. The sword, found on the body of a Japanese officer after the war, had been returned to Wainwright in 1949.

The horse was led down the street by another old soldier, a sergeant of the old army, the man who had polished the general's boots that morning and saddled the horse. Grief was evident on his face but he carried himself stiff and straight, as a soldier should. His name was Hubert Carroll.

The procession reached the Grayson Street gate of the post and the marching men came to a halt. The band played "Auld Lang Syne," and the hearse drove away.

There was one last ceremony for Skinny, one final mark of respect from a grateful nation. Flown to Washington, escorted by Col. L. A. "Pick" Diller, a former staff officer from Fort McKinley in the Philippines, his body lay in state in the Trophy Room of the Amphitheater at Arlington Cemetery. Not since the burial of the unknown soldier in 1921 had an American fighting man been given such an honor.

At 11:00 A.M. on September 8 the body was brought to the

---

*Mrs. Wainwright died at Emory John Brady Hospital in Colorado Springs, Colorado, in 1970.

Memorial Gate entrance to the cemetery. Four companies of the Third Infantry Regiment from Skinny's old post, Fort Myer, stood at attention. The coffin was placed atop a jet-black gun caisson drawn by six matched gray horses. A riderless black horse with boots reversed in the stirrups followed the caisson as the procession slowly marched along the roads of the cemetery to the heights behind the Custis-Lee Mansion. The army band played an old cavalry song, "Brave Rifles," that Skinny had loved to sing. It was the song of the Third Cavalry, which he once commanded.

Gens. George Marshall and Omar Bradley, followed by Gen. Matthew Ridgway, the Army Chief of Staff, and Adm. Arthur Radford, chairman of the Joint Chiefs, led more than 2,000 mourners. Scores of high-ranking military and civilian leaders attended, including nine of Wainwright's West Point classmates and many of his fellow officers from the Philippines, but MacArthur was not among them. "A previous engagement," he said. President Truman couldn't come either. He was meeting a visiting dignitary from "America's strongest ally in the Pacific," the Crown Prince of Japan.

An old man in civilian clothes walked with some difficulty up the hill to the gravesite. He appeared to have a problem with his hip, the result of a fall in a Japanese prison camp, but he gamely kept up with the rest. He was retired Maj. Gen. Edward P. "Ned" King, come to share a final moment with Skinny.

The caisson stopped. The distinguished guests, civilians, and veterans of Wainwright's war gathered around the empty grave. Some of them noticed the name on the nearest headstone, several feet away: Robert Powell Page Wainwright, Major, U.S. Cavalry—Skinny's father.

The army band played "Ruffles and Flourishes." The chaplain read a brief prayer while soldiers held the American flag taut above the coffin. Cannon boomed a seventeen-gun salute. The Honor Guard fired three rifle volleys. "Taps" rang out in the still air.

> Halfway down the trail to Hell
> In a shady meadow green
> Are the souls of all dead troopers camped
> By a good old time canteen,
> And their eternal resting place
> Is known as Fiddler's Green.

Skinny loved to recite that poem, with a glass in his hand and good cavalry friends around. He knew it by heart, this hundred-year-old cavalry chant. It quickened his pulse to think of the long line of cavalry, ghosts now, men like Jeb Stuart and Phil Sheridan and Phil Kearney and George Custer and Black Jack Pershing and Georgie Patton and Clint Pierce, all chanting it with him around a campfire.

> Marching down straight through to Hell
> The Infantry are seen
> Accompanied by the Engineers
> Artillery and Marine
> For none but the souls of Cavalrymen
> Dismount at Fiddler's Green.

God, how he loved it. The smell and the sound and the sight of a line of cavalrymen advancing across an empty plain. "There's no freer man alive," he said, "than a captain of cavalry in command of his own troop." How he reveled in the great cavalry stories of the past, of lightning charges with sabers flashing, of grounded infantry giving way in terror to the mounted giants leaping at them. He was the last of a breed of tough, lean cavalrymen. Wainwright's like won't pass our way again.

> Some go curving down the trail
> To seek a warmer scene
> But no Cavalryman ever gets to Hell
> Ere he's emptied his canteen.
> And so rides back to drink again
> With friends at Fiddler's Green.

How he loved to party at the club and sing those old-time cavalry songs—"The Girl I Left Behind Me," "Garry Owen," "She Wore a Yellow Ribbon"—dreaming as a young man of his own glory, someday. It came to him, of course, but not in the way he wanted.

> And so when a horse and man go down
> Beneath a saber keen
> Or in a roaring charge or fierce melee
> You stop a bullet clean

When his big chance came, on Bataan and on Corregidor, he had to fight a static war, a war of strong lines of defense. It was not the war he had trained for, the war of dashing and daring raids, of canteens clicking on leather and a strong horse beneath him. It was a war in a jungle where a man could barely walk, a war of foxholes and trenches. War in a concrete tunnel, dank and dark, that shook from bombs and shells. There were no cavalry charges for Wainwright when he was finally given command of an army. How he must have hated that.

> And the hostiles come to get your scalp.
> Just empty your canteen

In the end his beloved horses were eaten by his starving men. What silent, invisible tears Wainwright must have shed.

> And put your pistol to your head
> And go to Fiddler's Green.

WAINWRIGHT'S PEOPLE

MY WIFE AND I have spent the last eighteen months among old army people, and I say "old army" in both senses of the phrase—people of the old army between the wars, and army people whose ages range from almost seventy to ninety-five. Their warmth and generosity were overwhelming as they welcomed us into their homes and made us feel a part of their lives. "You're just like family," one said, and nothing could have pleased us more. These are vigorous, alert, and interesting people, and their friendship will remain with us long after the book is finished.

We quickly came to admire these men and women for their intelligence, erudition, and selflessness, and for their dedication to their country and to the cause of peace. They are all heroes, these people of Bataan and Corregidor, and the wives who waited and worried through their long years of captivity. They deny it, of course, and say they were simply professional soldiers doing their job. But they are much more. Like Wainwright, they felt a sense of dedication to the country and an obligation to serve it. Ideas like "duty," "honor," and "country" are more than mere words to them.

Many of the older ones had fought in World War I before Wainwright's war came upon them; many of the younger ones went on to serve in Korea; a few lost sons in Vietnam. In 1942 they were soldiers on the line, the very thin line America had then. They did their duty and held that line for as long as they could, giving us a chance to prepare, belatedly, for war. Because they know so directly and forcefully the meaning of war, they believe devoutly in peace, a peace maintained by a strong America. They know all too personally the consequences of unpreparedness. They paid a terrible price for it.

Their heroism and sacrifice deserve to be celebrated and remembered. They have opened for us a world we shall never forget. There are scores of vignettes, sidelights to Wainwright's story, that could not be included in the book, images of living rooms and hospital rooms; of voices, laughter, and tears; of strong drink and good conversation; of lined but animated faces. Meet a few of these

436

people. I won't use their names; they will know who they are.

A man places a saucer of milk on the back steps of his house every day for a stray neighborhood cat. "I know what it is to be hungry," he says.

A once tall and vigorous officer, confined, in his nineties, to a wheelchair in a nursing home, opens a drawer and brings out the citation for his DSC. "I keep it here," he says, "so that when I go they'll know what I did."

Another breaks down while talking about Christmas in the prisoner-of-war camps, so far from home and loved ones. "It'll be all right," his wife explains. "I've seen them all cry." Even so many years later they cannot forget.

A tall, lean, ex-cavalryman who has served with distinction in three conflicts—a hard-drinking, tough, no-nonsense commander —never lets a day pass without telephoning a buddy who was blinded in the war nearly forty years before.

An army nurse sends a tape recording of her experiences in the Philippines. Her husband—a soldier of Bataan—adds his comments. He recites the beautiful poem of praise to the nurses, "The Angels of Bataan." I hear the emotion in his voice and can share it. He is talking about extraordinary women.

An unusually capable Bataan officer, recovering from a serious illness, agrees to answer a few questions if we will keep our visit short. "When did you first meet General Wainwright?" we ask. The man delivers a three-hour, nonstop presentation of his association with the general, a thorough, well-organized briefing on the Bataan campaign that leaves us breathless with admiration.

At a hotel where officers are billeted for rest and rehabilitation, one tells the dining-room waiter, "You see that man over there? I want you to bring him a bowl of ice cream every day. That's all he's talked about for the last three years!"

An eighty-four-year-old officer, one of many involved in civic activities since the war, works tirelessly for thirty years to improve health-care services in his community, to atone, he says, for having surrendered and let his country down.

A brigadier general is offered a second star, but it means a tour of duty in Japan. He chooses to retire. "I've had enough of the Japanese," he says.

A man in his nineties, an officer in a rival branch of the service, recalls a visit to San Antonio after his liberation from the camps. "The best moment was when Wainwright greeted me with open arms, like a brother. That's the kind of guy he was."

A politically active four-star general, a dignified and imposing figure, bursts into song at the mention of a fellow officer from the prewar days on Corregidor. They had written a cabaret sketch together for the officers' club and he recalls every word of it.

A Bataan general is hospitalized at Walter Reed. He phones to make sure he has answered all my questions, done all he could to help, before he undergoes surgery. I tell a former sergeant who served as an orderly in the POW camps. He has not seen the general in thirty-five years. "I'll be down there like a shot," he says. "I'll do anything I can for him."

The general faces his lengthy hospital ordeal with tremendous dignity and courage. He is still a fighter. Sadly, he loses this battle, and we watch his wife face her ordeal with an equal measure of dignity and courage. She, too, is a fighter.

A wife writes to her husband every day of his captivity. She is told to stop; the letters will not be delivered. She continues to chronicle her daily life for him—Red Cross work, the escapades of their two young sons—and saves the letters, tying them in bunches with ribbon. To this day they lie untouched in the attic. He won't read them. He can't. "Those years are missing from my life," he says.

Another wife hears nothing for more than a year. There has been no word about her husband—one of Bataan's fighting generals—since the surrender. One night she has a dream. He is there, leaning down to kiss her as she sleeps. She knows now he is alive; and he is.

Four young army wives meet for dinner each week, to console one another and to share their loneliness. Yet each keeps silent on those rare occasions when she has received a postcard from her husband, in case another friend has gotten bad news.

The men return to women who had summoned almost superhuman strength to keep their families going and to lend their efforts to war work. Now the wives must cope with these strangers; men whose bodies and minds have undergone terrible abuse; men who suffer nightmares and claustrophobia and lethargy. Doctors are unprepared for patients who have known such deprivations for so long a time. "Thank God our wives understand," says one Wainwright staff officer. "How awful for the men who don't have a family to help them now." There are a few divorces, a few suicides, but these men and women are fighters. They are tough. They stick it out.

Every home has the photographs, a wall covered with portraits and snapshots, a graphic record of a lifetime of service. West Point cadets—sometimes two or three generations. Astride a horse . . . posing with the new Garand rifle . . . the first platoon or company or battalion . . . the happy family in prewar Manila . . . the joyous reunion. And pictures of Wainwright. The formal autographed portrait . . . with MacArthur on Bataan . . . commanding the Third Cavalry at Fort Myer.

After the photos, out come the diaries, the small brown notebooks, the impressions of prison-camp life recorded on the insides of flattened cigarette packs, kept all these years. They are treasured possessions.

The liquor flows freely. "The sun's up," says one. "It's time for Bloody Marys." "How about a 'heel tap,'" urges a cavalry officer. There is a long evening full of stories and pictures and the unearthing of a diary in which a Corregidor colonel, whose bravery as a prisoner of war is legendary, recorded each item he received from the Red Cross packages. Early the next morning, slightly hung over, I stagger to the window to be greeted by the sight of the officer planting marigolds in his garden, in military-straight rows.

Amidst the exhilaration of the homecoming in 1945 was the anxiety about the future. Many would retire on disability, some wanted at least one more post, others were young enough for a long career in the service. In 1945 the navy promotes its captains one grade; the Marine Corps follows suit and promotes its colonels. There is nothing from the army. Men who were colonels in 1942 remain colonels in 1945 and until their retirement; nothing for the men who fought so bravely in the jungles of Bataan or the shell-torn island of Corregidor.

Wainwright submits lists of citations, decorations, promotions. Many are reduced or denied. There is a subtle prejudice against the Philippines defenders for having surrendered. Even those who continue in the military feel it.

They are not bitter about their lot. "We're professional soldiers." "It was our job." "It's just the luck of the draw." They served their country well, and, for the most part, the army served them well. Their sons tell a different story. For them the army is paperwork, administrators, politicians, a lack of discipline—and they take early retirement. "It's not the same, Dad," they say. "It's no fun anymore." Gone are the camaraderie, the kinship, the spirit of service and dedication. The old army, Wainwright's army, is gone.

They shrug, and one officer in his eighties confides the secret of a long life. "Three things," he says. "Plenty of Ancient Age bourbon, Camel cigarettes, and blondes." I pass his philosophy along to the others and they laugh and raise their glasses. "I'll drink to that."

ACKNOWLEDGMENTS

I AM GRATEFUL TO the many individuals who graciously gave of their time and their recollections of General Wainwright, along with their official papers, diaries, notebooks, photographs, and other memorabilia. Some of the retired officers chose to express their views "off the record"; this caveat has been respected. The following persons, among others, have contributed material to the book either in person, by telephone, or by letter.

James H. Belote, William M. Belote, Albert J. Bland, Col. and Mrs. Joseph L. Chabot, the Honorable Malcolm M. Champlin, Col. William E. Chandler, Brig. Gen. Bradford G. Chynoweth, John S. Coleman, Col. and Mrs. Wibb E. Cooper, Stephen H. Crosby, Brig. Gen. and Mrs. LeGrande A. Diller, Col. Thomas Dooley, Col. and Mrs. Roy Doran, Brig. Gen. Charles C. Drake, Col. George G. Elms, Col. Bryan Evans, Mr. & Mrs. Joseph Farmer (Sallie Durrett), Brig. Gen. and Mrs. Arnold J. Funk, Col. and Mrs. Nicoll F. Galbraith, Whitney Galbraith, Samuel A. Goldblith, Julien M. Goodman, Jack D. Gordon, Richard M. Gordon, Harry B. Greenleaf, Brig. Gen. E. L. Harrison, Frank Hewlett, Brig. Gen. and Mrs. Willard A. Holbrook, D. Clayton James, Col. and Mrs. William F. Lawrence, Brig. Gen. Steve Mellnik, Col. George H. Millholland, Maj. and Mrs. Thomas D. Moffitt, Col. James E. Mrazek, Paul Nagurney, Danny Nugent, Maj. Gen. William H. Nutter, Walter Odlin, the Reverend H. Paul Osborne, Richard F. Palmer, Maj. Gen. George S. Patton, Jr., Forrest C. Pogue, Rear Adm. Lyle J. Roberts, Mrs. Harry A. Skerry, John Toland, Lt. Gen. and Mrs. T. J. H. Trapnell, Col. and Mrs. John R. Vance, Col. Lee Vance, Gen. John K. Waters, Gen. Albert C. Wedemeyer, Maj. John W. Whitman, Col. and Mrs. Stuart Wood, Lt. Gen. W. H. S. Wright.

Every writer on the Philippines in World War II is indebted to Louis Morton for the official army history of the campaign, *The Fall of the Philippines;* to John Toland for his analysis of the six months following Pearl Harbor, *But Not in Shame;* and to D. Clayton James for his biography, *The Years of MacArthur.* Toland and James made available to me their research materials and offered their comments

441

on the Wainwright-MacArthur relationship. Forrest Pogue, Gen. George C. Marshall's biographer and director of the Eisenhower Institute at the Smithsonian, described for me Wainwright's situation on Corregidor from the point of view of the chief of staff.

Frank Hewlett made available his file of United Press dispatches, bearing the blue pencil marks of the army censor, as well as the news summaries prepared by Carlos Romulo's office on Corregidor.

Brig. Gen. Arnold J. Funk provided me with a copy of the USAFFE-USFIP report and several excellent maps.

Col. Nicoll F. Galbraith supplied a report of his North Luzon mission and allowed me to read the letters he wrote to his family just after his liberation, providing me with insight into the condition, thoughts, and feelings of the army officers at that time.

Col. Thomas Dooley loaned me his complete wartime diaries, as did Walter Odlin and Col. John R. Vance, who also supplied a detailed handwritten account of the Philippines campaign, prepared while he was a POW. The Vance volume is meticulously illustrated, colored in crayons inexplicably provided by the Japanese. An astute historian in his own right, Colonel Vance offered cogent comments on the social, political, and economic climate of the Philippines, providing valuable background information for the Wainwright story.

Many archives and libraries provided prompt and generous assistance. These institutions are staffed by dedicated and knowledgeable people; a researcher could not ask for greater cooperation. I am especially indebted to Hannah M. Zeidlik and Kim Holien of the U.S. Army Center of Military History, Richard J. Sommers and Michael J. Winey of the U.S. Army Military History Institute, Edward J. Boone of the MacArthur Memorial library and archives, Robert E. Schnare and Kenneth Rapp of the U.S. Military Academy library and archives, Col. Morris Herbert of the Association of Graduates of the U.S. Military Academy, and John N. Jacob of the George C. Marshall Research Foundation.

I also wish to thank the staff of the Modern Military Records Division of the National Archives (Bill Cunliffe and Tom Trudeau), the Still Picture Branch of the National Archives, the Defense Audiovisual Agency/U.S. Army Still Photographic Library (Nora Edgington, Marilou Noakes, and Audrey Green), the Washington National Records Center, the Army Library, the Office of the Adjutant General (Paul Taborn), the Library of Congress for the

John Toland papers, the Fort Myer (Virginia) library, the Fort Sam Houston (Texas) museum, the Skaneateles (New York) Library Association (Jean T. Beers), the Yale University Library for the Stimson papers, and the Mississippi State University Library for the MacArthur Oral History Collection.

Benson Guyton of the American Defenders of Bataan and Corregidor supplied several good leads and a list of the Wainwright Travelers, the informal association of officers from the Philippines campaign organized after the war. Manny Lawton, Jerry McDavitt and Joe Vater of the ADBC also provided assistance, as did Col. J. R. Spurrier, Howard W. Palm, and George Petrach of the U.S. Horse Cavalry Association, and Lt. Col. Stanley D. Sagan of the San Antonio Retired Officers' Association.

At St. Martin's Press, Tom Dunne and Bob Miller offered enthusiastic support.

A special debt of gratitude is due my wife, Sydney Ellen Schultz. The imprint of her tireless contribution is evident on every page of this book and in every step of its writing. She tracked down people and papers with unerring accuracy, examined thousands of pages of archival materials, skillfully helped in the interviewing of scores of people, edited and sharpened my sometimes purple prose, and took charge of the proofreading and the construction of the index. And all the while took care of a sometimes moody author. Without her, this book would still be an idea.

—DUANE SCHULTZ

SOURCES

Because of the blockade of the Philippines garrison and its ultimate capitulation, official records of the conduct of the campaign are incomplete. Some USAFFE–USFIP records were sent out by submarine and small aircraft, but not all of this material can be accounted for. Louis Morton of the Office of the Chief of Military History undertook an exhaustive search of the files in the preparation of the U.S. Army monograph *The Fall of the Philippines* (1953). In addition, he corresponded with more than 100 officers who took part in the campaign. His research materials are on file with the U.S. Army Military History Institute at Carlisle Barracks, Pennsylvania, and I have drawn on his massive efforts. The Morton papers contain letters, interview transcripts, radiograms, and daily action reports.

During General Wainwright's years in captivity he ordered his commanders and their staff officers to prepare an operations report, from memory, on the fighting. Wainwright and his staff ultimately assembled this material in 1946 at Fort Sam Houston. The report, entitled "Report of Operations of USAFFE and USFIP in the Philippine Islands, 1941–1942," is on file at the Center of Military History and other army depositories. It includes eighteen annexes, organized as follows.

I. USAFFE Staff

II. Plan of Induction of Philippine Army; Arrival of Units from the United States

III. Headquarters Philippine Department Staff

IV. Report of Operations of North Luzon Force and I Philippine Corps in the Defense of Luzon and Bataan, 8 December 1941–9 April 1942

V. Report of Operations of South Luzon Force, Bataan Defense Force and II Philippine Corps in the Defense of South Luzon and Bataan from 8 December 1941–9 April 1942

VI. Report of Operations of Luzon Force, 12 March 1942–9 April 1942

VII. USFIP Staff

VIII. Report of Philippine Coast Artillery Command and the Harbor Defenses of Manila and Subic Bays, 14 February 1941–6 May 1942

IX. Report of Operations of Provisional Coast Artillery Brigade in the Philippine Campaign

X. Report of Operations of the Provisional Tank Group, 1941–1942

XI. Historical Report, Visayan-Mindanao Force, Defense of the Philippines, 1 September 1941–10 May 1942

XII. Report of Operations of the Philippine Division

XIII. Report of Operations Quartermaster Corps, United States Army in the Philippine Campaign, 1941–1942

XIV. Medical Department Activities in the Philippines, 1941–6 May 1942, and Including Medical Activities in Japanese Prisoner of War Camps

XV. Report of Operations, Finance Officer, USFIP, 8 December 1941–6 May 1942

XVI. United States Forces Stationed in the Philippines, 7 December 1941

XVII. Report of Operations, Signal Corps, United States Army, 8 December 1941–6 May 1942

XVIII. Citations

In October 1945 General and Mrs. Wainwright spent a month at a cottage on the grounds of the Ashford General Hospital in White Sulfur Springs, West Virginia. There, newsman Bob Considine, assisted by Brig. Gen. Lewis Beebe, helped Wainwright write his story of the Philippine campaign and the POW years. The forty-two-part newspaper serialization commenced nationwide in late 1945, and the following year a similar version was made available in book form as *General Wainwright's Story,* published by Doubleday. Wainwright autographed a copy of the book for Considine "To the Ghost."

It has been suggested that the Wainwright material was rushed into print to capitalize on the public interest in the returning prisoners of war. Also, by being the first to tell his story, Wainwright may have forestalled the publication of other versions of events. The book is interesting reading, but it is not without its errors— names and dates recalled inaccurately, for example—and, like many autobiographies, it does have its self-serving moments. Its usefulness for the biographer, therefore, is understandably limited, and where accounts of particular events have been called into question, confirmation has been sought from other sources.

Additional records consulted include reports and radiograms of the War Plans Division (WPD) and Operations Division (OPD) of the General Staff (RG 319); the Philippine Islands File (381); JAG case files (153); the papers of GHQ SWPA, HQ USAFFE, and HQ USFIP (407); and the papers of Maj. Gen. Richard K. Sutherland; all at the Modern Military Records Division of the National Archives and the Washington National Records Center at Suitland, Maryland. The National Archives also has Wainwright's personal file (Navy and Old Army Branch), and the Public Trial Records, *U.S.A. v. MASAHARU HOMMA,* which includes depositions and testimony from Wainwright, Pugh, Bluemel, Jones, and Tisdelle, among others.

The U.S. Army Center of Military History collection includes official and unofficial unit histories and operations reports, correspondence, and diaries, and the manuscripts of Bunker, Drake, Jones, and Parker, among others. The Center also has reports of the American Prisoner-of-War Information Bureau, *Japanese Studies in World War II,* and the four-volume *Triumph in the Philippines, 1941-1946,* prepared by the Combat History Division.

The U.S. Army Military History Institute at Carlisle Barracks, Pennsylvania, contains, in addition to the Morton papers, the papers of Beebe, Braly, Chynoweth, Pierce, and others.

The Special Collections Division of the U.S. Military Academy Library at West Point, New York, contains the Bluemel papers, among others, and several reports written about the Philippines campaign, including Cooper's medical report on USFIP and the POW years. The Association of Graduates office at West Point contains both personal and class files on Wainwright. The Mac-Arthur Memorial archives and library at Norfolk, Virginia, contains a wealth of material, especially RG 2 (HQ USAFFE), RG 3 (HQ SWPA), and RG 10 (MacArthur correspondence). The George C. Marshall Research Foundation in Lexington, Virginia contains material relating to Wainwright as commanding general, USFIP, and to the Medal of Honor issue, as well as the correspondence between Marshall and Mrs. Wainwright. The Toland papers (letters and interview notes used in the preparation of *But Not in Shame*) are at the Manuscript Division, Library of Congress. The Stimson diary is at the Yale University Library, New Haven, Connecticut. The MacArthur Oral History Collection at Mississippi State University, State College, Mississippi, contains the transcripts of interviews conducted by D. Clayton James for his definitive, 3-volume biography of MacArthur, *The Years of MacArthur.* James also edited Brougher's prisoner-of-war diary for publication, *South to Bataan, North to Mukden.*

As noted in the Acknowledgments, many persons assisted in the preparation of this book by consenting to interviews or providing information by letter, telephone, or tape recording. These men and women supplied anecdotes, diaries, letters, clippings, photographs, radiograms, operations reports, and other materials, and put me in touch with additional Wainwright people. Some of them requested anonymity when discussing sensitive military and political issues, generally because they have relatives still serving in the armed forces. Their experiences cover Wainwright's career from about 1910 to his death in 1953.

BOOKS

Ambrose, Stephen E. *Duty, Honor, Country: A History of West Point.* Baltimore: Johns Hopkins University Press, 1966.

Andrews, P. *In Honored Glory.* New York: Putnams, 1966.

Baldwin, Hanson. *Battles Lost and Won: Great Campaigns of World War II.* New York: Harper & Row, 1966.

Beck, John Jacob. *MacArthur and Wainwright: Sacrifice of the Philippines.* Albuquerque: University of New Mexico Press, 1974.

Belote, James H., & Belote, William M. *Corregidor: The Saga of a Fortress.* New York: Harper & Row, 1967.

Bergamini, David. *Japan's Imperial Conspiracy.* New York: William Morrow, 1971.

Blumenson, Martin. *The Patton Papers: 1940–1945.* Boston: Houghton Mifflin, 1974.

Brougher, William E. *Baggy Pants and Other Stories.* New York: Vantage Press, 1965.

Brougher, William E. *The Long Dark Road.* Privately printed, 1946.

Brougher, William E. *South to Bataan, North to Mukden: The Prison Diary of Brigadier General W. E. Brougher.* D. Clayton James, Ed. Athens: University of Georgia Press, 1971.

Burns, James MacGregor. *Roosevelt: The Soldier of Freedom.* New York: Harcourt Brace Jovanovich, 1970.

Buxton, G. E. *Official History of the 82nd Division, AEF: "All American" Division.* Indianapolis, 1919.

Chase, William C. *Front Line General.* Houston: Pacesetter Press, 1975.

Chunn, Calvin Ellsworth, Ed. *Of Rice and Men: The Story of Americans Under the Rising Sun.* Los Angeles: Veteran's Publishing Co., 1946.

Chynoweth, Bradford G. *Bellamy Park.* Hicksville, N.Y.: Exposition Press, 1975.

Coffman, Edward M. *The War to End All Wars: The American Military Experience in World War I.* New York: Oxford University Press, 1968.

Coleman, John S. *Bataan and Beyond: Memories of an American POW.* College Station: Texas A. & M. University Press, 1978.

Considine, Robert. *It's All News to Me: A Reporter's Deposition.* New York: Meredith, 1967.

Craig, William. *The Fall of Japan.* New York: Dial Press, 1967.

Davis, Kenneth S. *Experience of War: The United States in World War II.* Garden City, N.Y.: Doubleday, 1965.

Dupuy, Richard Ernest. *Men of West Point.* New York: Sloane, 1951.

Dyess, William E. *The Dyess Story: The Eye-Witness Account of the Death March From Bataan and the Narrative of Experiences in Japanese Prison Camps and of Eventual Escape.* New York: Putnam, 1944.

Eichelberger, Robert L. *Dear Miss Em: General Eichelberger's War in the Pacific, 1942–1945.* Jay Luvass, Ed. Westport, Conn.: Greenwood Press, 1972.

Eisenhower, Dwight David. *At Ease: Stories I Tell To Friends.* New York: Doubleday, 1967.

Eisenhower, Dwight David. *Crusade in Europe.* Garden City, N.Y.: Doubleday, 1948.

Eisenhower, Dwight David. *Eisenhower Diaries.* Robert H. Ferrell, Ed. New York: Norton, 1981.

Eisenhower, Dwight David. *Papers of Dwight David Eisenhower: The War Years.* Alfred D. Chandler, Ed. Baltimore: Johns Hopkins University Press, 1970.

Elman, Robert. *Fired in Anger.* New York: Doubleday, 1968.

Falk, Stanley L. *Bataan: The March of Death.* New York: Norton, 1962.

Farago, Ladislas. *Patton: Ordeal and Triumph.* New York: Dell, 1965.

Fleming, Thomas J. *West Point: The Men and Times of the United States Military Academy.* New York: William Morrow, 1969.

Ford, Corey. *Donovan of OSS.* Boston: Little, Brown, 1970.

Fortier, M. *The Life of a P.O.W. under the Japanese, in Caricature, as Sketched by Col. Malcolm Vaughn Fortier, P.O.W., from April 9, 1942 to August 30, 1945.* Spokane: C. W. Hill, 1946.

Frazer, Robert W. *Forts of the West.* Norman: University of Oklahoma Press, 1965.

Ganoe, William Addleman. *The History of the United States Army*. Ashton, Md.: Eric Lundberg, 1964.

Glines, Carroll V. *Four Came Home*. Princeton, N.J.: D. Van Nostrand, 1966.

Greenfield, Kent Roberts, Ed. *Command Decisions*. New York: Harcourt Brace, 1959.

Gunnison, Royal Arch. *So Sorry, No Peace*. New York: Viking Press, 1944.

Halsey, William F., and Bryan, J. *Admiral Halsey's Story*. New York: McGraw-Hill, 1947.

Hart, Scott. *Washington at War: 1941–1945*. Englewood Cliffs, N.J.: Prentice-Hall, 1970.

Herr, John K., and Wallace, Edward S. *The Story of the United States Cavalry: 1775–1942*. Foreword by J. M. Wainwright. Boston: Little, Brown, 1953.

Hersey, John. *Men on Bataan*. New York: Knopf, 1942.

Hinkel, John V. *Arlington: Monument to Heroes*. Englewood Cliffs, N.J.: Prentice-Hall, 1965.

Hough, F. O., Ludwig, V. E., and Shaw, H. I. *Pearl Harbor to Guadalcanal*. History of U.S. Marine Corps Operations in World War II. Volume I. Washington, D.C.: Government Printing Office, 1958.

Huff, Sidney. *My Fifteen Years With General MacArthur*. New York, 1964.

Hunt, Frazier. *The Untold Story of Douglas MacArthur*. New York: Devin-Adair, 1954.

Ind, Allison. *Bataan: The Judgment Seat*. New York: Macmillan, 1944.

James, D. Clayton. *The Years of MacArthur: 1880–1941*. Volume I. Boston: Houghton Mifflin, 1970.

James, D. Clayton. *The Years of MacArthur: 1941–1945*. Volume II. Boston: Houghton Mifflin, 1975.

Janowitz, Morris. *The Professional Soldier: A Social and Political Portrait*. Glencoe, Ill.: Free Press, 1960.

Keats, John. *They Fought Alone*. Philadelphia: Lippincott, 1963.

Kennedy, Milly Wood. *Corregidor*. Privately printed, 1971.

Kent Hughes, W. S. *Slaves of the Samurai*. Melbourne, Australia: Geoffrey Cumberlege, 1946.

Lee, Clark. *They Call It Pacific: An Eye-Witness Story of Our War Against Japan*. New York: Viking Press, 1943.

Lee, Clark. *Clark Lee's Bataan Bylines: The Story of a Gallant Defense*. New York: Associated Press, 1942.

Lee, Clark, and Henschel, Richard. *Douglas MacArthur*. New York: Holt, 1952.

Lee, Henry G. *Nothing but Praise*. Culver City, Cal.: Murray and Gee, 1948.

Liddell Hart, B. H. *The Real War: 1914-1918*. Boston: Little, Brown, 1930.

Lingeman, Richard. *Don't You Know There's A War On?* New York: G.P. Putnam's Sons, 1970.

Lyon, Peter. *Eisenhower: Portrait of the Hero.* Boston: Little, Brown, 1974.

MacArthur, Douglas. *Reminiscences.* New York: Fawcett, 1965.

Mallonée, Richard C. *The Naked Flagpole: Battle for Bataan.* R. C. Mallonée II, Ed. San Rafael, Cal.: Presidio Press, 1980.

Manchester, William. *American Caesar.* Boston: Little, Brown, 1978.

Marquardt, Frederic S. *Before Bataan and After: A Personalized History of Our Philippine Experiment.* New York: Bobbs-Merrill, 1943.

Marshall, S. L. A. *World War I.* New York: American Heritage Press, 1964.

Mellnik, Steve. *Philippine Diary: 1939–1945.* New York: Van Nostrand Reinhold, 1969.

Miller, Ernest B. *Bataan Uncensored.* Long Prairie, Minn.: Hart Publications, 1949.

Morison, Elting E. *Turmoil and Tradition: A Study of the Life and Times of Henry L. Stimson.* Boston: Houghton Mifflin, 1960.

Morison, Samuel Eliot. *The Rising Sun in the Pacific.* Volume III. Boston: Little, Brown, 1948.

Morton, Louis. *The Fall of the Philippines.* U.S. Army in World War II. Washington, D.C.: Government Printing Office, 1953.

Mydans, Carl. *More Than Meets the Eye.* New York: Harper, 1959.

Pogue, Forrest C. *George C. Marshall: Education of a General: 1880–1939.* New York: Viking, 1963.

Pogue, Forrest C. *George C. Marshall: Ordeal and Hope: 1939–1942.* New York: Viking, 1966.

Poweleit, Alvin, C. *USAFFE.* Privately printed, 1975.

Quezon, Manuel L. *The Good Fight.* New York: Appleton-Century, 1946.

Quinn, Michael A. *Love Letters to Mike: Forty Months as a Japanese P.O.W.* New York: Vantage Press, 1977.

Redmond, Juanita. *I Served on Bataan.* Philadelphia: Lippincott, 1943.

Romulo, Carlos. *I Saw the Fall of the Philippines.* Garden City, N.Y.: Doubleday, 1946.

Romulo, Carlos. *I Walked With Heroes.* New York: Holt, 1961.

Rosenman, Samuel I., Ed. *The Public Papers and Addresses of Franklin D. Roosevelt: Humanity on the Defensive, 1942.* New York: 1950.

Rovere, Richard, and Schlesinger, Arthur M., Jr. *The General and the President.* New York: Farrar, Straus and Young, 1951.

Rutherford, Ward. *Fall of the Philippines.* New York: Ballantine Books, 1971.

Sayre, Francis B. *Glad Adventure.* New York: Macmillan, 1957.

Sherwood, Robert E. *Roosevelt and Hopkins.* New York: Harper and Row, 1948.

Smyth, John. *Percival and the Tragedy of Singapore.* London: Macdonald, 1971.

Smythe, Donald. *Guerrilla Warrior: The Early Life of John J. Pershing.* New York: Scribner's, 1973.

Strong, Paschal, and Strong, Mary. *Sabers and Safety Pins.* Privately printed, 1954.

Tasaki, Hanama. *Long the Imperial Way.* Boston: Houghton Mifflin, 1950.

Toland, John. *But Not in Shame: The Six Months After Pearl Harbor.* New York: Random House, 1961.

Toland, John. *The Rising Sun: The Decline and Fall of the Japanese Empire.* New York: Random House, 1970.

Tolley, Kemp. *Cruise of the Lanikai.* Annapolis: Naval Institute Press, 1973.

Truman, Harry S. *Off the Record: The Private Papers of Harry S. Truman.* Robert H. Ferrell, Ed. New York: Harper and Row, 1980.

Tuchman, Barbara W. *The Proud Tower.* New York: Bantam, 1967.

Underbrink, Robert L. *Destination Corregidor.* Annapolis: Naval Institute Press, 1971.

Uno, Kazumaro. *Corregidor: Isle of Delusion.* Shanghai, China: Mercury Press, 1942.

Vance, John R. *Doomed Garrison: The Philippines (A POW Story).* Ashland, Ore.: Cascade House, 1974.

Wainwright, J. M. *General Wainwright's Story.* New York: Doubleday, 1946.

Watson, Mark S. *The War Department. Chief of Staff: Prewar Plans and Preparations.* U.S. Army in World War II. Washington, D.C.: Government Printing Office, 1950.

Wedemeyer, Albert C. *Wedemeyer Reports!* New York: Devin-Adair, 1958.

Weinstein, Alfred A. *Barbed-Wire Surgeon.* New York: Macmillan, 1948.

Whitney, Courtney. *MacArthur: His Rendezvous With History.* New York: Knopf, 1956.

Willoughby, Amea. *I Was on Corregidor.* New York: Harper, 1943.

Willoughby, Charles A., and Chamberlain, John. *MacArthur: 1941–1951.* New York: McGraw-Hill, 1954.

Wormser, Richard. *The Yellowlegs: The Story of the United States Cavalry.* New York: Doubleday, 1966.

NEWSPAPERS AND PERIODICALS

Pertinent issues of newspapers were scanned for material on Wainwright, including *The New York Times, The Washington Post,* the *Manila Tribune,* and other papers from Washington, D.C., San Francisco, San Antonio, and Syracuse. The newspaper clipping bureau employed by the Association of Graduates, U.S. Military Academy, yielded a useful file of articles from newspapers throughout the country. The *Congressional Record* was searched, along with wartime issues of popular magazines such as *Newsweek, Time, Life, Coronet, Saturday Evening Post, Collier's,* and postwar issues of such journals as *American Heritage* and *American Historical Review.* Also helpful were such periodicals as *Foreign Affairs, The Nation, Armored Cavalry Journal,* and *U.S. Naval Institute Proceedings,* along with West Point's *Assembly* and *Howitzer,* the Cavalry School's *Rasp,* and the Naval Academy's *Shipmate.* Special mention is made of the wartime newsletter published by Marie Grimes and Harriett Diller, *Philippine Postscripts,* and the postwar veterans' organization publications *Chit-Chat,* prepared by Col. Ray O'Day of Seattle, and *Quan,* the official publication of the American Defenders of Bataan and Corregidor, Inc. (Joseph A. Vater, Ed., 18 Warbler Drive, McKees Rocks, Pennsylvania 15136).

Armold, H. The lessons of Bataan: the story of the Philippine and Bataan quartermaster depots. *Quartermaster Review,* November 1946, pp. 12–15, 60, 63.

Babcock, C. Philippine campaign. *Cavalry Journal,* March 1943, pp. 5–7; May 1943, pp. 28–35.

Baldwin, H. The Fourth Marines at Corregidor. *Marine Corps Gazette,* November 1946, pp. 13–18, 50–54; December 1946, pp. 27–35; January 1947, pp. 23–29; February 1947, pp. 39–43.

Battle on Bataan. *Infantry Journal,* March 1942, pp. 4–5.

Bell, J. Corregidor. *Military Engineer,* March 1942, pp. 131-132.

Braly, W. Corregidor: a name, a symbol, a tradition. *Coast Artillery Journal,* July 1947, pp. 2–9, 36–44.

But not forgotten. *Collier's,* July 10, 1943, p. 16.

Champlin, M. Bataan, February 1942. *Shipmate,* February 1972, pp. 3–9; Escape from Corregidor. *Shipmate,* March 1972, pp. 3–6.

Chandler, W. 26th Cavalry (PS) battles to glory. *Armored Cavalry Journal,* March-April 1947, pp. 10–16; May-June 1947, pp. 7–15; July-August 1947, pp. 15–22.

Drake, C. I surrendered Corregidor. *Collier's,* January 8, 1949, p. 12.

Drake, C. No Uncle Sam. Center of Military History Files.

Fall of Bataan commemorated. *Army-Navy-Air Force Register,* April 12, 1952, pp. 3775–3776.

Flag of Corregidor. *Coast Artillery Journal,* May 1942, pp. 2–3.

Fleeger, H. Brief regimental history: 26th Cavalry, World War II, Bataan, from the diaries of Major H. J. Fleeger. *Cavalry Journal,* November 1945, pp. 6–9.

Hewlett, F. Quartermasters on Bataan performed heroic feats. *Quartermaster Review,* May 1942, pp. 64, 92.

Hill, M. Lessons of Bataan. *Infantry Journal,* October 1942, pp. 8–21.

Hogaboom, W. Action report: Bataan. *Marine Corps Gazette*, April 1946, pp. 25–33.

Jacoby, M. Corregidor cable no. 79, from Melville Jacoby, February 17, 1942. *Field Artillery Journal*, April 1942, pp. 263–267.

Jacoby, M. Taking care of the wounded on the Bataan front. *Command and General Staff School Quarterly*, April 1942, p. 41.

Japanese campaign on Luzon. *O.N.I. Weekly*, January 31, 1945, pp. 391–394.

Japanese propaganda on Bataan. *Infantry Journal*, October 1942, pp. 34–37.

Japanese tactics in the Philippines, 1942. *Tactical and Technical Trends*, 1942, No. 6.

Johnson, H. Defense along the Abucay line. *Military Review*, February 1949, pp. 43–52.

Junod, M. I found Wainwright in prison camp. *Coronet*, September 1952, pp. 94–98.

Kutz, H. Ordnance on Bataan. *Army Ordnance*, November 1942, p. 481.

Lanza, C. Bataan. *Field Artillery Journal*, May 1942, pp. 359–360; Corregidor. *Field Artillery Journal*, July 1942, pp. 553–556; Final—Bataan. *Field Artillery Journal*, July 1942, pp. 550–553.

Lee, C. Battle of Bataan. *Infantry Journal*, April 1943, pp. 19–23.

Lee, C. The fighting 26th. *Cavalry Journal*, March 1943, pp. 3–4.

Lewis, C. Luzon diary. *Field Artillery Journal*, April 1942, pp. 260–262.

Lopez, A. The fall of the Philippines. *Military Review*, August 1946, pp. 10–16.

MacArthur, D. Remarks of General Douglas MacArthur concerning his field artillery on Bataan. *Field Artillery Journal*, June 1942, p. 418.

McCarthy, Joe. The lost battalion. *American Heritage*, October 1977, pp. 86-93.

Mellnik, S. How the Japanese took Corregidor. *Coast Artillery Journal*, March 1945, pp. 2–11, 17.

Miller, E. Bataan uncensored. *National Guardsman*, March 1949, pp. 2–5; April 1949, pp. 10–13; May 1949, pp. 14–17.

Morton, L. The American surrender in the Philippines, April-May 1942. *Military Review*, August 1949, pp. 3–14.

Morton, L. Bataan diary of Major Achille C. Tisdelle. *Military Affairs*, Fall 1947, pp. 131–148.

Morton, L. The battling bastards of Bataan. *Military Affairs*, Summer 1951, pp. 107–113.

Observations during the campaign on Luzon, by a United States military observer. *Command and General Staff School Quarterly*, October 1942, pp. 14–15.

Palmer, B. Covering the withdrawal into Bataan. *Infantry School Quarterly*, July 1950, pp. 42–65.

Parker, T. The epic of Corregidor–Bataan, December 24, 1941–May 4, 1942. *U. S. Naval Institute Proceedings,* January 1943, pp. 9–22.

Siege of Corregidor. *Military Reports on the United Nations,* November 15, 1943, pp. 37–52.

Strobing, I. Corregidor's last breath. *Coast Artillery Journal,* August 1942, pp. 2–3.

Underbrink, Robert L. Mindanao gun. *Guns,* November 1970, pp. 24–25, 59.

Wachtel, J. 26th Cavalry (PS) of today. *Armored Cavalry Journal,* May-June 1947, pp. 16–17.

Wainwright, J. M. This is my story. *King Features Weekly* and various newspapers, 1945-1946.

Wheeler, J. Rearguard in Luzon. *Cavalry Journal,* March 1943, pp. 5–6.

Whitehead, A. Mounted attack in West Bataan–1942. *Cavalry Journal,* January 1945, p. 51.

Whitehead, A. With the 26th Cavalry (PS) in the Philippines, December 7–22, 1941. *Cavalry Journal,* May 1944, pp. 34–43; July 1944, pp. 34–41; September 1944, pp. 42–47.

NOTES

CHAPTER 1. "An Old–Fashioned Hero"

Two types of military leaders, the managers and the fighters: Janowitz, *The Professional Soldier*, pp. 154, 161. Comparison of MacArthur to Moses and Wainwright to King Saul: Beck, *MacArthur and Wainwright*, p. 241.

CHAPTER 2. "Back in Harness"

Voyage to the Philippines: various interviews, including Richard M. Gordon. Eisenhower on war in the Atlantic theater: Eisenhower, *At Ease*, p. 244. Fort Clark: Farago, *Patton*, p. 119. Wainwright family: *Dictionary of American Biography*, pp. 316–318; *Time*, May 8, 1944. Spanish–American war and manifest destiny: Tuchman, *The Proud Tower*, pp. 173–178. Arthur MacArthur and Philippine insurrection: D. MacArthur, *Reminiscences*, p. 25.

West Point: James, *The Years of MacArthur I*, pp. 74, 83; Eisenhower, *At Ease*, p. 4; Ambrose, *Duty, Honor, Country*, pp. 226, 241–245, 271; Fleming, *West Point*, pp. 288–289; issues of the yearbook, *Howitzer;* publications of the Association of Graduates, *Annual Reports* and *Assembly;* the two–volume *Centennial History of the U.S. Military Academy;* Cullum's *Biographical Register of the Officers and Graduates of the U.S. Military Academy.*

Wainwright at West Point: various cadet records, class of 1906, U.S. Military Academy library and archives; *Decennial Book Class of 1906;* personal and class files of the Association of Graduates.

Wainwright's early career: 201 file, Navy and Old Army Branch, National Archives, and various interviews. Wainwright "arriving in heaven": Brougher, *Baggy Pants*, pp. 74–75. War in the Moro province: Smythe, *Guerrilla Warrior*, p. 161. Army promotions: Ganoe, *The History of the United States Army*, pp. 438, 441.

General Staff College in France: Blumenson, *Patton Papers*, pp. 544–545. Eighty-second Division: Buxton, *Official History of the 82nd Division;* McCarthy, "The Lost Battalion"; Coffman, *The War to End All Wars*, pp. 275, 320–325, 357–359; Liddell Hart, *The Real War*, pp. 449–469; Marshall, *World War I*, pp. 421–431; and various interviews.

Army life between the wars and Fort Riley: Strong and Strong, *Sabers and Safety Pins;* and various interviews. Army War College (Patton quotation applied to Wainwright): Blumenson, *Patton Papers*, p. 893.

Wainwright at Forts Riley, Myer, and Clark from various interviews, including Chabot, Elms, Millholland, Moffitt, Nutter, Trapnell, and the United States Army, pp. 438, 441.

General Staff College in France: Blumenson, *Patton Papers*, pp. 544–545. Eighty-second Division: Buxton, *Official History of the 82nd Division;* McCarthy, "The Lost Battalion"; Coffman, *The War to End All Wars*, pp. 275, 320–325, 357–359; Liddell Hart, *The Real War*, pp. 449–469; Marshall, *World War I*, pp. 421–431; and various interviews.

Army life between the wars and Fort Riley: Strong and Strong, *Sabers and Safety Pins;* and various interviews. Army War College (Patton quotation applied to Wainwright): Blumenson, *Patton Papers*, p. 893.

Wainwright at Forts Riley, Myer, and Clark from various interviews, including Chabot, Elms, Millholland, Moffitt, Nutter, Trapnell, and Wright. The cavalry: Herr and Wallace, *The Story of the U.S. Cavalry*, p. 254.

CHAPTER 3. "Days of Empire"

Prewar life in the Philippines: various interviews and diaries, including Bland, Chabot, Cooper, Diller, Dooley, Funk, Galbraith, Goodman, Gordon, Millholland, Odlin, Skerry, Trapnell, Vance, Wood; issues of the Manila *Tribune* and Manila *Bulletin;* Eisenhower, *At Ease*, p. 236; Vance, *Doomed Garrison*, pp. 20–21; Mellnik, *Philippine Diary*, pp. 5–6, 13; Tolley, *Cruise of the Lanikai*, p. 135.

The Philippine Division, prewar planning, and Grunert's communications with the War Department: Marquardt, *Before Bataan and After*, pp. 253–254; Morton, *The Fall of the Philippines*, pp. 21, 64; James, *The Years of MacArthur I*, pp. 578–581; Baldwin, *Battles Lost and Won*, p. 115; Belote and Belote, *Corregidor*, p. 26.

Evacuation of dependents: various interviews, including Mrs. Cooper, Mrs. Funk, Mrs. Skerry, Mrs. Vance; *Time*, May 8, 1944; Brougher, "The Final Despedida," *Baggy Pants*, p. 163.

Marshall on the Philippines, assumption of command by MacArthur, U.S. preparations for war: James, *The Years of MacArthur I*, pp. 596, 610–612, 617; Morton, *The Fall of the Philippines*, pp. 26–29, 31, 34–42, 64, 69; Pogue, *George C. Marshall*, and Pogue interview.

Homma and Japanese war preparations: Toland, *The Rising Sun*, pp. 214, 313; Morton, *The Fall of the Philippines*, pp. 56–59; Belote and Belote, *Corregidor*, p. 36; *U.S.A. v. Masaharu Homma*.

Wainwright–Miller meeting: Miller, *Bataan Uncensored*, pp. 49–50. Marshall with newsmen: Pogue, *George C. Marshall* (1939-1942), pp. 201–205; Baldwin, *Battles Lost and Won*, p. 117. Marshall–MacArthur messages: War Plans Division, National Archives, and MacArthur Memorial. MacArthur–Sayre meeting: Sayre, *Glad Adventure*, p. 221. Quezon speech: Lee, *They Call It Pacific*, pp. 30–31. Lee letter: H. Lee, *Nothing but Praise*, pp. 77–79. Jacoby cables: Hersey, *Men On Bataan*, p. 16. Mydans' comments: Mydans, *More Than Meets the Eye*, p. 61.

the Fall of the Philippines, pp. 29, 40–43, 55; Redmond, *I Served on Bataan,* pp. 15–16, 21–23, 27; Mallonée, *The Naked Flagpole,* pp. 27, 52; Toland, *But Not in Shame,* pp. 43–46, 55–56, 65, 87, 92; Toland, *The Rising Sun,* pp. 292–293, 297; Morton, *The Fall of the Philippines,* pp. 80–92, 98, 104–106, 108, 120, 122–131; Lee, *They Call It Pacific,* pp. 34, 67–68; Lyon, *Eisenhower,* pp. 87–88, 91–94. Twenty-sixth Cavalry Regiment: Chandler, "26th Cavalry." *Pensacola* convoy: Beck, *MacArthur and Wainwright,* p. 18; Burns, *Roosevelt,* pp. 172–173; Stimson diary. Lingayen Gulf battle: Toland, *But Not in Shame,* p. 84; Morton, *The Fall of the Philippines,* p. 107; Mydans, *More Than Meets the Eye,* p. 66.

CHAPTER 5. "A Bold Gamble"

Withdrawal to Bataan: various interviews and diaries; USAFFE–USFIP report; Wainwright, *General Wainwright's Story,* pp. 35–40; James, *The Years of MacArthur II,* pp. 41–43; Morton, *The Fall of the Philippines,* pp. 136–138, 174–177, 180–187. Twenty-sixth Cavalry: Chandler, "26th Cavalry"; Morton, *The Fall of the Philippines,* pp. 133–136; Rutherford, *Fall of the Philippines,* p. 69.

Japanese invasion: Toland, *But Not in Shame,* pp. 92–94; Rutherford, *Fall of the Philippines,* pp. 67–69; Morton, *The Fall of the Philippines,* pp. 128–131.

USAFFE–War Department messages: War Plans Division, National Archives, and MacArthur Memorial. MacArthur's delay in implementing WPO–3: James, *The Years of MacArthur II,* p. 36. Quotation on difficulties facing Wainwright in advance of withdrawal: James, *The Years of MacArthur II,* pp. 38–39.

Movement of supplies into Bataan: Drake interview; Drake, "No Uncle Sam"; Underbrink, *Destination Corregidor,* p. 12; James, *The Years of MacArthur II,* pp. 31–37. Christmas 1941: various interviews and diaries; Hersey, *Men on Bataan,* p. 51; Morton, *The Fall of the Philippines,* p. 164; Romulo, *I Saw the Fall of the Philippines,* pp. 62, 64; Redmond, *I Served on Bataan,* pp. 29–32; Hart, *Washington At War,* pp. 50–53. Lee poem: H. Lee, "Incomplete Epitaph," *Nothing but Praise,* p. 38.

San Fernando: Toland, *But Not in Shame,* p. 125; Vance, *Doomed Garrison,* p. 81. Roosevelt message: Hersey, *Men on Bataan,* pp. 255–258. Jones–Wainwright incident: Toland, *But Not in Shame,* pp. 139–140; Morton, *The Fall of the Philippines,* pp. 205–207. Calumpit bridge: Toland, *But Not in Shame,* pp. 141–143; Morton, *The Fall of the Philippines,* pp. 209–210; and various interviews.

CHAPTER 6. "A Symbol of Forlorn Hope"

General: various interviews and diaries; USAFFE–USFIP report; Wainwright, *General Wainwright's Story,* pp. 45–50. USAFFE–War Department messages: War Plans Division, National Archives, and MacArthur Memorial. Romulo's experiences: Romulo, *I Saw the Fall of the Philippines,* pp. 90–102, 149.

San Fernando: Vance, *Doomed Garrison,* p. 83. Twenty-sixth Cavalry: Chandler, "26th Cavalry"; and various interviews. Stimson's comments: Stimson diary. Eisenhower's messages: Lyon, *Eisenhower,* pp. 97–98. Gerow's memorandum: War Plans Division, National Archives. Yale Bowl remark: Mallonée, *The Naked Flagpole,* p. 79. Layac bridge: Toland, *But Not in Shame,* pp. 148–149; and various interviews. Description of Bataan: Hersey, *Men on Bataan,* pp. 77–78. Food and supplies on Bataan: Mellnik, *Philippine Diary,* pp. 71–72; Mallonée, *The Naked Flagpole,* p. 85; Drake, "No Uncle Sam"; Toland, *But Not in Shame,* p. 158; and various interviews.

I and II Corps actions: Morton, *The Fall of the Philippines,* pp. 212–231, 245–280 (Morioka quotation, p. 218; Homma quotation, p. 269); Rutherford, *Fall of the Philippines,* pp. 96–97. Mt. Natib force: Toland, *But Not in Shame,* p. 162.

MacArthur visit to Bataan: Beck, *MacArthur and Wainwright,* pp. 67–68; Morton, *The Fall of the Philippines,* p. 268; Toland, *But Not in Shame,* pp. 153–154; James, *The Years of MacArthur II,* p. 53; and various interviews.

CHAPTER 7. "And Nobody Gives a Damn"

General: various interviews and diaries; USAFFE–USFIP report. USAFFE–War Department messages, and Wainwright–MacArthur messages: War Plans Division, National Archives, and MacArthur Memorial.

The fighting on Bataan: Morton, *The Fall of the Philippines,* pp. 284, 290, 295–296, 300–301, 305–309, 313–315, 325–330, 338–339. Wainwright at the front: Toland, *But Not in Shame,* pp. 162, 171; and various interviews. Bulkeley story: Toland, *But Not in Shame,* pp. 164–165. Lee poem: H. Lee, *Nothing but Praise,* pp. 20–26. MacArthur on Corregidor: James, *The Years of MacArthur II,* pp. 57–58. Homma story: Toland, *But Not in Shame,* pp. 173–174; *U.S.A. v. Masaharu Homma.*

Food and supplies on Bataan: Morton, *The Fall of the Philippines,* pp. 367–376; Falk, *Bataan,* pp. 33–35; Redmond, *I Served on Bataan,* p. 47; Mallonée, *The Naked Flagpole,* p. 85; and various interviews. Medical conditions on Bataan: Morton, *The Fall of the Philippines,* pp. 376–381; Falk, *Bataan,* pp. 36–38; Redmond, *I Served on Bataan,* pp. 68–69; and various interviews. Morale on Bataan: Morton, *The Fall of the Philippines,* p. 385; Mallonée, *The Naked Flagpole,* p. 108; C. Lee, *They Call It Pacific,* p. 3; Champlin, "Bataan"; and various interviews.

CHAPTER 8. "The End Here Will Be Brutal and Bloody"

General: various interviews and diaries; USAFFE–USFIP report; Wainwright, *General Wainwright's Story,* p. 57. USAFFE–War Department messages, and MacArthur–Roosevelt messages: War Plans Division, National Archives, and MacArthur Memorial.

The fighting on Bataan: Morton, *The Fall of the Philippines*, pp. 309–312, 315–319, 321–324, 339–340, 343, 347–352, 387–389, 408–410; Falk, *Bataan*, pp. 63-66.

Champlin's experiences: Champlin interview, and *Shipmate* articles. Clark Lee's experiences: C. Lee, *They Call It Pacific*, pp. 3, 248–252; Lee and Henschel, *Douglas MacArthur*, p. 157. Dyess' experiences: Dyess, *The Dyess Story*, pp. 44–45. Romulo's experiences: Romulo, *I Saw the Fall of the Philippines*, pp. 141–145. Redmond's experiences: Redmond, *I Served on Bataan*, pp. 73–74.

Bulkeley's PT boats: Toland, *But Not in Shame*, p. 178. Jones and the reduction of the pockets: Morton, *The Fall of the Philippines*, pp. 341–342; Toland, *But Not in Shame*, pp. 182–183, 193. Homma: Toland, *But Not in Shame*, pp. 184, 186; *U.S.A. v. Masaharu Homma*. Robenson story: Underbrink, *Destination Corregidor*. Van Oosten and Stewart stories: Bataan research files of Maj. John Whitman. White House meeting (February 22): Sherwood, *Roosevelt and Hopkins*, pp. 505, 509; Beck, *MacArthur and Wainwright*, pp. 122-123. Roosevelt speech and reaction to it: Burns, *Roosevelt*, p. 212; Brougher, *Baggy Pants*, p. 31; Mallonée, *The Naked Flagpole*, p. 111; H. Lee, *Nothing but Praise*, p. 33; and various interviews.

CHAPTER 9. "They Are Leaving Us One by One"

General: various interviews and diaries; USAFFE–USFIP report; Wainwright, *General Wainwright's Story*, pp. 2–6, 64, 67–69. USAFFE–War Department messages: War Plans Division/Operations Division, National Archives, and MacArthur Memorial.

MacArthur departure for Australia: Morton, *The Fall of the Philippines*, pp. 356–358, 360–361; Toland, *But Not in Shame*, pp. 269–270; Beck, *MacArthur and Wainwright*, pp. 133, 137–140; Huff, *My Fifteen Years with General MacArthur*, p. 50; and various interviews.

Romulo's experiences: Romulo, *I Saw the Fall of the Philippines*, pp. 188, 219, 224–226, 228, 244. Champlin's experiences: Champlin interview, and *Shipmate* articles. Redmond's experiences: Redmond, *I Served on Bataan*, p. 88.

Homma's army: Belote and Belote, *Corregidor*, p. 65. Japanese surrender ultimatum: *U.S.A. v. Masaharu Homma*.

Food and medical situation on Bataan: Morton, *The Fall of the Philippines*, pp. 381–384; James, *The Years of MacArthur II*, pp. 62–63; Redmond, *I Served on Bataan*, pp. 54–57; Belote and Belote, *Corregidor*, p. 101; Dyess, *The Dyess Story*, p. 48; and various interviews.

Baldwin story: Beck, *MacArthur and Wainwright*, p. 138. Considine story: Considine, *It's All News To Me*, pp. 275–276. Pugh quotation: Beck, *MacArthur and Wainwright*, p. 172. "Dugout Doug": James, *The Years of MacArthur II*, p. 66. "The Lost Leader": Chunn, *Of Rice and Men*, pp. 196–197.

CHAPTER 10. "The Troops on Bataan Are Fast Folding Up"

General: various interviews and diaries; USAFFE–USFIP report; Wainwright, *General Wainwright's Story*, pp. 73, 77–78, 82; *Congressional Record*. SWPA–War Department messages, USFIP–War Department messages, and SWPA–USFIP messages: GHQ SWPA files, National Archives, and MacArthur Memorial.

Description of Corregidor: Morton, *The Fall of the Philippines*, pp. 472–474, 481–482, 532; Belote and Belote, *Corregidor*, pp. 5–14, 66, 70–71, 75–77; Braly, "Corregidor."

Four–part command arrangement: James, *The Years of MacArthur II*, pp. 142–143; Beck, *MacArthur and Wainwright*, pp. 176–177; Morton, *The Fall of the Philippines*, pp. 363–365; and various interviews.

Coleman's experiences: Coleman, *Bataan and Beyond*, p. 39. Redmond's experiences: Redmond, *I Served on Bataan*, pp. 100–103, 121–125, 127. Romulo's experiences: Romulo, *I Saw the Fall of the Philippines*, pp. 241, 250–251, 271–273, 279–284, 289–296. Dyess' experiences: Dyess, *The Dyess Story*, pp. 63–65. Stimson's comments: Stimson diary. Funk, Tisdelle, and Pugh quotations: Beck, *MacArthur and Wainwright*, pp. 274–276.

The Fourth Marines: Baldwin, "The Fourth Marines at Corregidor," p. 134. Food on Corregidor: Morton, *The Fall of the Philippines*, p. 375; Belote and Belote, *Corregidor*, p. 102; and various interviews. Homma's testimony: Morton, *The Fall of the Philippines*, pp. 414–416; *U.S.A. v. Masaharu Homma*. Ability of MacArthur to send help from Australia: Morton, *The Fall of the Philippines*, pp. 401–404. Quotation on importance of Bataan battle: Hough *et al.*, *Pearl Harbor to Guadalcanal*, p. 155. Wainwright's visit to Bataan: Toland, *But Not in Shame*, p. 285; and various interviews. Wainwright's speeches: International News Summary, HQ USFIP, Press Relations Section, various dates.

Final Japanese offensive and the fall of Bataan: Morton, *The Fall of the Philippines*, pp. 421, 427–429, 440, 442, 447–453; Toland, *But Not in Shame*, p. 283, 291–292, 298–299, 301–302; Beck, *MacArthur and Wainwright*, p. 191; Hough *et al.*, *Pearl Harbor to Guadalcanal*, p. 183; Baldwin, "The Fourth Marines at Corregidor"; and various interviews.

CHAPTER 11. "All Hell's Gonna Break Loose"

General: various interviews and diaries; USAFFE–USFIP report; Wainwright, *General Wainwright's Story*, pp. 87–91, 96, 99, 104–105. SWPA–War Department messages, USFIP–War Department messages, Wainwright–Roosevelt messages, and SWPA–USFIP messages: GHQ SWPA files, National Archives, and MacArthur Memorial.

Stimson's comments: Stimson diary. Romulo's experiences: Romulo, *I Saw the Fall of the Philippines*, pp. 300–306. Redmond's experiences: Redmond, *I Served on Bataan*, pp. 141–142, 144–145. Considine's story: Considine, *It's All News To Me*, pp. 273–274.

Escapes to Corregidor: Redmond, *I Served on Bataan,* pp. 127–131; Belote and Belote, *Corregidor,* pp. 106–107; Morton, *The Fall of the Philippines,* pp. 460–461; Baldwin, *Battles Lost and Won,* p. 138; and various interviews.

Bataan Death March: Falk, *Bataan,* pp. 194–200; Toland, *But Not in Shame,* pp. 311, 329. Corregidor artillery: Belote and Belote, *Corregidor,* p. 108; Mellnik, *Philippine Diary,* pp. 107, 110–113. Pugh quotation: Beck, *MacArthur and Wainwright,* p. 276. Conditions on Corregidor: Belote and Belote, *Corregidor,* p. 123. Wainwright's speeches: International News Summary, HQ USFIP, Press Relations Section, various dates.

No-surrender orders: Considine, *It's All News To Me,* p. 277; James, *The Years of MacArthur II,* p. 147; Morton, *The Fall of the Philippines,* pp. 563–564. Beach defense troops: Belote and Belote, *Corregidor,* p. 135; Morton, *The Fall of the Philippines,* p. 529. Homma: Belote and Belote, *Corregidor,* p. 115. Food on Corregidor: Morton, *The Fall of the Philippines,* p. 543. Flag incident: Morton, *The Fall of the Philippines,* p. 538.

Malinta Tunnel under Japanese bombardment: Morton, *The Fall of the Philippines,* pp. 538–539, 542–543; Lee, *They Call It Pacific,* pp. 2–3; Baldwin, *Battles Lost and Won,* pp. 139–141; Belote and Belote, *Corregidor,* pp. 113, 114, 124; and various interviews.

CHAPTER 12. "Goodbye, Mr. President"
General: various interviews and diaries; USAFFE–USFIP report; Wainwright, *General Wainwright's Story,* pp. 102, 108, 110, 113–115, 119. SWPA–War Department messages, USFIP–War Department messages, Wainwright–Roosevelt messages, SWPA–USFIP messages, and Beebe–Sutherland messages: GHQ SWPA files, National Archives; Sutherland papers, National Archives; MacArthur Memorial; and Marshall Foundation.

Redmond's experiences: Redmond, *I Served on Bataan,* pp. 148–151. Wainwright's gun: Wood interview; Elman, *Fired in Anger,* pp. 464–466; Underbrink, "Mindanao Gun." Hoeffel quotation: Beck, *MacArthur and Wainwright,* p. 218. Homma: Morton, *The Fall of the Philippines,* pp. 525–527, 552–557, 559–560; Belote and Belote, *Corregidor,* pp. 133–134; Toland, *But Not in Shame,* p. 338; *U.S.A. v. Masaharu Homma.*

The fall of Corregidor: Morton, *The Fall of the Philippines,* pp. 539–551, 557–561, 564–566; Parker, "The Epic of Corregidor-Bataan," p. 12; Belote and Belote, *Corregidor,* pp. 124–127, 129, 142, 145–148, 170, 171; Vance, *Doomed Garrison,* pp. 132–135; Baldwin, *Battles Lost and Won,* pp. 141–142, 146–148; Beck, *MacArthur and Wainwright,* pp. 211–212; Underbrink, *Destination Corregidor,* pp. 2, 25; Mellnik, *Philippine Diary,* pp. 137, 140–141; Kennedy, *Corregidor,* p. 1; Toland, *But Not in Shame,* pp. 340–341, 343–347; Braly, "Corregidor"; and various interviews.

CHAPTER 13. "I Have Taken a Dreadful Step"

General: various interviews and diaries; USAFFE–USFIP report; Wainwright, *General Wainwright's Story*, pp. 124–156; Galbraith, "Report on the North Luzon Episode Following the Corregidor Surrender"; various U.S. newspapers.

Stimson's comments: Stimson diary. Uno's experiences: Uno, *Corregidor*, pp. 23–30. Eichelberger's comments: Eichelberger, *Dear Miss Em*, p. 238. Considine's story: Considine, *It's All News To Me*, p. 274. Mrs. Wainwright: New York *Herald Tribune*, May 6, 1942. Homma: *U.S.A. v. Masaharu Homma*.

Surrender and aftermath: Morton, *The Fall of the Philippines*, pp. 566–567, 575; Toland, *But Not in Shame*, pp. 349, 354–357, 360; Belote and Belote, *Corregidor*, pp. 172–173, 178–179, 182–183; Vance, *Doomed Garrison*, pp. 166–167; Mellnik, *Philippine Diary*, pp. 144–145, 148; James, *The Years of MacArthur II*, p. 150; Pogue, *George C. Marshall* (1939–1942), p. 258; Mydans, *More Than Meets the Eye*, p. 2; Gunnison, *So Sorry, No Peace*, pp. 1–2; Hough *et al.*, *Pearl Harbor to Guadalcanal*, p. 199; and various interviews.

CHAPTER 14. "Sold Down the River"

General: various interviews and diaries; Wainwright, *General Wainwright's Story*, pp. 158–159, 162, 168–175.

Medal of Honor: Stimson diary; Marshall papers (includes McNarney report); Pogue, *George C. Marshall* (1939–1942), p. 258, and Pogue interview; James, *The Years of MacArthur II*, pp. 129–133, 150–151; Sutherland papers.

Correspondence between Marshall and Mrs. Wainwright: Marshall papers.

Homma: Toland, *But Not in Shame*, pp. 365–366; Toland, *The Rising Sun*, pp. 396–400; quotation in Falk, *Bataan*, pp. 230–232.

POW accounts: papers or recollections of Beebe, Bland, Bluemel, Brougher, Davis, Dooley, Drake, Funk, Galbraith, Greenleaf, Odlin, Pierce, Roberts, Vance, Wood, among others; Vance, *Doomed Garrison*, pp. 184–191; Brougher, *Baggy Pants*, p. 32; Quinn, *Love Letters To Mike*, p. 1. *Nagara Maru* voyage: Odlin manuscript; Mallonée, *The Naked Flagpole*, pp. 171–172.

CHAPTER 15. "I Am Hungry All the Time"

POW accounts: papers or recollections of Beebe, Bland, Bluemel, Brougher, Davis, Dooley, Drake, Funk, Galbraith, Greenleaf, Odlin and Odlin manuscript, Pierce, Roberts, Vance, Wood, among others; Wainwright, *General Wainwright's Story*, pp. 181–183, 188, 198–199, 204–205; Vance, *Doomed Garrison*, pp. 194–203; Brougher, *Baggy Pants*, pp. 48–49;

Mallonée, *The Naked Flagpole,* pp. 183–184; postwar newspaper interviews with Wainwright and King (especially *The New York Times,* September 1945); Considine, *It's All News To Me,* p. 275; *U.S.A. v. Masaharu Homma.* Chynoweth quotation: Beck, *MacArthur and Wainwright,* pp. 239–240.

CHAPTER 16. "How Long, Oh Lord, How Long?"

POW accounts: papers or recollections of Beebe, Bland, Bluemel, Brougher, Davis, Dooley, Drake, Funk, Galbraith, Greenleaf, Odlin and Odlin manuscript, Pierce, Roberts, Vance, Wood, among others; Mallonée, *The Naked Flagpole,* p. 194; Quinn, *Love Letters To Mike,* p. 235; Brougher, *The Long Dark Road,* pp. 65-76, 142-152; Wainwright, *General Wainwright's Story,* pp. 208–219, 226, 234-242, 250-259; Smyth, *Percival and the Tragedy of Singapore,* p. 274, *U.S.A. v. Masaharu Homma.*

On the home front: various newspapers and magazines; *Collier's,* July 10, 1943; *Time,* January 3, 1944 and May 8, 1944; New York *Post,* October 20, 1944 (quotation from Mrs. Holley); *Philippine Postscripts,* March 1, 1944 and other issues. Correspondence between Marshall and Mrs. Wainwright: Marshall papers.

MacArthur messages: RG3 SWPA Official Correspondence, MacArthur Memorial. Stimson's comments: Stimson diary.

The Japanese position: Craig, *The Fall of Japan,* pp. 274–275; and various newspapers.

CHAPTER 17. "Day of Glory"

General: various interviews and diaries; various newspapers, especially *The Washington Post* and *The New York Times; U.S.A. v. Masaharu Homma; Vital Speeches of the Day,* vol. 11, pp. 712–714; Wainwright, *General Wainwright's Story,* pp. 259–269, 274–285, 288–290, 296.

OSS mission: Craig, *The Fall of Japan,* pp. 233–234, 276–278. Meeting with MacArthur: James, *The Years of MacArthur II,* pp. 787–788; Manchester, *American Caesar,* pp. 525, 527–530; Whitney, *MacArthur,* p. 217; MacArthur, *Reminiscences,* pp. 311–316; Considine, *It's All News To Me,* pp. 273, 276. Brougher, *Baggy Pants,* pp. 186–191. Medal of Honor: Stimson diary; Marshall papers; Truman, *Off the Record,* pp. 47, 101. Surrender ceremonies: Halsey, *Admiral Halsey's Story,* p. 281; Chase, *Front Line General,* p. 128; Smyth, *Percival and the Tragedy of Singapore,* pp. 274–275, 278.

CHAPTER 18. "Alone in His Hero's Cage"

General: various interviews and diaries; *Congressional Record; Vital Speeches of the Day; The New York Times, The Washington Post;* San Antonio *Express; Newsweek; Time; Assembly,* January 1954 (obituary by classmate Charles G. Mettler); MacArthur Memorial; Manchester, *American Caesar,* pp. 619–620.

Index

Because of the frequency of promotions in wartime, military ranks have not been included in this index.

472

ABOUT THE AUTHOR

Duane Schultz is Adjunct Professor at the University of South Florida. His latest World War II books are *Wake Island: The Heroic Gallant Fight,* a feature of the Military Book Club, and *Sabers in the Wind,* a novel about the forced repatriation of the Cossacks. He divides his time between Washington, D.C., and Clearwater Beach, Florida.